# Communication
# Between Cultures

# FROM THE WADSWORTH SERIES IN COMMUNICATION STUDIES

| Adler/Proctor/Towne | *Looking Out/Looking In*, Eleventh Edition |
| Backlund/Williams | *Readings in Gender Communication* |
| Baxter/Babbie | *The Basics of Communication Research* |
| Benjamin | *Principles, Elements, and Types of Persuasion* |
| Bettinghaus/Cody | *Persuasive Communication*, Fifth Edition |
| Borchers | *Rhetorical Theory: An Introduction* |
| Braithwaite/Wood | *Case Studies in Interpersonal Communication: Processes and Problems* |
| Brummett | *Reading Rhetorical Theory* |
| Campbell/Huxman | *The Rhetorical Act*, Third Edition |
| Conrad/Poole | *Strategic Organizational Communication*, Sixth Edition |
| Cragan/Wright/Kasch | *Communication in Small Groups: Theory, Process, Skills*, Sixth Edition |
| Crannell | *Voice and Articulation*, Third Edition |
| Dwyer | *Conquer Your Speech Anxiety*, Second Edition |
| Freeley/Steinberg | *Argumentation and Debate: Critical Thinking for Reasoned Decision Making*, Eleventh Edition |
| Geist-Martin/Ray/Sharf | *Communicating Health: Personal, Cultural and Political Complexities* |
| Goodall/Goodall | *Communicating in Professional Contexts: Skills, Ethics, and Technologies*, Second Edition |
| Griffin | *Invitation to Public Speaking*, Second Edition |
| Hall | *Among Cultures: The Challenge of Communication*, Second Edition |
| Hamilton | *Essentials of Public Speaking*, Third Edition |
| Hamilton | *Communicating for Results: A Guide for Business and the Professions*, Seventh Edition |
| Hoover | *Effective Small Group and Team Communication*, Second Edition |
| Huglen/Clark | *Argument Strategies from Aristotle's Rhetoric* |
| Isaacson/Saperstein | *The Art and Strategy of Service-Learning Presentations*, Second Edition |
| Jaffe | *Performing Literary Texts: Concepts and Skills* |
| Jaffe | *Public Speaking: Concepts and Skills for a Diverse Society*, Fifth Edition |
| Knapp/Hall | *Nonverbal Communication in Human Interaction*, Sixth Edition |
| Larson | *Persuasion: Reception and Responsibility*, Eleventh Edition |
| Littlejohn/Foss | *Theories of Human Communication*, Eighth Edition |
| Lumsden/Lumsden | *Communicating in Groups and Teams: Sharing Leadership*, Fourth Edition |
| Lumsden/Lumsden | *Communicating with Credibility and Confidence: Diverse People, Diverse Settings*, Third Edition |
| Metcalfe | *Building a Speech*, Sixth Edition |
| Miller | *Organizational Communication: Approaches and Processes*, Fourth Edition |
| Morreale/Spitzberg/Barge | *Human Communication: Motivation, Knowledge, and Skills*, Second Edition |
| Natalle/Bodenheimer | *The Woman's Public Speaking Handbook* |
| Rothwell | *In Mixed Company: Communicating in Small Groups and Teams*, Sixth Edition |
| Rubin/Rubin/Piele | *Communication Research: Strategies and Sources*, Sixth Edition |
| Samovar/Porter/McDaniel | *Communication Between Cultures*, Sixth Edition |
| Samovar/Porter/McDaniel | *Intercultural Communication: A Reader*, Eleventh Edition |
| Sellnow | *Confident Public Speaking*, Second Edition |
| Sprague/Stuart | *The Speaker's Compact Handbook* |
| Sprague/Stuart | *The Speaker's Handbook*, Seventh Edition |
| Verderber/Verderber | *The Challenge of Effective Speaking*, Thirteenth Edition |
| Verderber/Verderber | *Communicate!*, Eleventh Edition |
| VerLinden | *Critical Thinking and Everyday Argument* |
| West/Turner | *Understanding Interpersonal Communication: Making Choices in Changing Times* |
| Williams/Monge | *Reasoning with Statistics: How to Read Quantitative Research* |
| Wood | *Communication in Our Lives*, Fourth Edition |
| Wood | *Communication Mosaics: An Introduction to the Field of Communication*, Fourth Edition |
| Wood | *Communication Theories in Action: An Introduction*, Third Edition |
| Wood | *Gendered Lives: Communication, Gender, and Culture*, Seventh Edition |
| Wood | *Interpersonal Communication: Everyday Encounters*, Fifth Edition |
| Wood | *Relational Communication: Continuity and Change in Personal Relationships*, Second Edition |
| Wood/Duck | *Composing Relationships: Communication in Everyday Life* |

# Communication Between Cultures

## SIXTH EDITION

**LARRY A. SAMOVAR**

*San Diego State University,
Emeritus*

**RICHARD E. PORTER**

*California State University,
Long Beach, Emeritus*

**EDWIN R. McDANIEL**

*Aichi Shukutoku University*

THOMSON

WADSWORTH

---

Australia • Brazil • Canada • Mexico • Singapore • Spain
United Kingdom • United States

**THOMSON**
**WADSWORTH**

**Communication Between Cultures, Sixth Edition**
Larry A. Samovar, Richard E. Porter, Edwin R. McDaniel

**Publisher:** Holly Allen
**Acquisitions Editor:** Jaime Perkins
**Assistant Editor:** John Gahbauer
**Editorial Assistant:** Laura Localio
**Senior Technology Project Manager:**
Jeanette Wiseman
**Senior Marketing Manager:** Kimberly Russell
**Marketing Assistant:** Alexandra Tran
**Senior Marketing Communications Manager:**
Shemika Britt
**Project Manager, Editorial Production:**
Catherine Morris
**Creative Director:** Rob Hugel

**Executive Art Director:** Maria Epes
**Print Buyer:** Rebecca Cross
**Permissions Editor:** Roberta Broyer
**Production Service:** Melanie Field/Interactive
Composition Corporation
**Compositor:** Interactive Composition Corporation
**Text Designer:** Ellen Pettengell
**Photo Researcher:** Stephen Forsling
**Copy Editor:** Lunaea Weatherstone
**Cover Designer:** Laurie Anderson
**Cover Images:** Keren Su/Getty Images, Adalberto
Rios Szalay/Sexto Sol/Getty Images
**Text and Cover Printer:** Malloy Incorporated

For more information about our products, contact us at:
**Thomson Learning Academic Resource Center**
1-800-423-0563
For permission to use material from this text or product,
submit a request online at http://www.thomsonrights.com.
Any additional questions about permissions can be submitted
by e-mail to thomsonrights@thomson.com.

Thomson Higher Education
10 Davis Drive
Belmont, CA 94002-3098
USA

**Library of Congress Control Number:** 2005937106
**ISBN:** 0-495-00727-7

# CONTENTS

Preface  xi

**CHAPTER 1**

## Communication and Culture: The Voice and Echo  1

The Challenge of Intercultural
    Communication  1

Intercultural Contact  3

International Contact  4
*New Technology and Information
    Systems  4*
*Evolving Populations  4*
*The Global Economy  6*

Domestic Contact  7

Defining Our Terms  9
*Intercultural Communication  9*
*The Dominant Culture  10*
*Co-culture  11*

Essentials of Human Communication  11
*Defining Communication  12*
*Principles of Communication  12*

Culture  16
*The Basic Functions of Culture  17*
*The Elements of Culture  18*
*Defining Culture  19*

Characteristics of Culture  20
*Culture Is Learned  21*

Culture Is Shared  27
*Culture Is Transmitted from Generation
    to Generation  28*

Culture Is Based on Symbols  28

Culture Is Dynamic  29

Culture Is an Integrated System  30

Studying Intercultural Communication  31
*Individual Uniqueness  31*
*Stereotyping  31*
*Objectivity  32*

Preview of the Book  32

Summary  33

Activities  34

Discussion Ideas  34

**CHAPTER 2**

## The Deep Structure of Culture: Roots of Reality  35

The Deep Structure of Culture  36
*Deep Structure Institutions Carry a Culture's Most
    Important Beliefs  37*
*Deep Structure Institutions and Their Messages
    Endure  37*
*Deep Structure Institutions and Their Messages Are
    Deeply Felt  38*
*Deep Structure Institutions Supply Much of Our
    Identity  38*

Family  39
*The Importance of Family  39*
*Definition of Family  40*
*Forms of Family  40*
*The Functions of the Family  41*
*Communication, Culture, and Family  42*

Cultural Variants in Family Interaction 43
Gender Roles 44
Individualism and Collectivism 46
Age 49
Social Skills 51

History 52
United States History 55
Russian History 58
Chinese History 59
Japanese History 61
Mexican History 64
History of Islamic Civilization 66

Summary 70

Activities 71

Discussion Ideas 71

## CHAPTER 3

# Worldview: Cultural Explanations of Life and Death 72

Worldview 72
Importance of Worldview 72
Manifestations of Worldview 73

Religion as a Worldview 75
Importance of Religion 75
Religion and the Study of Intercultural Communication 77
Selecting Religious Traditions for Study 77
Religious Similarities 78
Sacred Scriptures 78
Authority 79
Traditional Rituals 80
Ethics 81
Security 81

Six Religious Traditions 81
Christianity 82
Judaism 85
Islam 88
Hinduism 95
Buddhism 99
Confucianism 104

Religion: A Final Thought 107

Summary 107

Activities 108

Discussion Ideas 108

## CHAPTER 4

# Culture and the Individual: Cultural Identity 109

The Need to Understand Identity 110

Defining Identity 111

A Typology of Identities 113
Racial Identity 113
Ethnic Identity 113
Gender Identity 115
National Identity 115
Regional Identity 116
Organizational Identity 116
Personal Identity 117
Cyber and Fantasy Identity 118

Acquiring and Developing Identities 119

Establishing and Enacting Cultural Identity 121

Cultural Identity and Intercultural Communication 123

Identity and Multiculturalism 124

Summary 125

Activities 126

Discussion Ideas 126

## CHAPTER 5

# Alternative Views of Reality: Cultural Values 127

Perception 128
Defining Perception 128
Perception and Culture 129

Beliefs 130

Values 131

Studying Cultural Patterns 132
Obstacles in Studying Cultural Patterns 132
Selecting Cultural Patterns 134

Dominant U.S. Cultural Patterns 135
Individualism 135
Equality 137
Materialism 137
Science and Technology 138
Progress and Change 138
Work and Leisure 139
Competition 140

Diverse Cultural Patterns 140

Hofstede's Value Dimensions 140
   *Individualism/Collectivism 141*
   *Uncertainty Avoidance 145*
   *Power Distance 146*
   *Masculinity/Femininity 148*
   *Long- and Short-Term Orientation 150*

The Kluckhohns and Strodtbeck's Value
   Orientations 151
   *Human Nature Orientation 151*
   *Person/Nature Orientation 153*
   *Time Orientation 154*
   *Activity Orientation 156*
   *Relational (Social) Orientation 157*

Hall's High-Context and Low-Context
   Orientations 158
   *High Context 158*
   *Low Context 160*

Face and Facework 160

Summary 162

Activities 163

Discussion Ideas 163


**CHAPTER 6**

**Words and Meaning: Language
and Culture 164**

Language and Communication 164
   *Communicative Functions of Language 166*
   *Conversation 166*
   *Expression of Affect 167*
   *Thinking 167*
   *Control of Reality 167*
   *Keeping of History 167*
   *Socialization and Enculturation 168*
   *Expression of Identity 168*

Language and Culture 168
   *Verbal Processes 169*
   *Word and Pronunciation Diversity 170*
   *Language, Culture, and Meaning 171*

Language and Thought 173
   *Contextualization 175*

Culture and the Rules of Interaction 175
   *Directness and Indirectness 176*
   *Maintaining Social Relationships 177*
   *Expressions of Affect 179*
   *Value of Conversation 179*

Language Diversity in the United States 182

Languages of Co-cultures 183
   *Spanish-Speaking Americans 184*
   *African-American English 184*
   *Women and Language 186*
   *Female vs. Male Communication Patterns 187*

Understanding Diverse Message Systems 188
   *Try to Learn the Languages of Other Cultures 188*
   *Understand Cultural Variations in the Use of
      Language 189*
   *Remember That Words Are "Culture Bound" 190*
   *Be Sensitive to Diverse Coding Systems 191*
   *Achieving Clarity 191*

Summary 192

Activities 192

Discussion Ideas 193


**CHAPTER 7**

**Nonverbal Communication:
The Messages of Action, Space,
Time, and Silence 194**

Nonverbal Communication in Everyday Life 195
   *Nonverbal Communication Is Universal 196*
   *Judging Internal States 196*
   *Creating Impressions 196*
   *Managing Interaction 197*

Defining Nonverbal Communication 197

Functions of Nonverbal Communication 198
   *Repeating 198*
   *Complementing 198*
   *Substituting 198*
   *Regulating 199*
   *Contradicting 199*

Studying Nonverbal Communication: Guidelines
   and Limitations 199
   *Nonverbal Communication Is Often Ambiguous 199*
   *We Are More than Our Culture 200*

Nonverbal Communication and Culture 200

Classifications of Nonverbal Communication 201
   *Body Behavior 201*
   *Facial Expressions 208*
   *Eye Contact and Gaze 209*
   *Touch 212*
   *Paralanguage 214*
   *Space and Distance 216*

Time  219
Silence  225

Summary  227

Activities  228

Discussion Ideas  228

## CHAPTER 8

# Cultural Influences on Context: The Business Setting  229

Culture and Context  229

Communication and Context  230
Communication Is Rule Governed  230
Context Specifies Communication Rules  231
Communication Rules Are Culturally
Diverse  231

Assessing the Context  231
Formality and Informality  232
Assertiveness and Interpersonal Harmony  233
Status Relationships  235

Intercultural Communication in an Evolving
Business Context  237

The Multinational Business Context  238
Business Protocol  238
Greeting Behaviors  240
Personal Appearance  242
Gift Giving  242
Management Styles  243
Negotiation Styles  245
Decision Making  249
Conflict Management  251
The Influence of Information Technology
on International Communication  252

The Domestic Business Context  253

Summary  254

Activities  254

Discussion Ideas  255

## CHAPTER 9

# Cultural Influences on Context: The Educational Setting  256

Culture and Education  258
Globalization  258
Multiculturalism  258

Cultural Diversity and Education  259
What Cultures Teach  259
How Cultures Teach  262

Education in a Multicultural Society  264
Challenges of Multicultural Education  265
Culture and Learning  266

Language Diversity in Multicultural
Education  275
Degree of Diversity  275
Language and Identity  276
Limited English Proficiency Students  276

Multicultural Competency in the Classroom  277
Developing Multicultural Proficiency  278
Multicultural Classrooms  279
Multicultural Communication Competence  280
Multicultural Communication Strategies  281

Summary  282

Activities  283

Discussion Ideas  283

## CHAPTER 10

# Cultural Influences on Context: The Health Care Setting  284

Culture, Health Care, and Communication  284

Culture and Health Care: Diverse
Worldviews  286
Dualistic and Holistic Worldviews  286
Mechanistic and Non-mechanistic Worldviews  287

Health Belief Systems  288
Scientific/Biomedical System  288
Magico-Religious System  289
Holistic System  289
Alternative Health Care Systems  289

Cultural Diversity in the Causes of Illness  290
Scientific/Biomedical Causes  290
Magico-Religious Causes  290
Holistic Causes  291

Cultural Diversity in the Treatment
of Illness  292
Scientific/Biomedical Treatments  292
Magico-Religious Treatments  293
Holistic/Naturalistic Treatments  294

Cultural Diversity in the Prevention
of Illness  295

Religion, Spirituality, and Health Care  297

Health Care Considerations for a Culturally Diverse
        Population 299
  *Family Roles 300*
  *Language Barriers 303*
  *Nonverbal Messages 304*
  *Formality 306*

Becoming a Better Intercultural Health Care
        Communicator 306
  *Recognize Diverse Medical Systems 307*
  *Recognize Ethnocentrism 308*

Summary 309

Activities 310

Discussion Ideas 310


**CHAPTER 11**

# Becoming Competent: Improving Intercultural Communication 311

A Philosophy of Change 313
  *Language Is an Open System 313*
  *We Have Free Choice 313*
  *Communication Has a Consequence 314*

Becoming Competent 314
  *Defining Intercultural Competence 314*
  *Basic Components of Communication
    Competence 314*

Potential Problems in Intercultural
        Communication 316
  *Seeking Similarities 316*
  *Withdrawal 317*
  *Anxiety 318*
  *Uncertainty Reduction 318*
  *Stereotyping 319*
  *Prejudice 323*
  *Racism 326*
  *Power 329*
  *Ethnocentrism 331*
  *Culture Shock 333*

Improving Intercultural Communication 338
  *Know Yourself 338*
  *Employ Empathy 341*
  *Cultural Differences in Listening 344*
  *Develop Communication Flexibility 346*
  *Understand Intercultural Conflict 347*
  *Learn About Cultural Adaptation 351*

Ethical Considerations 354
  *A Definition of Ethics 355*
  *Relativism 356*
  *Universalism 356*

Guidelines for an Intercultural Ethic 357
  *Be Mindful That Communication Produces
    a Response 357*
  *Respect the Worth of the Individual 358*
  *Seek Commonalities Among People and
    Cultures 358*
  *Recognize the Validity of Differences 360*
  *Take Responsibility for Your Actions 360*
  *Be Motivated 360*

Summary 361

Activities 362

Discussion Ideas 362


**EPILOGUE**

# Where Have We Been? Where Are We Going? 363

Where Have We Been? 363

Where Are We Going? 365
  *International Problems 365*
  *Technology 366*
  *Ethnic and Cultural Identity 368*


Notes 370

Photo Credits 406

Index 407

# PREFACE

*If one finger is sore, the whole hand will hurt.*

**CHINESE PROVERB**

*Our lives are all different and yet the same.*

**ANNE FRANK**

We approached the occasion of a sixth edition with three very different responses: gratification, excitement, and caution. Our pride and egos are delighted that our previous efforts were successful enough to warrant this new edition. It means that during the last thirty-five years our messages regarding improving intercultural communication appear to have some merit—and an audience. Our excitement centered on the realization that we were going to be allowed to tinker with what we had done in the five earlier editions. We knew, however, that we had to be cautious and prudent when advancing additional perspectives and material. We did not want to abandon the orientation that contributed to the popularity of the earlier editions. We believe that in this new edition we have been able to balance the past, present, and future of intercultural communication. We have retained the core of the field, added current thinking and research, and staked out some new territory.

This book is still about the unique relationship between communication and culture. More specifically, it is about what happens when people from different cultures come together to share ideas, feelings, and information. Because communication and culture work in tandem, we have tried to incorporate the basic principles from both topics throughout this book. Because intercultural interaction is a growing daily occurrence for many people, we have designed this text for all those whose professional or private life brings them into contact with people from cultures or co-cultures different from their own. We, therefore, treat communication among international cultures and communication among domestic co-cultures in the United States.

## Rationale

Worldwide interest in intercultural communication grows out of two assumptions. First, you live in an age when changes in technology, travel, economic and political systems, immigration patterns, and population density have created a world in which you increasingly interact with people from different cultures. And whether or not you welcome those changes, they will continue to grow in both frequency and intensity. Huston Smith said much the same thing when he wrote: "When historians look back on our century they may remember it most, not for space travel or the release of nuclear energy, but as the time when the peoples of the world first came to take one another seriously."[1]

Second, more and more people are now aware that culture affects communication in subtle and profound ways. Your cultural backgrounds and experiences help determine how the world looks to you and how you interact in that world.

## Approach

Fundamental to our approach to intercultural communication is the belief that all forms of human communication involve action. Put in slightly different terms, *communication is an activity that affects you as well as other people*. Whether you are generating or receiving words or movements, you are creating and producing messages. Any study of communication, therefore, must include information about the choices that you make in selecting your messages, as well as a discussion of the consequences of those choices. Hence, this book takes the view that engaging in intercultural communication is pragmatic (you do something), philosophical (you make choices), and ethical (your selected actions have a consequence).

## Philosophy

A dual philosophy has guided us in the preparation of this book. First, it is to the advantage of all seven billion of us who share the planet's limited resources to improve our interpersonal and intercultural communication skills. The world has grown so small that we all depend on each other now—whether we want to or not. As simple as it sounds, it is nevertheless true that what happens in one place in the world affects other places. Second, most of the obstacles to understanding can be overcome with motivation, knowledge, and appreciation of cultural diversity. We hope to supply you with all three. Culture and communication, we have come to believe, involve personal matters, and as the authors we have evolved our own philosophy about intercultural interaction. It is our contention that the First Commandment of any civilized society must be: Allow people to be different as long as those dissimilarities do not create hardships for others. At times, as you read this book, you will observe that we have openly stated our own positions, and we make no apologies for them. We have at the same time made a conscious effort to keep our own ethnocentrism in check, but for those instances in which it has accidentally emerged, we apologize.

## New Features

The sixth edition of *Communication Between Cultures* brings a number of significant changes and new features. One of the most obvious changes in the new edition is the inclusion of a new author—Dr. Edwin R. McDaniel from Aichi Shukutoku University in Japan. We feel fortunate to have Ed join us in our efforts to present the best research and ideas on intercultural communication. Before earning his doctorate at Arizona State University, Ed spent more than twenty-five years traveling all over the world gaining firsthand knowledge of a wide range of cultures. His expertise in the areas of globalization, anthropology, Asian history, and business has infused a new perspective into the book.

In addition to a new co-author, the sixth edition has numerous other modifications and elements that are worth noting. We should add that much of the new content has been guided by the excellent feedback provided by our readers and reviewers. We have, of course, incorporated a great deal of current material that reflects our own interpretation and vision of the field of intercultural communication.

- One of the major new additions to the sixth edition is a chapter on cultural identity and its influence on intercultural communication. Because your cultural identity tells you about yourself and your place in your culture, we believe it is instrumental in shaping both perceptions and communication patterns.
- It is now apparent that the world is experiencing serious clashes based on religious differences. Therefore, we deemed it appropriate to have an entire chapter on the topic of religion. Our main approach in this chapter is to demonstrate how one's worldview gets translated into daily life—including interactions with people from different cultures.
- Because the Middle East has grown in significance since the last edition, we have added the topic of Islamic civilization to our chapter on history.
- A new section in the chapter on language is presented that offers specific advice as to how you can adapt your language to various intercultural settings.
- Since intercultural conflicts seem to have intensified in recent years, we have expanded our treatment of stereotypes, prejudice, and racism.
- The chapter on values and cultural patterns has been revised and also augmented to include a new section on the Asian notion of "face saving."
- Our treatment of the influence of information technology and mass media has been greatly expanded and placed in various locations throughout the book.
- Because gender differences are so much a part of the intercultural process, the new edition weaves this important topic into every chapter. From religion to the workplace to the use of language and nonverbal communication, gender comparisons are presented.
- Because of the increased interest in intercultural contexts, all three chapters dealing with intercultural settings have been completely revised. New material on improving your intercultural communication skills in these environments has been added to each of the three chapters that examine intercultural business, education, and health care.
- Due to our strong conviction that communication produces a reaction that has a consequence, we have greatly expanded our discussion of ethics.
- As with prior editions, we have integrated fresh examples throughout the book. We have also added hundreds of new references to this current volume.

# Acknowledgments

No book is the sole domain of the authors. Many people contributed to this new edition, and we would like to acknowledge and thank them. We begin by thanking our publisher, Wadsworth Publishing Company, and on editors, Annie Mitchell and Jaime Perkins. They have always encouraged us and given us the freedom to advance new ideas. We are especially pleased with our long affiliation with Wadsworth Publishing Company. In this day of fads and short-lived associations, we greatly appreciate a relationship that spans nearly forty years and includes eighteen books. For the current edition, we want to acknowledge the editorial and production support provided by Catherine Morris, Douglas Thompson, Melanie Field, Stephen Forsling, and Lunaea Weatherstone. Many thanks to Alan Heisel for writing the Instructor's Resource Manual and for his diligent work producing the website quizzes.

We are grateful to our manuscript reviewers for their many helpful suggestions:

Anita Bailey, Macon State College
Cynthia Bone, Spokane Community College
Edward Borgens, Southeast Community College
Deborah A. Cai, University of Maryland
Carrie Chrisco, McNeese State University
Jay Danley, San Bernardino Valley College
Richard M. Drucker, Peirce College
Luke S. Fetters, Huntington College
Melanie Finney, DePauw University
Lisa Flores, University of Utah
Scherrie Foster, Fond du Lac Tribal and Community College
Tanya Gardner, Peirce College
Salma Ghanem, University of Texas–Pan American
Melissa Gibson Hancox, Mercyhurst College
Deborah Godwin-Starks, Indiana University–Purdue University
Elizabeth Goering, Indiana University–Purdue University
Denis Grimes, University of Wisconsin, Milwaukee
Sandra Hochel, University of South Carolina
Suda Ishida, Hamline University
Nancy Jackson, Clemson University
Pamela Kaylor, Ohio University
James Keaton, University of Northern Colorado
Su Il Kim, Metropolitan State College
Sandra King, Anne Arundel Community College
Charles J. Korn, Northern Virginia Community College
Celeste Lacroix, College of Charleston
Diane Lennard, New York University
Yang Lin, University of Akron
Deborah K. London, Merrimack College
Andrew Lovato, College of Santa Fe
Ulrich Luenemann, California State University, Sacramento
Thomas A. Marshall II, Robert Morris University
Polly McMahon, Spokane Falls Community College
Nicki L. Michalski, Lamar University
Margaret Miller Butcher, Fort Hays State University
Joanne Mundorf, University of Rhode Island
George Musambira, Western Kentucky University
Vicki H. Nelson, Curry College
Sister Rosemary O'Donnell, Aquinas College
Susan Opt, Salem College
Lisa M. Orick, Albuquerque TVI Community College
Daniel M. Paulnock, Saint Paul College
Nancy Pearson, Minot State University

Steven M. Rashba, University of Bridgeport
Ken Robol, Halifax Community College
Moira Rogers, Eastern Mennonite University
Joanna M. Sanchez, SUNY at Alabama
Sandra E. Schmidt, Greenville College
Sarah Schroeder, Northern Kentucky University
Pamela D. Schultz, Alfred University
Kathleen Siskar, Mesabi Range College
Kara Smith, College of Saint Rose
Cynthia A. Strong, Simpson University
Deatra H. Sullivan-Morgan, Elmhurst College
Robert L. Terrell, Cal State Hayward
Vanessa R. Thompson, Mountain State University
J. D. Turner, Methodist College
Steve Vrooman, Texas Lutheran University
Lisa A. Wallace, Ohio University, Chillicothe
S. Catherine Walsh, Mt. St. Mary College
Sylvia Walters, Davidson County Community College
John Warren, Bowling Green State University
Wendy West, Kentucky Christian College
Dennis L. Wignall, Dixie State College
Kathie Wilcox, Lewis-Clark State College
Richard Wiseman, California State University, Fullerton
Samuel Zalanga, Bethel University
Mei Zhong, San Diego State University
Merle Wm. Ziegler, Mississippi College

Finally, we express our appreciation to the thousands of students and the many instructors who have read past editions. They have enabled us to "talk to them" about intercultural communication, and, by finding something useful in our exchange, we have been allowed to produce yet another edition of *Communication Between Cultures*.

LARRY A. SAMOVAR

RICHARD E. PORTER

EDWIN R. MCDANIEL

## CHAPTER 1

# Communication and Culture: The Voice and Echo

*In some ways, September 11th was a harrowing reminder of how truly we all live in the same neighborhood now, even if the differences and distances between us remain as great as ever.*

PICO IYER

*Human beings draw close to one another by their common nature, but habits and customs keep them apart.*

CONFUCIUS

## The Challenge of Intercultural Communication

The beginning of this chapter affords us the simplest assignment we will face in this entire book. It is basically to remind you of the obvious conclusion that you now live in an age when all of the people on earth, regardless of their background or culture, are interconnected. Some of the connections might be obvious as you interact with neighbors who might speak a "strange" language or a business partner who stops and prays in the middle of a meeting. Others more subtle, such as China's emerging economy or North Korea's nuclear program, have a ripple effect on the stock market and the security of the world. It seems that now more than ever what happens in one part of the world touches all parts of the world. This book is about your adapting, adjusting, and taking part in this "new world."

It is our belief that because most significant values, beliefs, attitudes, and behaviors are rooted in culture it behooves you to understand how cultural experiences help explain the way people perceive the world and carry out the business of living in the world. Specifically this book seeks to answer some of the following questions:

- Why are you often uncomfortable when confronted with people who are different from yourself?
- Why do people from different cultures behave in ways that seem strange to you?

*The Internet now allows people almost anywhere in the world to exchange ideas and information on a regular basis.*

- How do cultural differences influence communication?
- Which cultural differences are important and which are inconsequential?
- Why is it difficult to understand and appreciate cultural differences?

Intercultural communication, as you might suspect, is not new. Since the beginnings of civilization when the first humans formed tribal groups, intercultural contact occurred whenever people from one tribe encountered others and discovered that they were different. These ideas of cultural differences have long been recognized, but in the absence of accompanying cultural knowledge, this recognition most often elicited the human propensity to respond malevolently to those differences. This reaction to the unfamiliar was well expressed over two thousand years ago by the Greek playwright Aeschylus, who wrote, "Everyone is quick to blame the alien." This penchant to blame the alien is still a powerful element in today's social and political rhetoric. For instance, it is not uncommon in the United States and elsewhere to hear charges that immigrants are responsible for all of the perceived social and economic problems affecting society.

We fear that, from a historical perspective, successful intercultural communication has been the exception rather than the rule. The history of humankind details an on-going antipathy and hostility toward those who are different. The twentieth century, for instance, suffered two world wars and witnessed the introduction and use of chemical, biological, and nuclear weapons with the potential to destroy humankind. The world also endured the Holocaust and various smaller-scale conflicts such as those in Korea, the Sudan, Vietnam, Kuwait, Iraq, Chechnya, Afghanistan, and Angola, and the various dissident clashes in many Latin American nations. Now the world is faced with the daily threat of terrorism. It appears that in every part of the world, and within the United States itself, people and societies must learn to cope with one another. This is what intercultural communication is about: dealing with changes in the world's fabric of social relationships and the challenges of managing the changes at both the international and domestic level. In short, with or without our consent, the last four decades have thrust you into social and professional situations with people who often appear alien, exotic, and perhaps even wondrous.

## Intercultural Contact

Here, early in the book, we explore some of the changes that have taken place in the United States and elsewhere that clearly underscore both the regularity and intensity of intercultural contacts. Many of you will be able to verify the examples we offer to document these alterations in intercultural contact, for you have had firsthand experiences

© Gloria Thomas

*Low-cost fares and the speed of modern aircraft have made tourism a major factor in intercultural contact.*

with people whose cultures are different from your own. Our rationale for looking at these changes is threefold. First, as the familiar gives way to a new and different world, the entire human race is affected. Second, many of the events that have brought diverse groups together are often subtle and difficult to detect. Hence, we believe that many of these events may have been overlooked. Finally, by learning about these changes, you will begin to understand the role and impact of culture on communication and (we trust) rise to meet the intercultural challenges posed in the twenty-first century.

We begin our inquiry by examining the places and circumstances under which you may find yourself engaging in communication with people from diverse cultural backgrounds. In rather general terms we can say that your intercultural interaction will have two distinct points of contact: *international* and *domestic*.

# International Contact

Because of international contacts, it is becoming obvious that a symbiotic relationship ties all people together. In today's world no nation, group, or culture can remain aloof or autonomous. Three international developments have made intercultural contact more axiomatic and pervasive: (1) *new technology and information systems*, (2) *changes in the world's population*, and (3) *rapid movement toward a global economy*.

## NEW TECHNOLOGY AND INFORMATION SYSTEMS

Shattuck is right when she writes that "modern technology in the last 25 years—from the Boeing 747 to the world wide web—has made our globe seem a much smaller place."[1] You can board a plane and fly anywhere in the world in a matter of hours. You can attend a breakfast meeting in Paris and a dinner conference in San Francisco on the same day. Reduced airfares make the tourist industry one of the largest producers of revenue in the world with global receipts in the trillions and number of travelers now over a billion.[2] One result of these expanded travel opportunities is that you may routinely encounter cultures that seem bizarre or mysterious. Sources of diversity now go far beyond eating utensils, traditional attire, and modes of travel. You can be exposed to cultural idiosyncrasies in the perception of time and space, the treatment of women and the elderly, the ways and means of conducting business, and even the discovery and meaning of truth.

New and advanced information systems continue to encourage and facilitate cultural interaction. As the RAND organization points out, "Technology's promise is here today and will march forward. It will have widespread effects across the globe."[3] Communication satellites, sophisticated television transmission equipment, and fiber-optic or wireless connection systems permit people throughout the world to share information and ideas instantaneously. The growth in wireless telephone systems, for example, is expanding rapidly with well over fifty thousand new subscribers each day. And, of course, the impact of the Internet on communication exchanges is phenomenal. You can now, with the simple click of a mouse, "talk" to anyone almost anywhere in the world.

## EVOLVING POPULATIONS

The second impetus to international communication is a rapid increase in and redistribution of the world's population. The world's population increases at a rate of approximately 200,000 people a day. Simple arithmetic will tell you that is almost 80 million people a year. In 2005, the world population was estimated to be 7.1 billion, with projections of it reaching 9.3 billion by 2050. Not only is the world's population growing rapidly, it is also on the move. More than 100 million people are living outside the country of their birth. A recent United Nations study concluded that the "surge in global migration at the end of the twentieth century shows no sign of letting up.[4]

This increase in movement of the world's population has produced numerous problems that make competent international contact more important than ever before. Let us touch on some of the problems.

**Natural Resources.** Oil, water, and food are the three most vivid examples of the world's population needing to cooperate on issues relating to natural resources. Violence and instability in much of the Middle East has created a situation where oil production is extremely unpredictable. Demands for this finite resource are now compounded by the fact that China and India, with a combined population of well over two billion people, are moving toward increased industrialization. For example, in the last ten years China's demand for oil has nearly doubled.[5]

Water as well as oil has become a natural resource that produces a need for the people of the world to discuss their common problems. Over the next half century, it is predicted that water, our most vital natural resource, will replace oil as the prime trigger for international conflict. Swomley points out the problem in the following manner:

> A worldwide water crisis looming on the horizon is expected to reach dire proportions within the next ten to thirty years. . . . It takes 1,000 tons of water to raise one ton of grain. At this rate, the 2.4 billion people projected to be added to the world's population over the next thirty years would require a quantity of water equal to twenty Nile Rivers or ninety-seven Colorado Rivers.[6]

Some Middle Eastern countries as well as parts of Asia, Africa, and even the southwestern United States are already experiencing water shortages and threats of water wars. These conflicts are an early sign of the approaching water crisis.[7]

A decrease in food sources, both from the ground and the sea, is another example of how limited resources can produce intercultural friction and the need to resolve that friction. Shortages of productive land to grow crops and disputes over fishing rights have generated serious problems throughout the world. For example, Tomlinson writes, "Nearly 40 million Africans are short of food, left to rely on aid to stave off hunger and even starvation."[8] Further, the United Nations estimates that each year more than forty thousand children die of malnutrition.[9]

**The Environment.** Environmental problems do not observe geographic or cultural boundaries and therefore represent yet another impetus for improved intercultural communication. A recent United Nations–sponsored study of the earth's health concluded, "Growing populations and expanding economic activity have strained the planet's ecosystems over the past half century, a trend that threatens international efforts to combat poverty and disease."[10] From China to Central America, weather-related flooding events have resulted from deforestation that left many hillsides bare, causing rainfall to run quickly into rivers rather than being absorbed, thus leading to devastating landslides and floods. In addition, as Schmidt has suggested, an African drought may be partly responsible for a decline in Caribbean Sea coral because of coral-damaging fungi found in the dust blown across the ocean.[11] Again, you can observe a world without environmental borders.

The environmental crisis produces a long and somber list of problems that touch all cultures. Destruction of the rain forests, famine, the pollution of air and water, the growing list of endangered plants and animals, toxic dumping, and the greenhouse effect are just a few of the many conundrums we all face as we try to balance population demands with the health of the planet.

**International Conflict.** Conflicts among nations and peoples provide yet another reason to encourage effective intercultural communication. It is estimated that there are more than twenty-seven armed conflicts taking place around the world.[12] The toll of this violence on human life is difficult to comprehend. Not only are thousands of soldiers being killed and wounded, but millions of innocent people have been drawn into the fighting—many of them children. The United Nations Children's Fund concluded that "nearly half the estimated 3.6 million people killed in wars since 1990 have been children, reflecting the fact that civilians increasingly have become the victims in contemporary conflicts."[13]

The widespread proliferation of nuclear weapons also underscores the need for cultures to interact in a civil manner. Mattern emphasizes the seriousness of the nuclear problem when he writes, "The year 2000 began with over 30,000 nuclear weapons stockpiled around the world."[14] Specter and Robbins spell out the most devastating news about these weapons in the following paragraph:

> Simply stated, nuclear, biological, and chemical weapons of mass destruction pose the greatest single threat to the United States and the world. Some twenty-five nations today have such weapons. North Korea has developed long-range missiles that could reach Alaska and Hawaii. Some weapons capable of decimating continents can cross international borders in a suitcase. The knowledge needed to turn common industrial materials into a death cloud is no longer the province of just a few scientists. Even the Internet carries how-to guides.[15]

Recent events have given credence to the axiom that hostility anywhere has the potential to become hostility everywhere. Distance no longer matters. The terrorist attacks against the World Trade Center have shown that the United States, although geographically fairly isolated, is not immune to conflict. Continued tensions in Iraq, North Korea, Iran, Israel, Chechnya, Palestine, parts of Africa, the Philippines, and Indonesia are all "hot spots ready to explode."[16]

## THE GLOBAL ECONOMY

A Russian proverb states, "Boris has one custom and Sergei another." This saying can easily be extended to the global economy, where people from diverse cultures come together to engage in commerce and, of course, communicate. Beamer and Varner underscore this point when they note that "organizations are finding themselves involved in communication across cultures, between cultures, among cultures—because they are doing business in foreign countries, perhaps, or because they are sourcing from another country, seeking financing from another country, or have an increasingly multicultural workforce."[17] What Beamer and Varner are pointing out is that the world is now under the influence of what has come to be known as "a global economy." The extent of the global economy is aptly stated by Cowin: "The world economy is 'borderless' and markets are becoming essentially one. Corporations are looking at the free flow of goods and services, capital and human resources as well as information as the pathway to growth."[18] And, as Goldsmith, Walt, and Doucet indicate, "The trend toward globally connected markets is likely to become even stronger in the future."[19]

These new economic ties mean that it would not be unusual for you to work for an organization that has a multicultural workforce and that does business in many countries. For that reason, we will have more to say in Chapter 8 about your possible role in the culturally diverse business setting.

# Domestic Contact

As changes have taken place throughout the world so too has the cultural landscape of the United States been altered. Within the boundaries of the United States people are redefining and rethinking the meaning of being a member of the U.S. population. What once was considered a homogeneous group has changed.

Recognition that the U.S. population comes in different colors and from diverse cultural backgrounds has had a profound effect on national identity. From all over the world, people from a large variety of cultures are now calling the United States their home. Simultaneously, groups that, for a host of reasons, remained silent for years, now ask—and at times demand—to be heard. The members of these groups, like the members of the dominant culture, share perceptions, values, modes of communication, and lifestyles that make them unique. Let us now briefly look at some of these groups.

We begin our analysis of domestic contact with an examination of immigration in the United States. U.S. immigration policies have created a country that leads Guerrière to conclude that "America is the most successful poly-racial, poly-ethnic, and poly-religious society in history."[20] Historically, the United States has made it relatively easy for people from other countries to move here. The United States permits more legal immigration than the rest of the world combined. As a consequence, the U.S. population contains a higher proportion of foreign-born individuals than at any time in the past hundred years. According to the 2000 U.S. Census, "The nation's foreign-born population numbered 34.2 million, accounting for 12 percent of the total U.S. population."[21] While these numbers appear to be high they do not even reflect the nation's estimated 10.3 million undocumented population.[22] Many observers believe that immigration to America will continue to increase because the rest of the world does not welcome foreigners to the degree the United States does. Data from the 2000 census reveals that "one out of every four Americans is a minority, with minority defined as anyone who is not a non-Hispanic white."[23] In California, non-Hispanic whites (what at one time were called Caucasians) are now a minority.[24] When you consider immigrants' American-born children, "births are becoming the most important source of [immigrant] population growth."[25]

To help you understand the cultural dynamics and numerical prominence of the non-Hispanic white in the United States, we will briefly mention the four co-cultures that you are most likely to come in contact with if you are a member of the dominant culture: *Latinos, African Americans, Asian Americans,* and *Muslim Americans.*

*Latinos* (which normally include people from Mexico, Puerto Rico, Cuba, and Central and South America) are the fastest growing population in the United States.

*Immigration has produced millions of new American citizens from a host of different cultures.*

© Jeff Greenberg/PhotoEdit

Rodriguez and Olswang offer the following summary of the demographics of this group:

> The nation's Hispanic population grew much faster than the population as a whole, increasing from 35.3 million in 2000 to 38.8 million in 2002 (U.S. Census Bureau, 2003). The official population estimates now indicate that the Hispanic community is the nation's largest minority community.[26]

Many members of the dominant culture resent the millions of Latinos now moving to the United States—either legally or illegally—each year. This large number of immigrants from a single location has created calls for everything from walling off the U.S.-Mexican border to a more rigid immigration policy with Mexico. Some of the bitterness arises because many Latinos have retained their native language rather than adopting English. For example, only the countries of Mexico and Colombia exceed the United States in the number of people who speak Spanish.[27] Spanish-language broadcast and print media have proliferated in recent years in both major and minor markets. The realm of politics has also recognized the importance of the Spanish-speaking population. Gamboa has reported that "candidates for Congress and governor aired more than 16,000 Spanish-language television spots during the 2002 campaign, and politicians seeking federal, statewide, or legislative office spent at least $16 million on such advertisements."[28] The mayor of New York paid for an advertisement on television showing him taking Spanish lessons. Not only are Latino voters the target of politicians, they are becoming the politicians. In California, the Los Angeles 2005 mayoral election was won by Antonio Villaraigosa—a Latino.

*African Americans* now account for approximately 13 percent of the total U.S. population.[29] Prior to the Civil Rights Act of 1964, African Americans and members of the dominant culture had only limited contact. Since that time, the groups have interacted with much greater regularity. As is often the case, however, when two diverse cultures come into contact, not all the encounters are successful. Even today, racism is a major cause of economic disparity between many African Americans and members of the dominant culture. As Estrin explains, "Race continues to play a powerful role in the chances for success in the United States from job opportunities to education to housing, at least in the metropolitan areas of Boston, Atlanta, Detroit, and Los Angeles."[30]

*Asian Americans* (particularly those of Chinese and Japanese ancestry) have been present in the United States since the late 1800s. Recent census data indicates they are the second fasting growing minority in the United States. There are more than 12.5 million residents who claim Asian-only ancestry.[31] First-generation immigrants face many communication problems. Imagine the adjustment problems faced by a refugee from Thailand who immigrated to the United States at the age of four. In a cultural sense, she is not quite Asian, and she is not quite American. She speaks the Mien language at home, English with her friends, and a blend of the two languages to her children. Not only are these people finding it difficult to cope with living in the United States so far away from both their homelands and their cultures, but they also can create difficult and unique communication problems for those who must interact with them.

*Muslim Americans* number an estimated 6 to 7 million and are increasing steadily.[32] The American Muslim community constitutes what Ostling calls "a growing and maturing community that worships at over 1,200 mosques across the United States."[33] The rapid growth of this group is not the only reason we have included them in our discussion of co-cultures. They have also been incorporated into our discussion because of all the news and false information surrounding Muslims and Muslim Americans since the events of 9/11 and the involvement of the United States in Iraq.

Until recently Arab Americans were the least studied of all the ethnic groups living in the United States. But as we noted, all of that has changed in the last few years. Before the unwanted publicity about Arab Americans they were a group that was both pious and modern as they attempted to blend traditional ways with American institutions. Their children might know it is time to pray, not by a muezzin's call from a mosque minaret, but because his or her Power Mac has chimed. Now, as El-Badry points out, "The lack of information, coupled with the media's tendency to use broad strokes to associate Arab-Americans with Arabs in the Middle East, has at times put the community in a defensive position."[34]

There are of course many additional co-cultures in the United States that we could have included in this early analysis: women, American Indians, gays and lesbians, the deaf, the incarcerated, gangs, prostitutes, the disabled, and various ethnic groups. In many cases members of these groups do not subscribe to all of the mainstream beliefs, values, and attitudes shared by the dominant culture.

# Defining Our Terms

## INTERCULTURAL COMMUNICATION

Because we have been using the term *intercultural communication* from the beginning, it only seems appropriate that we pause at this time and give meaning to those two words. We have also employed the phrases *dominant culture* and *co-culture* and believe it would be of value to define those concepts in this section of the book. Let us begin with intercultural communication. For us, intercultural communication occurs when a member of one culture produces a message for consumption by a member of another culture. *More precisely, intercultural communication involves interaction between people whose cultural perceptions and symbol systems are distinct enough to alter the communication event.*

## THE DOMINANT CULTURE

When we refer to a group of people as a *culture* we are applying the term to the dominant culture found in most societies. In discussions of the United States, many terms have been employed to represent this group. In the past, terms such as *umbrella culture, mainstream culture, U.S. Americans,* or *European Americans* have been applied when speaking of this collection of people. We prefer the term *dominant culture* because it clearly indicates that the group we are talking about is the one in power. This is the group that usually has the greatest amount of control over how the culture carries out its business. This group possesses the power that allows them to speak for the entire culture while setting the tone and agenda others will usually follow. As indicated, the power is not necessarily found in numbers, but in control. The people in power are those who historically have controlled, and who still control, the major institutions within the culture: church, government, education, military, mass media, monetary systems, and the like. As McLemore notes:

> The dominant group in American society was created as people of English ethnicity settled along the Atlantic seacoast and gradually extended their political, economic, and religious control over the territory. This group's structure, values, customs, and beliefs may be traced to (a) the English system of law, (b) the organization of commerce during the sixteenth century, and (c) English Protestant religious ideas and practices.[35]

In the United States, adult white males generally meet the requirements of dominance—and have since the establishment of this country. Although white males constitute only 34 percent of the U.S. population,[36] it is their positions of power, not their numbers, that foster this degree of control. White males are at the center of the dominant culture because their positions of power enable them to determine and manipulate the content and flow of the messages produced by various political, economic, and religious institutions. By controlling most of the cultural messages, they are thus able to control the images presented to the majority of the population. Whether it is the church, mass media, or government, the dominant culture sets goals, perpetuates customs, establishes values, and makes the major decisions affecting the bulk of the population. Their power allows them to influence what people think, what they aspire to be, how they behave, and even what they talk about. As Folb has noted, "Power is often defined as the ability to get others to do what you want."[37] It should be noted that a dominant group that greatly influences perceptions, communication patterns, beliefs, and values marks all cultures. What these groups use as the bases for their power (money, fear, the military, etc.) may differ from culture to culture, but they all lead the way. Folb made the same point when she wrote:

> High status and attendant power may be accorded those who are seen or believed to be great warriors or hunters; those invested with magical, divine, or special powers; those who are deemed wise; or those who are in possession of important, valued and/or vital societal resources and goods.[38]

Regardless of the source of power, certain people within every culture have a disproportionate amount of influence, and that influence gets translated into how other members of the culture behave.

## CO-CULTURE

We have just pointed out that within each society you will find a dominant culture. However, it should be noted, this culture is not monolithic. That is to say, within the dominant culture you will find numerous co-cultures and specialized cultures. As Victor suggests, "A national culture is never a homogeneous thing of one piece. In every culture there are internal contradictions or polarities. U.S. culture is no exception."[39] We believe that the best way to identify these groups is through the use of the term *co-cultures*. For a number of years the groups we are referring to were called *subcultures*. We prefer the word co-culture not so much out of political correctness, but because it calls attention to the idea of dual members. That is to say, it should be obvious that people often belong to more than one culture and therefore share some of the perceptions and communication patterns found within the larger, dominant culture. We will, therefore, use the word *co-culture when discussing groups or social communities exhibiting communication characteristics, perceptions, values, beliefs, and practices that are sufficiently different to distinguish them from the other groups, communities, and the dominant culture.*

As we have just noted, some co-cultures share many of the patterns and perceptions found within the larger, dominant culture, but they also have distinct and unique patterns of communication that they have learned as part of their membership in the co-culture. As you will see later in this chapter when we discuss culture in detail, most of the co-cultures in the United States meet many of the criteria and characteristics that we will apply to describe culture. For example, as Lane notes, "Deaf culture provides its members with traditions, values, and rules for behavior that are handed down from generation to generation."[40] Gays and lesbians as well, Goodwin points out, have their own language, traditions, and behavioral codes.[41] What is important about all co-cultures is that being gay, disabled, Latino, African American, Asian American, or female exposes a person to a specialized set of messages that helps determine how he or she perceives some aspects of the external world. It also significantly influences how members of that co-culture communicate those perceptions. As we already noted, these co-cultural affiliations can be based on race, ethnic background, gender, age, sexual preference, and so forth.[42] For example, as Hecht, Ribeau, and Sedano have shown, African Americans have evolved language and behavior characteristics that constitute a co-culture. This leads us to reach the same conclusion with regard to the Mexican American co-culture.[43]

Before we apply the three definitions we have just examined (intercultural communication, dominant culture, and co-culture) to the study of intercultural communication, we need to pause and talk about human communication. Our rationale for beginning with communication is a simple one. While this book is about the role of culture in communication, it is also about what the phrase *intercultural communication* implies about human interaction. By understanding some principles inherent in communication, you will be able to observe how these principles get acted out in the intercultural setting.

# Essentials of Human Communication

The importance and sway of communication on human behavior is dramatically underscored by Keating when she writes, "Communication is powerful: It brings companions to our side or scatters our rivals, reassures or alerts children, and forges consensus or battle lines between us."[44] What she is saying is that communication—your ability to share your beliefs, values, ideas, and feelings—is the basis of all human contact. Whether you live in a city in Canada, a village in India, a commune in Israel, or the Amazon jungles of Brazil, you participate in the same activity when you communicate. The results and the methods might be different, but the process is the same.

## DEFINING COMMUNICATION

There was good reason for the English statesman Benjamin Disraeli to say "I hate definitions." While definitions are necessary, they can also be troublesome. For example, it is nearly impossible to find a single definition of *human communication*. Over thirty years ago, Dance and Larson canvassed the literature on communication and found 126 definitions of communication;[45] since then, countless others have been added to their list. Isolating the commonalities of those definitions, and wishing to select one that is all-encompassing, we hold that *human communication is the process through which symbols are transmitted for the purpose of eliciting a response*.

## PRINCIPLES OF COMMUNICATION

For you to better understand this definition and the process of communication itself, we will examine some of the basic principles of communication that are in operation whenever you attempt to share your internal states with someone else.

There are a few points to keep in mind before we catalog some of the basic principles of communication. First, communication has more characteristics than we can discuss in the next few pages. Just as a description of a forest that mentions only the trees and flowers but omits the wildlife and lakes does not do justice to the entire setting, our inventory is not exhaustive. We, too, are forced to leave out some of the landscape. Second, while the linear nature of language forces us to discuss one principle at a time, keep in mind that in reality the elements of communication continuously interact with one another.

**Communication Is a Dynamic Process.** The statement *communication is a dynamic process* carries more than one meaning. First, it means that communication is an ongoing activity and unending process;[46] it is not fixed. Communication is like a motion picture, not a single snapshot. A word or action does not stay frozen when you communicate; it is immediately replaced with yet another word or action. As participants in communication, you too experience its dynamic nature. You are constantly affected by other people's messages and, as a consequence, are always changing. From the moment of conception through the instant of death (and some cultures believe even after death), you experience an almost endless variety of physical and psychological changes, some too subtle to notice, others too profound to ignore. As you shall see later in the chapter, culture too is dynamic.

**Communication Is Symbolic.** Inherent in our definition of communication is the fact that humans are symbol-making creatures. It is this symbol-making ability that allows for everyday interaction. You employ symbols both verbal (saying "Good morning") and nonverbal (smiling as a greeting) to share your internal states. It is the use of symbols that enables culture to be passed on from generation to generation. Through millions of years of physical evolution, and thousands of years of cultural evolution, you are now able to generate, receive, store, and manipulate symbols. This sophisticated system allows you to use a symbol—be it a sound, a mark on paper, a statue, Braille, a bodily movement, or a painting—to represent something else. Reflect for a moment on the wonderful gift you have that allows you to hear the words "The kittens look like little cotton balls" and, like magic, have an image in your head. Or what about the joy you experience when you are touched by your dearest friend? These two sets of symbols—words and actions—help you let other human beings know how you experience the world and what you think or feel about that world.

In terms of intercultural communication, it is important for you to realize the symbols you use are discretionary and subjective. As Gudykunst and Kim remind us, "The important thing to remember is that symbols are symbols only because a group of people agree to consider them as such. There is not a natural connection between symbols and their referents: the relationships are arbitrary and vary from culture to culture."[47] What is being said here is that although all cultures use symbols, they usually assign their own meanings to the symbols. Not only do Mexicans say *perro* for dog, but the mental image they form when they hear the sound is probably quite different from the one the Chinese may form. In addition to having different meanings for symbols, cultures also use these symbols for different purposes. In North America and much of Europe, the prevalent view is that communication is used to get things done. Trenholm and Jensen manifest this Western orientation when they note, "Communication is a powerful way of regulating and controlling our world."[48] In contrast, people in Japan, Taiwan, and China believe that most members of the culture internalize information and possess a common pool of information, so not much needs to be coded. Because symbols are at the core of communication, we will be discussing them throughout the book.

**Communication Is Systemic.** To say communication is *systemic* means "Communication occurs in particular situations or systems that influence what and how we communicate and what meanings we attach to messages."[49] Put in slightly different terms, communication does not occur in isolation or in a vacuum, but rather is part of a larger system. According to Littlejohn, "Communication always occurs in context, and the nature of communication depends in large measure on this context."[50] What this implies is that setting and environment help determine the words and actions you generate and the meanings you give the symbols produced by other people. Context provides what Shimanoff calls a "prescription that indicates what behavior is obligated, preferred, or prohibited."[51] Dress, language, topic selection, and the like are all adapted to context. For example, under most circumstances, males would not, even in hot weather, attend a university lecture without wearing a shirt. The rules for each context, be it boardroom, classroom, or courtroom, are culturally based and therefore relative. Many of these contextual rules are directly related to your culture. For example, in the business setting, all cultures have stated and unstated rules regarding who takes part in the decision-making process during meetings. In the United States, the rule tells us it is the boss. The simple American maxim "The buck stops here" gives us a clue as to the operational rule regarding decision making in the United States. In Japan, nearly everyone is consulted as part of the decision-making process. The Japanese proverb "Consult everyone, even your knees" demonstrates the Japanese approach to decision making.

When we speak of communication being systemic, we are referring to a host of variables. Let us pause and look at some other elements associated with the systemic nature of communication.

**Location.** People do not act the same way in every environment. Whether in an auditorium, restaurant, or office, the location of your interaction provides guidelines for your behavior. Either consciously or unconsciously, you know the prevailing rules, many of which are rooted in your culture. Nearly all cultures, for example, have religious buildings, but the rules of behavior in those buildings are culturally based. In Mexico, men and women go to church together and remain quiet. In Iran, men and women do not worship together, and chanting instead of silence is the rule.

**Occasion.** The occasion of a communication encounter also controls the behavior of the participants. You know from your own experience that an auditorium can be the occasion for a graduation ceremony, pep rally, convocation, play, dance, or memorial service. Each of these occasions call for distinctly different forms of behavior, and each culture has its own specifications for these behaviors. For example, a solemn U.S. protestant funeral calls for solitude and silence while an Irish wake calls for lively music, dancing, and a great deal of merriment.

**Time.** The influence of time on communication is so subtle that its impact is often overlooked. To understand this concept, you must answer these questions: How do you feel when someone keeps you waiting for a long time? Do you respond to a phone call at 2:00 A.M. the same way you do to one at 2:00 P.M.? Do you find yourself rushing the conversation when you know you have very little time to spend with someone? Your answers to these questions reveal how the clock often controls your actions. Every communication event takes place on a time-space continuum, and the amount of time allotted, whether it is for social conversation or a formal speech, affects that event. Cultures as well as people use time to communicate. In the United States, schedules and time constraints are ever present. As Hall and Hall note, "For Americans, the use of appointment-schedule time reveals how people feel about each other, how significant their business is, and where they rank in the status system."[52] Because time influences communication and the use of it is culture-bound, we treat the topic in greater detail in Chapter 7, which deals with nonverbal communication.

**Number of People.** The number of people with whom you communicate also affects the flow of communication. You know from personal experience that you feel and act differently if you are speaking with one person, in a group, or before a great many people. Cultures also respond to changes in number. For example, people in Japan find group interaction much to their liking, yet they often feel extremely uncomfortable when they have to give a formal public speech.

**Communication Involves Making Inferences.** Because there is no direct mind-to-mind contact between people, you cannot access the thoughts and feelings of other human beings but can only infer what they are experiencing. You make these inferences from a single word, from silence, from long speeches, from simple head nods, and from glances in your direction or when eyes are averted away from you. This characteristic of communication has always frustrated human beings, because, in a very real sense, everyone is isolated from one another by the enclosure of their skin. What you know and feel remains inside of you unless you symbolically express it—this is communication. It is as if you lived in a house with doors and windows that never opened. Perhaps the day will come when one of the futuristic devices from *Star Trek* becomes a reality, and another human being can have direct access to what you are experiencing, but for now you must live in a kind of solitary confinement. An African proverb makes this point figuratively: "The earth is a beehive; we all enter by the same door but live in different cells." Although the inability to have direct mind-to-mind contact is universal, the methods used to adjust to this limitation are culturally based. Some cultures believe that because they share a common pool of history and many similar experiences, they do indeed know what their cultural cohorts are feeling and thinking. Yet in many Western cultures, the lack of direct access to another's mind places great demands on such communication behaviors as asking questions, engaging in self-disclosure, and over-verbalizing.

**Communication Has a Consequence.** Earlier when we spoke of communication being a process we were preparing you for this next principle—a principle that states the act of sending and receiving symbols influences all the involved parties. As West and Turner note, "The process nature of communication also means that much can happen from the beginning of the conversation to the end. People may end up at a very different place once the discussion begins."[53] What West and Turner are saying is that when messages are exchanged something happens to you and your communication partner(s). The responses you have to messages vary in degree and kind. It might help you to visualize your potential responses as forming a continuum (see Figure 1.1). At one end of the continuum lie responses to messages that are overt and easy to understand. Someone sends you a message by asking directions to the library. Your response is to say, "It's on your right." You might even point to the library. The message from the other person has thus produced an overt observable response.

A little farther across the continuum are those messages that produce only a mental response. If someone says to you, "The United States doesn't spend enough money on higher education," and you only think about this statement, you are still responding, but your response does not have to be an observable action.

As you proceed across the continuum, you come to responses that are harder to detect. These are responses to messages you receive by imitating, observing, and interacting with others. Generally, you are not even aware that you are receiving these messages. Your parents act out their gender roles, and you receive messages about your gender role. People greet you by shaking hands instead of hugging, and without being aware of it, you are receiving messages about forms of address.

At the far end of the continuum are the responses to messages that are received unconsciously. That is, your body responds even if your cognitive processes are kept to a minimum. Messages that you receive can alter your glandular secretions, your heart

**FIGURE 1.1** Communication Responses

| 1 | 25 | 50 | 75 | 100 |
|---|---|---|---|---|
| Overt | Covert | Unconscious | Biological | |

rate, or the temperature of your skin, modify pupil size, and trigger a host of other internal responses. These chemical and biological responses are not outwardly observable, and they are the most difficult to classify. They do, however, give credence to our assertion that communication has a consequence. If your internal reactions produce chaos in your system, as is the case with severe stress, you can become ill. Regardless of the content of the message, it should be clear that the act of communication produces change in people.

The response you make to someone's message does not have to be immediate. You can respond minutes, days, or even years later. For example, your second-grade teacher may have asked you to stop throwing rocks at a group of birds. Perhaps the teacher added that the birds were part of a family and were gathering food for their babies. She might also have indicated that birds feel pain just like people. Perhaps twenty years later, you are invited to go quail hunting. You are about to say yes when you remember those words from your teacher and decide not to go. It is important to remember the power of your messages and to consider the ethical consequences of your communication actions. For whether or not you want to grant those consequences, you are changing people each time you exchange messages with them. In Chapter 11, we offer some guidelines that you can employ as you evaluate your ethical responsibilities.

We conclude this section on communication by reminding you of a point that should be obvious by now: *communication is complex,* and becomes even more complex when the cultural dimensions are added. Although all cultures use symbols to share their realities, the specific realities and the symbols employed are often quite different. In one culture you smile in a casual manner as a form of greeting, whereas in another you bow formally in silence, and in yet another you acknowledge your friend with a full embrace.

From our discussion you should now have an understanding of the concept of communication and the role it plays in normal everyday interaction. With this background in mind, we now want to turn your attention to the topic of culture.

# Culture

Moving from communication to culture provides us with a rather seamless transition, for as Hall points out, "Culture is communication and communication is culture."[54] Put into slightly different terms—when looking at communication and culture, it is hard to decide which is the voice and which is the echo. The influence of culture on perception, behavior, and communication can seen in following questions:

- Some people in the Philippines and China put dogs in their ovens, but people in the United States put them on their couches and beds. Why?
- People in Kabul or Kandahar sit on the floor and pray five times each day, but people in Las Vegas sit up all night in front of video poker machines. Why?
- Some people speak Tagalog; others speak English. Why?
- Some people paint and decorate their entire bodies, but others spend millions of dollars painting and decorating only their faces. Why?
- Some people talk to God, but others have God talk to them. And still others say there is no God. Why?

The general answer to all of these questions is the same: a major reason people learn to think, feel, believe, and act as they do is the messages that have been communicated to them—messages that bear the stamp of culture. Granting that culture is not the only stimulus behind your behavior, its omnipresent quality makes it the most powerful. As Hall concluded, "There is not one aspect of human life that is not touched and altered by culture."[55] In a very real sense your culture is part of who you are. What makes culture so unique is that you share your culture with other people who have been exposed to similar experiences. Hofstede clearly underscored this point when he noted, "Culture is to a human collective what personality is to an individual."[56] Nolan reaffirms this idea when he suggests that culture is a *group worldview*, the way of organizing the world that a particular society has created over time. This framework or web of meaning allows the members of that society to make sense of themselves, their world, and their experiences in that world.[57]

Notice that Nolan is talking about making sense of the world. Remember, you are born with all the anatomy and physiology needed to live in the world, but you are also born into a world without meaning. You do not arrive in this world knowing how to dress, what toys to play with, what to eat, which gods to worship, what to strive for, or how to spend your money and your time. Culture is both teacher and textbook. From how much eye contact you employ in conversations to explanations of why you get sick, culture plays a dominant role in your life. As we have noted, this book is about how different cultures produce different lives. In short, when cultures differ, communication practices also differ, as Smith pointed out:

> In modern society different people communicate in different ways, as do people in different societies around the world; and the way people communicate is the way they live. It is their culture. Who talks with whom? How? And about what? These are questions of communication and culture. A Japanese geisha and a New England librarian send and receive different messages on different channels and in different networks. When the elements of communication differ or change, the elements of culture differ or change. Communication and culture are inseparable.[58]

Because culture conditions you toward one particular mode of communication over another, it is imperative that you understand how culture operates as a first step toward improving intercultural communication. Although we will try to convince you that culture is a powerful force in how you see the world and interact in that world, later in the chapter we will remind you that a combination of elements contributes to the manner in which you communicate. But for now let us primarily focus on culture as we (1) *explain why cultures develop*, (2) *highlight the essential features of culture*, (3) *define culture*, and (4) *discuss the major components of culture*.

## THE BASIC FUNCTIONS OF CULTURE

In its most basic explanation, cultures exist so that people, living collectively, can adapt to their surroundings. As Triandis notes, culture "functions to improve the adaptation of members of the culture to a particular ecology, and it includes the knowledge that people need to have in order to function effectively in their social environment."[59] A more detailed explanation as to the functions of culture is offered by Sowell:

> Cultures exist to serve the vital, practical requirements of human life—to structure a society so as to perpetuate the species, to pass on the hard-learned knowledge and experience of generations past and centuries past to the young and inexperienced in order to spare the

next generation the costly and dangerous process of learning everything all over again from scratch through trial and error—including fatal errors.[60]

What is being said is that culture serves the basic need of laying out a predictable world in which each of you is firmly grounded and thus enables you to make sense of your surroundings. As Haviland notes, "In humans, it is culture that sets the limits on behavior and guides it along predictable paths."[61] The English writer Fuller echoed the same idea in rather simple terms when he wrote two hundred years ago, "Culture makes all things easy." It makes things easy because culture shields people from the unknown by offering them a blueprint for all of life's activities. While people in all cultures might deviate from this blueprint, they at least know what their culture expects from them. Try to imagine a single day in your life without having the guidelines of your culture. From how to earn a living to a systematic economic system, to how to greet strangers, to explanations of illness, to how to find a mate, culture provides you with structure. We might even go so far as to agree with Harris that "our primary mode of biological adaptation is culture, not anatomy."[62]

Anthropologists now suggest that in addition to making the world a less perplexing place, cultures have now evolved to the point where they are people's primary means of satisfying three types of needs: basic needs (food, shelter, physical protection), derived needs (organization of work, distribution of food, defense, social control), and integrative needs (psychological security, social harmony, purpose in life).[63]

## THE ELEMENTS OF CULTURE

Before we define culture, it is important that we pause and answer the following question: *What elements mark a collection of people as a culture?* We will answer this question by looking at five constituents found in every culture. Understanding these elements will enable you to appreciate the notion that while all cultures share a common set of components, these components often distinguish one culture from another.

**History.** All cultures seem to believe in the idea that history is a kind of chart that guides its members into the future. What is interesting about a culture's history is that, like most of the important elements of culture, it gets transmitted from generation to generation. These stories of the past offer the members of a culture part of their identity while highlighting the culture's origins, what is deemed important, and the accomplishments of which it can be proud. As you shall see in the next chapter, while all cultures pass on a history that helps shape their members, each history is unique to a particular culture and carries a specific cultural message. The "lessons" of the Spanish conquest of Mexico tell a different tale than the building of the Great Wall of China or the American Revolution.

**Religion.** Another feature of all cultures is their religion. More specifically, according to Parkes, Laungani, and Young, all cultures possess "a dominant, organized religion within which salient beliefs and activities (rites, rituals, taboos, and ceremonies) can be given meaning and legitimacy."[64] The influence of religion can be seen in the entire fabric of a culture. Both consciously and unconsciously religion impacts everything from business practices (the puritan work ethic) to politics (the link between Islam and government) to individual behavior (a code of ethics). Because religion is so powerful and pervasive we shall examine it in greater detail in Chapter 3.

**Values.** Values are another feature of every culture. The connection between values and culture is so strong that it is hard to talk about one without the other. As Macionis notes, values are "culturally defined standards of desirability, goodness, and beauty that serve as broad guidelines for social living."[65] The key word in any discussion of cultural values is "guidelines." In other words, values help determine how people ought to behave. To the extent that cultural values differ, you can expect that intercultural communication participants will tend to exhibit and to anticipate different behaviors under similar circumstances. For example, while all cultures value the elderly, the degree of this value is often very different as you move from culture to culture. In the Korean and Native American cultures, the elderly are highly respected and revered. They are even sought out for advice and counsel. This is, of course, in stark contrast to the United States, where the emphasis is on youth. We will return to a detailed comparison of cultural values in Chapter 4.

**Social Organizations.** Another feature found in all cultures is what we call "social organizations." These organizations (sometimes referred to as social systems or social structures) represent the various social units contained within the culture. Such units and institutions—including the family, government, schools, and tribes—help the members of the culture organize their lives. These social systems establish communication networks and regulate norms of personal, familial and social conduct.[66] How these organizations function and the norms they advance are unique to each culture. Nolan underscores the nature of these organizations in the following illustration:

> Social structures reflect our culture, for example, whether we have kings and queens, or presidents and prime ministers. Within our social structure, furthermore, culture assigns roles to the various players—expectations about how individuals will behave, what they will stand for, and even how they will dress.[67]

So important are the social organizations within a culture that we will make them the central focus of the next chapter.

**Language.** Language is yet another feature that is common to all cultures. As we shall see later in this chapter, and again in Chapter 6, not only does language allow the members of a culture to share ideas, feelings, and information, but it is also one of the chief methods for the transmission of culture. Whether it is English, Swahili, Chinese, or French, most words, meanings, grammar, and syntax bear the identification mark of a specific culture.

## DEFINING CULTURE

The preceding discussion of the functions and features of culture should enable you to see how culture is ubiquitous, complex, all-pervasive, and—most of all—difficult to define. As Harrison and Huntington note, "The term 'culture,' of course, has had multiple meanings in different disciplines and different contexts."[68] The elusive nature of the term is perhaps best reflected in the fact that as early as 1952 a review of the anthropology literature revealed 164 different definitions of the word culture.[69] As Lonner and Malpass point out, these definitions "range from complex and fancy definitions to simple ones such as 'culture is the programming of the mind' or 'culture is the human-made part of the environment.'"[70] For our purposes, we are concerned with a definition that contains the recurring theme of how culture and communication are linked. A definition that meets our needs is one advanced by Triandis:

> Culture is a set of human-made objective and subjective elements that in the past have increased the probability of survival and resulted in satisfaction for the participants in an ecological niche, and thus became shared among those who could communicate with each other because they had a common language and they lived in the same time and place.[71]

We like this definition because it includes what Harrison and Huntington call the "subjective" elements of culture—elements such as "values, attitudes, beliefs, orientations, and underlying assumptions prevalent among people in a society."[72] Think for a moment of all the subjective cultural beliefs and values you hold that influence your interpretation of the world and interactions in it. Your views about the American flag, work, immigration, freedom, age, ethics, dress, property rights, etiquette, healing and health, death and mourning, play, law, individualism, magic and superstition, modesty, sex, status differentiation, courtship, formality and informality, bodily adornment, and the like are all part of your cultural membership.

## Characteristics of Culture

Regardless of how many definitions we could have examined, there would have been a great deal of agreement concerning the major characteristics of culture. Examining these characteristics will help you become a better communicator for two reasons.

*Much of culture is transmitted unconsciously by observation and imitation.*

© Gloria Thomas

First, as we move through these characteristics, the strong connection between culture and communication will become apparent. You will discover that culture deals with matters of substance that influence communication. As Huntington notes, "The heart of culture involves language, religion, values, traditions, and customs."[73]

Second, this might be the first time you have been asked to examine your own culture or been exposed to the theory of culture. As Brislin points out, "People do not frequently talk about their own culture or the influence that culture has on their behavior."[74] People are often so close to their culture that there is no need to examine or discuss it, and because much of human behavior is habitual, they are unaware of the influence it has on their perceptions and interaction patterns. Remember, most of culture is in the taken-for-granted realm and below the conscious level. Learning about culture can therefore be a stimulating awakening as you give meaning to your actions and the actions of others. Shapiro offered much the same pep talk when he wrote:

> The discovery of culture, the awareness that it shapes and molds our behavior, our values and even our ideas, the recognition that it contains some element of the arbitrary, can be a startling or an illuminating experience.[75]

## CULTURE IS LEARNED

We begin with perhaps that most important characteristic of culture—*it is learned*. From the moment of birth to the end of your life, you seek to define the world that impinges on your senses. This idea is often difficult to comprehend, for most of you cannot remember a world without definitions and meanings. Yet perhaps you can imagine what a confusing place this world must be to a newborn infant. After living in a peaceful environment, the child, with but a brief transition, confronts sights, sounds, tastes, and other sensations that, at this stage of life, have no meaning. It must be, as the psychologist William James noted, a bubbling, babbling mass of confusion that greets the newborn.

As you move from word to word, event to event, and person to person, you seek meaning in everything. The meanings you give to these experiences are learned and culturally based. In some ways, this entire book is about how different cultures teach their members to define the circumstances and people that confront them. Without the advantages of learning from those who lived before, you would not have culture. In fact, "the group's knowledge stored up (in memories, books, and objects) for future use" is at the core of the concept of culture.[76] You are born with basic needs—needs that create and shape behavior—but how you go about meeting those needs and developing behaviors to cope with them is learned. As Bates and Plog note:

> Whether we feed ourselves by growing yams or hunting wild game or by herding camels and raising wheat, whether we explain a thunderstorm by attributing it to meteorological conditions or to a fight among the gods—such things are determined by what we learn as part of our enculturation.[77]

The term *enculturation* denotes the total process of learning one's culture. More specifically, enculturation is, as Hoebel and Frost say, "conscious or unconscious conditioning occurring within that process whereby the individual, as child and adult, achieves competence in a particular culture."[78] In social psychology and sociology, the term *socialization* is often used synonymously with enculturation. Regardless of which word is applied, the idea is the same. From infancy, members of a culture learn their patterns of behavior and ways of thinking until most of them become internalized and habitual.

When we speak of learning we are using the word in a rather broad sense. We are talking about learning that is both informal and formal.[79] *Informal learning* normally takes place through interaction (your parents kiss you and you learn about kissing—whom, when, and where to kiss), observation (you watch your mom do the laundry and your dad mow the lawn and you learn about gender roles—what a man does, what a woman does), and imitation (you laugh at the same jokes your parents laugh at and you learn about humor).

The *formal learning* of the culture is far more structured and often left to the institutions of the culture such as schools and churches. When a school system teaches American history or mathematics, they are giving the members of culture the tools the culture deems important. When a child has a Sunday school lesson focusing on the Ten Commandments, he or she is learning about ethical behavior. As you might suspect, it is often difficult to distinguish between informal and formal learning.

Because culture influences you from the instant you are born, you are rarely aware of many of the messages that it sends. As Keesing says, "It is a tenet of cultural anthropology that culture tends to be unconscious."[80] This unconscious or hidden dimension of culture leads many researchers to claim that culture is invisible. Ruben, for example, writes that "the presence of culture is so subtle and pervasive that it simply goes unnoticed. It's there now, it's been there as long as anyone can remember, and few of us have reason to think much about it."[81] Most of you would have a difficult time pointing to a specific event or experience that taught you about such things as direct eye contact, your use of silence and space, the importance of attractiveness, your view of aging, your ability to speak one language instead of another, and your preference for activity over meditation or for one mode of dealing with conflict over another. While you would readily recognize that you had to learn how to solve a science problem, you are apt to overlook the lessons of culture that are far more subtle. Reflect for a moment on the learning that is taking place in the following examples: A little boy in the United States whose grandfather tells him to shake hands when he is introduced to a friend of the family is learning good manners. An Arab father who reads the Koran to his one-day-old son is teaching him about God. An Indian child who lives in a home where the women eat after the men is learning gender roles. A Jewish child who helps conduct the Passover ceremony is learning about traditions. An Egyptian child who is told by his uncle that his behavior brings shame to his family is learning cultural values. A Japanese girl who attends tea ceremony classes is learning about patience. A fourth-grade student watching a film on George Washington crossing the Delaware River is learning about patriotism and fortitude. In these examples, people are learning their culture.

A number of points should be clear by now. First, learning cultural perceptions, rules, and behaviors usually goes on without your being aware of it. Second, the essential messages of a culture get reinforced and repeated. And third, you learn your culture from a large variety of sources. Family, church, and state are the three most powerful carriers of culture. We will examine these three in the next few chapters, and in Chapter 9 we discuss how schools are also a conduit for culture. But for now, let us touch on some of the more invisible "instructors" and "instructions" that are part of every culture.

**Learning Culture Through Proverbs.** In nearly every culture, proverbs—communicated in colorful and vivid language—offer an important set of values for members to follow. Proverbs are so important to the learning process that there is even a German proverb that notes "A country can be judged by the quality of its proverbs."

Proverbs are learned easily and repeated with great regularity. Because they are brief (a line or two), their power as a teacher is often overlooked. Yet many great Chinese philosophers such as Confucius, Mencius, Chung Tzu, and Lao-tzu used proverbs and maxims to express their thoughts to their disciples—thoughts that still endure in the Chinese culture. These words of wisdom survive so that each generation learns what a culture deems significant. As Sellers tells you, "Proverbs reunite the listener with his or her ancestors."[82] Seidensticker notes that "they say things that people think important in ways that people remember. They express common concerns."[83] Hence, "proverbs are a compact treatise on the values of culture."[84]

Because all people, regardless of their culture, share common experiences, many of the same proverbs appear throughout the world. For example, in nearly every culture some degree of thrift and hard work is stressed. Hence, in Germany the proverb states, "One who does not honor the penny is not worthy of the dollar." In the United States people are told, "A penny saved is a penny earned." In Japan and China, where silence is valued, you find the Japanese proverb that states, "The quacking duck is the first to get shot" and the Chinese proverb "Loud thunder brings little rain." However, in spite of numerous universal proverbs, there are also thousands of proverbs that cultures use to teach lessons that are unique to that particular culture. The importance of proverbs as a reflection of a culture is underscored by the fact that "interpreters at the United Nations prepare themselves for their extremely sensitive job by learning proverbs of the foreign language" they will be translating.[85] As Mieder notes, "Studying proverbs can offer insights into a culture's worldview regarding such matters as education, law, business, and marriage."[86] They are, as Mieder adds, "the true voice of the people."[87]

The following are a few of the hundreds of proverbs and sayings from the United States, each of which attempts to teach an important value held by the dominant culture.

**Strike while the iron is hot.** *He who hesitates is lost.* Both of these proverbs underscore the idea that, in the United States, people who take quick action are highly valued.

**Actions speak louder than words.** As we note later in this chapter, Americans are a "doing" culture; hence, activity and getting things done are important to the dominant culture.

**God helps those who help themselves.** *Pull yourself up by your bootstraps.* These sayings call attention to the strong belief in America that people should show individual initiative.

**A man's home is his castle.** This expression not only tells us about the value of privacy, but it also demonstrates the male orientation in the United States by implying the home belongs to the man.

**The squeaky wheel gets the grease.** In the United States, people are encouraged to be direct, speak up, and make sure their views are heard.

The following are some teaching proverbs from places other than the United States. You may see some of these proverbs again elsewhere in this book as we use them to explain the beliefs, values, and communication behavior of the cultures from which they are drawn.

**One does not make the wind but is blown by it.** This saying, found in many Asian cultures, suggests that people are guided by fate rather than by their own devices.

**Sweep only in front of your own door.** This German proverb reflects the very private nature of the Germans and their strong dislike of gossip. There is a somewhat similar proverb found in the Swedish culture: *He who stirs another's porridge often burns his own.*

**A zebra does not despise its stripes.** From the Maasai of Africa, this saying expresses the value of accepting things as they are. There is a similar proverb found in the Mexican culture: *I dance to the tune that is played.*

**A man's tongue is his sword.** With this saying, Arabs are taught to value words and use them in a powerful and forceful manner.

**Those who know do not speak and those who speak do not know.** This famous doctrine, in the *Analects* of Confucius, stressing silence over talk, is very different from the advice give in the previous Arab proverb.

**Even in paradise it's not good to be alone.** This Jewish proverb reaffirms the collective nature of that culture and the importance placed on interaction. The Mexican culture, with its long tradition of collectivism and interaction among friends and family, has a similar proverb. *Conversation is food for the soul.*

**When spider webs unite they can tie up a lion.** This Ethiopian proverb teaches the importance of collectivism and group solidarity. In the Japanese culture the same idea is expressed with the following proverb: *A single arrow is easily broken, but not in a bunch.* For the Yoruba of Africa, the same lesson is taught with the proverb that notes, *A single hand cannot lift the calabash to the head.*

**A harsh word dropped from the tongue cannot be brought back by a coach and six horses.** This Chinese proverb stresses the importance of monitoring your anger. The Japanese have a similar proverb regarding anger: *The spit aimed at the sky comes back to one.* The Koreans, who also believe that anger should be kept in check, offer the following proverb: *Kick a stone in anger and you harm your own foot.*

**Learning Culture Through Folktales, Legends, and Myths.** While folktales, legends, and myths are slightly different, we use the three words interchangeably because they all tell stories that are intended to transmit the important aspects of the culture. Anthropologists Nanda and Warms highlight the importance of this form of cultural learning as follows:

> Folktales and storytelling usually have an important moral, revealing which cultural values are approved and which are condemned. The audience for folktales is always led, through the ways the tale is told, to know which characters and attributes are a cause for ridicule or scorn and which characters and attributes are to be admired.[88]

Haviland confirms that the subject matter of these cultural stories concerns "the fundamentals of human existence: where we and everything in our world came from, why we are here, and where we are going."[89] Whether it be Pinocchio's nose growing larger because of his lies, Columbus being glorified because he was daring, Captain Ahab's heroics as he seeks to overcome the power of nature, Abraham Lincoln learning to read by drawing letters on a shovel by the fireside, or Robin Hood helping the poor, folklore constantly reinforces fundamental values.

As noted, every culture has hundreds of tales, each stressing a fundamental value. Americans revere the tough, independent, fast-shooting cowboy of the Old West; the English admiration of good manners, courtly behavior, and dignity is reflected in *The*

*Canterbury Tales*; the Japanese learn about the importance of duty, obligation, and loyalty in the ancient story of "The Tale of the Forty-Seven Ronin"; the Sioux Indians use the legend of "Pushing Up the Sky" to teach what people can accomplish if they work together. And the Chinese teach the folly of impatience by telling the tale of a farmer who did not like the slow growth of his plants so he tugged on them an inch each day until he proceeded to uproot them.

When it comes to superhuman heroes, Greeks learn about Hercules, Jews learn about Samson, the Norwegians learn about Thor, and Americans learn about Superman. In Zaire, children are told the Myth of Invincibility. In this story young boys learn that if they wrap green vines around their head, the enemies' weapons cannot hurt them.[90] Shiite Muslims pass on a seventh-century tale of how the prophet Mohammed's grandson, knowing he was going to die, fought to his death. In the story of Hanukkah it is told how, in the second century, a small band of Jews defeated a much larger army.

Legends, folktales, and myths do more than accent cultural values: "They confront cosmic questions about the world as a whole."[91] In addition, they can tell you about specific details of life that might be important to a group of people. Writing about Native American myths and legends, Erdoes and Ortiz make the following point concerning what stories can tell us about what was, and is, important to the Native American culture:

> They are also magic lenses through which we can glimpse social orders and daily life: how families were organized, how political structures operated, how men caught fish, how religious ceremonies felt to the people who took part, how power was divided between men and women, how food was prepared, how honor in war was celebrated.[92]

As you have seen, myths, folktales, and legends are found in every culture and are useful tools for teaching some major cultural values. Perhaps their most significant contribution is that they deal with the ideas that matter most to a culture—ideas about life, death, relationships, nature, and the like. Campbell maintains that "myths are stories of our search through the ages for truth, for meaning, for significance. We all need to tell our story and to understand our story."[93] Because myths offer clues into culture, Campbell urges us not only to understand our story but also to read other people's myths.[94] We strongly concur with Campbell—when you study the myths of a culture, you are studying what is important to that culture.

**Learning Culture Through Art.** A trip to any museum in the world quickly reveals how art, in addition to being a creative expression of beauty, is also a method of passing on the culture. As Haviland and his associates point out, "art often reflects a society's collective ideas, values, and concerns."[95] Nanda underscores this important idea, noting that "art is a symbolic way of communicating. One of the most important functions of art is to communicate, display, and reinforce important cultural themes and values."[96] The Chinese, for centuries, have seen the link between art and the transmission of cultural values. According to the art historian Gombrich, the Chinese have long "thought of art as a means of reminding people of the great examples of virtue in the golden ages of the past."[97]

You can learn about one of those Chinese virtues by examining the subject matter of Chinese paintings. In Asian cultures, most art depicts objects, animals, and landscapes, less often than focusing on people. It even attempts to highlight spiritual concerns. According to Hunter and Sexton, Chinese art often represents "Buddhist and Taoist concerns with the mind in meditation, with the relative insignificance of human striving in the great cosmos, and with the beauty of nature."[98] American and European

*While Western art focuses on the individual, much of Asian art is concerned with various aspects of nature.*

art, however, often emphasizes people. This difference reflects a difference in views: Asians believe that nature is more powerful and important than a single individual, whereas Americans and Europeans consider people as the center of the universe. In addition, in Western art, the artist tries to create a personal message. This is not the case with most Asian artists. As Campbell notes, "Such ego-oriented thinking is alien completely to the Eastern life, thought, and religiosity."[99] The rule of the Asian artist is not to "innovate or invent."[100]

As we already indicated, art is a relevant symbol, a forceful teacher, and an avenue for cultural values. A few more examples will further illustrate this point. We need only look at the art on totem poles to see what matters to Native Americans of the northwest U.S. The carvings on these poles tell the story of a people who are concerned about their ancestors, family, history, identity, wildlife and nature.[101] Keesing adds that Native American carvings show the relationships "between humans and animals, plants, and inanimate objects."[102] This emphasis on art to tell stories is very different when compared to the art of Islam. Since the Koran forbids the depiction of human figures, it is calligraphy that is perceived as fine art.[103]

It should be clear from our brief discussion of art in culture that Haviland and his colleagues are correct when they write, "Through the cross-cultural study of art and creativity, we discover much about different worldviews, religious beliefs, political ideas, social values, kinship structures, economic relationships, and historical memory as well."[104]

**Learning Culture Through Mass Media.** When we speak of mass media we are talking about those forms of media that are created, designed, and used to reach very large audiences. The impact of these devices on a population is now common knowledge. As Thompson points out, the mass media do much more than supply entertainment:

> Few people would deny that the nature of cultural experience in modern societies has been profoundly affected by the development of mass communication. Books, magazines and newspapers, radio, television, the cinema, records, tapes and videos: these and other forms of mass communication occupy a central role in our lives.[105]

When we add the Internet with its millions of websites, as well as CDs, e-books, and even video games, to Thompson's list you can begin to appreciate the power of media on shaping a culture. While granting the importance of printed media and the computer, it is television that is most influential. Whether it is Arab television reporting the news of Iraq to millions of people, or young children in the United States watching *Teletubbies*, television contributes to what Williams calls "mass social learning."[106] In the United States, where children average eight and a half hours of television exposure a day, it is easy to see how these images affect attitudes toward sex, leisure time, and people of different ethnic, gender, and/or age groups. Delgado offers an excellent summary of the power of mass media by noting that they "help constitute our daily lives by shaping our experiences and providing the content for much of what we talk about (and how we talk) at the interpersonal level."[107]

As we have said elsewhere, cultural messages are repeated, reinforced, and come from various sources. We are now looking at media as one of those sources. While it is difficult to make a direct cause and effect link, many social critics, including the American Psychological Association, believe that "violent programs on television lead to aggressive behavior by children and teenagers who watch those programs."[108] In the United States, films, police stories, and many documentaries glorify violence. The language we use in sports mirrors and sanctions violence. Watching a sporting event on television, you'll hear statements like "he has that killer instinct," "he is a headhunter," "it's war on that court," and "they are playing smash defense."

In the United States you can also find countless mass media examples that stress the importance of individualism—a key American value. Think for a moment of the thousands of ways you have been told the importance of not being like everyone else. Burger King says "Sometimes you just have to break the rules." Dodge sells its trucks by telling you "Rules are for fools," and Ralph Lauren pronounces "There are no boundaries."

We conclude our description of the first characteristic of culture by reminding you of two key points. First, most of the behaviors we label as cultural are automatic and invisible and are usually performed without you being aware of them. For example, in American culture, women smile more often than men,[109] a behavior learned unconsciously and performed almost habitually. Second, it is important that we remind you that we have mentioned only some of the many ways we learn our culture. Space constraints have forced us to leave out many subtle yet powerful "teachers." For example, in every culture sports is much more than simple play. As Nanda and Warms tell us, "Football in America and bull fighting in Spain are both popular because they illustrate important themes of the respective cultures. They are exciting in part because they tell stories loaded with cultural meaning."[110] According to Gannon, we can see these stories and their cultural meanings in everything from Japanese gardens to Parisian gothic architecture, from German symphony to Italian opera.[111] These cultural metaphors represent and teach, according to Gannon "the underlying values expressive of the culture itself."[112]

## Culture Is Shared

As you saw in our first characteristic, the means of transmitting the culture can take a variety of forms (proverbs, stories, art) and can have numerous "carriers" (family, peers, media, schools, church), but the key elements of culture (values, ideas, perception) must be shared by other members of the culture. This means that "culture is the common denominator that makes the actions of individuals intelligible to the other members of society."[113] Discovering those common behaviors is what this book is all about.

## CULTURE IS TRANSMITTED FROM GENERATION TO GENERATION

The American philosopher Thoreau once wrote, "All the past is here." As it regards culture, Thoreau is correct. For, if a culture is to endure, it must make certain that its crucial messages and elements are not only shared, but they also must be passed on to future generations. In this way the past becomes the present and helps prepare for the future. As Brislin said, "If there are values considered central to a society that have existed for many years, these must be transmitted from one generation to another."[114] According to Charon, this process of transmitting culture can be seen as a kind of "social inheritance."[115] Charon elaborates on this idea when he writes:

> Culture is a social inheritance; it consists of ideas that may have developed long before we were born. Our society, for example, has a history reaching beyond any individual's life, the ideas developed over time are taught to each generation and "truth" is anchored in interaction by people long before dead.[116]

The bonding together of generations reveals the clear connection between culture and communication. It is communication that makes culture a continuous process, for once cultural habits, principles, values, attitudes, and the like are formulated, they are communicated to each member of the culture. So strong is the need for a culture to bind each generation to past and future generations that, Keesing says, "Any break in the learning chain would lead to a culture's disappearance."[117]

# Culture Is Based on Symbols

All we have said to this point leads to the characteristic of culture that states *culture is based on symbols*. The portability of symbols allows people to package and store them as well as transmit them. The mind, books, pictures, films, religious writings, videos, computer disks, and the like enable a culture to preserve what it deems to be important and worthy of transmission. This makes each individual, regardless of his or her generation, heir to a massive repository of information that has been gathered and maintained in anticipation of his or her entry into the culture. Culture is therefore accumulative, historical, and perceivable

While cultural symbols can take a host of forms, encompassing gestures, dress, objects, flags, or religious icons, "the most important symbolic aspect of culture is language—using words to represent objects and ideas."[118] Notice the link between symbols and culture in the definition of the word *symbol* advanced by Macionis: "A symbol is anything that carries a particular meaning recognized by people who share culture."[119] Symbols conveyed through language are so important to a culture that the anthropologist Kluckhohn once wrote, "Human culture without language is unthinkable."[120] It is language that enables you to share the speculations, observations, facts, experiments, and wisdom accumulated over thousands of years—what the linguist Weinberg called "the grand insights of geniuses which, transmitted through symbols, enable us to span the learning of centuries."[121] Through language it is "possible to learn from cumulative, shared experience."[122] Bates and Plog offer this excellent summary of the importance of language to culture:

> Language thus enables people to communicate what they would do if such-and-such happened, to organize their experiences into abstract categories ("a happy occasion," for instance, or an "evil omen"), and to express thoughts never spoken before. Morality, religion, philosophy, literature, science, economics, technology, and numerous other areas of human knowledge and belief—along with the ability to learn about and manipulate them—all depend on this type of higher-level communication.[123]

# Culture Is Dynamic

The Greek philosopher Heraclitus might well have been talking about culture when, more than two thousand years ago, he observed: "You cannot step twice into the same river, for other waters are continually flowing in." What he was telling us then is true even today—cultures do not exist in a vacuum; because of "other waters continually flowing in," they are subject to change. As Ethington notes, cultures are in a never-ending "process of reinvention."[124] That reinvention stems from a host of reasons. Haviland and his associates write of that reinvention in the following observation: "Changes take place in response to such events as population growth, technological innovations, environmental crisis, the intrusion of outsiders, or modifications of behavior and values within the culture."[125]

While cultures have been subject to change since the earliest hunter-gatherers moved from place to place, never in recorded history have these changes been so widespread. As we demonstrated earlier, because of the spread of Western capitalism and the advancement of information technology systems, cultures are being bombarded with new ideas that are often being presented by a host of strangers. These "foreigners" may live next door or across the globe, but contact and change, whether in small increments or dramatic bursts, are now inevitable. Cultures are subject to fluctuations and seldom remain constant. Luckmann makes this point in the following manner:

> Although culture provides strength and stability, it is never static. Cultural groups face continual challenges from such powerful forces as environmental upheavals, plagues, wars, migration, the influx of immigrants, and the growth of new technologies. As a result, cultures change and evolve over time.[126]

We conclude this section on the dynamic nature of culture by pointing out that although many aspects of culture are subject to change, *the deep structure of a culture resists major alterations,* or as Beamer and Varner note, "Culture appears to remain unchanged at deep levels and only change on the surface. This is front-stage behavior, where popular culture thrives."[127] Changes in dress, food, transportation, entertainment, housing, and the like are normally compatible with the existing values of the culture. However, values associated with such things as ethics and morals, work and leisure, definitions of freedom, the importance of the past, religious practices, the pace of life, and attitudes toward gender and age are so deeply embedded in a culture that they persist generation after generation—a point Barnlund makes when he writes:

> The spread of Buddhism, Islam, Christianity, and Confucianism did not homogenize the societies they enveloped. It was usually the other way around: societies insisted on adapting the religions to their own cultural traditions.[128]

In the United States, studies conducted on American values show that most contemporary core values are similar to the values of the last two hundred years. In short, when assessing the degree of change within a culture, you must always consider what is changing. Do not be fooled because people in Beijing dress much like people in Paris or New York or that millions of Japanese watch American baseball to cheer for their "hometown" hero—these are "front stage behaviors." Most of what we call culture is below the surface, like an iceberg. You can observe the tip, but there are other dimensions and depths that you cannot see—that is the subterranean level of culture.

## Culture Is an Integrated System

Throughout this chapter we have isolated various pieces of culture and talked about them as if they were discrete units. The nature of language makes it impossible to do otherwise; yet in reality, culture functions as an integrated whole—it is, like communication, systemic. In fact, it has been said that if you touch one part of a culture you touch all that culture. The reason is that culture "is composed of parts that are related to each other."[129] The interrelationship of these various parts is so important that Haviland states, "All aspects of culture must be reasonably well integrated in order to function properly."[130]

Think of all the important ingredients of culture that are functioning when families take children to church, where they learn some of the key cultural values that they act out at school and even outside in the playground. As Hall said, "You touch a culture in one place and everything else is affected."[131] Values toward materialism will influence family size, the work ethic, spiritual pursuits, and the like. A complex example of the interconnectedness of cultural elements is the civil rights movement in the United States, which began in the 1960s. This movement has brought about changes in housing patterns, discrimination practices, educational opportunities, the legal system, career opportunities, and even communication. This one aspect of culture has altered American attitudes, values, and behaviors.

We conclude this section on the characteristics of culture by reminding you that the pull of culture begins at birth and continues throughout life. Using the standard language of her time (sexist by today's standards), anthropologist Ruth Benedict offered an excellent explanation of why culture is such a powerful influence on all our lives:

> The life history of the individual is first and foremost an accommodation to the patterns and standards traditionally handed down in his community. From the moment of his birth the customs into which he is born shape his experience and behavior. By the time he can talk, he is the little creature of his culture, and by the time he is grown and able to take part in its activities, its habits are his habits, its beliefs his beliefs, its impossibilities his impossibilities. Every child that is born into his group will share them with him, and no child born into the opposite side of the globe can ever achieve the thousandth part.[132]

The important point to take away from our entire discussion of culture is eloquently expressed in the following sentence: "God gave to every people a cup, a cup of clay, and from this cup they drank life. . . . They all dipped in the water, but their cups were different."[133] This book is about how those "different cups" influence how people perceive the world and behave in that world.

# Studying Intercultural Communication

If we have been successful in our endeavors thus far, you have been convinced of two important points. First, learning how to become successful in your future intercultural interactions is a necessary and worthwhile pursuit. Second, culture plays a significant role in how people perceive reality and communicate that reality. In our zeal to convince you of these two premises, we might have unintentionally been guilty of overstating the significance of culture in human behavior. Hence, we shall pause for a moment and alert you to some of the problems you will face as you make culture the centerpiece in the study of intercultural communication. Specifically, we will examine problems associated with (1) *the uniqueness of each individual*, (2) *stereotyping*, and (3) *objectivity*.

## INDIVIDUAL UNIQUENESS

The English statesman Lord Chesterfield once wrote, "There never were, since the creation of the world, two cases exactly parallel." He might have also said that there have never been two people exactly alike. The reason is simple: behavior is shaped by a multitude of sources, and culture is just one of those sources. Or put in slightly different terms, *we are more than our cultures*. Although culture offers people a common frame of reference, they are not captives of their culture subject to all the lessons of that culture. In fact, it is even a myth to think of people in terms of being blank slates. As Pinker points out, "The mind cannot be a blank slate, because blank slates don't do anything."[134] Instead, people are thinking, feeling individuals whose biology and ecology play crucial roles in their social behavior.[135] Consequently, the values and behaviors of a particular culture may not be the values and behaviors of all the individuals within that culture. Reflect for a moment on all the potential responses that could be generated by the simple phrase "going to the racetrack." It can elicit a wide variety of responses depending on the listeners' background. One person might believe horse racing is an evil form of gambling, while another maintains that horse racing is animal abuse, yet another, reading the same words, could respond by saying, "I love horse races." As Sitaram and Cogdell remind you, "Reality is not the same for all people."[136] One reason it is not the same is that your genetic makeup, your social group experiences, your gender, age, individual and family history, political affiliation, perceptions of others, current circumstances, and many other factors are at play every moment of your life. As the Roman playwright Terence noted more than two thousand years ago, "As many men, so many minds; every one his own way." Because every person has their own way, you must be cautious and prudent when making cultural generalizations. What we said earlier is worth repeating—as you study intercultural communication, always keep in mind that *people are more than their culture*.

## STEREOTYPING

Scarborough clearly highlights our next problem when he writes, "When we generalize about a group of people, as we do in describing a culture, we confront the issue of stereotyping."[137] While we would grant that stereotyping can be a problem when studying intercultural communication, you can take certain precautions to minimize the damaging effects of stereotyping. First, cultural generalizations must be viewed as approximations, not as absolute representations. Your personal experiences have taught you that people often do not follow the prescribed and accepted modes of cultural behavior. You may read about conformity as a trait of the Japanese people and while in Tokyo see a group of motorcycle riders dressed like the Hell's Angels. In instances such as these, remember the admonition of the English writer Robert Burton: "No rule is so general, which admits not some exception."

Second, when you make generalizations they should deal with what Scarborough refers to as "core values."[138] These are the values and behaviors that occur with enough regularity, and over a long enough period of time, that they clearly mark the members of a particular culture. If you examine the dominant culture of the United States, you would have little trouble noticing the importance of the individual. In the same manner, you could begin to get insight into the role of women in Saudi Arabia by noticing the complete absence of women in public demonstrations. What is true of the two core cultural values used in these examples is also a worthy guideline for generalizing about behavior. While there might be exceptions, greeting behavior in Mexico (men embracing) is different from greeting behavior in India (men bowing) or in the United States (men shaking hands). These kinds of behavior are recognizable because of their consistency over an extended period of time—usually involving generation after generation.

## OBJECTIVITY

Our final qualification for the study of intercultural communication involves the issue of objectivity. Simply put, you study other cultures from the perspective of your own culture and therefore your observations and your conclusions are tainted by your personal and cultural orientations. It is difficult, if not impossible, to see and to give meaning to words and behaviors with which you are not familiar. How, for example, do you make sense of someone's silence if you come from a culture that does not value silence? You might make the mistake of thinking, "How could someone be so insensitive as to be silent at a time like this?" Your ethnocentrism can therefore impede intercultural communication.

Objectivity also requires the elimination of both overt and subtle hostility. Negative behavior not only is contrary to the ideals of most cultures but cripples both the perpetrators of the behavior and the target. To discriminate against someone simply because he or she has skin of a different color, lives in a different country, prays to a different god, has a dissimilar worldview, or speaks a different language diminishes everyone. Our view about appreciating and accepting differences is clearly expressed in the following: ". . . diversity need not divide; that the fear of difference is a fear of the future; that inclusiveness rightly understood and rightly practiced is a benefit and not a burden."[139] To achieve those benefits, it will take all the people of the world working together to achieve a truly multicultural society, a world in which you endeavor to follow the advice of Weinberg when he exhorts you to learn to value discrete groups of people regardless of race, ethnicity, religion, country of origin, gender, or sexual preference.[140]

# Preview of the Book

Now that you have learned the basics of intercultural communication, you are ready to begin a more serious study, and this book is designed to assist you in that study. We have divided this book into eleven interrelated chapters. In Chapter 1, we introduced you to the challenges facing anyone who seeks to study intercultural communication. This first chapter also established the connection between human communication and culture. We conclude by alerting you to some problems inherent in studying intercultural communication. In Chapter 2, we will move to the topic of social organizations. Specifically we examine the role of the family and community in social perception and communication. Chapter 3 explores the deep structure of culture by looking at how a culture's worldview (religion) influences the manner in which members perceive matters related to gender, ethics, suffering, life, death, and the like. In Chapter 4, the issue is cultural identity—the way it is formed and its impact on perception and communication. Chapter 5 examines the cultural patterns and values that shape human behavior. Numerous cultural comparisons are presented to illustrate the link between cultural patterns and intercultural interaction.

In Chapters 6 and 7, we move from the theoretical to the practical by analyzing the symbols of intercultural interaction—both verbal and nonverbal. Chapter 6 looks at how language is developed and ways it is often employed differently depending on the culture. Chapter 7 canvasses the effect of cultural diversity on nonverbal communication and how nonverbal messages support verbal communication in a variety of cultures.

Chapters 8, 9, and 10 acknowledge the importance of two communication principles: first, that communication is rule-governed, and second, that those rules are often tied to a particular cultural context. Our investigation looks at cultural variations in the business (Chapter 8), education (Chapter 9), and health care (Chapter 10) settings.

Chapter 11, the final chapter in the book, is concerned with the improvement of intercultural communication skills. In a sense, our entire study focuses on the issue of improvement, but in Chapter 11 specific advice and recommendations are set forth. In addition, the final chapter examines the ethical implications of intercultural interaction.

The book concludes with an epilogue that seeks to discuss the future of intercultural communication.

# Summary

- Intercultural communication presents you with a challenge you must meet if you are to become an effective communicator in today's world.
- New and improved technology, growth in the world's population, and shifts in the global economic arena have contributed to increased international contacts. Everyone worldwide will be affected by and need to communicate about finite natural resources and the environment to help reduce and avoid international conflict.
- Domestic contacts are increasing because new immigrants and co-cultures are growing in numbers.
- Intercultural communication is communication between people whose cultural perceptions and symbol systems are distinct enough to alter the communication event.
- All cultures have a dominant or national culture that is normally defined by examining the people who control the power within the culture.
- Co-cultural communication is communication between members who hold two or more cultural experiences that might influence the communication process.
- Human communication is the process through which individuals—in relationships, groups, organizations, and societies—respond to and create messages and adapt to the environment and one another.

- Communication is dynamic; it is ongoing and changing, symbolic, systemic, relies on inferences, and has a consequence.
- Culture and communication are so intertwined that it is easy to conceive that culture is communication and communication is culture.
- Culture seeks to tell its members what to expect from life, and therefore it reduces confusion and helps us predict the future.
- The basic elements of culture are history, religion, values, social organizations, and language.
- Culture is shared learned behavior that is transmitted from one generation to another for purposes of promoting individual and social survival, adaptation, and growth and development.
- The characteristics of culture that most directly affect communication are that culture is (1) learned, (2) shared, (3) transmitted from generation to generation, (4) based on symbols, (5) dynamic, and (6) an integrated process.
- The problems associated with studying intercultural communication involve individual uniqueness, stereotyping, and a lack of objectivity.

## Activities

1. Explain the following statement: "In studying other cultures, we do so very often from the perspective of our own culture."
2. Explain how changes in technology, the new global economy, and increases in the world's population might affect you.
3. Explain how and why communication and culture are linked.
4. Attend a meeting or social function of a culture or co-culture different from your own. Try to notice the various ways that you can see specific cultural characteristics of that culture being acted out.
5. Explain the following statement: "When studying intercultural communication, you should be aware of the problems associated with individual uniqueness, stereotyping, and objectivity."

## Discussion Ideas

1. In small groups, discuss national or domestic news stories from the past week to determine under what circumstances cultures coming in contact with one another display communication problems. Cite both the cultures and the problems.
2. In small groups, identify your culture or co-culture. Discuss with other members of the group the types of communication problems that have occurred when you have interacted with people from cultures different from your own. Explain how these difficulties have made you feel.
3. In small groups, discuss the various ways in which the dominant culture influences and controls the values, attitudes, and behavior of co-cultures.
4. In small groups, discuss the following topic: "We are alike and we are different." Have the group produce a list describing how two different ethnic groups are alike and another list that specifies how they are different.
5. In small groups, discuss how changes in the demographics of the United States have affected you. How do you believe these changes will ultimately affect society?

## CHAPTER 2

# The Deep Structure of Culture: Roots of Reality

*The family is the nucleus of civilization.*

**WILL AND ARIEL DURANT**

*History is a pact between the dead, the living, and the yet unborn.*

**EDMUND BURKE**

Let us begin with a series of questions. Why do members of some cultures seek solitude, whereas those of other cultures feel despondent if they are not continuously in the company of other people? Why do some cultures frantically cling to youth, whereas others welcome old age and even death? Why do some cultures worship the earth, whereas others molest it? Why do some cultures seek material possessions, while others believe they are a hindrance to a peaceful life? These and countless other such questions need to be answered if you are to understand how people from different cultures communicate. It is not enough to know that some people bow whereas others shake hands or that some value silence whereas others value talk. Although these behaviors are significant, you also need to know what motivates them. We believe the source of how a culture views the world can be found in its *deep structure*. It is this deep structure that unifies a culture, makes each culture unique, and explains the how and why behind a culture's collective action. The three most influential social organizations that make up a culture's deep structure are (1) *family*, (2) *state* (community), and (3) *worldview* (religion). These three social organizations, working in combination, define, create, transmit, maintain, and reinforce the basic elements of every culture. Not only do these three institutions have a long history, but as Houseknecht and Pankhurst note, even today they remain the "essential components of modern life."[1]

We should add before we begin that these institutions often go by a variety names. For example, the notion of worldview, while normally transmitted by religion, also includes views of the world that do not have religious underpinnings. And when we speak of community in the cultural sense it also includes concepts that are related to country, state, and the history of culture. Regardless of the name that is applied to the three deep structure elements, they form the roots of every culture. In this chapter, we look at how family and state help shape the social perceptions and communication behaviors of members in a particular culture. In the next chapter, our topic will be worldview and religion.

## The Deep Structure of Culture

Although many intercultural communication problems occur on the interpersonal level, most serious confrontations and misunderstandings can be traced to cultural differences that go to the basic core of what it means to be a member of a specific culture. In the United States when members of the racist sect the Aryan Nations engage in violence against Jews on the Fourth of July,[2] when "a lunchroom fight pitting Arab and non-Arab students turns into an all-out brawl,"[3] and when thousands of American Indians protest the use of Indian names for mascots or nicknames,[4] it is the deep structure of culture that is being manifested. Elsewhere we find the same strife because of cultural collisions. News reports abound with stories of "ethnic clashes between Han Chinese and the Muslim Hui."[5] In Turkey, truck bombs exploded and killed Jews at two synagogues.[6] And, in Africa, tens of thousands are caught up in fighting that is "fueled by ethnic hatreds."[7] We continue to read where Christians face oppression around the world[8] and that cultural and ethnic unrest has come to places such as Indonesia, the Philippines, Chechnya, and Fiji. In each of these instances it is the deep structure of culture, not interpersonal communication, that is at the heart of these problems.

What we are suggesting is that when there are ethnic and cultural confrontations in Boston, Belfast, Beirut, Burundi, and Bombay, the deep structure of culture is being acted out. Although some of our examples are drawn from the past, Huntington speaks to the future of intercultural contact and the potential problems that can arise when cultural beliefs clash: "The great divisions among humankind and the dominating sources of conflict will be cultural."[9] Huntington's reasoning reminds us of the basic theme of this book, as well as the rationale for this chapter:

> The people of different civilizations have different views on the relations between God and man, the individual and the group, the citizen and the state, parents and children, husband and wife, as well as differing views of the relative importance of rights and responsibilities, liberty and authority, equality and hierarchy.[10]

It is important to notice that all the issues Huntington cites penetrate into the very heart of culture. They are what we call in this chapter the deep structure of a culture. Such issues (God, loyalty, family, community, state, allegiance, etc.) have been part of every culture for thousands of years. In fact, anthropologists believe that since the conception of the world's first cultures over forty thousand years ago, these same elements were at the core of those cultures. Haviland and his associates note that during the Upper Paleolithic period the earliest expressions of culture started to appear. These primitive manifestations indicated an interest in spiritual practices, "the importance of kinship," and "communities."[11] To better understand any culture it is our contention that these three deep structure elements need to be studied. As Delgado points out, "Culture produces and is reproduced by institutions of society, and we can turn to such sites to help recreate and represent the elements of culture."[12] The aim of this chapter is to look at those "sites" so that we might better understand how and why cultures have different visions of the world.

We would suggest four interrelated reasons as to why family, community, and worldview hold such a prominent sway over the actions of all cultures. Let us look at these four so that you might be able to appreciate the importance of a culture's deep structure to any study of intercultural communication.

## DEEP STRUCTURE INSTITUTIONS CARRY A CULTURE'S MOST IMPORTANT BELIEFS

The three institutions of family, state, and religion carry the messages that matter most to people. Your parents, community, and religion are given the task of teaching you what is important and what you should strive for. Whether you seek material possessions to attain happiness or choose a life that seeks spiritual fulfillment, the three deep structure institutions help you make those major decisions and choices regarding how to live your life. These institutions tell you how you fit into the grand scheme of things, whether you should believe in fate or the power of free choice, why there is suffering, what to expect from life, where your loyalties should reside, and even how to prepare for death. In short, these and other consequential issues fall under the domain of family, community, and church.

## DEEP STRUCTURE INSTITUTIONS AND THEIR MESSAGES ENDURE

These institutions are important because they endure. From the early Cro-Magnon cave drawings in southern France until the present, we can trace the strong pull of family, community, and religion. Generation after generation of children is told about Abraham, Moses, the Buddha, Christ, Muhammad, and the like. Whether it is the Eightfold Path, the Ten Commandments, or the Five Pillars of Islam, the messages of

*Cultural traditions help establish and maintain cultural identity.*

these writings survive. And just as every American knows about the values contained in the story of the Revolutionary War, every Mexican is aware of the consequences of the Treaty of Guadalupe Hidalgo.

The enduring quality of the major institutions of culture, and the messages they carry, is one of the ways in which cultures are preserved. Each generation is given the wisdom, traditions, and customs that make a culture unique. As students of intercultural communication, however, you need to be aware of the fact that often deep-seated hatreds that turn one culture against another also endure. We see a vivid example of the longevity of bitterness and revenge in the following *U.S. News & World Report* caption: "For 600 years, violent nationalism has bloodied the Balkans."[13] And in the Middle East we see the enduring nature of culture and conflict reaching back a thousand years. In short, whether it be the violent clashes in the Sudan, the ongoing religious disputes in the Holy Land, or seeing Pakistan name its first nuclear bomb after a sixth-century martyr who fought against India, scorn and distrust also endure.

## DEEP STRUCTURE INSTITUTIONS AND THEIR MESSAGES ARE DEEPLY FELT

The content generated by these institutions, and the institutions themselves, arouses deep and emotional feelings. Look around the world and you can observe deeply rooted loyalty and nationalism on every continent. Think for a moment about the violent reactions that can be produced by taking God's name in vain, calling someone's mother a dirty name, or burning the American flag. Countries and religious causes have been able to send young men to war, and politicians have attempted to win elections, by arousing people to the importance of God, country, and family. Regardless of the culture, in any hierarchy of cultural values we would find love of family, God, and country at the top of the list.

## DEEP STRUCTURE INSTITUTIONS SUPPLY MUCH OF OUR IDENTITY

One of the most important responsibilities of any culture is to assist its members in forming their identities. You are not born with an identity. Through countless interactions you discover who you are. Charon makes much the same point when he notes, "We learn our *identities*—who we are—through socialization."[14] And remember that socialization takes place within a cultural context. As you come in contact with other people, you begin to develop a variety of identities. Even now your identity, who you are, is composed of many facets. As Huntington points out, "Everyone has multiple identities which may compete with or reinforce each other: kinship, occupational, cultural, institutional, territorial, educational, partisan, ideological, and others."[15] These and countless other memberships help define you. However, the identities that mean the most are gained through deep structure institutions. At some point in your life you move from identities only based on the "I" to identities linked to the "we." As Gudykunst and Kim note, ethnic and cultural identities are "those views of ourselves that we assume we share with others in our in-groups."[16] What is important is that you begin to see yourself as part of a larger unit. Kakar explains this transition in the following manner:

> At some point of time in early life, the child's "I am!" announces the birth of a sense of community. "I am" differentiates me from other individuals. "We are" makes me aware of

the other dominant group (or groups) sharing the physical and cognitive space of my community.[17]

As you can see, this "we" identity connects the individual to cultural groups and the main institutions of the culture. According to Huntington, "People define themselves in terms of ancestry, religion, language, history, values, customs, and institutions."[18] You can observe that Huntington's catalog is the same as our list of family, church, and state. Put in slightly different terms, when you think about yourself, you most likely conclude that you are a member of a family (my name is Jane Smith), that you have a religious orientation (I am a Mormon), and that you live in the United States. Regardless of the culture, each individual identifies himself or herself as a member of these cultural organizations. Those identities are important to the study of intercultural communication in that identities, according to Guirdham, "can be used to identify similarities and differences in behaviors, interpretations, and norms."[19] Lynch and Hanson agree with Guirdham when they point out, "A person's cultural identity exerts a profound influence on his or her lifeways."[20] In Chapter 4, we will provide a more in-depth examination of how your cultural identity is developed and influenced.

# Family

The Chinese say that if you know the family, you do not need to know the individual. There is a Jewish adage that states, "God could not be everywhere and therefore he made mothers." In Africa the saying is, "A person who has children does not die." And in the United States children are told, "The apple does not fall far from the tree." Although these ideas might differ slightly, they all call attention to the importance of family to every human being's life. The family is among the oldest and most fundamental of all human institutions. It is also a universal experience—found in every culture.[21] Kim endorses these same notions when she notes, "The family is the basic unit of society and it is at the heart of its survival."[22] Although you can constantly see governments change and disappear in places like Iran, China, the old Soviet Union, and numerous countries in Africa, "families survive."[23] Because they have survived for thousands of years, the family unit "is a very effective means of providing social regulation and continuity."[24] Nye and Berardo even suggest that "without the family human society as we know it could not exist."[25]

## THE IMPORTANCE OF FAMILY

The American author William Thayer offers an excellent introduction to the importance of family when he notes, "As are families, so is society." It is clear what he is saying is that the individual and the culture both need the institution of family. Smith and Mosby underscore this point when they write, "The family is the most prominent social group that exists. It prepares its members for the various roles they will perform in society."[26] The reason family is such a crucial social organization is highlighted by Galvin and Brommel: "We are born into a family, mature in a family, form new families, and leave them at our death."[27] Perhaps the importance and power of this union is most manifest in the idea that the family is charged with transforming a biological organism into a human being who must spend the rest of his or her life around other human beings. It is the family that greets you once you leave the comfort of the womb.

*Extended families connect a great many relatives (grandparents, aunts, uncles, etc.) into a single unit.*

© Patrick Olear/PhotoEdit

Swerdlow, Bridenthal, Kelly, and Vine eloquently state this idea: "Here is where one has the first experience of love, and of hate, of giving, and of denying; and of deep sadness. . . . Here the first hopes are raised and met—or disappointed. Here is where one learns whom to trust and whom to fear. Above all, family is where people get their start in life."[28]

## DEFINITION OF FAMILY

Because family patterns change and evolve over time it has been difficult to arrive at a single definition of what constitutes a family. As Haviland, Prins, Walrath, and McBride note, "Historical and cross-cultural studies of the family offer as many different family patterns as the fertile human imagination can invent."[29] The problem is that when you define what family is, it is important to do so in a way that avoids ethnocentrism. That is to say, judgments of what is correct or normal are often rooted deep in a culture's history and value systems. From the acceptance of polygamous spouses to demands of same-sex marriages, a single definition of family, from a multicultural perspective, should be broad enough to be non-ethnocentric. Hence, we believe the definition advanced by Noller and Fitzpatrick meets that condition when they say that a family is "a group of intimates, who generate a sense of home and group identity, complete with strong ties of loyalty and emotion, and an experience of a history and a future."[30]

## FORMS OF FAMILY

As we have indicated, while all cultures deem family as a major and important institution, the form and type of the family is, as Haviland notes, "related to particular social, historical, and ecological circumstances."[31] Yet even with some cultural variation, most people encounter two families during the course of their life: the family they are born into (the family of orientation) and the family that is formed when and if they take a mate. Kinship bonds link these two families into more complex family systems.

In recent years, descriptions of family have begun to portray two major types—*nuclear* ("typically identified as a parent or parents and a child or children") and *extended* ("typically includes grandparents and relatives").[32] Nuclear families, which are common in North America, reflect child-rearing practices that highlight many of the values of that culture. For example, in nuclear families, according to Triandis, "there is less regimentation and less emphasis on obedience, while exploration and creativity are encouraged."[33] Even the values toward and the treatment of the elderly are replicated in nuclear families. In these families, older members of the family are not normally taken care of. As Haviland, Prins, Walrath, and McBride point out: "Retirement communities and nursing homes provide these services, and to take aged parents into one's home is commonly regarded as not only an economic burden but also a threat to the household's privacy and independence."[34] In extended families (such as those found among American Indians, Mexicans, Indians, Filipinos, Japanese, Chinese, and Koreans) you can observe almost the opposite behavior. For instance, "extended families insist on obedience and are more organized around rules than are nuclear families."[35] Regardless of the culture or the configuration, it is the family that teaches you culture and also "provides you with the foundation of your self-concept and communication competencies."[36]

## THE FUNCTIONS OF THE FAMILY

Families, of course, do much more than simply nurture the child. Schneider and Silverman offer you a list of some specific functions and duties that face every family:

> Families regulate sexual activities, supervising their members to be sure they conform to sexual norms. Families are in charge of reproduction to keep the society going, and they socialize the children they produce. Also families provide physical care and protection for the members. They also provide emotional support and caring.[37]

Barry and associates offer yet another cataloguing of the tasks usually relegated to the family. These include training in obedience, responsibility, nurturance, achievement, self-reliance, and general independence.[38]

While the two lists we have just presented are reasonably complete, we would like to add three additional functions that are relevant to intercultural communication.

**Families Transmit Important Culture Values.** As you observed in Chapter 1, a culture's core values and worldview come from a variety of sources, yet it is the family, as the first and primary caretaker, that first exposes the child to these important ideas. As Gudykunst notes, "Originally, children learn about their cultures from their parents. Parents begin to teach their children the norms and communication rules that guide behavior in their cultures"[39] Not only are norms and values diffused by the family to the child, but they also "give them their initial exposure to questions of faith."[40] In short, we agree with Al-Kaysi when he writes, "The family provides the environment within which human values and morals develop and grow in the new generation; these values and morals cannot exist apart from the family unit."[41]

*Families are instrumental in teaching important traditions and social skills.*

© HIRB

**Families Transmit Identity.** Families, working in tandem with other institutions, are important because they supply you with a large portion of your identity. Burguiere makes this point in the following way: "Before we become ourselves, we are a son or daughter of X or of Y; we are born into a family, and are identified by a family name before becoming a separate social being."[42] In this sense "family is not only the basic unit of society but also affords the individual the most important social identity."[43] The family does this by giving children knowledge about their historical background, information regarding the permanent nature of their culture, and specific behaviors, customs, traditions, and language associated with their ethnic or cultural group.[44]

**Families Transmit Communication Proficiencies.** Not only does family introduce you to the language of your culture, but it is the family that first tells you about communication. By observation, imitation, and practice you are first introduced to the topic of communication. As Gamble and Gamble note, "It is in the family that we first learn how to create, maintain, and end relationships; how to express ourselves; how to argue; how to display affection, how to choose acceptable topics for mixed company . . . "[45] What is interesting about Gamble and Gamble's observation is that while cultures train their young people in nearly all of the behaviors they mention, cultures differ in how these behaviors are executed. Whiting and Child state this important point in the following manner: "Child training the world over is in certain respects identical . . . in that it is found always to be concerned with certain universal problems of behaviour. Second, child training also differs from one society to another."[46]

## COMMUNICATION, CULTURE, AND FAMILY

To this point we have treated the topic of family in somewhat general terms and have not called out specific cultural differences in child-rearing practices. We are ready now, however, to discuss some specific cultural variations regarding the family. As Anderson notes, "The different cultures of our world have bequeathed to us a variety of forms of the family and specific roles that the family plays in society."[47] This subtle and yet powerful link between your culture and how you develop communication patterns and social roles is clearly highlighted by the anthropologist Margaret Mead:

> At birth, babies can grow up to be members of any society. . . . It depends on how they are trained and taught, loved and punished, whether they turn into one kind of person or another. So, if we make a study of this and find out the steps by which these human babies become one kind of grown-up person instead of another, we learn a great deal about them . . . the details of a bath, or the way the baby is fed, the way it's punished or rewarded give us a great many clues about the way character is formed in that society.[48]

What Mead is saying is one of the basic themes of this section. A human being's development can take any number of paths, and culture is one of the major determinants of that path. A child in India who lives with many people in one house learns about extended family. A Mexican child who is raised in a home with many elderly people learns about the treatment of the elderly. A child in Egypt who observes his parents praying five times a day is learning about Allah. These seemingly insignificant experiences, when combined with thousands of other messages from the family, shape and mold the way children communicate and interact with members of their own culture and with strangers. McGoldrick makes much the same point when she writes:

> Families do not develop their rules, beliefs, and rituals in a vacuum. What you think, how you act, even your language, are all transmitted through the family from the wider cultural context. This context includes the culture in which you live, and those from which your ancestors have come.[49]

What McGoldrick is saying is that families, like cultures, vary in everything from "their definition of family" to "their definition of the timing of life cycle phases and the tasks appropriate at each phase."[50] Let us look at some other family differences so that we can appreciate their specific impact on intercultural communication.

## CULTURAL VARIANTS IN FAMILY INTERACTION

Before we begin this section on the role of family in cultural interaction patterns, we need to cite three disclaimers. First, we remind you that all the major institutions of a culture are tied together. So while we might be treating the concept of family as a single social organization, you should be aware that they work in tandem with other aspects of a culture. As Houseknecht and Pankhurst note, "Family and religion must be viewed in terms of their interactions with other institutions."[51] When a family sits down to dinner and says grace before eating, the child is learning about the importance of both God and family at the same time. And when that same child helps his mother display the American flag for a Fourth of July picnic he or she is also learning about two deep structure institutions while engaging in a single activity.

Second, although it should be obvious, we nevertheless need to remind you that there are not only cultural differences in family interaction, but that families within a culture also display differences. Speaking to the point of variations between and within cultures Rodriguez and Olswang observe, "Societies differ, between and within cultures, in their conceptions of the desired traits in children, and therefore, parental beliefs and values might reasonably differ as parents seek to develop culturally defined traits in their children."[52]

Finally, because of space considerations, we do not present an in-depth exploration of the family. We simply want to make you more conscious of the cause-and-effect relationship existing between growing up in one's family and the manner in which one perceives and interacts with other people. The basic assumption of this section is simple: the interaction patterns in the family offer clues as to communication patterns found outside the family, or as the Swedish proverb tells you, "Children act in the village as they have learned at home."

## GENDER ROLES

One of the most important of all family patterns, and one that is found in all cultures, is the teaching of appropriate gender roles. As Wood notes, "Among the people who influence our gender identities, parents are especially prominent."[53] Early in life, family interactions teach children how to differentiate between masculine activities and feminine activities. In fact, studies reveal, "At 24 months children were aware that labels, such as boy, girl, mommy and daddy, applied to certain classes of people."[54] These perceptions are learned and influence how members of a culture interact with both sexes. Researchers now know a great deal about those interactions and the specific role culture plays in the learning process. As Berry and his colleagues note, "The issue of sex differences in child-rearing has received rather extensive treatment in the recent cross-cultural literature."[55] Knowing these differences usually offers clues as to how interaction is carried out. For example, with regard to the gender roles in a health care setting, Purnell and Paulanka note, "An awareness of family dominance patterns is important for determining with whom to speak when health-care decisions have to be made."[56]

What is intriguing about gender roles is that like all important aspects of a culture, specific perceptions can be traced to the deep structure issues we talked about earlier in the chapter. For example, historical events and "changing conditions have profoundly influenced our ideas about gender as well as our family."[57] From the start of the twentieth century to the early 1960s, most girls were raised to be wives and assume the general roles associated with staying at home. This of course is no longer the case. From being a member of the Supreme Court to being a part of a police SWAT team or a wartime army truck driver, females are now socialized to assume a host of different roles. Historical changes have also influenced how males in the United States see their roles in the family. As Wade and Tavris point out, "It is no longer news that many men, whose own fathers would no more have diapered a baby than jumped into a vat of boiling oil, now want to be involved fathers."[58]

You can also see the relationship between the deep structure of culture and gender interpretations in cultures such as the Japanese, Vietnamese, Chinese, and Korean. The history of these roles can be traced to the influence of Confucianism. Kim says of Korea: "Confucianism made men alone the structurally relevant members of the society and relegated women to social dependence."[59] In early Confucian families, boys studied the classics and played, while "girls were confined to the inner quarters of the house where they received instruction in womanly behavior and tasks, such as domestic duties, embroidery, and cooking."[60] Jankowiak maintains that at the core of these gender attitudes, at least for the Chinese, is the belief that both biological and cultural forces contribute to these differences.[61]

Even today, in Asian families, according to Davis and Proctor, "Males are primarily responsible for task functions, while females attend to social and cultural tasks."[62]

Children see the father get served first at meals, get the first bath, and receive nods and deep bows from the rest of the family. What is interesting about gender roles in most Asian cultures, Hendry says, is that although the family system perceives men as being superior to women, "the duty of care within the family falls almost automatically to women, whether it is in times of sickness, injury, or senility."[63] This is exemplified in the Chinese saying, "Strict father, kind mother."

In most of Latin America you can also find cultures that make sharp distinctions in how the family defines gender roles. As Beamer and Varner point out, "The Latin tradition is male orientated and based on a strong authoritarian leader."[64] The Mexican culture also places the father in the dominant role and the mother in the domestic role. As was the case with Confucian philosophy in the shaping of Asian gender roles, the conception of female roles within Christianity derives, in part, from the masculine representation of God as the Father.[65] You see this view toward gender roles being acted out when Mexican children learn very early in life that "within the family unit the father is the undisputed authority figure. The father makes all of the major decisions, and he sets the disciplinary standards. His word is final and the rest of the family looks to him for guidance and strength."[66] So strong is the influence of masculinity in the Mexican culture that "when the father is not present, the oldest son assumes considerable authority."[67] Not being the leader in one's home can even cause negative consequences. Think for a moment what is being implied by the Spanish proverb that states, "Woe to the house where the hen crows and the rooster is still." The female role within the Mexican and Spanish family is an important one that is clearly defined by tradition and religion. As Schneider and Silverman write, "Women, as mothers, belong to the City of God, set apart in the protected and protecting home. Motherhood is a sacred value in Mexico."[68] You can observe the same view of women in Spain. There, "the Spanish husband accords his wife due respect as stronghold of the family; he thinks of her as if she were a saint."[69] Female children observe this value and early in life begin "to play the role of mother and homemaker."[70] Both children observe yet other female roles within the home. They see a mother who is willing to sacrifice, is strong, and has great perseverance. As Dana notes, these "behaviors ensure survival and power through the children."[71]

In India, males are also considered the superior sex. Male children are believed to be entrusted to parents by the gods. Gannon offers the following summary of this view of gender in India:

> The preference for a son when a child is born is as old as Indian society. A son guarantees the continuation of the generations, and he will perform the last rites after his parent's death. This ensures a peaceful departure of the soul to its next existence in the ongoing cycle of life. The word *putra*, or son, literally means "he who protects from going to hell."[72]

The Indian perception of gender is reflected in the fact that "men make most of the important decisions, inheritance is through the male line, and a woman lives in her husband's village after she marries."[73] Very early in life, children begin to see how this belief is acted out: Boys are given much more freedom of expression than are girls; boys are encouraged to take part in the religious festivals and activities as a means of introducing them to the spiritual world, and girls are asked to help with the chores that keep the family functioning.

One of the clearest delineations of gender roles can be found in the Arab culture, which also treats males as the preferred sex. This partiality, as was the case with Confucianism and Christianity, can be traced to religious issues. While the Koran has a great deal to say about women, as Anderson notes, "The Koran addresses men only"[74] and tells them "that wives should obey their husbands."[75] There are countless more specific messages in the Koran ranging from not using cosmetics or perfume outside the house to rules about avoiding bathing in public places.[76] Family desire for a male heir is so strong that, on the wedding day, friends and relatives of the newly-weds wish them many sons. An Arab proverb states, "Your wealth brings you respect, your sons bring you delight." Sait points out just how strong the preference for males is when he writes that "traditional Palestinian society views women largely through the prism of family, honor, and chastity, and those violating those traditional social norms face reprisals."[77] This polarized notion about the sexes in Arab cultures even extends to weaning; as Patai says, "Weaning comes much earlier in the life of a girl than of a boy."[78] Through these and other practices, roles begin to evolve, and women learn to be subservient to men. Patai points out: "The destiny of women in general, and in particular of those within the family circle, is to serve the men and obey them."[79]

In Pakistani culture, which also has deep Islamic roots, you can see gender differences in the perception and treatment of boys and girls. Irfan and Cowburn explain the Pakistani family and gender in the following manner:

> In Pakistani culture males are more highly valued. They act as the head of the household, the primary wage earners, decision-makers, and disciplinarians. Elder brothers, or on some occasions even younger brothers, take over the role of father and never get challenged by the parents.[80]

It is important to note that gender roles, like all aspects of culture, are subject to change. While change is often slow, you can observe shifts in gender roles throughout the world. In Africa young women are starting to question the notion of female circumcision, and in parts of the Middle East women are asking for the right to vote. The notion of a global economy has also contributed to a reevaluation of females' roles within the family. As Nanda and Warms note, "Women are being increasingly incorporated into the world economy, especially working in multinational corporations in developing countries."[81] As we have indicated, these new economic roles, of course, influence what happens in the family. For example, studies have shown that as Mexican-American women secure employment outside the home, there is, within the family, "joint decision making and greater equality of male and female roles."[82]

## INDIVIDUALISM AND COLLECTIVISM

Of great importance to the study of intercultural communication is the notion of individualism and collectivism. These two ideas will, in fact, occupy a large portion of Chapter 5. However, we introduce the terms now for they play a significant role in child-rearing practices. Before we begin, it is important to realize that although the terms *individualism* and *collectivism* seem to be two ends of a continuum, they are actually dimensions of two points of reference along which cultures can be placed. As Triandis points out, "Most cultures include a mixture of individualistic and collective elements."[83] And what are these elements? In general terms, cultures classified as individualistic value the individual over the group. The individual is perceived as a sovereign and stand-alone entity. As West and Turner note, "Individualism involves self-motivation, autonomy, and independent thinking."[84]

Collective cultures have a view of the world that is somewhat different than cultures that value individualism. For example, Thomas and Inkson summarize collectivism in the following manner:

> In collective cultures, people primarily view themselves as members of groups and collectives rather than as autonomous individuals. They are concerned about their actions on their groups. Their activities are more likely to be taken in groups on a more public basis.[85]

If a family favors individualism over collectivism it is not a matter of chance, but rather, part of the enculturation process. That is to say, within each family, children begin to learn if they are from a culture that values individualism or one that stresses collectivism. The manifestations of these lessons take a variety of forms. Let us look at some of those forms as a way of understanding how our communication partners, and ourselves, might view other people.

**Individualism and the Family.** As we have stressed throughout this chapter, most cultural characteristics have their roots in the deep structure of a culture. For Americans, individualism, as it applies to families, is linked to the history of the United States. From America's western European heritage to the earliest colonial times and through the industrialization period, the nuclear family has been at the center of American culture. In these first nuclear families, early travelers to the United States would report that parents were proud of their "wildly undisciplined, self-assertive offspring."[86] We suggest that not much has changed during the last two hundred years. As Moghaddam, Taylor, and Wright point out, "In modern North America, 'family' is often described in terms of the isolated nuclear family."[87] As we have already noted, this kind of family tends to "emphasize independence and individual autonomy."[88] Triandis underscores this North American attitude toward child rearing when he writes, "In individualistic cultures independence is expected and valued, and self-actualization is encouraged. Mother and child are distinct and the child is encouraged to leave the nest."[89] As you would suspect, this independence and autonomy encourages self-reliance. As Nomura and his colleagues point out, "children in America appear to be encouraged to 'decide for themselves,' 'do their own things,' 'develop their own opinion,' or 'solve their own problems.'"[90] Althen buttresses this view when he writes that "the parents' objective in raising a child is to create a responsible, self-reliant individual who, by the age of 18 or so, is ready to move out of the parents' house and make his or her own way in life."[91] Still speaking about American families, he adds, "Notions about independence, individuality, equality, and informality are all embodied in what takes place in families."[92] As you will see in Chapter 5 when we discuss cultural patterns and values in detail, many of the "notions" mentioned by Althen have their origins within the structure of the family.

**Collectivism and the Family.** There is an Indian proverb that states "An individual could no more be separated from the family than a finger from the hand." We see the proverb being acted out when Wolpert tells us that, in India, family members "share property, all material possessions, food, work, and love, perform religious rituals together, and often live under the same roof."[93] This collective view of family is very different from the ideas just examined when we looked at the United States. The contrast is vivid when we turn to the culture of Mexico where we see families that offer their members lifelong support, emotional security, and a sense of belonging. In the

United States, one might say, "I will achieve mainly because of my ability and initiative"; the emphasis in Mexico on the extended family, close attachments, and tight bonds leads the Mexican to say, "I will achieve mainly because of my family, and for my family, rather than myself."[94] This strong idea of living and functioning within an extended family is also clear when we turn to Mexican Americans. Speaking of Mexican-American families, Sanchez notes that "While it often consists of a household of husband, wife, and children, people of Mexican origin are more likely to live in an extended family context, which includes parents, grandparents, brothers and sisters, cousins, and other blood relatives—commonly referred to as *la familia,* the greater family."[95] The idea of collectivism among Mexican families is further strengthened by a system of godparenting called *compadrazgo.* These godparents in most instances are not blood related, but add to the idea of an extended family. Zinn and Pok explain this further broadening of the Mexican family in the following manner: "The *compadrazgo* system of godparents established connections between families and in this way enlarged family ties"[96] Godparenting is also an important social institution in Brazilian culture.[97]

The Puerto Rican culture is another example of how the socialization process involves a collective orientation. According to Carrasquillo, "For the Puerto Rican, the family is an extended social unit that encompasses a wide variety of relationships. The extended family functions as a primary agent of socialization, as a safety net for its members in times of need, and as a means for obtaining protection, companionship, and social and business contact."[98]

France is yet another culture where the extended family is a major influence in the individual's life. Writing about French families, Asselin and Mastrone note that "The extended family serves as an active support network. Relatives, including godparents, are resources for finding jobs, an apartment, a car, and any number of products and services."[99]

Directly linked to collectivism in the family is the notion of dominance—who controls the child? In the Arab world, children learn that God controls them and must be listened to. In the United States, children learn to answer mainly to themselves or their parents. Among most African tribes, children are raised and nurtured by a series of adults. For example, according to Peltzer, child-rearing practices include "mothering by several adults during infancy and early childhood."[100] The Maasai of Africa even have a proverb that says, "The child has no owner." The meaning, of course, is that all members of the tribe are responsible for the socialization process. Families in Russia have a somewhat similar view with regard to the collective nature of child rearing. For example, according to Triandis, in Russian culture, "The scolding and interference by any adult who happens to be present is in striking contrast with a lack of intervention prevalent in individualistic societies."[101]

While learning such characteristics as self-reliance and responsibility, the child, through the extended family, is also being taught the parameters of loyalty. In the Bedouin tribes of Saudi Arabia, "Intense feelings of loyalty and dependence are fostered and preserved" by the family.[102] You find much the same attitude toward loyalty in the extended families of Africa. Richmond and Gestrin note, "The African extended family is extended indeed. Among its members are parents and children, grandparents, uncles and aunts, in-laws, cousins of varying degrees, as well as persons not related by blood."[103] There are large networks of loyalty in other cultures. Mexicans are also "intensely loyal to their families and pride themselves on their willingness to put their families first."[104] So important is this value toward family loyalty that even

Mexicans living in the United States, as Valenzuela tells us, have a "strong sense of loyalty."[105]

The Japanese also "hold loyalty in the highest esteem."[106] This means that children are brought up "to seek fulfillment with others rather than individually."[107] The Chinese family also takes this approach to loyalty. For historical and geographical reasons, most Chinese have always felt detached from their central government. Hence, family loyalty comes first for them, as this Chinese proverb makes clear: "Heaven is high and the Emperor is far away." So strong is the value of loyalty that ethnographic studies suggest that children in China are raised in a manner that teaches them that they should not bring shame to their family—which would be perceived as a lack of devotion. Hence, in China, "Children are socialized to be conscious of what others think of them and are expected to act so as to get the most out of approval of others while trying to avoid disapproval."[108] Chu and Ju make much the same point: "An important Chinese cultural value is filial piety. Traditionally Chinese children felt a lifelong obligation to their parents, ideally exemplified by an unreserved devotion to please them in every possible way."[109] You can also observe the value of collectivism influencing loyalty in the Arab family. As Nydell notes, for Arabs, "Family loyalty and obligations take precedence over loyalty to friends or the demands of the job."[110]

## AGE

The family is the first institution to introduce the child to the notion of age-grouping, an important perceptual attribute that greatly influences the way individuals perceive youth as well as old age. Classifying people by age is common in all cultures. As Haviland and his associates note, "Age grouping is so familiar and so important that it and sex have been called the only universal factors that determine a person's position in society."[111] As you would suspect, there are vast cultural differences in how age is perceived and responded to. These differences are particularly obvious with regard to the elderly. In the United States, at least among most members of the dominant culture, we find a culture that prefers youth to old age. Using remedies ranging from hair dye to plastic surgery, Americans seek to look younger, encouraged by a media that extols the values of youth and warns of the consequences of growing old. So extreme is the negative view toward the elderly that, according to Nussbaum, Thompson, and Robinson, "Studies have shown, for instance, that young people in the United States are sometimes unwilling to interact with elderly individuals."[112] The negative treatment in the United States is so blatant that during retirement years the elderly are often "segregated from the rest of society"[113] via retirement communities and convalescent homes.

The conditions we have just described with regard to the dominant culture in the United States do not exist in all cultures. In fact, Gardiner and Kosmitzki point out that "It is interesting to note how North American stereotypes of the elderly have influenced societal views of the aging process, especially when we consider how the elderly are perceived and treated in other countries."[114] Let us pause for a moment and look at some of the other countries and cultures.

In the Arab culture, Lutfiyya says, a very different socialization process exists:

Children are often instructed to kiss the hands of older people when they are introduced to them, to be polite in the presence of elders, and to stand up and offer them their seats. Young people are encouraged to listen to and to learn from their elders. Only from the older people who have lived in the past can one learn anything of value, they are told.[115]

Respect for the elderly is reflected in the Arab proverb that states, "A house without an elderly person is like an orchard without a well."

This same respect for the elderly is taught in most Asian cultures where "children read stories of exemplary sons and daughters who care for their parents through good times and bad."[116] One of the main reasons behind this great respect and revered attitude toward the elderly is that, in such places as China, the appreciation of the past is highly valued. When this devotion to the past is transferred to humans, you get proverbs such as "When eating bamboo sprouts, remember who planted them." Elderly people are not only venerated, they are also influential—both in and out of the family. As Wenzhong and Grove note, "Perhaps the chief determinant of relative power . . . is seniority."[117] You can find a similar attitude toward age in Malaysia, where, according to Gannon, "Malaysians frequently defer to the more senior or elderly member of the organization, who will generally be the first to speak at a meeting."[118] The hierarchy associated with age in this culture is clear. After the father, the eldest male has most of the authority. Because of the influence of Confucian principles in Japan, Hendry says, the younger members of the house are taught to be "indebted to the older members for their upbringing."[119] Carlson and his colleagues point out that this indebtedness creates a situation in Japan where there is great "obedience and deference to senior persons."[120] The Filipino culture is yet another in which the family teaches admiration and respect for the elderly. Says Gochenour, "There is an almost automatic deference of younger to older, both within the family and in day-to-day interaction in school, social life, and work."[121]

The French culture teaches young people that "mature age is preferred to youth."[122] As Curtius notes, "The values which French civilization prefer are the values of age."[123]

Within the Mexican-American culture you can observe "respect for one's elders is a major organizing principle."[124] We pointed out some of the ties between children and their elders when we discussed the role of godparent (compadrazgo) in the Mexican family. Godparents are held in high esteem because they enter the child's life while the child is an infant—usually at the time of baptism and confirmation ceremonies. Not only does the godparent enter the child's life early, but they serve a multitude of life-long purposes that bring them respect. As Sanchez notes, "Compadrazgo, or godparents, who have a moral obligation to act as guardian, provide financial assistance in time of need, and substitute as parents in the event of death."[125] The Brazilian culture also has the same respectful attitude toward the elderly. Kindness, duty, and obligation are some of the features of this way of thinking about age.[126]

Among American Indian families, the same positive attitude toward the elderly that we have seen in other extended families is taught early in life. As Still and Hodgins note, "The elderly Navajo are looked on with clear deference."[127] This reverence for the elderly is part of the culture's deep structure. According to Yellowbird and Snipp, "Historically, elderly American Indians have occupied a special role in the decision-making of American Indian families."[128] The special place allotted to the elderly comes from the fact that "American Indian elders transmit 'wisdom' and 'order' with the 'extended family' system."[129] Being a transmitter of the culture is part of the strong oral tradition found in this culture. That is to say, because most tribes do not have a system of writing, the elderly are the "carriers" of much of the knowledge that is deemed important. Commenting as an American Indian, Arnold notes, "Elders are responsible for passing on the collective and personal knowledge that our people have accumulated through thousands of years."[130]

African Americans represent yet another co-culture in the United States that has a view toward the elderly which differs from the one held by the dominant culture. Campinha-Bacote offers an excellent summary of this position: "The elders in an African-American community are valued and treated with respect. The role of grandmother is one of the most central roles in the African-American family."[131] Much of this respect stems from the strong African tradition of honoring age and seniority.[132]

## SOCIAL SKILLS

Earlier in this chapter we discussed how families were important to all cultures for a host of reasons. The reason that is most germane to this book is succinctly stated by Charon: "A family is a primary group living in one household that is expected to socialize children."[133] The key word in Charon's definition is *socialize*. Or put in slightly different terms, he is talking about teaching the child how to employ the language of the culture as well as how to interact with other human beings. DeFleur and her colleagues clearly identify the connection between family and communication in the following paragraph:

> The family is the most basic of all human groups. It is the context within which the first steps toward communication take place. The family is a great teacher of the symbols and rules of meaning that are the foundation of social life. Thus, the family has always been the principal source for learning vocabulary and linking symbols, meanings, and referents so the new members of society could take the first steps in communicating.[134]

As you must realize from personal experience, the family teaches much more than language. Galvin and Brommel point out that among other variables the family introduces the child to notions of power, assertiveness, control, negotiation styles, role relationships, and feedback rules.[135] Anderson adds to the list by noting that "Through socialization the family teaches the child to integrate into the community, to develop his potentials, and to form stable and meaningful relationships."[136] What Anderson is saying is that while children are very young and primarily under the influence of their immediate family, they acquire an understanding of basic social skills. They are learning about politeness, how to communicate and make friends, and even "what subjects can be discussed, and ways of expressing anger or affection."[137] Learning about these social skills comes from children observing and participating in family interactions. As Turner and West note, "We tend to understand and create our sense of family through our perceptions of our family interaction patterns. Thus, we characterize our family as quiet, extroverted, jovial, and so forth, based on how we think we talk to one another."[138]

Many of the same social skills are taught in all cultures. For example, instructions in good manners are stressed in every culture, for without some degree of civility you would have chaos and confusion. Yet the emphasis cultures place on universal child-rearing values differs in degree and intensity as you move from culture to culture. A good example of cultural differences in a common behavior can be found in the "teaching" of aggression, which of course is influenced "through culturally mediated childhood experiences."[139] For instance, some studies of family life have shown that parents encourage, approve, and reward aggressive behavior.[140] In the Puerto Rican culture, particularly among boys, being aggressive and extroverted is often taught.[141] Many cultures take an opposite view toward aggressive behavior. In the traditional Mexican family, which highly values respect, the child is taught to avoid aggressive behavior and to use, says Murillo, "diplomacy and tactfulness when communicating with another individual."[142] One study found that "the Mexican parents were the most punitive for aggression against other children, while the American parents stand out as particularly tolerant of aggression against other children."[143] As we have already indicated, non-aggressive behavior is a part of the Chinese family experience. In Chinese families, children learn the social skills necessary for group harmony, family togetherness, interdependence in relationships, respect for their place in the line of generations, and saving face.[144] And in Arab culture, aggression within families is overcome by requiring conformity from early childhood on.[145]

Another vivid example of how each family teaches various social skills can be seen among Thai families. Cooper and Cooper offer an excellent summary of the Thai family's role in teaching patterns of interaction:

> The child quickly learns that by behaving in a way that openly demonstrates consideration for the feelings of others, obedience, humility, politeness and respect, he can make people like him and be nice to him. This behavior may be summed up in one Thai word, *krengjai*. *Krengjai* is usually translated as consideration.[146]

You can also observe cultural differences in the teaching of communication skills when you look at family patterns regarding how children are taught about the value placed on vocal interaction. As Kim notes, "From an early age, Americans are encouraged to talk whenever they wish. American parents tend to respect children's opinions and encourage them to express themselves verbally."[147] As you would suspect, such a view toward the value placed on oral expression is not universal. For example, "From childhood Asians quickly learn the importance of reticence, modesty, indirection, and humility: a person should be quiet unless he is absolutely confident about what he has to say."[148] One study even suggested that Chinese infants, compared to children brought up in Caucasian households, are less vocal and active.[149] In the Native American Sioux culture, says McGoldrick, "talking is actually proscribed in certain family relationships."[150] The rationale for this behavior, she continues, is that "the reduced emphasis on verbal expression seems to free up Native American families for other kinds of experience—of each other, of nature, and of the spiritual."[151]

We hope the examples we have provided have demonstrated the prominence of the family in the enculturation process. It is an institution that not only helps shape each generation to the values and beliefs of the culture, but it is an institution that endures. In some ways the Chinese proverb that states "To forget one's ancestors is to be a brook without a source, a tree without a root" can be used to describe a view held by all cultures.

Let us now move to yet another deep structure institution that endures, gives a culture its strength, and has "deep roots." That institution is the larger community called the country or nation.

# History

> History is the witness that testifies to the passing of time; it illumines reality, vitalizes memory, provides guidance in daily life, and brings us tidings of antiquity.
>
> **Cicero**

The importance of history to the study of culture is clearly demonstrated in Cicero's statement. His declaration takes on added meaning for students of intercultural communication when you realize that the word *culture* can be substituted for the word *history*. In a very real sense both are the conduits that carry the essential messages that a culture deems important. Smith offers a more specific motivation for the study of history:

> For when we immerse ourselves in the flow of time, in the ebb and flow of cultures, in the immense drama of human life on our planet, we acquire a sense of vision of our earth as one small planet among many; so the study of history recognizes that our contemporary culture is but one expression of human life within a vast panorama of different communities and societies.[152]

Before beginning our discussion of how history and culture are interwoven, however, we remind you that our intention is simply to expose you to some historical examples that will enable you to understand why we strongly advocate that the study of

© Photodisc/Getty Images

*What a culture seeks to remember and pass on to future generations tells you about the character of the culture.*

intercultural communication go hand-in-hand with the study of history. The importance of this connection is underscored by Yu's recommendation that "we need to recognize that the history of every society or people deserves to be studied not only as part of world history but also on account of its intrinsic values."[153]

The influence of history is hard to pin down and define. As we said elsewhere, all the deep structure elements (family, religion, and history) are integrated. In addition, when we talk about history in this section of the book, we are talking about much more than historical events and specific dates. Granted, these are important, but when we refer to history as one of the deep structure elements of a culture, we are also talking about a culture's formal and informal government, its sense of community, its political system, its key historical heroes, and even its geography. All of these, working in combination, provide the members of every culture with their identity, values, goals, and expectations. For example, the history of the United States teaches young people that almost anything is possible—one can even become president. U.S. history books are full of stories about Abraham Lincoln's log-cabin background and the simple clothing-store clerk Harry Truman. Future texts will describe Bill Clinton's path from rural Arkansas to the White House. Such history is an integral part of the American psyche.

The penetrating effect of a culture's history on perception and behavior can be seen in countless examples. The roots of the deep-seated hatred and killing that occurred in the 1990s in the Balkan states can be traced back at least to the fourteenth century.[154] You can also see the long arm of history influencing current events in the Middle East. The existing disputes in that area become more understandable—if mistrust, animosity, and violence can be understood—when you realize that for centuries this area has been the site of conflict over territory considered sacred to Christians, Muslims, and Jews alike.[155] In Iraq, the contentious relations between Sunni and Shiite Muslims is not a product of Saddam Hussein's twentieth-century rule. The differences between these two sects can be traced all the way back to the seventh century.[156] The recent movie *Hotel Rwanda* increased our awareness of the 1994 ethnic conflict between the Hutus and Tutsis, which claimed as many as 800,000 lives, according to a U.S. State Department report.[157] The roots of that conflict extend back to the fifteenth century.[158] The continuing turmoil in the southern Russian state of Chechnya began in the mid-eighteenth century, when local Muslim tribes rose up to resist armies sent by the Moscow government to conquer the area.[159] Within the United States, a continuing source of tension between the major minority groups and the dominant culture can be attributed to a long and agonizing history. The brutal subjugation of Native Americans and African Americans is well known, and in the Southwest, Mexican Americans were similarly disposed of their property and inherent rights. It was not until the civil rights movement in the early 1960s that these minority groups began to gain a rightful degree of equality and self-determination.

Our interest in the study of history is predicated on two assumptions. First, historical events help explain the character of a culture. As the historian Basile noted, "For all people, history is the source of the collective consciousness."[160] From the earliest westward movement away from the east coast settlements of the early colonies to the contemporary explorations of outer space, Americans have agreed on a history of conquest. Second, what a culture seeks to remember and pass on to the next generation tells us about the character of that culture. U.S. history books and folktales abound with examples of how one person can make a major difference in the world. We have all learned how Rosa Parks began the civil rights protest which Martin Luther King, Jr., almost singlehandedly shaped into the civil rights movement, Cesar Chavez united the farmworkers, Bill Gates revolutionized modern technology, and Elvis Presley introduced us to rock and roll.

## UNITED STATES HISTORY

Any discussion of American history must begin with an analysis of the people who created the United States. It is these *first immigrants* who set the tone for what was to follow from 1607 to the present. The power and influence of these first settlers is clearly pointed out by McElroy when he notes, "Never before in history has a society made up chiefly of self-determining, self-selected immigrants and their descendants come into being in a place that offered so much opportunity for gain for those who would work for it."[161] McElroy also maintains that "primary American cultural beliefs derive from" these initial settlers and that they "began the process of distinguishing American behavior from European behavior, which during the next eight generations led to the formation of a new American culture."[162] What McElroy is suggesting is that much of what we now call American culture can be traced to a distinctive population that arrived at the outset of this country's history—a population that arrived believing in many of the values that continue to endure in the U.S., such as hard work, improvement, practicality, freedom, responsibility, equality, and individuality.[163]

These first settlers, who were predominantly Anglo-Saxons, brought with them some English values, the English system of law, and the basic organization of commerce that was prevalent during the sixteenth century. Just as these first settlers were beginning to stake out a culture, they were almost immediately confronted with a wave of non-Anglo-Saxons arriving through migration. And as we noted earlier, these "new citizens" continue to arrive even today. This ongoing influx of immigrants, both legal and illegal, has produced what is sometimes referred to as the first multicultural nation in the world.

Although cultural integration did not come easily during the early stages of the formation of the United States, the shared desire of the American people to be separated from what was known as the Crown and Divine Right, as well as from the Church of England, provided the impetus to seek unity. This impetus led, in part, to the binding of the English settlers with Germans, Irish, and other ethnicities into a social fabric ample enough to contain Catholics, Congregationalists, and Methodists and to unite North, South, East, and West within a national framework. Americans wanted to separate alienable rights—those that could be voluntarily surrendered to the government—from inalienable rights, those that could not be surrendered or taken away, even by a government of the people.[164] The fundamental American proposition became "life, liberty, and the pursuit of happiness" for each individual, whose liberties had to be secured against the potentially abusive power of government. The desire to escape the Crown and the Church of England also gave rise to what is commonly referred to as the doctrine of separation of church and state, which prohibits the government from supporting any single form of religion or from blocking anyone from practicing their desired religion.[165] This doctrine is currently at the forefront of U.S. political activity, as questions of abortion rights, school prayer, and governmental-sponsored displays of the Ten Commandments are debated at the highest levels of government.

As we have already noted, the people who settled the colonies quickly combined some English values with a new set of beliefs. Chief among them were *individuality, a lack of formality, and efficient use of time*. Centuries later, these values still endure. Historically, individualism was perhaps the first value that emerged in the new country.

As McElroy notes, "The self-selecting emigrants who left Europe for America manifested individualism by their emigration. When they got on the ships, they were already individualists."[166] This sense of individualism was also a strong influence in the nation's early political formation. According to Cohen, the founding fathers sought to establish a nation based on "political freedom, personal liberty, rule of law, social mobility, and egalitarianism."[167] The result was a government structured to facilitate economic, religious, and political freedom. A spacious land rich in natural resources encouraged implementation of these ideals, and personal liberty continues to be a hallmark of contemporary U.S. society. The value placed on individuality in the U.S. has been heightened through folklore and the popular media. For instance, there is a tale of how Daniel Boone's father knew it was time to move whenever a new neighbor was so close he could see smoke from the neighbor's fireplace. The rugged individual is readily exemplified by the lasting popularity of the American cowboy image—someone unencumbered by restrictive obligations or personal ties, free to roam the spacious American West at will, and able to surmount all challenges single-handedly. Stewart and Bennett, however, have pointed out that the early frontier individualism was more myth than reality.[168] Early settlers actually came together in loosely formed, informal groups to help each other accomplish a specific task and disbanded upon completion.

Distaste for formality and the wasting of time was also part of the colonial experience. Settling a new, undeveloped land required a great deal of attention to the daily activities of surviving, a situation that did not lend itself to formality or dependency. There was no time to waste on what was perceived to be the nonsense of rigid European and British rules of formality. Only the resourceful and determined survived. The difficult geographical factors of the U.S. western frontier also had psychological effects on the settlers. After developing habits of survival based on individualism, a lack of formality, and efficiency, they soon developed thought patterns, beliefs, values, and attitudes attuned to that environment. In this way, individualism became even more important for the American culture. Anything that might violate the right to think for yourself, judge for yourself, or make your own decisions was considered morally wrong.

U.S. history is also filled with instances of *violence and wars,* an aspect that has helped shape our culture. The early history of the United States saw the forced immigration and enslavement of Africans, the taking of Native American lands by force, and numerous wars—War of Independence, the War of 1812, the Civil War, and the Mexican-American War. There are, of course, many other examples that reflect the American attitude toward military action. McElroy offers an excellent summary of this aspect of contemporary American history: "The most remarkable cultural feature of American behavior in the twentieth century is repeatedly deploying huge armies and other military forces on far-distant continents and seas and in transferring colossal quantities of war supplies to distant allies."[169] Any review of U.S. history should lead you to recall that we employed force in Europe in 1917 and again in 1942. We went to Korea in the 1950s, Vietnam in the 1960s, and until the fall of the Berlin Wall in 1989, sent troops all over the world to "fight" the cold war. Grenada, Panama, Desert Storm, Kosovo, and now Afghanistan and Iraq followed those encounters. Guns are so much a part of U.S. culture and history that the Constitution guarantees your right to bear arms—a right no other nation grants. It is not our intention here to debate the merit of this heritage but only to point out its influence on the development of our culture.

Americans have historically believed in the principle of *Manifest Destiny*, a philosophy applied in the early 1800s to justify an aggressive campaign of westward expansion and territorial acquisition. Although originally used to dispossess Mexicans and Native Americans, this philosophy stressed that we were the people "who would inevitably spread the benefits of democracy and freedom to the lesser peoples inhabiting the region."[170] One might well imagine how easily it would be to construe the Bush administration's call for greater democracy among Arab nations as another example of U.S. application of Manifest Destiny.

Notions of freedom and independence were continually reinforced during the United States' formative period as settlers restlessly moved westward into new territories. The challenge of developing a sparsely populated land also produced a culture with a strong love of *change and progress*. Today, change is commonly associated with progress, especially when economically driven.[171] The ability to conceive new ideas and innovative ways of accomplishing tasks is regarded as a highly desirable attribute. Consistency lies in the expectation of frequent changes designed to improve products, processes, and individual conditions. The expectation, and indeed desire, for change and innovation that pushed early settlers across the vast wilderness of the U.S. has produced a national restlessness that now sends men and women on explorations of space. This can be seen as a continuing manifestation of a cultural heritage that emphasizes egalitarianism, independence, frequent change, and a willingness to deal with the unknown.

*All cultures highly value their historical traditions.*

© Gloria Thomas

## RUSSIAN HISTORY

Formerly the leading republic in the Union of Soviet Socialist Republics, the Russian Federation has been an independent nation since the disbanding of the Soviet Union in 1991. With an area almost twice the size of China or the United States, Russia is the largest country in the world. In addition, it has the longest border of any country on Earth. This extensive border, contiguous to many Asian and European nations, has played a major role in shaping both the history and culture of the Russian people.

The Russians, like so many European peoples, have been subjected to war, persecution, and suffering. For thousands of years Russia has been invaded and occupied time and time again by the Mongols, Germans, Turks, Poles, Swedes, French, Japanese, and English. Russian cities have been brutally occupied and tightly governed, with the population of entire towns and villages slaughtered. Consequently, Russians have developed a perception of the world that incorporates the plundering of "Mother Russia." While it is difficult for most Americans to understand this national paranoia toward outsiders, Daniels summarizes these differences in perception and history:

> It is of greatest importance for Americans to appreciate how different was Russia's international environment from the circumstances of the young United States. Russia found itself in a world of hostile neighbors, the United States in secure continental isolation. Living under great threats and equally great temptations, Russia had developed a tradition of militarized absolutism that put the highest priority on committing its meager resources to meet those threats and exploit those temptations.[172]

As is the case with all countries and cultures, historical and political heritage have helped mold the Russian people. Esler depicts those heritages in the following manner: "Russia's political tradition has historically been autocratic, from the legacy of the Byzantine emperors and Tartar khans, through the heavy-handed authoritarianism of Peter the Great, to the totalitarian regime of Joseph Stalin."[173]

The cultural experiences described by Esler instilled the Russian peoples with traits that made it easy for them to follow orders, accept the dictums of their leaders, and endure incredible hardship. One of the most vivid examples of the Russian people being dominated by harsh and authoritarian rulers had its beginning in the 1917 Bolshevik Revolution. This revolution was supposed to free the Russian people from the economic inequities and oppression of the Czarist regimes and give the working class a political voice. Instead, much of the country was destroyed and the entire sociocultural structure was changed in the name of Communism, which brought additional hardships to the populace. Stalin's program of state agricultural and industrial collectivization disrupted the lives of "tens of millions . . . Millions more died in the political purges, the vast penal and labor system, or in state-created famines."[174] The Second World War brought added suffering when some 27 million Soviet citizens lost their life in the struggle against Fascist Germany.[175] The repressive Communist regime lasted until 1991 before collapsing from economic stagnation and the people's demand for greater freedom.

The link between the Russian *people and their land* is also an essential component in appreciating this culture. As Kohan tells us, "Any understanding of the Russian character must inevitably begin with the land, which covers roughly one-sixth of the globe."[176] The vast harshness of Russia's steppes and forests and the sheer enormousness of their country created a people who "would rather settle down by a warm stove, break out a bottle of vodka, and muse about life."[177]

The Russian historical legacy is also marked by a deep appreciation of, and devotion to, the *performing and cultural arts*. From its beginning in the early 1700s, the world-famous Bolshoi Ballet has been a source of great pride and esteem among the Russian people. In the area of classical music, for over 100 years, the entire world as well as the Russian people have admired the work of such masters as Tchaikovsky and Stravinsky. In the field of literature, Russia has produced such giants as Chekov, Dostoevsky, Pushkin, and Tolstoy. Boris Pasternak, author of *Dr. Zhivago*, was awarded the Nobel Prize for Literature in 1958, and Alexander Solzhenitsyn received the award in 1970.

*Today Russia is a country in transition*. Over a decade has passed since the old Soviet Union ended its rule over the people of Russia, and the transition into the "new world" has been a difficult one for the people of this great nation. With very little history of democracy or capitalism to draw upon, Russia faces many problems. In the new century, President Vladimir Putin is struggling with a social revolution, the privatization of many state enterprises, widespread corruption, ethnic unrest, and, in Chechnya, armed rebellion. Moreover, there are growing signs of movement away from recent liberal democratic reforms and back to a more authoritarian central government,[178] which has long characterized Russia's history.

## CHINESE HISTORY

The Chinese proverb "Consider the past and you will know the present" clearly states how important history is to the study of their culture. Each Chinese derives his or her strongest sense of identity from history. Whatever people's qualities or quirks, whatever their circumstances or political allegiance, and whether they are part of the 3.2 billion that live in China itself or are scattered to distant lands as members of the Overseas Chinese community, *pride in China's history* weaves all members of the culture into a common fabric. According to Mathews and Mathews, one reason behind this intense pride is, "The past obsessed the Chinese in part because there is so much of it."[179] And there is indeed quite a lot of Chinese history. According to archeological findings, the prehistoric origins of Chinese society extend back some 5,000 years. The Chinese began documenting their historical record 3,500 years ago, during the Shang Dynasty (1523–1027 B.C.), which makes China the world's oldest continuous civilization.[180] For the student of intercultural communication, an examination of Chinese history is important not only because it is a source of such great pride to the Chinese people, but, as Matocha points out, "Many of the current values and beliefs of the Chinese remain grounded in the tradition of their history."[181] Let us now look at some of those beliefs.

A number of specific aspects of China's history contribute to the shaping of their worldview. First and foremost is China's long history of *physical and cultural isolation*. For centuries, immense natural barriers isolated China. To its north lie the vast open spaces of the desolate Siberian and Mongolian plateaus and the Gobi Desert. To the west, high mountain ranges, sometimes called "the roof of the world," separate the country from Russia and the nations of Central Asia. The towering Himalayas form the southwestern border, secluding China from Pakistan and India. And high mountains and deep valleys separate the country from its southern neighbors of Burma, Laos, and Vietnam. To the southeast and east, China is bounded by the ocean. This geographical remoteness contributed to the formation of a number of familiar Chinese characteristics and to China's sense of cultural superiority. Bond provides us an insightful summary of Imperial China's worldview:

> Traditionally the Chinese aptly described their mother country as the "middle kingdom" or more broadly "the centre of the earth". Indeed, before the age of imperialism China had no contestants for that position within its geographical area and could rightly regard itself as the seat of learning, invention, culture, and political sovereignty in East Asia.[182]

China's *self-perception of superiority* was predicated on their belief that their language, political institutions, and artistic and intellectual creativity were unsurpassed. This idea of superiority was related to the Chinese preoccupation with remaining aloof from the rest of the world. Bordering states were expected to send periodic "tribute" missions to the capital, and all other nations were considered barbarians. The Chinese government believed that the barbarian nations had little to offer and contact would "threaten the integrity of China's own values."[183] It was only after forcible incursions by the Western powers in the nineteenth century that China began a "process of cultural self-examination focused on the issue of how to cope with the fruit and passion of outside cultures."[184] According to Esler, modern-day China continues to be influenced by its imperial past:

> This combination of isolation and predominance has fostered distinctive patterns of behavior and attitude among the Chinese. The unique combination, for instance, contributed substantially to the cultural continuity that marks Chinese history. In fact, twentieth century China is still governed to a striking degree by ideas that first emerged two or three thousand years ago.[185]

Another historical value that has lasted throughout China's history is the notion of the *Chinese clan and family being more important than the state*. The significance of the family to the Chinese offers another example of the bond that exists between a culture's history and its perception of the world. Since inception, Chinese society has been built on agriculture, as Wenzhong and Grove note: "Generations of peasants were tied to the land on which they lived and worked. Except in times of war and famine, there was little mobility, either socially or geographically."[186] This labor-intensive agrarian lifestyle, extending over thousands of years, explains the Chinese cultural orientation toward collectivism, with the family or clan comprising the basic social unit. According to Chu and Ju, even the excesses of the Cultural Revolution in the late 1960s, which often pitted family members against each other, did not diminish the stability of the Chinese family, although the structure has been altered.[187] The importance of the family is best seen in Bond's statement that the "Chinese culture is no place to be alone."[188]

The *values of merit and learning*, two traits that mark modern China, also have a long historical tradition. During the Han Dynasty (206 B.C.–220 A.D.), an Imperial University was established and a system of civil service examinations instituted. The examinations, which continued to be held until the early 1900s, negated the influence of family or political connections and based advancement on individual merit. This provided an avenue for even the most humble peasant to advance to the highest social levels. Quite naturally, education became a highly valued part of early Chinese society. Because success in the examination system was the basis of social status and because education was the key to success in the system, education was highly regarded in traditional China. If a person passed the provincial examination, his entire family was raised in status to that of scholar gentry, thereby receiving prestige and privilege.[189]

Education continues to play a prominent role in Chinese society and while more students can now attain a university degree, competition remains a central aspect of the school system. Bond provides us a picture of Hong Kong classrooms:

> Class sizes are large because resources are often scarce, but more importantly because the Chinese believe that "On one mountain, there cannot be two tigers." A wide competition will better enable the best student to claw his or her way to the top, thereby proving that the best choice has been made.[190]

China's current worldview is strongly shaped by historical events of the past two hundred years. By the 1800s, the Western colonial powers had established themselves in the East Asian region and began to demand that China be opened to unrestricted trade. These demands, coupled with the ineffectiveness of a weak and corrupt Chinese Imperial Court, ultimately led to the Western nations establishing individual "spheres of influence" in China. In effect, these spheres resembled colonies, where the foreign residents enjoyed special privileges and extraterritoriality. It took World War II to rid China of the forced presence of the foreign powers.

Since the end of the Second World War, China's history has been one of internal strife and turmoil. Left with a backward and underdeveloped nation, the postwar Communist leaders initiated a series of reform programs—the Great Leap Forward and the Cultural Revolution—which had disastrous effects on the nation and the populace. During this period, under the leadership of Mao Zedong, China broke ties with the Soviet Union and, as Huntington notes, "saw itself as the leader of the Third World against both the [Soviet and U.S.] superpowers."[191] In reality, China became somewhat isolated from the developed world and suffered from a stagnant economy, which brought added hardships and suffering to the Chinese people.

In the early 1970s, China began to move away from the debilitating "revolutionary" programs and responded to political overtures from the U.S., which led to President Nixon's historic visit to Beijing in 1972. The death of Mao Zedong in 1976 provided China with pragmatic leaders who recognized the need for economic and political reforms.[192] With these reforms, China began to open itself to the rest of the world as it moved toward modernization. In the early 1990s, Chinese leaders opted for a market-driven economy, which has proven enormously successful and improved the lives of millions of Chinese citizens. By 2004, China's gross domestic product (GDP, purchasing power parity) had risen to the third largest in the world, following only the U.S. and the European Union.[193] As a result of China's growing economy and a demonstrated desire to play a larger role on the international stage, other nations have experienced a major increase in the amount of intercultural contact with the Chinese people. China's expanding military power is also a source of concern for its neighbors as well as the U.S.[194] China's re-emergence as a modern great power is reflective of its historical influence in Asia. The desire for increased military strength can be seen, in part, arising from the humiliating experience at the hands of the Western powers in the 1800s and 1900s. The Chinese take great pride in their long history, and they well remember the lessons of the past.

## JAPANESE HISTORY

Although the histories of Japan and China are closely intertwined and both were strongly influenced by Confucianism and Buddhism, the two countries exhibit quite different cultural characteristics. One important reason for these differences is the *link between Japan's geography and its culture*. Japan is a relatively small nation consisting of four major islands and several thousand smaller ones, which made it accessible only by sea until the early years of the twentieth century. This geographical seclusion has been a major influence on the development of Japan's cultural distinctiveness and how the Japanese view themselves. As Reischauer and Jansen note:

> Thus natural geographic isolation, magnified later by human design, forced the Japanese to live more separately from the rest of the world than any other comparably large and advanced group of people . . . this combination of natural and artificial isolation enabled them more than most other peoples to develop on their own and in their own way. [195]

Geographical features also made Japan relatively immune to large-scale immigration from the Asian mainland, and invading armies were often stymied by the sea. The resulting demographic isolation created a relatively homogeneous society characterized by cultural distinctiveness. This homogeneity promoted the development of a "Japanese way" of doing things. In other words, the Japanese formed a culture where there was a single right way to perform a task, be it writing, eating, dressing, living, or even thinking, and any other type behavior was viewed as incorrect.[196]

Another expression of Japanese cultural homogeneity can be seen in their view of foreigners. As a result of the country being closed to outsiders until the mid-nineteenth century, when it was forcibly opened by Western powers, the Japanese developed a strong allegiance to their country and an uncertainty toward foreigners. Their demographic and geographic separation and isolation "produced in the Japanese a strong sense of self-identity and also an almost painful self-consciousness in the presence of others."[197] This self-consciousness persists today and can sometimes be encountered by foreigners traveling outside the major urban areas, where they may find themselves treated as curiosities or even ignored. This behavior is a result of the Japanese uncertainty about how to interact with non-Japanese. While their culture specifies the appropriate behavior for working and socializing with other Japanese, no established "correct" way of dealing with foreigners has evolved.

Another important link between Japan's long history and some of its contemporary cultural values is the historical legacy of the *Tokugawa*, or *Edo*, period (1600–1867). In the early 1600s, following a period of debilitating civil wars, Japan was politically unified under the leadership of a military-style governor (*shogun*). All of Japanese society, most of which resided in or around castle towns, was divided into four specific, hierarchical groups—*samurai*, farmer, artisan, and merchant—each with its own set of subgroups and hierarchy. The central government specified strict codes of behavior to regulate the conduct of every aspect of personal and public life. The objective of these protocols was to ensure external peace and internal group stability by subordinating the individual to the greater social order. Social stability was the paramount objective, and this remains a central focus of Japanese social activity, demonstrated by an adherence to established norms and a resistance toward rapid change.

The castle town residences relied on benevolent feudal lords for protection and civil administration. In return for these benefits, the people professed a strong sense of loyalty toward the warlords. This cultural characteristic is evident in modern Japanese social relationships, where workers continue to demonstrate dedication and loyalty to their school, company, and other in-groups. Today's commercial companies and government organizations, taking the place of the castle town, frequently offer lifetime employment, although current economic considerations are forcing changes to this practice. Feudalism also inculcated the Japanese with an acceptance of discipline, sacrifice, and conformity. During the feudal era, people were required to conduct every aspect of their lives in a highly proscribed manner, depending on their social class membership. These conditions have been translated into contemporary Japanese dedication to social and organizational formality and an acceptance of higher authority, status differentials, and conformity to group expectations.[198]

As we have said throughout this chapter, a culture's history is but one of many sources that contribute to the character of the people of that culture. This concept is clearly demonstrated with regard to the Japanese attitude toward *collectivism*, or group orientation. Here again, we look to the link between culture and geography. In total land area, Japan is slightly smaller than California, but over 70 percent of the country is mountainous. Since people began to inhabit the islands, the rugged topography has forced the majority of the population to live in the narrow valleys and along the few coastal flood plains, where today some 127 million people are crowded together.[199] Japanese premodern society consisted of semi-isolated villages, where the people were forced to depend on cooperative efforts to carry out labor-intensive wetland (rice) cultivation. As Reischauer and Jansen point out, "Probably such cooperative efforts over the centuries contributed to the notable Japanese penchant for group identification and group action."[200] Group affiliations were further inculcated by the feudal system of government, which begin in the twelfth century and lasted until the Meiji Restoration in 1868. The rigid class system instituted by Tokugawa rulers in the early seventeenth century further strengthened group delineation and membership. This group orientation continues to guide contemporary Japanese society, where one's status is based more on the school attended, profession, or employer than on individual achievement.

The Second World War (1941–45) was yet another historical event that greatly impacted the Japanese culture. Strongly affected by their inability to resist Western powers in the mid-1800s, Japan immediately instituted a program designed to modernize and industrialize the nation in the image of the U.S. and European nations. Along with economic industrialization, Japanese leaders also sought to build a powerful military, capable of not only defending the island nation but also with the ability to give Tokyo a voice in international affairs. This produced a national sense of militarization in the first half of the twentieth century, which ultimately resulted in Japan's entry into World War II. At the end of the war, Japan's industrial and military capacity was virtually nonexistent. Almost one hundred years of modernization and industrialization efforts had been completely and comprehensively destroyed. However, demonstrating their cultural traits of discipline, the ability to endure hardship, and strong national identity, the Japanese began a wide-reaching program of reconstruction, aided by the Allied Occupation Forces.[201] Because of its long history of tenacity, hard work, determination, and loyalty to country, by the mid-1980s, Japan had become one of the world's leading economies. Even though the economy has experienced some ups and downs in the past fifteen years, the Japanese people continue their dedication to ensuring Japan remains an important economic and political player on the global stage. But the aftermath of World War II, especially the impact of the atomic bombs dropped on Hiroshima and Nagasaki, did leave the Japanese with a strong feeling of pacifism[202] and an unwillingness to engage in military operations not directly related to national self-defense.[203] The point we are making is really quite simple. The cultural characteristics we have discussed in this section have endured in Japan for centuries. They have guided the social organization and conduct of the Japanese people for several thousand years, through periods of prosperity and periods of devastation, and they remain a constant influence in Japanese society, even in this era of globalization.

## MEXICAN HISTORY

We agree with Griswold del Castillo when he writes, "Within the last few years Americans have become more aware of the importance of studying Mexico and its relationship to the United States."[204] Part of that study should include Mexican history. As we have noted throughout this chapter, the deep structure of a culture (religion, family, history) offers valuable insights into the makeup of the members of that culture. This is particularly true for Mexicans. As McKiniss and Natella note, "Mexicans tend to be very conscious of their past, to the extent of speaking of historical events as current issues."[205] Schneider and Silverman reiterate the same theme when they write, "Mexicans themselves believe that their history holds the key to their character."[206] Let us now turn to some of that history so that you might better understand the Mexican culture.

The history of Mexico, and how that history has influenced the Mexican people, can be divided into six major periods: (1) *the pre-Columbian period*, (2) *the invasion by Spain*, (3) *independence from Spain*, (4) *the Mexican-American War*, (5) *the revolution*, and (6) *modern Mexico*.

Although there is now evidence of human existence in Mexico and Central American as far back as fifty thousand years ago, most historians begin the story of the Mexican people with what is called the *pre-Columbian period*.[207] This period of Mexican history lasted from around 300 B.C. to 1519 A.D. when the great cultures of the Olmec, Maya, Toltec, and Aztec tribes flourished in different parts of what is now Mexico. Though each tribe made its own unique contribution to contemporary Mexican culture, collectively they are an important part of the Mexicans' view of the world and of themselves. These groups produced civilizations that were equal to anything in Europe.[208] Even today their legends, artistic heritages, architecture, and foods "are an integral part of the national identity."[209]

It is important to remember that Mexicans are extremely proud of this period of their history. Not only for achievements in agriculture, creative arts, and the establishments of human settlements, but also because tribes such as the Mayas were advanced in astronomy and mathematics. They developed the concept of zero before it was discovered in Europe, and they created one of the world's first calendars.[210] Mexicans are also well aware of the accomplishments of the Aztecs, whose art and social and religious structure have survived for thousands of years. The Aztecs were a very proud people and considered themselves the chosen people of the sun and war gods. Feelings of great pride in their national history, their historical legacy, and their nation itself remain common traits among Mexicans even today.

The pre-Columbian period of Mexican history ended with the *Spanish Conquest*. On April 22, 1519, with cries of "God, Glory, and Gold," Cortes invaded Mexico. As Cockcroft notes, "The European colonization of the original peoples of Mexico and Latin America was a violent affair."[211] The attempt at colonization was, as Foster says, "a collision of two totally foreign civilizations, each previously unknown to the other."[212] Cortes, because of his use of horses, guns, and interpreters, had very little trouble brutalizing and defeating the indigenous people of Mexico. It is estimated that killings, starvation, disease, and overwork affected about 90 percent of the native population by 1650.[213] The Spanish occupation of Mexico, and subsequent subjugation of the Mexican Indians, would change the country and the people forever.

Let us look at three of the major changes brought about by the Spanish military victory. The first was the introduction of Catholicism in Mexico. In the beginning it was left to the Spanish army to demolish Indian idols and replace them with crosses. It was the Spanish friars, however, not the soldiers, who "fanned out across the country" converting the conquered Indians.[214] Actually the conversions were rather easy. The Indians adapted the new religion to meet their needs. In addition, both cultures "believed in an afterlife and a world created by god(s)."[215]

The second outgrowth of the Spanish domination was the development of a rigid social class that many historians believe had negative consequences on the Indian people. As Foster observed, "The Spanish caste system spread illiteracy, racism, and official corruption through the land, setting one group against the others."[216] Third, Spain's occupation of Mexico resulted in large tracts of land being turned over to Spanish nobles, priests, and soldiers. This created a large gap between the upper and lower classes in much of Mexico—a characteristic that has been part of Mexican history for hundreds of years.

For almost three hundred years Mexico suffered under Spanish rule as a feudal and deeply Catholic country where landed aristocrats dominated a population of peasants.[217] In the summer of 1810, Miguel Hidalgo y Costilla, a Creole parish priest, formed a group of his followers and started working and fighting for the *independence of Mexico*. Although Hidalgo was executed in 1811, he is known as the "Father of Mexican Independence," an independence that came on February 24, 1821, in the form of the Plan of Iguala.[218] Final freedom did not arrive until 1824 when Mexico became a federal republic under its own constitution. During this period Mexico abolished noble titles and attempted to introduce measures that would produce a more democratic society. However, as Johns points out, "Neither independence from Spain nor the Mexican revolution changed the basic structure of social relations in which a small, largely Hispanic elite presided over the exploitation of the impoverished populace."[219]

The next twenty years was a time of great upheaval in Mexico as the people attempted to adapt to a new form of government. It is during this period that the territory of Texas declared its independence from Mexico. This event proved to be a major cause in the *Mexican-American War*, which began on May 13, 1846, when President Polk declared war on Mexico. In addition to Texas, Polk, with the backing of the American people, wanted to acquire what amounted to half of Mexico's territory. The two countries fought over the land for two years in a war "that Americans hardly remember and that Mexicans can hardly forget."[220] The war ended with the Treaty of Guadalupe Hidalgo.

On February 2, 1848, the treaty was signed in Guadalupe Hidalgo, a city north of the capital where the Mexican government had fled as U.S. troops advanced. Its provisions called for Mexico to cede 55 percent of its territory (present-day Arizona, California, New Mexico, Texas, and parts of Colorado, Nevada, and Utah) in exchange for fifteen million dollars in compensation for war-related damage to Mexican property.[221]

> For Mexicans the war was a bitter defeat. But for the United States it was an example of Manifest Destiny—"spreading the benefits of democracy to the lesser peoples of the continent."[222]

The war between these neighbors had an impact that is felt even today. Historians Samora and Simon speak of that impact when they write, "The Mexican-American War created unparalleled bitterness and hostility toward the United States, not only in

Mexico but throughout Latin America."[223] They add, "Even today, Latin American relationships with the United States are often marred by suspicion and distrust"[224] that go back over a hundred years.

The next important phase of Mexico's history deals with the *Revolution of 1910*. After a long and tiring dictatorship under President Porfirio Diaz, the Mexican people revolted. At the time of the revolution "90 percent of Mexico's *mestizos* and Indians were still desperately poor on the ranches and haciendas of a handful of wealthy landowners."[225] While the revolution "was an effort to bring about social change and equality for all Mexicans," it was also an attempt to return to local customs and tradition and to break away from European "culture and standards."[226] Under new leadership a constitution marked by a high degree of social content was approved in 1917. The revolution "ended feudalism and peonage and created labor unions and redistributed land."[227]

The last phase of Mexican history that is important to students of intercultural communication is called "*Modern Mexico*." Huge oil and natural gas reserves, manufacturing, agriculture, tourism, and the hundreds of *maquiladora* factories along the Mexican-U.S. border have made Mexico a major economic force in the world. And, of course, with the passage of the North American Free Trade Agreement (NAFTA) Mexico, the United States, and Canada are free-trade partners.

Although the passage of time and the implementation of economic agreements have improved relations between the governments of Mexico and the United States, there are still historical wounds that influence intercultural interactions. Two recent wounds are worth noting. First, there are different perceptions concerning undocumented immigrants. Many Mexicans resent the physical barriers that some border states have erected to keep out illegal immigrants. The events of September 11, 2001, have only increased the calls among many U.S. citizens for Washington to become more resolute in its efforts to restrict the flow of illegal Mexican immigrants into the United States. Second, hostility toward Americans increased again when "A majority of Californians voted in 1994 to deny education and health services to immigrants who enter the state without proper documentation."[228] The proposition was immediately challenged in court and made its way through the legal system before finally being killed by a new governor in 1999. Although the proposition never took effect, many Mexicans perceived this vote as a sign of racism. The issue of providing health and educational benefits to illegal immigrants remains a topic of heated debate in the U.S. Here again, many Mexicans find this activity to be racist. The Mexican-U.S. relationship remains a troubled one, marked by events in the past, contemporary problems, and, of course, cultural differences.

## HISTORY OF ISLAMIC CIVILIZATION

Our previous sections on history have dealt with individual nations and how past events have influenced the cultural characteristics of those nations. For our last section, however, we will take a much broader perspective and examine the sweeping history of Islamic civilization and how it continues to be a major factor in the lives of well over a billion people. The tragedy of September 11, 2001, and subsequent Middle East events are motivation enough for you to acquire an understanding of Islamic history and culture. But there are many additional reasons for learning about Islam. For example, Muslims now constitute approximately one-fifth of the world's population.[229] Today, Islam is the predominant religion of most nations of North Africa, the Middle East, and several in South Asia and Southeast Asia. Islam is the world's second largest religion, exceeded only by Christianity, and will soon be the "second largest religion in America."[230] Muslims are part of the U.S. fabric. They are your co-workers, your neighbors, your sports stars, and, significantly, they form an integral part of our society.

With its beginning in the seventh century, the story of Islamic civilization encompasses more than thirteen centuries, far more than space and time allow us to examine here. We will focus, therefore, on the rise of Islam in the Middle East, its spread westward, and ensuing interactions with European states. We urge you, however, to keep in mind that this is but a small part of the story of Islam. In the east, Islam spread across India and Central Asia to Western China and as far as Indonesia and the southern Philippines, where it remains a significant presence today. The world's fourth most populous nation, Indonesia, is home to almost 200 million Muslims.[231]

Since Chapter 3 discusses the establishment of Islam as a religion by Muhammad early in the seventh century, we will start our examination of Islamic history with his death. When Muhammad died in 632, no one had been designated to take his place nor was there a clear line of succession since he had no male heir.[232] This void was filled by a series of caliphs, from the Arabic word for "successor" or "representative,"[233] a role assumed by successive leaders of Islam until the demise of the Ottoman Empire in 1922, at the end of the First World War. The first caliphs were drawn from those who had directly served Muhammad and were known as the "Rightly Guided Caliphs" (632–661 A.D.).[234] Soon after his death, many of the Arab groups that had previously submitted to Muhammad's teachings and leadership sought to remove themselves from the control of the new caliphs. Armed groups of "believers" were quickly dispatched to suppress the dissenters and within two years the Arabian Peninsula had been completely subdued. By the middle of the seventh century, the "believers" held control of most of the modern Middle East.[235] As Donner points out, these conquests "established a large new empire in the Near East," with a leadership "committed to a new religious ideology."[236] The new empire, or state, provided the political order and organizational structure necessary for the proliferation of the Islamic religion.

Despite this structure, this period was not without internal problems. Questions of leadership succession continued to plague the caliphate and ultimately led to civil wars and the division of Islam into its two major factions—Sunni and Shiite. Today, Sunnis represent over 85 percent of all Muslims and Shiites compose 13–14 percent,[237] with the latter concentrated in Iran and Iraq. The basic difference separating these two divisions has its roots in the historical question of leadership of the Muslim community. Sunnis believe the leader of Islam should be determined by who is best qualified to lead. The Shiites, however, contend that leadership should be a function of heredity, through lineage traced back to Muhammad. The two groups see themselves divided not by ideology but by a question of politics.[238] However, since the Shiites have always been a minority, they have developed an interpretation of history quite different from the Sunni. Esposito provides an insightful summation of the two groups' worldviews:

> While Sunni history looked to the glorious and victorious history of the Four Rightly
> Guided Caliphs and then the development of imperial Islam . . . , [Shiite] history was the
> theater for the struggle of the oppressed and disinherited. Thus, while Sunnis can claim a
> golden age when they were a great world power and civilization, which they believe is
> evidence of God's favor upon them and a historic validation of Muslim beliefs, [Shiites] see
> in these same developments the illegitimate usurpation of power by Sunni rulers at the

expense of a just society. [Shiites] view history more as a paradigm of the suffering, disinheritance, and oppression of a righteous minority community who must constantly struggle to restore God's rule on earth under His divinely appointed Imam.[239]

These two contrasting perspectives provide us a greater understanding of the historical enmity influencing relations between Sunnis and Shiites in Iraq as they endeavor to set religious interpretations aside and unite under a banner of nationalism.

With the death of the last of the caliphates who had known Muhammad, the era of the "Rightly Guided Caliphs" ended and the Omayyad Caliphate (661–750 A.D.) began. The Omayyad Caliphate brought many changes to Islam, one of which was to relocate the capital from Medina, in Arabia, to Damascus, Syria. Of greater importance, consolidation of the Middle East enabled Muslims to embark on the conquest of more distant lands. Soon the forces of Islam were moving into Central Asia and to the Indus River in modern-day Pakistan. To the west, Muslim armies marched across North Africa and crossed into southern Spain in 710, where they remained a significant presence until 1492, when Christian armies forced the Muslims to abandon Granada, their last bastion on the Iberian Peninsula.[240]

In the mid-eighth century, the Omayyad Caliphate passed to the Abbasid Caliphate (749–1258) and the seat of government was moved to Baghdad. Under the Abbasids, the empire that had previously been controlled by an Arab hierarchy was changed into a multiethnic theocracy, dominated by "Muslims of non-Arab origin." With Islam as the uniting force, all "believers," regardless of ethnicity or place of origin, were considered equal.[241] Under the Abbasids, Baghdad became one of the world's most important cities, and its wealth enabled Muslim emissaries to continue to expand Islamic influence.[242] But this preeminence could not be sustained. As a result of political decline, agriculture failure, and the rise of numerous independent Islamic dynasties in other regions, by the tenth century Baghdad's control of the Islamic empire had become decentralized. These new powers further increased the spread of Islamic culture as the new dynasties sought to emulate Baghdad, becoming centers for learning, art, and craftsmanship.[243]

Although Muslims had occupied Jerusalem, the seat of both Christianity and Judaism, in 638, they ruled the city without religious prejudice and the city remained open to Christian and Jewish pilgrims.[244] This tolerance was ended in the early eleventh century, with the arrival of the Seljuk Turks, a nomadic people originally from the steppes near the Aral Sea, who sacked Baghdad and took control of Jerusalem. Pilgrims returning to Europe brought reports of the desecration of holy Christian sites and persecution of Christians. Seljuk forces also drove the Byzantines from their lands in Asia Minor, or what is now Turkey. The Byzantine rulers appealed to Rome for assistance, hoping for trained armies. In response, Pope Urban II, in 1095, called for the masses to help in "saving fellow Christians" and liberating the Holy Land.[245] Thus the Crusades were launched. Christian forces, consisting of nobles, mercenaries, and adventurers, were able to gain control of isolated pockets in the Holy Land before finally being defeated by the Arab ruler Saladin, in the late twelfth century. Of interest, Smith notes that "Saladin's treatment of the Christian population [in Jerusalem] was humane and reasonable, in notable contrast to the way in which Christians had earlier dealt with Muslims and Jews upon their arrival in Jerusalem."[246]

The final era of the caliphates, and indeed that of a united Islam, began with the Mongol invasion of Islam. Mongol warriors reached Baghdad during the mid-thirteenth century and set about destroying the city and all its inhabitants. The devastation brought by the Mongol armies pushed the Turkish nomads into the eastern regions of modern Turkey, where they met and defeated the last of the Byzantine forces. These nomads became known as the Ottomans, and they ruled Islam for more than six hundred years. During their reign, Ottoman armies pushed into Europe as far as Vienna, Austria, and took control of the Balkans, where large communities of Muslims remain today. By the seventeenth and eighteenth centuries, the European powers began to confront Ottoman rule, which was plagued by internal decay and could no longer contain the Christian nations. As the Ottoman Empire retreated, the European powers rushed in to fill the void. The extent of this change is pointed out by Bernard Lewis:

> By the early twentieth century—although a precarious independence was retained by Turkey and Iran and by some remoter countries like Afghanistan, which at the time did not seem worth the trouble of invading—almost the entire Muslim world had been incorporated into the four European empires of Britain, France, Russia, and the Netherlands.[247]

The final defeat of the Ottomans at the end of the First World War brought an end to more than thirteen centuries of a unified Islam and replaced it with nation-states, many of which remained under the domination of Western colonial masters until after the Second World War.[248] Since that time, relations between the West and the Muslim world have traveled a bumpy road, with the greatest focus on the oil-exporting nations of the Middle East and Indonesia.[249]

This brief chronology illustrates the richness of Islamic history, which shapes the identity and worldview of modern Muslims. History is particularly important to Muslims, and they are often exposed to it in daily life, as noted by Lewis:

> Middle Easterners' perception of history is nourished from the pulpit, by the schools, and by the media, and, although it may be—indeed, often is—slanted and inaccurate, it is nevertheless vivid and powerfully resonant.[250]

From the Muslim perspective, the early era of the caliphates represents a period of one ruler over a single state. The perception of unity persisted even after the caliphate had splintered into a variety of dynastic states, and the people of this Islamic domain identified themselves not by nationality or ethnicity but as Muslims.[251] But since the fall of the last Ottoman caliphate, in the early 1900s, the history of the Muslim world has been dominated by interaction with the West and characterized by near continual change and transformation.[252] Often this change was unilaterally imposed by an occupying power or an autocratic ruler.

These events help you to understand why Muslims today look on Islamic history with a sense of both pride and humiliation. Pride is taken in the fact that while Europe was mired in the Middle Ages, Islam represented "the most advanced civilization in the world"[253] and extended from the Pyrenees Mountains, along the French and Spanish border, to the islands of Indonesia and the southern Philippines. But since the middle of the nineteenth century, Muslims have seen continued Western encroachment on their lands. They also harbor perceptions of continuing unfair treatment from the Western powers, especially in regard to the Palestinian problem. With few exceptions, most Muslim nations are today characterized by poverty and autocratic rule.[254] Many Muslims see this as a failure of modernization,[255] and, rightly or wrongly, modernization is often associated with the West and Western values.[256] This has given rise to some groups calling for a return to the golden age of Islamic civilization, to include the reinstitution of strict Islamic law, values, and principles, and the exclusion of

Western ways. So strong is the influence of history that these groups romanticize the past as the way to a better future.[257]

To conclude our discussion, we feel it important to point out that the history of Islamic civilization can easily be misinterpreted as being one of simply conquest and colonization. However, one can also use that same lens to view the history of Western civilization. As Lewis tells us:

> From the end of the fifteenth century, the peoples of Europe embarked on a vast movement of expansion—commercial, political, cultural, and demographic—which by the twentieth century had brought almost the whole world into the orbit of European civilization.[258]

Space limitations preclude us from discussing the lasting achievements in the sciences, arts, literature, philosophy, and architecture that are a product of Islam. These accomplishments came from the early Islamic centers of civilization where art, scholarship, craftsmanship, and intercultural borrowing were encouraged. Because of its unification, advancement in a particular field was quickly spread throughout Islam.

Whatever your own history and culture, it bears an Islamic influence. Muslims have been coming to the U.S. since before the nineteenth century. They were among the early explorers, traders, and settlers. It is also estimated that Muslims constituted 14–20 percent of the slaves brought from Africa.[259] Words we use every day, such as *algebra*, *average*, *lemon*, or *magazine* have Arabic origins. And the next time you visit your favorite coffeehouse, recall that coffee was introduced to the West, along with coffeehouses, through Islam.

As we conclude this chapter, we again remind you that there are thousands of examples of the tandem relationship between history, worldview, family, and culture. We have offered but a handful. In each instance, our aim was to demonstrate that the study of intercultural communication must include a study of what Wolfe calls "the sacred trinity—God, family, and country."[260]

# Summary

- The deep structures of a culture, which include such elements as family, history (country), and religion (worldview), are important because they carry a culture's most important beliefs. Their messages endure, are deeply felt, and help supply much of a culture's identity.
- The family is instrumental in transmitting important values, cultural identity, and communication proficiencies.
- Family teaches gender roles, views toward individualism and collectivism, perceptions toward aging, and social skills.
- History and culture are interwoven.
- The study of intercultural communication and the study of history go hand in hand.
- History is the witness that testifies to the passing of time; it illumines reality, vitalizes memory, provides guidance in daily life, and brings us knowledge of antiquity.
- The influence of history is difficult to explain as it contains all of the deep structure elements of culture.
- A culture's history affects individual perception and behavior and how people relate to other cultures.
- Historical events help explain the character of a culture.
- History is a key element in developing a culture's identity, values, goals, and expectations.

# Activities

1. Ask someone from a different culture some specific questions about child-rearing practices. You might inquire about methods of discipline, toys, games, stories, topics discussed at the dinner table, and so forth.
2. Find out as much as you can about the history of your informant's culture. Try to isolate examples of how your informant's cultural values have been determined by historical events.
3. Form a small group of people from a variety of cultures and try to answer the following questions:
   a. What sort of family interactions influence gender roles?
   b. How do family interaction patterns influence interactions between young people and the elderly?

# Discussion Ideas

1. How are a culture's historical roots linked to current perceptions and behaviors of that culture?
2. Describe some of the relationships between family and history.
3. What are some ways a person's family influences their cultural identity?
4. Examine the deep structure of your culture(s) and explain how it influences intercultural communication.

## CHAPTER 3

# Worldview: Cultural Explanations of Life and Death

*Every religion is good that teaches man to be good; and I know of none that instructs him to be bad.*

THOMAS PAINE

*There is only one religion, though there are a hundred versions of it.*

GEORGE BERNARD SHAW

In the introduction to the last chapter we pointed out that family, community (country), and worldview (religion) were three of the earliest markers in the evolution of what we now call culture. We noted that these three social organizations working in combination transmit the most important beliefs of a culture, endure, are deeply felt, and help shape cultural identity. Having earlier explained family and community in detail, we now turn our attention to the topic of worldview.

## Worldview

### IMPORTANCE OF WORLDVIEW

The importance of worldview to the study of intercultural communication cannot be overstated. A culture's worldview helps its members make sense out of reality. It is, according to Haviland, Prins, Walrath, and McBride, "the collective body of ideas that members of a culture generally share concerning the ultimate shape and substance of their reality."[1] It is a culture's worldview that members of each culture use "in constructing, populating, and anticipating social worlds."[2] What is unique about these "social worlds" is that they are linked directly to social perception. As Hoebel and Frost note, worldview is an "inside view of the way things are colored, shaped, and arranged according to personal cultural preconceptions."[3] What is important to this book is that these preconceptions are rooted in culture. Kraft makes the same point in the following manner: "Every social group has a worldview—a set of more or less systematized beliefs and values in terms of which the group evaluates and attaches meaning to the reality that surrounds it."[4] This connection to culture is even more obvious if you remember that culture is automatic and unconscious—so is most worldview. Hall reinforces this point when he writes:

> Often, worldviews operate at an unconscious level, so that we are not even aware that other ways of seeing the world are either possible or legitimate. Like the air we breathe, worldviews are a vital part of who we are but not a part we usually think much about.[5]

Dana further underscores the importance of worldview to the study of intercultural communication by noting:

> Worldview provides some of the unexamined underpinnings for perception and the nature of reality as experienced by individuals who share a common culture. The worldview of a culture functions to make sense of life experiences that might otherwise be construed as chaotic, random, and meaningless. Worldview is imposed by collective wisdom as a basis for sanctioned actions that enable survival and adaptation.[6]

## MANIFESTATIONS OF WORLDVIEW

What is interesting about worldview is that it is the basic foundation of both cosmic issues revolving about the nature of reality at the same time it governs life in small ways. As Hoebel writes, "In selecting its customs for day-to-day living, even the little things, the society chooses those ways that accord with its thinking and predilections—ways that fit its basic postulates as to the nature of things and what is desirable and what is not."[7]

The pervasive impact of our worldview has led Olayiwola to conclude that a culture's worldview even influences the social, economic, and political life of a nation.[8] Because worldviews deal with the topics that penetrate all phases of human existence, they start with questions about what we commonly call the meaning of life. *Worldview, therefore, is a culture's orientation toward God, humanity, nature, questions of existence, the universe and cosmos, life, moral and ethical reasoning, suffering, death, and other philosophical issues that influence how its members perceive their world.*[9] The importance of examining these crucial issues has been identified by Pennington: "If one understands a culture's worldview and cosmology, reasonable accuracy can be attained in predicting behaviors and motivations in other dimensions."[10] The dimensions of worldview take a host of forms. For instance, the Islamic worldview provides insight into the Islamic culture's perception of women. As Bianquis points out, "Generally speaking, woman as an individual was subordinated to man both by the Quran and the Hadith. God created woman from a fragment of man's body that she might serve him."[11]

You can also observe a culture's worldview as it applies to the perception of nature. For example, while Native Americans believe one should live in harmony with nature, many environmentalists disavow the biblical tradition which tells people that God wants them to be masters over the Earth. They say that the following admonition from

Genesis promotes a worldview toward nature that may encourage a disregard for the environment: "Then God blessed them, and God said to them, be fruitful and multiply, fill the earth and subdue it; have dominion over the fish of the sea, over the birds of the air, and over every living thing that moves on the earth."[12] As noted, other worldviews produce different attitudes toward nature. The Shinto religion encourages an aesthetic appreciation of nature in which the focus is on reality and not heaven— a reality that makes nature supreme. Shintoism prescribes an aesthetic love of the land, in whole and in part. Every hill and lake, every mountain and river is dear. Cherry trees, shrines, and scenic resorts are indispensable to a full life. People perceive them as lasting things among which their ancestors lived and died. Here their ancestral spirits look on and their families still abide. People thus preserve nature so that nature can preserve the family.[13]

Another link between worldview and behavior can be seen in how a culture perceives the business arena. In two classic textbooks, Weber's *The Protestant Ethic and the Spirit of Capitalism* and Tawney's *Religion and the Rise of Capitalism*, the bond between religion, commerce, and production is examined. Both authors concluded there was a direct link. Bartels reaffirms that link to contemporary times when he tells us, "The foundation of a nation's culture and the most important determinant of social and business conduct are the religious and philosophical beliefs of a people. From these beliefs spring role perceptions, behavior patterns, codes of ethics and the institutionalized manner in which economic activities are performed."[14]

Even the manner in which a culture conducts its business can be reflected in its worldview. For example, if a culture values "out-of-awareness" processes and intuitive problem solving, it might reach conclusions in a manner much different from that of a culture valuing the scientific method. Howell made this same point with a specific example:

> A Japanese manager who is confronted with a perplexing problem studies it thoroughly; once he feels he understands what the problem is, he does not attempt to collect data and develop hypotheses. He waits. He knows that his "center of wisdom" is in his lower abdomen, behind and somewhat below the navel. In due time a message will come from the center, giving him the answer he desires.[15]

What is interesting about Howell's example is that in the Buddhist tradition, where meditation is stressed, a common meditation technique is watching one's breath as it originates in the abdomen. Here again you can see the tie between worldview and behavior.

We have attempted in this introduction to make it clear that worldview, perception, and communication are bound together. Gold clearly illustrates this crucial link between one's spiritual view and how that worldview determines the manner in which people live:

> Ask any Tibetan or Navajo about one's place in the scheme of things and the answer will inevitably be that we must act, speak, and think respectfully and reasonably toward others. Navajos say that we are all people: earth-surface walkers, swimmers, crawlers, flyers, and sky and water people. Tibetans know that we are humans, animals, worldly gods and demi-gods, ghosts and hell beings, and a host of aboriginal earth powers. Regardless of category or description, we're all inextricably connected through a system of actions and their effects, which can go according to cosmic order or fall out of synchrony with it.[16]

*Religion attempts to help its members understand and cope with both life and death.*

# Religion as a Worldview

We have already said that your worldview originates in your culture, is transmitted via a multitude of channels, is composed of numerous elements, and can take a variety of forms.[17] Helve maintains that basically these forms can be classified into three types—*scientific, metaphysical,* and *religious.*[18] Scientific worldviews are based on the rules of exact science that people take to be "the truth." A metaphysical worldview is predicated on what the believers hold to be sound theoretical and abstract reasoning devoid of an empirical base. The third type of worldview is religion. It is found in every culture and has for thousands of years given people their perception of the world. As Haviland and his colleagues specify, "worldview is intricately intertwined with religious beliefs and practices."[19] And this link between worldview and religion is found in every culture. As Nanda and Warms note, "Religion is a human universal."[20] The human need to confront important issues is so universal that, as Haviland points out, "We know of no group of people anywhere on the face of the earth who, at any time over the past 10,000 years, have been without religion."[21] And, as is the case with all deep structure elements, the long history of religion is directly linked to culture. Coogan repeats the same important point when he writes, "A belief in the existence of a reality greater than the human has served as a definer and creator of cultures."[22]

## IMPORTANCE OF RELIGION

For some unexplainable reason, the responsibility of generating and preserving the elements of worldview has rested with either religious institutions such as the Catholic Church or spiritual leaders like the Buddha. Whether it is the teachings of the Bible, Vedas, Koran, Torah, or I Ching, people have always felt a need to look outside themselves for the values they use to manage their lives and guidance on how to view and explain the world. As we have already mentioned, in a host of ways, since antiquity religion has provided the people of the world with advice, values, and guidance. It appears that for thousands of years billions of people have agreed with the Latin proverb that tells you that "A man devoid of religion is like a horse without a bridle." Most experts agree that religions have endured because they perform a variety of essential needs of life, attempt to address questions about mortality and immortality, suffering, the origins of the universe, and countless other events. As Malefijt notes, "Religion provides explanations and assigns values to otherwise inexplicable phenomena."[23] Religions also sanction a wide range of human conduct by providing notions of right and wrong, setting precedents for accepting behavior, and transferring the burden of decision making from individuals to supernatural powers.

Nanda presents a more specific listing of what religion provides the individual when she observes that culture "deals with the nature of life and death, the creation of the universe, the origin of society and groups within the society, the relationship of individuals and groups to one another, and the relation of humankind to nature."[24] You will notice that the items highlighted by Nanda offer credence to the basic theme of this chapter: the deep structure of culture deals with issues that matter most to people.

Whether it is conceptions of the first cause of all things, or natural occurrences such as comets, floods, lightning, thunder, drought, famine, disease, or an abundance of food, many people rely on religious explanations. Smith eloquently expresses the steadfast importance of religion to the psychological welfare of most people:

> When religion jumps to life it displays a startling quality. It takes over. All else, while not silenced, becomes subdued and thrown into a supporting role. . . . It calls the soul to the highest adventure it can undertake, a proposed journey across the jungles, peaks, and deserts of the human spirit.[25]

*For thousands of years, people have turned to religion for guidance and counsel.*

© Photodisc/Getty Images

## RELIGION AND THE STUDY OF INTERCULTURAL COMMUNICATION

Religion is not only important because it deals with "cosmic" issues, but it also is important to your study of intercultural communication because it focuses on personal matters. This significance can be found in the words of Smith when he writes, "The surest way to the heart of a people is through their religion."[26] We would add to his statement by observing that the surest way to gain insight into the important perceptions, values, and behaviors of a people is through their religion. Gurdjieff, the Greek-Armenian religious teacher, stated it this way: "Religion is doing, a man does not merely think his religion or feel it, he lives his religion." By studying that "living" you will learn about other cultures. For example, religion offers you clues into the social aspects of a culture. Grondona makes the same point when he asserts, "Throughout history, religion has been the richest source of values."[27] What Grondona is suggesting is that religion concentrates on social interaction as well as spiritual matters. McGuire advances this same idea when she writes: "Religion is one of the most powerful, deeply felt, and influential forces in human society. It has shaped people's relationships with each other, influencing family, community, economic, and political life."[28] Haviland expands on McGuire's conclusions in the following paragraph:

> The social functions of religion are no less important than the psychological functions. A traditional religion reinforces group norms, provides moral sanctions for individual conduct, and furnishes the substratum of common purpose and values upon which the equilibrium of the community depends.[29]

What we want you to take away from this section is the realization that religion involves both theology and everyday experiences. As Lamb observes, "It is clear that religion and culture are inextricably entwined."[30] Guruge takes much the same stance when he observes that "religion and civilization seem to have gone hand in hand in the evolution of human society to an extent that one could conclude that they are co-equal and coterminous."[31] Studying religious distinctions can be helpful in that they often represent "a set of differences that make a difference."[32] We strongly believe that Paden was correct when he wrote: "The study of religion . . . prepares us to encounter not only other centers and calendars, and numerous versions of the sacred and profane, but also to decipher and appreciate different modes of language and behavior. Toward that end, knowledge about others plays its indispensable role."[33] We would only add that this role is more important than ever before. From globalization to domestic changes in demographics, to debates between secularists and evangelical Christians, you are confronted with the importance of religion at every turn. As Richtere and his co-authors note, "The chances are that the new neighbor who moves next door may be a Christian, Jew, Hindu, Muslim, or Jain. Thus learning about religions new to us may, in our global society, be simply inevitable."[34]

## SELECTING RELIGIOUS TRADITIONS FOR STUDY

With thousands of religions, cults, movements, philosophies, and worldviews to choose from, how can we decide which orientations to examine? From agnostics to atheists, from Animism to Zoroastrianism, to approximately eight hundred religious denominations found in the United States,[35] how do we choose which worldviews to include and which to exclude? Drawing on the research of religious scholars, we have decided to examine Christianity, Judaism, Islam, Hinduism, Buddhism, and Confucianism. And while we grant the importance of other religious traditions and worldviews, our decision was based on three criteria—numbers, diffusion, and relevance.

First, while statistics of the world's religions are only approximations, most statistical studies reveal that worldwide, Christianity, Islam, and Hinduism each have over a billion followers.[36] And while Buddhists and the other Chinese traditional religions are more difficult to calculate, these traditions are practiced in much of Southeast Asian, China, and Japan. Hence, regarding our first criteria (numbers), Carmody and Carmody note: "When we speak of the great religions we mean the traditions that have lasted for centuries, shaped hundreds of millions of people, and gained respect for their depth and breadth."[37]

Second, by including *diffusion* as a criterion we are referring to the notion of dispersion of a religion throughout the world. For example, while the Jewish population is numerically small (14 million worldwide), Jews are spread throughout the world. In fact, only one third of the world's Jews live in Israel. Christianity and Islam, because of their missionary zeal, are also diffused throughout the world. In fact, although many Africans such as the Yoruba and the Neur, still follow traditional religions, however, most Africans, because of colonization and missionaries, are Christians or Muslims.[38]

Finally, the six traditions are worthy of serious study because they are as *relevant today* as they were thousands of years ago. As Smith states, these "are the faiths that every citizen should be acquainted with, simply because hundreds of millions of people live by them."[39] Not only are they important because they have historical significance, but as we noted, they have a domestic and global impact. We need only look at the worldwide reach of Islam and the political influence of the religious groups in the United States to see how information about religion can be helpful in understanding some of the actions of people within religious groups.

Before we treat each of the major religious traditions in detail, we need to mention the similarities among these spiritual paths, for as we have said repeatedly, it is often similarities rather than differences that lead to intercultural understanding.

## RELIGIOUS SIMILARITIES

It should not be surprising that there are numerous similarities among the world's great religions. Most human beings, from the moment of birth to the time of their death, ask many of the same questions and face many of the same challenges. For example, all religious traditions try to answer the same three questions: Where did I come from? Why am I here? What happens when I die? It falls on a religion to supply the answers to these universal questions. Although there are many similarities among all religious traditions, we have selected several parallel points that illustrate how in many ways cultures, like people, are somewhat alike in their search for the meaning of life and explanations for the experience of death.

## SACRED SCRIPTURES

At the heart of all the world's main religious traditions lies a body of sacred wisdom. As Crim points out, "Sacred scriptures express and provide identity, authorization, and ideals for the people of the tradition."[40] Each of these scriptures, whether oral or written, enables a culture to pass on the insights and traditions from generation to generation. As Coogan notes, "A religion's scriptures are the repository of its essential principles and the touchstone for its formulations of doctrine."[41] Although we say more about sacred writings later in the chapter, for now, let us briefly touch on some important religious texts as a means of underscoring the notion of commonality.

The Bible, consisting of the thirty-nine books of the Old Testament, written in Hebrew, and the twenty-seven books of the New Testament, written in Greek, serves as the written centerpiece of Christianity. For Jews, the Hebrew Bible, or Old Testament, is an important document that has lasted thousands of years and offers guidance even today. The Koran, which Muslims believe was dictated to the prophet Muhammad by God, is written in classical Arabic. For Muslims, according to Crystal, "the memorization of the text in childhood acts simultaneously as an introduction to literacy."[42] In Hinduism, the sacred writings are found in the Vedas, including the Bhagavad Gita. These divine wisdoms cover a wide range of texts and are written in Sanskrit. The Pali Canon, based on oral tradition, contains the teaching of the Buddha. "Pali became the canonical language for Buddhists from many countries, but comparable texts came to exist in other languages, such as Chinese and Japanese, as the religion evolved."[43] For the Confucian tradition, people will turn to the *Analects*. This collection has for centuries helped shape the thoughts and actions for billions of people.

## AUTHORITY

In nearly all cases, religious orientations have one or more individuals who are recognized as having special significance. These individuals are often called the founders of the religion. They are usually authority figures who provide guidance and instruction. For Jews it is Abraham and Moses. In the Muslim faith it is a supreme all-knowing God, called Allah in Arabic, who used Muhammad to deliver his important message. In some cases the wise counsel comes from a philosopher such as the Buddha or a

*Ritual is an important part of every religion.*

Religion as a Worldview **79**

prudent sage such as Confucius. For Christians the authority is Jesus—"the Son of God." It is important to remember that these authorities are significant "because they found or heard some message or teaching from God, from gods, or from human wisdom deeper and more profound than most people have ever experienced."[44] Regardless of the person, all traditions have someone greater than the individual who can be turned to for emotional and spiritual direction.

## TRADITIONAL RITUALS

We begin our discussion of the importance and commonality of religious ritual by turning to one of the "authorities" we have just mentioned—Confucius. In *Analects* 8.2, Confucius noted the value of ritual when he said, "Without ritual, courtesy is tiresome; without ritual, prudence is timid; without ritual, bravery is quarrelsome; without ritual, frankness is hurtful."[45] Just what are these religious rituals that Confucius, and all authorities, counsel their followers to practice? In their strictest form, "Ritual consists of symbolic actions that represent religious meaning."[46] The function of ritual to a religion and culture is clearly spelled out by Malefijt: "Ritual recalls past events, preserving and transmitting the foundations of society. Participants in the ritual become identified with the sacred past thus perpetuating traditions as they re-establish the principles by which the group lives and functions."[47]

Rituals, like so many aspects of culture, are not instinctive and, therefore, need to be passed on from generation to generation if they are to endure. Haviland expands on the importance of rituals when he notes, "Not only is ritual a means for reinforcing a group's social bonds and for relieving tensions, but it is also one way many important events are celebrated and crises, such as death, made less socially disruptive and less difficult for individuals to bear."[48] As you can observe, rituals serve an assortment of purposes. From reaffirming a culture's beliefs to expressing identity to providing structure, ritual is a key component of all religions.

Rituals take a variety of forms. They include traditions dealing with the lighting of candles or incense, the wearing of certain attire, or deciding whether to stand, sit, or kneel when you pray. There are rituals dealing with space (Muslims turning toward Mecca when they pray) and others that call attention to time (Christians celebrating Christmas and Easter). For some groups the rituals surrounding sacred times can be "the cosmic rhythms of the sun, moon, planets, and stars."[49] There are rituals concerning death, as in the case of Hindus who "believe cremation on the banks of the Ganges ensures purification and good rebirth."[50]

The most common of all rituals are rites of passage. According to Angrosino, "rites of passage are social occasions marking the transition of members of the group from one important life stage to the next. Birth, puberty, marriage, and death are transition points that are important in many different cultures."[51]

Rituals can also be indirect. A good example of an indirect ritual is the Japanese tea ceremony. At first glance, it would appear that the tea ceremony is simply the preparation and drinking of tea, but the importance of the ritual to Buddhism is far greater. As Paden notes:

> Every detailed act, every move and position, embodies humility, restraint, and awareness.
> This framing of ordinary action in order to reveal some deeper significance—in this
> example the values are related to the Zen Buddhist idea of imminence of the absolute in
> the ordinary—is a common element of ritual behavior.[52]

## ETHICS

Regardless of the tradition, "religion is bound to concepts of what a person should or should not do (an ethic)."[53] In Matthew 19:16, you can see the link between ethics and religion when the question is asked, "Teacher, what good deed must I do to have eternal life?" In addition, as Scarborough points out, these ethical teachings about what is right and wrong also have much to say about a culture's core values.[54] In many instances the link between religion and ethics can be seen in specific religious laws. In Judaism, for example, there is "not merely the Ten Commandments but a complex of over six hundred rules imposed upon the community by a Divine Being."[55] And when you turn to Islamic ethics the bond between religion, law, and behavior is even more apparent. Smart makes this very clear when he writes:

> Islamic life has traditionally been controlled by the Law, or *sharia*, which shapes society as both a religious and a political society, as well as shaping the moral life of the individual—prescribing that he should pray daily, give alms to the poor, and so on, and that society should have various institutions, such as marriage, modes of banking, etc.[56]

What is intriguing about ethical standards is that many of them are the same for all cultures. According to Smith, the message "pretty much tells a cross-cultural story."[57] For example, all religions say you should avoid murder, thieving, lying, and adultery.[58] In addition, they all stress the virtues of "humility, charity, and veracity."[59] According to Coogan, what they all seek to accomplish by the formation of ethical principles is to "enable their adherents to achieve the ultimate objective of the tradition—the attainment of salvation, redemption, enlightenment, and the 'liberation of the soul.'"[60]

## SECURITY

All religions, as we have noted elsewhere, provide their members with a sense of identity and security. Religion unites people by asking them to share symbols, values, and norms. There is a strong feeling of security to know that you are part of a religious family that is feasting on the same day, wearing the same attire when they pray, bowing in one direction or another, or taking Holy Communion. Part of the similarity of security can be found in the fact that all traditions provide meaning and purpose. Macionis summarizes this sense of refuge and security found in all religious traditions:

> Religious beliefs offer the comforting sense that the vulnerable human condition serves a great purpose. Strengthened by such beliefs, people are less likely to collapse in despair when confronted by life's calamities.[61]

# Six Religious Traditions

As we begin our discussion of the great religions of the world, it is important to keep a few points in mind. First, we need to once again remind you that religion is but one kind of worldview, and even the person who says "There is no God" has answers to the large questions about the nature of truth, how the world operates, life, death, suffering, and social relationships. What they possess is called a secular worldview. A clear example of a secular worldview would be an extreme form of nationalism. According to Smart, nationalism as a worldview "has many of the same appurtenances of a religion."[62] That is to say, they have rituals, ethical dimensions, and the like. The important point, as noted by Ridenour, is to "realize that everyone has a worldview whether or not he or she can recognize or state it."[63]

Second, as Hendry says, "Religion pervades many spheres which we might call secular and it cannot easily be separated from them."[64] It is often difficult to draw a line between religion and a subtle manifestation of religion. What one person might call religion or worldview another might call philosophy. For example, when a group of people believe in intuitive wisdom over "scientific facts" as a means of discovering reality, they may do so without evoking the teachings of Buddhism or Hinduism. For our purposes, the labeling is not nearly as important as the notion that a culture's heritage includes ways of dealing with timeless and fundamental questions.

Finally, it is not our intent to offer a course on world religion but rather to isolate those aspects of worldview and religion that are most important to the study of intercultural communication. Hence, we have left out much of theology and dogma of the world's great religions and concentrated on ways in which religion "gets acted out." As Coogan notes, "The world's major religious traditions have both reflected and shaped the values of the societies of which they have been an inseparable element."[65] In short, we, like Smith, believe that the locus of religion is in the person and in human interaction.[66]

## CHRISTIANITY

We start with Christianity, a religion of over two billion people—which makes it the largest religious tradition on earth. In a relatively short period of time, Christianity has scattered throughout the world. It is also the dominant worldview found in North America. There are thousands of groups or denominations that can be classified as Christian. For example, the *World Christian Encyclopedia* now lists 33,800 different Christian denominations worldwide.[67] While Catholics, Protestants, Pentecostals, Latter-day Saints, and Jehovah's Witnesses each have some unique features, they nevertheless have specific rituals, beliefs, traditions, basic characteristics, and tenets that are called Christianity. One of the strengths of Christianity throughout the centuries has been its ability to maintain its basic core while being adaptive and varied. As Wilson points out, "Christianity can be seen for what it was historically and what it continues to be today: a living, ever-changing religion which, like any other religion, owes its vitality to its diversity."[68]

**Basic Assumptions.** At its core, Christianity is a set of beliefs, a way of life, and a community of people. These three common features have their roots in a theology of Christianity. These basic assumptions are summarized by Hale:

> Essentially, Christianity is a monotheistic tradition centered on faith in God (the eternal creator who transcends creation and yet is active in the world) and in Jesus Christ as the savior and redeemer of humankind. Christianity holds that God became incarnate—fully human—as Jesus of Nazareth. Christians believe that Jesus died on a cross and was resurrected, physically rising from the dead. The belief in the Trinity, the sacred mystery of Father, Son, and Holy Spirit as one, triune ("three-in-one") God is central to the Christian tradition.[69]

As you can observe from the above summary, at the heart of Christian faith is the assertion "that the crucified Jesus was resurrected by God and present in the church as 'the body of Christ.'"[70] Noss and Noss further underscore the importance of Jesus to Christianity when they note, "In the belief that Jesus is the clearest portrayal of the character of God all the rest of Christian doctrine is implied."[71]

So important is the notion of a single omnipresent, omnipotent God to Christians that they see the creator as the source of all that is good and loving. Christians believe salvation is possible only through their caring and loving creator. As Wilson points out, "The Christian churches teach that the human soul is immortal and was originally destined to spend eternity in the presence of God in heaven."[72] Angrosino describes this important link between God and heaven in the following manner:

> The aim of the Christian is to be with God in heaven for all eternity. To that end, Christians have focused on three theological virtues, so called because they derive from God, are defined in relation to God, and are believed to lead to God. These virtues are faith, hope, and charity.[73]

Of the thousands of directives that Jesus and his apostles carried to the world, let us select a few of those that have most shaped the Christian tradition and also most directly apply to the study of intercultural communication. It should be noted that many of the teachings of Jesus, like so many religious doctrines, have been modified over time. For example, since the Reformation of the sixteenth century, Martin Luther and the Protestant movement have influenced much of modern Christianity. Yet we can still point to earlier characteristics of Christianity developed prior to the Reformation that help demonstrate the link between religion, perception, and behavior.

**Organized Worship.** For Christians the church serves a variety of purposes. Not only is it a "house of worship" and a place of great reverence, it is also a kind of community—a place where people gather in groups and share a common identity. For our purposes it is the social dimension of Christianity that offers insight into the communication aspects of that tradition. Simply stated, Christian theology believes in organized worship as a means of proclaiming God's message.[74] As Carmody and Carmody note, "Jesus's view of the self was relational. The self was not a monad existing in isolation."[75] Jesus believed, "The closer people drew to God, the closer they could draw to one another."[76] Remember, even at the Last Supper, Jesus shared his final meal with his twelve disciples rather than be alone. Our point is that this notion of organized worship has contributed to the social dimension of Western cultures. Americans are social creatures and belong to numerous clubs, committees, and organizations. The French historian de Tocqueville pointed out over two hundred years ago that Americans had a large series of networks and associations that went well beyond their family unit. Perhaps the stimulus for such behavior can be found in Christianity. In the East, one's spiritual life is conducted in solitude; in the West, God's "message" is shared with others.

**Ethics.** For the two thousand years of Christian history, starting with Jesus, this religion advanced ethical principles intended to give direction to the followers of the faith. These ethical injunctions are found in the Ten Commandments and scattered throughout the Bible. Perhaps the most powerful ethical teachings are found in the manner in which Jesus lived his life and preached about the importance of love. As Fisher and Luyster note, "The central ethic Jesus taught was love."[77] The word *love* appears with astonishing frequency in the New Testament. We would even suggest that the following ethic regarding love might be the most repeated in Christian history:

"Love your neighbor as yourself. What you would like people to do to you, do to them."[78]

If you look carefully, however, there are countless other examples that demonstrate the ethic expressed by Jesus. Think for a moment of the ethical implications of some of the following paraphrased admonitions advanced by Jesus: the Golden Rule; turn the other cheek; before all else, be reconciled; forgive seventy times seven; I was hungry and you gave me food; and let the sinless cast the first stone."[79] You can clearly observe the ethical manifestations of these ideas of love and compassion reflected in everything from the large amounts of charitable contributions Americans make to their willingness to go to foreign countries to improve the lives of strangers.

**Individualism.** The Western concept of the importance of the individual, which we have discussed throughout this book, can be linked partially to Christianity. Most scholars maintain that Christianity, along with Judaism, were the first religions that placed "greater emphasis on the autonomy and responsibility of the self."[80] As McGuire points out, Christianity "is characterized by an image of the dynamic multidimensional self, able (within limits) to continually change both self and the world."[81] In short, while membership in a church community is important to Christians, it is this religious tradition that "discovered the individual."[82] An example of the power of self can be seen in the view of salvation, particularly for Protestants. Salvation "is achieved by our own efforts alone and there is a tendency for deeds to count more than prayers."[83] Even the Bible carries examples of individualism. As Woodward notes, "The Gospels are replete with scenes in which Jesus works one on one healing this woman's sickness, forgiving that man's sins, and calling each to personal conversion."[84] Summarizing this important point, Woodward adds, "Christianity discovers individuality in the sense that it stresses personal conversion."[85]

You also can see the importance of the individual in that part of Christian theology that begins with the assumption that the world is real and meaningful because God created it. Human beings are significant because God created them in his image. The Christian God is a personal God, who desires a relationship with his creation.[86] In a culture that values individualism, Christianity is perhaps the perfect religion in that each person can have a one-on-one bond with God.

**Doing.** Much of the Western "doing" orientation (which we will discuss in Chapter 5) can be found in Christianity and in the manner in which Jesus lived his life. From the very beginning "the Jesus movement began to send out emissaries" to bring the news about Jesus to all who would listen.[87] Peter, one of Jesus' disciples, once said of Jesus, "He went about doing good."[88] This example set by Jesus was translated into action. For instance, the Romans would cast out people into the streets at the first sign of sickness because they were afraid of dying. Christians would take an active role and try to nurse the sick.[89] This is not an isolated example. Anyone who has studied Christianity knows that Jesus was an active man who urged his followers to be vigorous and active. The Bible is full of accounts of how he traveled from place to place healing the sick and counseling misfits and ordinary people.

**Future.** Throughout this book we will discuss cultural attitudes toward time. From those discussions, and from your own observations, you can conclude that Americans are future oriented—they are always concerned with what will happen next rather than living in the present. We are suggesting that one of the reasons behind this behavior might have its roots in Christianity. Put in slightly different terms, in comparison to other religions, one of the lessons of Christianity is that the future is important. As Muck points out, for Christians "no matter what happened in the past, it is the future that holds the greatest promise."[90] God forgives mistakes, regret, and remorse. As Blanche and Parkes note, "Christians hold that those who repent of their sins and turn to Jesus Christ will be forgiven and will join him in heaven after death."[91] In this sense, the individual is to move on. Hence, even the notion of a heaven places emphasis on the future.

**Gender.** The enduring legacy for Christian women is, of course, the Garden of Eden story found in Genesis. This is not the only view of women used to define their place in both the family and society. For example, when Paul speaks in 1 Timothy, he advises: "I permit no woman to teach or to have authority over men; she is to keep silent. For Adam was formed first, then Eve; and Adam was not deceived, but the woman was deceived and became the transgressor."[92] Paul also writes that wives should remain "busy at home" and be "subject to their husbands."[93] While these sorts of examples are often used to justify placing women in second-class positions, recent events and a new interpretation of the Bible reveal a view of women that is more consistent with current perceptions—and perhaps accurately reflects the beliefs of Jesus. For example, with the exception of the Catholic Church, the number of women who are becoming priests is growing at a rapid rate. Some biblical scholars are asserting that Jesus might well have been a feminist and offer examples to justify their claim. First, prior to the coming of Jesus, Roman society regarded women as inherently inferior to men. Husbands could divorce their wives, but wives could not divorce their husbands. Jesus banned all divorce. Roman men could marry girls as young as ten or eleven years old. Jesus challenged these practices. Wrote one biblical scholar, "The new religion offered women not only greater status and influence within the church, but also more protection as wives and mothers."[94]

Second, "although he called only men to be apostles, Jesus readily accepted women into his circle of friends and disciples."[95] Defying custom, Jesus even invited women to join him at meals. All of this leads Murphy to note, "Women were often prominent in the accounts of his ministry, and he acknowledged the oppression they face."[96]

Finally, Jesus helped define a new role for women by giving them greater responsibility. For example, they "shared with men the cultural responsibility for teaching children, as reflected in the proverb: 'My son, keep your father's commandment, and forsake not your mother's teaching.'"[97]

**Courage.** A strong message in Christianity is courage and bravery. As Carmody and Carmody note, "Jesus was courageous."[98] A careful reading of the life of Jesus reveals a man who would not be intimidated by his opponents. On occasion after occasion, we have accounts of Jesus' strong personality emerging. His strength and courage are traits that all Christians are reminded of repeatedly. As you know from your own experience, these are also two powerful values in the American culture. Here again, you can see the link between worldview and communication styles.

## JUDAISM

Although Jews represent less than one-half of 1 percent of the world's population (approximately 14 million Jews), and approximately 2 percent of the entire population of the United States,[99] their geographical distribution and their interest in politics, the arts, literature, medicine, finance, and the law have, for thousands of years, made them important and influential. As Smith notes, "It has been estimated that one-third of our Western civilization bears the marks of its Jewish ancestry."[100] Judaism is the oldest of the organized religions being practiced today and the smallest of all the major religious traditions. Judaism is believed to have been founded in approximately 1300 B.C. when twelve Israelite tribes came to Canaan from Mesopotamia. Later, many of them settled in Egypt where they were held as slaves until they fled to Jerusalem in about 1200 B.C. Under the guidance and leadership of Moses, the Jewish religion began to take shape. In this nearly four thousand years of historical development, the Jewish religion and the people who practice it have exhibited not only a penchant for continuity but also a remarkable adaptability. In their encounters with other civilizations and religions, the Jewish people have endured many attempts to purge them of their beliefs—and at times their very existence. Yet they have managed to assimilate, integrate, and survive while maintaining an unbroken line of both their culture and their religion.

**Basic Assumptions.** As we have indicated, Judaism is one of the three great monotheistic world religions, the others being Christianity and Islam. Judaism has as its theology the belief that the people of Israel are God's chosen people, having made a covenant with God. Banks says it this way: "At the heart of the Jewish religion lies the existence of a covenant between God and his people."[101] Although Jews believe that God's providence extends to all people, they also hold to the notion God entered into this special covenant (solemn agreement) with them through four of their prophets—Abraham, Isaac, Jacob, and Moses. In this agreement God promised to make Israel a great nation; in response the Jewish people were to be obedient to God and to carry God's message by example. From circumcision to the keeping of the Sabbath, signs of the covenant abound in Jewish culture and religion.[102] It is this covenant that is at the heart of why Jews consider themselves God's "chosen people." In Jewish theology, this special "consideration never meant advantages for the Jews, only increased responsibilities and hardships."[103]

The Jewish worldview is expressed through a number of concepts basic to the faith: (1) Jews "believe in one universal and eternal God, the creator and sovereign of all that exists,"[104] (2) no human ever will be divine, (3) humans are free, (4) "the afterlife depends largely upon the behavior of the individual during his life on earth,"[105] (5) humans are the pinnacle of creation, (6) Jews belong to a group or nation whose goal is to serve God, (7) humans must be obedient to the God-given commandments in the Torah (first five books of the Bible) and assume personal responsibility, and (8) "culturally approved behavior will be rewarded after death; disapproved behavior will be punished."[106] These eight concepts compose a belief system stressing the secular notion that order must be maintained if Jews are to have a collective life. The Ten Commandments in the Torah therefore give structure to and make possible a social world.[107]

The Jewish faith is unique in that it is both a culture and a religion. It is common, for example, to find nonreligious Jews who identify fully with the culture but not with the theology. Fisher and Luyster elaborate on this point: "Judaism has no single founder, no central leader or group making theological decisions; Judaism is a people, a very old family. This family can be defined either as a religious group or a national group."[108] Judaism penetrates every area of human existence, providing humankind with a means of communicating with both the secular and transcendental worlds.[109] It

**Family.** As you saw in the last chapter, all societies value the family, but for Jews the family is the locus of worship and devotion. On nearly every occasion, be it in the home or the synagogue, the family is an active participant in Jewish life. From circumcisions to Passover seders, to bar or bat mitzvahs, to marriage and death, the family and religion are strongly bound together. Rosten offers a clear digest of this link in the following paragraph:

> For 4,000 years, the Jewish family has been the very core, mortar, and citadel of Judaism's faith and the central reason for the survival of the Jews as a distinct ethnic group. The Jewish home is a temple, according to Judaic law, custom, and tradition.[122]

## ISLAM

We agree with Smith when he says, "Islam is a vital force in the contemporary world."[123] The statistical impact of Islam is highlighted by Belt when he writes, "Some 1.3 billion human beings—one person in five—heed Islam's call in the modern world, embracing the religion at a rate that makes it the fastest growing on Earth, with 80 percent of believers now outside the Arab world."[124] Islam will soon be the second-most-commonly practiced religion in the United States[125] with nearly 7 million members.[126] Yet, in spite of these numbers, Islam is, as Belt notes, the "most misunderstood religion on earth."[127] The events of September 11, 2001, along with a series of other conflicts involving a small yet visible group of Muslims, seem to have only added to the incomplete or false information many Americans have about this religion. As Noss and Noss point out:

> The heart of Islam is well hidden from most Westerners, and the outer images of Islamic countries present bewildering contrasts: stern ayatollahs ordering the lash for prostitutes, camel drivers putting down prayer mats in the desert, a sophisticated royal prince discussing international investments, and fiery national liberators proclaiming equality and denouncing Western values.[128]

**Basic Assumption.** While the basic beliefs of Islam are complex and numerous, there is one article of faith that is at the heart of this religion. Simply stated, it is the idea that Muslims believe in one, unique, incomparable God. Calverley summarizes this fundamental notion in the following manner: "Islam always has taught that Allah is One, that there is only One God. The first half of the Muslim creed says: 'There is no god at all but Allah.'"[129] In the Koran the idea is stated as follows: "He is God, the One. God to Whom the creatures turn for their needs. He begets not, nor was He begotten, and there is none like Him."[130] There are two other assumptions that grow out of the overarching precept of one God. They are the notion of *submission* and the belief in *divine decrees* (predestination). As Scarborough notes, "Islam means submission to the will of God. A Muslim is one who submits. Islam holds that man's purpose is to serve the will of God."[131] Part of that service is to consider that events in life are predestined by the will of Allah. Perhaps the most repeated statement among committed Muslims is "if God wills it." Farah points out that "The sayings of the Prophet are replete with his insistence on God's role as preordainer and determiner of all that takes place."[132] For example, in the Koran you can read some of the following admonitions:

> No soul can ever die except by Allah's leave and at a term appointed . . .[133]

> Thy God hath created and balanced all things, and hath fixed their destinies and guided them . . .[134]

is not simply a religion that serves spiritual needs but a guide to worship, ceremonies, justice, friendship, kindness, intellectual pursuits, courtesy, and diet.

**Oppression and Persecution.** The entire history of Judaism has been one of oppression and persecution. As Ehrlich notes, "All too often the story of Jews has been presented as a litany of disasters."[110] Van Doren confirms the same idea: "The history of Judaism and the Jews is a long complicated story, full of blood and tears."[111] Even today anti-Semitism is on the rise in parts of Europe. Through the belief that God is using them "to introduce insights into history that all people need," suffering, oppression, and persecution seem to be built into the Jewish faith.[112] Prager and Telushkin offer an excellent summary of the long-standing persecution of Jews:

> Only the Jews have had their homeland destroyed (twice), been dispersed wherever they have lived, survived the most systematic attempt in history (aside from that of the Gypsies) to destroy an entire people, and been expelled from nearly every nation among whom they have lived.[113]

What we have is a religious group who, for thousands of years, has experienced murder, exile, and discrimination. The residue of these experiences is that even today many Jews have a difficult time trusting non-Jews. Some additional results of religious persecution of the Jewish people are quite nicely summarized by Van Doren:

> With all that, the Jews are still essentially the same stubborn, dedicated people, now and forever maybe, affirming the same three things. First, they are a people of the law as given in the only books of Moses. Second, they are the chosen people of God, having a covenant with him. Third, they are a witness that God is and will be forevermore.[114]

**Learning.** Of additional interest is the importance the Jewish religion places on learning. So strong is this value that the Jewish essayist Elie Wiesel quotes a Jewish saying that "Adam chose knowledge instead of immortality." This attitude helps determine how Jews perceive the world and function in it. For thousands of years Jews have made the study of the Talmud (a holy book that is over five thousand pages long) an important element of Jewish life.[115] Some Hebrew translations of the word *Talmud* actually contain the words "learning, "study," and "teaching."[116] So strong is the value of learning for Jews that the Jewish prayer book speaks of "the love of learning" as one of three principles of faith.[117] References to the importance of education are sprinkled throughout Jewish holy books. "As early as the first century, Jews had a system of compulsory education."[118] Jews have a proverb that states, "Wisdom is better than jewels." Occupations using the mind (teacher, lawyer, doctor, writer, and so on) are popular professions in the Jewish community.

**Justice.** The Jewish faith also teaches a strong sense of justice. An individual's responsibility and moral commitment to God and other people are clearly spelled out in detail in all Jewish religious writings. Novak notes, "the promotion of justice is a paramount concern" for the Jew.[119] In fact, one of the four categories of Jewish law is actually "to ensure moral treatment of others."[120] You can see this concern for justice in everything from ancient Jewish writings to the active role Jews played during the civil rights movement in the 1960s. So deep-seated is this basic precept that Smith believes much of Western civilization owes a debt to the early Jewish prophets for establishing the notion of justice as a major principle for the maintenance of "social order."[121]

behavior might have its roots in Christianity. Put in slightly different terms, in comparison to other religions, one of the lessons of Christianity is that the future is important. As Muck points out, for Christians "no matter what happened in the past, it is the future that holds the greatest promise."[90] God forgives mistakes, regret, and remorse. As Blanche and Parkes note, "Christians hold that those who repent of their sins and turn to Jesus Christ will be forgiven and will join him in heaven after death."[91] In this sense, the individual is to move on. Hence, even the notion of a heaven places emphasis on the future.

**Gender.** The enduring legacy for Christian women is, of course, the Garden of Eden story found in Genesis. This is not the only view of women used to define their place in both the family and society. For example, when Paul speaks in 1 Timothy, he advises: "I permit no woman to teach or to have authority over men; she is to keep silent. For Adam was formed first, then Eve; and Adam was not deceived, but the woman was deceived and became the transgressor."[92] Paul also writes that wives should remain "busy at home" and be "subject to their husbands."[93] While these sorts of examples are often used to justify placing women in second-class positions, recent events and a new interpretation of the Bible reveal a view of women that is more consistent with current perceptions—and perhaps accurately reflects the beliefs of Jesus. For example, with the exception of the Catholic Church, the number of women who are becoming priests is growing at a rapid rate. Some biblical scholars are asserting that Jesus might well have been a feminist and offer examples to justify their claim. First, prior to the coming of Jesus, Roman society regarded women as inherently inferior to men. Husbands could divorce their wives, but wives could not divorce their husbands. Jesus banned all divorce. Roman men could marry girls as young as ten or eleven years old. Jesus challenged these practices. Wrote one biblical scholar, "The new religion offered women not only greater status and influence within the church, but also more protection as wives and mothers."[94]

Second, "although he called only men to be apostles, Jesus readily accepted women into his circle of friends and disciples."[95] Defying custom, Jesus even invited women to join him at meals. All of this leads Murphy to note, "Women were often prominent in the accounts of his ministry, and he acknowledged the oppression they face."[96]

Finally, Jesus helped define a new role for women by giving them greater responsibility. For example, they "shared with men the cultural responsibility for teaching children, as reflected in the proverb: 'My son, keep your father's commandment, and forsake not your mother's teaching.'"[97]

**Courage.** A strong message in Christianity is courage and bravery. As Carmody and Carmody note, "Jesus was courageous."[98] A careful reading of the life of Jesus reveals a man who would not be intimidated by his opponents. On occasion after occasion, we have accounts of Jesus' strong personality emerging. His strength and courage are traits that all Christians are reminded of repeatedly. As you know from your own experience, these are also two powerful values in the American culture. Here again, you can see the link between worldview and communication styles.

## JUDAISM

Although Jews represent less than one-half of 1 percent of the world's population (approximately 14 million Jews), and approximately 2 percent of the entire population of the United States,[99] their geographical distribution and their interest in politics, the arts, literature, medicine, finance, and the law have, for thousands of years, made them important and influential. As Smith notes, "It has been estimated that one-third of our Western civilization bears the marks of its Jewish ancestry."[100] Judaism is the oldest of the organized religions being practiced today and the smallest of all the major religious traditions. Judaism is believed to have been founded in approximately 1300 B.C. when twelve Israelite tribes came to Canaan from Mesopotamia. Later, many of them settled in Egypt where they were held as slaves until they fled to Jerusalem in about 1200 B.C. Under the guidance and leadership of Moses, the Jewish religion began to take shape. In this nearly four thousand years of historical development, the Jewish religion and the people who practice it have exhibited not only a penchant for continuity but also a remarkable adaptability. In their encounters with other civilizations and religions, the Jewish people have endured many attempts to purge them of their beliefs—and at times their very existence. Yet they have managed to assimilate, integrate, and survive while maintaining an unbroken line of both their culture and their religion.

**Basic Assumptions.** As we have indicated, Judaism is one of the three great monotheistic world religions, the others being Christianity and Islam. Judaism has as its theology the belief that the people of Israel are God's chosen people, having made a covenant with God. Banks says it this way: "At the heart of the Jewish religion lies the existence of a covenant between God and his people."[101] Although Jews believe that God's providence extends to all people, they also hold to the notion God entered into this special covenant (solemn agreement) with them through four of their prophets—Abraham, Isaac, Jacob, and Moses. In this agreement God promised to make Israel a great nation; in response the Jewish people were to be obedient to God and to carry God's message by example. From circumcision to the keeping of the Sabbath, signs of the covenant abound in Jewish culture and religion.[102] It is this covenant that is at the heart of why Jews consider themselves God's "chosen people." In Jewish theology, this special "consideration never meant advantages for the Jews, only increased responsibilities and hardships."[103]

The Jewish worldview is expressed through a number of concepts basic to the faith: (1) Jews "believe in one universal and eternal God, the creator and sovereign of all that exists,"[104] (2) no human ever will be divine, (3) humans are free, (4) "the after-life depends largely upon the behavior of the individual during his life on earth,"[105] (5) humans are the pinnacle of creation, (6) Jews belong to a group or nation whose goal is to serve God, (7) humans must be obedient to the God-given commandments in the Torah (first five books of the Bible) and assume personal responsibility, and (8) "culturally approved behavior will be rewarded after death; disapproved behavior will be punished."[106] These eight concepts compose a belief system stressing the secular notion that order must be maintained if Jews are to have a collective life. The Ten Commandments in the Torah therefore give structure to and make possible a social world.[107]

The Jewish faith is unique in that it is both a culture and a religion. It is common, for example, to find nonreligious Jews who identify fully with the culture but not with the theology. Fisher and Luyster elaborate on this point: "Judaism has no single founder, no central leader or group making theological decisions; Judaism is a people, a very old family. This family can be defined either as a religious group or a national group."[108] Judaism penetrates every area of human existence, providing humankind with a means of communicating with both the secular and transcendental worlds.[109] It

This orientation of fatalism can also be seen in the saying *"in sha'a Allah"* (if God wills it). The word *inshalle* is also used with great frequency and translates as "God willing." These usages are important, for they represent the Islamic theological concept that destiny unfolds according to God's will.

**Origins.** Although we looked at Islamic history in the last chapter, this religious tradition also needs to be examined from a religious perspective. The early origins of Islam, dating back thousands of years, are summarized by Woodward:

> The Arabs were mostly polytheists, worshiping tribal deities. They had no sacred history linking them to one universal god, like other Middle Eastern peoples. They had no sacred text to live by, like the Bible; no sacred language, as Hebrew is to Jews and Sanskrit is to Hindus. Above all, they had no prophet sent to them by God, as Jews and Christians could boast.[135]

This early animistic polytheism period, with its images of carved gods and blood sacrifices, was fertile ground in which to bring forth a new religion. The process of beginning a new theology was greatly expedited by the arrival of Muhammad. For Muslims, Muhammad (570–632) was the messenger of God. Muslims believe that their God, Allah, spoke to human beings many times in the past through other prophets. But it was Muhammad who delivered a religious message and established a social order that was to become Islam. Muhammad was troubled by the idolatry of the Arabs. He was also concerned about the fate of his people on judgment day. These two issues caused Muhammad to suffer a kind of "spiritual stress." After a series of revelations, however, Muhammad became persuaded that there was only one God, and that God was Allah. From that point on Muhammad began to preach about the power of Allah. Because he believed that community and religion were one and the same, Muhammad established the city-state that became known as Medina. This fusion of church and state was unique to Muhammad's time. This and other accomplishments marked him, according to Muslims, as "one of the most remarkable and charismatic men in history."[136]

Along with "God's message" Muhammad was able to preach what was to become known as "particularism." According to McGuire, "Religious particularism seems to require a sense of opposition: one's own religion is seen as triumphant over some other."[137] This strong element of religious particularism in Muhammad's message encouraged missionary expansion. Muhammad's' message was so powerful that when combined with missionary zeal Islam, within a few centuries, as Gordon points out, had expanded to north Africa, Persia, Jerusalem, Damascus, the Caucasus, central Asia, Europe, Egypt, and Turkey.[138] The growth and popularity of Islam as a religion has continued until today where Muslims "form the majority in more than fifty countries and a substantial minority in many others."[139]

**Pillars of Faith.** Islam, like Christianity and Judaism, is monotheistic. It believes in one God, and that God is Allah. The two major forms of Islam—Sunni and Shiite—both accept that Muhammad was the heir to the religious mantle passed down by the prophets of the Bible. According to Elias, "Muslims are supposed to believe in five cardinal points, which are so central to the religion that they are called the "Pillars of Faith."[140] To better understand how Muslims perceive the world we will now pause and briefly examine these Pillars.

*Divine Unity.* The first Pillar is called *tawhid*. Central to Islamic belief is the oneness or unity (in Arabic, *tawhid*) of Allah.[141] So strong is this commitment to the "one true

God" that Muslims believe that every other deity is false and that "it is a grievous sin to worship any other force or being in the universe."[142] A Muslim, then, is one who accepts and submits to the will of Allah. So powerful is this belief in Allah that, according to Fisher and Luyster, "The first sentence chanted in the ear of a traditional Muslim infant is the *Shahadah*—'La ilaha illa 'llah."[143] This saying literally means, "There is no god but God." To utter this allegiance to a single God is also one way a person can become a Muslim. You only have to declare, "I testify that there is no god but God, and that Muhammad is the Prophet of God."[144]

***Prophecy.*** According to Elias, "Muslims are supposed to believe that God wishes to communicate with human beings, and he uses prophets for this purpose."[145] These "messengers of God" included, among others, Adam, Noah, Abraham, Moses, and Jesus. However, Muslims "consider Jesus to have been the second to last prophet, who foretold the coming of Muhammad."[146] That is, Muslims believe that his final prophet—Muhammad—revealed God's eternal message.

***Revelation.*** Muslims hold that God revealed scriptures to humanity as guidance for them. According to Elias, "Four such scriptures are recognized: the Torah as revealed to Moses, the Psalms of David, the New Testament of Jesus, and the Koran of Muhammad."[147] Muslims believe that all the scriptures before the Koran were tampered with and corrupted by humans. Hence, they hold that the Koran is God's final word and "supersedes and over rules all previous writings."[148] Because of the importance of the Koran to the followers of the Islamic faith, we will expand our discussion of this book a little later in this section.

***Angelic Agency.*** Muslims believe in the existence of angels. As Fisher and Luyster note, for Muslims "angels are everywhere; they come to our help in every thought and action."[149] Elias speaks of the two most important angels in Islamic theology and the function they serve:

> The most famous angel is Gabriel, who served as an intermediary between God and Muhammad in the revelation of the Qur'an. Another important figure is Iblis, who used to be the chief of all angels but was punished for disobeying God by being cast out of Heaven. After that he turned into Satan and now not only rules Hell but also tries to tempt human beings from the path of goodness.[150]

***Last Judgment and Afterlife.*** The concept of the "final judgment" and the notion of an afterlife are linked because the ending of the earth determines what happens to each person on the Day of Judgment. Let us explain. Muslims, like Jews and Christians, believe in the Day of Judgment (the Day of Resurrection) when all people will be resurrected for God's judgment according to their beliefs and deeds. Put in slightly different terms, "Islam says that what we experience in the afterlife is a revealing of our tendencies in this life. Our thoughts, actions, and moral qualities are turned into our outer reality."[151] The notion of a moral code, and its tie to an afterlife, is one of the most fundamental and crucial elements of Islamic doctrine. Elias writes, "Judgment, reward, and punishment are central points in Islam and are the foundation upon which its entire system of ethics is based."[152] The result of Allah's judgment determines whether each person will be sent to heaven or hell. The Islamic teaching makes it very clear that these two places are poles apart.

Speaking of heaven, Elias notes, "The Qur'an paints an extremely vivid picture of Heaven as a garden with streams and fruit trees, where we will live a lavish and comfortable life."[153] The picture of hell, for those who oppose Allah and his prophet Muhammad, is very different. For example, in hell, according to Islam "infidels, or unbelievers, will experience the torments of Hell, fire fueled by humans, boiling water, pus, chains, searing winds, food that chokes, and so forth."[154] While many Muslims may see these two descriptions as only metaphors for an afterlife, the two depictions nevertheless underscore the importance of good and evil, and the consequences of each, in Islamic teaching.

**Five Pillars of Practice.** Having looked at the Five Pillars of Faith, we are now ready to see how these Pillars are put into practice. The acting out of these Pillars is referred to as the Five Pillars of Practice (statement of belief, prayer, alms, fasting, and pilgrimage). Many Muslims follow a sixth Pillar—*Jihad*—which we will include in our analysis. All Muslims are expected to learn and perform these duties and rituals as part of their practice. Referring to these Pillars, Fisher and Luyster maintain that they "outline specific patterns for worship as well as detailed prescriptions for social conduct, to bring remembrance of God into every aspect of daily life and practical ethics into the fabric of society."[155]

*Repetition of the Creed.* Repetition of the creed, often called *Shahada,* literally means uttering the following creed: "There is no God but Allah, and Muhammad is the Prophet of Allah." The first part of this pronouncement expresses the primary principle of monotheism, and the second element reinforces the Muslim belief in Muhammad, thus validating the Koran. These words in Arabic are heard everywhere Muslims practice their faith.

*Prayer.* Prayer (*Salat*) is a central ritual, performed five times a day: on rising, at noon, in the mid-afternoon, after sunset, and before retiring. The prayer ritual is very structured: one must face Mecca, recite a prescribed prayer, and be prostrate, with the head to the ground. These prayers can be offered in a mosque, at home or work, or even in a public place. According to tradition the worshipper concludes each session by uttering a phrase known as the *taslim:* "Peace be on you, the mercy and blessing of God."[156] When observing someone in prayer, you should "avoid staring at, walking in front of, or interrupting" the person.[157]

*Almsgiving.* Almsgiving (*Zakat*) began as a voluntary activity and has since become codified. This pillar is predicated on the belief that one is expected to share his possessions with the poor of the community. Muslims are required to give about 2.5 percent of their income to support Muslims in need and the Islamic faith. There is, like so much of religious ritual, a deeper meaning behind the act of almsgiving. Schneider and Silverman offer part of the rationale for almsgiving when they write: "Consideration for the needy is part of Islam's traditional emphasis on equality. In the mosque, all are equal; there are no preferred pews for the rich or influential—all kneel together."[158]

*Fasting.* Fasting (*Sawm*) is a tradition observed during the holy month of Ramadan, which is the ninth month of the Islamic lunar calendar. Ramadan is not only a religious experience for Muslims, but during the period there is "a great emphasis upon social and family ties."[159] During this period, Muslims do not eat, drink, engage in sexual activity, or smoke between sunrise and sunset.[160] Exceptions are of course made for the sick, nursing mothers, small children, and those who are traveling.[161] The act of fasting is believed to serve a number of purposes. First, it eliminates bodily impurities and initiates a new spiritual awakening. Second, as Nydell notes, "The purpose of fasting is to experience hunger and deprivation and to perform an act of self-discipline, humility, and faith."[162]

*Pilgrimage.* The pilgrimage (*Hajj*) means that once in a lifetime every Muslim, if financially able, is to make a pilgrimage to Mecca (in Saudi Arabia) as evidence of his or her devotion to Allah. During the official three days of Great *Hajj* the individual visits a number of holy sites. The trip involves a series of highly symbolic rituals designed to bring each Muslim closer to Allah. For example, the rituals begin "with the donning of the *ihram*, a white garment; this is a rite of ritual purification that symbolizes a turning away from worldly concerns."[163] The pilgrims also circle the *Kabha* (a simple square stone building believed to be built by Abraham) seven times.[164]

*Jihad.* The Pillar of *Jihad* is, as Ilias points out, "one of the most misinterpreted concepts in Islam."[165] Part of the misinterpretation is self-induced by Islamic extremists when they use the word as a rhetorical device to inflame the passions of their followers. This was the case when Yasser Arafat called for a "jihad to liberate Jerusalem"[166] and when the word became the rallying call of the September 11th fanatics who attacked the United States.

Another contributing factor to this misunderstanding can be traced to a lack of knowledge about Islam on the part of Westerners. Gordon speaks of all these misinterpretations in the following manner: "*Jihad* is a complex term that has too often been reduced in the Western media and popular imagination to but one of its meanings, namely 'holy war,' the slogan of modern radical Islamic movement."[167] Part of the misunderstanding stems from the fact that through the centuries the idea of *Jihad* has come to have two meanings—both of which are used by followers of the faith. One deals with the individual (inner *Jihad*), which is "the function of the individual who must strive constantly to live up to the requirements of the faith,"[168] and the other focuses on the entire Islamic tradition (outer *Jihad*). In the wake of 9/11 and subsequent events, we need to fully comprehend exactly what is meant by *Jihad*. Let us look at both of these meanings so that you might better understand this complex subject.

We begin with the inner *Jihad*, what Novak calls "the struggle with oneself."[169] For a more detailed summary of this first interpretation we turn to Sheler when he writes, "Islamic scholars say *Jihad*—literally 'to struggle'—pertains first and foremost to mastering one's passions and leading to a virtuous life."[170] Gordon states the same idea in a slightly different manner when he notes that *Jihad* "is working to achieve a perfect moral order in society as well as in each individual life."[171] What should be clear is that this first view of *Jihad* is concerned with "the battle all individuals wage against their own baser instincts."[172]

As we have already noted, it is the second interpretation of the word (the outer *Jihad*) that causes problems both in and out of the Islamic faith. As Belt points out, many Muslims see this meaning to imply an "armed struggle." It is this version of *Jihad* that "gives the radicals of today a pretext, however twisted, for waging a holy war against nonbelievers."[173] The second meaning, according to Elias, "covers all activities that either defend Islam or else further its cause."[174] Hence, early wars that Muslims engaged in that brought new lands or people under Islam were known as *Jihad* wars. Muslims often suggest that these wars were similar to the Christian crusades. One of the most famous of these wars is discussed by Armstrong when she points out that Arabs, under the name of Islam, "waged a *Jihad* against their imperial masters the Ottoman, believing that Arabs, not Turks, should lead the Muslim peoples."[175] As we noted, even today some Arabs believe that when Muslim lands or the Islamic faith are in danger, "they are bound by Islamic tradition to wage a '*Jihad* of the sword.'"[176] It is easy to see how this orientation contributes to a militant vision of the Islamic tradition.[177] Regardless of the merits of this line of reasoning, it behooves you to understand the importance that *Jihad* carries in the Islamic tradition and to try to discover which of the two meanings is being employed by the person speaking about a *Jihad*. Are they speaking of internal striving and wisdom or advocating violence against non-Muslims?

**The Koran.** For Muslims the Koran is the most sacred of all texts. It is the "last revealed word of God" and "the primary source of every Muslim's faith and practice."[178] When Allah spoke to Muhammad, the prophet wrote down, in what is now classical Arabic, the divine words in the Koran, the holy book of Islam. To a Muslim, this 114-chapter book represents the unique and exact words of Allah. It is a map, a manual on how to live. It treats topics ranging from how to lead a holy life to proper conduct in both social and economic matters. A superb capsule of the significance of the Koran to all Muslims is put forth by Belt:

> For Muslims the Koran is also a poetic touchstone, a source of the pure Arabic language memorized by Muslim school-children and recited by Muslim adults on very important occasions—weddings, funerals, holidays. In a religion that forbids statuary and icons, this book is the physical manifestation of the faith, and small, tattered copies of it are found tucked into the pockets of every shopkeeper in the Muslim world.[179]

Unlike the Hebrew Bible and the Christian New Testament, the Koran has very little narrative. As we noted, it deals with themes "regarding legal and social matters and the general conduct of life."[180] The reason the Koran offers counsel in both spiritual and practical topics is that like so much of Islam, the Koran does not distinguish between religious, social, and political life. The eclectic nature of the Koran has encouraged some observers to suggest that the Koran is the most memorized book in the world. Ilias notes, "To this day there is great prestige in memorizing the text, and one who knows it in its entirety is called *hafiz* (literally 'guardian')."[181]

In summary, for Muslims, Allah has spoken completely in the Koran, and he will not speak again. Hence, the book, says Wilson, is "seen as a perfect revelation from God, a faithful reproduction of an original engraved on a tablet in heaven which has existed from all eternity."[182]

**A Complete Way of Life.** It must be remembered that Muhammad, who was Allah's messenger, was both a political and a religious prophet. In Islam, religion and social membership are therefore inseparable. In this sense it touches all aspects of the Arab's life. As Richter and his colleagues note: "Islamic law makes no distinction between religion and society, but governs all affairs, public and private."[183] Nydell further develops this idea in the following manner: "An Arab's religion affects his whole way of life on a daily basis. Religion is taught in school, the language is full of religious expressions, and people practice their religion openly, almost obtrusively, expressing it in numerous ways.[184] Novak said it quite clearly when he wrote, "Contained within its teaching of the path to God is guidance for the entire range of human life—social, political, and economic."[185]

Simply put, Islam is "a total way of life, pervading every aspect of a believer's day-to-day behavior in the narrow sense."[186] Viewed from this perspective, Islam is a codification of all values and ways to behave in every circumstance, from child rearing to eating, to preparing for bed, to the treatment of homosexuals, to views toward modesty.[187] As Smith noted, Islam is a religion that guides human thought and practice in unparalleled detail.[188]

The channeling of most behavior through religion can be seen in the interaction between Muslims and non-Muslims. For example, Angrosino points out how "The Islamic revolution in Iran is perhaps the most conspicuous example of religion as a political force in the modern world. It is, indeed, the prototype of the 'political Islam' (sometimes referred to as 'fundamentalist Islam') that has become such a major force in our own time."[189] The same link between Islam and so-called non-religious activity is even manifested in the manner by which some Muslims perceive the business arena. For example, because Muslims are forbidden by Islamic law to charge interest on loans, banking practices can be problematic when Westerners attempt to do business in Islamic countries.[190]

Like so many worldviews that are a complete way of life, Islam is taught from infancy. You will recall that we mentioned that the first sentence chanted in the ear of a Muslim infant is "*La ilaha illa 'llah*" (There is no god but God). Lutfiyya summarizes Islam as a religion that stresses "(1) a feeling of dependency on God; (2) the fear of God's punishment on earth as well as the hereafter; and (3) a deep-seated respect for tradition and for the past."[191] This religious orientation provides its members with specific guidelines that need to be followed. Says Esler, the Islamic tradition has resulted in "an immense body of requirements and prohibitions concerning religion, personal morality, social conduct, and political behavior. Business and marital relations, criminal law, ritual practices, and much more were covered in this vast system."[192] What Islam did from its beginnings until today is bind "all its millions to a religion, a civilization, and pattern of history."[193]

**Gender.** The topic of gender differences is a difficult one for a number of reasons. First, as Westerners we are examining this subject as "outsiders." Hence we must be careful not to apply Western models to the Muslim perception and treatment of women. Second, worldwide attitudes regarding gender roles are constantly in a state of flux—particularly as they apply to Islamic women. Within Iraq, women are now taking an active role in the new National Assembly and women in Kuwait recently were granted voting rights. And third, broad generalizations regarding gender often overlook regional differences. For example, as Farah notes, "A village woman of rural Afghanistan is very different from a well-educated Palestinian who is socially and politically active in the struggle to assert her Palestinian identity."[194]

Even granting certain limitations on our discussion of gender, we agree with Gordon when he notes, "The role of women in Islamic society is a hotly debated topic both within and outside the Islamic world."[195] Contributing to the debate is the fact that the Koran and other religious teachings offer a variety of interpretations on the subject of women. For instance, Islamic scholars point to the Koran to demonstrate that women must give their consent in marriage, are included in inheritance, and even "teach that men and women have equal religious rights and responsibilities."[196] Yet the Koran also contains several verses that make it apparent that "men are clearly depicted as superior to women."[197]

The way Muslim women dress makes an obvious cultural statement about the role of gender in Islamic culture. For example, the Koran instructs women to "cover their adornments" and to "draw their veils over their bosoms."[198] They are also called upon "to be modest in public and conceal their charms from all but their own men."[199] This attitude is expressed today with the following proverb: "A woman is like a jewel: You don't expose it to thieves." It must be remembered that when evaluating gender differences, it is important to keep the host culture in mind and not let ethnocentrism color your evaluation. Ilias makes the same point when he writes: "Despite the egalitarian social structure that dominates the majority of Islamic societies, women from all backgrounds usually embrace rather than reject their religious tradition."[200]

**Art and Architecture.** The tandem relationship that Islam has to all phases of life has helped create a remarkable and brilliant civilization that is "as distinctive in its way as those of China or the Greco-Roman Mediterranean."[201] Part of that civilization is seen in the art and architecture associated with Islam. Many Arab countries are, as Crim notes, "rich in painting, sculpture, and the decorative arts."[202] What is interesting about the artistic magnificence of Arab art is that it reflects Islamic religion. The Koran "teaches that an object and its image are united."[203] This would, in part, help explain why so little Arab art is representational rather than illustrative. By this we mean that in most Arab art forms the emphasis is on shapes, form, design, style, and even calligraphy—not people, landscapes, and other representations of reality.

## HINDUISM

Hinduism, with over a billion followers, is the world's oldest known religion, and in some ways the most profound of all religions.[204] In spite of its many followers and long history, Hinduism remains the most difficult of all religious orientations for the Westerner to understand. As Esler notes, "The Hindu religion is extremely ancient, very complicated, and more than a little exotic to Western eyes."[205] Scarborough repeats this same idea when, discussing the West's view of Hinduism, he writes, "Defying straightforward explanations of Westerners, it is neither a creed nor an institution, and it includes a vast array of beliefs and deities."[206] Some of the reasons for the differences between Western views and Hinduism are mentioned by Narayanan: "Hinduism is somewhat difficult to define. The religion has no single founder, creed, teacher, or prophet acknowledged by all Hindus as central to the religion, and no single holy book is universally acclaimed as being of primary importance."[207] Boorstin buttresses this view when he writes:

> Western religions begin with a notion that One—One God, One Book, One Son, One Church, One Nation under God—is better than many. The Hindu, dazzled by the wondrous variety of the creation, could not see it that way. For so multiplex a world, the more gods the better! How could any one god account for so varied a creation? [208]

As you can see, this "thing" called Hinduism is difficult to pin down. As Smart points out, "Even to talk of a single something called Hinduism can be misleading, because of the great variety of customs, form of worship, gods, myths, philosophies, types of rituals, movements, and styles of art and music contained loosely within the bounds of a single religion."[209] However, "despite the diversity, there is a general Hindu worldview."[210] Let us now examine that worldview.

**Origins.** Providing an accurate history for the development of Hinduism is difficult. The lack of a single founder and text, which we just discussed, makes it problematical when we attempt to point to a specific chronology. Yet most historical theories trace the origins of this religion back to a time almost four thousand years ago when a group of light-skinned Aryan Indo-European tribes invaded what is now northern India.[211] These conquerors brought their religion with them and combined it with the beliefs of the indigenous people of the Indus Valley.[212] Hence, the early stages of Hinduism saw both a mixing of cultures and of gods.[213] The mixing of religious ideas and civilizations created a worldview that was as much a social system as it was a religious orientation.[214] Even today Hinduism is often referred to as a complete way of life.

The origins of Hinduism history were "marked not by remarkable personalities (although there must have been many) and great proselytizing movements, but rather by the composition of orally transmitted sacred texts expressing central concepts of what we now call Hinduism."[215] Because of the message contained in these texts, and their significance to Hinduism, we now pause and examine a few of them.

**Sacred Texts.** Earlier we mentioned that in Hinduism there was not a single text such as the Bible or the Koran. This does not mean, however, that Hinduism is without some holy books. The oldest and in some ways most fundamental scripture of these books are the Vedas. The Vedas are actually "four collections of ritual materials."[216] So important are these four books that Richter and his associates have noted that "in the difficult process of defining 'Hinduism,' one possible point to note is the acceptance of the Vedas."[217] The Vedas "transmit the ancient revelations in a series of hymns, ritual texts, and speculations composed over a period of a millennium beginning *ca 1400* B.C."[218]

Another important group of primary texts are the Upanishads. Written in Sanskrit between 800 and 400 B.C., "The Upanishads teach the knowledge of God and record the spiritual experiences of the sages of ancient India."[219] Prabhavananda and Manchester make the same point with the following description: "The literal meaning of Upanishad, 'sitting near devotedly,' brings picturesquely to mind an earnest disciple learning from his teacher."[220]

Written around 540 to 300 B.C., the Bhagavad Gita is a poem in dialogue form between a warrior Arjuna and the God Krisna.[221] This eighteen-chapter book "teaches how to achieve union with the supreme Reality through the paths of knowledge, devotion, selfless work, and meditation."[222] One of the most important characteristics of the text strikes at the very core of Hinduism. It is that God is an exalted, inspiring, and sublime force *within us*. Because God is within us, say the Hindus, we can rise above our mortal limitations and be liberated. The Bhagavad Gita also speaks of three courses you can follow to accomplish this liberation. Shattuck offers an excellent summary of those paths:

> In the Bhagavad Gita, Krishna outlines three paths that lead to liberation: (1) the discipline of knowledge, *jnana-yoga,* (2) the discipline of action, *karma-yoga,* and (3) the discipline of devotion, *bhakti-yoga.*[223]

**Important Teachings.** As is the case with all religions, the messages and lessons advanced by the sacred texts, teachers, and prophets of Hinduism are numerous, and most are beyond the scope of this chapter. However, Hinduism does contain some important teachings that you will find useful when interacting with someone who is a Hindu.

**Divine in Everything.** In many respects, Hinduism is a conglomeration of religious thought, values, and beliefs. Not only is there not a single founder, it also does not have an organizational hierarchy, such as that of the Catholic Church. Among the Hindus, one may find magic, nature worship, animal veneration, and an unlimited number of deities. This view of a vast number of deities makes Hindus among the most religious people in the world because they find the divine in everything. As Boorstin notes, "The Hindu is dazzled by a vision of the holy, not merely holy people but places like the Himalayan peaks where the gods live, or the Ganges which flows from Heaven to Earth, or countless inconspicuous sites where gods or goddesses or unsung heroes showed their divine mettle."[224] Rituals are important for showing that God is in everything, and ritual significance can be found in everyday activities such as the lighting of incense, bathing, eating, and marriage ceremonies.

**A Complete Way of Life.** As is the case with so many religions, Hinduism pervades every part of existence. Radhakrishnan, a former Oxford don and second president of India, observed: "Hinduism is more a culture than a creed."[225] This creed "forms the basis of a social system, and thereby governs the types of modalities of interaction even in contemporary society."[226] In this sense, as Venkateswaran points out, "Hinduism is not merely a religion. It encompasses an entire civilization and a way of life, whose roots date back prior to 3000 B.C.E."[227] As Narayana notes, "The boundaries between the sacred and non-sacred spheres do not apply to the Hindu traditions."[228]

**Another Reality.** Hinduism is based on the fundamental assumption that the material world, the one we can touch and see, is not the only reality. Instead, they hold that there are other realities that lead to spiritual advancement, and reveal the true nature of life, the mind, and the spirit. Guidance from the Bhagavad Gita offers the following advice: "A man of faith, intent on wisdom, His senses restrained, will wisdom win."[229] This advice is based on the Hinduism view that "What we see as reality is the merest illusion, a game, a dream, or a dance."[230] Hindus are not satisfied with what they see or hear, as reflected in the Hindu saying, "Him the eye does not see, nor the tongue express, nor the mind grasp." This notion of other realities stems from the Hindu idea of deliverance from the misleading appearances and experiences of the physical world. Hindus believe that finding satisfaction in the material and physical world might gratify us for many lifetimes, but eventually the satisfaction will "wear out." To experience nirvana, or liberation, one needs to discover the spiritual existence found outside traditional concepts of reality. For Hindus, "Nirvana releases man from the cycle of birth, suffering, death, and all other forms of worldly bondage."[231] Nirvana is, therefore, "a state of spiritual enlightenment."[232] And that "enlightenment" is another reality.

**Brahman.** The notion of Brahman is actually an extension of our last point regarding different realities. While the word Brahman has several meanings, at its foundation is the Hindu belief in a sort of cosmic principle of an ultimate reality. According to Smart this definitive reality is seen as "the sacred Power which is both the sacrificial process and in the cosmos."[233] It is a special knowledge about "the truth of things" that allows someone to be enlightened. As Usha notes, Brahman is the "all-pervading transcendental Reality."[234] Jain and Kussman offer a summary of this important concept:

> Brahman is the ultimate level of reality, a philosophical absolute, serenely blissful, beyond all ethical or metaphysical limitations. The basic Hindu view of God involves infinite being, infinite consciousness and infinite bliss.[235]

***Discovery of Self.*** Hindu philosophy, says Hammer, begins with the premise that "the ultimate cause of suffering is people's ignorance of their true nature, the Self, which is omniscient, omnipotent, omnipresent, perfect, and eternal."[236] The Upanishads speak of the self at the starting point in the following poem:

> Know this:
> The Self is the owner of the chariot,
> The chariot is the body,
> Soul (buddhi) is the (body's) charioteer,
> Mind the reins (that curb it).[237]

To help one discover "the Self," Hinduism offers its followers some specific recommendations. Non-Hindus can gain insight into this worldview by looking at some of these guidelines. First, *intellect is subordinate to intuition.* Truth does not come to the individual; it already resides within each of us. The same point is made in the Bhagavad Gita: "Meditation excels knowledge." Second, *dogma is subordinate to experience.* One cannot be told about God; one must experience God. Third, *outward expression is secondary to inward realization.* Communication with God cannot take place through outward expression; it must occur through internal realization of the nature of God. Fourth, *the world is an illusion because nothing is permanent.* All of nature, including humankind, is in an unending cycle of birth, death, and rebirth or reincarnation. Fifth, *it is possible for the human to break the cycle of birth, death, and reincarnation and experience an internal state of bliss called nirvana.* One achieves nirvana by leading a good life and thus achieving higher spiritual status in the next life. Holding materialism in abeyance and practicing introspection and meditation can advance this spiritual status. The path toward nirvana is also influenced by one's karma, an ethical standard that asserts, "Every act we make and every desire we have, shapes our future experiences and influences the path toward Nirvana."[238] As Jain and Kussman point out: "The present condition of each individual life is a product of what one did in the previous life, and one's present acts, thoughts, and decisions determine one's future states."[239]

***Dharma.*** The ideas and beliefs behind *dharma* represent an important concept of Hinduism. As DeGenova points out, "*Dharma*, perhaps the most influential concept in Indian culture and society, refers to actions characterized by consideration of righteousness and duty."[240] As you can observe from this definition, *dharma* pertains to both religious and communal responsibilities. So powerful is *dharma* to Hindus that many believe it is the main pattern underlying the cosmos and is reflected in both the "ethical and social laws of humankind."[241] An extension of the belief and command of *dharma* is the idea that if you go against *dharma*, which is seen as a cosmic norm, you will be producing bad karma. Because karma affects this life and subsequent lives (reincarnation) most Hindus seek to live a virtuous life and follow their *dharma.*

***Multiple Paths.*** One of the enduring qualities of Hinduism has been its ability to offer various paths and to adapt to diverse needs. As Swami Prabhavananda noted, "God can be realized in many ways."[242] Prabhavananda is referring to the famous Hindu expression that states "Truth is one, but sages call it by various names."[243] McGuire offers an excellent summary of the eclectic nature of Hinduism in the following paragraph:

> Indeed, Hinduism is a way of life that encourages acceptance of multiple representations of deity, multiple religious functionaries and multiple authorities, multiple understandings of duty and proper devotion, multiple allegiances to autonomous congregations, and multiple (and changeable) devotional practices and holy places.[244]

# BUDDHISM

A fifth major religious tradition that can influence intercultural communication is Buddhism. Although the followers of Buddhism are small in numbers (about 400 million followers) when compared to Christianity, Islam, or Hinduism, its impact on all civilization has been profound. As de Bary points out, "By extending itself over so many cultural areas in South and East Asia, Buddhism has established a greater universality than any other religion in that part of the world."[245] In spite of its recognition in Asia many Westerners find it difficult to understand Buddhism. Thera, quoting the philosopher T. H. Huxley, mentions some of these differences when he writes:

> Buddhism is a system which knows no God in the Western sense, which denies a soul to man, which counts the belief in immortality a blunder, which refuses any efficacy to prayer and sacrifice, which bids men look to nothing but their own efforts for salvation.[246]

**Origins.** Buddhism was founded by an Indian prince named Siddhartha Gautama in about 563 B.C. The story of how this man became known as the Enlightened One has three essential features that are crucial to the study of Buddhism. First, it is important to note that Prince Siddhartha was born into great luxury. His father was a king who had numerous mansions. As Siddhartha himself wrote, "I wore garments of silk and my attendants held a white umbrella over me."[247]

Second, in spite of all the lavish surroundings the prince felt a deep discontentment with his life. When he was twenty-nine he awoke to the recognition that man's fate was to suffer. As Van Doren notes, "Overwhelmed with the sadness, he began to seek some means of allaying the pain of life."[248] Through meditation he found the solution and became known as the Buddha (the Enlightened One). This Great Renunciation produced two emotions that some say formed the core of Buddhism. According to Robinson, Johnson, and Thanissaro, "The first is *samvega*, the emotion the prince felt on his first encounter with aging, illness, and death."[249] The next was the feeling of complete calm and "sense of serene confidence (*prasada*) the prince experienced when he discovered there was a way to overcome the suffering of life."[250]

Third, "After this momentous event the Buddha spent the next forty-five years of his life wandering up and down the Ganges Valley preaching the message to ascetic and lay persons alike."[251] Around 230 B.C. Buddhist missionaries were sent into Sri Lanka (previously called Ceylon).[252] Over the next 600–700 years, Buddhism spread across Southeast Asia, China, and Korea. By the time it reached Japan in the sixth century, Buddhism was firmly established across most of what we now call Asia.[253]

**Basic Assumptions.** As was the case with Christianity, there are numerous forms of Buddhism. And while the most popular of these (Theravada, Mahayana, and Tibetan Buddhism) have some specific differences, they nevertheless share the same basic assumptions. Let us look at some of those assumptions.

At the center of this worldview are two key concepts. First, *Buddha taught that he was not a god but simply a man.* While he could in some ways be perceived as a savior for helping people, his "powers" were not that of a Supreme Being. As de Bary points out, Buddha's "salvific powers are understood quite differently from the Judeo-Christian conception of God the Messiah and attributes of the latter as Creator, Judge, Redeemer of chosen people, Father, Son, etc., are largely absent in Buddha."[254] When the Buddha was asked if he was God, the answer he offered his followers demonstrates the importance of this crucial concept to the practice of Buddhism:

"Are you a god?" they asked.

"No."

"An angel?"

"No."

"A saint?"

"No."

"Then what are you?"

Buddha answered, "I am awake."[255]

That simple response, "I am awake," tells all those who seek Buddha that the answer to life can be found in the simple act of "waking up" and becoming aware to the truths that accompany being enlightened.[256]

Second, Buddha *taught that each individual has the potential to seek the truth on their own.* As Rahula notes, "He taught, encouraged, and stimulated each person to develop himself and to work out emancipation, for he has the power to liberate himself from all bondage through his own personal effort and intelligence."[257] Fisher and Luyster express the same idea in the following manner: "In its traditional form, it holds that our salvation from suffering lies only in our own efforts. The Buddha taught us that only in understanding how we create suffering for ourselves can we become free."[258] It is often difficult for Westerners to understand this orientation. While many Western religions stress community and direction from the clergy, Buddhism, on the contrary, challenges each individual to do their own religious seeking. A famous Buddhist saying is "Be lamps unto yourselves."

**The Four Noble Truths.** Much of the Buddha's message can be found in the Four Noble Truths. Scholars maintain that from these Truths "we get a fairly good and accurate account of the essential teaching of the Buddha."[259] Definitions of what

*Buddhism teaches that each individual has the potential to seek "the truth" on their own.*

© Photodisc/Getty Images

constitutes the Truths range from simple recipes for understanding what is wrong with the world to explanations of how it works.[260] Smith notes that these Noble Truths "stand as the axioms of his (Buddha's) system, the postulates from which the rest of his teachings logically derive."[261]

The First Noble Truth is that life is *dukka*, usually translated as "suffering." As the Buddha said in his early writings: "Birth is suffering, aging is suffering, illness is suffering, worry, misery, pain, distress, and despair are suffering; not attaining what one desires is suffering."[262] The notion of suffering is not as narrow as the word would suggest. For example, "It includes not only acute or manifest states of mental or physical suffering, but also any degree of unpleasantness, discomfort, dissatisfaction, anxiety, or unease."[263] The teachers of Buddhism would point out that if your life is not characterized by some degree of suffering, you only need look around the world to see the suffering of others. Contrary to Western interpretation, the Buddha's philosophy is not pessimistic. As Rahula notes, "First of all, Buddhism is neither pessimistic nor optimistic. If anything at all, it is realistic, for it takes a realistic view of life and the world.[264]

The Second Noble Truth (*tanha*) concerns the basis and origins of suffering. The Buddha taught that much of the suffering is caused by craving, self-desire, envy, greed, and ignorance. Suffering could also come from seeking great wealth and status to "being ignorant to the nature of reality."[265] The Buddha taught that overcoming craving and ignorance could be solved by developing the mind, thinking carefully, and meditating. These three practices would lead to true happiness and enlightenment.[266]

The Third Noble Truth, often referred to as "the End of Suffering," states that the cessation of suffering is possible. Smith summarized this Third Truth in the following manner:

> The Third Noble Truth follows logically from the Second. If the cause of life's dislocation is selfish craving, its cure lies in the overcoming of such craving [desire]. If we could be released from the narrow limits of self-interest into the vast expanse of universal life, we would be relieved of our torment.[267]

The Fourth Noble Truth is often called "the remedy" in that it is maintained that by following the Eightfold Path you could remove suffering and achieve nirvana.[268] For Buddhists, nirvana is "described in part as the perfectly peaceful and enlightened state of transformed consciousness in which passions and ignorance are extinguished."[269] Crim explains that "Nirvana was simply, directly, and absolutely the end of problems of ordinary human existence."[270]

The importance of the Fourth Noble Truth and its relationship to the Eightfold Path is highlighted by Rahula: "Practically the whole of teaching of the Buddha, to which he devoted himself during 45 years, deals in some way or other with this Path."[271] Because of their importance to the Buddhist worldview we turn to a brief discussion of the tenets of the Eightfold Path.

**The Eightfold Path.** If the Four Noble Truths deal with the symptoms that created unhappiness and suffering, the Eightfold Path is the treatment. The Buddha made it clear that it was not "an external treatment, to be accepted passively by the patient as coming from without."[272] Instead, the Buddha made it apparent that the eight steps of the path involved training—they needed to be learned and practiced simultaneously. As Solé-Leris notes, "It must be clearly understood that, although the eight factors of the path are enumerated one after the other for purposes of explanation, the idea is not that they should be cultivated successively."[273]

1. *Right view* is achieving a correct understanding and accepting the reality and origins of suffering and the ways leading to the cessation of suffering. Often referred to as "right knowledge" or "complete view," this first principle implies an awareness or a type of "intellectual orientation" of the Four Noble Truths.[274] An example of this cerebral orientation before you arrive at a meditative stage (eighth step) is made clear by the famous Buddhist teacher Anzan Hoshin, "To have Complete View, we must look very thoroughly indeed, hear very thoroughly indeed, live very thoroughly, question completely."[275]

2. *Right thought* is being free from ill will, cruelty, and untruthfulness toward the self and others. Buddha believed that right thought would "tend to purify the mind."[276]

3. *Right speech* "means abstaining from four unskilled verbal deeds: lying, divisive tale-bearing, harsh or abusive language, and idle chatter."[277] Buddha stressed that people should "use communication in the service of truth and harmony."[278]

4. *Right behavior*, some have said, is Buddha's version of the Ten Commandments, for his fourth principle "aims at promoting moral, honourable and peaceful conduct."[279] Among other things this path called for abstaining from the taking of life, from stealing, from sexual misconduct, from lying, and from drinking intoxicants. What this step is asking you to do is learn self-control and be mindful of the rights of others.

5. *Right livelihood*, for the Buddha, meant refraining "from occupations that harm living beings—for example, selling of weapons, liquor, poison, slaves, or livestock."[280] The Buddha believed that these forms of livelihood were not conducive to a spiritual progress.

6. *Right efforts* are "summarized in four terms: *avoiding* and *overcoming* unwholesome states of mind while *developing* and *maintaining* wholesome states of mind."[281] Buddha believed this right effort also called for "cultivating mindfulness and concentration."[282]

7. *Right mindfulness* is, as Solé-Leris notes, "the mindful, unbiased observation of all phenomena in order to perceive them and experience them as they are in actual fact, without emotional or intellectual distortions."[283] This step goes to the heart of the Buddhist idea that liberation is said to be through a mind that is aware of the moment. Hoshin offers some excellent examples of mindfulness in the following paragraph:

   Complete Mindfulness is to be mindful of the present. Mindfulness of body, mindfulness of environment, of feelings, of mind; mindfulness of seeing, hearing, touching, tasting, smelling, and thinking; mindful of form, basic reactivity, symbolization, patterning and consciousness.[284]

8. *Right concentration* is complete concentration on a single object and the achievement of purity of thought, free from all hindrances and distractions. As Smith and Novak point out, "Buddha counsels patient, persistent attempts at sustaining one's full attention on a single point."[285] When the mind is still, according to the Buddha, "the true nature of everything is reflected."[286]

## Important Teachings

***The Improbability of Language.*** One of the most important teachings of the Buddha, and one that can influence intercultural communication, centers on Buddha's views toward language. *Buddhism requires abandonment of views generated by the use of ordinary words and scriptures.* In Buddhism "language is considered deceptive and misleading with regard to the matter of understanding the truth."[287] Brabant-Smith offers much the same idea when he notes, "Ordinary language tends to deal with physical things and experiences, as understood by ordinary man; whereas Dharma language (Buddha's teaching) deals with the mental world, with the intangible non-physical world."[288] This notion finds expression in two famous Buddhist statements: "Beware of the false illusions created by words," and "Do not accept what you hear by report."[289] These sayings reflect Buddhists' belief that there is a supreme and wonderful truth that words cannot reach or teach—that is transmitted outside of ritual and language. A Buddhist teacher expressed it this way: "A special transmission outside the scriptures; No dependence upon words or letters; Direct pointing at the mind of man; Seeing into one's nature and the attainment of Buddhahood."[290]

***Self-Enlightenment.*** The Buddha believed you could find enlightenment within yourself. That is to say, Buddhism is *directed at the individual.* The assumption is that each person has the ability to find both truth and peace in this lifetime. Two very celebrated Buddhist maxims note: "Betake yourself to no external refuge. Work out your own salvation with diligence" and "You are your own refuge; there is no other refuge."[291] Bodhi explains the same idea in the following manner:

> The Buddha rests his teaching upon the thesis that with the right method man can change and transform himself. He is not doomed to be forever burdened by the weight of his accumulated tendencies, but through his own effort he can cast off all these tendencies and attain a condition of complete purity and freedom.[292]

***Impermanency.*** The Buddha once wrote, "Snow falls upon the river, white for an instant then gone forever."[293] It was his way of stressing the *impermanent nature of all things.* He taught that everything, both good and bad, was always changing—always in a state of flux. Buddha believed that recognizing that nothing was permanent would encourage his followers to appreciate the moment, accept the tentative nature of life, and treat other people with kindness. Moving the notion of impermanency to a code of ethics, Buddha told his followers that "People forget that their lives will end soon. For those who remember, quarrels come to an end."[294] This idea regarding the unpredictable character of life is eloquently stated by the second-century Buddhist philosopher Narajuna: "Life is so fragile, more so than a bubble blown to and fro by the wind. How truly astonishing are those who think that after breathing out, they will surely breathe in again, or that they will awaken after a night's sleep."

***Karma.*** The Buddha's teaching regarding karma is important because it sets the tone for ethical standards. Karma is concerned with action and reaction and with cause and effect: good deeds bring good results; corrupt deeds bring corrupt results. As is the case with so much of this religion, "Buddhism teaches that individuals have within themselves the potential to change their own Karma."[295] Hence, Buddha rejected the notion of divination and appealing to a higher source for good karma. The Buddha stated: "All beings are the owners of their deeds (Karma), the heirs of their deeds; their deeds are the womb from which they sprang. . . . Whatever deeds they do—good or evil—of such they will be the heirs."[296]

**Humanism.** Finally, in Buddhism we see a worldview more concerned with *humanism and the art of living daily life* than supernatural authority or even metaphysical speculation. De Bary speaks of the humanistic approach of Buddhism when he writes:

> Human virtues such as wisdom, compassion, courage, equanimity, selflessness, etc., are exemplified by the Buddha and his followers, and the Buddhist art, especially in painting and sculpture, has inspired people of different cultures in the common human ideal of aspiration, contemplative detachment, and compassionate action.[297]

The reason for Buddha's humanistic appeal is clearly explained by Smith:

> Buddha preached a religion that skirted speculation. He could have been one of the world's great meta-physicians, but the thicket of theorizing was not for him. Whether the world is eternal or not eternal, whether it is finite or infinite, whether the Buddha exists after death or not—on such questions the Buddha maintains a noble silence.[298]

## CONFUCIANISM

As is the case with all religious traditions, Confucianism, for thousands of years, has had a major role in shaping the culture and history of the people who followed this religion.[299] Even today "many analysts who have studied the East Asian economic miracle over the past three decades have concluded that Confucian values like emphasis on the future, work, achievement, education, merit, and frugality have played a crucial role in their development."[300] The importance of Confucianism to the study of intercultural communication is made clear by Gudykunst and Kim when they write, "Confucianism influences behavior in most Asian cultures and influences the behavior of Asians living in non-Asian cultures."[301]

We begin by noting Confucianism is more than a religion. In fact, "Confucius discouraged prayer."[302] It appears that "The teachings of Confucius were never intended to be a religion. It has no revelatory sacred writings, no priesthood, no doctrine of an afterlife, and frowned on asceticism and monasticism."[303] If not a religion, then what is it? Crim gives a partial answer to the question when he points out: it is "the system of social, political, ethical, and religious thought based on the teachings of Confucius and his successors." Notice the words "religious thought" instead of the word "religion."[304] Although Confucianism has had a profound influence on the cultures of Korea, Vietnam, and Japan, its greatest impact for thousands of years has been on the people of China. As Barry, Chen, and Watson note, "If we were to describe in one word the Chinese way of life for the last two thousand years, the word would be 'Confucian.'"[305] The roots of Confucianism are planted so very deep in China that even during the antireligious period of Communism the leaders borrowed the Confucian notions of selflessness, allegiance, and deference to help accomplish their purpose of controlling the masses.[306] In some ways this control was made easy. As we noted, "Confucianism has no priests, no temples, no religious rituals."[307] It is "a rational, ethical system with strict norms, stressing loyalty to the ruler, obedience toward one's father, and proper behavior."[308]

**Confucius the Man.** As was the case with Buddhism, Confucianism centers on the teachings of a single man: Confucius. The importance of this man is noted by Scarborough when he writes, "Confucius is perhaps the most influential individual in

Asian history, not so much for his views on government as for his teachings on the proper relationships and conduct among people."[309] Confucius was born in 551 B.C. in the small feudal state of Lu, which is now the Shantung province in China. Confucius dabbled at various careers early in his life; however, at the age of thirty he turned to teaching. According to McGreal, "People were impressed by his integrity, honesty, and particularly his pleasant personality and his enthusiasm as a teacher. Three thousand people came to study under him and over seventy became well-established scholars."[310] What Confucius taught grew out of his observations about "the human condition" in China during his lifetime. As Crim notes, "Confucius was witness to the political disintegration of the feudal order, an era characterized by the hegemony of various states and almost constant internecine warfare."[311] In response to these observations, "Confucius asserted that government must be founded on virtue, and that all citizens must be attentive to the duties of their position."[312]

**Basic Assumptions.** As has been pointed out, at the core of Confucianism you *do not* find a deep conviction in a God. But instead it is a deep commitment to social harmony. According to Dragga, Confucianism "emphasizes the individual's social relations and social responsibility over self-consciousness: people perceive themselves according to their social relationships and responsibilities as opposed to their individual being."[313] The rationale for this point of view is that "order does not reside in some cosmically transcendent force, but in the bonds of society."[314] As Yum notes, "Confucianism is a philosophy of human nature that considers proper human relationships as the basis of society."[315] These "proper" relationships involved such things as the protection of "face," dignity, self-respect, reputation, honor, and prestige.

**The Analects.** Confucius did not write down his philosophy. Therefore, the details of his teaching have come to us through his disciples. The most influential and far reaching of these collections is the Analects—which literally means "discussion over Confucius' words." These books were not written in a systematic and structured fashion. In fact, the Analects were written over a fifty-year period and consist of twenty books. Today these books continue to be a considerable influence on Chinese and East Asian values and behavior. What they contain are the aphorisms, sayings, stories, proverbs, and the like that the disciples believed to be the most salient ideas of Confucian philosophy.[316]

**Important Teachings.** As we have already indicated, Confucianism teaches that the proper and suitable foundation for society is based on respect for human dignity. That respect stressed the proper hierarchy in social relationships between family members, community, and superiors. Confucius set forth a series of ideals that structured much of his thought about these relationships. An understanding of these teachings will help you appreciate something about Asian perception and interaction.

*Jen (humanism).* Most scholars agree that the idea of *Jen* is the cornerstone of what Confucius taught. *Jen* "can be translated as human-heartedness, humanity, virtue, benevolence, morality, etc."[317] Confucius taught that *Jen* was the ultimate guide to human behavior and all people should act according to the principles of *Jen*. These meant that regardless of one's status or personality, conflicts can be avoided and harmony achieved if *Jen* was extended to others.

***Chun tzr (perfect person).*** A person who possesses *Chun tzr* is thought to be the ideal person, the kind of person in who cultivated feeling has maximum development.[318] The trait is often referred to as the "superior man" in that it "is someone fully adequate and poised to accommodate others as much as possible rather than to acquire all that he or she can acquire selfishly."[319]

***Li (rituals, rites, proprieties, conventions).*** *Li* is the outward expression of good manners—the way things should be done. "Confucius believed there must be defined rules that society will comply with in such matters as social relationships, religious ceremonies, and other general customs."[320] In contemporary times, *li* could be something as straightforward as a handshake or a bow as a correct greeting.

***Te (power).*** *Te* literally means power. But for Confucius it was power that was properly used. He strongly believed that "leaders must be persons of character, sincerely devoted to the common good and possessed of the character that compels respect."[321]

***Wen (the arts).*** Confucius had great reverence for the arts. As Gannon points out, Confucius saw the "arts as a means of peace and as an instrument of moral education."[322] We can further observe that veneration in the following paragraph:

> By poetry the mind is aroused; from music the finish is received. The odes quicken the mind. They induce self-contemplation. They teach the art of sensibility. They help to retrain resentment. They bring home the duty of serving one's parents and one's prince.[323]

**Confucianism and Interpersonal Communication.** As is the case with all the worldviews we have examined, Confucianism influences perception and communication in a variety of ways. First, Confucianism teaches, both directly and indirectly, the notion of *empathy*. For example, *Jen*, which we just discussed, is often thought of as "the capacity to measure the feelings of others by one's own."[324] This, of course, is the definition of empathy.

Second, when communicating, those that follow Confucian philosophy would be concerned with *status relationships*. Remember, it was the goal of Confucius "to make social relationships work without strife"[325] and part of that working is manifested in proper status relationships. You can see this in everything from differentiated linguistic codes (words showing respect and rank)[326] to "paternalistic leadership" in business and educational settings.[327]

Third, Confucian principles manifest great concern for *ritual and protocol*. As we noted early, social etiquette was an important part of Confucian teaching. Novak reminds us that "in Confucius's view, attentive performance of social ritual and everyday etiquette shapes human character in accordance with archetypal patterns."[328] In the business context, according to Beamer and Varner, ritual and protocol can be seen in the fact that when negotiating with the Chinese they "have a preference for form."[329] The penchant for form and correct manners, the Chinese believe, will preserve harmony among the participants.

Fourth, in Confucian philosophy *interaction within the family* is the model for most social relationships.[330] These relationships have well-defined hierarchical order concerning father and son, husband and wife, and old and young members of the family.[331]

Finally, Confucian philosophy would tend to encourage *the use of indirect instead of direct language*. In North America, people often ask very direct questions, are sometimes blunt, and frequently use the word "no," and like it when people get to the point rather quickly. Confucian philosophy, on the other hand, encourages indirect communication. For example, "In Chinese culture, requests often are implied rather than stated explicitly for the sake of relational harmony and face maintenance."[332] Yum makes much the same point while demonstrating the link between Confucianism and talk:

> The Confucian legacy of consideration for others and concern for proper human relationships has led to the development of communication patterns that preserve one another's face. Indirect communication helps to prevent the embarrassment of rejection by the other person or disagreement among partners.[333]

As we conclude our discussion of Confucianism we once again remind you of its importance to Chinese culture. As a way of life as much as a religion, it has survived for thousands of years and as a philosophy it is "firmly entrenched in Chinese culture, and its values still can be seen today."[334]

## Religion: A Final Thought

One of the key points of this chapter has been the idea that there are a variety of approaches to dealing with cosmic questions about life and death. Friedman makes the same point when he notes "that God speaks multiple languages."[335] Yet because of space constraints we are able to look at only some of those "languages." As we noted at the outset of this chapter, there were numerous worldviews and religions we had to omit from our analysis. For example, in the West there are millions of people who are Mormons, Jehovah's Witnesses, and Unitarians. There are also people who follow New Age philosophies as a worldview or practice Wicca (witchcraft). Turning to Asia and East Asia we did not include Taoism and Shintoism or Zen Buddhism. And we omitted primal religions practiced in parts of Africa, Australia, the Pacific Islands, and the native Indian cultures of North and South America. Should you find the time and opportunity to learn about these religions and worldviews, you will discover more about the crucial link between worldview and communication. You will once again learn one of the central messages of this section—simply that religion, for thousands of years, has had a pronounced impact on the life of every culture and the lives of the members of those cultures. And today, perhaps more than ever before, that impact cannot be ignored.

The question is clear—can the world's great religions learn to live together? Friedman poses the same question in the following paragraph:

> Can Islam, Christianity, and Judaism know that God speaks Arabic on Fridays, Hebrew on Saturday, and Latin on Sundays, and that he welcomes different human beings approaching him through their own history, out of their own history, out of their language and cultural heritage?[336]

## Summary

- Worldview is a culture's orientation toward God, humanity, nature, the universe, life, death, sickness, and other philosophical issues concerning existence.
- Although worldview is communicated in a variety of ways, religion is the predominant element of culture from which your worldview is derived.

- Although all religions have some unique features they share many similarities. These include, among other things, sacred scriptures, a specific authority, traditional rituals, a set of ethics, and providing a sense of security to their members.
- The six most prominent religious traditions are Christianity, Judaism, Islam, Hinduism, Buddhism, and Confucianism.

## Activities

1. In a small group, try to answer the following question: Why has religion been so relevant to humankind for more than ten thousand years?
2. Attend a church that is very different from your own, and try to determine the rituals and messages that might influence perceptions of members of that church.
3. In a small group, discuss what aspects of religion are most directly related to perception and communication.

## Discussion Ideas

1. Explain how understanding the religious aspect of a particular culture's lifestyle might help you understand that culture's worldview.
2. Explain the phrase "religion is only one kind of worldview."
3. What is the link between religion and the values of a culture?
4. What common set of ethics could you locate from the six religious traditions discussed in this chapter?

## CHAPTER 4

# Culture and the Individual: Cultural Identity

*The particular human chain we're part of is central to our individual identity.*

ELIZABETH STONE

*The value of identity of course is that so often with it comes purpose.*

RICHARD GRANT

*Who am I?* Stop for a minute and reflect on that question. Jot down a few of your thoughts. Some of you will find the question relatively easy and be able to produce a lengthy list of identifiers. Others will struggle and be able to write down only a few items. Regardless of the length of your list, the answers provided in response to the question will offer insight into some of your many identities.

Identity is an abstract and multifaceted concept that plays a significant role in all communication interactions. Globalization, intercultural marriage, and immigration patterns promise to add greater complexity to cultural identities in the twenty-first century.[1] With this in mind, we use this chapter to discuss some of the various aspects of identity, which becomes particularly important during intercultural communication. In Chapters 2 and 3, we examined how the deep structures of culture contribute to your identities. So important is the topic of identities that we will return to it throughout the book.

Since the concept is so pervasive, it is necessary to have a good appreciation of exactly what identity entails. To provide that understanding, we begin by pointing out the expanding need to understand the role of identity in our culturally diverse society. This is followed by a theoretical definition of identity, a typology of some of your various identities, and an examination of some of the many different ways identity is acquired. We then address the assortment of ways you establish and enact your cultural identities and the role of identity in communication. Our final section will look at the growing phenomena of bicultural and multicultural identities that are being produced by globalization.

# The Need to Understand Identity

The necessity of understanding your sense of identity is self-evident. Identity development is considered a critical aspect of everyone's psychological well-being. According to Pinney, a principal objective of one's adolescence years is the formation of an identity, and "those who fail to achieve a secure identity are faced with identity confusion, a lack of clarity about who they are and what their role is in life."[2]

An understanding of identity is also an essential aspect in the study and practice of intercultural communication.[3] Increased international contact driven by the processes of globalization, armed conflicts (which are partly based on cultural differences), and domestic diversity arising from immigration, interracial marriages, and divergent values add to the importance of identity in intercultural situations.

The growing awareness of identity among U.S. Americans was demonstrated in the 2000 census, which was the first time respondents were allowed to select more than one category to report their racial identity. Some 2.4 percent of the respondents, representing almost 7 million U.S. Americans, identified themselves as being of two or more races.[4] Another question on Census 2000 allowed individuals to write in their "ancestry or ethnic origin." That question produced about 500 different categories[5] and more than 90 of the categories had populations in excess of one hundred thousand.[6] The Census Bureau reports that the information is needed to "tailor services to accommodate cultural differences" and to "address the language and cultural diversity of various groups."[7] It is also a good measure of U.S. diversity and the level of awareness that people have about their identity.

The unsettled world that we all live in is in part influenced by adherence to varying perceptions of identity. Writing in the *New York Times*, Brooks talks of a "great reshuffling of identities, and the creation of new, often more rigid groupings."[8] He contends that despite the influence of information technologies and the forces of globalization, "old national identities are proving surprisingly durable."[9] Brooks sees people becoming more self-segregated and distancing themselves, socially and physically, from groups that exhibit different cultural traits, which can encompass political views, religious beliefs, and lifestyle choices. The uncertainty resulting from the rapidly changing world order and upheaval of traditional social structures is creating a high degree of uncertainty among many people. In reaction to these changes, "Many millions of people believe that their best haven of certainty and security is a group based on ethnic similarity, common faith, economic interest, or political like-mindedness."[10] In other words, as people struggle to adapt to the dynamics of modern social life, identity is becoming an important factor in how they live their lives and with whom they associate.

Of immediate concern to the study of intercultural communication is how identity influences and guides expectations about your own and others' social roles, as well as providing guidelines for your communication interaction with others.[11] For example, the U.S. cultural model for classroom interactions between a professor and students is very well defined. During lectures, students are free to ask questions and respectfully challenge the professor's assertions. Students are aware that the professor may call on them to answer questions about the lesson, and this anticipation instills a motivation to be prepared. Identity as professor or student provides the blueprint for classroom behavior. But the blueprint described here is designed for a U.S. classroom. In collective cultures, such as Japan, the identity roles are the same, but the expectations are quite different. Japanese students do not normally expect to be called on to answer questions, and they seldom ask their professor questions during class. This example is somewhat oversimplified, but it demonstrates the importance of understanding the role of identity in an intercultural situation.

There are many more reasons behind the need to gain an awareness of identity and its influence on intercultural interactions. However, we believe the above discussion should convince you of the need to become better acquainted with both your own identity and that of others. To help you with that task, we will begin with a definition of identity.

# Defining Identity

As we mentioned earlier, identity is an abstract, complex, and dynamic concept. As a result of those characteristics, identity is not easily defined, and therefore communication scholars have provided a variety of descriptions. Yep, for example, sees identity as "a person's conception of self within a particular social, geographical, cultural, and political context. . . . Identity gives the individual a sense of self and personhood."[12] Ting-Toomey considers identity to be the "reflective self-conception or self-image that we each derive from our family, gender, cultural, ethnic, and individual socialization process. Identity basically refers to our reflective views of ourselves and other perceptions of our self-images."[13] In a more concise definition, Martin and Nakayama characterize identity as "our self-concept, who we think we are as a person."[14] For Mathews, "Identity is how the self conceives of itself, and labels itself."[15] While all of these definitions treat identity in its broadest sense, some scholars address cultural identity more specifically.

Fong contends that "culture and cultural identity in the study of intercultural relations have become umbrella terms that subsume racial and ethnic identity."[16] She defines cultural identity as:

> The identification of communications of a shared system of symbolic verbal and nonverbal behavior that are meaningful to group members who have a sense of belonging and who share traditions, heritage, language, and similar norms of appropriate behavior. Cultural identity is a social construction.[17]

Lustig and Koester look at cultural identity as "one's sense of belonging to a particular cultural or ethnic group."[18] Ting-Toomey and Chung see cultural identity as "the emotional significance that we attach to our sense of belonging or affiliation with the larger culture."[19]

This blizzard of definitions is not meant to confuse you but instead to demonstrate the abstractness of identity, which makes it difficult to construct a single, concise description agreeable to all. Part of the difficulty stems from identity being an early topic of interest in the fields of psychology and sociology,[20] and only later becoming a subject of investigation for intercultural communication scholars, who began to examine the cultural components of identity. As a result, some definitions address "identity" and others speak of "cultural identity." As we will demonstrate throughout the chapter, we believe that culture influences every facet of all your identities.

Identity is dynamic and multiple. By this we mean that identity is not static, but changes as a function of your life experiences.[21] In addition you have more than one identity. Consider how you identified yourself in grade school, in high school, and after you entered college. During that time you acquired some new identities and set aside some old ones. For example, you left behind your identity of being a high school student and assumed that of a college student. However, you did retain the regional identity of your hometown and state and your racial identity. Perhaps you gave up your identity of being a member of a high school sports team, such as swimming or volleyball, and took on the identity of a sorority or fraternity member. As you can see, your identity is a composite of multiple identities, which are integrated—they do not work in isolation but in combination based on the situation.[22] As an illustration, when you are in the classroom, your identity as a student is salient, but you are still a male or female, a friend of some of your classmates, a part-time employee, a son or daughter, and perhaps even a wife or a husband, to list just a few.

To help reduce some of the complexity and better understand peoples' multiple identities, some researchers have constructed categories to classify the different identities. Turner offers three similar categories of classification.[23] *Human* identities are those perceptions of self that link you to the rest of humanity and set you apart from other life forms. *Social* identities are represented by the various groups you belong to, such as race, ethnicity, occupation, age, hometown, and others. Social identity is a product of the contrast between membership in some social groups but not others (i.e., the in-group/out-group dichotomy). *Personal* identity arises from those things that set you apart from other in-group members and mark you as special or somewhat unique. This may be some innate talent, such as the ability to play a musical instrument without formal training, a special achievement, like sailing around the world solo, or something as intangible as your personality.

Hall offers a similar categorization of identity. He says, "Each of us has three levels of identity that, depending on the context, may or may not be salient in our interactions with others. These three levels are *personal*, *relational*, and *communal*."[24] *Personal* identities are those which make you unique and distinct from others. *Relational* identities are a product of your relationships with other people, such as husband/wife, teacher/student, and executive/manager. *Communal* identities are "typically associated with large-scale communities, such as nationality, ethnicity, gender, or religious or political affiliation."[25]

Hall's communal identity is essentially the same as Taylor's social identity, and Gudykunst provides a further classification of that type of identity, which is the most important during intercultural communication.

> Our social identities can be based on our memberships in demographic categories (e.g., nationality, ethnicity, gender, age, social class), the roles we play (e.g., student, professor, parent), our membership in formal or informal organizations (e.g., political parties, social clubs), our associations or vocations (e.g., scientists, artists, gardeners), or our memberships in stigmatized groups (e.g., homeless, people with AIDS).[26]

This section has provided a theoretical understanding of identity as an abstract concept and attempted to show that an individual's identity is "made up of numerous overlapping aspects or subidentities."[27] We also discussed some ways of organizing your multiple identities into broad categories. Since they are the most relevant to intercultural communication interaction and study, we will now look at some different social identities and examine how they are influenced by culture.

# A Typology of Identities

Although we use the terms *identity* and *identities* interchangeably, we have also pointed out that in actuality one's identity consists of multiple identities, which act in concert. The importance and saliency of any single identity is a function of the situation. As the context varies, you may choose to emphasize one or more of your identities. While attending class, your identity as a student will be in the forefront, but when you arrive at work, your occupational identity will become paramount. In both environments, however, some of your identities, such as racial and biological sex, will also be present, albeit in a secondary role. Regardless of the identity or identities that are on display, all are tempered, to various degrees, by culture. In this section, we will examine a few of your many identities and illustrate how culture influences each.

## RACIAL IDENTITY

We should begin by explaining that race is a social construct arising from efforts to categorize people into different groups. According to Collier, race has been used by academic, government, and political agencies to identify groups of people as outsiders.[28] Researchers employing this perspective approach race as a socially constructed term related to issues of power. Allport indicates that anthropologists originally designated three separate races—Mongoloid, Caucasoid, and Negroid, but added others later.[29] These categories divided people into groups based solely on physical appearances. Today, racial identity is commonly associated with external physical traits such as skin color, hair texture, facial appearance, or eye shape.[30] Modern science, however, has found that there is very little genetic variation among human beings, which belies the precision of racial categorization as a means of classifying people. The concept is further eroded by centuries of genetic intermixing,[31] which is becoming an increasing occurrence in contemporary society through interracial marriage. The concept of racial identity persists in the U.S. as a socially constructed idea, no doubt abetted by the historical legacy of events such as slavery, the early persecution of Native Americans, issues of civil rights, and most recently, a growing influx of immigrants.

## ETHNIC IDENTITY

Because "the difference between the terms *race* and *ethnicity* has not been clarified adequately in the literature"[32] the variation between racial and ethnic identity can also be unclear and confusing. The problem is further compounded because people frequently delineate their ethnic identity in "highly individual ways according to their particular situation and circumstances."[33] From our perspective, however, racial identity is tied to a biological heritage that produces similar, identifiable physical characteristics. Ethnicity or ethnic identity is derived from a sense of shared heritage, history, traditions, values, similar behaviors, area of origin, and in some instances, language.[34]

Some people derive their ethnic identity from a regional grouping, such as:

- The Basque, who are located along the Spanish-French border
- The Bedouin, who are nomadic Arab groups that range from the eastern Sahara across North Africa and the Arabian Peninsula, to the eastern coast of Saudi Arabia
- The Kurds, a large ethnic group in northeast Iraq, with communities in Turkey, Iran, and Syria

- The Roma (commonly called Gypsies), who are scattered across eastern and western Europe

In each of these groups, their sense of ethnicity transcends national borders and is grounded in common cultural beliefs and practices.

The ethnicity of many U.S. Americans is tied to their ancestors' place of origin prior to their coming to the U.S., from places such as Germany, Italy, Mexico, or China. After the arrival of the original immigrants, subsequent generations often refer to themselves as German-American, Italian-American, Mexican-American, or Chinese-American. As Chen explains, the hyphen both separates and connects the two cultural traditions.[35]

During the early years of the United States, immigrants often grouped together in a particular region to form ethnic communities. In these areas the people's sense of ethnic identity remained strong as traditional cultural practices and beliefs were followed and perpetuated. But as time passed, members of younger generations moved to areas of greater ethnic diversity and often married into other ethnic groups. For some, this tended to dilute their feeling of ethnic identity, and today, it is not uncommon to hear U.S. Americans refer to their ethnicity by providing a lengthy historical account of their family's ethnic merging. Others will often simply refer to themselves as "just an American" or "a White American." Frequently, they are members of the U.S. dominant culture, which originally grew out of Judeo-Christian religious traditions imported from Western Europe, whose historical lineage is characterized by an extensive mixing of interethnic marriages over the years. Martin and Nakayama write that many cultural practices associated with "whiteness" are beyond the awareness of the actual participants, but are move discernible by members of minority culture groups.[36] Thus, "whiteness" is often associated with positions of privilege.

*Gender identity refers to the ways particular cultures differentiate between masculine and feminine roles.*

© Dennis MacDonald/PhotoEdit

## GENDER IDENTITY

Gender identity is quite different from biological sex or sexual identity. Gender refers to how a particular culture differentiates masculine and feminine social roles. As Ting-Toomey tells us, "Gender identity, in short, refers to the meanings and interpretations we hold concerning our self-images and expected other-images of 'femaleness' and 'maleness.'"[37]

Culture influences on what constitutes gender beauty and how it is displayed vary between cultures. In the U.S., despite the threat of skin cancer, many young women consider having a good tan to be part of their summer beauty regimen. In Northeast and Southeast Asian cultures, however, dark skin is considered a mark of lower socio-economic status and exposure to the sun is avoided. Some cultures express gender differences through language usage. In Japanese, certain words are traditionally used exclusively by women, and men employ different words to express the same meaning. In English, there is little or no distinction among words used by women and men. Cultural variations in gender identity can also be evident in fashion. James found that in Denmark:

> The men are more concerned with their weight than the women, who wear loose-fitting clothes, and hardly a miniskirt is to be seen—even among teenagers. This is because being extravagantly sexy is not the main way for women to advance themselves in Denmark.[38]

This is quite in contrast to fashion in the U.S. and many Western European nations.

## NATIONAL IDENTITY

National identity refers to your nationality. For the majority of people, it is the nation where they were born. But national identity can also be acquired by immigration and naturalization. People who have taken citizenship in a different country from their birthplace will eventually begin to adopt some or all aspects of national identity, depending on the strength of attachment to their new homeland. Alternatively, people residing permanently in another nation may retain a strong attachment to their homeland. One of the authors knows many expatriates who have lived and worked in Japan for an extended time, yet they continue to consider their national identity to be their country of birth—e.g., Australian, U.S. American, or Peruvian. National identity usually becomes more pronounced when a person is away from their home country. When asked where they are from, international travelers normally respond with their national identity—i.e., "We are from Canada." There are, however, many instances where local affiliation outweighs national affiliation. Texans, for instance, are noted for identifying themselves as being from Texas rather than from "the States." International sporting events or periods of international crisis can also stimulate strong feelings of national identity.[39]

As we have indicated, identity is dynamic and can change contextually over time. A particularly interesting example of this dynamism is occurring in the European Union, where younger generations are moving away from the national identity of their parents and adopting what might be termed a transnational identity. Thomas Reid reports that the young adults from EU nations tend to "think of 'Europe' as their native land."[40] To test this assertion, one of the authors asked two international graduate students—one from Austria and one from Germany—attending a U.S. university about their national identity. The student from Austria considered herself to be a

"European" rather than Austrian. The other indicated she still referred to herself as German, but she had many friends who were confused about their national identity.

Most nations are home to a number of different cultural groups, but one group usually exercises the most power and is often referred to as the dominant culture because its members maintain control of economic, governmental, and institutional organizations. This control leads to the establishment of a "national character," which has been defined by Allport:

> "National character" implies that members of a nation, despite ethnic, racial, religious, or individual differences among them, do resemble one another in certain fundamental matters of belief and conduct, more than they resemble members of other nations.[41]

In the U.S., the dominant culture is considered to be members of Western European ethnicity, and cultural traits arising from that heritage are ascribed to the nation as a whole and referred to as the "national character."

## REGIONAL IDENTITY

With the exception of very small nations like Monaco or the Holy See (i.e., Vatican City), every country can be divided into a number of different geographical regions, and often these regions reflect varying cultural traits. The cultural contrasts between these regions may be manifested through ethnicity, language, accent, dialect, customs, food, dress, or different historical and political legacies. Residents of these regions use one or more of those characteristics to demonstrate their regional identity.

In the U.S., many regional identities are delimited by state boundary lines, and almost everyone is proud of their home state. Residents of Texas and California offer prime examples of pride in regional identity. Louisiana is marked by a distinct cultural tradition derived from its French historical heritage. Regional identity can also be based on a larger geographical area, such as New England, the South, "back East," or the Midwest.

In Japan, regional identity is marked by a variety of different dialects (e.g., Tokyo, Kansai, Kyoto), some of which are difficult to understand (e.g., Kagoshima and Okinawa) by individuals from outside the area. Japanese living overseas often form clubs based on their home prefecture and hold periodic gatherings to celebrate their common traditions. Despite reunification, East and West German identity remains a reality. Mexicans demonstrate their regional identity when they tell people they are from Sinaloa, Michoacan, Oaxaca, or Mexico City. Political division resulting from war has imposed regional identities on residents in North and South Korea.

## ORGANIZATIONAL IDENTITY

In some cultures, a person's organizational affiliation can be an important source of identity. This is especially true in collectivistic cultures, but far less so in individualistic cultures. To illustrate this dichotomy we will contrast organizational identity practices in Japan, a collectivistic culture, and the U.S., an individualistic culture.

While the practice is becoming less prevalent among younger employees, Japanese businessmen employed by large corporations have traditionally worn a small lapel pin to signal their company affiliation. There is no similar practice among U.S. managers and executives. Although some in the U.S. occasionally may wear polo shirts or ties with a company logo, this is not a common or habitual practice. In Japan, a person's organizational identity is so important that during introductions the company's name

*Organizational affiliation can be an important source of identity.*

is given before the individual's name. For example, Mrs. Suzuki, an employee at the Tokyo Bank, would be introduced as *Tokyo Ginkōno Suzuki san* (translation: Tokyo Bank of Suzuki Mrs.).[42] In the U.S., an individual is introduced by their name first and then the organization. On business cards, the Japanese businessperson's company and position are placed above his or her name. On U.S. business cards, the company name is normally at the top, followed by the individual's name in large, bold letters, and the organizational position is under the name in smaller type. These rather simplistic and seemingly mundane examples offer insight into how collective cultures stress group membership and individualistic cultures emphasize the individual.

## PERSONAL IDENTITY

Earlier in this chapter we noted that personal identity consists of those characteristics that set one apart from others in their in-group, those things that make one unique, and how one sees oneself. There are also cultural influences at play when determining

*Personal identity arises from those things that help set you apart from the dominant culture and that you believe mark you as unique.*

© Rudi Von Briel/PhotoEdit

personal identity. Markus and Kitayama report that "people in different cultures have strikingly different construals of the self, of others, and of the interdependence between the two."[43] People from individualistic cultures like the U.S. and Western Europe, work to exemplify their differences *from* others, but members of collectivistic cultures tend to emphasize their membership or connection *to* others. While still slaves to fashion, most U.S. Americans try to demonstrate their personal identity in their dress and appearance. In collective cultures, like Japan, people tend to dress in a similar fashion because it is important and, often even necessary, to blend in.

## CYBER AND FANTASY IDENTITY

The Internet allows you to quickly and easily access and exchange information on a worldwide basis. As Suler, a psychologist, informs us, the Internet also provides an opportunity to escape the constraints of everyday identities:

> One of the interesting things about the Internet is the opportunity it offers people to present themselves in a variety of different ways. You can alter your style of being just

slightly or indulge in wild experiments with your identity by changing your age, history, personality, physical appearance, even your gender. The username you choose, the details you do or don't indicate about yourself, the information presented on your personal web page, the persona or avatar you assume in an online community—all important aspects of how people manage their identity in cyberspace.[44]

The Internet allows individuals to select and promote what they consider the positive features of their identity and omit any perceived negative elements, or even construct entirely new identities. According to Suler, some online groups require participants to assume an "imaginary persona," and infatuation with these invented identities can become so strong they can "take a life of their own."[45] For some online gamers, the allure of their fantasy identity has become so compelling that they become addicted and suppress their actual persona.[46]

Another form of fantasy identity extending across cultures centers on characters from science fiction movies, comic books, and *anime*. Every year, people attend domestic and international conventions devoted to these subjects. For example, the 2005 Hong Kong Game Fair and Comics Festival was expected to draw 400,000.[47] Comic-Con International has been held annually in San Diego, California, since 1970, and in 2005 attracted more than 104,000 attendees, including exhibitors.[48] At these gatherings, some attendees come dressed, individually or in groups, as their favorite fantasy character or characters. For a few hours or days, they assume and enact the identity of their favorite media character.

There are many additional forms of identity that play a significant role in the daily lives of people. For example, we have not examined the functions of age, religion, socio-economic class, physical ability, or minority status, all of which are part of some individuals' identity and are influenced by culture.

# Acquiring and Developing Identities

As we discussed earlier, identities are largely a product of group membership. This is echoed by Ting-Toomey when she writes: "Individuals acquire and develop their identities through interaction with others in their cultural group."[49] Identity development then becomes a process of familial and cultural socialization, exposure to other cultures, and personal development. We have already looked at the family in Chapter 2, but the influence of family on identity is so great that we need to touch on a few points here. The initial exposure to your identity came from your family, where you began to learn the culturally appropriate beliefs, values, and social roles.[50] Guidance from family members begins at a very young age by teaching the proper behavior for boys and girls, which instills gender identity. Interacting with extended family members teaches the different age-appropriate behaviors. And it is the family which first begins to inculcate the concept of an individual- or group-based identity.

Upon entering school, you were required to learn and demonstrate the behaviors that are culturally ascribed for a student. The media also plays a considerable role in identity development. The near constant exposure to media stereotypes creates a sense of how we should look, dress, and act in order to present age and gender appropriate identities. Media is used to recruit people to join different groups, such as those for or against a specific activity like gay marriage, abortion, or the war in Iraq—and inclusion into a group imparts another identity.

From a theoretical perspective, Phinney offers a three-stage model to help understand identity development.[51] Although her model focuses on ethnic identity among adolescents, it can also be applied to the acquisition and growth of cultural identity. *Unexamined ethnic identity*, the initial stage, is "characterized by the lack of exploration of ethnicity."[52] During this stage, the individual is not particularly interested in exploring or demonstrating their personal ethnicity. For members of minority cultures, this lack of interest may result from the desire to suppress their own ethnicity in an effort to identify with the majority culture. Majority members in the U.S., on the other hand, seem to take for granted that their identity is the social norm and give little thought to their own ethnicity.[53]

The second stage, *ethnic identity search*, begins when the individual becomes interested in learning and understanding their own ethnic identity. Movement from stage one to stage two can result from a variety of stimulations. An incident of discrimination might move a minority member to reflect on his or her own ethnicity. This could lead to a realization that some beliefs and values of the majority culture can be detrimental to minority members,[54] and stimulate a movement toward one's own ethnicity. Dolores Tanno grew up in northern New Mexico and had always considered herself Spanish. After leaving New Mexico, she discovered that some people saw her as Mexican rather than Spanish, and this motivated her ethnic identity search.[55] Increased interest in ethnic identity could come from attending a cultural event, taking a culture class, or some other event that produces a greater awareness of one's cultural heritage. *Ethnic achievement*, Phinney's final stage of identity development, is reached when you have a clear and confident understanding of your own cultural identity. For minority members, this usually comes with an ability to effectively deal with discrimination and negative stereotypes.[56] Identity achievement can also provide one with greater self-confidence and feelings of personal worth.

Martin and Nakayama have constructed separate, four-stage identity development models for minority and majority members. In the minority model, *unexamined identity*, the initial stage, is similar to Phinney's model, where individuals are not really concerned with issues of identity. During stage two, *conformity*, minority members endeavor to fit in with the dominant culture and may even possess negative self-images. *Resistance and separatism*, stage three, is usually the result of some cultural awakening that stimulates a greater interest and adherence to one's own culture. Concurrently, rejection of all or selected aspects of the dominant culture may occur. In the final stage, *integration*, individuals have a sense of pride and identity with their own cultural group and demonstrate an acceptance of other cultural groups.[57]

The model for majority identity development follows a similar first stage, *unexamined identity*, where identity is not a concern. *Acceptance*, the second stage, is characterized by acquiescence to existing social inequities, even though such acceptance may be at an unconscious level. At the next stage, *resistance*, the dominant culture member becomes more aware of existing social inequities, begins to question her or his own culture, and increases association with minority culture members. Achievement of the fourth and final stage, *redefinition and reintegration*, brings an increased understanding of one's dominant culture identity and an appreciation of minority cultures.[58]

Based on how they were achieved, your identities can also be classified as ascribed or avowed.[59] Simply stated, this refers to whether your identities were obtained involuntarily or voluntarily. Your racial, ethnic, and sexual identities were assigned at birth and are considered ascribed, or involuntary. In hierarchical cultures where social status is often inherited, such as Mexico, a person's family name can be a strong source of ascribed identity. Your identity as a university student is avowed because you voluntarily elected to attend the school. Although being a university student is a voluntary identity, your culture has established expectations for delineating appropriate and inappropriate social behavior for college students. When enacting your college student identity, you will normally try to conform to those socially appropriate expectations, sometimes consciously and at other times subconsciously.[60]

# Establishing and Enacting Cultural Identity

By now, you should have a clear understanding of what constitutes identity, an awareness of some of your many identities, and the difference between ascribed and avowed identities. This background will help you better understand how cultural identities are established and acted out.

As you go about your daily routine, stepping through various contexts, different identities are established, re-established, and displayed. By interacting with others you continually create and recreate your cultural identity through communication.[61] As Molden tells us, "It is through communication that we are able to express and (hence make known) our similarities and dissimilarities to others."[62] The communication employed to create and enact identity can take a variety of forms, including "conversation, commemorations of history, music, dance, ritual, ceremonial, and social drama of all sorts."[63]

As noted earlier, initial identity development and display is a product of interaction with family members. Families are the source of stories that tie us to the past and provide us with a "sense of identity and connection to the world."[64] These stories are also infused with cultural beliefs and values, which become part of one's identity.

*Identities can be displayed in cultural rites of passage.*

© Gloria Thomas

Culture's influence in establishing an individual's identity is demonstrated by contrasting student interaction styles in U.S. and Japanese schools. In the U.S., individualism is stressed and even young children are taught to be independent and develop their personal identity. U.S. schools encourage competition in the classroom and on the playing field. Students quickly learn to voice their opinion and feel free to challenge the opinions of others as a means of asserting their own identity. Being different is a common and valued trait. This is in contrast to the collective societies found in South America, West Africa, and Northeast Asia, where children learn the importance of family dependence and interdependence, and identity is "defined by relationships and group memberships."[65] This produces activities that promote identity tied to the group. In Japanese elementary schools, homeroom teachers divide classes into groups of four or five students, who are encouraged to solve problems collectively rather than individually.[66] The young Japanese students' identity is drawn from their study group and the school they attend. They are taught to avoid being different and to adhere to the Japanese proverb "A tall tree catches much wind."

Identities are also established and displayed in cultural rites of passage, which are used to help adolescents gain an increased awareness of who they are as they enter adulthood.[67] In some underdeveloped societies, the rite can involve a painful physical experience, such as male or female circumcision, but in developed nations, the rite is usually less harsh and is often a festive celebration. The bar mitzvah, for instance, is used to introduce Jewish boys into adulthood, where they become more responsible for religious duties. In the Mexican culture, girls look forward to their *Quinceañera*, held on their fifteenth birthday. The celebration is a means of acknowledging that a young woman has reached sexual maturity and is now an adult, ready to assume additional family and social responsibilities. In addition, the celebration is intended to reaffirm religious faith, good morals, and the virtues of traditional family values.[68] In the Euro-American culture, rites of passage into adulthood are generally not as distinct, but are often associated with the individual attaining a greater degree of independence.[69] Graduation from high school or college, for example, brings increased expectations of self-sufficiency and a new identity.

Once established, identities are enacted in many ways beginning in childhood and progressing through adolescence into the adult years. Individuals in almost every culture have ways of displaying their religious or spiritual identity. Many Jews wear yarmulkes or other distinctive clothes, and among Christians it is common to see a cross being worn as an item of personal jewelry. Muslim women wear the traditional headscarf (*hijab*) because it is considered part of their religious identity.[70] Some men and women wear a red dot (*pottu*) on their forehead as a sign of their devotion to the Hindu religion. Each of these symbols identifies the wearer as belonging to a specific religious group—a sign of both inclusion and exclusion.

Identity is often signaled by involvement in commemorative events. The Fourth of July in the U.S., Bastille Day in France, and Independence Day in Mexico are celebrations of national identity. The annual Saint Patrick's Day parade in New York City is an opportunity for people of Irish heritage to take pride in their ethnic identity. *Oktoberfest* celebrations allow people to rekindle their German identity, and the Lunar New Year is a time for the Chinese and many other Asian cultures to observe traditions that reaffirm their identities. Every summer, villages and cities all across Japan hold *matsuri* festivals, which are based on ancient Shinto traditions. These celebrations serve as a symbol of unity within the community and offer an opportunity for the participants to evince their regional identity.

While many customs of identity enactment are tradition-bound, evolving circumstances can bring about new ways. This type of change was discovered by David and Ayouby, who conducted a study of Arab minorities in the Detroit, Michigan, area. They found that a division existed between how early immigrants and more recent arrivals understood Arab identity.[71] Immigrants who arrived in the U.S. years earlier were satisfied "with meeting and enacting their ethnicity in a ritualistic fashion by eating Arabic food, perhaps listening to Arabic music, and even speaking Arabic to their limited ability."[72] The more recent Arab immigrant arrivals, however, had a "more politicized identity,"[73] resulting from their experiences in the civil wars and political turmoil of the Middle East. They felt that being an Arab involved taking a more active role in events in their native land, such as sending money back or becoming politically active.[74]

There are certainly many more ways of establishing and enacting your identity than we have discussed here. For instance, we did not address the obvious cultural identity markers of language, accents, or family names. But this overview should convince you of the complexity of your identities and how they are shaped by culture.

# Cultural Identity and Intercultural Communication

We have pointed out that your identity is established through communicative interaction with others. According to Hecht and his colleagues, identity is also "maintained and modified through social interaction. Identity then begins to influence interaction through shaping expectations and motivating behavior."[75] As was previously discussed, you are constantly moving in and out of different identities as you interact with other people, and with each identity, you employ a set of communicative behaviors appropriate for that identity and setting. Your culture has shaped your understanding and expectations as to what are the correct communication practices for various social settings—e.g., classroom, hospital, or sales meeting. However, these understandings and expectations are culture-bound,[76] and what is appropriate in one culture may be inappropriate in another. We have already illustrated how student/teacher interaction differs in the U.S. and Japan. Students and teachers in the two countries have quite different culturally established standards for how they should act and communicate in the classroom. But what if a Japanese student were placed in a U.S. classroom or vice versa?

In an intercultural meeting, the varying expectations for identity display and communication style carry considerable potential for creating anxiety, misunderstandings, and even conflict. This is why Imahori and Cupach consider "cultural identity as a focal element in intercultural communication."[77] Continuing with our student/teacher example, try to imagine how a student from a culture that does not value communicative assertiveness would feel in a typical U.S. classroom. Being unaccustomed to having the instructor query students, they would probably be reluctant to raise their hand and would likely consider U.S. students who challenged the teacher to be rude or even arrogant. To avoid potential problems during intercultural interaction, you need to develop what Collier calls intercultural competence.

Intercultural competence occurs when the avowed identity matches the identity ascribed. For example, if you avow the identity for an assertive, outspoken U.S. American and your conversational partner avows himself or herself to be a respectful, nonassertive Vietnamese, then each must ascribe the corresponding identity to the conversational partner. You must jointly negotiate what kind of relationship will be mutually satisfying. Some degree of adjustment and accommodation is usually necessary.[78]

Collier is saying that in order to communicate effectively in an intercultural situation, an individual's avowed cultural identity and communication style should match the identity and style ascribed to him or her by the other party. But since the communication styles are likely to be different, the participants will have to search for a middle ground, and this search will require flexibility and adaptation. As a simple illustration, the Japanese traditionally greet and say goodbye to each other by bowing. However, in Japanese/U.S. business meetings, the Japanese have learned to bow only slightly while shaking hands. In doing this, they are adjusting their normal greeting practice to accommodate those individuals from the U.S. Longtime U.S. business representatives to Japan have learned to emulate this behavior. Thus, a mutually satisfying social protocol has evolved. In achieving this, the participants have demonstrated the principal components of intercultural communication competence—motivation, knowledge, and skills—which will be examined in Chapter 11.

# Identity and Multiculturalism

Between 1989 and 2003, international adoptions in the U.S. increased from 8,102 to 21,616.[79] In a survey of the U.S., *The Economist* reported that one in every fifteen marriages was classified as interracial in 2000,[80] and ethnic minorities now represent 25 percent of the population in new suburbs.[81] In Chapter 8, we will talk about how global business is now being conducted in a transnational environment. These examples further illustrate the claim that forces such as globalization, immigration, and intercultural marriage are bringing about an increased mixing of cultures, and this mixing is producing people who possess multiple cultural identities. Chuang notes that "cultural identity becomes blurry in the midst of cultural integration, bicultural interactions, interracial marriages, and the mutual adaptation processes."[82] Martin, Nakayama, and Flores further support this idea by reporting that "increasing numbers of people are living 'in between' cultural identities. That is, they identify with more than one ethnicity, race, or religion."[83] To explore this further, we will look at the change in attitude toward identity in international adoption, the growth phenomenon of "ethnic shopping," and the rise of what is called intercultural transients.

In the past, it was not uncommon for children of international adoption to be raised by their U.S. families with little or no appreciation of the culture of their native land.[84] This was evident in the 2002 Academy Award–nominated documentary *Daughter from Danang*, which related the trials of a mixed Vietnamese and American woman who returned to Vietnam in search of her identity after twenty-two years in the U.S.[85] She was driven by a desire to find out more about her birth family and herself, but because she had never been exposed to the Vietnamese culture, the reunion ended in disaster. The potential for such unfortunate meetings should be reduced in the future as a greater awareness of the importance of cultural identity is moving many parents to recognize and promote the cultural traditions of their adopted children.[86] While it is perhaps an extreme example, the media provided considerable coverage of actress Angelina Jolie's decision to build a home in Cambodia so that her adopted son could stay in touch with his cultural heritage.

Immigration, interracial marriage, and mixed-race births are creating a social environment where many U.S. youths consider cultural diversity as a normal part of social life.[87] Kotkin and Tseng contend that in the U.S. there is "not only a growing willingness—and ability—to cross cultures, but also the evolution of a nation in which personal identity is shaped more by cultural preferences than by skin color or ethnic heritage."[88] Hitt points out that sociologists call this evolving trend "ethnic shifting" or "ethnic shopping," and that "more and more Americans have come to feel comfortable changing out of the identities they were born into and donning new ethnicities in which they feel more at home."[89] To illustrate this bending of ethnic identities, he relates that the 2004 Irish-Canadian parade queen in Montreal was half Irish and half Nigerian.[90] The Internet has afforded people an opportunity to conduct in-depth genealogical research, and one result is a growing number of U.S. Americans who now consider themselves Native Americans.[91] According to Wynter, the blurring of racial and ethnic boundaries has also been promoted by U.S. corporations.[92] This can be seen in many entertainment genres, such as hip-hop and rap music, which enjoys fans from every racial and ethnic category. Products, especially clothes, endorsed by prominent sports figures are worn by members of all cultural groups. U.S. sports fans identify with team members from China, Cuba, the Caribbean, Latin America, Japan, Korea, Lithuania, and many other nations, as well as those from a variety of U.S. ethnic groups.

The global marketplace is giving rise to what Onwumechili and his colleagues have termed "intercultural transients." These are "travelers who regularly alternate residence between their homeland and a host foreign country,"[93] and must manage frequent cultural changes and identity renegotiations.[94] Over the past decade, a growing number of nations have made dual citizenship available, which has added to the number of intercultural transients. Carlos Ghosn serves as a model example of an intercultural transient. Ghosn was born in Brazil, attended schools in Lebanon and France, and speaks five languages. A citizen of Lebanon, he is the CEO of Nissan (a Japanese company) and CEO of Renault, positions he holds concurrently.[95] To fulfill his responsibilities, Ghosn has to divide his time between Japan, France, and the U.S. and must adjust to the intricacies of each culture. In explaining his ability to make these transitions, Ghosn says, "I have always believed that you can learn the most from people who are not just like you. Seeing issues from someone else's perspective can be very instructive."[96] As transportation technology continues to make access to distant lands easier, the ranks of intercultural transients will expand. Even one of the authors of this textbook is required to manage issues of cultural readjustment and identity renegotiation as he moves back and forth between Japan and the U.S. three or four times each year.

Issues of identity can be expected to remain—and perhaps become more—complex as multiculturalism increasingly characterizes contemporary society. It is clear, however, that the old understanding of a fixed cultural identity or ethnicity is outdated, and identity is rapidly becoming more of an "articulated negotiation between what you call yourself and what other people are willing to call you."[97] But regardless of what form they may take or how they are achieved, your identities will remain a consequence of culture.[98]

## Summary

- There are many reasons behind the need to understand identity, including personal psychological well-being. Identity is also a focal point of intercultural communication, which is becoming increasingly important as a result of globalization and U.S. domestic diversity.

- Identity is a highly abstract, dynamic, multifaceted concept that defines who you are. Turner places identities into three general categories—human, social, and personal. Hall uses three similar categories—personal, relational, and communal.
- Every individual has multiple identities—e.g., race, ethnic, gender, national, regional, organizational, personal, cyber/fantasy—that act in concert. The importance of any single identity is a result of the situation.
- Identity is acquired through interaction with other members of one's cultural group. The family exerts a primary influence on early identity formation. Identity development models have been constructed by Phinney and Martin and Nakayama.
- Identities are established through group membership and are enacted in a variety of ways, including rites of passage, personal appearance, and participation in commemorative events. Concepts of identity within the same group can change over time.
- Identity plays a critical role in intercultural communication. Competent intercultural communication is achieved when the participants find commonality in ascribed and avowed identities.
- As society becomes increasingly multicultural, new concepts of cultural identity are evolving.

## Activities

1. Construct a list of as many of your identities as you can. Using the list, draw a pie chart with each identity receiving space proportional to that identity's importance to you. Compare your chart with other classmates' charts. Minority members often afford more space to their ethnicity than do majority members.
2. Pair up with a classmate and ask each other the following questions:
   A. Describe your ethnic background.
   B. What aspects of your ethnicity give you the greatest feeling of pride?
   C. Describe some of the customs, rituals, and/or ceremonies associated with your ethnic group.
   D. Excluding members of your family, describe a member of your ethnicity who is a good role model for others in that cultural group.
   E. Describe a situation in which you felt out of place as a result of being different from others.[99]
3. Select an ethnicity other than your own and try to answer the five questions from the previous activity.[100]

## Discussion Ideas

1. Why is an awareness of identity important in your personal life? What are some of the situations where this awareness would be beneficial?
2. How would you define identity? How would you explain your identities to another person?
3. What are some of your different identities and how did you acquire them? What are some differences between your identities and the same identities in another culture?
4. How did you establish some of your identities? How do you enact those identities?
5. What are some of the factors common to your identities that might create problems during intercultural interaction?

## CHAPTER 5

# Alternative Views of Reality: Cultural Values

*Your beliefs become your thoughts. Your thoughts become your words. Your words become your actions. Your actions become your habits. Your habits become your values. Your values become your destiny.*

MAHATMA GANDHI

*On a group of theories one can found a school; but on a group of values one can found a culture, a civilization, a new way of living together among men.*

IGNAZIO SILONE

P revious chapters have provided you with an understanding of the basic components of culture, explained some of the many different ways you acquire your culture, and examined many of the factors that contribute to how members of a culture see the world. By now, you should have a general appreciation of just how extensively your daily life is guided by culture. Influences such as family, history, religion, and cultural identity contribute to your decisions as to what you think about and how you should act. It may be something as mundane as what you consider to be an appropriate snack—a hamburger or a ball of rice wrapped in seaweed. It can be as complex as how you should view and react to the issues of school prayer and abortion rights in the U.S. or AIDS prevention in the underdeveloped world. What you think and do about something is in part based on the beliefs and values that have been instilled in you by your culture.

Because of the importance of values to the study of intercultural communication, we will examine (1) how culture shapes your perception, (2) how culture inculcates a set of values, and (3) how these values differ across cultures. We will spend considerable time studying how different cultural patterns influence intercultural communication, but first we will look at perception, beliefs, and values.

# Perception

To steer your attention toward the topic of perception, we will begin with a few questions. The moon is a rocky, arid physical sphere that orbits the Earth; yet when looking at this object, many Americans often see a man in the moon, many Native Americans as well as Japanese perceive a rabbit, the Chinese claim a lady is fleeing her husband, and Samoans report a woman weaving—why? In Japan and China people fear the number four, in the United States it is the number thirteen. For Americans, a "V" sign made with two fingers usually represents victory or peace. Japanese high school students see it as a sign of happiness or good luck. But, when given with the palm facing inward, Australians and the British equate the gesture with a rude American sign usually made with the middle finger—why? Most Asians respond negatively to white flowers because white is associated with death. For Peruvians, Iranians, and Mexicans, yellow flowers often invoke the same reaction—why?[1] In all these examples, the external objects (moon, hands, flowers) were the same, yet the responses were different. The reason is perception—how diverse cultures have taught their members to look at the world in different ways. To this end we will (1) define perception, (2) link perception to culture, (3) briefly discuss beliefs and values, and (4) look at how cultural differences in perception influence intercultural communication.

## DEFINING PERCEPTION

Perception is the means by which you make sense of your physical and social world. As the German novelist Hermann Hesse wrote, "There is no reality except the one contained within us"—and we will add that that reality has been placed in us, in part, by our culture. The world inside of us, says Singer, "includes symbols, things, people, ideas, events, ideologies, and even faith."[2] Your perceptions give meaning to external forces.

*Your perceptions and responses to external events are in part determined by your culture.*

© Photodisc/Getty Images

As Gamble and Gamble state, "Perception is the process of selecting, organizing, and interpreting sensory data in a way that enables us to make sense of our world."[3] In other words, perception is the process whereby people convert the physical energy of the world outside of them into meaningful internal experiences. Because that outside world encompasses everything, we can never completely know it. As Singer notes, "We experience everything in the world not as it is—but only as the world comes to us through our sensory receptors."[4] Although the physical dimension is an important phase of perception, you must realize it is the psychological aspects of perception that help you understand intercultural communication.

## PERCEPTION AND CULTURE

Whether you feel delighted or ill at the thought of eating the flesh of a cow, pig, fish, dog, or snake depends on what your culture has taught you about food. Whether you are repulsed at the sight of a bull being jabbed with short, barbed steel spears and long sharp swords, consider it as a traditional sport, or see it as dramatic art depends on culture. By exposing a large group of people to similar experiences, culture generates similar meanings and similar behaviors. This does not mean, of course, that everyone in a particular culture is exactly the same, as we discuss in a later section of this chapter.

Because this is a book about culture, we offer an example of how culture affects perception and communication. In a classic study by Bagby, Mexican children from a rural area and children from the dominant culture in the United States viewed, for a split second, stereograms in which one eye was exposed to a baseball game while the other was exposed to a bullfight. Overall, the children reported seeing the scene according to their culture; Mexican children tended to report seeing the bullfight, and American children tended to report the baseball game.[5] What should be obvious is that the children made selections based on their cultural background; they were inclined to see and to report what was most familiar.

In yet another experiment demonstrating how culture influences perception, Caucasian mothers tended to interpret as positive those aspects of their children's speech and behavior that reflected assertiveness, excitement, and interest. Navajo mothers who observed the same type of behavior in their children reported them as being mischievous and lacking discipline. To the Navajo mothers, assertive speech and behavior reflected discourtesy, restlessness, self-centeredness, and lack of discipline; to the Caucasian mothers, the same behaviors reflected self-discipline and were, therefore, beneficial for the child.[6]

Personal credibility is another perceptual trait that is shaped by culture. People who are credible inspire trust, know what they are talking about, and have good intentions. Americans usually hold that expressing one's opinion as openly and forcefully as possible is an admirable trait. Hence, someone is perceived as being highly credible if he or she is articulate and outspoken. In Japan, a person who is quiet and spends more time listening than speaking is seen as more credible because the Japanese regard constant talking as a sign of shallowness. Among Americans, credible people seem direct, rational, decisive, unyielding, and confident. Among the Japanese, a credible person is perceived as being indirect, sympathetic, prudent, flexible, and humble.[7] In Japan, social status is a major indicator of credibility, but in the United States it carries only modest importance. Even the perception of something as simple as the blinking of one's eyes is affected by culture, as Adler and Rodman note: "The same principle causes people from different cultures to interpret the same event in different ways. Blinking while another person talks may be hardly noticeable to North Americans, but the same behavior is considered impolite in Taiwan."[8]

As we highlighted in Chapter 2, how the elderly are perceived is also a product of culture. In the United States, culture "teaches" the value of youth and rejects growing old. In fact, "young people view elderly people as less desirable interaction partners than other young people or middle-aged people."[9] This negative view of the elderly is not found in all cultures. For example, in the Arab, Asian, Latin American, and American Indian cultures, older people are perceived in a very positive light. And notice what Harris and Moran tell us about the elderly in Africa:

> It is believed that the older one gets, the wiser one becomes—life has seasoned the individual with varied experiences. Hence, in Africa age is an asset. The older the person, the more respect the person receives from the community, and especially from the young.[10]

It is clear from these few examples that culture strongly influences our subjective reality and that there are direct links among culture, perception, and behavior. As Triandis noted, "cultural factors provide some of the meaning involved in perception and are, therefore, intimately implicated with the process."[11]

We are now ready to summarize in two ways how culture is involved in the perception process. First, perception is selective. This means that because there are too many stimuli competing for the attention of your senses at the same time, you "allow only selected information through [y]our perceptual screen to [y]our conscious mind."[12] What is allowed in is, in part, determined by culture. Second, your perceptual patterns are learned. As we have pointed out a number of times, everyone is born into a world without meaning, and it is culture that assigns meaning to most of our experiences. As Adler notes, "perception is culturally determined. We learn to see the world in a certain way based on our cultural background."[13] As is the case with all of culture, perceptions are stored within each human being in the form of beliefs and values. These two concepts, working in combination, form what are called *cultural patterns*.

# Beliefs

The Spanish poet Antonio Machado once noted that "Under all that we think, lives all we believe, like the ultimate veil of our spirits." According to Rogers and Steinfatt, "Beliefs serve as the storage system for the content of our past experiences, including thoughts, memories, and interpretations of events. Beliefs are shaped by the individual's culture."[14] Beliefs are important, as noted by Purnell and Paulanka, because they are "something that is accepted as truths."[15] Beliefs are usually reflected in your actions and communication behavior. If, for instance, you believe that snakes are slimy, you avoid them. On the other hand, if you believe that only through the handling of snakes can you find God (as do some religious sects), you handle them and believe your faith will protect you from venomous bites. You might embrace the *New York Times*, CNN, FOX News, or even MTV as an arbiter of the truth because you respect them. If you value the Islamic tradition, you will believe that the Koran is an infallible source of knowledge and thus accept the miracles and promises that it offers. Whatever you trust as a source of truth and knowledge—the *Times*, the Bible, the Koran, the entrails of a goat, tea leaves, the Dalai Lama, visions induced by peyote, the changes specified in the Taoist I Ching, or Paris Hilton—depends on your cultural background and experiences. If someone believes that sitting quietly for long periods of time can guide him or her along the right and true path, you cannot throw up your hands and declare the belief wrong just because it disagrees with your convictions. You must be able to recognize that cultures have different realities and belief systems. People who grow up in cultures where Christianity is the predominant religion usually believe that salvation is attainable only through Christ. People who are Jewish, Islamic, Buddhist, Shinto, or Hindu do not subscribe to that conviction. They hold their own beliefs about salvation or what happens to the human spirit when the body dies. What is enthralling about beliefs is that they are so much a part of culture that in most instances we do not question them or even demand proof. We simply accept them because we "know they are true."

## Values

One of the most important functions of beliefs is that they form the basis of your values. Values are, according to Rokeach, "a learned organization of rules for making choices and for resolving conflicts."[16] As Nanda and Warms point out, "Values are shared ideas about what is true, right, and beautiful that underlie cultural patterns and guide society in response to the physical and social environment."[17] Because this is a book about culture, it is essential that you note that Nanda and Warms used the word *shared* in their description, for values are not only held by individuals, they are also the domain of the collective.[18] Albert highlights the significance of values when he notes that "a value system represents what is expected or hoped for, required or forbidden. It is not a report of actual conduct but is the system of criteria by which conduct is judged and sanctions applied."[19] While any list concerned with "conduct" would be incomplete, Hofstede offers a short list of some topics that deal with values:[20]

- Evil versus good
- Dangerous versus safe
- Ugly versus beautiful
- Abnormal versus normal
- Irrational versus rational
- Dirty versus clean
- Decent versus indecent
- Unnatural versus natural
- Paradoxical versus logical
- Moral versus immoral

Your cognitive structure consists of many values. These values are highly organized and, as Rokeach says, "exist along a continuum of relative importance."[21] Values can be classified as primary, secondary, and tertiary. Primary values are the most important: they specify what is worth the sacrifice of human life. In the U.S., democracy and the protection of oneself and close family members are primary values. Secondary values are also quite important. Alleviation of the pain and suffering of others and securing material possessions are secondary values to most people in the U.S. You care about such values, but do not hold the same intense feeling toward them as you do with primary values. Tertiary values are at the bottom of our hierarchy. Examples of tertiary values in the U.S. are hospitality to guests and cleanliness. Although you strive to carry out these values, they are not as profound or consequential as values in the first two categories.

As we pointed out in Chapter 2, values, like all important aspects of culture, are transmitted by a variety of sources (family, proverbs, media, school, church, state, etc.) and therefore tend to be broad-based, enduring, and relatively stable. In addition, Hofstede reminds us that, as is the case with most aspects of culture, "values are programmed early in our lives" and therefore are often nonrational.[22]

As you saw from the list of sample values offered by Hofstede, values generally are normative and evaluative. In other words, values inform a member of a culture what is normal by identifying what is good and bad, and right and wrong. Cultural values define what is worthwhile to die for, what is worth protecting, what frightens people, and what are proper subjects to study and which deserve ridicule. As already indicated, values are learned within a cultural context. For example, the outlook of a culture toward the expression of affection is one of the many values that differ among cultures. In the United States, people are encouraged to express their feelings openly and outwardly and are taught not to be timid about letting people know they are upset. Think for a moment about what message is carried by the proverb "The squeaky wheel gets the grease." This U.S. positive value toward the expression of emotion is very different from the one found in China. As Gao and Ting-Toomey note, "Chinese are socialized not to openly express their own personal emotions, especially strong negative ones."[23] Bond points out that among the Chinese, "Uninhibited emotional display is a disruptive and dangerous luxury that can ill be afforded."[24] There is even a Chinese proverb that states, "A harsh word dropped from the tongue cannot be brought back by a coach and six horses." What is important about values is that they get translated into action. For instance, being aware that the Japanese value detail and politeness might cause you to follow their custom and carefully examine the business card offered by a Japanese business representative, rather than giving it a quick glance before tucking it away in your coat pocket or purse.

Attentiveness to cultural values might also offer partial insight into a culture's approach to business. Huntington found data from the 1960s that showed the economies of South Korea and Ghana to be remarkably similar. By the 1990s, however, South Korea's economy had risen to the fourteenth largest in the world, but Ghana's had remained static. According to Huntington, the reasons for this change were clear: "South Koreans valued thrift, investment, hard work, education, organization and discipline. Ghanaians had different values. In short, culture counts."[25] This is an excellent example of the link between values and cultural characteristics.

# Studying Cultural Patterns

People and cultures are extremely complex and consist of numerous interrelated cultural orientations. A useful umbrella term that allows us to talk about values, beliefs, and other orientations collectively is *cultural patterns*. You should think of cultural patterns as a system of beliefs and values that work in combination to provide a coherent, if not always consistent, model for perceiving the world. These patterns contribute not only to the way a people perceive and think about the world, but just as importantly for our purposes, the manner in which they live in that world. As you would suspect, these cultural patterns are useful in the study of intercultural communication because they are systematic and repetitive instead of random and irregular.[26] Because of this systematic and recurring characteristic of cultural patterns, they can be isolated and investigated.

## OBSTACLES IN STUDYING CULTURAL PATTERNS

Before opening our discussion of cultural patterns we need to offer a few cautionary remarks that will enable you to better use the cultural patterns presented in the remainder of this chapter.

**We Are More than Our Culture.** We begin by repeating an important point made in Chapter 1. Simply stated, the dominant values of a culture may not be the values of all individuals within that culture. Factors as divergent as age, gender, and co-cultural affiliations, along with "socioeconomic status, educational level, occupation, personal experience,"[27] also shape your view of your environment. Although we recognize the complexity of human behavior and individual prerogative, we feel that culture has the strongest influence on your communication behavior because all of your other experiences take place within a cultural context. In addition, as we noted previously, cultural learning occurs very early in life. As pointed out by Lynch and Hanson, "Lessons learned at such early ages become an integral part of thinking and behavior."[28]

**Cultural Patterns Are Interrelated.** Due to the linear nature of language, we are forced to talk about only one cultural pattern at a time. It is important, however, to realize that the patterns do not operate in isolation—they are interrelated and integrated. It might be helpful to visualize these patterns as a large stone being cast into a pond that creates ripples. For example, a pattern that stresses a spiritual life as being more important than materialism (a large stone) also directs values toward age, status, social relationships, and the use of time (the ripples). Another example of patterns being linked could be found in a culture's view of formality (large stone). Values toward dress, language, greeting behavior, the use of space, and age (ripples) would grow out of the key pattern.

**Heterogeneity Influences Cultural Patterns.** Any attempt to delineate a national culture or typical cultural patterns for any culture is extremely hazardous because of the heterogeneity of almost all societies. For example, it is estimated that together the United States and Russia contain over 125 ethnic groups. The *Encyclopedia of American Religions* identifies nearly 1,200 different religions in the United States. And, of course, the United States is home to numerous co-cultures that do not share many of the values associated with the dominant culture. Lynch makes this point clear in the following paragraph:

> In the United States, competition is highly prized; however, the reverse is true in many Native American, Hispanic/Latino, Asian, Pacific Island, and Southeast Asian cultures. Competition is viewed as self-serving; and the emphasis is on cooperation and teamwork. Because competition is a negative trait in these cultures, being viewed as competitive rather than cooperative would bring shame rather than pride.[29]

The U.S. is well known for its extensive cultural diversity, but we can assure you that many other nations also have large and varied ethnic populations. *The CIA World Factbook* tells us that Romania has populations of Hungarians, Romas, Ukrainians, Germans, Russians, and Turks. Peru has Amerindians, *mestizos* (mixed Amerindian and white), whites, blacks, Japanese, Chinese, and others. While the Han Chinese make up the majority of China's population, there are also Zhuang, Uygur, Hui, Yi, Tibetan, Miao, Manchu, Mongol, Buyi, and Korean ethnic groups. Even Japan, noted for its relative homogeneity, has significant populations of Koreans, Chinese, Brazilians, and Filipinos. In Afghanistan, Goodson notes, "Islam is divided by hundreds of variations," regional politics, and "tribal social groupings" based on communal loyalties that make it difficult to speak of a single nation or culture.[30] And the division between Sunni, Shiite, and Kurds in Iraq is now well known. Hence, common cultural patterns that could be said to hold for the whole country must be limited to the dominant culture in each country.

**Cultural Patterns Change.**  Your scan of world events—or remembering what we wrote in Chapter 1—will tell you cultures change and therefore so do the values of the culture. The women's movement, for example, has greatly altered social organizations and some value systems in the United States. With more women than men now earning college degrees, we can see how the workplace and classrooms have changed in the United States during the last twenty years.[31] As globalization brings Western capitalism and culture to nations throughout the world, it is common to see young people in some traditional countries now wearing Levi's and dancing to American pop music. However, even granting the dynamic nature of culture and value systems, we again remind you that regardless of the culture, the deep structures always resist change.

**Cultural Patterns Are Often Contradictory.**  In many instances, we find contradictory values in a particular culture. In the United States, we speak of "all people being created equal," yet we observe pervasive racial prejudice toward minorities and violence directed against gays. Individualism is at the heart of American culture, yet the United States is the most humanitarian country in the world, as was demonstrated in the wake of the December 2004 tsunami that struck many Indian Ocean nations. Americans claim to be a moral and honorable group of people, yet the United States is one of the world's most violent societies. Indeed, the most divisive political issues now facing the U.S. are related to contrasting values—e.g., abortion, gay marriage, separation of religion and the state. These sorts of contradictions are found in all cultures. In China, where Confucianism and Buddhism stress interpersonal harmony, you will witness human rights violations. The Koran teaches brotherhood among all people, yet in many Arab cultures there is a vast gulf between the rich and the poor. Even with the reservations we have just offered, it is our contention that the study of cultural patterns is a worthwhile endeavor that can provide considerable insight into the values, behaviors, and communication styles of other cultures.

## SELECTING CULTURAL PATTERNS

Deciding on what cultural patterns to discuss is not an easy assignment. We have already mentioned the idea that culture is composed of countless elements. This fact influenced our decision regarding what patterns to examine and which to exclude from our analysis. We are not the first writers who have had to decide what to include and what to exclude. Leading scholars in the area of intercultural communication have advanced numerous classifications and typologies. While there is obviously a great deal of overlap in these systems, it might help you appreciate the problems associated with isolating key patterns if we pause for a moment and mention what four different scholars have developed to help investigate and explain different cultures. For Gannon, cross-cultural understanding can best be achieved through the use of his four-stage model, which employs cultural metaphors to help understand a culture.[32] Trompenaars and Hampden-Turner believe that you must examine and compare cultures along eight different categories that they have established.[33] Although Grondona is writing about economic development, he nevertheless presents an excellent typology of seventeen cultural patterns (which he calls *values systems*) that can offer significant insight into a culture.[34] Weaver maintains that cultures can be studied and compared along eight separate cultural dimensions, which can be divided into numerous subsets.[35]

This brief overview of four different cultural pattern typologies developed by different scholars should provide you an appreciation of the complexity and difficulty related to the study and understanding of other cultures. However, two points are readily apparent. First, for most scholars of intercultural communication, cultural patterns are points lying on a continuum. The rationale is a simple one—cultural differences are usually a matter of degrees. Second, there is a great deal of duplication and overlap in any discussion of cultural patterns. In fact, many of the patterns we have selected to discuss in detail are also part of the taxonomies developed by Gannon, Trompenaars and Hampden-Turner, Grondona, and Weaver.

# Dominant U.S. Cultural Patterns

We have already alluded to many of the difficulties in allowing a specific cultural pattern to characterize an entire culture. This problem is even more transparent when dealing with the United States and its diverse multiracial and ethnic culture. As Charon notes, "Listing American values is a difficult task because there are so many exceptions and contradictions."[36] However, Charon adds, "On a general level, Americans do share a value system."[37] Kim echoes this same notion when she writes, "There are similar characteristics that all Americans share, regardless of their age, race, gender, or ethnicity."[38]

Although this book tends to focus on explaining other cultures, we nevertheless believe that a section on American cultural patterns would be helpful for all of our readers. For people who are not members of the dominant culture, we trust that our discussion of cultural patterns will provide insights into that culture. For those who are members of the dominant culture, we offer our analysis of cultural patterns for three reasons. First, as we have said throughout this book, people carry their culture wherever they go, and that culture influences how they respond to the people they meet. To understand the communication event in which you are involved, you must appreciate your role in that event. Second, examining one's own cultural patterns can reveal information about culture that is often overlooked. As the anthropologist Edward T. Hall once observed, "culture hides more than it reveals, and strangely enough what it hides, it hides most effectively from its own participants." Finally, one's cultural patterns can serve as a reference point for making comparisons between cultures.

We limit our discussion of American cultural patterns to the dominant culture as defined in Chapter 1. You will recall we said that the dominant culture is that part of the population, regardless of the culture being studied, that controls and dominates the major economic and social institutions and determines the flow and content of information. In the United States, that group has been, and continues to be, white, male, and of European heritage.[39]

## INDIVIDUALISM

The single most important cultural pattern in the United States is individualism. Broadly speaking, individualism refers to the doctrine, spelled out in detail by the seventeenth-century English philosopher John Locke, that each individual is unique, special, completely different from all other individuals, and "the basic unit of nature."[40]

*One indication of individualism is how North Americans use space.*

© Larry Samovar

Locke's view is a simple one: The interests of the individual are or ought to be paramount, and all values, rights, and duties originate in individuals. The value of individualism is so commanding that many other imperative American values spring from individualism. Gannon underscores the link between individualism and other values when he writes:

> Equality of opportunity, independence, initiative, and self-reliance are some of the values that have remained as basic American ideals throughout history. All of these values are expressive of a high degree of individualism.[41]

As Gannon noted, this emphasis on the individual, while found elsewhere in the world, has emerged as the cornerstone of American culture. Huntington points out that this "sense of individualism and a tradition of individual rights and liberties is unique among civilized societies."[42] The origin of this value has had a long history and a variety of champions. Benjamin Franklin told Americans that "God helps those who help themselves" and Herbert Hoover reminded them that "the American system was based on rugged individualism." Whether it is in sexual, social, or ethical matters, the self for Americans holds the pivotal position. So strong is this notion that some Americans believe that there is something wrong with a person who fails to demonstrate individualism. Think of the power of the concept as stated by former Supreme Court justice Felix Frankfurter: "Anybody who is any good is different than anybody else." Whether it is literature, art, or American history, the message is the same: individual achievement, sovereignty, and freedom are the virtues most glorified and canonized.

American role models, be they the cowboys of the Old West or action heroes in today's movies, videos, or computer games, are all portrayed as independent agents who accomplish their goals with little or no assistance. The result of these and countless other messages is that most Americans believe that each person has his or her own separate identity, which should be recognized and reinforced. As Kim points out, "In America, what counts is who you are, not who others around you are. A person tends to be judged on his or her own merit."[43]

## EQUALITY

Closely related to individualism is the American value of equality. As Hanson observes, "The United States was founded on the principle that 'all men are created equal.'"[44] You can see examples of equality being emphasized in everything from government (everyone has the right to vote) to social relationships ("Just call me by my first name"). Americans believe that all people have a right to succeed in life and that the state, through laws and educational opportunities, should ensure that right. The value of equality is prevalent in both primary and secondary social relationships. For instance, most of the primary social relationships within a family tend to advance equality rather than hierarchy. Formality is not important, and children are often treated as adults. In secondary relationships, you find that most friendships and coworkers are also treated as equals. People from cultures that have rigid, hierarchical social structures often find it disconcerting to work with Americans, who they believe negate the value of hierarchical structures within a society. We do not mean to imply that Americans completely ignore hierarchy. According to Althen, Americans rely on more subtle ways to mark status, such as "tone of voice, order of speaking, choice of words, [and] seating arrangements."[45]

We would be remiss, when describing the dominant culture in the United States, if we did not once again remind you of some of the contradictions that often exist when we speak of individualism and equality. As Macionis points out, "Despite prevailing ideas about individualism and freedom, many people in the United States still evaluate others according to their sex, race, ethnicity, and social class."[46] He adds, "Although we describe ourselves as a nation of equals, there is little doubt that some of us rank as 'more equal than others.'"[47] While granting that many Americans have experienced periods of inequality, Hanson is correct when she writes, "Not all citizens have had equal rights throughout the course of the country's history, but Americans nevertheless value the notion highly and strive toward this ideal."[48]

## MATERIALISM

Materialism has always been an integral part of life for most Americans. As Stewart and Bennett note, "Americans consider it almost a right to be materially well off and physically comfortable."[49] Althen echoes the same idea when he writes that for Americans materialism "is natural and proper."[50] This ideal is even displayed on a popular bumper sticker which proclaims, "The person who dies with the most toys wins." Americans expect to have swift and convenient transportation (preferably controlled by themselves), a large variety of foods at their disposal, clothes for every occasion, and comfortable homes equipped with environmental controls and countless labor-saving devices.

## SCIENCE AND TECHNOLOGY

For most Americans, science and technology, or what Clark calls "the value of know-how,"[51] take on the qualities often associated with a god. The following inscription, found on the National Museum of American History in Washington, D.C., expresses the same idea: "Modern civilization depends on science." Clark maintains that Americans think that scientific and technical knowledge is linked to their very survival.[52] This strong belief gives rise to the notion among most Americans that nothing is impossible when scientists, engineers, and inventors put their minds to a task. From fixing interpersonal relationships to walking on the moon, science has the answer. The American respect for science is based on the assumptions that reality can be rationally ordered by humans and that such an ordering, using the scientific method, enables people to predict and control much of life. Very broadly, this emphasis on science reflects the values of the rationalistic-individualistic tradition that is so deeply embedded in Western civilization. From John Locke to Francis Bacon, René Descartes, Bertrand Russell, and Albert Einstein, Western cultures have long believed that all problems can be solved by science. This emphasis on rationality and science, according to Macionis, helps "explain our cultural tendency (especially among men) to devalue emotion and intuition as sources of knowledge."[53] While Westerners tend to prize rationality, objectivity, empirical evidence, and the scientific method, these views often clash with cultures that value and believe in fatalism, subjectivity, mysticism, and intuition.

## PROGRESS AND CHANGE

In the United States, as Hanson reminds you, "Change, newness, and progress are all highly valued."[54] From altering their personalities with the assistance of self-help gurus, to changing where they live at a faster rate than any other people in the world, Americans do not value the status quo. Nor have they ever. "Early Americans cleared forests, drained swamps, and altered the course of rivers in order to 'build' the country. Contemporary Americans have gone to the moon in part to prove they could do so."[55] The French writer Alexis de Tocqueville, after visiting the United States in the early 1800s, reached much the same conclusion when he wrote that the people in the United States "all consider society as a body in a state of improvement, and humanity as a changing scene." From the culture's earliest establishment as a distinct national entity, there has been a diffuse constellation of beliefs and attitudes that may be called the cult of progress. Various aspects of this orientation are optimism, receptivity to change, emphasis on the future rather than the past or present, faith in an ability to control all phases of life, and confidence in the perceptual ability of the common person. You can observe this strong conviction in change and progress in how Americans view the environment. Hanson offers a summary of this point when she notes: "This belief also has fostered a use of force in interactions with the environment and other people that is evident in phrases such as 'taming the wilderness,' 'winning the West,' and 'conquering space.'"[56]

A passion for progress cultivates not only the acceptance of change but also the conviction that changes move in a definite direction and that the direction is good. Each new generation in the United States wants its opportunity to be part of that change. So strong is the belief in progress and change that Americans seldom fear taking chances. The writer Henry Miller clearly captured this American spirit when he wrote, "Whatever there be in progress in life comes not through adaptation but through daring, through obeying blind urge." As we discuss later in the chapter, many older and more traditional cultures, which have witnessed civilizations rise and fall and believe in fatalism, do not easily embrace change, progress, and daring and often have difficulty understanding the way Americans behave. As Althen notes:

> This fundamental American belief in progress and a better future contrasts sharply with the *fatalistic* (Americans are likely to use that term with a negative or critical connotation) attitude that characterizes people from many other cultures, notably Latin, Asian, and Arab, where there is a pronounced reverence for the past. In those cultures the future is considered to be in the hands of "fate," "God," or at least the few powerful people or families that dominate the society. The idea that people in general can somehow shape their own futures seems naïve, arrogant, or even sacrilegious. [57]

## WORK AND LEISURE

Work, like all major cultural patterns, has a long history in the U.S. McElroy speaks to that history, and to the importance of work in the United States, when he writes:

> The primary American cultural beliefs derive from the initial experience of European settlers in the future United States. They all relate to work, the first necessity for survival in a wilderness. It was the peculiar experiences of work—what kind was done, who did it, how much it was rewarded—that began the process of distinguishing American behavior from European behavior, which led during the next eight generations to the formation of a new American culture.[58]

The value associated with work is so important in the United States that people who meet each other for the first time often ask the common question "What do you do?" Embedded in this simple query is the belief that working (doing something) is important. For most Americans, work represents a cluster of moral and affective conditions of great attractiveness, while at the same time voluntary idleness often constitutes a severely threatening and damaging social condition. A major reward for hard work, and an important American value, is leisure. Most Americans seem to have embraced the words of the poet and philosopher George Santayana: "To the art of working well a civilized race would add the art of playing well." For Americans, play is something they have earned. It is relief from the regularity of work; it is in play that we find real joy. This emphasis on recreation and relaxation takes a variety of forms. Each weekend people rush to get away in their recreational vehicles, play golf or tennis, go skiing, ride their mountain bikes, or "relax" at a gambling casino or race track.

## COMPETITION

The late professional football coach Vince Lombardi once said, "Winning isn't everything, it's the only thing."[59] This attitude toward competition is part of an American's life that is taught from early childhood on. Whether it be through the games they play or their striving to receive a higher grade than the person they are sitting next to in class, a competitive nature is encouraged in the United States. People are ranked, graded, classified, and evaluated so that everyone will know if they are the best. Young people are even advised that if they lose and it does not bother them, there is something wrong with them. As Kim points out, "For competitive Americans, who hate losing, everything in life is a game to win."[60] As is the case with all the patterns found in a culture, the origin of a specific pattern has a long history. Notice the call for competition in the following proverb—written at the beginning of the first century by the Roman philosopher Ovid: "A horse never runs so fast as when he has other horses to catch up and outpace." The message was clear then and it is clear now—you need to "outpace" all the other horses. "In its purest form," notes Kim, "competition challenges Americans to become even better."[61]

Competition is yet another pattern that often causes problems for Americans when they interact with people who do not espouse this value. For instance, "Asians believe that it is neither necessary nor beneficial to be obsessed with winning."[62] Harris and Moran offer yet another example of differing perceptions of competition as it applies to the French: when confronted with individuals with a competitive drive, the French may interpret them as being antagonistic, ruthless, and power-hungry. They may feel threatened, and overreact or withdraw from the discussion.[63]

## Diverse Cultural Patterns

So far we have discussed some cultural characteristics as they applied to the dominant U.S. culture. We are now ready to make some cultural comparisons. As we mentioned earlier in this chapter, many anthropologists, social psychologists, and communication scholars have devised taxonomies that can be used to analyze key behavioral patterns found in every culture. While these patterns are numerous, there are four taxonomies that seem to be at the core of any study of intercultural communication. The first classification, developed by Hofstede, identifies five value dimensions (individualism/collectivism, uncertainty avoidance, power distance, masculinity/femininity, long-term/short-term orientation) that are influenced and modified by culture. The second four orientations grow out of the anthropological work of the Kluckhohns and Strodtbeck (human nature, person/nature orientation, time, activity, relational orientation). Hall advanced our third taxonomy, which looks at how high context and low-context cultures respond to various message systems. Our final cultural pattern was developed from research by intercultural communication scholar Ting-Toomey, whose work has highlighted the role of "face" and "face-work" in intercultural communication.

## Hofstede's Value Dimensions[64]

Hofstede, in the preface to the second edition of his book, clearly articulates the rationale behind his study:

> This book explores the differences in thinking and social action that exists among members of more than 50 modern nations. It argues that people carry "mental programs" that are

developed in the family in early childhood and reinforced in schools and organizations, and that these mental programs contain a component of national culture. They are most clearly expressed in the values that predominate among people from different countries.[65]

Hofstede's work was one of the earliest attempts to use extensive statistical data to examine cultural values. In carrying out his research, Hofstede ultimately surveyed more than one hundred thousand managers in multinational organizations in fifty countries and three geographical regions. After careful analysis, each country and region was assigned a rank of one through fifty in each of his studies, using four identified value dimensions (individualism/collectivism, uncertainty avoidance, power distance, masculinity/femininity). Subsequent research involving participants from twenty-three nations identified a fifth dimension (long-term/short-term orientation) and these countries were ordered one through twenty-three. These rankings not only offer a clear picture of what was valued in each culture, but also help you see comparisons across cultures.

## INDIVIDUALISM/COLLECTIVISM

We first mentioned the cultural dimensions of individualism and collectivism in Chapter 2 when we examined the topic of social organizations. We will now return to that topic for a more comprehensive discussion. For many years, researchers have maintained "self-orientation versus collective orientation as one of the basic pattern variables that determine human action."[66] As Ting-Toomey notes, "Individualistic and collective value tendencies are manifested in everyday family, school, and workplace interactions."[67]

Although Hofstede is often given credit for investigating the concepts of individualism and collectivism, he is not the only scholar who has researched these crucial intercultural dimensions. Triandis, for example, has derived an entire cross-cultural research agenda that focuses on these concepts.[68] Although we speak of individualism and collectivism as if they are separate entities, it is important to keep in mind that all people and cultures have both individual and collective dispositions. Brislin helps clarify this point when he notes, "Although no culture totally ignores individualistic or collective goals, cultures differ significantly on which of these factors they consider more critical."[69]

Andersen and his colleagues offer us an excellent summary of the traits which define the individualism-collectivism continuum:

> Collectivistic cultures emphasize community, collaboration, shared interest, harmony, tradition, the public good, and maintaining face. Individualistic cultures emphasize personal rights and responsibilities, privacy, voicing one's own opinion, freedom, innovation, and self-expression.[70]

With this synopsis in mind, we will now look at the two dimensions in more detail.

**Individualism.** Having already discussed individualism when we looked at American culture, we need only touch on some of its components: (1) the individual is the single most important unit in any social setting, (2) independence rather than dependence is stressed, (3) individual achievement is rewarded, and (4) the uniqueness of each individual is of paramount value.[71] According to Hofstede's findings (see Table 5.1), the United States, Australia, Great Britain, Canada, the Netherlands, and New Zealand

**TABLE 5.1** Individualism/Collectivism Values for Fifty Countries and Three Regions

| RANK | COUNTRY | RANK | COUNTRY |
|------|---------|------|---------|
| 1 | United States | 28 | Turkey |
| 2 | Australia | 29 | Uruguay |
| 3 | Great Britain | 30 | Greece |
| 4/5 | Canada | 31 | Philippines |
| 4/5 | Netherlands | 32 | Mexico |
| 6 | New Zealand | 33/35 | Yugoslavia |
| 7 | Italy | 33/35 | Portugal |
| 8 | Belgium | 33/35 | East Africa |
| 9 | Denmark | 36 | Malaysia |
| 10/11 | Sweden | 37 | Hong Kong |
| 10/11 | France | 38 | Chile |
| 12 | Ireland | 39/41 | Singapore |
| 13 | Norway | 39/41 | Thailand |
| 14 | Switzerland | 39/41 | West Africa |
| 15 | Germany | 42 | Salvador |
| 16 | South Africa | 43 | South Korea |
| 17 | Finland | 44 | Taiwan |
| 18 | Austria | 45 | Peru |
| 19 | Israel | 46 | Costa Rica |
| 20 | Spain | 47/48 | Pakistan |
| 21 | India | 47/48 | Indonesia |
| 22/23 | Japan | 49 | Colombia |
| 22/23 | Argentina | 50 | Venezuela |
| 24 | Iran | 51 | Panama |
| 25 | Jamaica | 52 | Ecuador |
| 26/27 | Brazil | 53 | Guatemala |
| 26/27 | Arab countries | | |

The lower the number the more the country promotes individualism. A higher number means the country can be classified as collective.

Source: Adapted from Geert Hofstede, *Cultures Consequences: Comparing Values, Behavior, Institutions and Organizations Across Nations*, 2nd ed. (Thousand Oaks, CA: Sage Publications, 2001).

all tend toward individualism. Goleman highlights some of the characteristics of these and other cultures that value individualism:

> People's personal goals take priority over their allegiance to groups like the family or the employer. The loyalty of individualists to a given group is very weak; they feel they belong to many groups and are apt to change their membership as it suits them, switching churches, for example, or leaving one employer for another.[72]

In cultures that tend toward individualism, competition rather than cooperation is encouraged; personal goals take precedence over group goals; people tend not to be emotionally dependent on organizations and institutions; and every individual has the right to his or her private property, thoughts, and opinions. These cultures stress individual initiative and achievement, and they value individual decision making. When thrust into a situation that demands a decision, people from cultures that stress this trait are often at odds with people from collective cultures. This point is made by Foster:

> At the negotiating table, differences in this dimension can clearly cause serious conflict. Individual responsibility for making decisions is easy in individualistic cultures; in group

*Collective cultures value the group as the most important social entity.*

oriented cultures this can be different. Americans too often expect their Japanese counterparts to make decisions right at the negotiating table, and the Japanese are constantly surprised to find individual members of the American team promoting their own positions, decisions, and ideas, sometimes openly contradicting one another.[73]

Remembering our earlier analogy regarding the stone in the pond that creates ripples, it should be clear that the cultural pattern of individualism creates a host of "ripples" that are discernible in a variety of ways. In small groups, "individuals are motivated to work for themselves."[74] In the use of space, Andersen notes that "people from individualistic cultures are more remote and distant proximally."[75] Within the family context, Hanson tells us that individualism is stressed through self-determination, self-reliance, and an emphasis on privacy.[76] In the business setting, according to Lewis, individualistic Americans "like going it alone."[77] When moving to the classroom, Hofstede suggests that you find teachers dealing with individual pupils and encouraging pupil initiative.[78]

**Collectivism.** A rigid social framework that distinguishes between in-groups and out-groups characterizes collectivism. People count on their in-groups (e.g., relatives, clans, organizations) to look after them, and in exchange they believe they owe loyalty to the group. Triandis suggests some of the following behaviors are found in collective cultures:

> Collectivism means greater emphasis on (a) the views, needs, and goals of the in-group rather than oneself; (b) social norms and duty defined by the in-group rather than behavior to get pleasure; (c) beliefs shared with the in-group rather than beliefs that distinguish self from in-group; and (d) great readiness to cooperate with in-group members.[79]

In collective societies, such as those in Pakistan, Colombia, Venezuela, Taiwan, Peru, and much of Africa and Asia, people are born into extended families or clans that support and protect them in exchange for their allegiance. Triandis offers an excellent summary of the role and power of the family as a starting point for collective cultures:

> The prototypical collectivist social relationship is the family, where people have strong emotional ties and feel that they "obviously belong together," the link is long-term (often for life) and there are many common goals. Cooperation is natural and status is determined by position within the group.[80]

As you can imagine, a *we* consciousness prevails instead of an *I* orientation. In African societies, as pointed out by Richmond and Gestrin, "Individual needs and achievement, in contrast to the West, take second place to the needs of the many."[81] This perception of community is explained by Etounga-Manguelle:

> If I had to cite a single characteristic of the African culture, the subordination of the individual by the community would surely be the reference point to remember. African thought rejects any view of the individual as an autonomous and responsible being.[82]

In African and other collective cultures, identity is based on the social system. The individual is emotionally dependent on organizations and institutions, and the culture emphasizes belonging to organizations. Organizations invade private life and the groups to which individuals belong, and individuals trust group decisions even at the expense of individual rights. Characterizing China as a collective culture, Meyer notes, "With individual rights severely subordinated, group action has been a distinctive characteristic of Chinese society."[83] Collective behaviors have deep historical roots. Look at the message of collectivism in these words from Confucius: "If one wants to establish himself, he should help others to establish themselves first." You can also notice this view about working as a group in the Chinese proverb "No matter how stout, one beam cannot support a house."

Numerous co-cultures in the United States can be classified as collective. The research of Hecht, Collier, and Ribeau, for example, concludes that African Americans also have the characteristics of collective societies.[84] And, according to Luckman, "Hispanics—including Mexican-Americans, Cubans, Salvadorans, Guatemalans, Puerto Ricans, and others—greatly value the family, and often place the needs of the family members above the needs of individuals."[85]

As is the case with all cultural patterns, collectivism influences a number of communication variables. Kim, Sharkey, and Singles, after studying Korean culture, believe that traits such as indirect communication, saving face, concern for others, and group cooperation are linked to Korea's collective orientation.[86] Research has established that individualism/collectivism also imparts an influence on the style of conflict management used by a culture.[87]

Collectivism is also contextual. For example, in collective classrooms, such as those found in Mexico, harmony and cooperation in learning are stressed instead of competition.[88] Think of what is being implied in the Mexican saying "The more we are, the faster we finish." The medical environment also reflects the pattern of individualism and collectivism. Schneider and Silverman offer the following view of the health care context in Egypt: "Even in illness, Egyptians prefer company. A stream of friends and relatives who bring him soda, food, aspirin, and advice will surround a man who has a headache or a fever. Hospitals are crowded with residents and friends visiting patients."[89] In the business context, Marx maintains that "Negotiations in collective cultures are often attended by a group of people" and "decision making takes longer."[90]

# UNCERTAINTY AVOIDANCE

At the core of uncertainty avoidance is the inescapable truism that the future is unknown. Though you may try, you can never accurately predict the next minute, hour, day, year, or decade. As American playwright Tennessee Williams once noted, "The future is called 'perhaps,' which is the only possible thing to call the future." As the term is used by Hofstede, *uncertainty avoidance* "defines the extent to which people within a culture are made nervous by situations which they perceive as unstructured, unclear, or unpredictable, situations which they therefore try to avoid by maintaining strict codes of behavior and a belief in absolute truths."[91]

**High Uncertainty Avoidance.** High uncertainty-avoidance cultures try to avoid uncertainty and ambiguity by providing stability for their members, establishing more formal rules, not tolerating deviant ideas and behaviors, seeking consensus, and believing in absolute truths and the attainment of expertise. These cultures are also characterized by higher levels of anxiety and stress. People with this orientation believe that life carries the potential for continuous hazards.

To avoid or mitigate these hazards, there is a strong need for written rules, planning, regulations, rituals, ceremonies, and established communication protocols, which add structure to life. Nations with a strong uncertainty-avoidance tendency are Portugal, Greece, Peru, Belgium, and Japan (see Table 5.2).

**Low Uncertainty Avoidance.** At the other end of the continuum, we find countries like Sweden, Denmark, Ireland, Norway, the United States, Finland, and the Netherlands, which have a low uncertainty-avoidance need. They more easily accept the uncertainty inherent in life, tend to be tolerant of the unusual, and are not as threatened by different ideas and people. They prize initiative, dislike the structure associated with hierarchy, are willing to take risks, are flexible, think that there should be as few rules as possible, and depend not so much on experts as on themselves. As a whole, members of low uncertainty-avoidance cultures are less tense and more relaxed.

As was the case with our other value dimensions, differences in uncertainty avoidance affect intercultural communication. In a classroom composed of children from low uncertainty-avoidance cultures, we might expect to see students feeling comfortable in unstructured learning situations and also being rewarded for innovative approaches to problem solving.[92] As Hofstede points out, the opposite is the case in high uncertainty-avoidance cultures. Here you find "students expect structured learning situations and right answers."[93]

Approaches to uncertainty avoidance would also affect negotiation sessions involving members from either orientation. High uncertainty-avoidance members would most likely want to move at a rather slow pace and require a greater amount of detail and planning. Some older members might also feel uncomfortable with younger members of the opposite group. There would be differences in the level of formality with which each culture would feel comfortable. In addition, Lewis notes that in high-uncertainty business situations there is a "preference for agendas and sticking to them."[94] The negotiation process would see differences in the level of risk taking on each side. Americans, for example, would be less constrained by the unknown and more willing to take a risk. Writing about American business practices, Harris and Moran point out, "In light of their history, their perceptions of their rugged individualism, and the rewards of capitalism, Americans have embraced risk and are not risk avoidant."[95]

**TABLE 5.2** Uncertainty Avoidance Values for Fifty Countries and Three Regions

| RANK | COUNTRY | RANK | COUNTRY |
|------|---------|------|---------|
| 1 | Greece | 28 | Ecuador |
| 2 | Portugal | 29 | Germany |
| 3 | Guatemala | 30 | Thailand |
| 4 | Uruguay | 31/32 | Iran |
| 5/6 | Belgium | 31/32 | Finland |
| 5/6 | Salvador | 33 | Switzerland |
| 7 | Japan | 34 | West Africa |
| 8 | Yugoslavia | 35 | Netherlands |
| 9 | Peru | 36 | East Africa |
| 10/15 | Spain | 37 | Australia |
| 10/15 | Argentina | 38 | Norway |
| 10/15 | Panama | 39/40 | South Africa |
| 10/15 | France | 39/40 | New Zealand |
| 10/15 | Chile | 41/42 | Indonesia |
| 10/15 | Costa Rica | 41/42 | Canada |
| 16/17 | Turkey | 43 | United States |
| 16/17 | South Korea | 44 | Philippines |
| 18 | Mexico | 45 | India |
| 19 | Israel | 46 | Malaysia |
| 20 | Colombia | 47/48 | Great Britain |
| 21/22 | Venezuela | 47/48 | Ireland |
| 21/22 | Brazil | 49/50 | Hong Kong |
| 23 | Italy | 49/50 | Sweden |
| 24/25 | Pakistan | 51 | Denmark |
| 24/25 | Austria | 52 | Jamaica |
| 26 | Taiwan | 53 | Singapore |
| 27 | Arab countries | | |

The lower the number, the more the country can be classified as one that does not like uncertainty. A higher number is associated with a country that does not feel uncomfortable with uncertainty.
Source: Adapted from Geert Hofstede, *Cultures Consequences: Comparing Values, Behavior, Institutions and Organizations Across Nations*, 2nd ed. (Thousand Oaks, CA: Sage Publications, 2001).

## POWER DISTANCE

Another cultural value dimension offered by Hofstede is power distance, which classifies cultures on a continuum of high and low power distance. In this case, he is talking about the distance between power and the members of a particular culture. He summarizes the concept of power distance in the following manner: "Power distance as a characteristic of a culture defines the extent to which the less powerful person in society accepts inequality in power and considers it as normal."[96] The premise of the dimension deals with the extent to which a society prefers that power in relationships, institutions, and organizations be distributed equally or unequally. Although all cultures have tendencies for both high- and low-power relationships, one orientation seems to dominate. Foster offers a clear explanation of this dimension:

> What Hofstede discovered was that in some cultures, those who hold power and those who are affected by power are significantly far apart (high power distance) in many ways, while in other cultures, the power holders and those affected by the power holders are significantly closer (low power distance).[97]

**High Power Distance.** Gudykunst tenders a concise summary of high power distance cultures when he writes, "Individuals from high power distance cultures accept power as part of society. As such, superiors consider their subordinates to be different from themselves and vice versa."[98] People in high power distance countries such as India, Africa, Brazil, Singapore, Greece, Venezuela, Mexico, and the Philippines (see Table 5.3) believe that power and authority are facts of life. Both consciously and unconsciously, these cultures teach their members that people are not equal in this world and that everybody has a rightful place, which is clearly marked by countless vertical arrangements. Social hierarchy is prevalent and institutionalizes inequality. Etounga-Manguelle underscores this point as it applies to Africa when he notes, "In more vertical societies, Africa among them, subordinates consider their superiors to be different having a right to privilege."[99]

In organizations within high power distance cultures, you find a greater centralization of power, more importance placed on status and rank, a larger proportion of supervisory personnel, a rigid value system that determines the worth of each job, and subordinates adhering to a rigid hierarchy.[100]

**TABLE 5.3** Power Distance Values for Fifty Countries and Three Regions

| RANK | COUNTRY | RANK | COUNTRY |
|------|---------|------|---------|
| 1 | Malaysia | 27/28 | South Korea |
| 2/3 | Guatemala | 29/30 | Iran |
| 2/3 | Panama | 29/30 | Taiwan |
| 4 | Philippines | 31 | Spain |
| 5/6 | Mexico | 32 | Pakistan |
| 5/6 | Venezuela | 33 | Japan |
| 7 | Arab countries | 34 | Italy |
| 8/9 | Ecuador | 35/36 | Argentina |
| 8/9 | Indonesia | 35/36 | South Africa |
| 10/11 | India | 37 | Jamaica |
| 10/11 | West Africa | 38 | United States |
| 12 | Yugoslavia | 39 | Canada |
| 13 | Singapore | 40 | Netherlands |
| 14 | Brazil | 41 | Australia |
| 15/16 | France | 42/44 | Costa Rica |
| 15/16 | Hong Kong | 42/44 | Germany |
| 17 | Colombia | 42/44 | Great Britain |
| 18/19 | Salvador | 45 | Switzerland |
| 18/19 | Turkey | 46 | Finland |
| 20 | Belgium | 47/48 | Norway |
| 21/23 | East Africa | 47/48 | Sweden |
| 21/23 | Peru | 49 | Ireland |
| 21/23 | Thailand | 50 | New Zealand |
| 24/25 | Chile | 51 | Denmark |
| 24/25 | Portugal | 52 | Israel |
| 26 | Uruguay | 53 | Austria |
| 27/28 | Greece | | |

The lower the number, the more the country can be classified as one that has a large power distance. A higher number is associated with a country that demonstrates small power distance.

Source: Adapted from Geert Hofstede, *Cultures Consequences: Comparing Values, Behavior, Institutions and Organizations Across Nations*, 2nd ed. (Thousand Oaks, CA: Sage Publications, 2001).

**Low Power Distance.** Low power distance countries such as Austria, Finland, Denmark, Norway, the United States, New Zealand, and Israel hold that inequality in society should be minimized. Or as Brislin notes, "Cultures referred to as 'low power distance' are guided by laws, norms, and everyday behaviors that make power distinctions as minimal as possible."[101] People in these cultures believe they are close to power and should have ready access to that power. To them, a hierarchy is an inequality of roles established for convenience. Subordinates consider superiors to be the same kind of people as they are, and superiors perceive their subordinates the same way. People in power, be they supervisors, managers, or government officials, often interact with their constituents and try to look less powerful than they really are.

We can observe signs of this dimension in nearly every communication setting. Within the educational context, Calloway-Thomas, Cooper, and Blake offer the following summary:

> In large power distance societies, the educational process is teacher centered. The teacher initiates all communication, outlines the path of learning students should follow, and is never publicly criticized or contradicted. In large power distance societies, the emphasis is on the personal "wisdom" of the teacher, while in small power distance societies the emphasis is on impersonal "truth" that can be obtained by any competent person.[102]

According to Hofstede, in a business context with low power distance you might observe decisions being shared, subordinates being consulted, bosses relying on support teams, and status symbols being kept to a minimum.[103]

## MASCULINITY/FEMININITY

Hofstede uses the words *masculinity* and *femininity* to refer to the degree to which masculine or feminine traits are valued and revealed. His rationale, and one that is supported by most anthropologists, psychologists, and political scientists, is that many masculine and feminine behaviors are learned and mediated by cultural norms and traditions. Adler feels that the terms *masculinity* and *femininity* do not adequately convey the full meaning behind this dimension and chooses to use the terms *career success* and *quality of life*.[104] While we agree with Adler's assessment, we will adhere to Hofstede's original titles and suggest you refer to Adler's labels if they help you to better understand the dimension.

**Masculinity.** Masculinity is the extent to which the dominant values in a society are male oriented. Hofstede advances an excellent summary of these values when he notes:

> Masculine cultures use the biological existence of two sexes to define very different social roles for men and women. They expect men to be assertive, ambitious, and competitive, and to strive for material success, and to respect whatever is big, strong, and fast.[105]

Ireland, the Philippines, Greece, Venezuela, Austria, Japan, Italy, and Mexico are among countries where you can find many of the masculine values described by Hofstede (see Table 5.4). For example, in Ireland, despite the high level of economic development, in 2002 women were elected to only 32 of the 226 combined seats available in the Upper and Lower House.[106]

Adler reports that masculine cultures have highly defined gender roles and promote career success. "Assertiveness and the acquisition of money and things (materialism)"[107] are emphasized and often take precedence over interpersonal relationships.

**TABLE 5.4** Masculinity Values for Fifty Countries and Three Regions

| RANK | COUNTRY | RANK | COUNTRY |
|---|---|---|---|
| 1 | Japan | 28 | Singapore |
| 2/3 | Austria | 29 | Israel |
| 2/3 | Venezuela | 30/31 | Indonesia |
| 4/5 | Italy | 30/31 | West Africa |
| 4/5 | Switzerland | 32/33 | Turkey |
| 6 | Mexico | 32/33 | Taiwan |
| 7/8 | Ireland | 34 | Panama |
| 7/8 | Jamaica | 35/36 | Iran |
| 9/10 | Great Britain | 35/36 | France |
| 9/10 | Germany | 37/38 | Spain |
| 11/12 | Philippines | 37/38 | Peru |
| 11/12 | Colombia | 39 | East Africa |
| 13/14 | South Africa | 40 | Salvador |
| 13/14 | Ecuador | 41 | South Korea |
| 15 | United States | 42 | Uruguay |
| 16 | Australia | 43 | Guatemala |
| 17 | New Zealand | 44 | Thailand |
| 18/19 | Greece | 45 | Portugal |
| 18/19 | Hong Kong | 46 | Chile |
| 20/21 | Argentina | 47 | Finland |
| 20/21 | India | 48/49 | Yugoslavia |
| 22 | Belgium | 48/49 | Costa Rica |
| 23 | Arab countries | 50 | Denmark |
| 24 | Canada | 51 | Netherlands |
| 25/26 | Malaysia | 52 | Norway |
| 25/26 | Pakistan | 53 | Sweden |
| 27 | Brazil | | |

The lower the number, the more the country can be classified as one that favors masculine traits; a higher score is a country that prefers feminine traits.

Source: Adapted from Geert Hofstede, *Cultures Consequences: Comparing Values, Behavior, Institutions and Organizations Across Nations*, 2nd ed. (Thousand Oaks, CA: Sage Publications, 2001).

**Femininity.** Cultures that value femininity as a trait stress nurturing behaviors. A feminine worldview maintains that men need not be assertive and that they can assume nurturing roles; it also promotes sexual equality and holds that people and the environment are important. In addition, in feminine cultures there tend to be "overlapping social roles for the sexes."[108] Interdependence and androgynous behavior are the ideal, and people sympathize with those less fortunate. Nations such as Sweden, Norway, Finland, Denmark, and the Netherlands tend toward a feminine worldview. For example, in Sweden, which had the highest ranking in Hofstede's femininity category, women occupied 45 percent of the 349 legislative positions following the 2002 election.[109]

You can also observe the role of gender in the workplace. In masculine societies, women are expected to stay home and society doesn't encourage a professional career. As Kim points out:

> In Japan, Germany, and other European and Asian countries, women face serious obstacles to achieving work place equality. They are expected to assist men and are given lower wages, less stable employment, and fewer opportunities for advancement.[110]

*Many cultures make strong distinctions between male and female roles and rituals within the society.*

© Robert Fonseca

In contrast, feminine societies expect women to work and often provide the necessary social support systems. In Sweden, for example, parents are offered "the option of paternity or maternity leave to take care of newborn children and the state provides day-mothers to care for older children."[111]

## LONG- AND SHORT-TERM ORIENTATION

Over the years, there has been some condemnation of Hofstede's work. One major criticism dealt with the Western bias Hofstede used to collect his data.[112] As a means of overcoming this problem, Hofstede offered a new orientation called long- versus short-term orientation. This new research, involving twenty-three countries, used an assessment called the Chinese Value Survey (CVS), "an instrument developed by Michael Harris Bond in Hong Kong from values suggested by Chinese scholars,"[113] often called Confucian dynamism.[114] Hofstede summarizes the link between this fifth orientation and Confucianism:

> The long-term/short-term orientation dimension appears to be based on items reminiscent of the teachings of Confucius, on both poles. It opposes long-term to short-term aspects of Confucian thinking: persistence and thrift to personal stability and respect for tradition.[115]

It is easy to see how these patterns would influence interaction in a variety of settings. For example, in business organizations, cultures that rank high on long-term orientation (China, Hong Kong, Taiwan, Japan, South Korea) would most likely have employees who reflect a strong work ethic and show great respect to their employers. We would also expect individuals who are members of these cultures to value social order and long-range goals. Those cultures that rank low on the long-term orientation index (the United States, Great Britain, Canada, Philippines), according to Hofstede, often do not place a high priority on status, try to postpone old age, are concerned with short-term results, and seek quick gratification of their needs.[116]

# The Kluckhohns and Strodtbeck's Value Orientations

Our next taxonomy is from the Kluckhohns and Strodtbeck, who were cultural anthropologists (see Table 5.5). They based their research on the notion that every individual, regardless of culture, must deal with five universal questions. Although the Kluckhohns and Strodtbeck used the phrase "value orientations" to describe these five questions, they were in fact talking about what we have to this point called cultural patterns. These patterns tell the members of the culture what is important and also offer guidance for living their lives.[117] Since the completion of the Kluckhohns and Strodtbeck's work, other researchers have added to their findings.[118] As we indicated, after examining numerous cultures, they came to the conclusion that all people turn to their culture to answer the same five basic questions:

1. What is the character of human nature?
2. What is the relation of humankind to nature?
3. What is the orientation toward time?
4. What is the value placed on activity?
5. What is the relationship of people to each other?[119]

Two important points need to be made before we turn to a specific explanation of the five dimensions advanced by the Kluckhohns and Strodtbeck. First, as was the case with Hofstede's ranking from one to fifty, the Kluckhohns and Strodtbeck's five orientations are best visualized as points along a continuum. Second, as you move through these five orientations, you will undoubtedly notice some of the same characteristics discussed by Hofstede. This is understandable in that both approaches are talking about meaningful values found, with varying degrees, in all cultures. Hence, both sets of research were bound to track many of the same patterns.

## HUMAN NATURE ORIENTATION

Nearly all judgments about human behavior, be they moral or legal, begin with this core question: What is the character of human nature? Was Anne Frank right when she wrote in *The Diary of a Young Girl*, "In spite of everything, I still believe that people

**TABLE 5.5** Five Value Orientations from Kluckhohn, Kluckhohn, and Strodtbeck

| ORIENTATION | VALUES AND BEHAVIOR | | |
|---|---|---|---|
| Human nature | Basically evil | Mixture of good and evil | Basically good |
| Humankind and nature | People subjugated to nature | People in harmony with nature | People the master of nature |
| Sense of time | Past oriented | Present oriented | Future oriented |
| Activity | Being | Being in becoming | Doing |
| Social relationships | Authoritarian | Group oriented | Individualism |

Source: F. R. Kluckhohn and F. L. Strodtbeck, *Variations in Value Orientations* (New York: Row and Peterson), 1960.

are really good at heart"? Or was the philosopher Immanuel Kant correct when he observed, "Out of the crooked timber of humanity no straight thing can ever be made"?

Questions concerning human nature have concerned religious leaders and philosophers for centuries. You can observe the importance of these questions when reading Borrowman's brief catalog of some questions related to human nature:

> What are the relative effects of "grace," "will," genetic heredity, geographical conditions, social institutions, and historical accident on the behavior of an individual? Would the "natural" man tend toward love and altruism in his treatment of others, or would he be dominated by greed and brutality? Is reason capable of dominating the behavior of man or merely a tool which he uses to mediate between demands of an insatiable id and an uncompromising super-ego?[120]

Your answers to the questions posed by Borrowman represent a powerful force in how you live your life. As Stevenson and Haberman tell us, "Different conceptions of human nature lead to different views about what we ought to do and how we can do it."[121] Although all people on an individual basis answer questions about human nature, there are also cultural explanations for why people act as they do.

Most discussions of human nature usually deal with divisions of evil, good and evil, and good. Let us look at each of these issues and how they often differ from culture to culture.

**Evil.** Some cultures begin with the premise that people are intrinsically evil. In the United States, this orientation, which was inherited from Puritan ancestors, was the prevailing view for many years. In the last hundred years, however, Americans have come to see themselves as a mixture of good and evil. That is, most Americans now believe they are "perfectible." By following certain rules, we can change, improve, and "be saved." According to this view, with constant hard work, control, education, and self-discipline, we can achieve goodness. You can also see this self-help approach to life in Christianity. For Christians, God is the father and humans are his children. As is the case with all children, you get guidance but must also make choices. According to Christianity, "We are rational beings, we have self-consciousness, and we have free choice."[122] Through those choices, we can move from being corrupt to being good.

A more restrictive view of the goodness or evilness of human nature is found in other parts of the Arab world. Where Islam is strong, you can find cultures that are imbued with the notion that people have a penchant for evil and therefore cannot, when left to their own resources, be trusted to make a correct decision. Hence, to help control the actions of their members, numerous institutions, ranging from the religious to the political, are designed to monitor and manage behavior. As discussed in Chapter 3, Islam came to the Middle East at a time when the Bedouin culture was plagued with immorality and hedonism. Allah was needed, the people thought, to save these sinners.

**Good and Evil.** People who hold the Taoist worldview believe that the universe is best seen from the perspective of yin and yang, an infinite system of opposing elements and forces in balanced dynamic interaction, and two of the forces present in this universe are good and evil. Since humanity is part of the universe, these forces are naturally present in humankind. This idea is clearly seen in the notion of yang and yin. Yang and yin are cyclic; they go through natural periods of balanced increase and decrease. Periodic increases in yang are accompanied by corresponding decreases in yin—this is followed by an opposite cycle in which yin increases while yang decreases. This view of the good and evil nature of humanity extends the position that people cannot eliminate evil, because it is a natural and necessary part of the universe. That is, good can only be recognized against a background of evil, and evil is only recognizable against a background of good.

We should add that many Europeans, for very different reasons, also have a duality (good/evil) approach to human nature. However, they believe that while we might be born with a propensity for evil, through learning and education people can become good.

**Good.** Perhaps the most extreme view of innate goodness of human nature can be found in the philosophies of Confucianism and Buddhism. Most interpretations of the writings of Confucius maintain that he was "very optimistic" about human nature.[123] Hundreds of years later we see this same view toward the innate goodness of people in the words of the Chinese philosopher Lu Wang: "Human nature is originally good." Buddhism also maintains that you are born pure and are closest to what is called "loving kindness" when you enter this world. Hence, people are good, but their culture often makes them evil.

Cutting across the arguments concerning the good and evil of human nature has been the question of the essential rationality of human nature. Throughout history, there has been tension between those who believe in fate or mystic powers and those who believe that the intellect can solve any problem and discover any truth. Imagine for a moment your perceptions of reality if you are French and take the rational approach characteristic of Descartes's philosophy, or if you are Native American and believe that forces external to you control much of your thinking and behavior. And for the Hindu, mysticism, intuition, and spiritual awareness are needed to understand the nature of reality. A belief in fate, as opposed to one that stresses free will, is bound to yield different conclusions.

## PERSON/NATURE ORIENTATION

**Human Beings Subject to Nature.** The differences in conceptions of the relationship between humanity and nature produce distinct frames of reference for human desires, attitudes, and behaviors. At one end of the scale devised by the Kluckhohns and Strodtbeck is the view that maintains human beings are subject to nature. Cultures that hold this orientation believe that the most powerful forces of life are outside their control. Whether the force be a god, fate, or magic, a person cannot overcome it and must therefore learn to accept it. This orientation is found in India and parts of South America. For the Hindu, because everything is part of a unified force, "the world of distinct and separate objects and processes is a manifestation of a more fundamental reality that is undivided and unconditional."[124] This "oneness" with the world helps create a perceptual vision of a harmonious world. In Mexico and among Mexican Americans, there is a strong tie to Catholicism and the role of fate in controlling life and nature. As Purnell notes, at the heart of this worldview is "a stoic acceptance of the ways things are."[125]

**Cooperation with Nature.** The middle or so-called cooperation view is widespread and is associated with East Asians. In Japan and Thailand, there is a perception that nature is part of life and not a hostile force waiting to be subdued. This orientation affirms that people should, in every way possible, live in harmony with nature. The desire to be part of nature and not control it has always been strong among Native Americans. As Joe and Malach note, "Tribal groups continue to teach respect for the land and to forbid desecration of their ancestral lands. These groups also carry out various ceremonies and rituals to ensure harmony with as well as protection of the land (Mother Earth)."[126] This orientation is eloquently summarized in a statement attributed to Chief Seattle, leader of the Suquamish Native Americans of Washington State: "Humankind has not woven the web of life. We are but one thread within it. Whatever we do to the web we do to ourselves. All things are bound together—all things connect."

**Controlling Nature.** At the other end of the scale is the view that compels us to conquer and direct the forces of nature to our advantage. This value orientation is characteristic of the Western approach, which, as we noted earlier in the chapter, has a long tradition of valuing technology, change, and science. Americans have historically believed that nature was something that could and had to be mastered. The early immigrants to North America found a vast, harsh wilderness that they needed to "tame." Even our language reflects this orientation. In earlier years, dams were built to "tame" rivers, and today we talk about "conquering" space. For people with this orientation there is a clear separation from nature.

We can often find examples of cultures clashing because of divergent views on how to relate to nature. A case in point is the ongoing controversy between the dominant American culture and some American Indian tribes who object to widespread strip mining of coal because it disfigures the earth and displaces spirits worshipped by the tribes. Our cultural orientation of controlling nature can be seen in a host of other instances. Adler highlights some of these:

> Other examples of the North Americans' dominance orientation include astronauts' conquest (dominance) of space, economists' structuring of markets, sales representatives' attempts to influence buyers' decisions; and, perhaps most controversial today, biotechnology and genetic programming.[127]

## TIME ORIENTATION

As a species, our fixation with time and the power we give it are rather obvious. Over two thousand years ago, the Greek playwright Sophocles observed, "Time is a kindly God." As is the case with most of the issues discussed in this book, cultures vary widely in how much they want to give in to that "God." Where they differ is in the value placed on the past, present, and future and how each influences interaction. So important is a culture's use of time that we develop the subject in detail in Chapter 7, but for now let us simply highlight some of the major cultural differences in the perception of time.

**Past Orientation.** Past-oriented cultures believe strongly in the significance of prior events. History, established religions, and tradition are extremely important to these cultures, so there is a strong belief that the past should be the guide for making decisions and determining truth. You can see this orientation in China, which because of its long and resplendent history continues to respect the past. Chu and Ju found that respect for their historical heritage was considered the most important traditional value among Chinese.[128] There is even a famous Chinese proverb that states, "The past is as clear as a mirror, the future as dark as lacquer." In Japan, where Shintoism is strong and reverence toward ancestors is important, the past still remains paramount. Great Britain, because of its extensive devotion to tradition, including the continuation of a monarchy, resists change as it attempts to cling to the past. France is yet another culture that can be understood by exploring its view of the past. The French, on many levels, venerate the past. As Hall and Hall tell us:

> The importance of French history to the average French person can hardly be overstated. The French live surrounded by thousands of monuments to their glorious past. Every quarter in Paris has its historically important statues, buildings, or fountains, daily reminders of past achievements. French villages have statues to local heroes and important political leaders. As a result of this constant immersion in history, the French tend to see things in their historical context and relate contemporary events to their origins.[129]

Within the United States, American Indians—in part because of their strong oral tradition—also value the past. Many Native American stories in fact use the past to set examples and to "provide moral guidelines by which one should live."[130]

A culture's judgment about the past is evident in a variety of situations. For example, when conducting business with a past-oriented culture, Trompenaars and Hampden-Turner suggest you "talk about history" and "show respect for ancestors, predecessors, and older people."[131] Lewis adds to the list by telling you that there should be "exploration of all issues before decisions are sought."[132]

**Present Orientation.** Present-oriented cultures hold that the moment has the most significance. For them, the future is vague, ambiguous, and unknown, and what

*Past-orientation cultures place a high value on traditions.*

is real exists in the here and now. For these cultures, enjoyment comes in the present. People of the Philippines and most Latin American countries usually hold these beliefs. Mexican Americans also "prefer to experience life and people around them fully in the present."[133] Luckmann suggests that this view is also characteristic of the African-American co-culture.[134]

**Future Orientation.** Future-oriented cultures, such as the U.S. dominant culture, emphasize the future and expect it to be grander than the present. What is going to happen holds the greatest attraction for most Americans because whatever we are doing is not quite as good as what we could be doing. This does not mean that Americans have no regard for the past or no thought of the present, but it is certainly true that most of them, in thought or action, look to the future.

Like many other orientations, our view of time is related to a host of other values. For example, Americans' view of the future makes them optimistic. This is reflected in the common proverb "If at first you don't succeed, try, try again." This optimistic view of the future also sees Americans believing they can control the future. The power to control the future was clearly spelled out by former President Lyndon Johnson when he told all Americans that "Yesterday is not ours to recover, but tomorrow is ours to win or to lose."

## ACTIVITY ORIENTATION

Activity orientation is the way a culture views activity. Three common modes of activity expression, as detailed by the Kluckhohns and Strodtbeck, are being, being-in-becoming, and doing.

**Being Orientation.** A being orientation refers to spontaneous expression of the human personality. As Adler and Jelinek point out, "People in being-orientated cultures accept people, events, and ideas as flowing spontaneously. They stress release, indulgence of existing desires, and working for the moment."[135] Most Latin cultures have the view that the current activity is the one that matters the most. In Mexico, for example, people take great delight in the simple act of conversation with family and friends. Mexicans will talk for hours with their companions, for they believe that the act of "being" is one of the main goals and joys of life. Gannon observes that Saudis have much the same approach to life. He points out that "several customers may be helped at the same time, or different business negotiations might be managed at once in the same office. This behavior exemplifies the Being orientation."[136]

**Being-in-Becoming Orientation.** The being-in-becoming orientation stresses the idea of development and growth. It emphasizes the kind of activity that contributes to the development of all aspects of the self as an integral whole. This usually correlates with cultures that value a spiritual life more than a material one. For example, in both Hinduism and Buddhism, people spend a portion of their lives in meditation and contemplation in an attempt to purify and fully advance themselves.

**Doing Orientation.** The doing orientation describes activity in which accomplishments are measurable by standards external to the individual. The key to this orientation is your trying to visualize a value system that stresses activity and action. It is the doing orientation that most characterizes the dominant American culture. Think of the high value placed on "doing" and "action" in the following two well-known proverbs: "No sooner said than done—so acts your man of worth," and "Idle hands are the Devil's workshop."

Kim offers an excellent synopsis of Americans' attitude toward doing and activity in the following paragraph:

> Americans are action oriented; they are go-getters. They get going, get things done, and get ahead. In America, people gather for action—to play basketball, to dance, to go to a concert. When groups gather they play games or watch videos. Many Americans don't have the patience to sit down and talk. . . . Life is in constant motion.[137]

According to Gannon, Israel is also a doing culture. He notes, "Israel is a classic 'doing' society in which action is taken proactively to control situations and overcome environmental problems."[138]

The doing orientation of a culture impinges on many other beliefs and values. Your definition of activity affects your perception of work, efficiency, change, time, and progress. Even the pace at which you live your life—from how fast you walk to the speed at which you reach conclusions—is related to where you land on the being/doing scale. Americans have long admired and rewarded people who can make rapid decisions and "speak up" quickly, and they even become impatient with people who are too reflective. Writing about American education, Newman notes:

> The child who speaks when the teacher requests a response is rewarded. The one who ponders is often considered withdrawn, problematic. The educational system appears to favor students who have the immediate answer, not those who take time to consider other questions.[139]

This attitude toward activity contrasts with that fostered by the Taoist tradition, where the individual is not the active agent; he or she is to remain calm, and truth eventually will make itself apparent. Imagine members of these two cultures sitting down together at a business meeting—or occupying the same classroom. African Americans are also a doing culture. Emotional vitality, activity, openness of feelings, and being expressive, which are part of the African-American experience, all involve forms of doing.[140]

## RELATIONAL (SOCIAL) ORIENTATION

This value orientation is concerned with the ways in which people perceive their relationships with others. Having already discussed, in some detail, the basic ideas behind relational orientations when we examined Hofstede's dimensions of individualism and power distance, our explanations here are rather brief.

**Authoritarian Orientation.** The value orientations in this category are on a continuum ranging from authoritarianism to individualism. Although most Americans find it difficult to believe, many cultures have had only authoritarian leaders, and therefore believe this type of social relationship to be the norm. In parts of Africa and in much of the Arab world, people believe that there are some individuals who are born to lead while others must follow. In these cultures, authoritarian relationships—from those with the ruling family to those with the leaders of the church—are accepted. The Arab proverb "The eye cannot rise above the eyebrow" demonstrates this accepting attitude.

**Collective Orientation.** As we noted elsewhere, collective cultures (such as the Chinese, Indian, African, Native American, Korean, and Latin American cultures) see the group as the most important of all social entities. Group affiliations take precedence over individual goals. In India, for example, the family influences a person's education, marriage, and occupation choice. So strong is the collective nature of some African tribes that "attempts to get Maasai students to raise their hands and participate in formal classrooms are often futile."[141] This behavior of remaining passive so that one does not call attention to themselves is also prevalent in Japanese classrooms.

**Individualism Orientation.** Having already spent a number of pages on the topic of individuals, we now simply remind you that those cultures that value individualism believe all people should have equal rights and complete control over their own destiny. Anything else, as most Americans hold, violates the will of God and the spirit of the Constitution.

# Hall's High-Context and Low-Context Orientations

The anthropologist Edward Hall offers us another effective means of examining cultural similarities and differences in both perception and communication. He categorizes cultures as being either high or low context, depending on the degree to which meaning comes from the settings or from the words being exchanged.[142] The assumption underlying Hall's classifications is that "one of the functions of culture is to provide a highly selective screen between man and the outside world. In its many forms, culture therefore designates what we pay attention to and what we ignore."[143]

The word *context* needs to be understood if you are to appreciate the link between context and communication. Context can be defined as "the information that surrounds an event; it is inextricably bound up with the meaning of the event."[144] Although all cultures contain some characteristics of both high and low variables, most can be placed along a scale showing their ranking on this particular dimension (see Table 5.6). To call your attention to this fact, we have placed various cultures on a continuum rather than using only two rigid categories. The Halls define high and low context in the following manner:

> A high context (HC) communication or message is one in which most of the information is already in the person, while very little is in the coded, explicitly transmitted part of the message. A low context (LC) communication is just the opposite; i.e., the mass of the information is vested in the explicit code.[145]

## HIGH CONTEXT

In high-context cultures (Native American, Latin American, Japanese, Arab, Chinese, African American, and Korean), many of the meanings being exchanged during the encounter do not have to be communicated through words. One reason that meanings often do not have to be stated verbally in high-context cultures is that the people are very homogeneous. They have similar experiences, information networks,

**TABLE 5.6** Cultures Arranged Along the High-Context and Low-Context Dimension

**High-Context Cultures**
|
Japanese
|
Chinese
|
Korean
|
African American
|
Native American
|
Arab
|
Greek
|
Latin
|
Italian
|
English
|
French
|
North American
|
Scandinavian
|
German
|
German/Swiss
|
**Lower-Context Cultures**

Source: Based on the work of Edward T. Hall. See notes for Chapter 5 at the end of the book.

and the like. High-context cultures, because of tradition and history, change very little over time. According to Hofstede, high-context cultures are "more often found in traditional cultures."[146] These are cultures in which consistent messages have produced consistent responses to the environment. "As a result," the Halls say, "for most normal transactions in daily life they do not require, nor do they expect, much in-depth, background information."[147] Because meaning is not necessarily contained in words, in high-context cultures information is provided through inference, gestures, and even silence. High-context cultures tend to be aware of their surroundings and can express and interpret feelings without verbally stating them.

Andersen points out, "High-context cultures are more reliant on and tuned in to nonverbal communication."[148] Meaning in high-context cultures is also conveyed "through status (age, sex, education, family background, title, and affiliations) and through an individual's informal friends and associates."[149] Because of all the subtle "messages" used by high-context cultures, members of these groups, according to Gudykunst, often "communicate in an indirect fashion."[150]

## LOW CONTEXT

In low-context cultures (German, Swiss, Scandinavian, and North American), the population is less homogeneous and therefore tends to compartmentalize interpersonal contacts. This lack of a large pool of common experiences means that "each time they interact with others they need detailed background information."[151] In low-context cultures, the verbal message contains most of the information and very little is embedded in the context or the participants. This characteristic manifests itself in a host of ways. For example, the Asian mode of communication (high context) is often vague, indirect, and implicit, whereas Western communication (low context) tends to be direct and explicit. In addition, as Lynch notes, "Low-context communicators talk more, speak more rapidly, and often raise their voices."[152] Althen offers an excellent summary of Americans' fascination with language in the following paragraph:

> Americans depend more on spoken words than on nonverbal behavior to convey messages. They think it is important to be able to "speak up" and "say what's on their mind." They admire a person who has a moderately large vocabulary and who can express him- or herself clearly and cleverly.[153]

Differences in perceived credibility are yet another aspect of communication associated with these two orientations. In high-context cultures, people who rely primarily on verbal messages for information are perceived as less credible. They believe that silence often sends a better message than words, and anyone who needs words does not have the information. As the Indonesian proverb states, "Empty cans clatter the loudest." Differences in this communication dimension can even alter how conflict is perceived and responded to. Ting-Toomey has observed that the communication differences between high-context and low-context cultures are also apparent in the manner in which each approaches conflict. For example, because high-context cultures tend to be less open, they hold that conflict is harmful to most communication encounters. For them, Ting-Toomey says, "Conflict should be dealt with discreetly and subtly."[154]

Harris and Moran summarize the low-context dimension as it applies to the business setting in the following manner:

> Unless global leaders are aware of the subtle differences, communication misunderstandings between low- and high-context communicators can result. Japanese communicate by not stating things directly, while Americans usually do the opposite—"spell it out." The former is looking for meaning and understanding in what is not said—in the nonverbal communication or body language, in the silences and pauses, in relationships and empathy. The latter places emphasis on sending and receiving accurate messages directly, usually by being articulate with words.[155]

## Face and Facework

Our last cultural pattern is called "face" and "facework." Here we are using the term *face* as a metaphor for the self-image you want to project to other people. Since it is how you want others to see you, it is a product of social interaction and, as such, can be either lost or gained.[156] Facework is the construction and communication of face. In other words, facework is the various actions you engage in to acquire face for yourself or give face to someone else. For a job interview, you will probably wear your best dress or suit and be sure to arrive a few minutes before the scheduled time. During the interview you will remember to sit erect, maintain eye contact, respond to questions with thoughtful answers, use more formal terms of address, and avoid slang. These efforts amount to self-directed facework because you want to make a positive impression on the personnel manager. As the old adage goes, you will "put on your best face." Complementing a friend on their new haircut or swimsuit is an example of other-directed facework.

Ting-Toomey has conducted extensive research into the role of face and facework in intercultural communication, especially in conflict situations. Her work assumes that people from all cultures strive to "maintain and negotiate face in all communication situations."[157] Face and facework, however, are influenced by cultural values and vary from one culture to the next.[158] In individualistic cultures, for example, people are more concerned with maintaining their own face. Stewart and Bennett tell us that in the U.S., "Self-definition is determined primarily by personal achievement."[159] This means that a person's face is usually derived from their own self-effort and is normally independent of others. Since U.S. Americans do not normally rely on group affiliation for their identity or social support, they are less concerned with how they influence someone else's face. This produces a rather direct, forthright communication style. Common U.S. expressions such as "don't beat around the bush," "tell it like it is," and "be honest with me" demonstrate the value placed on open, candid communication. In some instances, positive interpersonal relations may take a backseat to frankness. Gudykunst and Nishida tell us that "North Americans see threats to their credibility or self-image as face threats," and actual loss of face is a result of personal failure.[160]

In collectivistic cultures, group membership, which includes family, clan, school, and workplace, is normally the primary source of identity and status. Considerable value is placed on establishing and sustaining stable, harmonious relationships with members of these in-groups. This is evident in what constitutes face in collectivistic societies. For the Japanese, face involves "honor, appearance of propriety, presence, and the impact on others."[161] Among the Chinese, according to Gao and Ting-Toomey, "gaining and losing face is connected closely with issues of social pride, honor, dignity, insult, shame, disgrace, humility, trust, mistrust, respect, and prestige."[162] As you would suspect, extreme politeness is also part of face saving in that being rude or disrespectful would cause the other person to feel shame and experience a lack of pride.

These varying attitudes as to what represents face have a very noticeable impact on how a culture views and approaches conflict. Kim tells us that in collective cultures in-group conflict "is viewed as damaging to social face and relational harmony, so it should be avoided as much as possible,"[163] As a result, in collectivistic cultures maintenance of mutual and other face receives greater emphasis than self-face. In Japan, for instance, an individual's actions that discredit or bring shame to in-group members or disturbs smooth interpersonal relations will result in a loss of face.[164]

The different value placed on face, what constitutes face, and how it is managed has a very noticeable influence on facework. Drawing on the individualism/collectivism cultural pattern, Ting-Toomey posits that when confronted with the potential for conflict, collectivists will be more inclined toward avoidance and obligating measures.[165] This is a result of concern for both mutual- and other-face, and how one's actions may affect others. March illustrates this concern for others' face when he relates that a widespread practice in Japan is to pay the bill without first checking it. To examine the bill would create a loss of face for the store personnel and the store itself.[166] Individualists, however, are concerned primarily with self-face and tend to favor confrontational and solution-oriented approaches to resolve conflicts.[167] In the U.S., therefore, it is quite common to closely examine the bill before paying.

These contrasting attitudes toward conflict produce quite different culturally based communication styles. During intercultural communication events, these contrasting styles can produce confusion, misinterpretation, or even animosity among the participants. Adherence to an indirect communication style in order to sustain amicable relations can actually produce the opposite effect among individualistic participants. Conversely, the use of open, direct forthright communication can be perceived as rude and inconsiderate by collectivistic participants, who will consider the interaction as face threatening.

The difference between face and facework across cultures is a function of different cultural values. Just as we have discussed throughout this chapter, the variation in cultural values has a direct and continuing influence on how you perceive the world, behave, and communicate. As we conclude this chapter, we need to urge you to learn more about variations in cultural patterns so that you will be able to understand, predict, and even adapt to the behavior of people from cultures different from your own.

## Summary

- Culture and communication are so intertwined that it is easy to conceive that culture is communication and communication is culture.
- Culture seeks to tell its members what to expect from life, and therefore it reduces confusion and helps us predict the future.
- The basic elements of culture are history, religion, values, social organizations, and language.
- Culture is shared learned behavior that is transmitted from one generation to another for purposes of promoting individual and social survival, adaptation, and growth and development.
- Culture most directly affects communication because culture is (1) learned, (2) transmitted from generation to generation, (3) based on symbols, (4) dynamic, and (5) an integrated process.
- Perception is best defined as "the process of selecting, organizing, and interpreting sensory data in a way that enables us to make sense of our world."
- Perception is the primary mechanism by which you develop your worldview.
- Beliefs are our convictions in the truth of something—with or without proof.
- Values are enduring attitudes about the preferability of one belief over another.
- There are numerous cultural patterns that can be examined: Gannon's Four-Stage Model of Cross-Cultural Understanding, Trompenaars and Hampden-Turner's Basis for Cultural Differences, Grondona's Cultural Typology, and Weaver's Contrast Cultural Continuum.
- Dominant American cultural patterns include individualism, equality, materialism, science and technology, progress and change, work and leisure, and competition.
- The most prominent and diverse culture patterns that explain both perceptual and communication differences are Hofstede's Values Dimension, which includes (1) individualism and collectivism, (2) uncertainty avoidance, (3) power distance, (4) masculinity and femininity, and (5) long-term and short-term orientation.

- The Kluckhohns and Strodtbeck's Value Orientation includes (1) human nature, (2) the perception of nature, (3) time, (4) activity, and (5) relationships.
- In Hall's Context Orientation, (1) high context and (2) low context describe the degree to which individuals rely on internalized information.
- In Ting-Toomey's concept, face and facework take different forms and value in different cultures. Face is a function of group affiliation in collectivistic cultures and is self-derived in individualistic cultures. In conflict situations, collectivistic cultures focus on other- and mutual-face, while individualistic cultures focus on self-face.

## Activities

1. In small groups, list the American cultural values mentioned in this chapter. Try to think of other values that are not included in the text. Then find examples from American advertising campaigns that illustrate these values. For example, the advertising slogan from an athletic-shoe manufacturer, "Just do it," reflects the American value of accomplishment.
2. Working with others in a small group and using Hofstede's value dimensions, make a list of behaviors found in American culture that reflect individualism, uncertainty avoidance, and femininity.
3. Working in a small group, make a list of typical American behaviors that relate to evil, good and evil, and good. How widespread are these behaviors within the culture?
4. Examine your behavior and determine how well you fit into the various degrees of time orientation.

## Discussion Ideas

1. How does learning about one's culture help in understanding other cultures?
2. What are the differences in behavior exhibited by people who come from cultures that have different activity orientations?
3. Examine the concept of high- and low-context cultures. What problems can you anticipate when you are communicating with someone who holds a different context orientation?
4. How does cultural diversity in social perception affect the intercultural communication process?

## CHAPTER 6

# Words and Meaning: Language and Culture

*Language is so fundamental to our being that it is hardly possible to imagine life without it. It is so tightly woven into our human experience that anywhere on earth where two or more people gather together they likely will be communicating in some way.*

**STEVEN PINKER**

*A different language is a different view of life.*

**FEDERICO FELLINI**

## Language and Communication

The fact that language is the primary means people use to communicate with one another may seem patently obvious. Yet, the relational dynamics between language and communication are such a part of your everyday life and behavior that you probably do not consciously recognize them. This relationship is clearly identified by Bonvillain when she points out that language is

> the primary means of interactions between people. Speakers use language to convey their thoughts, feelings, intentions, and desires to others. Language links interlocutors in a dynamic, reflexive process. We learn about people through what they say and how they say it; we learn about ourselves through the ways that other people react to what we say; and we learn about our relationships with others through the give-and-take of communicative interactions.[1]

Language is not only our main link with the outside world, it is also a marker that distinguishes us from the other animal creatures we share the world with. The idea is eloquently expressed by Thomas:

> . . . the gift of language is the single human trait that makes us unique, setting us apart from the rest of life. Language is like nest building or hive making, the universal and biologically

specific activity of human beings. We engage in it communally, compulsively, and automatically. We cannot be human without it; if we were to be separated from it our minds would die, as surely as bees lost from the hive.[2]

What is being said by these two quotations is of significance to all students of intercultural communication. Because of your ability to use language, you can "reliably cause precise new combinations of ideas to arise in each other's minds."[3] Pinker notes, "In nature's talent show we are simply a species of primate with our own act, a knack for communicating information about who did what to whom by modulating the sounds we make when we exhale."[4] The ultimate usefulness of this knack or ability is cleverly suggested by Cartmill:

Language lets us get vast numbers of big, smart fellow primates all working together on a single task—building the Great Wall of China or fighting World War II or flying to the moon. It lets us construct and communicate the gorgeous fantasies of literature and the

*Symbol systems take a variety of forms, can be preserved, and help transmit the culture from generation to generation.*

© Photodisc/Getty Images

profound fables of myth. It lets us cheat death by pouring out our knowledge, dreams, and memories into younger people's minds. And it does powerful things for us inside our own minds because we do a lot of thinking by talking silently to ourselves. Without language, we would be only a sort of upright chimpanzee with funny feet and clever hands. With it, we are the self-possessed masters of the planet.[5]

## COMMUNICATIVE FUNCTIONS OF LANGUAGE

One thing that emerges from our analysis to this point is that language is the basic tool by which humans make society function. Orbe and Harris underscore this idea when they write that "in its most basic form, language is a tool humans have utilized, sometimes effectively, sometimes not so effectively, to communicate their ideas, thoughts, and feelings to others."[6] Saville-Troike furthers this notion by saying:

> At the level of individuals and groups interacting with one another, the functions of communication are related to participants' purposes and needs. These include such categories of functions as *affect* (conveying feelings or emotions), *directive* (requesting or demanding), *poetic* (aesthetic), *phatic* (empathy and solidarity), and *metalinguistic* (reference to language itself).[7]

Language also permits you to pool knowledge and to communicate with others who are beyond the reach of your voice in space and time so that you need not rediscover what others have already discarded. This capability is a key in making progress possible because it allows us to learn from the past, long after our predecessors have left us.[8]

Language serves a number of cultural, communal, and societal functions. First, from the cultural perspective, it is the primary means of preserving culture and is the medium of transmitting culture to new generations. Second, it helps establish and preserve community by "linking individuals into communities of shared identity."[9] Third, at the societal level, it is important to all aspects of human interaction because as Saville-Troike emphasizes, language

> . . . often relates to political goals, functioning to create or reinforce boundaries in order to unify speakers as members of a single speech community and to exclude outsiders from intragroup communication [as well as] serve a social identification function within a society by providing linguistic indicators which may be used to reinforce social stratification, or to maintain differential power relationships between groups.[10]

As you can see, language is a multifunctional tool that helps you satisfy a variety of needs. We will briefly look at several of these functions in order to demonstrate the important role language plays in daily interaction and the study and practice of intercultural communication.

## CONVERSATION

Conversation is the most fundamental form of communication because it provides you with the means of conducting human affairs. It is the process of blending thoughts and ideas without necessarily setting out to seek truth or to prove a point. As Drew notes, "It is largely through conversation that we are socialized, through which institutional organizations such as the economy and the polity are managed, and through which we manage our ordinary social lives."[11] The conversation function of language also reflects the accomplishments of human cultures and what is available for future societies to inherit.[12] Conversation, therefore, is a basis for many of the fundamental functions of language. As you will see in our discussion below, these functions serve a variety of individual and collective needs.

## EXPRESSION OF AFFECT

Language provides a means for you to express outwardly your internal affective states. This form of expression may range from a simple statement such as "I feel lousy" to loud cursing at something that is not functioning properly or to voicing personal surprise or happiness. Whether in the absence of others or in their presence, as Coertze asserts, this use of language serves as a means of getting rid of nervous energy when you are under stress.[13] What is interesting about the affective function of language is that while all cultures use language for this purpose, there is a wide range of differences in how emotional expressions are acted out. That is to say, some cultures, such as the people of Thailand, do not make excessive use of language when expressing most emotions. Yet many people who live in cultures of the Middle East and Latin America are extremely expressive in their use of language. Later in this chapter we make some cultural comparisons to emphasize this point.

## THINKING

Humans tend to be both visual and verbal thinkers and engage in both forms depending upon their activity as well as their preference. Yet, as Crystal indicates, verbal thinking plays an extremely important role in human communication because language functions as an instrument of thought when you speak your thoughts out loud as an aid to problem solving or thinking.[14] So important is this function of language that we will develop it in much greater detail later in the chapter.

## CONTROL OF REALITY

Communication also assists you in the control of reality. Prayers or blessings invoking supernatural beliefs use language to try and control the various forces that are believed to control or influence one's life. For instance, in the Roman Catholic mass, the speaking of the words "This is my body" is believed to identify the moment when the communion bread becomes the body of Christ.[15]

## KEEPING OF HISTORY

The American philosopher Emerson was correct when he wrote, "Language is the archives of history." That is why in Chapter 1 we pointed out how all cultures employ symbols to help pass on the culture from generation to generation. Language is used to record past events and achievements, a function represented by all kinds of record keeping ranging from historical records, geographical surveys, and business accounts to scientific reports, legislative acts, and public-record databases. This arena, Crystal points out, "is an essential domain of language because the material guarantees the knowledge-base of subsequent generations, which is a prerequisite of social development and the perpetuation of culture."[16]

## SOCIALIZATION AND ENCULTURATION

Socialization and enculturation, says Brislin, involve "the experiences in which children participate so that they will eventually become productive and responsible adults."[17] The link between language and culture is evident because language is the primary means of instructing members of a society in culturally acceptable practices and behaviors for social interaction, in the appropriate relationships to the physical environment, and to the sensed but unseen supernatural. It is, in short, the sharing of a common or similar worldview and system of values that not only results in a shared ability for verbal communication but also makes possible other forms of culturally determined ways of communication.[18]

## EXPRESSION OF IDENTITY

In Chapter 4 we dealt extensively with how culture contributes to the construction of an individual's many identities. Language, of course, is the major mechanism through which much of your culturally based individual and group identities are constructed. Identities do not exist until they are enacted through language. Language not only presents information about your identity, the linguistic expression of identity unites people by reinforcing your different group identities. Cheering at a football game, reciting the Pledge of Allegiance, or shouting names or slogans at public meetings can both reinforce your group identification and reveal a great deal about you—in particular your culture, regional origins, social background, education level, occupation, age, gender, and personality.[19]

Beyond shouting slogans or cheers, language also helps you express and maintain your sociolinguistic identity, which is derived from the way cultures organize themselves into hierarchically ordered social groups or classes. The way people talk can reveal a great deal about their social position and their level of education.[20] This is particularly evident in the Japanese language where juniors normally address seniors using polite forms of language. But when addressing the junior, the senior may choose to use a less polite form as a way of reinforcing his or her authority.

To this point we have talked about language in general terms and have said very little about the specific role language plays in diverse cultures. That is about to change—in the remaining pages of this chapter we will examine the link between language and culture in both the speaking and thinking processes, as well as language diversity among co-cultures in the United States.

# Language and Culture

Language usage and style reflect the personality of a culture in much the same way that they reflect the personality of an individual. Philipsen supports this view when he says:

> Cultural premises and rules about speaking are intricately tied up with cultural conceptions of persons, agency, and social relations—that is, rules and beliefs about speech articulate with a larger cultural code defining the nature of persons, whether and how it is that humans can act efficaciously in their world of practice, and what are the possible and appropriate ways in which individuals are linked together in social units.[21]

This relationship between language and culture is further emphasized by Saville-Troike when she writes, "There is no doubt, however, that there is a correlation between the form and content of a language and the beliefs, values, and needs present in the culture of its speakers"[22]

The relationship between language and culture has caused Edwards to believe that language and culture have the power to maintain national or cultural identity. For him, language is important in ethnic and nationalist sentiment because of its powerful and visible symbolism; it becomes a core symbol or rallying point.[23]

The impact of language as a strong symbol of national identity may be seen in the history of the Basques, an ethnic group in the north of Spain and southwestern France. According to Crystal, the Spanish government from 1937 to the mid-1950s made an active attempt to destroy the Basque culture by forbidding the use of Euskara, the Basque language. Euskara could not be taught in the schools or used in the media, church ceremonies, or in public places. Books in the language were publicly burned, and Basque names could not be used in baptism ceremonies. All Basque names in official documents were translated into Spanish, and inscriptions on public buildings and tombstones were removed.[24] However, the Basque sense of cultural identity was so strongly tied to their language that the Spanish government's attempts to ban Euskara ultimately failed. Today, more than a million Basque speak Euskara, and it is the first language of more than 700,000.

Because many political and civil leaders recognize that language and culture are inseparable, they often take steps to limit or prohibit any change in the language they perceive as a threat to their culture.[25] Costa Rica, for instance, in 1977 enacted a new law that restricts the use of foreign languages and imposes fines on those who break it. Under that law, companies that advertise in a foreign language were required to include a Spanish translation in larger letters.[26] Likewise, Iran has banned companies from using Western names. Turkey's government is considering fining anyone who uses foreign names on the airwaves. And France has a list of thirty-five hundred foreign words that cannot be used in schools, bureaucracies, or companies.[27] The French have actually carried this attempt to maintain a "pure" language to an extreme, as Andrews indicates:

> The French have an official language academy to watch over linguistic developments and try to regulate them. They're so alarmed by what they consider to be the "contamination" of French by foreign tongues (especially American English) that they've resorted to drastic measures.[28]

The current French strategy for language control "is to set up for all the mass media obligatory percentages of content created and produced entirely in France—that is, to set up *cultural quotas.*"[29]

In addition to recognizing these attempts to preserve languages and language usage, it is also important to realize that languages do acquire words from other languages. Languages around the world, for example, have acquired numerous words from indigenous American languages, such as *avocado, chocolate, coyote, sequoia, caribou, chipmunk, Chinook,* and *tomato.* Although these words had their origins in the Americas, they have made their way into a wide range of other languages.

## VERBAL PROCESSES

As we have already indicated, it is impossible to separate language from culture. In its most basic sense, Rubin says, language "is a set of characters or elements and rules for their use in relation to one another."[30] These characters or elements are language symbols that are culturally diverse. That is, they differ from one culture to another. Not only are the words and sounds for those symbols different, but so are the rules for using those symbols and sounds.

The words used to represent things are different in various languages. In English, for instance, you have a pet dog or cat, but in Spanish, your pet is a *perro* or a *gato*. While you live in a house, Thai people live in *bans*. Although this type of difference is obvious, there are other types of linguistic diversity that may not be so obvious. Phonology—the number and tonal qualities of speech sounds—is also culturally diverse. While in English there are twenty-one consonant sounds and five vowels that combine to form thirty-eight various phoneme sounds, the Filipino language has sixteen consonants and ten vowels forming twenty-six phonemes. The Arabic language has only twenty letters in its alphabet, which somewhat limits the number of available words. Hence, an Arab may need to use half a dozen words to convey the meaning of a single English word.

Grammatical structures are also unique to each language. In English, there are both singular and plural nouns and pronouns, but in Korean "the distinction between singular and plural is made by the context of the sentence."[31] In English, verb tenses express contrast between past, present, and future acts, but in Vietnamese, the same verb reflects all three and the time of the action is inferred from the context.[32] Syntax, the word order and structure of sentences, also varies depending on the language. In the normal word order of simple sentences for Filipinos, the predicate is followed by the subject.[33] For example, the English sentence "The teacher died" would be "*Namatay ang guro,*" or "Died the teacher," in the Filipino language. In Japanese, the predicate comes at the end of the sentence, so "I went to Tokyo" would be "*Watashi wa Tokyo ni ikimashita*" or "I Tokyo went to." In English, the possessive form is indicated by the use of an apostrophe: Rosemary's house. In Spanish, the apostrophe is not used and possession is shown in the form of *casa de Rosa Maria* (house of Rosemary). These examples tell you that if you want to communicate in another language, it is important to know not only the symbols (words) of that language but also the rules (syntax) for using those symbols.

## WORD AND PRONUNCIATION DIVERSITY

In situations where cultures share the same language, there are differences in word meanings and in word pronunciation. Language is much more than just a symbol and rule system that permits communication with another person; it is also the means by which people think and construct reality. As Nanda and Warms point out, "Language does more than just reflect culture: it is the way in which the individual is introduced to the order of the physical and social environment. Therefore, language would seem to have a major impact on the way in which the individual perceives and conceptualizes the world."[34]

Some excellent examples of word and pronunciation differences can be found by comparing American English with British English. Scott explains these differences in the following paragraph:

> American and British English vocabularies have diverged over time, resulting in lexical differences that have the potential to confound English-language intercultural communication. The differences derive from the need to adapt the meanings of existing expressions

or to find new expressions for different things and to borrow expressions from different cultures. Separation and slow means of communication also cause differences and encourage one side to retain archaic expressions that others have abandoned or modified. The differences in vocabulary can be grouped into four categories: the same expressions with differences in style, connotation, and/or frequency; the same expressions with one or more shared and different meanings; the same expression with completely different meanings; and different expressions with the same shared meaning. These differences in vocabularies affect understanding of all varieties of English.[35]

An example of how differences in American and British English may manifest themselves is provided in this conversation overheard in the heartland of the London financial district:

"Yes, it is a pity that Ian's in queer street."

"Too much hire purchase was the problem, wasn't it?"

"Yes, and too many purchases of bespoke clothes and other things."

"And now his personal and business current accounts are badly overdrawn?"

"Precisely. He's been forced to retain a solicitor, and his position as commercial traveler is in jeopardy."[36]

This conversation between two of Ian's acquaintances reveals that Ian has gotten into debt over his inability to pay, and he has had to hire a lawyer to try to get him out of his adverse circumstances.

In addition to confusion that can arise when two cultures share the same language, when a culture attempts to translate one language into another for purposes of informing the public, a number of comedic situations sometimes arise. Some examples are given from this selection of signs written in English discovered around the world:

**In a Japanese hotel:** *You are invited to take advantage of the chambermaid.*

**Outside a Paris dress shop:** *Dresses for street walking.*

**In a Rome laundry:** *Ladies, leave your clothes here and spend the afternoon having a good time.*

These few examples reveal the difficulties that may occur when appropriate word usage and rules of syntax are unknown or not followed.

Pronunciation diversity can also cause misperceptions and embarrassing situations. Swain tells of a woman who "wondered why Australians are happy about mothers dying. She said they always smile when they say 'mothers die.'"[37] The woman did not understand that the pronunciation of the word "day" in Australian English sounds like the word "die" in American or British English. Such differences, while sometimes amusing, illustrate just how language diversity can lead to misunderstanding, confusion, and embarrassment.

## LANGUAGE, CULTURE, AND MEANING

As children, you probably asked your parents quite frequently, "What does that word mean?" This question indicates that people tend to look for meaning to be inherent in words themselves. If you believe, however, that words actually possess meaning, you are taking a naïve view. It is far more accurate to say that meanings are internal (i.e., held inside our heads) and that words only bring those meanings to awareness as required. A word can elicit many different meanings depending on your background and the context in which the word is encountered. For instance, to one person, the word *cool* might mean something related to the weather. For another person, *cool* may mean something that is nice and very trendy or "with it." All people draw on their unique backgrounds to decide what a word means. People can ascribe similar meanings to words only if they have had or can anticipate similar experiences. For instance, if your past experiences include baseball, then a *rope* is a line drive. If your background lies in the world of rock music, the word *ax* is not the name of something used to chop wood but indicates a guitar. And, it is quite likely that a patient or a relative of a patient and a physician engaged in oncology research will possess different meanings for the word *cancer*.

A word, then, can potentially elicit many meanings. Linguists have estimated that the five hundred most-used words in the English language can produce over fourteen thousand meanings. The word *cat*, for example, can refer not only to a fuzzy domestic pet, but to a jazz musician, a type of tractor, a type of fish, a kind of sailboat, or even a kind of whip. And the simple word *lap* can stand for the distance around a track, a portion of your anatomy, the drinking method of a cat or dog, or the sound of water washing onto the shore. All of this simply means that there are many more ideas, feelings, and things to represent than there are words to represent them. Consequently, you must use your own personal background and experiences to abstract meaning from the words you encounter. As the English poet Tennyson said, "Words, like Nature, half reveal and half conceal the Soul within." We add that what is "half concealed" may often be more important than what is revealed.

Now, if culture is included as a variable in the process of abstracting meaning, the problems become all the more acute, for culture teaches us both the symbol (dog) and what the symbol represents (a furry, domesticated animal). When you are communicating with someone from your own culture, the process of using words to represent your experiences is much easier because within a culture people share many similar experiences. But when communication is between people from diverse cultures, different experiences are involved and the process becomes more troublesome. Objects, events, experiences, and feelings have the labels or names they do because a community of people arbitrarily decided to so name them. If this notion is extended to the intercultural setting, you can see that diverse cultures can have both different symbols and different responses. If you imagine shifting your cultural references for every word and meaning you know, you can begin to visualize the influence of culture on how we send and receive messages. Think for just a moment about the array of meanings various cultures have for words such as *freedom, sexuality, trespassing, wealth, nature, leadership, assertiveness, security, democracy, outer space,* or *AIDS*.

The Hawaiian and Sami languages offer some additional examples of the relationship between culture and meaning. The Hawaiian language contains only about twenty thousand words, and only fifteen thousand of those are in dictionaries. The Hawaiian language is very ambiguous to outsiders because some words have up to five different meanings, and some of the words can be used in a variety of ways and contexts. Reineke emphasizes the complexity of the Hawaiian language when he says: "Only knowledge of all the possible meanings of a word and the probable intent of the speaker enables one to arrive at the correct interpretation."[38]

Sloane points out that reindeer are a staple of the Sami economy, and snow is a prevalent weather condition in Kiruna, Sweden. Consequently the Sami language, spoken in northern Scandinavia, has five hundred words to explain *snow* and several thousand more to define *reindeer*, but no word for *computer*.[39] For example, in Sami language, one of the words used to describe snow means "where reindeer have been digging and eating in one place and then left, so it's no use to go there."[40] Because these words hold such significance for the Sami culture, their language has hundreds of words to represent them. Computers, however, play no part in the herding of reindeer, so the Sami language does not have words to represent such common English terms as *computer, printer,* or *hard drive.*

There are even differences between British and American usage in word meanings. Although some words are spelled and pronounced the same, they have different meanings. For instance, the words *boot, bonnet, lift,* and *biscuit* in British English translate into American English as *car trunk, car hood, elevator,* and *cookie.* In the area of business, there are also interesting differences. Ruch provides some examples: The British term *annual gunnel meeting* translates in American English as *annual meeting of shareholders.* The British word *billion* translates as *trillion,* and the British term *superannuation scheme* translates as *pension plan.*[41]

From these examples, you can see that culture exerts an enormous influence on language because culture teaches not only the symbols and rules for using those symbols, but, more importantly, the meaning associated with the symbols. Further, culture influences the way people think and perceive reality. In the next section, we will examine how culture influences language and thought.

# Language and Thought

You may easily assume that everyone speaks and thinks in much the same way—that they just use different languages. This is not the case. Just as verbal behavior differs from one culture to another, thought processes and perceptions of reality also differ. How people think and how they ultimately speak is determined largely by their culture. This cultural dynamic is known as linguistic relativity.

The essence of linguistic relativity is set forth in the theoretical formulations of Benjamin Lee Whorf, and suggests that language and thought are so intertwined that one's language determines the categories of thought open to him or her. As Whorf has indicated, "We cut up and organize the spread and flow of events as we do largely because, through our mother tongue, we are parties to an agreement to do so, not because nature itself is segmented in exactly that way for all to see."[42] What has become known as the Sapir-Whorf hypothesis argues that language is not simply a means of reporting experience, but, more important, it is a way of defining experience. Sapir, a student of Whorf, wrote:

> Human beings do not live in the objective world alone, nor alone in the world of social activity as ordinarily understood, but are very much at the mercy of the particular language which has become the medium of expression for their society. . . . The real world is to a large extent unconsciously built up on the language habits of the group. No two languages are ever sufficiently similar to be considered as representing the same social reality. The worlds in which different societies live are distinct worlds, not merely the same world with different labels attached.[43]

Kodish offers further insight into linguistic relativity when he writes that "linguistic relativity is a view of language that is intertwined with behavior, consciousness."[44] An outcome of linguistic relativity suggested by Bonvillain is what she calls cultural presuppositions:

> These presuppositions are collected by people during their lifetime of involvement in and learning through their experiences, that is, their enculturation. Because all human

experiences are cultural, a tremendous amount of accumulated but unstated knowledge is continuously carried with us.[45]

Rogers and Steinfatt provide yet another explanation of linguistic relativity when they point out that "Linguistic relativity is the degree to which language influences human thought and meanings. It proposes that in human thought language intervenes between the symbols and the ideas to which the symbols refer."[46] Nanda further explains how the Sapir-Whorf hypothesis might operate in practice:

> If my language has only one term—brother-in-law—that is applied to my sister's husband, my husband's brothers, and my husband's sisters' husbands, I am led by my language to perceive all of these relatives in a similar way. Vocabulary, through what it groups together under one label and what it differentiates with different labels, is one way in which language shapes our perception of the world.[47]

In a similar sense, in the Hindi language of India, there are no single words that are equivalent to the English words for *uncle* and *aunt*. Instead, as Rogers and Steinfatt relate, Hindi has different words for your father's older brother, your father's younger brother, your mother's older brother, your mother's older brother-in-law, and so forth.[48]

The Navajo language provides other instances of how language defines experience. For the Navajo, it is important to express both the nature and direction of movement.[49] Thus, instead of saying "One dresses," the Navajo would say, "One moves into clothing." Or instead of saying "One is young," the Navajo would say, "One moves about newly."[50] Both instances reflect the concern with movement inherent in the Navajo language. The Navajo hold a high concern for people's rights and individual autonomy.[51]

Bonvillain demonstrates this concern for individual autonomy in the following set of sentences:

**English speaker:** "I must go there."
**Navajo speaker:** "It is only good that I shall go there."
**English speaker:** "I make the horse run."
**Navajo speaker:** "The horse is running for me."[52]

Young adds to this linguistic view when he indicates that the English and Navajo languages "express different concepts presupposing people's (and other animate beings') rights to individual autonomy."[53] Young continues by indicating that English has numerous terms that express coercion, such as *cause, force, make, compel, order, must, have to, ought to.* In contrast, the Navajo language, spoken in Arizona, Colorado, New Mexico and Utah, does not contain such coercive and compelling verbs. Thus, instead of saying "I *must* go there" or I *have* to go there," a Navajo speaker would say "It is only good that I shall go there." This construction "lacks the force of compelling necessity."[54] Bonvillain adds to this point when she says that

> . . . whereas English readily expresses the idea that a person has a right to impose her or his will on another animate being, Navajo again does not express direct compulsion.[55]

Although complete acceptance of linguistic relativity is controversial, Crystal makes its application to culture and language clear: "There is the closest of relationships between language and thought. . . . Language may not determine the way we think, but it does influence the way we perceive and remember, and it affects the ease with which we perform mental tasks."[56] Thus, you can clearly see that culture influences language by way of its symbols and rules as well as your perceptions of the universe. Equally important is the fact that meaning takes different forms as you move from one culture to another.

## CONTEXTUALIZATION

Cultural differences in cognitive processes are also seen in the process of contextualization. Contextualization refers to how you create sense from fragmentary images of your environment by combining them to develop a larger mental image. Contextualization is akin to the psychological concept of closure. Shea explains this process by suggesting that seeing some fur, hind legs, and big ears may lead you to the larger image of a rabbit.[57] There are substantial cognitive differences between European Americans and East Asians in terms of how they employ words to contextualize their environment. According to Shea, "The cognitive differences between Americans and East Asians . . . [show] striking variation in how people brought up in the East and the West view the world."[58]

East Asians tend to be more holistic and make little use of categories and formal logic. Westerners tend to pay attention primarily to the object and the categories to which it belongs; they use rules, including formal logic, to understand the object.[59] On the other hand, "Asians exhibit greater 'attention to the field' than Americans."[60] Shea provides you with two examples of cultural differences in contextualizing. In the first situation, Asians and Americans were required to group together two of three words: *seagull, sky,* and *dog.* Americans chose to group *seagull* and *dog* together using the communality of both seagulls and dogs being animals. Asians, on the other hand, grouped *seagull* and *sky* indicating the relationship between birds and the sky. In the second example, choices were to be made between the word trio *pen, notebook,* and *magazine,* Asians grouped *pen* and *notebook* together while Americans grouped *notebook* and *magazine.*[61] Again, the reported relationships reflected the influence of culture on context.

# Culture and the Rules of Interaction

Human languages frequently seem to be the only communication system that combines apparently meaningless elements to create meaningful structures.[62] Yet, as Arensberg and Niehoff have correctly observed, "Nothing more clearly distinguishes one culture from another than its language."[63] A somewhat comedic example of how language usage reflects cultural diversity may be seen from the various ways in which a sign might announce a broken vending machine. In the United Kingdom, the sign might read "Please Understand this Machine Does Not Take 10p Coins." In the United States, the rendition would probably be "NO 10p COINS." The Japanese version would express regret at the inability to accept 10p coins and offer apologies to the consumer. Although the rules and uses of diverse languages often appear arbitrary and nonsensical to nonnative speakers, to the native speakers, the rules make perfect sense and seem more logical than those of other languages. To help you understand the degrees of diversity found in how cultures actually use language, we will examine four characteristics of language that include rules for (1) *directness and indirectness,* (2) the *maintenance of social customs and relationships,* (3) *expression of affect,* and (4) *the value of talk.*

## DIRECTNESS AND INDIRECTNESS

Language usage reflects many of the deep structure values of a culture. The degree to which a culture values directness or indirectness is reflected in that culture's language style. For instance, most Americans are familiar with direct language because that style marks the dominant cultural interaction form used in the United States. Your own experiences should tell you that Americans are rarely reserved. Indeed, the language style used by most Americans can be characterized as direct bluntness and frank, explicit expressions. Americans try to avoid vagueness and ambiguity and get directly to the point. If that means saying "no," they will say "no" without hesitation.

East Asian cultures view the American style of directness and bluntness as impolite and reflecting disregard for others, leading to embarrassment and injured feelings. In these cultures, indirect language styles are used in order to preserve the dignity, feelings, and "face" of others. The Buddha taught the virtue of indirectness when he advised his disciples to avoid "harsh speech." And the negative reaction to directness is reflected in an Asian proverb that states, "Once an arrow leaves the bow it cannot be retrieved."

The use of fewer words is also a characteristic of East Asian language styles. In many respects these cultures actually enjoy the aesthetics of vagueness. In fact, speakers are more concerned with the overall emotional quality of the interaction than with the meaning of particular words and sentences. Kashima and Kashima explain that, because of the collective nature of their cultures, many East Asian languages frequently do not reflect the use of personal pronouns in an effort to emphasize the importance of the group rather than the individual. They further indicate that members of Chinese, Japanese, Korean, and Thai cultures tend to employ language cautiously because they favor moderate or suppressed expression of negative and confrontational messages.[64]

In most East Asian cultures, the primary function of speech is the maintenance of social harmony. This value is reflected in a Japanese saying that states, "The mouth is the cause of calamity." The use of indirect language, therefore, facilitates face-saving and helps maintain social harmony. Ma states that members of these high-context cultures expect their communication partners to be able to read between the lines or decode messages from a holistic, context-based perspective.[65]

The use and meaning of the word "yes" in direct and indirect languages frequently poses a major linguistic difficulty when North Americans interact with many East Asians, such as the Chinese. Most North Americans learn to say yes and no as a means of expressing their individual views. But, being a collective culture, the Chinese usually reserve the use of yes or no to express respect for the feelings of others. "In other words," says Ma, "to say yes for no or no for yes is largely a reflection of the indirect approach to communication, through which undesirable interpersonal consequences can be avoided."[66]

The use of indirect language is evident in ways other than the use of yes and no. For example, an American host or hostess, when complimented on his or her cooking, is likely to respond, "Oh, I'm so glad you liked it. I cooked it especially for you." In contrast, as Marks explains, the Chinese host or hostess will "instead apologize profusely for giving you nothing even slightly edible and for not showing you enough honor by providing proper dishes."[67]

The Chinese also employ indirect language in their use of offensive language. For many Americans the creation of an "immediate effect" is a major rhetorical goal. When you insult someone, they know its full impact immediately. The Chinese prefer a "corrosive effect" that is deferred and long lasting. Says Ma, for the Chinese, the most powerful insult is to leave the insulted person unable to fall asleep at a later time because the more he or she thinks about the words, the more insulting the words become.[68]

The Korean language also reflects a cultural propensity for the consideration of others. Face-saving is crucial, as Park and Moon-soo relate, because Koreans do not want to feel responsible for causing someone to experience shame.[69] The Korean philosopher Han Yongun maintained that interpersonal harmony is the key to virtuous "social action." From an American perspective, the interpersonal communication of Koreans in the presence of family, work associates, and friends may seem strange. As you learned in Chapter 3, Confucian ethics govern most interpersonal relationships, following a basic premise that proper human relationships are the foundation of society. Proper interpersonal communication includes the expression of warm feelings and the placement of interpersonal relationships before personal interests.[70]

Mexicans are very concerned about being respectful to others and preserving dignity, and this is reflected in how they use language. Direct arguments are considered rude. A Mexican usually attempts to make every interaction harmonious and in so doing may appear to agree with the other person's opinion. In actuality, a Mexican will retain his own opinion unless he knows the other person well or has enough time to explain his opinion without causing the other person to lose face. This indirect politeness is often viewed by North Americans as dishonesty and aloof detachment when in actuality it is a sign of individual respect and an opportunity for the other person to save face.

Among the many African tribal languages, indirectness, imprecision, and ambiguity are often practiced as art forms. Speakers frequently employ indirect language styles in an attempt to preserve the dignity, feelings, and face of others. Richmond and Gestrin, writing about African language behavior, indicate:

> Africans speak naturally, with eloquence, and without hesitation or stumbling over words, but their language is often imprecise and their numbers inexact. Every personal interaction becomes a discussion that establishes a basis for the relationship between the two parties. Westerners should probe gently for specific details until they are reasonably satisfied that they understand what is meant even if not stated.[71]

Drawing upon her experiences gained living in Kenya, Miller adds to the understanding of African speaking styles when she indicates that:

> In collectivistic cultures like Kenya, a public speech is more than a performance by a skilled actor; it is a shared experience. It drives home its message by allowing audience members to exert the mental effort to interpret and make connections for themselves, thereby creating an even stronger bond between speaker and audience through shared comprehension.[72]

## MAINTAINING SOCIAL RELATIONSHIPS

It is safe to say that in most cultures, language is the primary vehicle for maintaining and enhancing social status and relationships. This is yet another instance of how cultures preserve their deep structure values—be they formal or informal.

The Spanish language, for instance, expresses formality through separate verb conjugations for formal and informal speech. In Spanish, there are formal and informal pronouns for the English word *you*. In formal speech, the pronoun *usted* is used, whereas in familiar speech, the pronoun *tu* is appropriate.

The use of language to reflect social status is one of the most significant differences between Japanese and Western communication styles. In Japan, the very structure of the language emphasizes a focus on human relationships, whereas Western languages tend to focus on objects or referents and their logical relationships. For the Japanese there are rigid rules that govern both social relationships and social status in all aspects of life. According to Matsumoto and Assar, separate vocabularies are used for addressing superiors, peers, and inferiors. When a Japanese person is speaking to someone who occupies a lower social position, he or she must speak in a particular fashion. When a person is speaking to someone of higher status, he or she must use other appropriate language even though the message content is identical.[73]

In the Japanese language, a number of words take different forms for different situations, sometimes depending on relationships between the speaker and the listener or the person being discussed. For example, there are many words for "you": *omae*, *kimi*, *kisama*, and *anata-sama*. Also, some words in Japanese are used only by men while others are used only by women. As an illustration, a Japanese man will use the word *oame* (you) when speaking with close, personal acquaintances or if he wishes to address another person in a rude or angry manner. Thus, the same word, *omae*, can have opposite meanings depending on the context. In addition, some words are used only between a husband and wife to express their delicate conjugal relationship. *Anata*, for example, is generally translated into English as "you," but when used by a wife to call her husband, it has the meaning of "dear" or "darling."

In the Thai culture, a great deal of importance is placed on an individual's place in the social order. This concern is reflected in the Thai language, which contains many forms of address appropriate to the various levels of social hierarchy. Different classes use different pronouns, nouns, and verbs to represent rank and intimacy. There are at least forty-seven pronouns, including seventeen forms for *I* and nineteen for *you*. Because the language contains different forms for different social classes, it is possible to distinguish four distinct Thai languages: the royal, the ecclesiastic, the common or familiar, and slang.

Language is also used to define gender roles and relationships within a culture. There are many instances where males and females learn different styles of speech. Pronunciation, grammar, vocabulary, and context of use can all be affected by the gender of the speaker. This is especially evident in the Japanese language. Females use a style known as *joseino* or *onnakotoba* that evolved among upper-class women as a sign of their position in society. Japanese women have conscious control over their speech styles. Female speech forms are used when women wish to emphasize their femininity; on other occasions, they adopt a sexually neutral style. Crystal elaborates this point when he indicates that a Japanese woman may, therefore, use the feminine style when talking to other women about children and adopt the neutral style when talking to business colleagues.[74]

Male authority is a characteristic of Mexican culture, and is reflected in the Spanish language through the use of gendered nouns and pronouns. A group of men, for instance, would be referred to as *ellos*, and a group of women as *ellas*, the *o* ending being masculine and the *a* ending being feminine. But if a group contains several men and one woman, it is called *ellos*, using the masculine gender; if a group contains several women and one man, the group is still called *ellos*. A group of girls is called *niñas*, but a group of girls that includes a single boy is called *niños*.

## EXPRESSIONS OF AFFECT

The manner in which emotional affect is expressed is yet another example of diversity in language behavior. Koreans, for instance, are far more reserved than Americans; verbally, their feelings are neither freely nor openly expressed. Love is not expressed as openly, as warmly, or as sweetly as in the United States. As Park and Moon-soo point out, a Korean wife will maintain her reserve and not rush to embrace her husband at the airport even though he may have been absent for years.[75]

In British English, speech is interspersed with euphemisms that enable the speaker to avoid expressing strong feelings. For instance, when English speakers wish to disagree with someone, they are liable to preface their comments with such phrases as "I may be wrong, but . . ." or "There is just one thing in all that you have been saying that worries me a little." Another example of this subtleness is the frequent use of an expression of gratitude to preface a remark, as in "I'd be awfully grateful if . . ." or "Thank you very much indeed, but . . . ." This restraint is also evident in the differences between American and British word choice. Compare the following signs seen in the United States and England:

- United States: "No dogs allowed."
- England: "We regret that in the interest of hygiene, dogs are not allowed on the premises."
- United States: "Please keep hands off door."
- England: "Obstructing the door causes delay and can be dangerous."

The expression of anger also differs from culture to culture. Among American-English speakers, a conventional expression of anger is to raise the volume of the voice. In other cultures, however, anger may be expressed differently. As Saville-Troike notes, "A Navajo expressing anger uses enclitics [a special way of accenting a verb] not recognized as emotion markers by speakers of other languages, and a friendly greeting on the street between Chinese speakers may have surface manifestations corresponding to anger for speakers of English."[76]

## VALUE OF CONVERSATION

People in many cultures derive a great deal of pleasure from the art of conversation and public speaking. Knowing which cultures delight in verbal play and debate can give you an important insight into how oral interaction may differ from culture to culture.

Throughout Africa, the spoken word rather than the written word is generally the foremost means of communication. Richmond and Gerstin state: "As Tanzania's founding father, Julius Nyerere, has written, 'The very origins of African democracy lay in ordinary oral discussion—the elders sat under a tree and talked until they agreed.'"[77] Whatever language they speak, Africans seem to be natural orators. While visiting with Africans, you might well be called upon to give an extemporaneous speech, and it will pay for you to be prepared with a few appropriate points illustrated with amusing stories.[78]

Drawing from their oral tradition, Africans enjoy debate and exchanges of views. Miller points out that among the Kenyans, speaking in public is an unavoidable individual responsibility.[79] Life events are marked by ceremonies involving multiple public speeches. At a wedding, for example, speeches are expected from the best man, the

*People in many cultures derive a great deal of pleasure from the art of conversation.*

© A. Ramey/PhotoEdit

parents of both bride and groom, as well as from grandparents, aunts and uncles, and a host of others.[80]

As storytellers, African speakers seek to hold their audiences' attention through the prolific use of proverbs, which enrich their speech and provide insights on how they feel about particular issues.[81] Africans make extensive use of the proverb as a means of teaching and perpetuating culture as well as a powerful rhetorical device. Knappert illustrates this point in the following paragraph:

> In conversation, as in storytelling, proverbs and parables, which transmit the wisdom of past generations, play an important role. Nothing is closer to the heart of African society and thought than the proverb. More than any other African tradition, it expresses the essence of African wisdom.[82]

The force of the proverb among the Akan people of West Africa is illustrated by Yankah: "Part of the rhetorical power of the proverb derives from its authoritativeness, or rather its ascription to authoritative sources."[83] To the outsider, this can present a problem because knowledge of a tribe's cultural history and traditions is required to make sense of the proverbs.

Proverbs reveal the power and credibility of words when they are ascribed to elderhood and ancestry. They express universal truths that also have parallels in Western wisdom and experience. To facilitate intercultural communication, Westerners should embellish their speech with their own proverbs that the Africans will surely understand, appreciate, and in many cases, find similar to their own.[84]

Arabs share a deep love of language. They believe that Arabic is "God's language" and as such treat language with great respect and admiration. Both the Arabic word for eloquence and the word for male maturity come from the same root. In the words of Ahmad Hasan al-Zayyat, therefore, "strong manhood is co-extensive with strong rhetoric." An ancient Arab proverb notes, "A man's tongue is his sword." The Arab language contains a rich vocabulary and well-rounded, complex phrases that permit educated and illiterate alike to have a strong mastery of their language. Words are often used for their own sake rather than for what they are understood to mean. Whereas an American can adequately express an idea in ten words, the Arabic speaker may use one hundred. Arabs ordinarily do not publicly admit to personal deficiencies. They will, however, spend hours elaborating on the faults and failures of those who are not members of their clique.

Virtually every Saudi speaks Arabic, and those who engage in international activities are usually fluent in English as well. In social discourse, Arabs value what, by American standards, might appear to be an exaggerated speaking style. Because most intercultural communication between Saudis and Westerners is likely to be in English, it is necessary to know about the transference of Arabic communication patterns into English. The most frequently transferred are intonation patterns, a tendency toward over-assertion, repetition, exaggeration, and organizational logic. Certain intonation and stress patterns may make it difficult for the English-speaking listener to comprehend what is being said. If the patterns have unwanted affective meanings for the listener, speech can sound aggressive and threatening, or if the flat Arabic intonation pattern has been transferred, this monotonous tone can be interpreted as a lack of interest. Arabs expect over-assertion and repetition in almost all types of communication. For example, as Alaney and Alwan assert, a simple "no" by a guest to the host's request to eat more or drink more will not suffice. To convey the meaning that he (or she) is actually full, the guest must keep repeating "no" several times, coupling it with an oath such as "By God" or "I swear to God."[85]

Greek culture has a long and rich historical tradition that glorifies rhetorical techniques. The Greeks use a variety of key sayings to express much of their culture. In a sense, these sayings are proverbs because they reflect Greek morality and serve as generic forms of expression that convey much meaning in short phrases. For example, Greeks look harshly on lack of gratitude, and a Greek who feels thus slighted might respond, "I taught him how to swim and he tried to drown me." When a Greek is at fault and has no excuse, he or she is liable to say, "I want to become a saint, but the demons won't let me." If one succeeds in putting a halt to the bragging of another, he will say, "I cut out his cough."

Insights into the way that the Spanish language is used in Mexico can help you understand Mexican culture. First, Mexicans take great delight in verbal play. For example, as Condon illustrates, at a party in which Mexican and North American men are introduced to the wives of the guests, the North American man may say, "I am *pleased* to meet you." In contrast, the Mexican man may say, "I am *enchanted* to meet you." Mexicans make broad use of double entendres, come up with clever turns of phrases, and insert old quotations at the right moments in an otherwise ordinary conversation.[86] If there are opportunities to engage in talk, the Mexican is ready, even among casual acquaintances. And, as Riding reports, once an emotional bond is established, he or she is open and generous, willing to confide, and very hospitable.[87]

In the United States, the co-culture of African Americans also highly values talk and conversation. From engaging in verbal games such as playing the dozen, rappin', to runnin' it down, African Americans enjoy verbal interplay. As Weber points out, "Black language and the numerous styles that have been developed are indications of the African-American's respect for the spoken word."[88] It should be pointed out that the respect Weber is referring to should not be defined by the dominant culture, but rather by the definitions of language usage that apply in the African-American community.

Our goal in this section has been to convey the fact that language is inseparable from culture. Culture influences language symbols and rules for using those symbols. As you have also seen, meaning is culturally determined.

## Language Diversity in the United States

Language diversity presents a problem in the United States. Forty-seven million people residing in the United States speak a language other than English at home, and there are almost twelve million people who live in homes where no English is spoken. Areas of California, New Mexico, and Texas have the highest percentage of Spanish-speaking residents who do not speak English at home. But the spread of the Spanish-speaking population is not limited to those areas. Wallraff reports that "even Sioux City, Iowa, now publishes a Spanish-language newspaper."[89] In addition, there are 2.4 million Chinese speakers who live in the United States. Of these, 80 percent prefer to speak Chinese at home.[90] Speakers of Korean and Vietnamese permeate many areas of the United States as well. Wallraff suggests the severity of this problem when she states:

> Small American towns from Huntsville, Alabama, to Meriden, Connecticut, to Wausau, Wisconsin, to El Cenizo, Texas . . . have been alarmed to find that many new arrivals do not speak English well and some may not even see the point of going to the trouble of learning it.[91]

Because there are so many non-English or limited-English speakers, language diversity has become a subject of political concern in the United States. Politicians at all levels of government frequently make legislative proposals to make English the official language of the United States. While we do not endorse such proposals, we

*Language diversity is an important matter of concern in the United States.*

do believe, as Brown points out, that knowledge of English and the ability to communicate in English are essential in American society. Brown adds that the "inability to speak the language of the community in which one lives is the first step towards misunderstanding, for prejudice thrives on lack of communication."[92] The obvious solution to this issue is to ensure that all people have access to suitable English-language learning and yet be free to preserve their native cultures and languages, as they desire.

Not everyone agrees with making English an official language. Taking an opposite position, Elgin points out some inconsistencies in these proposals:

> . . . the U.S. government and some state governments are now working seriously to establish "English Only" laws that would drastically restrict the use of foreign languages in the United States. Isn't it a bit strange to spend tax money for classes to teach Spanish to English-speaking students in our schools while at the same time making it difficult (or illegal) for Spanish-speaking individuals to use Spanish there? This is just one of many curiosities resulting from the current confusion about language and languages.[93]

In the next section, we examine the notion that people living within the same geographic boundaries often use language in ways that differ from those of the dominant culture. Specifically, we will explore language usage of selected co-cultures in the United States.

# Languages of Co-cultures

During our earlier discussion of the Sapir-Whorf hypothesis, we indicated that language is a guide to dealing with and understanding social reality. From this belief comes the corollary thought that cultures evolve different languages to satisfy their own unique needs. As Nanda and Warms note:

> All human groups have language and all languages are equally sophisticated and serve the needs of their speakers equally well. A language cannot make its speakers more or less intelligent, sexist, sophisticated, or anything else. Individual knowledge of vocabulary may vary, as may the artfulness with which an individual communicates, but every human speaks with equal grammatical sophistication.[94]

What Nanda and Warms are implying is that although every human language community may have a variety of different linguistic symbols, the grammars that accompany those symbols are equally sophisticated. This is not meant to imply that everyone within a language community speaks equally well. As you must be well aware, some people speak with terrible grammar.

Co-cultures exist within nearly every society, but, as we indicated earlier, they function both within and outside the dominant culture. Members of most co-cultures live in two or more very distinct groups. Hence, their enculturation and cultural identity can be noticeably different from that of the dominant culture. A co-culture's language evolution tends to be influenced by the dominant culture's attitudes toward them. In many co-cultures, the name given to an experience clearly demonstrates how they perceive and interact with the dominant culture. Through the examination of a co-culture's language, you can learn a great deal about that group's experiences, values, and behaviors. To facilitate your understanding, we will examine some of the unique language behaviors found among the Spanish-speaking, African-American, and women's co-cultures in the United States.

## SPANISH-SPEAKING AMERICANS

The United States now has the third-largest Spanish-speaking population of any country in the world, exceeded only by Mexico and Colombia, and 70 percent of Latinos in the United States mainly speak Spanish at home.[95] Of these, many have limited or no fluency in English. Yet, as Arpan and Arpan relate, "While not all Hispanics have the same needs, the majority of them need transportation, driver's licenses, and language training."[96] Latinos have reported communication problems in dealing with such public institutions as hospitals and K–12 schools.[97] Students, as well, have reported language barriers and a shortage of suitable programs and materials.[98]

To facilitate integration of the Latino community and the dominant culture, there must be reciprocal acts on the part of both Latinos and the public institutions that serve them. Schools, hospitals, law enforcement agencies, and banks are some of the public institutions that must learn to accommodate the Latino community. Not only will this accommodation help Latino immigrants become productive members of society, it also benefits the dominant culture because this large segment of the population contributes large sums to the economic well-being of the country.

It is easy to stand back from the Spanish-speaking population and suggest that all they need to do is learn English. While this may be a laudable goal, it is not always a practical goal. Parents who are busy earning a living or caring for a household and children do not necessarily have the time or the energy to attend English classes. And some children attending public schools may not have English language training available to them. Yet the need for English-language education is clearly stated by Bron:

> Language, certainly, is a natural social prerequisite to communicating and functioning in social and personal life in the community and in society at large. This fact—often neglected or forgotten by those whose mother tongue is the only language sufficient to communicate in their own county, or in countries where the same language is spoken every day—becomes very clear and important to immigrants whose native languages are different from the language of the country they have chosen to live in.[99]

## AFRICAN-AMERICAN ENGLISH

It should be quite obvious that many African Americans speak different varieties of English than whites, thus creating different speech communities. Shade provides a cultural explanation for these differences:

> These communities employ different varieties of speech, follow different rules for interaction, possess different core cultural elements that influence white and black communication behaviors, and possess different worldviews, which account for the differences in communication and the way blacks and whites process and interpret messages.[100]

Over centuries, many African Americans have evolved a unique language style now recognized as African-American vernacular English (AAVE).[101] This linguistic style permits African Americans to create, maintain, and express their culture as well as deal with European American prejudices toward their culture.[102] Some African Americans use this form of speech for all of their communication. Others use it only in certain contexts, such as among friends and family, while speaking standard English at school or at work. African Americans may code switch from one form to the other during any speech event depending on circumstances such as topic, attitude, or co-participants.[103]

**Characteristics of AAVE.** African-American vernacular English is a vivid and imaginative language that involves much more than a vocabulary shift or the rhymed and accented lyrics of a rap artist. It is a distinctive language form with a unique syntax, semantic system, grammar, and rhythm. The grammar rules differ in many ways and form a logical system that is independent of mainstream English. African-American English contains a variety of terms denoting different ways of talking that depend on the social context. Its own style and function characterize each manner of speaking. But you must remember, as Nanda and Warms suggest, that African-American English "is in no way linguistically inferior. Like every other language, it is fully systematic, grammatical, symbolic, and certainly no barrier to abstract thought."[104]

Smitherman as well as Hecht, Collier, and Ribeau, point out that sentence structure and semantics in African-American vernacular English have been particularly influenced by early African tribal languages.[105, 106] This has led to the development of a language style with a number of readily identifiable characteristics. We will draw on the work of Rickford, Crystal, Bonvillain, and Smitherman to list some representative examples of African American linguistic expression.

- Shortening of the third-person present tense by dropping the s: *He walk, She go, He talk.*[107, 108]
- Use of the verb *to be* to indicate continuous action: *He be gone* for "He is gone frequently/all the time."[109]
- Deletion of the verb *to be* in the present indicative: *He tired* for "He is tired."[110] *She the first one started us off* for "She was the first one who started us off."[111]
- Use of *done* for completed (sometimes used with *been*): *They done been sitting there for a whole hour.*[112]
- Use of a stressed *been* to emphasize the duration of something: *He been married* for "He has been married for a long time (and still is)."[113]
- Use of *Uhm* and *Ima* for *am* and *am going to. Uhm really tired* for "I am really tired." *Ima show everybody up* for "I am going to outdo everyone else."[114]
- Use of double and triple negatives: *Won't nobody do nothing about that. He ain't got no money.*[115, 116]
- Reduction of word-final consonants: *door* becomes *do;*[117] *Last* becomes *las'.*[118]
- The final *ng* sound drops the *g: talking* becomes *talkin.*[119]
- The initial voiced *th* realized as *d: dem* for "them."[120]
- The final *th* is sometimes replaced with *f: with* becomes *wif.*[121]
- Substitution of the *x* sound for the *s* sound: *ask* becomes *axe.*
- Variation of /r/: *Carol* becomes *Ca'ol.* [122]

These are but a short sample of the linguistic characteristics of African-American language. You may consult the works we have cited above to learn more about this vivid and imaginative language, including street language that generates movement and power within its listeners.

## WOMEN AND LANGUAGE

Do men and women systematically use language in different ways? Bonvillain believes the following sentences contain clues that can tell you whether the speakers are men or women:

- "You're driving rather fast, aren't you?"
- "Well, I guess it's approximately four feet high."

Both sentences, says Bonvillain, "are more typical of the speech of women than of men."[123] In a general sense, women and men constitute two diverse linguistic groups "because women and men are socialized to express themselves in different ways in accordance with cultural norms that teach and reinforce differentiated gender roles."[124] Communication for women has different purposes and rules than communication for men.[125] Tannen eloquently expresses this point: "Different words, different worlds." Elium and Elium add, "Females put a greater and different emphasis on conversation."[126]

**Why Do Women Communicate?** Noting that women and men have different communication styles, we begin our exploration of female communication by identifying the purposes of communication for women. For most women, says Wood, communication is used as a primary means of establishing and maintaining relationships with others.[127] Wood, after intensive research into gender issues, has identified six features of women's communication that foster *connections, support, closeness,* and *understanding.*[128] These six features will be discussed below.

*Equality.* Equality is an important feature of communication for women. It helps them achieve symmetry and equality by matching experiences. For instance, in response to someone spilling their drink, a woman may say, "I've done the same thing so many times." This establishes equality in the sense that the individual who spilled the drink is not alone in how he or she feels. This creates an interactive pattern in conversations rather than rigid turn taking.

*Showing Support.* Showing support for other women is an essential interaction characteristic instilled by culture. Women tend to display support for others by the use of phrases characteristic of women's speech. Sentences like "Oh, you must feel terrible" and "I think you did the right thing" illustrate the propensity of women to display support, understanding, and sympathy.[129]

*Understanding Feelings.* A third cultural characteristic is the desire to express understanding and sympathy. In many instances this is accomplished through the asking of questions that probe for an understanding of feelings. Questions such as "How did you feel when it occurred?" and "Do you think it was deliberate?" address the content of the conversation while paying serious attention to the feelings involved.[130]

*Conversation Maintenance.* Women's speech is characterized by efforts to sustain a conversation by prompting others to speak or elaborate. Conversational maintenance involves women using phrases like "Tell me about your day" to prompt others to speak or elaborate. In addition, women tend to initiate topics for others using such phrases as "Was your faculty meeting interesting?" which serves to initiate and maintain interaction.[131]

**Responsiveness.** Another cultural characteristic of women is responsiveness to others. Women are usually socialized to care about others and to make them feel valued. This characteristic is frequently displayed in women's conversation through responding to what others have said. For example, during a conversation a woman might interject, "That's interesting," or she might nod to show she is actively engaged in the conversation.[132]

**Interpersonal Closeness.** Wood's last characteristic of women's communication behavior is a personal and concrete style that seeks to develop and maintain interpersonal closeness. Closeness is created by the use of "details, personal disclosures, anecdotes, and concrete reasoning."[133] This personal tone in women's conversation cultivates connection and identification so that communicators' feelings are emphasized and clarified.

**Tentativeness.** Tentativeness is an additional characteristic of women's communication style that has been identified by Holmes. Tentativeness can take the form of verbal hedges, qualifying terms, and tag questions. Verbal hedges are phrases like *I think, I believe, I feel, I guess, I mean,* and *I wonder.*[134] Qualifying terms include words like *well, you know, kind of, perhaps,* and *possibly.* An example of a qualifying statement is "I am probably not the best judge of this, but . . . ." Intonation also indicates tentativeness by turning the answer into what Bonvillain calls a tag question in which a speaker makes a declarative statement and then adds a question or "tag" about the assertion. Typical tag sentences could be "Jane looked nice today, didn't she?" or "It's cold in here, isn't it?"[135] Tag questions also serve to keep the conversation provisional. "That was a pretty great concert, don't you think?" leaves the door open for further conversation.

Much controversy exists about the purpose of tentativeness in women's speech. Prior research claimed that these tentative communication devices were evidence of inferiority and represented a lack of confidence, uncertainty, and low self-esteem. Lakoff calls this speech powerless, a reflection of women's socialization into subordinate roles.[136] Although there may be some validity to these assertions, more recent research indicates that there may be several different explanations for women's tentative speech.[137]

As evidenced by the seven features identified by Wood and Holmes, tentative communication, rather than reflecting powerlessness and inferiority, may instead "express women's desires to keep conversation open and include others."[138] Other researchers have found women's use of tentative communication to be context based. Although some women may use servile, submissive, or polite tentative communication, these traits are often a stereotype of how women are thought to talk and not the way they actually do talk. Instead, the way they communicate is heavily influenced by the context. For example, women may use more tentative communication when in the presence of men but less in the presence of women. A board meeting may be conducive to tentative communication in order to establish camaraderie, but the courtroom may not. Holmes reports that one study even found that men were just as likely to use tentative communication as women depending on the context.[139] As a result, it is a good idea to consider the context before affixing a stereotypic, negative label on women's tentative communication.

## FEMALE VS. MALE COMMUNICATION PATTERNS

The characteristics of female communication we have discussed stand in sharp contrast to those of male communication. Tannen helps explain these differences when she suggests the primary purpose of communication for men is to *exert control, preserve independence*, and *enhance status*.[140] Amid her gender research, Wood has identified five tenets of masculine speech. First, it focuses on instrumental activity and minimizes feelings. This communication style usually involves problem-solving efforts, data collection, and solution suggestions. Content, rather than feelings, is emphasized. Second, adds Wood, it "expresses superiority and maintains control."[141] Despite jokes about women's talkativeness, Aries believes that men usually maintain conversational dominance. They talk more and for longer periods,[142] and they redirect conversations for their own benefit and interrupt as a controlling or challenging device.[143] Third, Wood says men assert themselves in absolute ways. Their language is usually forceful and direct with infrequent use of tentative communication. Fourth, men tend to speak in abstract terms that are general and removed from personal experiences.[144] Finally, as Wood reveals, men's conversation tends not to be very responsive. Sympathy, understanding, and self-disclosure are rarely expressed because the rules of men's speech dictate that these responses are condescending and make one vulnerable.[145]

In summary, we must conclude that women are primarily concerned with personal relationships when they communicate, whereas men are concerned mainly with "getting the job done." Women seem to talk more about relationships and feelings than men. But, as Romaine indicates, whether this is a sign of actual gender differences or reflects the social context of the communication is open to question because "the most frequent venue for all female talk is domestic rather than public."[146]

Women tend to include everyone present in conversation; men, however, seek to establish dominance. Although women may engage in tentative speech, men's speech is characteristically assertive. Women's communication is decidedly responsive, while men's communication is distinctly unresponsive. From this perspective, you should easily see how the different rules and features of women's and men's speech create the potential for misunderstanding and conflict between women and men.

## Understanding Diverse Message Systems

Having learned about the nature of language and its relationship to culture, you should now have an impression of the important role language plays in intercultural communication. But simply having this knowledge is not enough for you to be an effective intercultural communicator. Your newfound knowledge must be applied in diverse cultural settings before you can develop effective language facility in intercultural communication situations.

The American poet Ezra Pound offers an excellent introduction to gaining intercultural competency when he reminds you, "The sum of human knowledge is not contained in any one language." While all cultures have both verbal and nonverbal codes, these codes bring to individual minds meanings that reflect the experiences and ideas of each person's particular culture. Thus, it is difficult to arrive at a common code if you and your communication partner speak different languages. To overcome this problem, we now offer some helpful advice regarding the use of both verbal and nonverbal codes.

### TRY TO LEARN THE LANGUAGES OF OTHER CULTURES

Our first piece of advice is rather obvious. With over six thousand different languages in the world, it would be ridiculous for us to suggest you learn all of them. What we are recommending is that if you plan to spend time interacting with people from a particular culture, learn what you can of their specific language. You would be far more effective, for example, if you could speak Spanish when doing business in Mexico. Because much of the world speaks English, many Americans have a tendency to assume they need not learn a foreign language. The fact that so many others have made an attempt to learn your language should motivate you to reciprocate. When visiting another country, knowing a few simple phrases such as "hello," "thank you," and "good-bye" can open many doors, because it signals your interest in the host culture.

Even within the United States there is a need to develop second-language skills. As Luckmann has pointed out, "Large communities of people who speak languages other than English are flourishing in Southern California, Texas, New Mexico, and Arizona. In Los Angeles alone, over 100 languages other than English are spoken."[147]

## UNDERSTAND CULTURAL VARIATIONS IN THE USE OF LANGUAGE

If you do not speak the language of your communication partner, there still are things you can do to facilitate understanding. Try to keep in mind that language is more than a vehicle of communication; it teaches cultural lifestyles, ways of thinking and perceiving the world, and different patterns of interacting. A few examples demonstrating some variations in how cultures use language might help you appreciate the variety of language patterns you might encounter as you seek to become a more competent communicator.

Much of Jewish culture is reflected in the wide use of stories, parables, and allegories. People, events, and circumstances are talked about in vivid narratives. For many Jews, the story is as important as the point being made by the story. If you are interacting with Arabs, it would be useful to understand some unique characteristics of their language code. As Nydell points out:

> There are many situations in which verbal statements are required by etiquette. Meeting someone's small child calls for praise, carefully mixed with blessings. The most common blessings are "May God keep him" or "This is what God wills." Such statements reassure the parents that there is no envy (you certainly would not add, "I wish I had a child like this!").[148]

The Chinese perceive and use language in a manner different from most Americans. As Geo and Ting-Toomey note, "Speech in Chinese culture is constantly exercised with caution and, consequently, perceived as less important."[149] This lack of emphasis on the spoken word means that the Chinese "believe that talk has limitations and that meanings reside beyond mere words."[150] Knowing this simple fact about Chinese language usage could help you in two ways. First, you could understand why "the ability to surmise and decipher hidden meanings is highly desirable in the Chinese culture."[151] Second, knowing the Chinese view of language could influence the manner in which you send and receive messages from members of the Chinese culture and also how you deal with silence. We will address the issue of silence as an aspect of nonverbal communication in Chapter 7.

Our final example of how cultures use language in ways that are distinctive to their culture comes from France. Asselin and Mastron reveal one of these distinctions when they write, "In conversation, French people prefer to make their points quite directly but in well-phrased, articulate arguments. The linguistic subtleties may be lost on Americans, who hear only the brutally frank (for them) opinions."[152]

# REMEMBER THAT WORDS ARE "CULTURE BOUND"

In much of the world, English is taught as a second language, and therefore you can face countless situations where you are speaking English with someone who does not share your fluency in the language. And remember, in the United States English is the second or third language for more than 31 million immigrants who now live in this country. We therefore will consider some ways to help you improve the manner in which you speak to people who are not native speakers. To this end, we will look at *idioms, ambiguity*, and *culturally based expressions*.

**Idioms.** An idiom is a group of words which, when used together, has a meaning different from the one which the individual words would have. For instance, *it is raining cats and dogs, give me a ring*, or *biting off more than you can chew* are all idiomatic phrases that have cultural meanings different from the literal meaning of the words. Hence, idioms are not capable of literal translations. Remembering that most words are culture-bound, you must be extremely careful when using idioms.

Now, using your imagination, try to create an image of someone who speaks English as a second language and is trying to discover literal meanings in the following examples of common American-English idioms:

- "Now just hold your horses, you are acting like a bull in a china shop."
- "Of course it is true, I had my eyes and ears peeled and got it from the grapevine."
- "Let's put this plan to the acid test by looking at the nuts and bolts of the deal."
- "If we stop beating our heads against a brick wall, we would not appear to be such wimps."
- "We need to be careful that the tail doesn't wag the dog."
- "Don't listen to John—he's got an ax to grind and often makes waves."
- "She's not the least bit funny—in fact, she's just laid an egg."
- "John dropped the ball on this one, and he's sure ticked off."
- "If you think we're on the same wavelength, just give me a buzz, or we can play it by ear."
- "We need to stop dilly-dallying and get off the dime."

**Ambiguity.** Ambiguity is another problem you face when interacting with someone for whom English is not their native language. Ambiguous terms are words, phrases, or sentences that have multiple meanings and can be interpreted in more than one way. Since the use of ambiguity tends to be culture-bound, multiple-meaning discourse can cause a great deal of confusion in the mind of the culturally inexperienced. Try to imagine the confusion in the mind of someone who is not a native speaker when he or she encounters some of the following sentences:

- "At our school we have cut dropouts in half."
- "It appears that red tape is holding up the new bridge."
- "The new vaccine may contain rabies."
- "At our school, kids make nutritious snacks."
- "The new study of obesity is looking for larger test groups."

**Culturally Based Expressions.** We remind you once again to keep in mind that the words you use and the meanings you give them are part of your cultural experiences. People with different experiences will use different words with different meanings.

Again, confusion can reign if you employ common American expressions that are not part of another culture's frame of reference. Numerous international students have told us they did not fully understand the meaning of such words or phrases as "dialoguing," "being stressed out," "affirmative action," "interfacing," "pro-life," "networking," "uptight," or "sexual harassment." To be a competent communicator and avoid confusion, you must be careful in selecting the words and phrases you use in intercultural communication.

## BE SENSITIVE TO DIVERSE CODING SYSTEMS

Being sensitive to your surroundings and to other people is one of the hallmarks of a competent intercultural communicator. According to Chen and Starosta, intercultural sensitivity is "an individual's ability to develop a positive emotion towards understanding and appreciating cultural differences in order to promote appropriate and effective behavior in intercultural communication."[153] We suggest that part of being sensitive means you must learn about diverse coding systems and develop code sensitivity toward the message systems used by other cultures. It would generally be inappropriate to use African-American vernacular English if you are white. If you interact with disabled people, you need to learn a list of what are called the "no-no words." *Crippled, gimp, deaf and dumb, deaf mute, abnormal, unfortunate,* or *victim* are examples of words that exhibit a lack of cultural awareness.[154]

Insensitivity also results when you refer to a co-culture using a term different from what members of that co-culture would use to refer to themselves. It reflects your respect of co-cultures if you use such words as *Asian* rather than *Oriental*, *gays* rather than *homosexuals*, *Latino* rather than *Mexican*, and *African Americans* rather than *Negroes*. We must remind you, however, that the names we have suggested above are not subscribed to by all members of co-cultures. Some homosexuals, for instance, do not like the term gay, and some Mexicans do not wish to be called Latino. What is important here is acknowledging what Lynch and Hanson tell you: "Defining and describing individuals from any culture, ethnic, linguistic, or racial group is similar to defining and describing families, that is, the words that are used should be those that the members prefer."[155]

## ACHIEVING CLARITY

As we have stressed throughout this section, the achievement of clarity in intercultural interaction is dependent upon your ability to understand diverse message systems. Guirgham offers a useful checklist to use as a guide when your message system is different from that of the people with whom you are communicating.[156]

- State your points clearly and precisely.
- Adjust to the other person's level of understanding without being demeaning.
- Explain jargon.
- Be careful in your use of idioms.
- Slow your speaking down without being insulting.
- Speak in smaller verbal units.
- Repeat key points.
- Encourage others to ask questions.
- Check for understanding.

# Summary

- Language is distinctly human; it is a faculty that separates us from other species of animals.
- Language is important to human activity because it is the means by which we reach out to make contact with others.
- Language functions to facilitate affective expression, thought, social interaction, the control of reality, the maintenance of history, and the expression of identity.
- Language is the primary means of preserving and transmitting culture.
- Symbols (words) and sounds for those symbols vary from culture to culture. The rules (phonology, grammar, syntax, and intonation) for using those symbols and sounds also vary.
- Language serves as a guide to how a culture perceives reality.
- The meanings we have for words are internal and are largely determined by the culture in which we have been raised.
- Cultures use language differently when applied to issues of directness, maintaining social relationships, affective expression, social customs and conversation.
- All cultures and co-cultures have special experiences that frame usage and meaning.
- Many African Americans speak a particular language style called African-American vernacular English.
- Women's communication patterns and practices differ in form and substance from those of men.
- Women communicate in order to foster connections, support, closeness, and understanding.
- When interacting with people from other cultures, you should attempt to learn some phrases of their language.
- It is important to understand cultural variations in the use of language.
- Idioms are groups of words which, when used together, have a different meaning from the meaning the words have individually.
- When speaking with someone for whom English is a second language, try to seek clarity and avoid the use of idioms, ambiguous words, culturally based expressions, or cultural insensitivity.

## Activities

1. Enroll in a foreign language class or check out foreign language instruction CDs from the library and begin to learn another language. Determine how the grammar and syntax of the new language differ from your native language.

2. Seek out someone whose native language is not English. Discuss with them the use of sayings, proverbs, and idiomatic expressions in their language. Compare sayings, proverbs, and idioms from that person's language that are difficult to translate into English. Also, try to discover whether both languages share similar expressions.

3. Talk with people whose language style reflects the indirect use of language. Attempt to discover how they perceive Americans' use of a direct communication style.

4. In conversations with women or men, try to use forms of speaking that align with those common to the gender of the person with whom you are speaking. Is using this communication style an easy task? Do you feel comfortable trying to use this style?

# Discussion Ideas

1. How does language diversity cause problems in the United States? What solutions can you propose to deal with these problems?
2. How does language influence our perceptions and our view of the universe?
3. How do cultural factors help determine the meanings for words? What cultural factors have the most impact on word meanings?
4. What can men and women in the United States do in order to communicate better with one another?
5. What cultural factors determine the manner in which affect is displayed orally?

## CHAPTER 7

# Nonverbal Communication: The Messages of Action, Space, Time, and Silence

*Silence is one of the great arts of conversation.*

**CICERO**

*Do not the most moving moments of our lives find us all without words?*

**MARCEL MARCEAU**

To move one's head from side to side in the United States is usually a sign of "no" and means disagreement, yet in India the same sign often represents agreement. In Western cultures, people normally greet by shaking hands. Arab men often greet by kissing on both cheeks. In Japan, men greet by bowing, and in Mexico they often embrace. In most Middle Eastern and Asian countries, pointing with the index finger is considered impolite. In Thailand, to signal another person to come near, one moves the fingers back and forth with the palm down. In the United States, you beckon someone to come by holding the palm up and moving the fingers toward your body. In Vietnam, that same motion is reserved for someone attempting to summon his or her dog. The Tongans sit down in the presence of superiors; in the West, you stand up. Crossing one's legs in the United States is often a sign of being relaxed; in Korea, it is a social taboo. In Japan, gifts are usually exchanged with both hands. Muslims consider the left hand unclean and do not eat or pass objects with it. Buddha maintained that great insights arrived during moments of silence. In the United States, people employ talk to arrive at the truth.

The above examples were offered for two reasons. First, we hoped to arouse your interest in the subject of nonverbal communication. Second, we wanted to demonstrate that although much of nonverbal communication is universal, many of your nonverbal actions are altered by culture. Hence, this chapter looks at the various ways culture and nonverbal communication work in tandem.

*Nonverbal messages can be used to express attitudes, feelings, and emotions.*

# Nonverbal Communication in Everyday Life

To appreciate the importance of nonverbal communication to human interaction, you should reflect for a moment on the countless times in a day that you send and receive nonverbal messages. Barnlund highlights some of the reasons why this form of communication is important to the study of intercultural communication:

> Many, and sometimes most, of the critical meanings generated in human encounters are elicited by touch, glance, vocal nuance, gestures, or facial expression with or without the aid of words. From the moment of recognition until the moment of separation, people observe each other with all their senses, hearing pause and intonation, attending to dress and carriage, observing glance and facial tension, as well as noting word choice and syntax. Every harmony or disharmony of signals guides the interpretation of passing mood or enduring attribute. Out of the evaluation of kinetic, vocal and verbal cues, decisions are made to argue or agree, to laugh or blush, to relax or resist, or to continue or cut off conversation.[1]

With just a handful of examples Barnlund makes it extremely clear why nonverbal communication is an indispensable and all pervasive element in human behavior. Perhaps its most obvious application is found in the fact that young children start comprehending words at around six months of age yet understand nonverbal communication well before that time. Hence, from the moment of birth to the end of life, nonverbal behavior is an important symbol system. This importance is made clear by Knapp and Hall, who conclude that any "list of all the situations where nonverbal communication plays an important role would be interminable."[2] While we agree with the position that nonverbal communication is omnipresent, we also maintain that there are some principal uses of nonverbal behaviors that are worth mentioning. Let us look at a few of these so that you will see why any study of intercultural interaction must include information about nonverbal communication.

## NONVERBAL COMMUNICATION IS UNIVERSAL

Although later in the chapter we will deal with specific nonverbal actions as they relate to particular cultures, it is essential that here at the outset of our analysis you realize that all human beings, regardless of their culture, utilize nonverbal communication. Regardless of the culture involved, nonverbal communication is the primary and most basic means of expressing affect. In spite of the culture or the person, feelings and messages related to projection, aggression, courtship and mating, emotional states, and the like are found in every culture. We might add that nonverbal communication is also universal in that many of the same actions make sense regardless of culture or country. A smile, a wave, a touch, or pointing are nonverbal expressions used in every culture to convey meaning. Even the look of confusion that might cross your face if you were lost in downtown Beijing might well bring a Chinese passerby to your aid as they assign meaning to your expression.

## JUDGING INTERNAL STATES

Heraclitus was correct when he noted more than two thousand years ago that one's "eyes are more accurate witnesses than ears." What he is telling us is that nonverbal communication is important because people use this message system to express attitudes, feelings, and emotions. Consciously and unconsciously, intentionally and unintentionally, people make important judgments and decisions concerning the internal states of others—states they often express without words. If you see someone with a clenched fist and a grim expression, you do not need words to tell you that this person is not happy. If you hear someone's voice quaver and see his or her hands tremble, you may infer that the person is fearful or anxious, despite what he or she might say. Your emotions are reflected in your posture, face, and eyes—be it fear, joy, anger, or sadness—so you can express them without ever uttering a word. For this reason, most people rely heavily on what they learn through their eyes. In fact, research indicates that you will usually believe nonverbal messages instead of verbal messages when the two contradict each other.[3]

You can even evaluate the quality of your relationships according to the interpretations assigned to nonverbal messages. From tone of voice to the distance between you and your partners, to the amount of touching in which you engage, you can gather clues to the closeness of your relationships. Nonverbal communication is so subtle that a shifting of body posture can also send a message. The first time you move from holding hands with your partner to touching his or her face, you are sending a message, and that message takes on added significance if your touch is returned.

## CREATING IMPRESSIONS

Nonverbal communication is important in human interaction because it is partially responsible for creating impressions. In most instances nonverbal messages arrive before the verbal and influence the flow of the interaction. It is suggested that in most employment interviews it is often the first ten seconds that counts the most. Pauronit conducted a study that demonstrated the effect of first impressions and race on a counseling session involving black and white subjects.[4] He found that counselors reacted differently to clients because of their color. Your personal experiences will show you how often your first judgments are based on the color of a person's skin, facial expression, manner of dress, or if he or she is in a wheelchair. Even how you select friends and sexual partners is grounded in first impressions. You often approach certain people because of how attractive you find them, and of course, avoid others because of some rapid decision you made concerning their appearance. Take a minute and recall your reactions the first time you encountered a homeless person living on the streets.

## MANAGING INTERACTION

A moment of reflection will reveal that managing interaction is another important use you make of nonverbal communication. Your nonverbal actions, whether intentional or unintentional, offer your partner clues about the conversation. Among other things, this would include "when to begin a conversation, whose turn it is to speak, how to get a chance to speak, how to signal others to talk more, and how to end a conversation."[5]

To better help you understand nonverbal communication and its role in intercultural communication, we will (1) define nonverbal communication, (2) list its functions, (3) offer some guidelines when studying nonverbal communication, (4) link nonverbal communication to culture, and (5) discuss the major classifications of nonverbal messages. It should be noted that we will begin our discussion of each category of nonverbal communication by noting some of the basic behaviors found in the dominant culture of the United States before relating the classification to other cultures. Knowing what behaviors Americans bring to a communication event can help you understand your response to the people you meet.

# Defining Nonverbal Communication

Because the central concern of this chapter is to examine how and why people communicate nonverbally, and with what consequences in the intercultural setting, we begin with a definition of nonverbal communication. As you discovered in earlier chapters, there is no shortage of definitions for *culture* and *communication*. The same proliferation is characteristic of the term *nonverbal behavior*. We shall, therefore, select a definition that is consistent with current thinking in the field and reflects the cultural orientation of this book. We propose that *nonverbal communication involves all those nonverbal stimuli in a communication setting that are generated by both the source and his or her use of the environment and that have potential message value for the source or receiver.* It is not by chance that our definition is somewhat lengthy; we wanted to offer a definition that would not only establish the boundaries of nonverbal communication but would also reflect how the process actually works. Our definition also permits us to include unintentional as well as intentional behavior in the total communication event. This approach is realistic because you send the preponderance of nonverbal messages without ever being aware that they have meaning for other people. In verbal communication, you consciously dip into your vocabulary and decide what words to use. Although you often consciously decide to smile or select a certain piece of jewelry, you also send countless messages that you never intend to be part of the transaction. For example, frowning because of the sun in your eyes may make someone mistakenly believe you are angry; leaving some shampoo in your hair could make someone think you look silly; and touching someone's hand for an extended period of time could cause that person to think you are flirting when that was not your intent. These are all examples of how your actions, without your blessing, can send a message to someone else.

The sociologist Goffman describes this fusing of intentional and unintentional behavior:

> The expressiveness of the individual (and therefore his capacity to give impressions) appears to involve two radically different kinds of sign activity: the expression that he gives and the impression that he gives off. The first involves verbal symbols or their substitutes which he uses admittedly and solely to convey the information that he and the other are known to attach to these symbols. This is communication in the traditional and narrow sense. The second involves a wide range of action that others can treat as symptomatic of the actor (communicator), the expectation being that the action was performed for reasons other than the information conveyed in this way.[6]

# Functions of Nonverbal Communication

One point should be clear by now—nonverbal communication is multidimensional. This multidimensional aspect is revealed in the fact that nonverbal communication often interacts with verbal messages. The interfacing of the verbal with the nonverbal carries over to the many uses and functions of nonverbal behavior.[7] We will examine five of those uses: (1) repeating, (2) complementing, (3) substituting, (4) regulating, and (5) contradicting.

## REPEATING

People often use nonverbal messages to repeat a point they are trying to make. If you were telling someone that what they were proposing was a bad idea, you might move your head from side to side while uttering the word "no." You might hold up a hand in the gesture signifying that a person should stop at the same time you actually use the word "stop." Or you might point in a certain direction after you have just said, "The new library is south of that building." The gestures and words have a similar meaning and reinforce one another.

## COMPLEMENTING

Closely related to repeating is complementing. Although messages that repeat can stand alone, complementing generally adds more information to messages. For example, you can tell someone that you are pleased with his or her performance, but this message takes on extra meaning if you pat the person on the shoulder at the same time.

Physical contact places another layer of meaning on what is being said. Many writers in the area of nonverbal communication refer to this type of message as "accenting" because it accents the idea the speaker is trying to make. You can see how an apology becomes more forceful if your face, as well as your words, is saying, "I'm sorry." You also can accent feelings of anger by speaking in a voice that is much louder than the one you employ in normal conversation.

## SUBSTITUTING

The substitution aspect of nonverbal communication is in operation when you perform some action instead of speaking. If you see a very special friend, you are apt to enlarge the size of your smile and throw open your arms to greet him or her, which is a substitute for all the words it would take to convey the same feeling. In reaction to a group of boisterous people, you might place your index finger to your lips as an alternative to saying, "Please calm down so that I can speak." Or you can offer someone the thumbs-up sign as a way of "saying" everything is "okay" or that they are doing a good job.

## REGULATING

You often regulate and manage your communication by using some form of nonverbal behavior. You nod your head in agreement to indicate to your communication partner that you agree and that he or she should continue talking, or you remain silent for a moment and let the silence send the message that you are ready to begin to give the other person a chance to talk. A parent might engage in stern, direct eye contact with a child as a way of "telling" him or her to terminate naughty behavior. In short, nonverbal behavior can help control the situation.

## CONTRADICTING

On some occasions, your nonverbal actions send signals opposite from the literal meanings contained in your verbal messages. You tell someone you are relaxed and at ease, yet your voice quavers and your hands shake. It also is a contradictory message when you inform your partner that you are glad to see him or her, but at the same time you are sulking and breaking eye contact. Because people rely mostly on nonverbal messages when they receive conflicting data, you need to be aware of the dangers inherent in sending opposing messages. As the German psychiatrist Sigmund Freud noted, "Though we may lie with our lips, betrayal oozes out of us at every pore."

# Studying Nonverbal Communication: Guidelines and Limitations

Because the study of nonverbal communication has been popularized in recent years, this complex and multifaceted subject is often misunderstood. Therefore, we need to pause before pursuing the topic any further and mention some potential problems and misconceptions associated with this important area of study.

## NONVERBAL COMMUNICATION IS OFTEN AMBIGUOUS

We alluded to the first problem earlier when we discussed the intentional and unintentional nature of nonverbal communication. Simply stated, nonverbal communication can be ambiguous. For example, you may engage in a random gesture (swatting a fly off your arm) and someone may see that action and assume you are waving at them. Wood clearly underscores the idea of ambiguity when she writes, "We can never be sure that others understand the meanings we intended to express with our nonverbal behavior."[8] Part of the ambiguity we have been talking about takes place because nonverbal communication can be contextual. The ambiguity of context is clearly seen if someone brushes against you in an elevator—was it merely an accident or an opportunistic sexual act? Our point should be obvious: when you use or interpret nonverbal communication, you need to be aware of the ambiguous nature of this form of interaction. Or as Osborn and Motley tell us, "Meanings and interpretations of nonverbal behaviors often are on very shaky ground."[9]

## WE ARE MORE THAN OUR CULTURE

The next problem relates to individual differences—a subject we treated in great detail in Chapter 1 when we discussed the idea that your behavior is often produced by dynamics other than your culture. With regard to nonverbal interaction Beamer and Varner note the following: "Nonverbal communication is influenced by a number of factors, including cultural background, socioeconomic background, education, gender, age, personal preferences and idiosyncrasies."[10] Simply stated, not all people in a particular culture engage in the same nonverbal actions, so interpretations of nonverbal communication must be carefully evaluated before generalizations can be made.

# Nonverbal Communication and Culture

We have already mentioned that while much of your nonverbal communication is "part of a universally recognized and understood code,"[11] there is still a great deal of your nonverbal behavior that is rooted in your culture. Rosenblatt expressed this important idea in the following manner: "What emotions are felt, how they are expressed, and how they are understood are matters of culture."[12] Therefore, we support the position that nonverbal communication "plays a crucial and necessary part in communicative interactions between people from different cultures."[13]

As students of intercultural communication, learning about the alliance between culture and nonverbal behavior will help you improve the manner in which you engage in intercultural interactions. Hall underscores the need to learn about nonverbal communication in the following manner:

> I am convinced that much of our difficulty with people in other countries stems from
> the fact that so little is known about cross-communication. . . . Formal training in the
> language, history, government, and customs of another nation is only the first step in a
> comprehensive program. Of equal importance is an introduction to the nonverbal language
> which exists in every country of the world and among the various groups within each
> country. Most Americans are only dimly aware of this silent language even though they use
> it every day.[14]

By understanding the important cultural differences in nonverbal behavior, you will be able to gather clues about underlying attitudes and values. You have already seen that nonverbal communication often reveals basic cultural traits. Smiling and shaking hands tells us that a culture values amiability. Bowing tells you that another culture values formality and rank and status. It is not by chance that Hindus greet each other by placing their palms together in front of them while slightly tilting their heads down; this salutation reflects the belief that the deity exists in everyone, not in a single form.

The connection between nonverbal communication and culture is made even more apparent if you recall from Chapter 1 that culture is invisible, omnipresent, and learned. Nonverbal communication has these same qualities. Hall alerts us to the invisible aspect of culture and nonverbal communication by employing phrases such as "silent language" and "hidden dimension." Andersen makes much the same point by telling you, "Individuals are aware of little of their own nonverbal behavior, which is enacted mindlessly, spontaneously, and unconsciously."[15] Both of these scholars are saying that much of your nonverbal behavior, like culture, tends to be elusive, spontaneous, and frequently beyond your awareness. We also remind you that culture is all-pervasive, multidimensional, and boundless; it is everywhere and in everything. The same is true of nonverbal behavior.[16]

Another parallel between culture and nonverbal behavior is that both need to be learned. Although much of outward behavior is innate (such as smiling, moving, touching, eye contact), you are not born with a knowledge of the communication dimensions associated with nonverbal messages. First, we offer a word about some exceptions to this notion before we develop this relationship between learning and nonverbal communication. Research supports the view that because people are all from one species, a general and common genetic inheritance produces universal facial expressions for most of your basic emotions (for example, fear, happiness, anger, surprise, disgust, and sadness).[17] Most scholars would agree, however, that "cultures formulate display rules that dictate when, how, and with what consequences nonverbal expressions will be exhibited."[18] Macaronis summarized this important principle in the following manner:

> People the world over experience the same basic emotions. But what sparks a particular emotion, how and where a person expresses it, and how people define emotions in general vary as matters of culture. In global perspective, therefore, everyday life differs not only in terms of how people think and act, but how they infuse their lives with feelings.[19]

# Classifications of Nonverbal Communication

Before we begin to break down nonverbal communication into a series of categories, we must once again remind you of the unified nature of the categories. As Richmond, McCracken, and Payne point out, "Messages generated by each category do not exist in isolation but rather exist in the company of messages from other categories, verbal messages, contexts, and people functioning as message receivers."[20] Most classifications divide nonverbal messages into two comprehensive categories: those that are primarily produced by the body (appearance, movement, facial expressions, eye contact, touch, smell, and paralanguage), and those that the individual combines with the setting (space, time, and silence).

## BODY BEHAVIOR

**General Appearance.** From hair sprays to hairpieces, from reducing diets to twenty-four-hour fitness centers, from false eyelashes to blue contact lenses, and from plastic surgery for all parts of the body to tanning salons that might contribute to skin cancer, people show their concern for how they appear to others. Keating underscores the sway your outer shell has on others when she writes, "The power of communication to draw others near or to drive them away derives as much from how we appear as from the language we deploy."[21] Very early in life most people realize that outward appearances, as revealed in "our sex, clothing style, race, age, ethnicity, stature, body type, and mood all reveal our physical persona."[22] Reflect for a moment on how you make judgments of other people based on personal appearance, dress, and the objects they carry around or place on their bodies. Studies show that being overweight in the United States reduces income, lowers the chances of getting married, and helps decrease the amount of education one receives.[23] When deciding whether or not to strike up a conversation with a total stranger, you are influenced by the way that person looks. One study pointed out that people made decisions about the future success of blind dates based completely on physical appearance.[24] According to Ruben, we tend to draw on a person's attractiveness, dress, and personal artifacts to make inferences (often faulty) about that individual's "intelligence, gender, age, approachability, financial well-being, class, tastes, values, and cultural background."[25]

***Skin Color.*** Skin color is perhaps the most obvious example of how general appearance is linked to perception and communication. As Vazquez points out, "skin color is the first racial marker children recognize and can be considered the most salient of phenotypic attributes."[26] This indicator is important to intercultural communication in that skin color draws attention to the idea of differences.[27] And as Knapp and Hall note, "In many respects, permanent skin colors have been the most potent body stimulus for determining interpersonal responses in our culture."[28] Skin color "may also be the basis of the allocation of economic and psychological privileges to individuals relative to the degree those privileges are awarded to valued members of the dominant culture."[29]

***Judgments of Beauty.*** Concern with personal appearance is both ancient and universal. As far back as the Upper Paleolithic period (about forty thousand years ago), your ancestors were using bones for necklaces and other bodily ornaments. From that period to the present, historical and archaeological evidence has shown that people are fixated on their bodies. They have painted them, fastened objects to them, dressed them, undressed them, and even deformed and mutilated them in the name of beauty. As the anthropologist Keesing has written, "The use of the body for decoration appears to be a cultural universal."[30] Face painting is still common in parts of Africa, in South America, and among some Native American tribes. In Ethiopia and Eritrea, many women still utilize facial tattoos as "beauty marks."[31] In India, most women place red dots on their forehead to show they are married. And of course, many women in the United States use various forms of makeup and even cosmetic tattoos to amend their appearance.

In intercultural communication, appearance is important because, as Gardiner and Kosmitzki note, "One's body image and the satisfaction with it result from comparisons with an implicit cultural ideal and standard."[32] And, as you would suspect, the ideal varies from culture to culture. In the United States, people tend to value the appearance of tall, slender women and men with muscular bodies.[33] This notion of lean and trim as a sign of attractiveness is not the rule in all cultures. In Japan, diminutive females are deemed the most attractive. In Africa, we can see yet another definition of physical attractiveness. Richmond and Gestrin observe:

> Ideas of pulchritude in Africa differ from those of Europe and the Americas. In traditional African societies, plumpness is considered a sign of beauty, health, and wealth, and slimness is evidence of unhappiness or disease or that a woman is being mistreated by her husband.[34]

Among the Chinese, you can see yet another cultural standard for female attractiveness. As Wenzhong and Grove note, "Many women keep their hairstyles simple (often one or two braids) and make little attempt to draw attention to themselves through self-decoration such as colorful scarves, jewelry, or makeup."[35]

As you might suspect, the judgment of beauty across cultures is a perception that is ripe for ethnocentrism. Remland offers an excellent example of this ethnocentrism when he reminds us that "what is seen as beautiful in one culture may look hideous to people from another culture."[36] Remland adds:

> The many exotic rituals we often see in PBS documentaries or in the pages of *National Geographic*, such as neck stretching, lip enlargements, earlobe plugs, teeth filing, and so on represent the beautifying practices common in many parts of the world. Of course, liposuction, hair implants, facelifts, laser surgery, and the like, while not the least bit extraordinary to many westerners, may seem abhorrent to people from other parts of the world.[37]

Because cultures are dynamic and always in a state of flux, it will be interesting to observe if perceptions of attractiveness begin to change in Japan, Africa, Russia, China, and even Afghanistan as these cultures come into greater contact with Western media.

***Attire.*** The use of clothing goes well beyond protection from the elements—it is often a form of communication. In the United States, as Adler and Rodman state, "Clothing can be used to convey economic status, education, social status, moral standards, athletic ability and/or interests, belief system (political, philosophical, religious), and level of sophistication"[38] From a cultural perspective we also add that clothing can be a reflection of a culture's value orientation. Attire, whether used as military dress, signs of status, or costumes, offers dues into a culture's view of the world.[39] For example, modesty is highly valued among Arabs. In most instances, "Girls are not allowed to participate in swimming classes because of the prohibitions against exposing their

*In much of the world, people still dress in their traditional attire.*

bodies."[40] Al-Kaysi develops this point in more detail when he speaks of the links between modesty and dress among Muslim women: "The main garment must be a 'flowing' one, that is, woman must avoid tight or clinging clothes which exaggerate her figure, or any part of it, such as breasts, legs or arms."[41] Arab women also cover their hair with scarves and in some very orthodox areas even their entire face. And Arab men do not wear shorts or unfastened shirts in public.

The link between cultural values and clothing is also seen among Filipinos. Gochenour tells us, "Values relating to status and authority are the root of the Filipino's need to dress correctly."[42] Of the German culture, Hall and Hall write:

> Correct behavior is symbolized by appropriate and very conservative dress. The male business uniform is a freshly pressed dark suit and tie with a plain shirt and dark shoes and socks. It is important to emulate this conservative approach to both manners and dress. Personal appearance, like the exterior appearance of their homes, is very important to Germans.[43]

The Spanish also link appearance to one's rank, as Ruch asserts: "Historically, dress has denoted social status."[44] In Spain, it is not uncommon to see people of high status wearing a suit and tie in very hot weather. Perhaps nowhere in the world is the merger between attire and a culture's value system more evident than in Japan. McDaniel makes the connection when he writes: "The proclivity for conservative dress styles and colors emphasizes the nation's collectivism and, concomitantly, lessens the potential for social disharmony arising from nonconformist attire."[45]

In much of the world, people still dress in their traditional garments. For Arab men, says Ruch, correct business attire would "include a long loose robe called a *dishdasha* or *thobe* and a headpiece, a white cloth *kaffiya* banded by a black egal to secure it."[46]

As we have noted, for Muslims clothing is much more than apparel to cover the body. As Torrawa points out, garments often reflect important values of the Arab culture.[47] As is the case with so many aspects of culture, there is often a "below the surface" reason for cultural behaviors. This deep structure and its tie to attire in the Arab world are eloquently explained by Torrawa:

> In all its guises, clothing inscribes ideologies of truth and deception, echoing the words of Scripture, and revealing—and unraveling—that honor can only be attained when every robe donned is a robe of honor and every garment a garment of piety.[48]

Whether it is Sikhs in white turbans, Japanese in kimonos, Hasidic Jews in blue yarmulkes, Africans in white dashikis, or the black attire of the Amish in the United States, you need to learn to be tolerant of external differences so that you do not let these differences impede communication.

**Body Movement: Kinesics.** People have always known that actions communicate. As Benjamin Franklin, using the ant as an example of industriousness, said, "None preaches better than the ant, and she says nothing." The study of how movement communicates is called *kinesics*. The basic assumption of this important message system is clearly highlighted by Morreale, Spitzberg, and Barge: "How people hold themselves, stand, sit, and walk communicates strong nonverbal messages. Whether you intend to send a message or not, every move you make potentially communicates something about you to others."[49] Kinesics cues are those visible body shifts and movements that can send messages about (1) your attitude toward the other person (standing face-to-face with a friend, called direct body orientation, or leaning forward may show that you are relaxed), (2) your emotional state (tapping on the table or playing with coins can mean you are nervous), and (3) your desire to control your environment (motioning someone to come closer means you want to talk to him or her).

Scholars have suggested that people can make as many as 700,000 distinct physical signs. Hence, any attempt at cataloging them would be both frustrating and fruitless. Our purpose is simply to call your attention to the idea that while all people use movement to communicate, culture teaches you how to use and interpret these movements. In the upcoming sections, we look at a few cultural differences in posture, sitting behavior, and movements of the body that convey specific meanings (gestures). Before we begin, we must once again remind you that in most instances the messages the body generates operate only in combination with other messages. People usually smile and say hello to a friend at the same time. In Mexico, this is illustrated when asking someone to wait for "just a minute" (*un momento, por favor*): the speaker also makes a fist and then extends the thumb and index finger so that they form a sideways U.

**Posture.** Posture offers insight into a culture's deep structure. We can see the bond between culture and values by simply looking at the Japanese, Thai, and Indian cultures. In Japan and other Asian cultures, the bow is much more than a greeting. It signifies that culture's concern with status and rank. In Japan, for example, low posture is an indicator of respect.[50] Although it appears simple to the outsider, the bowing ritual is actually rather complicated. The person who occupies the lower station begins the bow, and his or her bow must be deeper than the other person's. The superior, on the other hand, determines when the bowing is to end. When the participants are of equal rank, they begin the bow in the same manner and end at the same time. The Thai people use a similar movement called the *wai*. The *wai* movement—which is made by pressing both hands close together in front of one's body, with the fingertips reaching to about neck level—is used to show respect. The lower the head comes to the hands, the more respect is shown.[51] You can see yet another greeting pattern in India. Here the posture when greeting someone is directly linked with the idea that Hindus see God in everything —including other people. The *namaste* (Indian greeting) is carried out by a slight bow with the palms of both hands together, the fingertips at the chin.[52]

**Sitting.** As eccentric as it sounds, the way people sit is often a reflection of important cultural characteristics. In the United States, where being casual and friendly is valued, people, consciously or unconsciously, act out this value by the way they sit. As Novinger illustrates, the position for males "includes a slump and leaning back and a type of sprawl that occupies a lot of space."[53] In many countries, such as Germany and Sweden, where lifestyles tend to be more formal, slouching is considered a sign of rudeness and poor manners. In fact, according to Nees, "German children are still taught to sit and stand up straight, which is a sign of good character. Slouching is seen as a sign of a poor upbringing."[54] For the Samoan culture it is the idea of respect that is being acted out by how one sits. For example, people show respect by positioning themselves at a lower position than the person to whom they are junior.[55]

Even the manner in which you position your legs while sitting has cultural overtones. Remland offers an excellent example of this idea with the following example. "An innocent act of ankle-to-knee leg crossing, typical of most American males, could be mistaken for an insult (a showing of the sole of the foot gesture) in Saudi Arabia, Egypt, Singapore, or Thailand."[56] And according to Ruch, the same seemingly simple act is extremely offensive when doing business in Ghana and in Turkey.[57] People in

Thailand also believe there is something special about the bottoms of the feet. For them the feet are the lowest part of the body and they should never be pointed in the direction of another person.[58] For the Thai, the feet take on so much significance that people avoid stomping with them.

Within the United States, there are differences in how people move, stand, and sit during interaction. Women often hold their arms closer to their bodies than do men. They usually keep their legs closer together and seldom cross them in mixed company. Their posture is also more restricted and less relaxed than the posture of males. Most research in the area of gender communication concludes that these differences are related to issues such as status, power, and affiliation.[59] Posture and stance also play an important role in the African-American co-culture. This is most evident in the walk employed by many young African-American males. According to Hecht, Collier, and Ribeau, "The general form of the walk is slow and casual with the head elevated and tipped to one side, one arm swinging and the other held limply."[60] The walk, says the *San Diego Union-Tribune*, "shows the dominant culture that you are strong and proud, despite your status in American society."[61]

**Gestures.** The power of gestures as a form of communication is reflected in the fact that the co-culture of the deaf in the United States has a rich and extensive vocabulary composed of gestures. Another example of the power of gestures can be found in the hand signals used by various urban gangs. The slightest variation in performing a certain gesture can be the catalyst for a violent confrontation. You can see the importance of gestures in intercultural communication because some gestures that are positive, humorous, or harmless in some cultures can have the opposite meaning in other cultures.[62] For example, in the United States, pointing usually does not carry negative connotations. Yet, in China, pointing at someone can be taken as a sign of rudeness.

Because there are thousands of gestures found in every culture, we do not intend to offer a taxonomy that is all-inclusive or complete. Such a listing could fill the remaining pages of this book. Instead, it is our purpose to present but a few examples that will assist you in seeing the link between gestures and culture. Rather than presenting a random cataloging of these gestures, we will look at (1) *pointing*, (2) *idiosyncratic gestures*, (3) *beckoning*, (4) *acceptance and understanding*, and variations related to the (5) *amount and size of the gestures*.

In the United States *pointing* is a very common gesture. Americans point to objects and at people with the index finger. Directions are even given by pointing in one direction or another with the index finger. Germans point with the little finger, and the Japanese point with the entire hand, palms up. The Navajo use their chin, and in much of Asia, pointing with the index finger at a person is considered rude.[63]

As we have already indicated, there are a limitless number of *idiosyncratic* gestures found in each culture. These are the gestures whose meanings are the feature and property of a particular culture. In China, if you place your right hand over your heart it means you are making a sincere promise. For the French, pulling the skin down below the right eye can mean "I don't believe you." In Argentina, one twists an imaginary mustache to signify that everything is okay. In the United States, "making a circle with one's thumb and index finger while extending the others is emblematic of the word 'OK'; in Japan (and Korea) it traditionally signified 'money' (*okane*); and among Arabs this gesture is usually accompanied by a baring of teeth, and together they signify extreme hostility."[64] This same gesture to a Tunisian means "I'll kill you."

Many sexual connotation gestures are also tied to a certain culture. In the United States someone might use the middle finger to send an insulting obscene gesture. This sexual insult gesture is not universal. For example, the gesture we discussed in the last paragraph (forming an O with the thumb and index finger) is, according to Lynch and Hanson, "an obscene gesture among some Latino cultures."[65] In the Italian culture, the gesture referring to someone as a homosexual is moving the finger behind your ear.[66]

The taken-for-granted sign we make for *beckoning* is also culturally based. In the United States, when a person wants to signal a friend to come, he or she usually makes the gesture with one hand, palm up, fingers more or less together and moving toward his or her body. Koreans express this same idea by cupping "the hand with the palm down and drawing the fingers toward the palm."[67] When seeing this gesture, many Americans think the other person is waving good-bye. Filipinos often summon someone with a quick downward nod of the head. In Germany and much of Scandinavia, tossing the head back makes a beckoning motion. For many Arabs, holding the right hand out, palm upward, and opening and closing the hand perform nonverbally asking someone to "come here."[68] And in Spain, to beckon someone you stretch your arm out, palm downward, and make a scratching motion toward your body with your fingers.

Head movements denoting *acceptance and understanding* represent another example of how some gestures are rooted in culture. In the United States, moving your head up and down is seen as a sign of understanding and agreement. This same movement can have different meanings in different cultures. As Lynch and Hanson point out, "This same gesture is interpreted quite differently in many other cultures. Among Asian, Native American, Middle Eastern, and Pacific Island groups, it often means, 'I hear you speaking.' It does not signal that the listener understands the message nor does it suggest that he or she agrees."[69] Greeks express "yes" with a nod similar to the one used in the United States, but when communicating "no," they jerk their heads back and raise their faces. Lifting one or both hands up to the shoulders strongly emphasizes the "no."

There are also cultural differences regarding the *amount and size of gestures* employed during a communication encounter. It is generally accepted that Italians, South Americans, most Latinos, Africans, and people from the Middle East employ gestures with greater size and intensity than do cultures such as the Japanese, Chinese, Finns, and Scandinavians.[70] A few specific examples will help illustrate this point. As Falassi and Flower note, "Speaking with their hands—or all their bodies in fact—is in tune with the Italian love of theatrics, and their native gusto for social interaction."[71] Berry and his colleagues make much the same point with regard to the "exciting impression" Italians make "because of their lively movement patterns."[72] Novinger describes the animated style of gesturing in Brazil when she writes, "Brazilians say that if you tie their hand they cannot speak. They use hand gestures and broad arm gestures as they talk."[73] The same zeal toward gestures is found among Chileans. In that culture, according to Winter, gestures are used to help add meaning to conversations and to emphasize key points.[74] This use of gestures to contribute to meaning is also the case among Arab men. Here you can see gesturing and "the waving of arms used to accompany almost every spoken word."[75] Members of many Asian cultures perceive such outward activity quite differently, often equating vigorous action with a lack of manners and restraint.[76] And, according to Lewis, "Arms are used very little by Nordics during conversation."[77] Germans are also made uncomfortable by gestures that are, by their standards, too flamboyant. Ruch offers the following advice to American executives who work with German corporations:

> Hands should be used with calculated dignity. They should never serve as lively instruments to emphasize points in conversation. The entire game plan is to appear calm under pressure.[78]

You can also see the significance of gestures by looking at various co-cultures. For example, as compared to males, women tend to use fewer and smaller gestures.[79] African Americans value a lively and expressive form of communication and hence display a greater variety of movements than whites when interacting.[80]

## FACIAL EXPRESSIONS

The early Greek playwrights and the Noh actors of Japan were keenly aware of the shifts in mood and meaning that facial expressions conveyed. Both forms of drama use masks and extensive makeup to demonstrate differences in each actor's character and attitude. Whether it is the Mexican adage that "One's face is the mirror of one's soul," or the Yiddish proverb that states "The face tells the secret," people everywhere have been captivated by the face. What is fascinating about the study of the face is that you are talking about three faces. First, there is your "assigned" face, the one you are born with. While it is altered by age, health, and even cosmetics and surgery, this is your face at rest. Second is the face you are able to manipulate at will. You can decide to smile, wink, frown, and so on. Finally, you have the face that is changed by your surroundings and the messages you receive. This is that face that, with or without your blessing, can show fear, happiness, sorrow, and such.

Among scholars the importance of the three faces we just mentioned is well established. For example, facial cues can reflect course of action,[81] convey messages of "social submissiveness and dominance,"[82] tell others how interested you are, signal your degree of involvement, indicate your level of comprehension about the moment, and divulge whether or not your reactions are spontaneous or managed.[83]

While facial expressions play an important role in any study of intercultural communication, the specific implications of these expressions are often difficult to assess. At the core of a lingering academic debate lies this question: Is there a nearly universal language of facial expressions? One position holds that anatomically similar expressions may occur in everyone, but the meanings people attach to them differ from culture to culture.[84] The majority opinion, which we introduced earlier in the chapter, is that there are universal facial expressions for which people have similar meanings. Ekman advances this point of view: "The subtle creases of a grimace tell the same story around the world, to preliterate New Guinea tribesmen, to Japanese and American college students alike. Darwin knew it all along, but now here's hard evidence that culture does not control the face."[85] What is being presented is the theory that there is "a basic set of at least six facial expressions that are innate, universal, and carry the same basic meaning throughout the world."[86] These six pancultural and universal facial expressions are happiness, sadness, fear, anger, disgust, and surprise.

Despite the biological-based nature of facial expressions, there seem to be clear cultural expectations as to how cultural norms often dictate when, where, how, and to whom facial expressions are displayed.[87] As Matsumoto declares, "Different cultures recognize the power of the face and produce many rules to regulate not only what kinds of facial behavior are permitted in social interaction, but also how it may be even to attend to the faces of others during interaction."[88] A few specific examples will illustrate the role of culture in the production and interpretation of facial expressions.

In many Mediterranean cultures, people exaggerate signs of grief or sadness. It is not uncommon in this region of the world to see men crying in public. Yet in the United States, white males often suppress the desire to show these emotions. Japanese men even go so far as to hide expressions of anger, sorrow, confusion, or disgust by laughing or smiling.[89] In one study, Japanese and American subjects revealed the same facial expressions when viewing a stress-inducing film while they were alone. However, when viewing the film in the presence of others, the Japanese manifested only neutral facial expressions. Min-Sun Kim says that Koreans also withhold emotion and do not engage in animated facial expressions.[90] The Chinese also do not readily show emotion for reasons that are related to a cultural value—that value is the concept of saving face. For the Chinese, displaying too much emotion violates face-saving norms by disrupting harmony and causing conflict.[91]

The smile is yet another emotional display that is linked to one's culture. Everyone is born knowing how to smile. Yet the amount of smiling, the stimulus that produces the smile, and even what the smile is communicating often shift from culture to culture. As Kraut and Johnson note, culture can "influence smiling both by determining the interpretation of events, which affects the cause of happiness, and by shaping display roles, which determine when it is socially appropriate to smile."[92] In America, a smile can be a sign of happiness or friendly affirmation and is usually used with great regularity. In the German culture, according to Nees, a smile "is used with far more discretion, generally only with those persons one knows and really likes."[93] In the Japanese culture, the smile can also mask an emotion or be used to avoid answering a question.[94] People of lower status in Japan may also use the smile "to denote acceptance of a command or order by a person of higher status when in fact they feel anger or contempt for the order or the person giving the order."[95] In the Korean culture, too much smiling is often perceived as the sign of a shallow person. Dresser notes that this "lack of smiling by Koreans has often been misinterpreted as a sign of hostility."[96] Thais, on the other hand, smile much of the time. In fact, Thailand has been called the "Land of Smiles."[97]

There are, of course, countless idiosyncratic facial expressions that are the exclusive domain of a particular culture. Remland presents just a few of these that clearly illustrate the unique character of some facial expressions:

> In Saudi Arabia we can call someone a liar by rapidly moving our tongue in and out of our mouth; in Greece we can say no by raising and lowering our eyebrows once. If we speak out of turn in southern China and Tibet and want to apologize, we can protrude the tip of our tongue and then immediately withdraw it.[98]

Even within a culture, there are groups that use facial expressions differently from the dominant culture. Summarizing the research on gender differences, Pearson, West, and Turner report that, compared to men, women use more facial expressions and are more expressive, smile more, are more apt to return smiles, and are more attracted to others who smile.[99]

## EYE CONTACT AND GAZE

In drama, fiction, poetry, and music, eyes have always been a fascinating topic. You can see the power of eye contact, or the lack of it, as professional poker players try to hide behind their dark glasses during an important tournament. The reason for using the eyes as a form of communication is clearly seen in Emerson's admonition: "When the eyes say one thing, and the tongue another, a practiced man relies on the language of the second." Shakespeare also knew the power of the eyes when he wrote "Thou tell'st me there is murder in mine eye." And Bob Dylan underscored the same force of eyes in his lyrics "Your eyes said more to me that night than your lips would ever say." Even the "evil eye" is more than just an expression. In one study, Roberts examined 186 cultures throughout the world and found that 67 of them had some belief in the evil eye.[100] Zuniga highlights the power of the evil eye (*mal ojo*) in Mexico and Puerto Rico with the following observation: "*Mal ojo* is believed to be the result of excessive admiration and desire on the part of another. Mothers may isolate their children for fear of having one become victim of *mal ojo*."[101] The Korean culture also has a distinctive approach to eye contact that underscores its significance to human communication. They have the term *nunch'i*, which means communicating with the eyes. This style of eye contact is so important that Robinson maintains it causes "miscommunication between Westerners and all Asians."[102]

The reason the eyes are such an important communication tool is that the number of messages we can send with our eyes is nearly limitless. We have all heard some of the following words used to describe a person's eyes: *direct, sensual, sardonic, expressive, intelligent, penetrating, sad, cheerful, worldly, hard, trusting,* and *suspicious.* According to Leathers, in the United States, eyes serve six important communication functions: they "(1) *indicate degrees of attentiveness, interest, and arousal;* (2) *influence attitude change and persuasion;* (3) *regulate interaction;* (4) *communicate affect;* (5) *define power and status relationships;* and (6) *assume a central role in impression management.*"[103] There is also evidence that people alter their use of eye contact when they engage in deception.[104]

As in the case with most of the communication behavior discussed in this book, eye contact and all its variations represent an important variable in the study of culture and communication.[105] In the United States, as Triandis notes, looking another person directly in the eye is very common.[106] Not only is it the rule, for most members of the dominant culture eye contact is highly valued.[107] In fact, most people in Western societies expect the person with whom they are interacting to look them in the eye. There is even a tendency in North America to be suspicious of someone who does not follow the culturally prescribed rules for eye contact. So important is this interpersonal skill that one popular communication textbook offered the following advice to its readers: "You can improve your eye contact by becoming conscious of looking at people when you are talking to them. If you find your eyes straying away from that person, work to regain direct contact."[108] The key word in the above sentence is *direct.* For direct eye-to-eye contact is not a custom throughout the world. In many cultures direct eye contact is a taboo or an insult. In Japan, for example, prolonged eye contact is considered rude, threatening, and disrespectful.[109] For the Japanese it is not uncommon for them to look down, away, or even close their eyes while engaging in conversation. You can of course appreciate the problems that might arise if Americans are not aware of the Japanese use of eye contact. As Richmond and her associates point out, many Americans often interpret Japanese eye contact, or lack of it, "as signs of disagreement, disinterest, or rejection."[110] Among people from Mediterranean cultures you find yet another attitude toward eye contact. Some of these features are highlighted by Lewis:

> Mediterranean people use their eyes in many different ways for effect. These include glaring (to show anger), glistening eyes (to show sincerity), winking (very common in Spain and France to imply conspiracy) and the eyelash flutter (used by women to reinforce persuasion).[111]

Dresser notes that "people from Latin American and Caribbean cultures also avoid eye contact as a sign of respect."[112] This same orientation toward eye contact is found in Africa. Richmond and Gestrin tell us, "Making eye contact when communicating with a person who is older or of higher status is considered a sign of disrespect or even aggression in many parts of Africa where respect is shown by lowering the eyes."[113] There is even a Zulu saying that states, "The eye is an organ of aggression." Eye contact often reflects a cultural value. India and Egypt are two good examples of eye contact mirroring a cultural value. According to Luckmann, "In India, the amount of eye contact that is appropriate depends on one's social position (people of different socioeconomic classes avoid eye contact with each other)."[114] In Egypt, the issue is not social status but rather gender. "Women and men who are strangers may avoid eye contact out of modesty and respect for religious rules."[115]

Potential problems can arise when Asians and Westerners interact with cultures that practice prolonged eye contact with their communication counterpart. For example, Lonner and Malpass note, "In the Middle East, relatively extended gaze exchanges are considered appropriate during exchanges between men."[116] Members of these cultures believe such contact shows interest in the other person and helps them assess the truthfulness of the other person's words.[117] Germans also engage in very direct eye contact. This point and some of the problems that can arise from this behavior are noted by Nees: Germans will look you directly in the eye while talking, which some Americans find vaguely annoying or disconcerting. From the German point of view, this is a sign of honesty and true interest in the conversation. For Americans it can seem too intense and direct.[118]

In America, the prolonged stare is often a part of the nonverbal code that the co-culture of the male homosexual employs. An extended stare, along with other nonverbal messages, at a member of the same sex is often perceived as a signal of interest and sexual suggestion.[119] A few other differences in the use of eye contact in the United States are worthy of our consideration. The Hopi interpret direct eye contact as offensive and usually will avoid any type of staring. The Navajos dislike sustained eye contact so strongly that they have incorporated it into their creation myth. The myth, which tells the story of a "terrible monster called He-Who-Kills-With-His Eyes," teaches the Navajo child "a stare is literally an evil eye and implies a sexual and aggressive assault."[120] This same uncomfortable feeling toward direct and prolonged eye contact can be found among Mexican Americans. As Parnell and Paulanka note, "Mexican-Americans consider sustained eye contact when speaking directly to someone rude. Direct eye contact with superiors may be interpreted as insolence. Avoiding direct eye contact with superiors is a sign of respect."[121]

There also are gender variations among members of the dominant culture in how people use their eyes to communicate. For example, "Both sexes signal interest and involvement with others by making eye contact, but men also use it to challenge others or to assert their status and power."[122] In addition, research on the subject indicates that in most instances, women maintain more eye contact than do men; women look at other women more and hold eye contact longer with one another than do men.[123] We should add that gender characteristics regarding eye contact vary from culture to culture. As we noted earlier, in cultures where gender segregation is the norm (India, Saudi Arabia, etc.) direct eye contact between men and women is avoided.[124]

As you might imagine, eye contact is also an important consideration when communicating with a member of the deaf community. Without visual contact, American Sign Language could not be used. Turning your back to someone who is signing is

*Touch as a form of communication can send messages about your feelings and relationships.*

© Larry Samovar

essentially the same as ignoring him or her. So delicate is the use of eye contact that you seldom realize the modifications you make. For example, the next time you are talking with a disabled person, perhaps someone in a wheelchair, notice how little eye contact you make with him or her as compared with someone who is not disabled.

## TOUCH

Being touched or touching is a compelling communication device. The American playwright Tennessee Williams eloquently expressed the power of touch when he wrote, "Devils can be driven out of the heart by the touch of a hand on a hand, or a mouth on a mouth."

Whether your touch behavior is conscious or unconscious, the act of touching is a reflection of what you are feeling and experiencing at the moment. Hence, the meanings you assign to being touched, and your reasons for touching others, offer insights into the communication encounter, as the character Holden Caulfield vividly helps illustrate in the American classic *The Catcher in the Rye*:

> I held hands with her all the time. This doesn't sound like much, but she was terrific to
> hold hands with. Most girls if you hold hands with them their god damn hand dies, or else

they think they have to keep moving their hand all the time, as if they were afraid they'd bore you or something.[125]

Touch is the earliest sense to mature; it manifests itself in the final embryonic stage and comes into its own long before eyes, ears, and the higher brain centers begin to work. Soon after birth, infants begin to employ their other senses to interpret reality. During the same period, they are highly involved with touch. They are being nuzzled, cuddled, cleaned, patted, kissed, and in many cases breastfed. So important is touch to human communication that researchers now know that people who are denied "caregivers' touch" can develop serious biological and emotional problems.[126] As you move from infancy into childhood, you learn the rules of touching. You are taught whom to touch and where they may be touched. By the time you reach adolescence, your culture has taught you how to communicate with touch. You use touch out of social politeness, for sex, consolation, support, and control.[127] In the United States, people learn to shake hands with nearly everyone (making sure it is a firm shake), hug certain people (but not everyone with the same intensity), be intimate with still other people (knowing well in advance the zones of the body that you can touch), and make love to one person (being aware of the sexual regions defined by culture and sex manuals).

You need only watch the news on television or stand at an international airport to know that there are major differences in how cultures use touch, even in the simple act of greeting or saying good-bye. In a study involving touch behavior among culturally diverse couples at an international airport, Andersen offers the following narrative of some of their findings:

> A family leaving for Tonga formed a circle, wove their arms around each other's back, and prayed and chanted together. A tearful man returning to Bosnia repeatedly tried to leave his sobbing wife; each time he turned back to her, they would grip each other by the fingertips and exchange a passionate, tearful kiss and a powerful embrace. Two Korean couples departed without any touch, despite the prolonged separation that lay ahead of them.[128]

Let us look at a few other cultural examples so that you see the link between culture and touch. Arabs employ touching behavior as part of their communication style.[129] As we have said elsewhere, because of religious and social traditions, those Arabs who are Muslims eat and do other things with the right hand, but do not greet with the left hand—this is social insult. The left hand is used to engage in basic biological functions. Many Asians also see a link between touch and its religious meaning. Dresser offers the following observation regarding touching the head: "Many Asian people believe the head houses the soul. Therefore, when another person touches their head, it places them in jeopardy. It is prudent for outsiders to avoid touching the heads and upper torsos of Asians."[130] Many African Americans are also annoyed if a white person pats them on the top of their head. They believe it carries the same meaning as being told, in a condescending manner, that they are "a good little boy or girl."

The act of kissing as greeting and other social touching also differs from culture to culture. People in much of Eastern Europe, Spain, Greece, Italy, Portugal, Israel, and the Arab world will kiss when they meet their friends. There is also much more same-sex touching in Mexico and Spain. Men will greet each other with an embrace (*abrazo*). As Condon notes, "Hugs, pats on backs, and other physical contact are an important part of communication in Mexico."[131] And in Costa Rica, women greet each other with a kiss on one cheek and a hand on the shoulder.[132] In much of Southeast Asia, people not only avoid touching when meeting, but also have very little physical contact during the course of the conversation. In China, men and women seldom "show physical affection in public."[133] When describing business practices in Japan, Rowland asserts, "Touching fellow workers and associates is not common in Japan. Patting someone on the back or putting a friendly arm around them is not done."[134] Even the simple act of kissing has cultural overtones. Although mouth-to-mouth kissing, as a sexual act, is common in most Western cultures, it is not widespread in many parts of Asia. In fact, the Japanese have for centuries rhapsodized about the appeal of the nape of the neck as an erotic zone. The Japanese have no word for kissing, so they have borrowed from the English language for their word *kisu*.

There are gender and ethnic differences within the United States in how individuals use and react to touch. Generally speaking, males engage in less touch behavior than do females.[135] And, according to Morreale, Spitzberg, and Barge, "Men use touch to assert power or express sexual desire; and men tend to touch females more than females touch males."[136] There are, of course, other differences in how the two genders employ touch behavior. Bates notes, "Women initiate hugs and embraces far more often than men do, to other women, to men, and to children."[137]

There are also cultural differences regarding gender when you interact with other cultures. Novinger points out those differences when she writes, "An orthodox Jew or a fundamentalist Muslim will not shake hands with (touch) a woman as a greeting or when being introduced, because such touch of a non-family female is not culturally permitted."[138]

Co-cultures within the United States often employ touch in ways that are unique to their members. African Americans "give skin" and "get skin" when greeting each other, but they do not normally use "skinning" (touching) when greeting white people unless they are close friends. A limited number of studies reveal that African Americans engage in more interpersonal touch than do whites.[139] And, Leathers says, one study has shown that "black females touch each other almost twice as often as white females."[140]

## PARALANGUAGE

When the German poet Klopstock wrote, "The tones of human voices are mightier than strings or brass to move the soul," he knew that the sounds we generate, apart from the meaning contained in the word, often communicate more than the words themselves. Most of you probably have viewed a foreign film with subtitles. During those intervals when the subtitles were not on the screen, you heard the actors uttering an unfamiliar language but could essentially understand what was happening just from the sound of the voices. Perhaps you inferred that the performers were expressing anger, sorrow, joy, or even who the hero was and who was cast in the role of the villain. The rise and fall of voices also may have told you when one person was asking a question and another was making a statement or issuing a command. Whatever the case, certain vocal cues provided you with information with which to make judgments about the characters' personalities, emotional states, ethnic background, and rhetorical activity. To be sure, you could only guess at the exact meaning of the words being spoken, but sound variations still told you a great deal about what was happening. Shakespeare said the same thing with great style when he wrote, "I understand the fury in your words, but not the words." What we have just been considering is often referred to as *paralanguage*, which involves the linguistic elements of speech—how something is said and not the actual meaning of the spoken words. Most classifications divide paralanguage into three kinds of vocalizations, (1) *vocal qualifiers* (volume, pitch, rhythm, tempo, resonance, tone), (2) *vocal characterizers* (laughing, crying, yelling, moaning, whining, belching, yawning), and (3) *vocal segregates* ("uh-huh," "shh," "uh," "oooh," "mmmh," "hmmm").

**Vocal Qualities.** It is extraordinary how many inferences about content and character can be made just from the paralinguistic sounds people produce. For example, paralanguage cues assist you in drawing conclusions about an individual's emotional state, socioeconomic status, height, ethnicity, weight, age, intelligence, race, regional background, and educational level.[141] Let's pause for a moment and look at some of the paralanguage messages you send and receive that have message value for a particular culture.

While vocal qualities have numerous components, it is in the use of volume where cultural differences are most apparent. A few examples will illustrate this point. Arabs speak with a great deal of volume because volume for them connotes strength and sincerity. As Triandis notes, "Arabs believe that loud and clear is 'sincere' and soft is 'devious.'"[142] For Brazilians, speaking loudly signifies "interest and involvement."[143] Ruch says Germans conduct their business with a "commanding tone that projects authority and self-confidence."[144] On the other end of the continuum, there are cultures that have a very different view toward loud voices. Remland observes that "Britons generally prefer a quieter, less intrusive volume than persons from many other cultures."[145] A visitor from Thailand once asked one of the authors if the loud voices she was hearing in America meant Americans were upset or mad at something. Her question made a great deal of sense. For as Cooper and Cooper note, in Thailand "a loud voice is perceived as being impolite."[146] In Japan, raising one's voice often implies a lack of self-control. For them, a gentle and soft voice reflects good manners and helps maintain social harmony—two important values in Japanese culture.

Co-cultures also use vocal qualifiers in subtle and unique ways. For example, as part of their unique communication style, many African Americans use more inflection, are more intense and more dynamic, and have a greater emotional range in their use of voice than most white Americans.[147] Some members of the dominant culture view these characteristics in a negative light.[148] Differences in paralanguage also mark the communication patterns of males and females. In several studies, females evidenced a faster rate of speech than men and also had fewer silent pauses while speaking.[149] After reviewing numerous studies on gender differences in the use of voice, Pearson, West, and Turner concluded that females speak at a higher pitch than men, speak more softly, are more expressive, pronounce the complete "ing" ending to words, and come closer to standard speech norms.[150] Women also have greater variation in their voice when they speak than do men.[151]

**Vocal Characteristics.** As noted, vocal characteristics are vocalizations that for a specific culture convey a learned meaning. For example, the seemingly natural act of sneezing "is considered in Islam a blessing from God."[152] The rationale behind this sound having religious overtones goes to the heart of Islam. Because all actions are God's will, sneezing is an action triggered by God. In fact, after the sneeze a Muslim would say *Al-hamdu illah* (praise and thanks to God). Laughing also sends different messages, depending on the culture. Lynch and Hanson do an excellent job noting this difference when they write:

> Laughing and giggling are interpreted as expressions of enjoyment among most Americans—signals that people are relaxed and having a good time. . . . Among other cultural groups, such as Southeast Asians, the same behavior may be a sign of extreme embarrassment or discomfort or what Americans might call "nervous laughter" taken to the extreme.[153]

**Vocal Segregates.** This category of paralanguage, much like vocal characteristics, is sounds that are audible but are not actual words. In some occasions these sounds have very little meaning and are used for substitutes for words. A case in point in the overused "uh" sound produced by many Americans when they can't locate a specific word. However, in many cultures these sounds take on a special meaning. For instance, the Maasai also use a number of sounds that have special significance, the most common one being the "eh" sound, which the Maasai draw out and which can mean "yes," "I understand," or "continue."[154] In Kenya, the "iya" sound tells the other person that everything is okay; in Jamaica, the "kissing" or "sucking" sound expresses anger, exasperation, or frustration. The Japanese also make ample use of vocalics in their conversations. During interpersonal discussions, say Richmond, McCracken, and Payne, the "Japanese will often hiss or inhale one's breath while talking to others as a sign of respect."[155] They will also make small utterances to demonstrate their attentiveness, such as *hai* (yes, certainly, all right, very well), *so* (same as the English so), or *e* (well . . . or let me see . . .).[156]

During the first part of the chapter, we focused on nonverbal communication through body behavior. We now examine how people employ space, time, and silence as ways of communicating. Although these variables are external to the communicator, they are nevertheless used and manipulated in ways that send messages. For example, imagine your reaction to someone who stands too close to you, arrives late for an important appointment, or remains silent after you reveal some personal information. In each of these instances, you would find yourself reading meaning into your communication partner's use of (1) *space and distance*, (2) *time*, and (3) *silence*.

## SPACE AND DISTANCE

The flow and shift of distance between you and the people with whom you interact are as much a part of communication experiences as the words you exchange. Notice how you might allow one person to stand very close to you and keep another at a distance. The study of this message system, called *proxemics*, is concerned with such things as your (1) *personal space*, (2) *seating*, and (3) *furniture arrangement*. All three have an influence on intercultural communication.

**Personal Space.** Your personal space, that piece of the universe you occupy and call your own, is contained within an invisible boundary surrounding your body. As the owner of this area, you usually decide who may enter and who may not. When your space is invaded, you react in a variety of ways. You may back up and retreat, stand your ground as your hands become moist from nervousness, or sometimes even react violently. Your use of personal space, like so much of your communication behavior, is learned on both the conscious and unconscious level. The anthropologist Edward T. Hall

© Photodisc/Getty Images

*How you respond to space is linked directly to your culture.*

attempted to classify how personal space was used in North America by proposing four categories he labeled (1) intimate, (2) casual-personal, (3) social, and (4) public.[157] Each of these categories demonstrates how space can communicate. *Intimate distance* (actual contact to eighteen inches) is normally reserved for very personal relationships. You can reach out and touch the person at this distance. In *personal distance* (eighteen inches to four feet) there is little chance of physical contact and you can usually speak in your normal voice. *Social distance* (four to twelve feet) is the distance at which most members of the dominant culture conduct business. *Public distance* is usually used in public presentations and can vary from relatively close to a very large distance.

As is the case with most forms of communication, space is associated with culture. For example, cultures that stress individualism (England, the United States, Germany, and Australia) generally demand more space than do collective cultures and "tend to take an active, aggressive stance when their space is violated."[158] In collective cultures, according to Andersen, where people are more interdependent, "the members work, play, live and sleep in close proximity to one another."[159] According to Triandis, Arabs, Latin Americans, and U.S. Hispanics would fall into this category.[160] As Condon notes, in Mexico the "physical distance between people when engaged in conversation is closer than what is usual north of the border."[161] With regard to Arabs, Ruch writes, "Typical Arab conversations are at close range. Closeness cannot be avoided."[162] According to Richmond and Gestrin, "Africans get physically close to complete strangers and stand even closer when conversing."[163]

As you have just seen, a person's use of space is directly linked to the value system of their culture. In some Asian cultures, for example, students do not sit close to their teachers or stand near their bosses; the extended distance demonstrates deference and esteem. Extra interpersonal distance is also part of the cultural experience of the people of Scotland and Sweden, for whom it reflects privacy. In Germany, as Hall and Hall note, private space is sacred.[164] To the Germans, according to Gannon, "This distancing is a protective barrier and psychological symbol that operates in a manner similar to that of the home."[165] You find the opposite view toward space in the Brazilian culture where "closeness and human warmth is apparent," and hence, conversation takes place with less room between participants.[166]

**Seating.** In addition to seating being a practical matter, cultures also use seating arrangements as a form of nonverbal communication. Notice, for example, that Americans, when in groups, tend to talk with those opposite them rather than those seated or standing beside them. This pattern also controls how they select leaders when in groups: in most instances, the person sitting at the head of the table is chosen (or the leader will move directly to the head table position). In America, leaders usually are accustomed to being removed physically from the rest of the group and consequently choose chairs at the end of the table. In China, seating arrangements take on different meanings. The Chinese often experience alienation and uneasiness when they face someone directly or sit on opposite sides of a desk or table from someone. The Chinese prefer to sit next to others.[167] If you see a news story of American diplomats meeting with government officials from China, you might observe that the meeting is taking place with people sitting side by side on couches. In Korea, seating arrangements reflect status and role distinctions. In a car, office, or home, the seat at the right is considered to be one of honor.

For the Japanese, "Seating arrangements at any formal or semiformal function are also based on hierarchy."[168] When engaged in business or diplomatic negotiations, the Japanese will arrange themselves with the most senior person sitting in the middle and those nearest in rank to the left and right of this senior position. Extremely low ranking members will sit away from the table, behind the other representatives. Seating arrangements are also a way of demonstrating social hierarchy in the Fijian culture.[169] The seat near the central house post is the seat of honor. Status in this culture is also reflected in the fact that women sit "below" men in the home and seniors sit above junior members of the household.

**Furniture Arrangement.** Closely related to seating patterns is the concept of furniture arrangement. The importance of this form of communication is clearly seen in the Chinese traditional philosophy of *feng shui*. For the Chinese, and recently for many Westerns, *feng shui* "is the art of manipulating the physical environment to establish harmony with the natural environment to achieve happiness, prosperity, and health."[170] You can observe some of the signs of this philosophy in the way some Chinese arrange themselves at a table. In signing business agreements, the Chinese will often want to sit in a seat that they believe allows them to be in consonance with their surroundings.[171]

As is the case with all aspects of nonverbal communication, the arrangement of furniture is a reflection of cultural values. In the United States, furniture arrangement is used for privacy and "can be used to withdraw or avoid interactions."[172] This is not the situation in other parts of the world. For example, people from France, Italy, and Mexico who visit the United States are often surprised to see that the furniture in the living room is pointed toward the television set. For them, conversation is important, and facing chairs toward a television screen stifles conversation.

Even the arrangement of furniture in offices gives us a clue to the character and values of a people. According to Hall and Hall, "French space is a reflection of French culture and French institutions. Everything is centralized, and spatially the entire country is laid out around centers."[173] Hence, offices are organized around the manager, who is at the center. In Germany, where privacy is stressed, office furniture is spread throughout the office.[174] In Japan, where group participation is encouraged, many desks are arranged hierarchically in the center of a large, common room absent of walls or partitions.[175] The supervisors and managers are positioned nearest the windows. This organization encourages the exchange of information, facilitates multitask accomplishments, and promotes the Confucian concept of learning through silent observation.

Some co-cultures have their own special use of space. Prostitutes, for example, are very possessive of their territory. When they mentally mark an area as their own, even though it may be a public street or hotel lobby, they behave as if it were their private property and attempt to keep other prostitutes away.[176] In prisons, where space is limited, controlled, and at a premium, space and territory are crucial forms of communication. New inmates quickly learn the culture of prison by learning about the use of space. They soon know when to enter another cell, that space reduction is a form of punishment, and that lines form for nearly all activities. Women normally "establish closer proximity to others" than do men.[177] In summarizing other gender differences in the use of space, Leathers has concluded:

> Men use space as a means of asserting their dominance over women, as in the following:
> (a) they claim more personal space than women; (b) they more actively defend violations of their territories—which are usually much larger than the territories of women; (c) under conditions of high density, they become more aggressive in their attempts to regain a desired measure of privacy; and (d) men more frequently walk in front of their female partner than vice versa.[178]

Spatial distance is also a variable when interacting with members of the deaf culture. For example, when using American Sign Language, it is necessary for the person signing to be seen. It would not be uncommon for two signers to sit across from one another at a distance that hearing people might perceive as impersonal.[179]

## TIME

Three centuries ago, when the Dutch mathematician Christian Huygens built the first pendulum clock, which allowed people to keep track of hours and minutes, little did he know that his invention would have such an impact on people's lives. You now strap clocks to your wrists, hang them on your walls, see them on your computer screen, and give them power to control everything from your moods to your relationships. Anthropologists Rapport and Overing underscore the importance of time to human behavior when they write, "To cut up life into moments of being, in sum, is for the individual to possess a means by which that life can be filled, shaped and reshaped in significant ways."[180] Self-reflection will reveal how time communicates. If you arrive thirty minutes late for an important appointment and offer no apology, you send a certain message about yourself. Telling someone how guilty you feel about your belated arrival also sends a message. Studies even point out that one of the hallmarks of a successful and intimate relationship is the amount of time people spend together.[181] What is happening is obvious; how the parties are perceiving and using time is sending a message about how much they care for each other. Of course, there is much more to time than what it says about your relationships. Gonzales and Zimbardo accentuate this multidimensional aspect of time when they write, "Our temporal perspective influences a wide range of psychological processes, from motivation, emotion and spontaneity to risk taking, creativity and problem-solving."[182] Your own experience tells you that in North America, most members of the dominant culture adhere to the advice of Benjamin Franklin that tells them "Time is money." Think of what is being said about the use of time in the common expressions "He who hesitates is lost" and "Just give me the bottom line."

As in the case with all aspects of nonverbal communication, culture plays a substantial role in how you perceive and use time. As Lewis points out, "Fatalism, work ethic, reincarnation, *susu*, Confucianism, *Weltschmerz*, *dusha*, etc., all reveal different notions about time."[183] Ballard and Seibold establish much the same link between culture and time when they note: "The existence and proliferation of objective, independent time-measuring devices is itself a cultural by-product, and the uniform seconds, minutes, and hours that clocks appear to 'measure' also are culturally constructed."[184] Gannon highlights the bond between time and culture in the United States when he writes:

> Time is also limited in America because there are so many things to do in one's lifetime. The society develops technologically at horrendous speed, and it's difficult to keep up. One has to be continuously on the move. This is America: there is little time for contemplating or meditating.[185]

As you would suspect when cultures use time in dissimilar ways, problems can occur. As Novinger states, "When people of two different cultures 'use' time differently, their interaction can generate misunderstanding, misinterpretation, and ill will."[186] A culture's conception of time can be examined from three different perspectives: (1) *informal time*; (2) *perceptions of past, present, and future*; and (3) *Hall's monochronic and polychronic classifications*.

## Informal Time

**Punctuality.** In most instances, rules for informal time, such as *punctuality* and *pace*, are not explicitly taught. Like most of culture, these rules usually function below the level of consciousness. Argyle makes much the same point when he compares cultural differences in *punctuality* standards:

> How late is "late"? This varies greatly. In Britain and America one may be 5 minutes late for a business appointment, but not 15 and certainly not 30 minutes late, which is perfectly normal in Arab countries. On the other hand, in Britain it is correct to be 5–15 minutes late for an invitation to dinner. An Italian might arrive 2 hours late, an Ethiopian after, and Japanese not at all—he had accepted only to prevent his host from losing face.[187]

As the above example demonstrates, reaction to punctuality is rooted in our cultural experiences. In the United States, you have all learned that the boss can arrive late for a meeting without anyone raising an eyebrow; if the secretary is late, he or she may receive a reprimand in the form of a stern glance. A rock star or a physician can keep people waiting for long periods of time, but the warm-up band and the food caterer had better be on time. In Latin America, one is expected to arrive late to appointments as a sign of respect. In fact, in Chile it is even considered rude to be on time to social events.[188] This same notion of time is seen in Spain, where, according to Lewis, there is the belief that "punctuality messes up schedules."[189] In Africa, people often "show up late for appointments, meetings, and social engagements."[190]

There is even a Nigerian expression that says, "A watch did not invent man." These two views of tardiness would be perceived as rudeness in Germany. According to Hall and Hall, "Promptness is taken for granted in Germany—in fact, it's almost an obsession."[191]

**Pace.** We can determine a culture's attitude toward time by examining the *pace* at which members of that culture perform specific acts. Americans, because of the pace of life in the United States, always seem to be in a hurry. As Kim observes, "Life is in constant motion. People consider time to be wasted or lost unless they are doing something."[192] Conveniences help—from fast-food restaurants to one-stop gas stations to microwave ovens—as Andersen and Wang point out, "In the United States, time is viewed as a commodity that can be wasted, spent, saved, and used wisely."[193] The attitude toward time means that Americans want to get things done quickly. Americans are constantly seeking faster computers and cars. People in the United States grow up hearing others tell them not "to waste so much time" and "Actions speak louder than words." Other cultures see time differently and hence live life at a pace different from that of most people in the United States. Asselin and Mastron point out that "the French do not share the American sense of urgency to accomplish tasks."[194] The Japanese and Chinese cultures also treat time in ways that often appear at cross-purposes with American goals. The Chinese have a proverb that states, "He who hurries cannot walk with dignity." Drawing on the Japanese culture for his example, Brislin illustrates how pace is reflected in the negotiation process:

> When negotiating with the Japanese, Americans like to get right down to business. They were socialized to believe that "time is money." They can accept about 15 minutes of "small talk" about the weather, their trip, and baseball, but more than that becomes unreasonable. The Japanese, on the other hand, want to get to know their business counterparts. They feel that the best way to do this is to have long conversations with Americans about a wide variety of topics. The Japanese are comfortable with hours and hours, and even days and days, of conversation.[195]

Indonesians are yet another group that does not hurry. They perceive time as a limitless pool. According to Harris and Moran, there is even "a phrase in Indonesia describing this concept that translates as 'rubber time,' so that time stretches or shrinks and is therefore very flexible."[196] People in Latin America also have a view of time that sees them conducting their business at a slower pace than the one found in the United States. For these cultures there is belief "that there is always another day." In Africa, where a slow pace is the rule, "People who rush are suspected of trying to cheat," says Ruch.[197]

As we have mentioned elsewhere, nonverbal behavior is often directly linked to a culture's religious and value orientation. This notion is made manifest when you turn to the Arab culture. As we discussed in Chapter 3 when we looked at Islam, most Arabs believe that their destiny is a matter of fate. The Arab connection to the pace of life and time is clearly pointed out by Abu-Gharbieh:

> Throughout the Arab world, there is nonchalance about time and deadlines: the pace of life is more leisurely than in the West. Social events and appointments tend not to have a fixed beginning or end.[198]

Manifestations of pace assume a host of forms. One study, for example, pointed out that even the speed at which people walk reflects a culture's concept of time. People from England and the United States move much faster than people from Taiwan and Indonesia.[199]

**Past, Present, and Future.** How a culture perceives and uses the concepts of past, present, and future was discussed in Chapter 5 when we looked at cultural values. Let us review some of those findings so that you can see how time is tied not only to cultural values but also to nonverbal communication.

*Past Orientation.* As the word "past" tells you, cultures with this orientation attach great importance to the past and use what went before as a gauge for their current perception of people and events. Richmond, McCracken, and Paye offer an excellent summary of the link between the past and comprehending the present: "Cultures that have a past-oriented philosophy tend to apply past events to similar new situations. These societies have respect for the elderly and listen to what their senior citizens have to say regarding the past."[200] As we mentioned, knowing that a culture is past oriented can give you insight into how members of that culture view the world and other people. For example, the British place much emphasis on tradition and are often perceived as resisting change. A statement often heard in England when people ask about the monarchy is "We have always done it this way." The Chinese and Japanese, with their traditions of ancestor worship and strong pride in their cultures' persistence for thousands of years, are also cultures that use the past as a guide to how to live in the present. As a Chinese proverb advises, "Consider the past and you will know the present." The Irish and Irish Americans also take great pride in their past, making them yet another culture that is past oriented. As Wilson notes, "Irish-Americans, with their strong sense of tradition, are typically past oriented. They have an allegiance to the past, their ancestors, and their history. The past is often the focus of Irish stories."[201]

American Indians represent another culture that uses the past to help explain and understand life. Still and Hodgins explain this approach in the following manner:

> Most American Indian tribes are not future oriented. Very little planning is done for the future because their view is that many things are outside of the individual's control and may affect or change the future. In fact, the Navajo language does not include a future tense verb. Time is not viewed as a constant or something that one can control, but rather as something that is always with the individual. Thus, to plan for the future is something viewed as foolish.[202]

*Present Orientation.* In this orientation, the past is not nearly as important as the present. Present-oriented people see the future as ambiguous and capricious. Filipinos and Latin Americans are cultures that emphasize enjoying and living in the moment. These cultures tend to be more impulsive and spontaneous than others and often have a casual, relaxed lifestyle. Mexican Americans also have a culture that "tends to focus on the present and a more flexible attitude toward time."[203] Because of this outlook, "the quality of an interpersonal relationship, rather than the amount of time spent with someone, is of higher importance."[204] This approach to time frequently misinterprets a concern with the present as a sign of indolence and inefficiency.

*Future Orientation.* In future-oriented cultures, what is yet to come is most valued. Change, taking chances, and optimism are part of the hallmarks of cultures that hold to this orientation. This view toward the future is the one most Americans have. As a people, Americans are constantly planning for the future, and their children play with toys (dolls, cars, guns, and so on) that prepare them for adulthood. Many of you can hardly wait to finish what you are doing so that you can move on to something else. As we noted during our discussion of pace, having an eye to the future often produces a very low tolerance for extensions and postponements. What you want, you want now, so you can dispose of this moment and move on to the next. In addition, future-oriented cultures welcome innovation and "have less regard for past social or organizational customs and traditions."[205]

Distinctions in time orientations, like all aspects of nonverbal communication, can create communication differences. A business meeting involving these three orientations might look something like the following conversation:

**Past orientation:** Why don't we look at how much success we had with a similar merger with a Japanese company five years ago?

**Present orientation:** Just wait a second. It really doesn't matter what we did five years ago. The key is what we want to do now.

**Future orientation:** Only worrying about what is going on now is shortsighted. For this company to make money we need to think about what this merger will mean in the future.

**Monochronic (M-time) and Polychronic (P-time) Classifications.** Anthropologist Edward T. Hall advanced another classification of time as a form of communication. Hall proposed that cultures organize time in one of two ways: either monochronic (M-time) or polychronic (P-time).[206] Hall's classifications represent two distinct approaches to perceiving and utilizing time.

*M-time.* As the word *monochronic* implies, this concept explains time as lineal and segmented. More specifically, "A monochronic view of time believes time is a scarce resource which must be rationed and controlled through the use of schedules and appointments, and through aiming to do only one thing at any one time."[207] Novinger sums up the characteristics of monochronic cultures by noting, "Cultures that are monchronic have a predominantly linear and sequential approach to time that is rational, suppresses spontaneity and tends to focus on one activity at a time."[208] Cultures with this orientation would, of course, value punctuality, good organization, and the judicious use of time. The English naturalist Charles Darwin abstracted this view of time when he wrote, "A man who dares to waste one hour of time has not discovered the value of life." The time clock records the hours you must work, the school bell moves you from class to class, and the calendar marks important days and events in your lives.

Cultures that can be classified as M-time are people from Germany, Austria, Switzerland, and America. As Hall explains, "People of the Western world, particularly Americans, tend to think of time as something fixed in nature, something around us and from which we cannot escape; an ever-present part of the environment, just like the air we breathe."[209] According to Trompenaars and Hampden-Turner, you can see in the business setting how cultures that view time in a sequential pattern would schedule in advance and not run late and have "a strong preference for following initial plans."[210]

*P-time.* People from cultures on polychronic time live their lives quite differently than do those who move to the monochronic clock. People and human relationships are at the center of polychronic cultures. As Smith and Bond point out, "A polychronic view of time sees the maintenance of harmonious relationships as the important agenda, so that use of time needs to be flexible in order that we do right by the various people to whom we have obligations."[211] These cultures are normally collective and deal with life in a holistic manner. For P-time cultures, time is less tangible; hence, feelings of wasted time are not as prevalent as in M-time cultures. They can interact with more than one person or do more than one thing at a time. Gannon offers an excellent example of the multidimensional nature of P-time when he talks of the Turkish culture. "'Polychronism' best describes the Turkish ability to concentrate on different things simultaneously at work, at home, or in the coffee house."[212] Because P-time has this notion of multiple activities and flexibility, Dresser believes it "explains why there is more interrupting in conversations carried on by people from Arabic, Asian, and Latin American cultures."[213] Africans are yet another culture that takes great stock in the activity that is occurring at the moment and emphasize people more than schedules. As Richmond and Gestrin note, "Time for Africans is defined by events rather than the clock or calendar."[214] "For Africans, the person they are with is more important than the one who is out of sight."[215] This leads, of course, to a lifestyle that to outsiders appears to be spontaneous and unstructured.

Within the United States, there are co-cultures that use time differently from the dominant culture. Mexican Americans frequently speak of "Latino time" when their timing varies from that of the dominant culture. Burgoon and Saine have observed that the Polynesian culture of Hawaii has "Hawaiian time,"[216] a concept of time that is very relaxed and reflects the informal lifestyle of the native Hawaiian people. And among Samoans, there is a time perspective referred to as "coconut time," which is derived from the notion that it is not necessary to pick coconuts because they will fall when the time is right. African Americans often use what is referred to as "BPT" (Black People's Time) or "hang-loose time."[217] This concept, which has its roots in the P-time cultures of Africa, maintains that priority belongs to what is happening at that instant. Statements such as "Hey, man, what's happenin'?" reflect the importance of the here and now.

In Table 7.1, Hall and Hall summarize the basic aspects of monochronic and polychronic time. Their condensation takes many of the ideas we have mentioned and translates them into specific behaviors.

**TABLE 7.1** Comparison of Monochronic and Polychronic Cultures

| MONOCHRONIC TIME PEOPLE | POLYCHRONIC TIME PEOPLE |
| --- | --- |
| Do one thing at a time | Do many things at once |
| Concentrate on the job | Are easily distracted and subject to interruption |
| Take time commitments (deadlines, schedules) seriously | Consider time commitments an objective to be achieved, if possible |
| Are low context and need information | Are high context and already have information |
| Are committed to the job | Are committed to people and human relationships |
| Adhere to plans | Change plans often and easily |
| Are concerned about not disturbing others; follow rules of privacy | Are more concerned with people close to them (family, friends, close business associates) than with privacy |
| Show great respect for private property; seldom borrow or lend | Borrow and lend things often and easily |
| Emphasize promptness | Base promptness on the relationship |
| Are accustomed to short-term relationships | Have strong tendency to build lifetime relationships |

*Source:* Adapted from Edward T. Hall and Mildred Reed Hall, *Understanding Cultural Differences: Germans, French, and Americans* (Yarmouth, ME: Intercultural Press, 1990), 15.

## SILENCE

An African proverb states, "Silence is also speech." We contend that silence can send nonverbal cues concerning the communication situations in which you participate. Observe the poignant use of silence when the classical composer strategically places intervals of orchestration so that the ensuing silence marks a contrast in expression. Silence can indeed be a powerful message. There is a story of how the American philosopher Ralph Waldo Emerson "talked" in silence for hours to the famous English writer Thomas Carlyle. It seems that Emerson, on a visit to Europe, arranged to meet with Carlyle, who was his idol. Emerson maintains they sat together for hours in perfect silence until it was time for him to go, then parted company cordially, congratulating each other on the fruitful time they had had together.

Periods of silence affect interpersonal communication by providing an interval in an ongoing interaction during which the participants have time to think, check or suppress an emotion, encode a lengthy response, or inaugurate another line of thought. Silence also helps provide feedback, informing both sender and receiver about the clarity of an idea or its significance in the overall interpersonal exchange. Silence cues may be interpreted as evidence of agreement, lack of interest, injured feelings, or contempt. Silence can transcend the verbal channel, often revealing what speech conceals. The intercultural implications of silence as a means of interpreting ongoing verbal interactions are as diverse as those of other nonverbal cues, as Crystal helps to illustrate:

> Cross-cultural differences are common over when to talk and when to remain silent, or what a particular instance of silence means. In response to the question "Will you marry me?" silence in English would be interpreted as uncertainty; in Japanese it would be interpreted as acceptance. In Igbo, it would be considered a denial if the woman were to continue to stand there and an acceptance if she ran away.[218]

Knowing how various cultures use silence is an essential component for anyone who interacts with a culture different from their own. As Braithwaite points out:

> One of the basic building blocks of competence, both linguistic and cultural, is knowing when not to speak in a particular community. Therefore, to understand where and when to be silent, and the meaning attached to silence, is to gain a keen insight into the fundamental structure of communication in that world.[219]

Silence is not a meaningful part of the life of most members of the dominant culture in the United States. Talking, watching television, listening to music, and other sound-producing activities keep us from silence. Numerous studies have pointed out that most Americans believe that talking is an important activity and actually enjoy talking.[220] Beamer and Varner point out that Americans "often feel responsible for starting a conversation or keeping it going, even with strangers."[221] The assumption is that silence indicates a lack of attention and interest. Other cultures also have a similar positive view of talking over silence. Within the business context, Lewis notes that "a silent reaction to a business proposal would seem negative to American, German, French, Southern European and Arab executives."[222] It seems that there is a link between cultures that stress social interaction (Jewish, Italian, French, Arab, etc.) and their perception of and use of silence. In fact, talking in these cultures is highly valued. In the Greek culture, there is also a belief that being in the company of other people and engaging in conversation are signs of a good life. There are no references to concepts of solitude and silence; rather, history and literature are replete with allusions to rhetoric and dialogues. The culture that produced Aristotle, Plato, and Socrates is not one that will find silent meditation very appealing. This is in sharp contrast to cultures in which a hushed and still environment is the rule. We now look at a few cultural variations in the use of silence so that you might better understand how a lack of words can influence the outcome of any communication event.

In the Eastern tradition, the view of silence is much different from the Western view. Easterners do not feel uncomfortable with the absence of noise or talk and are not compelled to fill every pause when they are around other people. There is a belief in many Eastern traditions that words can contaminate an experience and that inner peace and wisdom come only through silence. Barnlund says of Buddhism, "One of its tenets is that words are deceptive and silent intuition is a truer way to confront the world; mind-to-mind communication through words is less reliable than heart-to-heart communication through an intuitive grasp of things."[223] Further, Buddhism teaches that "what is real is, and when it is spoken it becomes unreal." The Chinese philosopher Confucius had much the same view of silence when he counseled "Believe not others' tales, / Others will lead thee far astray"; "Silence is a friend who will never betray." For many Asian people silence is often used as a means of avoiding conflict. Chan explains this idea when he writes, "A typical practice among many Asian peoples is to refuse to speak any further in conversation if they cannot personally accept the speaker's attitude, opinion, or way of thinking about particular issues or subjects."[224]

Silence is very complex in the Japanese culture in that it can serve a variety of purposes. First, among family members silence is actually seen as a way of "talking." In the following example Kerr offers an interesting explanation of how silence takes the place of words for the Japanese:

> When people say "There's no communication between parent and children," this is an American way of thinking. In Japan we didn't need spoken communication between parents and children. A glance at the face, a glance back, and we understand enough.[225]

Second, silence is often linked to credibility. That is, someone who is silent is often perceived as having higher credibility than someone who talks too much. Jaworski makes this point when he notes, "Reticent individuals are trusted as honest, sincere, and straightforward. Thus silence is an active state, while speech is an excuse for delaying activity."[226] The Japanese also use silence to avoid both conflict and embarrassment.[227] The Japanese view of silence is also reflected in the following proverbs: "It is the duck that squawks that gets shot," "Numerous words show scanty wares," "A flower does not speak," and "The mouth is to eat with, not to speak with." Compare these perceptions of silence with the American saying "The squeaky wheel gets the grease." You can easily imagine how the use of silence might create communication problems when people representing these two divergent styles come together. For example, Adler says that during business negotiations between Japanese and Americans, each has a different rendering of the same silent period. The Japanese use the silence to "consider the Americans' offer; the Americans interpret the silence as rejection."[228]

Silence plays a dominant role in the Indian culture. The Hindu believes that "self-realization, salvation, truth, wisdom, peace, and bliss are all achieved in a state of meditation and introspection when the individual is communicating with himself or herself in silence."[229] As you would suspect, to accomplish these states you would have to remain still and avoid talk.

Many Scandinavian cultures, like Asian cultures, also have a view of silence that differs from the one found in the dominant culture in the United States. For example, in Finland, Sweden, Denmark, and Norway, silence conveys interest and consideration. In fact, your silence tells the other person that you want them to continue talking.[230]

Some co-cultures living in the United States also differ from the dominant American culture in the use of silence. Many American Indians believe that silence, not speaking, is a sign of a remarkable person. The famous Indian leader Chief Joseph is quoted as saying, "It does not require many words to speak the truth." Johannesen, in discussing the meaning of silence among American Indians, noted that for this co-culture "one derives from silence the cornerstone of character, the virtues of self-control, courage, patience and dignity."[231] American Indians use silence as a gesture of respect to persons of authority, age, and wisdom. Among Navajos, if someone does not use silence and responds too quickly when asked a question, they are considered immature.[232] In social settings, silence is the rule when a Native American is meeting a stranger, during periods of mourning, when dealing with someone who is exceptionally angry, or greeting someone who has been gone for a long period of time.[233]

Two points should be obvious from our discussion of silence. First, you must be careful not to assume that people are communicating only when they talk. As the American composer John Cage declared, "There is no such thing as empty space or an empty time. There is always something to see, something to hear. In fact, try as we may to make silence, we cannot." Second, because of cultural variations in this form of communication, it behooves you to know cultural attitudes toward talk, noise, and silence. This knowledge can save you from both anxiety and ethnocentrism in intercultural communication.

# Summary

- We make important judgments and decisions about others based on their nonverbal behavior and also judgments about their emotional states.
- Nonverbal communication is culture-bound.
- Nonverbal communication involves all nonverbal stimuli in a communication setting that are generated by both the source and his or her use of the environment and that have potential message value for the source or receiver.
- Nonverbal messages may be both intentional and unintentional.
- Nonverbal communication has five basic functions: to repeat, complement, substitute for a verbal action, regulate, and contradict a communication event.
- Nonverbal actions seldom occur in isolation.
- Nonverbal communication and culture are similar in that both are learned, both are passed on from generation to generation, and both involve shared understandings.
- Studying nonverbal behavior can lead to the discovery of a culture's underlying attitudes and values.
- Studying nonverbal behavior can also assist us in isolating our own ethnocentrism.
- Your body is a major source of nonverbal messages. These messages are communicated by means of general appearance and attire, body movements (kinesics), facial expressions, eye contact, touch, and paralanguage.
- Cultures differ in their perception and use of personal space, seating, and furniture arrangement.

- We can understand a culture's sense of time by learning about how members of that culture view informal time, the past, present, and future, and whether or not their orientation toward time is monochronic or polychronic.
- The use of silence varies from culture to culture.

# Activities

1. Locate pictures from magazines and newspapers that you believe are showing the following facial expression: (a) anger, (b) joy, (c) sadness, (d) fear, and (e) revulsion. Show these pictures to people from various cultures and see what interpretations they give to the facial expressions.
2. Ask your informant (from a culture different from your own) to demonstrate examples of his or her culture's use of communicative body movements (kinesics). What similarities are there between yours and your informant's? What differences are there? What are the potential areas for misunderstandings?
3. In small groups, produce an inventory of common American gestures. An example of one is the "OK" gesture: the thumb and forefinger of one hand form an "O," and the rest of the fingers on that hand arch above the "O." What other gestures can you think of? Compare your findings with those of the rest of the class and make a master list.
4. Watch a foreign film and look for examples of differences in proxemics, touch, and facial expressions. Compare these differences to the dominant culture of North America.
5. In a small group, read the following paragraph and explain what went wrong:

> Jan was in Brazil on business. Ciro, a Brazilian associate, invited her to a dinner party he and his wife were hosting. The invitation was for "around 8, this Friday night." Jan arrived at Ciro's house at exactly 8:00. Ciro and his wife were still dressing and had not even begun to prepare the food.

6. Select an airport, supermarket, or shopping mall where people from different cultural backgrounds might be interacting. Observe the interactions by referencing the items listed below:
   a. What are the average distances between the people you observed? Were there differences related to culture?
   b. What differences did you observe in touching behavior?

# Discussion Ideas

1. Why is it useful to understand the nonverbal language of a culture?
2. In what situations might you need to interpret the nonverbal behavior of someone from another culture? What problems could arise from not understanding differences in nonverbal behavior?
3. Give your culture's interpretation of the following nonverbal actions:
   - Two people are speaking loudly, waving their arms, and using a lot of gestures.
   - A customer in a restaurant waves his hand over his head and snaps his fingers loudly.
   - An elderly woman dresses entirely in black.
   - A young man dresses entirely in black.
   - An adult pats a child's head.
   - Two men kiss in public.
4. How can studying the intercultural aspects of nonverbal behavior assist you in discovering your own ethnocentrism? Give personal examples.
5. How late can you be for the following? (a) a class, (b) work, (c) a job interview, (d) a dinner party, (e) a date with a friend. Now ask these same questions of members of Latin American and Asian cultures.
6. What is meant by "Nonverbal communication is rule governed"?
7. In a small group, discuss the following topic: Are there more cross-cultural nonverbal behaviors that are alike or more that are different?

## CHAPTER 8

# Cultural Influences on Context: The Business Setting

*Live together like brothers and do business like strangers.*

**ARAB PROVERB**

*You will never know a man till you do business with him.*

**SCOTTISH PROVERB**

## Culture and Context

There is a well-known saying that everyone has to be someplace. The next three chapters are about those places—the settings or contexts in which communication events occur. Communication is not immune from external influence—it does not take place in a void. All human interaction, therefore, is influenced to some degree by the cultural, social, and physical settings in which it occurs. These settings are called the *communication context*.

To a large degree, your culture specifies the appropriate communicative behavior within a variety of social and physical contexts by prescribing rules that dictate correct deportment for specific communicative situations. When communicating with members of your own culture, you and your cohorts rely on internalized cultural rules that stipulate the appropriate behaviors for the specific communication situation. These rules enable you to communicate effectively with each other, and since they are a product of your enculturation, you do not have to consciously think about which rules to use—you intuitively know which rules to apply when communicating in a given context. But when engaging in intercultural communication, things can be different, because you and your communication partners may be operating from a set of very different rules. To be a competent intercultural communicator, you must be aware of how diverse cultural rules influence the communication context. Otherwise, you may encounter a variety of surprises—some of which could be embarrassing, detrimental, or both!

*The setting where business is conducted and the rules that are applied to the transaction are greatly influenced by culture.*

© Gloria Thomas

# Communication and Context

In order to help you understand just how important context is to intercultural communication, we will review three basic assumptions about human communication: (1) *communication is rule governed*, (2) *context prescribes appropriate communication rules*, and (3) *communication rules are culturally diverse*.

## COMMUNICATION IS RULE GOVERNED

Both consciously and unconsciously, people expect that their interactions will follow culturally determined rules and shared forms of behavior. Social settings usually stipulate which rules govern a particular situation, but it is culture that makes the rules. In Saudi Arabia, for instance, a contextual rule prohibits men and women, including married couples, from touching each other in public.[1] In the United States, however, such public displays of affection are quite acceptable and common. Communication rules govern both verbal and nonverbal behaviors and specify not only what should be said but also how it should be said. Nonverbal rules, as we saw in Chapter 7, apply to touch (who gets touched and where), facial expressions, (where and when to reveal a smile), eye contact (the appropriateness and inappropriateness of staring), and paralanguage (when to whisper, when to shout).

Verbal rules govern such things as turn taking, voice volume, and formality of language. Obviously, the rules differ depending on the context. In a job interview, you might use formal or respectful words such as "sir" or "ma'am" when responding to your potential employer. At a football or basketball game, your language would be far less formal, incorporating slang phrases and quite possibly good natured derogatory remarks about the opposing team or the officials. For the job interview, you might wear what

U.S. Americans call a "power suit" (i.e., a dark suit with white or blue shirt and conservative tie for men or a dark suit, possibly pin-striped, with a white or pastel blouse for women), whereas at the sports event, jeans or shorts and a T-shirt could be appropriate. Your nonverbal behavior would also be different. At the interview, you would probably shake hands with your prospective employer, but at the game, you might hug your friends, slap them on the back, or hit a "high-five" (a hand gesture) as a form of greeting.

## CONTEXT SPECIFIES COMMUNICATION RULES

Our second assumption about communication is that the context specifies the appropriate rules. Think for a moment about how such diverse contexts as a classroom, bank, church, hospital, courtroom, wedding, funeral, or a day at the beach determines which communication rules apply. Also, imagine the responses of others if your behavior deviates from expected norms. Extreme deviations can lead to social sanctions such as being ignored, being asked to leave a theater, or even being cited for contempt of court.

## COMMUNICATION RULES ARE CULTURALLY DIVERSE

A third assumption is that rules are culturally diverse. Although cultures have many of the same social settings or contexts, they frequently abide by different rules. Consequently, concepts of dress, time, language, manners, nonverbal behavior, and control of the communication ebb and flow can differ significantly among cultures. When doing business in Turkey, for example, your Turkish colleagues will insist on paying for all the entertainment. Turkish hospitality is legendary, and they will not permit you to pay for any part of the meal.[2] In the United States, the rules for business entertaining are very different. The cost of the meal or entertainment is often shared. Different cultures, different rules.

To be successful in intercultural communication, it is essential to be aware of your own culture's rules and also the cultural rules of the person with whom you are interacting. If you understand the rules, the other person's behavior will make greater sense to you, and you will be better prepared to control and modify your own behavior to meet his or her expectations.

In this chapter, we examine how culture influences communication in the *business setting*. In the next chapter, we will consider the *educational setting* context, and in Chapter 10, we will explore the *health care setting* context. We have selected these three arenas because they represent three common contexts in which you are likely to encounter people from cultures different from your own.

# Assessing the Context

Before moving to a detailed analysis of specific settings, we need to pause and examine three communication variables that are woven in and out of every communication setting. That is to say, regardless of the communication context, (1) *formality and informality*, (2) *assertiveness and interpersonal harmony*, and (3) *status relationships* play a major role in how people respond to their interpersonal and organizational environments.

# FORMALITY AND INFORMALITY

Cultures tend to range from very informal views of events and people to perceptions that are quite formal. The manifestations of informality and formality take many forms and include such diverse behaviors as the way people dress, their posture, how someone is addressed, and even the type of speech used.

**Informality.** Grounded in a strong belief in individualism and equality, the United States has long been considered an *informal* culture. As Javidi and Javidi have pointed out, "In North America people tend to treat others with informality and directness. They avoid the use of formal codes of conduct, titles, honorific, and ritualistic manners in their interactions with others."[3]

U.S. informality is manifested in a host of ways. For example, regardless of their social position, most U.S. Americans will quickly move to using first names when meeting strangers or beginning a business venture. Even the simple greeting "Hi" can be seen as a reflection of American informality in other cultures. Althen offers the following summary of how informality is commonly reflected in U.S. culture:

> Idiomatic speech and slang are liberally used on most occasions, with formal speech reserved for public events and fairly formal situations. People from almost any station in life can be seen in public wearing jeans, sandals, or other informal attire. People slouch down in chairs or lean on walls or furniture when they talk, rather than maintaining an erect bearing.[4]

The informality and openness displayed by U.S. Americans can be a source of confusion, misunderstanding, and embarrassment for people from more formal cultures. Steward and Bennett offer some examples to buttress this important point:

> The degree of informality found in American communication patterns is uncommon in other cultures. In most Latin American and European societies, for instance, there are levels of formality attached to status difference. In Asian cultures, formal communication may be demanded by greater age as well as by higher status. In Japan, formality is also extended to strangers with whom a relationship is demanded. This formality is no joking matter, since failure to follow appropriate form may suggest to others a severe flaw in character.[5]

**Formality.** In contrast to the high degree of informality found in the U.S., there are many examples of cultures that place a high value on formality. In Egypt, Turkey, and Japan, for instance, the student/teacher relationship is very formal. This may be seen in the Egyptian proverb "Whoever teaches me a letter, I should become a slave to him forever." In these countries, when the teacher enters the room, students are expected to stand. When students meet their teachers on the street, they are expected to bow to them. Contrast this with the relaxed, informal student/teacher relationships found in the United States.

Formality is also evident in how cultures use forms of address. Not knowing these differences can cause problems during intercultural exchanges. Germans, for example, address others and conduct themselves in a very formal manner, which many U.S. Americans would consider extreme. Hall and Hall note, "American informality and the habit of calling others by their first names make Germans acutely uncomfortable, particularly when young people or people lower in the hierarchy address their elders or their superiors by their first names."[6] The extensive use of titles to identify people and their positions in the social structure is another way the Germans exhibit their formality. For instance, if Helmut Schröder was both a professor and a medical doctor, he would be referred to as *Herr Professor Doktor* Schröder (i.e., Mr. Professor Doctor). Germany is not the only place where forms of address are directly linked to perception and values. Morrison, Conaway, and Borden report that titles play an important role in India, where first names are usually reserved for close friends.[7] Schneider and Silverman remind us that Mexicans are yet another culture that values formality:

> Mexicans also make heavy use of honorific titles to show respect. New acquaintances met at a party are addressed as *señor, señora,* and *señorita.* In business, people address managers with titles like director, doctor, *ingeniero* (engineer), or *licienciado* (someone who has a higher education degree).[8]

The significance of informality and formality in communication goes well beyond a culture's use of language. The number of friends you have, your closeness to those friends, and what you tell those friends are also affected. In a study on intercultural friendships, Gareis noted, "Whereas Americans are easily accessible," Germans tend to be formal and private even when dealing with their friends.[9] This is exemplified by a German proverb that states, "A friend to everyone is a friend to no one."

Kim uses a peach and a coconut as metaphors to contrast the differences in interpersonal relationships in the U.S. and Japan. U.S. informality tends to make people generally friendly toward everyone and forming relationships comes easy. But highly personal, deep feelings, which would make an individual vulnerable, are seldom revealed to others. This practice is likened to a peach, with a soft exterior and a hard center. The Japanese, in contrast, are characterized as being like a coconut, with a hard exterior that is difficult to penetrate. The Japanese use formality as a shell to keep people at a distance while deciding if a relationship is desired. Once the shell is penetrated, however, the Japanese are very affectionate, generosity is all encompassing, and personal vulnerability is not a concern.[10]

It is easy to imagine the outcome of a cross-cultural business venture if, at the initial meeting, the U.S. Americans were offering personal information about themselves, speaking in an informal manner, and using their counterparts' first names, while the Japanese were doing exactly the opposite.

## ASSERTIVENESS AND INTERPERSONAL HARMONY

The second important dimension of culture that affects the communication context is the manner in which people present themselves to others. While there are many aspects of communication styles, *assertiveness* and *interpersonal harmony* directly influence the intercultural setting—be it in a business meeting, classroom, or health care context.

**Assertiveness.** U.S. culture is known for its assertive communication style. It is not uncommon for U.S. Americans to enroll in assertiveness training classes, where they are encouraged and taught to be frank, open, and direct when dealing with other people. Think about the style of communication displayed on the MSNBC or Fox News television political talk shows, where participants frequently end up shouting at each other in an effort to make their point. In the sports arena, "trash talk" is commonplace between members of opposing teams, from high school to professional games. While the communication styles in these two settings tend to be exaggerations of the norm, they serve to illustrate the positive value that is placed on communicative assertiveness in the U.S.

The many signs of assertive and aggressive behavior among U.S. Americans, like all aspects of culture, did not develop by chance. A culture that has a long history of valuing nonconformity, individualism, competition, freedom of expression, and even some select forms of rebellion is bound to encourage assertive behavior. The reason Americans value assertive communication, according to Nadler, Nadler, and Broome, are obvious: "North American individuals are expected to stand up for their rights, and this often involves confrontation."[11] This idea is enforced by Wenzhong and Grove:

> In a culture where individualism is as highly valued as it is in the United States, people are expected to take the initiative in advancing their personal interests and well-being and to be direct and assertive in interacting with others. High social and geographic mobility and the comparatively superficial nature of many personal attachments create a climate where interpersonal competition and a modest level of abrasiveness are tolerated and even expected.[12]

**Interpersonal Harmony.** While the U.S. and some Western European cultures, such as Germany and Israel,[13] see assertiveness as an asset, other cultures see it as threatening and detrimental to harmonious interpersonal relations. Among Northeast and Southeast Asian cultures, mutual agreement, loyalty, and reciprocal obligation underlie the importance placed on harmonious relations.

To better understand the value some people assign to interpersonal harmony, we turn to the Filipino culture. According to Gochenour, for members of the Filipino culture, "The ultimate ideal is one of harmony—between individuals, among the members of a family, among the group divisions of society, and of all life in relationship with God."[14] Filipinos have two terms that express their conception of harmony: *amor propio* and *pakikisama*. *Amor propio* translates into English as "harmony" and refers to a very fragile sense of personal worth and self-respect. In interactions with others, it denotes being treated as a person rather than as an object. This value makes the Filipino especially vulnerable to negative remarks that may affect his or her standing in society. Consequently, Filipinos seldom criticize or verbally confront others, and if they do, it is in the most polite manner.[15] They see bluntness and frankness as uncivilized traits. Instead they value *pakikisama*, or smooth interpersonal relations.[16]

Maintaining harmonious relations is also a primary consideration among the Japanese, in both personal and professional settings. For the Japanese, harmony is more a product of adhering to accepted models of behavior than a compelling principle. Since deviance is considered threatening and disruptive, most Japanese willingly accept and adopt normative expectations during social and professional interactions. This ensures, on the surface, a smooth-running organization and presents the appearance of a homogeneous, cooperative collective.[17] As Schneider and Silverman point out, "in their society, values and norms forcefully promote self-control and the avoidance of direct personal confrontation."[18] Accordingly, to avoid disruption and maintain harmony within the organization, the market, or the nation, Japanese business executives will sometimes make corporate profit a subordinate consideration.[19] Gao and Ting-Toomey point out that, like the Filipinos and Japanese, the Chinese "tend to regard conflict and confrontation as unpleasant and undesirable."[20] Chen and Xiao underscore this same point when they state: "It is without a doubt that harmony is one of the primordial values of Confucianism and of the Chinese culture."[21]

For reasons different from those found in Asian cultures, Mexicans also value smooth interpersonal relationships and try to avoid face-to-face confrontations. This makes the concept of truth situational in Mexico, and in order to sustain positive relations or make the other person feel better, Mexicans may slightly alter the facts or withhold important negative information. Condon notes that the practice of shading the truth in Mexico is so pervasive that it has become institutionalized.[22] Mexican efforts to avoid discord are seen in a number of different settings. Ruch, for example, notes that in the business context, "When a visitor asks for information that a Mexican doesn't have, the Mexican does his best to say something that will please the visitor."[23]

From these examples, you can visualize the communication problems that can arise when people from a culture that promotes assertiveness come in contact with individuals from a culture valuing accord and harmony. Imagine what might happen when a group of culturally unaware German businessmen begin negotiations with a delegation of Chinese, who are also culturally uninformed.

## STATUS RELATIONSHIPS

The third communication variable that influences nearly all communication settings relates to a culture's view on differences in status. Every society and organization has specific culturally based values and protocols to guide the interaction between people of varying social positions. Using a broad classification scale, a culture can generally be categorized as either egalitarian, with a low level of concern for social differences, or hierarchical, where significant emphasis is placed on status and rank.

**Egalitarian.** Egalitarianism facilitates and encourages informal interaction between subordinates and seniors, minimizing the expectation or need for deference and formality. A person's status is usually acquired through individual effort, rather than ascribed by birth, appointment, or age. This creates an environment of social mobility by encouraging the belief that everyone has the opportunity to improve their social status. However, individuals who enjoy positions of power often make it a habit to downplay appearances of their increased power and prestige.

The United States, Australia, and New Zealand are considered highly egalitarian cultures. Most U.S. Americans are little concerned with differences in social status and power. This is partly the result of the U.S. frontier heritage, when early settlers were forced to rely on hard work to survive. The rigid social formality and protocol common in Europe at that time found little utility in the harsh landscape of the colonies or along the western frontier.[24] As a result, equality, or the appearance of equality, became a cultural value that persists today.

This value is easily illustrated by press reports on how U.S. presidents spend their leisure time. Ronald Reagan was noted for chopping wood; Bill Clinton would often stop off at McDonald's while jogging in a T-shirt and running shorts; George W. Bush is frequently photographed clearing brush at his Texas ranch. These activities allowed each president to downplay his status and demonstrate that, outside the Oval Office, he is just like anyone else.

Questioning authority figures, be it in the classroom, a staff meeting, or a presidential press conference, is another manifestation of an egalitarian society. In a U.S. business setting, equality can be seen in the use of first names rather than titles and the easy access workers have to their superiors. Also, individuals are assigned to positions of increased responsibility based on their ability, rather than age or longevity with the organization.

**Hierarchical.** Cultures that subscribe to a hierarchical view of social status are in marked contrast to egalitarian cultures. In countries like Japan and Spain, differences in status are made obvious through proscribed protocols that govern interpersonal and organizational activities and even by the language style used. Real power is held by a few individuals, who may have achieved their position by means of family connections, level of education, or simply age. Merit or ability is often a secondary consideration. Interactions between subordinates and seniors are conducted in a formal manner, and titles are always used. Seniors are often expected to assume a patriarchal role in response to the junior member's deference.

The hierarchical tradition of many Asian countries results from Confucian philosophy, which began in early China.[25] Confucianism provides a specific, hierarchical social structure and contains well-defined guidelines for relations between seniors and juniors. Expressions of Confucian social hierarchy are clearly evident in China, Japan, Korea, Taiwan, Vietnam, and Singapore, where teachers receive the utmost respect, and students are not expected to question their professors. When meeting in Japan, the junior person always bows lower than the senior. Also, the junior will use a formal, polite level of language, while the senior may elect to use an informal style. Variation in language among people from hierarchical cultures is not limited to Asia. For example, in Spain, Mexico, and many of the Spanish-speaking cultures, the informal *tu* (you) is used among family, friends, and close acquaintances, but when dealing with more distant relations, the formal *usted* is used. India also has a history of very distinct hierarchical divisions derived from its caste system. Although the system was dissolved by law,[26] the persistent "belief that there are qualitative differences between the castes"[27] continues to influence relationships in India.

In a business setting, discordant relations can quickly develop if the participants adhere to conflicting views on egalitarianism and hierarchy. The behaviors and actions of representatives from hierarchical cultures are frequently dictated by culture-bound rules relating to status,[28] quite in contrast to the free-wheeling activities exhibited by egalitarians. Members of egalitarian cultures, however, enjoy greater freedom of action and individuality and may view the structured, regimented procedures followed by their hierarchical counterparts as unnecessary and overly formal. But consider how members of a Japanese delegation, which equates status with age, would react to a youthful Australian serving as the leader of his negotiating party.

Having looked at the potential impact of the overarching variables of informality, formality, assertiveness, interpersonal harmony, and status relationships, we are now ready to apply these dynamics, and others, to various intercultural settings. We begin by looking at the international business context. We will examine how communication is effected by various aspects of international business, including protocol, management, negotiations, decision making, and conflict management. To demonstrate the impact of globalization, an illustration is provided of how information technology (IT) is influencing some culturally based business protocols in Japan. Finally, we provide a brief overview of the domestic business context to draw attention to cultural diversity found in the U.S.

# Intercultural Communication in an Evolving Business Context

The first instances of cross-cultural trade are lost in antiquity, but probably occurred well before the historical record began. Archeological evidence has revealed the existence of trade diasporas more than three thousand years ago in what is now Iran,[29] and recorded history is replete with examples of cross-cultural trade. Between 1200 and 700 B.C., the Phoenicians sailed from ports in present-day Lebanon and established trade routes throughout the Mediterranean, traveling as far as the Atlantic coast of Spain. Goods from China were carried through Central Asia, along the Silk Road, to the Roman Empire. Later, Marco Polo is believed to have traveled this route to China, returning to Italy in the late thirteenth century with tales of riches and exotic cultures.[30] Voyages by sixteenth-century Portuguese explorers opened India, Southeast Asia, and China to Western trade settlements. Indeed, trade and exploitation were principal motives for the establishment of European colonies in Africa, the Americas, Southeast Asia, and the Pacific Islands. The shift from an agrarian to an industrial society, brought about by the Industrial Revolution in the latter half of the nineteenth century, expanded and accelerated cross-cultural trade. Increased means of production raised the requirement for raw materials, and distribution of the finished products necessitated greater access to foreign markets. The first half of the twentieth century found the industrialized nations competing for international resources and markets on a global scale.

The end of the Second World War created a world divided into three political spheres—communist, democratic, and non-aligned. Despite these ideological differences, however, international trade continued to expand at an ever-accelerating rate. The fall of the Berlin Wall in 1989 concluded more than forty years of political bipolarism and ushered in a new multipolar political order, underpinned by economic convergence and driven by sophisticated technological innovation. Contemporary transportation systems, telecommunication technologies, and increasingly advanced product distribution has brought about what Cairncross[31] calls the "death of distance," by significantly reducing, or even eliminating, time- and distance-related barriers. The importance of national borders has been greatly reduced in an era characterized by international joint ventures, mergers, licensing agreements, foreign capital investment, and off-shore production, resulting in increasing economic interdependencies between nations.

All developed and developing nations are now tied directly to an international system of economic interdependence, and most countries have at least one asset within their borders that is needed by another country. In 2004, the United States alone exported 1.15 trillion dollars in goods and services to its major trading partners.[32] Imports, however, amounted to 1.76 trillion dollars, resulting in a 617.7-billion-dollar trade deficit, a more than 24 percent increase from 2003.[33] The 2004 U.S. trade deficit with China was over 161 billion dollars[34] and a combined 110 billion dollars with the 25 members of the European Union.[35] U.S. economic interdependency was demonstrated by a 35 percent increase in demand for foreign oil in 2004.[36]

But international interdependencies in the twenty-first century are not restricted to raw materials and finished goods. Today, if you decided to call about your phone bill or credit card application, you may talk to someone in India, Ireland, the Bahamas, or even the Philippines. If you use a U.S. accounting firm to prepare your taxes, the forms may be completed in Bangalore, India. Communication technologies have allowed service industries to outsource tasks ranging from accounting to reading medical x-rays.[37] Off-shore service centers have become so extensive that sometimes local employees are given "accent neutralization"[38] classes in an effort to suppress their native accents or are trained to affect a regional U.S. accent.[39]

U.S. corporations are increasingly dependent on the international market. For example, the Coca-Cola corporation has operations in more than two hundred countries, and the U.S. market produces less than 30 percent of the annual revenues.[40] McDonald's operates more than 28,000 outlets in 119 nations.[41] The new kid on the block, Starbucks, has already expanded to more than "1,500 coffeehouses in 31 markets outside North America."[42]

International corporations also enjoy a broad presence in the U.S. For example, the makers of Baby Ruth candy bars are owned by a Swiss company. Both Baskin-Robbins ice cream and Snapple are subsidiaries of British corporations. The parent company of Ray-Ban sunglasses is based in Italy. Radio Corporation of America is part of a German organization. News Corp., a United Kingdom–based company, owns the Los Angeles Dodgers. The next time you see a Plymouth, Dodge, Jeep, or Chrysler automobile going down the freeway, recall that it was made by Daimler Chrysler, a Germany-based company.[43] Your television, DVD player, computer, and iPod were probably assembled in China. Nokia cell phones are manufactured by a Finnish corporation, and the network provider Verizon is part of a British organization. To see how business is becoming more and more international, just look at the operating instructions for a new iPod nano. You will find that the operations can be set in more than twenty languages.

The examples just cited are representative of the rise of multinational corporations and reflect the increasing international integration of business. According to Thomas, "Virtually all business conducted today is global business,"[44] which has generated greater contact between cultures. This contact, in turn, has created a need for knowledge and understanding on how to conduct business in a manner that accommodates different cultural rules. In a globalized marketplace, cross-cultural teamwork and collaboration are essential for an organization's success. Moreover, globalization generally results in individuals from one culture working not only with, but also for, individuals from another culture. This situation often proves to be difficult because, as Harris and Moran reveal, there are many problems when working or living in a foreign environment. Communication across cultural boundaries is difficult. Differences in customs, behavior, and values result in problems that can be managed only through effective cross-cultural communication and interaction.[45]

# The Multinational Business Context

The development of business communicative skills in a multinational marketplace represents a challenging endeavor. Such seemingly universal concepts as management, negotiation, decision making, and conflict management are frequently viewed differently from one culture to another. We now turn our attention toward the multinational business context and the views various cultures hold regarding (1) *business protocol*, (2) *management*, (3) *negotiations*, (4) *decision making*, and (5) *conflict management*.

## BUSINESS PROTOCOL

A popular bumper sticker in the United States reads "Rules Are for Fools." While this may be expressive of the high value Americans place on individualism and independence, we urge you not to follow that admonition when doing business with people from other cultures. In most parts of the world, culturally correct protocol is both expected and respected. To introduce you to some of the variations in protocol, we start with the elements that help initiate business relationships: (1) *initial contacts*, (2) *greeting behavior*, (3) *personal appearance*, (4) *gift giving*, and (5) *office spatial design*.

**Initial Contacts.** When engaging in international business, the ways in which you establish initial contact and make an appointment can range from a brief, unsolicited telephone call to writing a formal letter of request or the use of a "go-between" or emissary. The manner in which the initial business contact is made and the amount of advance notice between the contact and appointment are key factors you must consider when doing business in another culture.

A few examples should help clarify this point. In El Salvador and much of Latin America, including Mexico, appointments must be made at least a month in advance by mail or telephone and then verified one week before the meeting. In Latin American cultures, you should establish your contacts as high up in the organization as possible. Morrison, Conaway, and Borden suggest you "use a local *persona bien colocada* (well-connected person) to make introductions and contacts for you."[46]

While the "cold call" is common in the U.S. and can also be used in India, the use of trusted intermediaries is common, and often required, in many other cultures. For example, if you want an appointment in Egypt, you must send a letter of introduction to an Egyptian contact who can facilitate arranging a meeting. The use of an intermediary who is willing to set up appointments with all the right people is essential in the Egyptian business world. Endicott suggests that "Business by 'who you know' has always been an influential force in Egypt."[47]

In Africa, the use of an intermediary is also essential, which is exemplified by the Congolese proverb that states, "The friends of our friends are our friends." Richmond and Gestrin relate that intermediaries can open doors, ensure a warm reception for your upcoming visit, and assess the prospects for the proposal you plan to present. An intermediary is an absolute must in Africa when approaching someone of a higher status.[48]

"Nothing is possible in China without contacts," according to Zinzius.[49] There is even a proverb that states, "The go-between wears out a thousand sandals." The Chinese rely heavily on interpersonal relations, called *guanxi*, built and maintained through mutual obligations beginning with family, relatives, friends, and extending to organizational acquaintances. An international business person coming to China will have to establish a *guanxi* network, which may take considerable time—even years. The process can be expedited through the use of a mediator, preferably someone who is already well known in the Chinese business community.[50] To do business in Saudi Arabia, you need a sponsor who will act as an intermediary, make appointments, and arrange meetings. In Italy, as well, strong contacts who can represent you and make appropriate introductions are preferred. Even with such a representative, it is important that your initial contact be written and in Italian.

When planning initial meetings with business representatives from other countries, it is particularly important to select an appropriate date. Most cultures have their own unique schedule of national and religious holidays, and the successful international business person is always aware of those dates. For example, in China, many businesses close the week before and the week after the Chinese (Lunar) New Year. In Saudi Arabia, no business is conducted during *Aid-al-Fitr*—the three-day festival of breaking fast at the end of the month of Ramadan—and *Aid-al-Adha*—the three-day feast of sacrifice.[51] In Japan, business is not conducted during New Year's holidays, Golden Week (late April and early May), or *Obon*, (mid-August), when many people travel to visit the graves of their ancestors. In Israel, the Jewish holy day—the Sabbath—begins at sunset on Friday and ends at sunset on Saturday. The business week, therefore, runs from Sunday through Thursday. Attempting to conduct business on the Sabbath would be considered highly inappropriate. Friday is also the Muslim holy day, and in many Muslim nations this is a non-work day.

## GREETING BEHAVIORS

Once a meeting has been arranged and an agreeable date set, it is important that an effort be made to use the greeting practices of the host culture. Americans tend to be informal and friendly. Both men and women shake hands on meeting and leaving. First names generally are used with the exception of very senior persons or formal situations. Business cards are exchanged in business settings but seldom in strictly social gatherings. These greeting behaviors, typical to U.S. and Canadians, are uncommon in many

*Greeting behaviors are rule governed and often vary from culture to culture.*

©Digital Vision/Getty Images

other cultures. For instance, in Saudi Arabia, greetings involve numerous handshakes and tend to be expressive and elaborate. Saudi men often embrace and kiss on both cheeks. Saudi women are rarely present for business meetings, but when they are, an introduction is unlikely. Titles are very important for Saudis and are always used. Business cards are routinely exchanged and are printed in both Arabic and English.

Doing business in the People's Republic of China offers some additional contrasting examples. The Chinese business community is more formal than the U.S., and the use of titles is essential and reflects the cultural emphasis on hierarchy. In fact, the use of titles by the Chinese is so pervasive it often extends to work positions such as Chief Engineer, Accountant, Department Manager, and even Foreman.[52] It is also important to remember that in China, the order of names is reversed from that in the West. The Chinese place their family name (surname) first and their given name last. For example, in the name Wang Jintao, Wang is the family name and Jintao is the given name, and in English the proper address would be Mr. Wang. Many culturally uninformed Westerners have made the mistake of addressing their counterpart by their first name, thinking it was his or her last name.

The Chinese have widely adopted the Western handshake for initial and subsequent greetings. However, this does not extend to the common Western practice of a slap on the back or an arm around the shoulder. As Harris and Moran indicate, a slight bow and a brief shake of the hands is most appropriate.[53] Nonverbal gestures in China can also carry different meanings from those assigned in the West. For instance, the head nod is used by the Chinese to acknowledge the speaker, not to signal agreement. Zinzius reports that during discussions with the Chinese one should keep both feet on the ground because "It is extremely improper and a sign of disrespect to point one's shoe soles toward the counterpart."[54] The hierarchical nature of Chinese society also dictates that direct eye contact should be avoided. Whereas in the West you are expected to maintain a high degree of eye contact during discussions, the Chinese consider this to be rude and disrespectful.[55]

In Finland, firm handshakes are the normal greeting for men and women. Among the Finns, it is customary for women to be greeted first. So important is a firm handshake to the Finnish that even children are encouraged to shake hands. However, hugs and kisses are reserved for greetings with close friends and family. Introductions include first and last names or a title and a last name. Unlike the Chinese, the Finns expect you to maintain direct eye contact during conversations.[56] Desai offers one final example of cultural variations in greeting behavior. In India, Bangladesh, and Nepal, a common social greeting is the *namaste*,[57] where one presses the hands together near the chest, as in prayer, and bows slightly toward the other person.

With few exceptions, international business representatives are encouraged to try and practice the cultural protocols of the host nation. We now need to address one of those exceptions. The Japanese are well known for their custom of bowing when meeting someone. What is less well known is that, among the Japanese, the bow is a highly refined practice filled with many subtle nuances as to who bows first, how low, and how long. These distinctions, which the Japanese begin learning as children, can be difficult if not impossible for a foreigner to master. According to Dunung, the complexity is so great that

> The Japanese recognize this truth and do not expect foreigners to bow. It is best not to try and imitate Japanese bows unless you have studied the art thoroughly, for your own good intentions may result in an improper bow that offends someone. For foreign men and women, a respectful slight nod of the head and shoulders will be considered appropriate in most situations.[58]

## PERSONAL APPEARANCE

We are often reminded of the importance of first impressions and how our personal appearance is usually the first thing that influences that impression. In international business, where language barriers may impede the ability to fully express yourself, personal appearance takes on added importance.

As we discussed earlier in this chapter, the U.S. is an informal culture. This informality is reflected by the policy of "casual Friday," which many U.S. organizations use to promote a relaxed dress code for employees. The dot-com organizations in Silicon Valley are noted for their very informal dress code, and young entrepreneurs can often be seen conducting business in polo shirts and jeans. Other cultures, as we have noted, are more formal, and this attitude also extends to their personal appearance, especially in business interactions. In Japan, for example, a dark blue, tailored suit is the standard uniform of a Japanese corporate employee. Dress that differentiates an individual from the majority is not readily accepted. Even though the younger generation of Japanese has started to wear more color and different styles, conservative clothes are still the norm among managers and executives.[59] German businessmen and businesswomen also dress conservatively, with dark suits and white shirts the norm.[60] In almost every instance of international business, conservative dress with coat and tie is expected, especially for the initial meetings. In fact, success in much of Latin America is tied to appearances. Business executives dress fashionably and expect their counterparts to embody this same aura of success. In Indonesia, the Philippines, and Malaysia, native businessmen and women have a relaxed standard of dress, which often omits a coat and tie. However, the international business representative should not adopt these practices until a strong relationship has been developed. Western businesswomen working in Islamic nations or with Muslim counterparts should dress conservatively and modestly with a high neckline, sleeves extending below the elbow, and hemlines past the knees. Pants and pantsuits should not be worn.

It is easy to imagine the consequences of a businessman from the U.S. dressing in slacks and an open-necked sports shirt arriving at a meeting with his German counterparts, who are wearing dark suits and ties. In this instance, the first impression would probably be less than positive.

## GIFT GIVING

An old adage says, "Beware of Greeks bearing gifts." However, among many cultures—particularly collectivistic cultures, which we have discussed throughout the book—gift giving is a common practice. It is used to sustain relations, repay past favors, and ensure preferable consideration in the future. The presents, which may include the direct payment of money, are seen as a means of creating or sustaining an obligation that must eventually be repaid.[61] Individualistic Western cultures, especially the U.S., often view these payments as a form of bribery. The U.S. anathema toward commercial bribery is so strong that it is prohibited by the Foreign Corrupt Practice Act, which "makes it unlawful to bribe foreign government officials to obtain or retain business."[62] China has also enacted legislation to prohibit bribery in business transactions. In 2002, regulations were established that designated gifts in excess of 180 U.S. dollars as bribery.[63]

The exchange of gifts remains a common business protocol, but the international business representative must be able to distinguish between what is considered a gift and what is seen as a bribe. From the U.S. perspective, suitable gifts among employees from international organizations are small, relatively inexpensive mementos presented to commemorate the event or as an expression of appreciation and solidarity. Acuff reports, "Small gifts—such as pens, cups, and key rings engraved with your company logo—are not only acceptable, but virtually essential in global business. Home and office decorations and books and magazines are also popular."[64]

For the business person going abroad, it is useful to know not only the views concerning gift giving, but also what gifts are appropriate in the culture where business will be conducted and when they should be given. In Japan, for example, Nishiyama reports that gifts are exchanged at the beginning of any new business relationship. "The value and type of gift depend on the size of future business and the status of the relationship."[65] In contrast, gifts are not given in Chile until the business relationship has become well established, and in Denmark they are not required at all.[66]

Understanding what constitutes an appropriate or inappropriate gift is as important as knowing when to give a present. In Guatemala and Japan, white flowers should not be given as a gift as they are normally associated with funerals, as are chrysanthemums in Italy.[67] Alcoholic beverages should not be given in Islamic countries or to a Muslim counterpart. Additionally, if giving a gift to a Muslim, you should not use your left hand, as this is considered the unclean hand. Dresser points out that in Japan, "To give a clock as a gift is equivalent to saying, 'I wish you were dead,'"[68] because it reminds the recipient that time is running out. While thirteen is an inauspicious number in the United States, gifts in numbers of four are inappropriate in Japan because the Japanese words for *four* and *death* are pronounced the same, though written differently.

As the preceding examples indicate, the rules for gift giving vary considerably across cultures. Prior to leaving for your international destination, it is important to learn as much as possible about the gift-related customs of your host nation. You will need to know if a gift is expected, what is appropriate, when to give a gift, and how it should be presented. While these seem like small, inconsequential considerations, without an understanding of what is proper and improper, you run the risk of destroying the international transaction before it even begins.

## MANAGEMENT STYLES

We begin our analysis of the influence of culture on management styles with the following case study:

James has been a manager with MicroTech, Inc., for eight years and is considered to be on a fast track to the executive ranks. Approximately six months ago, he was transferred from the home office in Seattle to take over as head of the Tokyo branch, his first international assignment. Soon after arrival in Japan, James began implementing some of the management programs that has made him a success in the U.S. In one program, the top performer from each department is designated every month. Each of the departmental awardees is presented a desk plaque at a ceremony in front of his co-workers, given a gift certificate worth $100, and has his picture placed in the lobby of the office building. Recently, James has noticed a sharp drop in productivity and office morale seems to be very low. Some of the workers have even started complaining about having to attend the monthly award presentations.

As the above case study indicates, the tasks of a business manager are multifaceted and varied. The ultimate objective is to motivate employees to work cooperatively and productively in the achievement of a specific goal.[69] For an international manager, the complexity of these tasks are compounded by the influence of culture,[70] which shapes our expectations of leadership styles, communication behaviors, decision-making processes, negotiation procedures, supervisor/subordinate relations, personnel recognition and reward, considerations for promotion, and all the many other aspects of the workplace. According to Early and Ang, an understanding of cultural differences will increase the ability to successfully meet the many demands placed on an international manager.[71]

In the short case study we presented, it was clear that James made very little effort to increase his cultural knowledge of the Japanese prior to departing on his international assignment. Even a brief examination would have disclosed that the Japanese culture is traditionally group-oriented and individual attention is avoided. James's program of recognizing and awarding individual employees was directly opposed to the Japanese perception that all achievements are a product of the entire workgroup's efforts, and no one individual should be singled out for recognition. The monthly award ceremony only served to embarrass the recipients and disgruntle the co-workers. The program that had worked so well for James in the U.S. only produced falling morale and lower productivity in Japan.

The Chinese also have a preference for group affiliation rather than individualism. Unlike the Japanese, who tend to focus on the workgroup, the extended family is considered the most important social unit among the Chinese. This value is often seen in Chinese family enterprises, where it is common to find many of the management and executive positions filled by family members and close friends.[72] What a U.S. manager would likely consider nepotism is a common, valued Chinese practice.

Business meetings are another context where international managers must consider cultural differences. In the U.S., meetings are designed to disseminate information and, when required, make decisions. Therefore, meetings should be held only when absolutely necessary, start on time, follow a predetermined agenda, and end on time. As you might expect, not all cultures view meetings from this perspective. The French, for example, consider meetings to be a forum for exchanging information, or to validate decisions that have already been decided by senior management. Compared to their U.S. counterparts, during meetings the French employ more formal conduct and language and adhere closely to the organizational hierarchy.[73]

Another important aspect of international management concerns presentations at meetings. U.S. and British managers are culturally conditioned to provide succinct, well-organized presentations that directly relate to the topic of discussion. Italians are schooled to speak eloquently, to thoroughly cover all possibilities, and do not feel constrained by scheduled times. English managers will normally understate their personal qualifications,[74] while U.S. managers go to great lengths to ensure their education and experience is known. It is easy to imagine the frustration and potential for misunderstanding at a cross-cultural business presentation involving representatives from these three cultures.

International managers are also confronted with cultural differences when preparing and executing business contracts. In the U.S., a highly individualistic and low context culture, a contract is considered a legally binding document, which should specify and explain every aspect of the agreement. As a result, U.S. contracts are normally lengthy, highly detailed tomes which state exactly the responsibilities of each participant, what can and cannot be done, and attempt to account for every contingency. Any deviation from the contract provisions requires the mutual agreement and consent by all involved parties, frequently calling for an addendum or a renegotiation of the entire document. Group-oriented, high context cultures, such as China, Japan, and South Korea, see contracts quite differently. In these cultures, the greatest concern is for the relationship of the parties involved rather than the specifics of the business deal. In these cultures, the contract is a much more informal, flexible document that simply outlines the general provisions of the agreement. The emphasis is placed on the establishment and exercise of mutual trust between the participants.

From the perspective of these three Northeast Asian cultures, a contract cannot account for every possibility and foresee changes that may be needed in the future. Events may arise that make it difficult for one or more of the contractual parties to meet a previously specified requirement. In these instances, the participants will take into account the circumstances and try to reach a solution that best serves the interests of everyone concerned. For the Chinese, Japanese, and Koreans, the contract is not a sterile document that binds the signers to a list of specific duties. Rather, it is the symbol of a relationship based on trust and a commitment to mutual obligations.[75]

As an international manager, you will be forced to deal with a wide variety of cultural expectations for business contracts. In Germany, for example, contracts will need to be excruciatingly detailed, and signers are expected to adhere precisely to the various provisions. In the Arab world, however, the word of the individual carries more weight than the written word, and in some cases, insisting on a contract may be perceived as an insult.[76] The successful resolution of these sometimes conflicting, culture-based views is through increased awareness and patient negotiation, and as we will see in the following section, cross-cultural negotiation can be a complex, demanding endeavor.

## NEGOTIATION STYLES

Visit the business section of any Barnes & Noble or Borders bookstore and you will find numerous texts on negotiations. Using "negotiation" to search Amazon.com will bring up more than three thousand selections. Narrow the search by using "international negotiation" and you will still find over one thousand entries. This is an easy way to discover the critical role that negotiation plays in international business. The process is so important that some estimates suggest international executives spend more than 20 percent of their time in negotiation activities.[77] This is probably a very conservative estimate, considering that negotiations are integral to all international mergers, joint ventures, import of raw materials, export of finished products, patent licensing agreements, and every other cross-cultural, commercial undertaking.

Both domestic and international business negotiations involve representatives from different organizations working to achieve mutually agreeable solutions, while concurrently trying to minimize differences, misunderstandings, and conflicts. To obtain these objectives, they rely on communication. The role of communication is so important that Drake calls it the "life-blood of negotiation" and considers it an area often overlooked in intercultural negotiation studies.[78]

As you might suspect, culture plays a critical role when representatives from different nations set out to try to reach an accord acceptable to both sides. Marked by the participants' varying cultural values, ideals, beliefs, and behaviors, international negotiations offer a rich medium for misunderstanding and friction. So demanding is the task, one experienced negotiator has characterized "cross-cultural and international settings as the most challenging."[79] This challenge arises because cross-cultural negotiation participants are influenced by their respective national bargaining style, which is often a product of contrasting historical legacies, different cultural values, dissimilar decision-making processes, and varying attitudes toward conflict. During negotiations, these differences can exacerbate, and often obscure, the actual commercial issues under consideration.

To best demonstrate culture's influence on international business bargaining, we will examine three aspects related to the negotiation process: (1) *participant perspective*, (2) *external factors*, and (3) *expected outcomes*.

**Participant Perspective.** Culture will affect how people view the negotiation process as a whole, their perception of their counterparts, and how they actually conduct the bargaining sessions. For example, the U.S. approach to negotiations is a product of the classical Greek tradition of rhetorical eloquence, argumentation, debate, and persuasion.[80] Drawing on this Aristotelian legacy, U.S. trade and corporate representatives frequently enter into negotiations with a direct, somewhat confrontational approach. They commonly view the bargaining process as adversarial in nature, driven by the underlying objective of winning. There is also an emphasis on quick results that maximize profits and produce a short-term perspective. Relationships with the other side, especially long-term relations, are a secondary consideration, if considered at all.

The U.S. outlook can easily create problems when negotiating with collective-based cultures. For example, Japanese and Chinese negotiators take a long-term view toward business ventures. Their first goal is to work on building a relationship, establishing a level of trust, and determining the desirability of entering into an extended association with the other organization. The approach is more collegial and the focus is on mutual interests, giving rise to a "win-win"[81] perspective, which is quite in contrast to the more aggressive U.S. view of "business is business." For the Russians, negotiations are simply a forum for debate, an opportunity to convince the other side of the rightfulness of their position. The Russians often interpret an offer to make concessions as an indication of weakness. Rather than compromise on an issue, they will simply reiterate their original arguments in the expectation that the other negotiating team will ultimately realize the correctness of the Russian position.[82]

The age of the negotiators can also be a factor. The Chinese have great respect for their elders and consider them to have more wisdom than younger people. But in Western societies, especially the U.S., age is less an issue than expertise or competency. A team of bright, young U.S. engineers sent to negotiate the specifics of a technology transfer project with a Chinese corporation may well encounter difficulties just because of their youthfulness. The Chinese negotiators, typically around fifty years of age, may have trouble seeing the U.S. team as credible or competent.[83] The gender of the team members can also play a role in negotiations, especially in Muslim countries. In Saudi Arabia, where women are considered subordinate to men and are subject to many culturally based social restrictions, Saudi negotiators may have difficulty interacting with a female negotiator. The issue is so sensitive that some experts advise against including women on the negotiating team when dealing with Saudis.[84]

**External Factors.** All negotiators hold culturally based expectations of how the bargaining process should proceed and what might be considered appropriate and inappropriate behaviors. This involves concepts such as the application of formality and informality, status of the members, view of time, role of government, ethical standards, display of emotions, and communication style.

Earlier in the chapter, we discussed how cultural values of formality and informality can influence people's dress, actions, and communication style. This becomes a particularly important aspect at the negotiation table. Negotiators from the U.S., a highly informal culture, tend to avoid titles and are quick to use first names soon after meeting someone. These actions can be quite disconcerting in European cultures, such as France, Germany, and England, where formality plays a greater role and titles are an important part of an individual's identity. Representatives from China, Japan, and Korea will also expect negotiations to be conducted on a more formal level than someone from Australia, an informal culture. Koreans prefer titles to names, even among themselves, according to Lewis.[85]

The social or organizational status of members of the negotiating teams is another important cultural consideration. The U.S., being strongly egalitarian, is prone to select members based on their proven managerial or technical abilities, with little concern for their position. In other cultures, however, the status of team members is of considerable importance. The inclusion of high-ranking company officers or individuals from influential families is often an indication that the company is serious about negotiations and wants to reach a successful agreement. In East Asia, the number of people assigned to the team will also signal the level of importance attached to the negotiations—the more participants, the greater the importance.

In the past, before becoming more culturally astute, U.S. businessmen were noted for arriving in Tokyo on Monday with hotel reservations booked for a one-week stay. Their plan was to begin negotiations on Tuesday and sign a contract by Friday so they could return home for the weekend. These expectations often doomed the business transaction before the parties even met. The U.S. participants were enculturated to view time as a fixed commodity—something that should not be wasted. Thus, they were impatient to quickly move from one objective to the next, with a minimum of inactivity between each event. This Western desire to move the negotiations along rapidly is not a popular approach in Japan and China. There is even an Asian proverb that states, "Patience is power; with time and patience the mulberry leaf becomes a silk gown." For these cultures time is perceived quite differently than in the West. In business, their first goal is to get to know the other party. The Japanese and the Chinese see entering into a commercial arrangement much like entering into a marriage. It is something that should last for a long time and be beneficial to both parties. Accordingly, they want to take time to ensure that relations with the other organization will be both compatible and productive. To achieve this, considerable time will be spent in entertainment and sightseeing activities in order to increase their knowledge of the members of the other negotiating team. Early meetings will focus more on the general background of the other organization and less on the specifics of the proposed business transaction.

The role that a nation's government plays in business is yet another factor in international negotiations. U.S. corporate negotiators consider government as separate and apart from the business transaction. The function of government is to establish and enforce laws designed to create a level playing field for economic activities. Active governmental involvement in commercial negotiations is seen as a potential obstruction to a successful conclusion between the involved parties. This is quite different from China, where the Communist Party is commonly involved in commercial events,[86] and some companies are owned and managed by the government.

Culture also shapes one's ethics, on both a personal and national level. As discussed earlier, in commercial dealings the U.S. has instituted laws prohibiting the payment of bribes or giving of gifts that exceed $180. However, in some countries, payments or gifts used to "grease the wheels" are considered a natural part of doing business and permeates all levels of society. Dissimilar opinions on the appropriateness of providing payment to facilitate an international business arrangement can easily result in failed negotiations.

Emotional displays by negotiators can also have a bearing on the outcome of an international business transaction. For example, Western business representatives often characterize their Asian counterparts as "inscrutable" due to a lack of facial expressions displayed at the bargaining table. In the U.S., it is normal and expected for people to use a wide range of nonverbal behaviors as outward signs of their feelings. The U.S. culture teaches that it is a natural part of social interactions to signal pleasure, disgust, anger, or any other emotion through nonverbal displays. In China, Japan, and Korea, however, outward demonstrations of emotions are felt to disturb the harmony and are studiously avoided. Thus, at a negotiation table a Korean representative would consider a frowning U.S. counterpart to be rather immature. In other cultures, such as Mexico and those in the Middle East, expressed emotions are expected and seen as a means of emphasizing and reinforcing one's negotiation position.[87] Beamer and Varner explain the role of emotion for a Kuwaiti negotiator, and the potential for an adverse reaction, this way:

> His love of verbal play and the importance of emotion in communication may make the Kuwaiti negotiator's wording of messages seem theatrical to a low-context communicator [e.g., U.S. or Canadian] who shuns ambiguity and strives for directness and simplicity.[88]

A negotiator's communication style can also be the source of difficulties in international business. Representatives from collective cultures such as China, Japan, Korea, and Indonesia place considerable value on maintaining positive relations with their negotiation counterparts. To accomplish this, they rely on an indirect communication style. Sensitive issues with the potential to create conflict or cause discord are handled with care and normally addressed in an indirect manner. The Chinese and Japanese are reluctant to give a direct negative reply, relying instead on equivocal statements such as "That may be difficult," "We need to study that more," or "We will think about it." The Indonesians are so concerned with maintaining harmonious relations they have "twelve ways to say 'no'."[89] Indirectness of this magnitude can be the source of consternation, confusion, and even misinterpretation to the Western negotiator, who is used to "getting to the point" and "not beating around the bush." For example, if a Japanese negotiator tells his U.S. counterpart that a request "will be difficult," he is actually saying no and there will be no further consideration of the issue. However, the U.S. business representative is likely to interpret the statement as an indication that the request will remain under consideration, with a possible reply at a later date. Waiting for a response that will not come can quickly lead to strained relations.

**Expected Outcomes.** As with every other aspect of negotiations, culture also instills participants with an expectation as to what the bargaining should achieve, what form the end result should take. The varying cultural perceptions of business contracts were discussed earlier in this chapter, but the importance of these issues is worth reviewing from the context of negotiations. Coming from a highly legalistic society,[90] U.S. negotiators see the final objective of successful negotiations as a signed and

The negotiation session is altered and modified by cultural rules for doing business.

binding contract. The amount of importance that U.S. negotiators attach to contracts is best described by Salacuse:

> For them [U.S.] the contract is a definitive set of rights and duties that strictly binds the two sides, controls their behavior in the future, and determines who does what, when, and how. According to this view, the parties' deal is their contract."[91]

These expectations give rise to lengthy, detailed contracts, frequently involving lawyers or legal experts as part of the negotiating team. This perception is quite in contrast to collectivistic cultures, where business negotiations are considered a means of establishing long-term relationships rather than producing a legal document restricted to governing a single, specific transaction. From the Chinese perspective, the negotiations are designed to establish the parameters of the relationship, and the contract should serve only an outline or a guide.[92] Like the Chinese, the Japanese and the Saudis also dislike detailed contracts.[93] The Japanese believe that since future events cannot be predicted, a contract must be flexible in order to accommodate situational and organizational changes.

## DECISION MAKING

Although negotiations involve a near-constant process of decision making, international executives are also required to make, manage, and implement decisions dealing with a variety of other business-related areas. These can include such diverse issues as personnel management, new product development, market expansion, sales initiatives, the acceptance or rejection of a proposal, and many, many more. To be effective, international business managers must be aware of who makes decisions and how those decisions are made across different cultures. In some cultures, like France,[94] a few high-level individuals are usually responsible for making all decisions, but in other cultures the group is actively involved in every step of the process. In some group cultures, like Japan, a true consensus is required, while in other group-oriented societies, such as Mexico, the members will rely on the responsible individual to make the decision.[95]

These cultural differences are especially evident when comparing U.S. and Japanese decision making. In the U.S. corporate sector, decisions are usually the product of a top-down process, disseminated downward through an authoritative or semi-authoritative structure. Decisions are generally made by a few individuals or a simple majority of executives after they have considered the influencing factors and various interest groups. This procedure is a result of a U.S. cultural heritage that emphasizes egalitarianism, independence, frequent change, and a willingness to deal with conflict. In U.S. companies, the authority to make strategic decisions resides with a few, top-level individuals, which allows for a quick process once the appropriate, and often legally mandated, studies (e.g., market analysis, environmental survey, etc.) have been finished. Although U.S. managers generally expect to be asked for their input, there is no guarantee this will occur or that their opinion will influence the final outcome. While the decisions are often made very quickly, implementation can take considerably longer. With no prior knowledge, affected employees usually need time to understand, accept, and adapt to the new requirements. If the workers do not agree with or understand the changes, their resistance can slow or even halt implementation.[96]

A strong group orientation and emphasis on social stability are salient considerations in Japan's consensus-based decision-making process. In contrast to the U.S. top-down model, decision making in large Japanese corporations, especially trading companies, usually begins with mid-level managers and follows a bottom-up procedure known as *ringi seido*. In this process, one or a few employees prepare a written proposal (*ringi sho*) which takes the form of "a subordinate respectfully consulting the opinion of a superior."[97] All of the involved organizational sections will subject the proposal to comprehensive discussions (*nemawashi*), often even before receiving the formal document. At each level, the merits and possible impact of the suggestion will be examined in depth, and if everyone is in agreement, the manager will endorse the proposal and forward it. If approved, the document will ultimately circulate to the upper management and executive levels. When a clear consensus emerges, the proposal becomes policy.

The key aspect of this process is that a consensus must be achieved. Everyone must be in agreement, or at least outwardly profess agreement. Quite naturally, getting everyone to agree can take considerable time and effort. Detailed and in-depth information relating to all aspects of the proposal must be obtained, disseminated, studied, and discussed. Should dissent arise, additional time is required for further discussions and consultations, which may take place in the workplace during the day and continue in restaurants and bars after scheduled working hours. Once a consensual decision is achieved, however, implementation is rapid and encompassing, a result of the broad employee involvement in the decision process from start to finish. Everyone is given the opportunity to voice their opinion and discuss the proposal before it is finally approved. As a result, employees are already familiar with the proposal, its impact, and actions needed for implication.

The difference between Japanese and U.S. decision making illustrates the influence of culture and the important role cultural awareness plays in international business. But an awareness of the difference is often insufficient to provide an international business with the necessary cultural competence, which requires both an awareness of differences and an understanding of the cultural factors motivating the dissimilarities. In Japanese and U.S. decision making, a primary cause for the wide difference lies in the two cultures' contrary attitudes toward conflict. The U.S. model involves accepting and dealing with confrontations, while the Japanese model works to avoid conflict. How conflict is managed differently across cultures is the subject of our next section.

## CONFLICT MANAGEMENT

Conflict is an inescapable aspect of relationships and if managed improperly can lead to irreparable breakdowns—separation or divorce at the interpersonal level, war on a national scale, or lost opportunities in commercial endeavors. As you might expect, culture determines how conflict is viewed and managed. Since the role of culture in conflict is examined in considerable detail in Chapter 11, we will limit our discussion here to the international business arena.

Cross-cultural business, marked by the participants' varying values, ideals, beliefs, and behaviors, offers a rich medium for discord. Collectivistic cultures have an aversion to open, direct conflict, which is seen as a threat to the harmony and stability of the relationship between group members. This is in contrast to individualistic cultures, where dissent and disagreement are a natural and valued part of life.[98] This dissimilarity can be illustrated by comparing the Chinese and the Australian approach to conflict management. Because conflicts are not openly dealt with in China,[99] a Western business representative may not realize a problem has developed when the Chinese begin withdrawing from the business relationship. This is very different from the individualistic Australians, who are comfortable with controversy. As Hendon, Hendon, and Herbig note:

> They [Australians] expect it in most transactions in life; they are familiar with it whenever they deal with unions; they are not at all put off by it; and they are quite capable of even enjoying it, to the point of intentionally creating conflict at times just to engage the other side. They admire people who can handle conflict with style. Negative reactions evoked by conflict do not bother them at all.[100]

This attitude toward conflict is similar to that found in the U.S. marketplace, where disagreement and debate are considered to be a natural and advantageous way of arriving at the best possible solution.

Being sensitive to the perils of disharmony, organizations in collectivistic countries have instituted a variety of means to obviate or reduce the incidence of disagreement. In Japan, these measures include programs to socialize employees to view the organization as part of "their professional and personal fulfillment."[101] Because the individual's identity is, in part, derived from the organization, there is little incentive toward disruptive organizational activities. Japanese companies also incorporate small group discussions and the use of trusted intermediaries to help preclude or resolve conflicts. Other means include the use of consultations prior to meeting formally and an unquestioning acceptance of authority. Criticism, a potent source of disagreement, is expressed indirectly, in passive, accommodating styles. Since conflict carries the potential loss of face, the Japanese and Chinese are likely to remain silent or use nonverbal behaviors to express disapproval. Complaints may be expressed through humor, jokes, or via a third person.

In contrast to collectivistic cultures, institutional disagreement in individualistic cultures, like the U.S., has promoted quite different methods of managing conflict. Majority rule and unilateral decisions, passed down vertically from higher authority, for example, are common management techniques in the U.S. If employees disagree with a decision, they have a variety of options—openly express their dissent to upper management, try to fight the decision through legal or arbitration channels, organize cohorts to act against the decision, or just quit and find another job. Obviously, none of these options is overly concerned with group harmony or organizational cohesion. In the U.S., individual self-interest overrides matters of group continuity and organizational stability. A common means of dealing with conflict in the U.S. is through legal measures. This is why U.S. contracts are usually drafted by lawyers and contain specifications for every conceivable potential.

## THE INFLUENCE OF INFORMATION TECHNOLOGY ON INTERNATIONAL COMMUNICATION

At the beginning of this chapter, we talked about how the forces of globalization, such as advanced transportation systems and communication technologies, had fostered a dramatic increase in cross-cultural trade and created ever-increasing international economic interdependencies. One of the most influential forces of globalization in the business world is the Internet. According to research by Cairncross, the "astonishing fall in the cost of transferring information around the world"[102] has forced businesses to think and act from a global perspective. This global perspective has brought about an emphasis on cross-border market penetration facilitated by organizational transparency and convergence. In other words, the Internet has helped create both a need and a demand for international businesses to adopt uniform standards and practices, irrespective of national borders and cultural differences. This raises the question as to whether business practices in the global market, which relies heavily on information technology (IT), are forcing some nations to change their culturally established organizational communication protocols. This question was answered in the affirmative by a recent pilot study investigating the influence of IT on Japanese organizational communication practices.[103] While the study focused only on one country (Japan), the insights gained from the results have application to other countries and cultures.

The investigation revealed that the dynamics of the global marketplace and increased reliance on IT were creating changes, although in small increments, in traditional Japanese corporate communication procedures. For example, the *nemawashi* process, which was discussed earlier, is being modernized by the use of IT systems. Corporate employees can use IT to promulgate and discuss relevant issues without the need for face-to-face interaction. Some organizations were also using IT to expedite the *ringi* decision-making process, with one company reducing the time to achieve a consensus from ten to six days. Additionally, the expanded use of e-mail among employees is creating a move away from the traditional Japanese indirect communication to a more direct practice. According to Fouser, some Japanese found that e-mail provided an anonymity which "encouraged people to use casual and blunt language."[104] This is, in part, because e-mail messages deprive the receiver of the broader context, including nonverbal cues, which is so critical to Japanese high-context communication. In some instances, this introduction of directness had created interpersonal conflict among workers. However, the study disclosed that younger Japanese workers preferred the more direct style. In addition to this source of workforce friction, the adoption and application of IT has created new communication challenges.[105] While e-mail has increased the speed of operations, this acceleration of communication can also create problems in multinational organizations due to varied language skills. This becomes particularly problematic when multiple e-mails on a specific topic are exchanged among a wide (multinational) employee audience—first-language users will read, comprehend, and respond much faster than second-language users. As the exchange proliferates, understanding by the second-language users will continue to lag, and they may ultimately find themselves excluded from the discussion.

From these examples it is easy to see that globalization, driven by technological innovation, is exerting pressure on many forms of culturally based corporate communication protocols. As we have continually stated, cultural changes occur very slowly, but to stay competitive in the international marketplace, organizations will have to either adapt to the dynamics of globalization or find themselves left behind.

By now, you have probably discovered just how difficult the communicative dynamics of international business can be. This is a field where well-developed intercultural communication skills are both required and demanded. But there is also an ever-increasing need for the development of intercultural competence at the domestic level, to which we now turn our attention.

## The Domestic Business Context

As we have noted throughout this book, through birthrates and immigration, the United States has become a nation characterized by an extensive cultural diversity, where almost 18 percent of the population speak a language other than English in their homes.[106] Minorities are now the fastest-growing segment of the U.S. demography.[107] The U.S. Census Bureau's 2003 American Community Survey disclosed that the number of U.S. Latinos had reached 39.9 million, which represents nearly 14 percent of the total population. The complexity of U.S. diversity is saliently illustrated by looking at the demographics of Los Angeles County, in Southern California, where the minorities collectively represent the majority,[108] over 55 percent of the population older than five years does not speak English in their homes,[109] and the school system struggles "to cope with children who speak some 92 different languages at home."[110]

As with the general population, minorities also constitute the fastest-growing segment of the U.S. labor force, according to U.S. Department of Labor reports.[111] Although white non-Latinos continue to represent the majority of U.S. workers, Mitra Toosi reports their share of the labor force has been decreasing and is expected to continue declining for the next fifty years. The share of white non-Hispanics is anticipated to decrease from 73 percent in 2000 to 53 percent in 2050. Over the same period, Hispanics are expected to more than double their share, from 11 percent in 2000 to 24 percent of the labor force in 2050. Blacks are also expected to increase their share, from 12 percent in 2000 to 14 percent in 2050. Asians, the fastest-growing group in the labor force, are projected to raise their share from 5 percent to 11 percent between 2000 and 2050.[112]

The number of minority entrepreneurs is also expanding. In 2001, the U.S. Department of Commerce found that "minority-owned businesses grew more than four times as fast as U.S. firms overall between 1992 and 1997."[113]

The meaning embedded in this wilderness of statistics is that the U.S. domestic workforce is presently characterized by a culturally diverse population that is expected to continue growing at a significant rate. Successful management of this diverse labor force will demand increased awareness and acceptance of varying cultural values and greater intercultural communication competence. All segments of the U.S. economy will have to be knowledgeable of and responsive to the many issues that hold potential for cross-cultural conflict. Managers in this culturally varied workplace will have to be constantly alert to the hazards of discrimination, discussed in detail in Chapter 11, which can come in many forms. As the workforce becomes more diverse, the opportunities for racial, ethnic, language, and religious intolerance will also expand.

Increased racial and ethnicity complexity brings varied cultural beliefs, values, and attitudes to the work center, and these cultural differences can increase the chance of gender and sexual harassment among employees. Some cultures hold very different attitudes toward women and freedom of sexual preference. These attitudes can sometimes translate into negative treatment of co-workers of the opposite gender or sexual preference. Many U.S. corporations have recognized the importance of cultural diversity among workers and instituted training programs designed to promote employee awareness of the many cultural differences. In the future, successful organizations will have to take added measures to ensure employees enjoy workplace equality, regardless of race, ethnicity, gender, or sexual preference.

We conclude this chapter by urging you to be aware of the important influence culture has on the conduct of business—both internationally and domestically. Part of that awareness is realizing that you may be unfamiliar with significant aspects of the business contexts as it relates to culture. Therefore, we implore you to heed the words of President John F. Kennedy: "The greater our knowledge increases, the greater our ignorance unfolds."

## Summary

- The communication context refers to the cultural environment in which communication occurs.
- Culturally diverse rules specify how communication is to take place by prescribing the appropriate behaviors in given contexts.
- Rules concerning informality, formality, assertiveness, interpersonal harmony, and social status can be found in every communication setting.
- In multinational business, cultures differ in their approach to protocol, management, negotiations, decision making, and conflict management.
- In international organizations, the use of information technology (IT) is creating changes to the established culturally based communication practices.
- Rapidly increasing cultural diversity in the U.S. business community will require greater intercultural understanding and skills.

## Activities

1. Visit several ATMs in different areas of your city and see what languages are available. In small groups, discuss why the ATMs might have two or more languages. If the languages vary between locations, try to decide why.

2. Select a controversial topic such as (1) the U.S. should adopt English as the official language, (2) affirmative action should be abolished, or (3) the U.S. should take stronger measures against illegal immigrants. Divide the class into small groups of

four or five. Have the members of each group work to arrive at a *true consensus* decision for the questions. Afterward, discuss the difficulties encountered in the group consensus process.
3. In a small group, list the different problems that can arise in a multinational workforce, either international or domestic. Discuss some measures that might help resolve or lessen these problems.
4. List as many words and phrases as you can that might create cultural or sexual harassment problems in the workplace.

## Discussion Ideas

1. What is meant by the phrase "communication is rule governed"? What are some of the rules that govern your communication in the classroom? What are some rules that govern your behavior when purchasing a new suit? How might these rules differ in another country?
2. What are some of the established communication protocols that govern U.S. business interactions? How might some of these protocols create a problem when dealing with business representatives from other cultures?
3. What are some common factors in the U.S. negotiation style that might create problems in a cross-cultural negotiation session? What recommendations would you offer for eliminating or solving these problem areas?
4. What changes has information technology (IT) brought to your life in the past ten years? How has it changed your interactions with businesses?
5. To accommodate the increasing U.S. demographic diversity, what changes (e.g., products offered, management style, advertising, etc.) will business have to make?

## CHAPTER 9

# Cultural Influences on Context: The Educational Setting

*Education helps one cease being intimidated by strange situations.*

**MAYA ANGELOU**

*It is in listening to the student that I learn how to speak with him or her.*

**PAULO FREIRE**

Culture is inseparably linked to education; people raised in diverse cultures are educated in accordance with the perceived needs of their cultures. Thus, while people may be biologically alike, they grow up to be socially different because of their cultural experiences; schools represent one of the most important of those experiences. Schools also provide a context in which both the socialization and the learning processes occur. Because of the profound impact that schools have on intercultural interaction, it is the main focus of this chapter.

Because the classroom is such an important intercultural setting, we believe it is worth study for several reasons. First, you can gain valuable insight into a culture by studying its perceptions of and approaches to education. The importance of education to the Chinese, for example, is expressed in the simple proverb "learning is a treasure which follows its owner everywhere." By contrast, many Latinos perceive education and schooling as being closely related yet different. For numerous Latinos, education is perceived to be more than formal schooling; it is recognized as an avenue to economic reward. As Tapia points out, Latinos believe that "education also has a moral evaluative connotation such that a well-educated child has respect for elders and authority, has good manners, and is considerate of other people."[1]

Second, schools teach the formal knowledge cultures deem necessary: language, history, government, science, art, music, and how to survive in society. This is true whether you are considering a country as large and complex as the United States or a

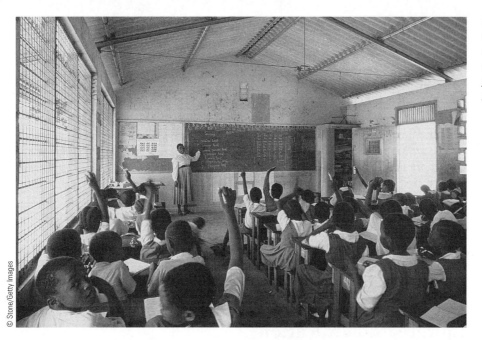

*Schools are a primary means by which a culture's history and values are transmitted from generation to generation.*

small tribal society in the midst of a South American rain forest. For instance, the basis of survival in the United States, as presented in our educational system, is to obtain the knowledge and skills necessary to secure employment that provides income sufficient to live comfortably. In the forest, survival skills may include how to set an animal snare, how to fashion a functional bow and arrow, how to make a fire, or how to recognize which plants are edible and which are toxic. By discovering how learning and knowledge differ from one culture to another, you can learn valuable insights into the backgrounds of people from other cultures.

A third reason you should know about the influence culture has on education is to become aware of the informal knowledge of a culture. Saville-Troike emphasizes this point for you by indicating that children are supposed to internalize the basic values and beliefs of their culture. They learn the rules of behavior that are considered appropriate for their role in the community and begin to be socialized into that community.[2] In school, children learn the rules of correct conduct, a hierarchy of cultural values, how to treat and interact with one another, gender-role expectations, respect, and all of the other informal matters of culture.

Fourth, education in all of its forms is one of the largest professions in the United States. Consequently, many of you may encounter members of diverse cultures, whether as a teacher in a traditional classroom, conducting business training seminars, or providing child-care guidance seminars to new parents. An awareness of the cultural diversity now inherent in education can help your understanding of specific communication behaviors in multicultural classrooms. Finally, as parents or potential parents, it behooves you to understand the dynamics of culturally diverse classrooms.

You should recognize that however large and different in symbolic and operational detail, most cultural communities are essentially identical in many of the most rudimentary elements of social structure, needs, and desires.[3] In essence, all cultures teach much the same thing: perpetuation of the culture and passing its history and traditions from generation to generation. A culture's system of formal and informal education seeks to meet the perceived needs of its society. Thus, in every culture, schools serve a multitude of functions. First, they help fashion the individual. As children grow, what they learn and the ways in which they learn influence their thinking and behavior. From a child's point of view, education provides a way to certainty. It offers every child a set of guidelines and values for living life. As the English social philosopher Herbert Spencer wrote, "Education has for its object the formation of character." Henry expands this notion by expressing the idea that children are shaped by their schools as they become aware of what they must know in order to lead productive, successful, and satisfying lives.[4]

Education is universally influenced by culture. But this influence is especially important in multicultural societies because of co-cultural diversity. Because of this connection, we believe that to be effective teachers, educators must also be effective intercultural communicators.

A first requisite to achieving competent multicultural communicative capabilities in the educational setting is to understand the dynamics associated with culture and education. To this end, we will examine (1) *the relationship between culture and education*, (2) *cultural diversity in education*, (3) *education in a multicultural society*, (4) *language diversity in multicultural education*, and (5) *becoming a multiculturally competent communicator*.

# Culture and Education

As we have observed throughout this book, globalization and multiculturalism are strong forces guiding and changing international and national relationships. These changes also impact education and create a need to revise and reform educational practices in order to accommodate new cultural dynamics as they manifest themselves in various educational forums.

## GLOBALIZATION

Globalization has the effect of eliminating or reducing traditional borders between people. Globalization, suggest Keohane and Nye, drives an evolution toward a world linked economically, militarily, environmentally, socially, and culturally at multicontinental distances.[5] Globalization results in an international flow of both capital and goods and of information and ideas. Globalization also promotes the free movement of people across national borders resulting in an influx of immigrants in the United States, both adults and children. Immigrant children come from culturally diverse backgrounds and consequently affect the way in which American schools must function because, as Brannon indicates, "dealing with the world means dealing with people from backgrounds and orientations other than our own."[6]

A recent effect of globalization on education in the United States is the outsourcing of tutoring to other countries. Many American high school students who work with tutors are finding their tutors reside in places like Cochin, India. So, instead of face-to-face interaction with their tutors, these American students now log onto a computer link that connects them with their tutor. Using headsets and microphones, students study with tutors who may be over seven thousand miles away.

## MULTICULTURALISM

Coming from a democratic perspective, multiculturalism is a philosophy or ideology that recognizes the personal worth and dignity of every individual regardless of culture, ethnicity, race, religion, gender, or national origin. In many respects, multiculturalism has evolved as a response to the immigration brought about by globalization. Thus, says Malveaux, multiculturalism is concerned with the impact of immigration on society and with the ways in which co-cultures interact with the dominant culture and with each other.[7]

Immigration leads to the formation of co-cultures within a society. Although, as Bruffee indicates, there are some universal societal values,[8] there also are unique values that generally are shared only within cultures and co-cultures. Co-cultures, says Singh, should be seen as a system of values, attitudes, modes of behavior, and lifestyles of a social group that is distinct from but related to the dominant culture.[9] These unique cultural characteristics, however, must be integrated into the American education system. Multiculturalism thus reflects what Singh refers to as an overarching perspective in which cultural diversity is accepted as a value shared by both the dominant culture and the various co-cultures of a society.[10]

Multiculturalism affects the educational process because it affects the cultural dynamics of the classroom. As members of immigrant co-cultures enter the education system, they bring a cultural diversity presence to the classroom. This presence cannot be ignored; it must be recognized and incorporated into the educational system. Holland thus believes that education in a multicultural society must give appropriate consideration to ethnic and racial diversity, native languages, physical and emotional disabilities, and poverty.[11] Such considerations, however, are not easily accomplished. Cultural inertia and economic factors are but two barriers to developing a true multicultural educational system. Society as a whole and educators especially must work toward the development of schools that meet the needs of everyone. As Singh emphasizes, everyone deserves equal respect and equal opportunity for self-realization by virtue of their humanity and human potential as rational beings.[12]

We, along with educators such as Singh, believe that educational systems must change to meet the challenges of multiculturalism. Schools will need to develop a primary goal of preparing students at all academic levels to participate fully in the ever-emerging global village. And as Stromquist and Monkman suggest, these changes are going to deeply affect how education is defined, whom it serves, and how it is assessed.[13]

# Cultural Diversity and Education

We believe the Chinese philosopher Tehyi Hsieh was correct when he wrote, "The schools of the country are its future in miniature." Consequently, it is important that you understand and appreciate these "schools," whether they be located in your community or elsewhere.

As you might suspect, cultures with formal educational systems tend to teach many of the same things—literacy, mathematics, science, history, religion, and so forth. Yet, significant differences may be found in (1) *what cultures teach* and (2) *how cultures teach*. Because these differences define the form of education within cultures, we will examine some of these issues.

## WHAT CULTURES TEACH

In order to help you understand how culture influences education, we will begin by looking at what cultures teach. An ancient Chinese proverb tells us that "by nature all men are alike, but by education widely different." This difference is mainly due to the influence of culture on the world's educational systems. In earlier chapters, we emphasized that cultures impress upon each generation their worldview, values, and perceptual filters. Yet, as writer Paul Goodman observed, "There is only one curriculum, no matter what the method of education: what is basic and universal in human experience and practice, the underlying structure of culture." What is taught in a culture, therefore, is crucial to the maintenance and perpetuation of that culture and usually is a major responsibility of the formal educational systems within a culture.

The teaching of history is common in all cultures, but cultures emphasize their own history. This natural tendency to emphasize one's past is succinctly expressed by the scholar Abba Eban, who noted, "A nation writes its history in the image of its ideal." In the United States that ideal involves events such as the Declaration of Independence, the American Revolution, the Industrial Revolution, and the many victories America has achieved on the battlefield. In Mexico, however, the focus might be on the cultural heritage of the pre-Columbian Indians and the Mexican Revolution. The teaching of language is also common in all cultures, but, as with history, cultures first teach their own

*In subtle and manifest ways, schools in all cultures impart ethnocentrism.*

© Frank Siteman/PhotoEdit

language. When schoolchildren are taught a culture's history and language, a society is passing on its culture and reinforcing its beliefs and values—as well as its prejudices.

Every culture, whether consciously or unconsciously, tends to glorify its historical, scientific, economic, and artistic accomplishments while frequently minimizing the achievements of other cultures. In this way, schools in all cultures impart ethnocentrism. For instance, the next time you look at a world map, notice that the United States is probably located in the center—unless, of course, you are looking at a map designed by a Chinese or Russian cartographer. Many students in the United States, if asked to identify the great books of the world, would likely produce a list of books authored mainly by dead, Western, white, male authors. This subtle ethnocentrism, or the reinforcing of a culture's values, beliefs, and prejudices of the culture, is not uniquely an American phenomenon. Studying only the Koran in Pakistani schools or only the Torah in Israeli classrooms is also a quiet form of ethnocentrism.

What a culture emphasizes in its curriculum can provide some insight into the character of that culture. Spanish students, for instance, are taught the basic skills of reading, writing, and arithmetic. In addition to these basics, Spanish students are also instructed in "formative" skills, "national spirit," and "complementary" skills. Formative skills are taught through religious education. Culture is a matter of great pride in Spain, and this pride is partially instilled by including "national spirit" as part of the educational process.

As you learned earlier, the Chinese culture is distinctively collectivist, hence, Chinese education emphasizes the goals of the group or society, fosters in-group belonging, demands cooperation and interdependence, stresses moral behavior, and pursues harmony. As Lu points out, Confucian tradition holds that teachers should not only teach knowledge but also cultivate in students a strong sense of moral and righteous conduct. Chinese teachers, consequently, hold a position of moral authority and instruct students in the culture's moral rules of conduct.[14]

Like the Chinese, the Japanese are strongly collectivist, a cultural value aptly expressed in the Japanese proverb that states, "A single arrow is easily broken, but not in a bunch." Like the Chinese, Japanese students are taught cooperation, harmony, and interdependence. The Japanese also believe that proper decorum and social behavior are absolutely essential to social harmony. Nemoto summarizes this position by indicating that the Japanese insist that education include the process of character formation and moral education, and they regard this as a fundamental part of school education.[15] Proper social behavior, according to White, is something that all students can and must attain and is paramount in the Japanese educational system.[16]

Reading, writing, and mathematics are emphasized in the Japanese curriculum, but, unlike the United States, little attention is paid to oral communication. A lack of effective oral communication skills frequently causes Japanese students serious problems if they attend school in the United States where oral proficiency is encouraged and expected.

The Japanese educational system is characterized by a high degree of uniformity. Following the Second World War, the Japanese realized that national prosperity depended on school outcomes. They, therefore, created a centralized ministry of education and standardized the school curriculum.[17] According to Nemoto, the education ministry sets national curriculum standards for all public schools, from kindergarten to high school, to ensure a standardized education.[18] Generally speaking, throughout Japan students in the same grade study essentially the same material in virtually the same kind of classroom at approximately the same time and pace.

Mexican schools present you with yet another insight of what a culture deems essential in the education of its people. Being familiar with Mexican educational practices is especially important to American educators because large numbers of students from Mexico now attend school in the U.S.

Mexican education practices differ in a number of ways from the educational systems found in the United States, China, Japan, Korea, or other countries. Mexico's educational system mandates completion of the twelfth grade, although the severe economic climate in parts of Mexico often precludes students from achieving this goal. While some Mexican classrooms appear similar to those in North America, many rural schools seldom have the luxury of individual textbooks or the use of videos and computers. According to Grossman, rural schoolteachers frequently may have to read from a single textbook while students recite after them or write down what is said in a notebook.[19]

As with most educational systems, history is emphasized in Mexico. But students are also taught Mexican cultural values as well as the arts, trades, and vocational skills. As Mexican children grow up within cooperative environments that emphasize strong family ties, schools reinforce this primary value by emphasizing cooperation over competition. So strong is the value of cooperation that "the Mexican student will tend to look down on overt competition because of his or her fear of arousing the envy and destructiveness of peers."[20]

As you can see from the examples we have discussed, cultures tend to teach what is essential for self-perpetuation and continuation from generation to generation. In many cases—particularly within industrialized cultures—there are close similarities in the areas of science and mathematics. But in other areas such as history, philosophy, and social values, there are frequently extensive differences in what is taught.

## HOW CULTURES TEACH

Since you now realize that what is taught in educational systems varies between cultures, you should not be surprised to find there are also differences in how students and teachers participate in the learning process. Being familiar with *what* a culture teaches can give you insight into that culture. Knowing *how* teaching occurs within a culture is just as important because it (1) *provides knowledge about the nature of the culture,* (2) *helps you understand interpersonal relationships among students and between students and teachers,* and (3) *helps you understand the importance a culture places on education.*

The formal education process prevalent in a culture is tied directly to the values and characteristics of that culture. It is common in some cultures for teachers to talk or lecture a great deal of the time, whereas in other cultures students do most of the talking. Silence and minimal vocal participation is characteristic of some classrooms, whereas others tend to be noisy and active. In many cultures, students listen and then write down what their teacher has said rather than using individual textbooks. This is particularly true in countries where the economy prohibits the luxury of individual textbooks. Also, as you shall see, the authority vested in the teacher differs from culture to culture. Even nonverbal aspects such as space, distance, time, and dress codes are cultural variables that are reflected in classroom behavior. We will pause for a moment to look at some of the diverse behaviors that reveal the uniqueness of some cultures' classrooms.

In Spain, classrooms are characterized by a lack of competition. Unlike American students, Spanish students do not compete for grades. Ideas and information are shared and not treated as if they were the domain of one person. Classrooms truly reflect the Spanish proverb that states, "Three helping one another will do as much as six men singly." Spanish schools do not emphasize extracurricular activities. Spanish students, therefore, tend to spend about twice as much time pursuing academic subjects than do American students. As we noted in Chapter 5 when we discussed cultural values, the Spanish culture has a high level of uncertainty. Spanish classrooms, therefore, tend to be very structured to reduce that uncertainty and make students feel comfortable. To this end, teachers outline specific objectives for the day, enforce rules of conduct, and explain assignments clearly. The Spanish culture considers teachers to be experts; students are expected to agree with their teachers at all times or be viewed as disloyal. On examinations and written assignments, students are expected to repeat the teacher's ideas rather than provide their own thoughts or creative answers.

Reward for student achievement is not immediate in the Spanish classroom. Students must complete their homework assignments and other projects on time, but they must wait until their final examination to receive a grade. Student evaluations do not emphasize how well the student did but rather what needs to be improved.

In Japan, social standing is determined largely by the attained level of education and the prestige of the schools attended. This has created a teaching system that is intensely competitive yet nourishes the cultural values of group solidarity and collaboration. One of the most important teaching methods in Japanese schools is rote memorization of factual knowledge. Classroom instructors spend most of their time giving lectures and writing on blackboards. Students copy down what teachers say and memorize facts and figures. In a geography class, for instance, students memorize the names and capital cities of all major countries, and the location of large rivers, mountains, islands, and oceans. In a world history class, students might memorize important facts about the United States such as the Civil War, the Emancipation Proclamation, and the Marshall Plan, but they do not analyze the causes or social implications of these events.[21]

In many collective cultures, conformity is stressed in the classroom.

Korean educational processes are similar to those in Japan. Teachers assume leadership roles in the areas of social values, civic awareness and duty, and academic preparation. Parents hold teachers responsible for disciplining their children, and children are often told that their teachers will be notified if they misbehave at home.

For most subjects, Korean students remain in their homerooms and teachers rotate among classes. This permits the homeroom teacher to be both the social and academic counselor who can easily deal with discipline problems. As group solidarity and conformity are important goals in the Korean educational system, having students take all of their classes together and wear uniforms leads to the achievement of these goals. These goals are further realized through rules governing appearance, such as hair length for boys and no makeup for girls, which are strictly enforced even on the way to and from school.

Numerous cultural values are also reinforced in the Mexican classroom. For example, Ting-Toomey believes that because Mexico is a collective culture it tends to deal with conflict in a manner that reflects consideration of the feelings of others.[22] Collectivism is also revealed by the high level of cooperation in the Mexican classroom. It is not uncommon, according to Grossman, for Mexican students to share their homework or answers with others in order to display group solidarity, generosity, and helpfulness.[23] In the Mexican classroom, group interaction is the primary learning mode, yet there are times when the teacher will talk and students will sit quietly at their desks. Because Mexican culture values conversation, when students are engaged in group interaction, they will participate enthusiastically in classroom discussion. Because it is not considered impolite for more than one person to speak at the same time, multiple conversations may occur simultaneously. Teachers move about the classroom during these periods, interact at very close distances, and offer pats on the back or touches as a means of praise and positive reinforcement.

Finally, as we have already indicated, Mexicans value the present. As the famous Latino writer Octavio Paz said, "Reality is a staircase going neither up nor down; we don't move, today is today, always is today." This focus on the present pervades the Mexican classroom. As Headden suggests, rather than moving from one subject area to another simply because the clock tells them it is time to change topics, Mexican students work at a relaxed pace even if it means taking longer to finish. Mexican students are more concerned with doing a job well, regardless of the amount of time required.[24]

From our discussion of these representative educational systems, it should be clear to you that culture dramatically affects the learning process. What a culture teaches exemplifies that culture's unique history and traditions. Cultures also differ in how they teach—lecture versus interaction, cooperation versus competition, silence versus noise, active versus passive, textbook versus recitation, and the like. Even the status of teachers and the esteem in which education is held are reflections of a culture's values. We will now turn our attention to the complex issue of multicultural education in the U.S. and the challenges inherent in meeting the educational needs of many culturally diverse students learning in the same classroom.

# Education in a Multicultural Society

As we indicated in Chapter 1, the world is experiencing a major population explosion with a predicted world population of 8.3 billion by 2025. The U.S. is not immune to the effects of this population explosion. The forces of globalization on immigration policies have made it possible for many people from diverse cultures to call the United States home. This means that the racial and ethnic composition of the U.S. population is changing dramatically. Demographer Harold Hodgkinson predicts that over the next twenty-five years the African-American population will increase slowly while the Asian, Latino, and Native American populations will increase rapidly.[25]

You should not be surprised to discover that cultural diversity has found its way into American classrooms. With the arrival of new immigrants, there is a corresponding group of immigrant children, and the schools become the recipients of these children.[26] In this section, we will explore how American schools are responding to the challenge of cultural diversity. First, we will examine the *challenges of multicultural education*. Next, we will look at *cultural learning styles*. And third, we will examine *cultural interaction styles*.

## CHALLENGES OF MULTICULTURAL EDUCATION

The need for effective multicultural education is a fact that must be faced by the educational establishment. Regardless of a student's native culture or co-cultural membership, the goal of multicultural education must be to prepare students to become useful, functioning members of society. This is a significant challenge because cultural diversity in the classroom produces a group of students who have different learning styles as well as different goals, expectations, and communication styles. Meeting this challenge requires that educational systems continually adapt to the ever-changing cultural dynamics found in U.S. classrooms. The nature of this challenge is provided by Gollnick and Chinn, who state:

> Educators today are faced with an overwhelming challenge to prepare students from diverse cultural backgrounds to live in a rapidly changing society and a world in which some groups have greater societal benefits than others because of race, ethnicity, gender, class, language, religion, ability, or age. Schools of the future will become increasingly culturally diverse. But it is not only ethnic and racial diversity that is challenging schools. During the past 35 years, new waves of immigrants have come from parts of the world unfamiliar to many Americans. With them have come their religions, which seem even stranger to Americans than these new people.[27]

Recognizing this challenge is a first step. But, as Gay indicates, meeting the challenge is a difficult assignment.

> People coming from Asia, the Middle East, Latin America, Eastern Europe, and Africa differ greatly from earlier generations of immigrants who came primarily from western and northern Europe. These unfamiliar groups, cultures, traditions, and languages can produce anxieties, hostilities, prejudices, and racist behaviors among those who do not understand the newcomers or who perceive them as threats to their safety and security.[28]

But, when faced with these problems, the spirit of multiculturalism demands that everyone's commonality be recognized and affirmed. To help achieve this objective, Banks and his colleagues believe that

> Schools can make a significant difference in the lives of students, and they are a key to maintaining a free and democratic society. Democratic societies are fragile and are works in progress. Their existence depends on a thoughtful citizenry that believes in democratic ideals and is willing and able to participate in the civic life of the nation.[29]

Bruffee further holds that "schools should be looking for ways to engage culturally dissimilar students in understanding and dealing with one another effectively."[30]

From these perspectives, if schools are to meet the challenge of multicultural education, they must provide students with intellectual awakening and growth. A multicultural student body is important to the experiences of both the dominant culture and co-cultures alike. Such an approach to education requires an educational strategy in which "students' cultural backgrounds are used to develop effective classroom instruction and school environments. It is designed to support and extend the concepts of culture, diversity, equality, social justice, and democracy in the formal school setting."[31]

The difficulties associated with educating students in a multicultural nation are not easily solved. The problems facing education in the United States are complicated by two interrelated factors. First, the American educational system, as Althen points out, "is based on the idea that as many people as possible should have access to as much education as possible."[32] This means that the educational system must accommodate all levels of student ability and all areas of interest. The second factor is the increasing student cultural diversity. Le Roux describes this dynamic when he says:

> Education can never be culturally neutral. No educational system anywhere develops or exists independently or remains unaffected by its social or historical roots. The policies, practices and perspectives of the prevailing dominant culture influence educational content and approach. Because no social structure is homogeneous, often minority "cultural goods" are sacrificed for the sake of maintaining and fostering the dominant culture.[33]

In order to achieve the goals described above, Gollnick and Chinn believe that the practice of multicultural education should be based on the following set of beliefs and assumptions:

- Cultural differences have strength and value.
- Schools should be models for the expression of human rights and respect for cultural differences.
- Social justice and equality for all people should be of paramount importance in the design and delivery of curricula.
- Attitudes and values necessary for the continuation of a democratic society can be promoted in schools.
- Schooling can provide the knowledge, dispositions, and skills for the redistribution of power and income among diverse groups.
- Educators working with families and communities can create an environment that is supportive of multiculturalism.[34]

Recognizing the goals of multicultural education is only a first step in learning to become a competent multicultural educator. In the next section we will turn our attention to the connection between culture and learning so that you can both understand that relationship and use that knowledge to help you better construct effective messages for the multicultural classroom context.

## CULTURE AND LEARNING

Aristotle once wrote, "To learn is a natural pleasure, not confined to philosophers, but common to all men." While learning itself may be natural to humankind, people differ in how they prefer to learn. Over time, cultures have adopted approaches to learning that best fit their unique needs. Consequently, the manner in which people prefer to learn is culturally diverse, and this diversity affects the way in which people learn and process information.[35] The strength of the link between culture and learning is shown by Hollins, King, and Haymen, who report that culture and ethnicity have a far greater influence on learning than social class.[36]

Although there are a variety of culturally influenced learning styles, it is important at this juncture to note that no learning style is better or worse than another.[37] In fact, diverse learning styles may be an advantage to education. As Gay believes, learning styles should be looked upon as tools to improve the school achievement of diverse students by creating more cultural congruity in the teaching/learning process.[38] Additionally, research has shown that "when students are permitted to learn difficult academic information or skills through their identified learning style preferences, they tend to achieve statistically higher test and aptitude scores than when instruction is dissonant with their preferences."[39]

Children entering the multicultural classroom come from culturally diverse backgrounds and bring with them different ideas about education. This gives rise to two subjects relevant to multicultural education: (1) *cultural styles* and (2) *learning and cognition*. Both of these issues affect how students learn and participate in the educational process.

**Cultural Styles.** Cultural styles describe overarching cultural orientations of ethnocultural groups. These orientations are expressed as behaviors reflecting a *modal personality*.[40] The modal personality or style of a group refers to behaviors that are most likely to be found in a sample of the population. You must remember that modal or most likely behavior does not necessarily mean that everyone or even most of the members of a particular culture reflect or share the same trait. As Shade, Kelly, and Oberg observe, "what we are describing are stylistic patterns that seem to be observed in a large percentage of a particular cultural or co-cultural population."[41]

Categorizing cultures runs the risk of stereotyping and trying to fit all members into a neat set of characteristics. Yehieli and Grey caution that attempting to fit the world's cultures and co-cultures into a handful of categories is difficult and not completely accurate. It can, however, help educators understand how cultures differ from one another.[42] Bearing this caution in mind, we will present you three general cultural styles and their characteristics identified by Lewis,[43] and reported by Yehieli and Grey, that have proven useful in describing cultural diversity in people's behavior. The three styles are *linear-active, multi-active,* and *reactive* cultures. These styles and their associated behavioral characteristics are outlined below.

### Linear-Active Cultures

- Value facts and figures
- Respect highly organized planners
- Think linearly
- Use a straightforward, direct communication style
- Take task-oriented approaches
- Prefer rationalism and science over religion

Typical examples of linear-active cultures include white mainstream Americans and Western Europeans.

### Multi-Active Cultures

- Value emotions, close relationships, compassion, warmth, and feelings
- Act more impulsively than people from linear-active or reactive cultures

- Prefer face-to-face interaction
- Use direct and animated communication style
- Feel uncomfortable with silence

Typical examples of multi-active cultures are African Americans, Africans, Arabs, Jews, and Latinos.

### Reactive Cultures

- Value subtle communication: listen first, then respond
- Honor harmony, humility, and agreement
- Use indirect communication style
- Tolerate silence and find it meaningful

Typical examples of reactive cultures are Asian Americans, Pacific Islanders, and Native Americans.[44]

If you consider these behaviors for a moment, you should see that they reflect deep structure cultural or co-cultural beliefs, values, and worldviews. These cultural styles also affect the way in which people learn because they influence learning and cognitive styles.

**Learning and Cognition Styles.** Education researchers have investigated learning styles and teaching methods in order to determine how children from diverse backgrounds prefer to learn. Below we will present brief descriptions of ten learning styles. Although each described style is unique, you will see some overlap between them. From this presentation, you should develop an enhanced sense of how people from different cultures and co-cultures prefer to learn.

*Field Independence versus Field Sensitivity.* This learning style reflects how people tend to perceive their environment and whether they focus on the field (the whole concept) or concentrate on parts of the field. This style is sometimes seen as referring to whether one sees the forest or the trees. In describing field-sensitive individuals, Gollnick and Chinn report these "individuals have a more global perspective of their surroundings; they are more sensitive to the social field. Field-independent individuals tend to be more analytical and more comfortably focused on impersonal, abstract aspects of stimuli in the environment."[45] Field-sensitive students prefer to work with others, seek guidance from their teachers, and receive rewards based on group relations. Field-independent students, however, prefer to work independently, are task oriented, and prefer rewards based on individual competition.

Low-context, highly industrialized, individualistic societies such as the United States are predominantly field-independent. High-context, traditional, collectivistic societies like Mexico and Japan tend to be field sensitive. According to Leung, African Americans, Asian Americans, Hispanic Americans, Native Americans, and Hmong students prefer a field-sensitive, holistic style.[46] Kush indicates, however, that while children raised in traditional Mexican settings tend to develop a more field-dependent learning style, children raised in Mexican-American families that have assimilated aspects of the Anglo culture seem to embrace a more field-independent learning style.[47]

*Cooperation versus Competition.* This learning style reflects whether students prefer to work together in a cooperative environment or to work independently in competition with one another. Students from collective cultures expect and accept group work;

in fact, they often work harder in a group than they do alone. Students in individualistic cultures expect to be graded more on individual work. Cultures, however, do vary in the degree to which they stress cooperation or competition. Latino cultures, says Grossman, teach their children to cooperate and work collectively in groups. North Americans, on the other hand, teach their young to work individually and to compete with one another.[48] In addition to the Latino culture, African Americans, Asian Americans, Pacific Rim Americans, Filipino Americans, and Hawaiians tend to raise their children cooperatively. Students working together on class assignments manifest this emphasis in the classroom. For example, in Hawaiian families, multiple caretakers, particularly older siblings, bring up children. According to Hollins, King, and Haymen, this behavior extends to the classroom and is evidenced by "high rates of peer interaction, frequently offering help to peers or requesting assistance from them."[49] In addition, Cleary and Peacock indicate that Native Americans tend to thrive in cooperative rather than competitive learning environments.[50]

***Trial and Error versus "Watch, Then Do."*** Some people prefer to learn by engaging themselves in a task and learning to do it by trial and error. Others desire demonstrations and want to observe first and then attempt the task. Many mainstream American students prefer to solve problems and reach conclusions by trial and error. This approach is not common in all cultures. As Grossman notes, in many cultures, "individuals are expected to continue to watch how something is done as many times and for as long as necessary until they feel they can do it."[51] According to Cleary and Peacock, many Native American students prefer to watch until they feel competent to engage in an educational activity.[52]

***Tolerance versus Intolerance for Ambiguity.*** This classification is concerned with how well people deal with ambiguous situations. Students from some cultures are open-minded about contradictions, differences, and uncertainty. Students from others, however, prefer a structured, predictable environment with little change. Although U.S. culture generally has a high tolerance for ambiguity, the classroom tends to be an exception. The U.S. school day is frequently quite structured with students moving from subject to subject and often room to room based on the clock. Tolerance or intolerance for ambiguity also affects what is taught in the classroom. For example, U.S. culture emphasizes right/wrong, correct/incorrect, yes/no answers with emphases on logic, rationalism, and cause and effect relationships. In contrast, many non-Western cultures are less tied to logic and rationalism. American Indian cultures, for instance, give little regard to seeking truth in absolute terms.

The remaining six learning styles reflect additional ways in which people learn. As you will see, the learning styles relate to different learning preferences and they do not apply to all students. They are, however, important when planning curricula for multicultural classrooms.

***Listening and Receiving.*** This is a passive learning style in which students rely on peers, family, or other authority figures to tell them what to think, what opinion to have, and how to respond. Asian and some Asian-American students may benefit from this learning approach. Shade, Kelly, and Oberg report that "this form of learning may be found in classrooms in which the teacher merely provides information to students who passively absorb it by listening and taking notes or completing worksheets."[53]

*Analytical Learning Approach.* In this learning style, students use deductive and/or inductive logic to discover knowledge. Students prefer to use certain formulas or algorithms that lead them to deduce certain facts, or experiment, discover a concept, or acquire knowledge through induction."[54]

*Intuition.* In this approach, students prefer to seek knowledge by developing insights into or about a situation or an idea. Bypassing the usual methods of discovery or proof, learners make cognitive leaps to conclusions or ideas they perceive as self-evident."[55] In some instances, this form of learning may be associated with mysticism or spirituality.

*Aesthetics.* Here students prefer to learn by experiencing visual images, rhythms, cadence, time, and patterns of their environment and thus gain a sense of the world around them. Learning or knowing comes through perception—seeing, feeling, touching, experiencing. This model of learning is sometimes defined as the basis for creativity or doing creative thinking.[56]

*Constructive Learning.* Students who prefer a constructive learning style tend to create their own models, theories, or representations of ideas. "They take what they perceive to be important information and integrate it and connect it with their own experiences or worldviews.[57]

*Tactile/Kinesthetic.* In this style, learners benefit from field trips, role-playing, hands-on training, using tools, and working in laboratory settings. These experiences provide the learner with the physical engagement that works best for them. Because of their need to touch things, these students may benefit from building tangible representations of lessons such as models.[58]

**Relational Styles for Learning.** Relational styles refer to the manner in which people relate to one another. As with other aspects of human behavior, how people interact with others is learned within a cultural context. Individual relational styles carry over into the classroom setting and can affect classroom interaction. Although there is an abundance of relational styles, we will discuss five such styles that are relevant to the multicultural education setting.

*Dependency/Independence.* This relational style reflects the degree to which students rely on the support, help, and opinions of their teachers. Grossman highlights some cultural differences regarding this relational style when he notes that "compared to European American students, many but not all non-European American students, especially Hispanic Americans, Native Americans, Filipino Americans, and Southeast Asian Americans, tend to be more interested in obtaining their teachers' direction and feedback."[59] If, as an educator, you are aware of this need for outside support, you can develop effective support strategies for students who seem to show little initiative or independence.

*Participation/Passivity.* Some students like to be actively engaged in the learning process, while others prefer to remain passive. Some cultures train their children to participate actively in the learning process by asking questions and engaging in discussion. In other cultures, the teacher holds all the information and disseminates it to the students, who are expected to be passive and merely listen and take notes. In many Latino, Asian, and Pacific Islander cultures, students are expected to learn by listening, watching (observing), and imitating. In the American school system, however, critical thinking, judgmental questioning, and active initiation of discussions are expected patterns of relational interaction.

***Impulsivity/Reflectivity.*** Students from different cultural backgrounds may differ in how long they think about a question or problem before arriving at a conclusion or stating an answer. In the United States, students are taught to make quick responses to questions. As Gollnick and Chinn observe, "Impulsive students respond rapidly to tasks; they are the first ones to raise their hands to answer the teacher's question and the first ones to complete a test."[60] In other cultures, such as the Japanese, students are reflective and arrive at answers slowly. Two Japanese proverbs underscore the idea of being reflective: "Add caution to caution" and "He who rushes after two hares will catch neither." In cultures that emphasize reflectivity, students who guess or err are perceived as guilty of not having taken enough time to find the correct answer. In many Asian cultures, such behavior can result in a painful loss of face. Asian and Native Americans, notes Grossman, are examples of students who are taught to examine all sides of an issue and all possible implications before answering.[61] Along the impulsivity/reflectivity dimension, Mexican and North American cultures are somewhat similar. Both cultures teach their children to think on their feet and make quick responses or guesses to questions. The major difference between these two cultures lies in their motivation to respond. According to Grossman, Latino students respond quickly because they wish to please their teachers and make the moment pleasant. North American students respond rapidly because they are motivated by individual success and achievement.[62]

***Aural, Visual, and Verbal Preferences.*** Students differ in terms of their preferences for aural, visual, or verbal stimulation. For example, Cleary and Peacock indicate that Native Americans tend to be both visual and oral learners and prefer to use a combination of visual and oral learning styles, although they lean toward visual learning.[63] This preference means that they learn through direct observation or by viewing images. In addition, the strong oral tradition of American Indian cultures predisposes many Indians to be oral learners. Cleary and Peacock describe the impact of an oral learning tradition among American Indians:

> The strong oral tradition of American Indian tribal groups remains a potent influence on the ways many of the students learn, despite the fact that many of these students are first language English speakers or the fact that many have not been directly influenced by traditional storytellers.[64]

This propensity for listening may seem like an advantage for Indian students, but because they listen without providing much feedback, teachers often perceive them as not paying attention or not being involved in learning. Other cultures prefer to relate in an aural mode over other forms. Grossman identifies several co-cultures that prefer this learning style: "Many students, including African Americans, Hispanic Americans, Haitian Americans and Hmong Americans tend to be aural learners."[65]

As educators, you should anticipate that multicultural classrooms will contain both visual and verbal learners. To create an effective learning environment, you must provide a multi-sensory approach to teaching.

***Energy/Calmness.*** Some students prefer a highly active and animated classroom. Others desire a calm and placid environment. Again, these preferences are in part

*Because of the challenges of multicultural education, teachers must learn to motivate students from a variety of backgrounds.*

© Michael Newman/PhotoEdit

culture based. African-American students, for instance, are used to more stimulation than is found in many schools. Franklyn explains this style:

> Many African American children are exposed to high-energy, fast-paced home environments, where there is simultaneous variable stimulation (e.g., televisions and music playing simultaneously and people talking and moving in and about the home freely). Hence, low energy, monolithic environments (as seen in many traditional school environments) are less stimulating. . . . Variety in instruction provides the spirit and enthusiasm for learning.[66]

With an understanding of these diverse learning and relational styles, by now you should realize the potential for chaos in a classroom if some or all of these preferred learning and relational styles were present simultaneously. Schools that provide a multicultural learning environment must find a way in which all students utilize learning and relational styles that best suit their cultural backgrounds.

**Cultural Motivation Styles.** In addition to cultures having specific learning styles, cultures emphasize specific reasons to engage in learning. These reasons are called motivation styles and are the underlying reasons why students want to learn. What motivates students to learn is a primary concern for the multicultural educator who must be aware of and employ a variety of motivational techniques that coincide with her or his students' cultural backgrounds. Here, we will discuss four types of motivational style that impact the multicultural classroom: *intrinsic motivation, extrinsic motivation, learning on demanded,* and *learning when interested.*

**Intrinsic Motivation.** Some students harbor an inner drive to succeed. This is called intrinsic motivation. Simply excelling at a task is sufficient reward to motivate these students. European-American students generally are motivated to learn for intrinsic reasons. North American students often desire to succeed academically so that they can secure a good position and earn a great deal of money—a manifestation of the value of materialism discussed in Chapter 5.

***Extrinsic Motivation.*** Other students lack this inner drive and need to be stimulated by outside rewards. Asian students are more likely to be extrinsically motivated. As Yao observes, "Asian children are often found to be motivated extrinsically by their parents and relatives. They study hard because they want to please their parents and impress their relatives."[67] American Indian students, says Grossman, are often externally motivated because they want to please others rather than offend or hurt them.[68]

***Learning on Demand.*** Learning on demand occurs in an environment that contains a set curriculum. Students are expected to study that which is scheduled without regard to their particular interest. Students from cultures with learning on demand orientations excel in this environment. Grossman captures this motivation style when he says, "All cultures require children to learn many things whether they want to or not."[69] In Japan, for instance, all students are required to memorize information such as dates, complex sequences, and lengthy formulas in mathematics, science, and social studies. Each student is also required to learn how to play a musical instrument, regardless of his or her musical ability, and instruction often begins in first grade.[70]

***Learning When Interested.*** In some cultures, people believe that they should learn what is useful and interesting to them rather than gaining information just for the sake of learning. Students from these cultures tend to thrive when they are permitted to learn about what is of interest and immediately relevant to them. Latino and Native American cultures, for example, stress the importance of learning what is relevant and useful. Walker, Dodd, and Bigelow describe the Native American approach to learning in the following paragraph.

> Native American students prefer to learn information that is personally interesting to them; therefore, interest is a key factor in their learning. When these students are not interested in a subject, they do not control their attention and orient themselves to learning an uninteresting task. Rather, they allocate their attention to other ideas that are more personally interesting, thus appearing detached from the learning situation.[71]

In light of the numerous examples we have just examined, it should be clear that multicultural educators must contend with a complex matrix of learning and motivational styles in their classrooms. It may be impossible to accommodate all of these styles simultaneously. But with teachers' awareness of these various learning styles, they can selectively employ styles that are most appropriate for their particular classroom.

**Cultural Interaction Styles.** In the educational process, communication is a significant activity because it is the mechanism through which learning occurs. As Le Roux notes, "No education can take place without interpersonal communication. Effective teaching can thus be qualified in terms of relating effectively in the classroom. Effective education thus also presupposes effective communication skills."[72] Yet students coming from different backgrounds may perceive and react differently to what a teacher says or does in the classroom because they have internalized culturally different interaction styles.

Shade, Kelly, and Oberg define interaction styles as the verbal, nonverbal, and communication rules that guide a community's use of language. Interaction styles are culturally diverse. Community members teach their children an accepted vocabulary, guidelines about what information is important, the appropriate way to listen, methods of getting attention, what represents an adaptable tone and voice level, and how to read kinetic codes.[73]

Recognition of interaction styles is important in the multicultural classroom because they govern the ways in which people communicate with one another. It is important for you to be familiar with cultural diversity in interaction styles because students bring their own learned ways of communicating to the classroom. Hence, we will discuss some of the most relevant styles found among co-cultures that are appropriate to the multicultural classroom.

In traditional American classrooms, students are expected to engage in a *passive-receptive* style of interaction where they listen quietly while teachers talk. Only when the teacher has finished do students respond, following some prearranged, stylized form—by asking or answering questions, validating or approving what was said, or taking individual, teacher-regulated turns at talking. Individual students gain the right to participate in the conversation only by permission of the teacher.[74]

In contrast to the passive-receptive interaction style, African American, Latino, and Native Hawaiian co-cultures make use of *participatory-interactive* interaction styles. In this particular style, speakers expect listeners to engage them actively through vocalized, motion, and movement responses as they are speaking. Both speakers and listeners are action-provoking partners in the construction of the conversation.[75] African Americans have an expressive or verbal communication style that is characteristic of their co-culture. "With tones, looks, gestures, signals and body language, African American children and adults engage in 'telling the truth' or 'telling it like it is.'"[76] To other cultures, this style may seem confrontational, insulting, and hurtful of people's feelings, but within the African-American community, the style reflects courage, honesty, and an unwillingness to comprise one's integrity.[77]

American Indians utilize a communication style that reflects the cultural dynamic of living with nature or living in harmony with people. Shade, Kelly, and Oberg indicate that "as such, individuals from this community pay close attention to every detail of the situation. They see and watch movement as reflected in gestures, facial expressions or changes in the physical setting. Even when engaged in conversations, individuals within this community are conducting long-distance scanning, noticing motions in the environment, and identifying objects and people from afar."[78]

The Athabaskan Indians of Alaska frequently experience problems interacting with whites because their communication style involves lengthy pauses between thoughts. A white speaker, report Nelson-Barber and Meier, may ask a question, then pause, waiting for the Indian speaker to reply. When it appears the listener has nothing to say, the white speaker will speak again. The Indian, who wishes to reply, but is accustomed to longer pauses between speakers, may not be given an adequate opportunity to speak. The implications for the white/Indian classroom interaction are obvious. If white teachers do not make a conscious shift from their own expectations to local notions about conversation, there will be little opportunity to engage students.[79]

Many Mexican Americans employ a communication style that involves verbal play with the use of jokes and humor similar to that found among African Americans. This approach provides release of tension and serves as a way of avoiding verbal disagreements, as arguing is considered rude and disrespectful. Diplomacy and tact are valued communication skills.[80]

One last example of co-cultural diversity in communication styles comes from Native Hawaiians who maintain many of their traditional cultural practices. According to Irvine, Native Hawaiians use a participatory-interactive style similar to the call-responses of African Americans. Known as "talk-story" or "co-narration," this style involves several students working collaboratively, or talking together to create an idea, tell a story, or complete a learning task.[81]

# Language Diversity in Multicultural Education

Language is an important and significant social dynamic in the multicultural classroom. As we indicated in Chapter 6, language is a system of symbolic substitution that enables you to share your experiences and internal states with others. In an ideal setting, the use of a communal language helps create mutual understanding, facilitates shared meanings, and permits communication with others on a similar level. The impact of immigration, however, has caused the use of a communal language to fade in American schools. As Gann indicates, students today arrive in schools with a variety of languages and dialects, determined by region, neighborhood, and social class.[82]

## DEGREE OF DIVERSITY

Nationally, in 2003, 19 percent of all students attending urban public schools did not speak English as their first language. Among this population of students, 64 percent of Asian and 68 percent of Latino children spoke a language other than English at home.[83] The U.S. Census has determined that of the estimated 45 million school-aged students in the nation's public schools, about 9.9 million, or approximately 22 percent, live in households in which languages other than English are spoken. In New York City public schools, children are taught in ten different languages; in Dade County, Florida, students speak no fewer than fifty-six tongues; and in California, one in three students speaks a language other than English at home.[84] According to Leppert, if existing trends continue, by 2040 one-half of the U.S. population will speak Spanish as a first language.[85] As a result of this changing population, some children come to school barely speaking English, some students are limited in their English-speaking ability, and other students are fully bilingual. In many urban schools, diversity has already eliminated the concept of an ethnic majority.

The lack of a common language in American classrooms is problematic as language diversity confounds the educational process. Abrams and Ferguson help detail the severity of this problem: "Students who arrive in the United States without basic reading and writing skills in English often experience an initial sense of frustration and failure in mainstream classes, finding themselves unable to cope with even simple texts and written assignments."[86]

Unfortunately, the educational system's response to this problem has not always been appropriate. Discrimination against students who use non-standard language is quite common in various policies and school practices, even among those that call for linguistic tolerance.[87] Le Roux summarizes this fault in the following paragraph:

> In schools the culture-bound use of language, which is often unevenly distributed among
> different ethnic or cultural groups represented in class, is frequently applied as the sole
> determinant when assessing the quality of student thought and performance. A lack of an

adequate English vocabulary severely affects the academic progress of many students from cultural and language groups other than the mainstream one. The danger is that language proficiency and not academic ability is being assessed in multicultural classrooms.[88]

If learners from diverse cultural backgrounds and languages are to succeed educationally, it is imperative that educators understand and respect students for whom English is a second language. King suggests this requires demonstrating patience and valuing students' contribution to the class. To this end, educators need to model respectful yet challenging communication and questioning skills that show respect for the diverse modes of language and student learning.[89] In addition, teachers must recognize that their students' ethnic identity is tied directly to their native language.

## LANGUAGE AND IDENTITY

In the educational setting, language performs the vital function of helping individuals construct and maintain their ethnic identity. As Dicker notes, "It is not surprising that our native language is often referred to as our 'mother tongue,' a term which recalls our earliest memories and influences."[90] A person's native language, thus, has deep significance because it is the seed of identity that blossoms as children grow.[91] Language helps individuals construct an identity that ties them to their in-group and at the same time sets them apart from other possible reference groups.[92] When non- or limited-English-speaking students enter the American school system, they are encouraged to assimilate into the English-speaking culture. This assimilation can act as a wedge between students' existing cultural identity and the social system into which they are entering. Teachers can mediate this difficult process by showing respect for their students' native languages and thus ease students' adaptation to an English-speaking culture.

## LIMITED ENGLISH PROFICIENCY STUDENTS

One thing that should be obvious to you by now is that limited English proficiency, or LEP, students have a hard time in school. Their difficulty involves both cognitive and linguistic issues. McKeon has identified four sources of their difficulty. First, LEP students must be concerned with both the cognitive aspects of learning subject matter and the linguistic problems of learning English. LEP students "must decipher the many structures and functions of the language before any content will make sense."[93] They must not only grasp the subject content but also make the new language express what they have learned. LEP students, therefore, must perform at a much higher cognitive and linguistic level than their English-speaking peers, who need only to deal with the cognitive aspects of learning.

A second problem faced by LEP students is academic insufficiency. Developing higher cognitive and linguistic levels is often difficult because of academic delays. Many students who first enter American schools are academically deficient in their native language. As a result, it is very difficult for them to function at prescribed grade levels, let alone at higher cognitive and linguistic levels.[94]

A third problem for LEP students is that they enroll in U.S. schools at various points in their academic career—kindergarten, second grade, eleventh grade, and so on. The problem this creates, according to McKeon, is that "the higher the grade level, the more limited-English-proficiency is likely to weigh on students because at higher levels of schooling, the cognitive and linguistic loads are heavier."[95]

The fourth complication for LEP students is that they arrive from countries that may emphasize different curricular sequences, content objectives, and instructional pedagogies. A deductive instructional approach generally is used in the United States, but many Asian cultures frequently use an inductive approach. U.S. schools emphasize written education, whereas African and Middle Eastern schools emphasize oral education. As we have noted before, the U.S. culture values argumentation, debate, directness, and assertiveness. Since many other cultures emphasize accord, harmony, and cooperation, students from these cultures may not possess the oral argumentative skills that are often required in North American classrooms.

## Multicultural Competency in the Classroom

We have highlighted several key issues in multicultural education. By so doing, it has not been our intent to generate an image of an educational system that is helplessly mired in problems. Instead, by identifying the impact of culture on educating a diverse society, illuminating the problematic issues, and considering the concerns of all those involved, we hope to extend the dialogue of multicultural education.

One important conclusion should have emerged by now: "Communication in the learning environment is influenced by cultural, psychological and contextual factors and it involves the application of interpersonal and intrapersonal values."[96] Before educators can create effective messages, they must possess a comprehensive understanding of the linguistic, ethnic, cultural, and social class diversity present in today's schools. Thus, as Banks and his colleagues indicate, "teachers should become knowledgeable about the cultural backgrounds of their students. They also must acquire the skills needed to translate that knowledge into effective instruction and an enriched curriculum."[97]

Teachers must understand that culture creates expectations about appropriate behaviors for teachers and students alike and prescribes the "best" ways to learn. Additionally, teachers must obtain a more coherent view of learning styles that will provide not only personal empowerment but also a social perspective truly reflective of the social reality in the larger world.[98] Educators must, as White-Clark specifies,

> learn specific communication strategies that will enhance the achievement of culturally diverse students. These messages will result in teachers being concerned individuals who command respect, respect students, are strict, although caring, in requiring all of their students to meet high academic and behavioral standards; they are concerned not only with the cognitive development which is taking place in their students, but also with their students; affective, social, and emotional development; they use a culturally relevant approach to literacy teaching.[99]

The development of these strategies, as White-Clark indicates, must be derived from a knowledge of ethnic-cultural diversity, a multiple-perspective outlook, knowledge about inequality in the multi-ethnic society and of values and skills to tackle inequality, holding values and skills aimed at safeguarding ethnic-cultural diversity, and holding values and skills necessary for living democratically in a multi-ethnic context.[100]

Because schools abound with cultural diversity, educators, students, and parents must learn to communicate with one another and work together seeking solutions to their problems. With this optimistic outlook in mind, we will consider four topics that we believe can lead to the development of culturally competent classroom communication: (1) *developing multicultural competence*, (2) *multicultural classrooms*, (3) *multicultural communication competence*, and (4) *developing multicultural communication strategies*.

## DEVELOPING MULTICULTURAL PROFICIENCY

When you enter a multicultural educational situation, you must be prepared to deal with the inherent conflicting cultural values and practices. You must also be prepared to help answer this question posed by Hollins: "In a culturally diverse society where a central purpose of school is cultural transmission, whose culture should be transmitted, and whose cultural values and practices should guide the schooling process for the nation?"[101] To equip yourself to fit into this environment, you must first *understand yourself* and, second, *understand diversity*.

**Understanding Self.** The Greek philosopher Socrates once wrote, "Know thyself." This is excellent advice for anyone working in a multicultural environment. Put into practical terms, educators must be aware of what they bring to the classroom. Hollins explains this need in the paragraph below:

> As a classroom teacher, you bring your own cultural norms into your professional practice. The extent to which your teaching behavior will become an extension of your own culture exclusively or will incorporate the cultures of the students you teach may be influenced by your perceptions of the relationship between culture and school practices, political beliefs, and conceptualization of school learning.[102]

This realization is important because, as Le Roux indicates, teachers are often not aware of their prejudices, which can lead to unintentional racism.[103] An honest, straightforward evaluation can be very helpful in discovering your prejudices. Rhine suggests several questions you might ask yourself, such as "What are my strengths?" "What are my weaknesses?" "How can I enhance my strengths and compensate for my weaknesses?" "Do I have any ethnic or gender biases?" "How do these biases manifest themselves in my classroom?" "Does my ethnic or gender identification affect my classroom?" "Am I prepared to handle attacks on my own racial background or those of my students?" "What new knowledge or experiences can I seek to assist in these issues?"[104] Your answers to these questions can be enlightening as you approach the multicultural learning environment. You will have a good idea of what you can do best, and more importantly, you will know the areas in which you need to improve.

**Understanding Diversity.** Anyone associated with education needs to be as unbiased as possible and know as much as they can about the cultural backgrounds of their students. This includes a familiarity with the educational structure of the students' cultural heritages as well as their particular learning-style preferences, linguistic rules, nonverbal behaviors, and gender-role expectations. As Banks and his colleagues say, "Teachers should become knowledgeable about the cultural backgrounds of their students. They should also acquire the skills needed to translate that knowledge into effective instruction and an enriched curriculum."[105] While this is an admirable goal, it is not easily attained. Wan describes some of the factors that can impede reaching this goal: "When people experience a new cultural environment, they are likely to experience conflict between their own cultural predispositions and the values, beliefs, and opinions of the host culture."[106] Although acquisition of this knowledge places an initial burden on you, such knowledge will facilitate understanding and learning in the classroom. Acknowledging diversity is consistent with the traditional educational goal of exploring alternatives that change students' lives.[107]

Robins, Lindsey, Lindsey, and Terrell detail for you some of the essential capabilities competent multicultural teachers must possess:

- *Assess culture.* Be aware of your own culture and the effect it may have on the people in your classroom. Learn about the culture of the school and the cultures of the students and you'll anticipate how they will interact with, conflict with, and enhance one another.
- *Value diversity.* Welcome a diverse group of learners into your classroom and appreciate the challenges diversity brings. You'll share this appreciation with the learners in your class, developing a community of learning with them.
- *Manage the dynamics of difference.* Recognize that conflict is a normal and natural part of life. Develop the skills to manage conflict in a positive way. Help learners understand that what appear to be clashes in personalities may in fact be conflicts in culture.
- *Institutionalize cultural knowledge.* Work to influence the culture of your school so that its policies and practices are informed by the guiding principles of cultural proficiency. Take advantage of teachable moments to share cultural knowledge about the instructors, their managers, the learners, and the communities from which they come. You'll create opportunities for these groups to learn about one another and to engage in ways that honor who they are and challenge them to be better still.[108]

In an educational context, where cultural competence guides the development of the social environment, a sense of community is essential. Nelson-Barber and Meier report that discussions with minority students about their schooling experiences have revealed a sense of not feeling at home in the classroom. Students' perceptions of nonmembership is one of the most fundamental issues for proficient multicultural teachers to understand.[109]

## MULTICULTURAL CLASSROOMS

It might be tempting to think of classroom communication as a verbal utterance such as "Open your math books to page 137 and solve problems one through eight." Effective communication in a multicultural classroom encompasses much more. A major goal in multicultural education is to make all students feel welcome and at home in their learning environment. Nelson-Barber and Meier emphasize this important point:

> In order for school to be a place that enables students to become whoever they want to be, it must first be a place where students are recognized and celebrated for who they are. Multicultural classrooms are successful only to the extent that they provide a context for students with different experiences to forge connections with one another, while allowing them to maintain their identity.[110]

One approach to communicating this message is to create a classroom that reflects a multicultural community.

**Classroom as Community.** You can begin to resolve students' feelings of nonmembership by creating a sense of community in the classroom. To attain this objective,

Ramsey suggests that educators must move away from teaching practices that exclude and ignore diversity and move toward teaching approaches that recognize and incorporate these differences in all aspects of their instructional approach.[111]

In discussing several important aspects of a classroom as a community, Leeman suggests that educators must create environments in which commonality among the members of the class is valued. He also recommends that teachers foster an atmosphere of trust and personal involvement between students and between students and teachers, utilize an open way of solving conflicts that students perceive as fair, encourage active participation of the students in the school, and emphasize interaction among students.[112] To create a classroom community, Shade, Kelly, and Oberg suggest several principles that must be fulfilled:

- A learning community must be inviting.
- The leader of the learning community must send personally inviting messages.
- An inviting classroom has firm, consistent, and loving control.
- An inviting learning community provides students with a sense that they can accomplish the tasks being asked of them.[113]

In a classroom with a successful sense of community, students should be able to say that "At school, I feel safe enough to . . ."

- Be myself
- Give my opinion
- Choose what I want to do and to do it
- Go wherever I want to[114]

Most of this chapter has dealt with issues of cultural diversity. The reason for devoting so much time to this topic is to give you the background and perspectives to (1) *develop multicultural communication competence* and (2) *create effective multicultural communication strategies*.


## MULTICULTURAL COMMUNICATION COMPETENCE

Teachers need to maintain an open dialogue with their students. This does not imply that students should be in charge of the learning environment. Instead, it means that teachers and students should discuss and negotiate learning styles, communication patterns, and expectations. This will require that students make connections between course content and their preferred learning method. Students' voices should be routinely honored in the classroom through open discussion or teacher/student dialogues.[115]

Communication competence, however, requires more than just opening the door to student/teacher dialogue. It requires an understanding of what determinants are active in a particular classroom. Le Roux offers several important ideas you can incorporate into your personality in order to be an effective multicultural communicator:

> Within-group differences within a cultural group may be as great as or greater than between-group cultural differences. It must be emphasized that culture is neither the only nor even the most important variable when differences or potentially conflicting situations arise in diverse settings. Socio-economic status, educational background, religion, gender, age, and worldview are some of the determinants that influence the *who* and *what* we are, but also *why* we react in a particular way in certain situations.[116]

# MULTICULTURAL COMMUNICATION STRATEGIES

Effective communication requires the development of appropriate communication strategies. The first consideration in developing effective strategies is to think about the culture in which messages are being constructed. For instance, in a traditional American classroom situation, when a teacher has a disciplinary problem with a student, he or she might warn the student that further inappropriate behavior will result in a trip to the vice-principal's office. In a remote Alaskan village, however, a different message such as "I'll be steaming with your mother tonight" might be appropriate. In this cultural situation, homes in the village have no running water and bathing takes place in a communal gender-specific steam room as a group activity. For the student, this message would translate as "I will be with your mother tonight, so stop misbehaving or I will talk with her about you."

In a more general sense, effective communication strategies should be based upon a number of factors and assumptions. We will limit our discussion to two specific factors: *immediacy* and *empathy*.

**Immediacy.** Teachers may employ the technique of immediacy, which uses approach and avoidance behaviors to optimize their teacher/student communication and enhance their credibility. According to Johnson and Miller, students are attracted to persons and things they like, evaluate highly, and prefer. They avoid or move away from things they dislike, evaluate negatively, or do not prefer.[117]

Research has revealed a positive relationship between immediacy and cognitive learning and between immediacy and credibility across numerous cultures. Even in high-power-distance cultures such as in Kenya, say Johnson and Miller, students seem to benefit from seeing their teachers as approachable.[118] Additionally, Jazayeri reports that immediacy is also related to students' perceptions of teacher effectiveness in Mexico, Norway, China, Japan, and Australia, as well as in the United States.[119]

**Empathy.** The development of empathic faculties on the part of both teachers and students is another requisite for the community classroom. Empathy is the ability to assume the role of another and, by imagining the world as the other sees it, predict accurately the motives, attitudes, feelings, and needs of the other. Empathy involves two steps. First, empathic teachers are able to imagine how it must be for immigrant students to adapt to a classroom where surroundings, language, and behavior are often different and unfamiliar. Second, empathy involves communicating in ways that are rewarding to the student who is the object of empathic prediction.[120]

Accurate prediction requires accepting people for who they are and thus understanding what can realistically be expected of them. Because you accept other people for who they are does not mean that you must agree with what they say or do. Although you accept students' feelings, ideas, and behavior as legitimate, you still do not have to agree with them. Students do, however, react positively to empathic understanding—to the realization that they are understood, not evaluated or judged, but understood from their own point of view rather than from someone elses.[121]

The ability to communicate empathy requires learning specific behaviors and practice; it does not happen automatically. Cooper and Simonds offer four guidelines that you may follow in order to become an empathic communicator:

- *Communicate a supportive climate.* Community classrooms are supposed to create a supportive climate. To nourish this climate, you must create messages that indicate you understand your students' feelings and needs rather than expressing judgments of student behavior.

- *Attend to a student's nonverbal behavior as well as their verbal communication.* Effective interpretation of messages requires that you respond to the cognitive content of the message as well as to the meta-communication expressed nonverbally.
- *Accurately reflect and clarify feelings.* There is a tendency to respond more to the content of what others say—the ideas, thoughts, opinions, and attitudes expressed—than to the feelings that the other is expressing. Feelings are more difficult to respond to because in the mainstream American culture most people have less experience responding to feelings than to ideas.
- *Be genuine and congruent.* You are not likely to foster a good relationship with students if you communicate in false or misleading ways. A truly constructive relationship is one in which the participants respond to each other in an honest and genuine fashion. Your communication is congruent when the things that you do and say accurately reflect your real thoughts and feelings.[122]

It is important to remember that children have the capacity to make rapid adaptations across vastly different cultural and linguistic systems. When teachers and students work together, learning is facilitated and enjoyable. As Malcolm points out, "We are underestimating teachers when we consider them to be captives to the invisible culture of the classroom and we are underestimating pupils when we consider them to be captives to their own cultural patterns which contradict it."[123]

We hope that at this point you understand and appreciate the impact cultural diversity has on the American classroom. And we want you to acknowledge that an education system that fails to understand cultural diversity will lose the richness of values, worldviews, lifestyles, and perspectives of the diverse American co-cultures.

## Summary

- Globalization and multiculturalism influence education.
- Systems of formal and informal education seek to meet the perceived needs of societies.
- Schools are a primary means by which a culture's history and traditions are passed from generation to generation.
- Schools teach the informal knowledge of a culture.
- Schools are a primary vehicle for teaching cultural values.
- Schools in the United States are becoming increasingly more diverse.
- Schools no longer teach only Eurocentric cultural values; instead, today schools routinely teach the experiences and values of many cultures.
- Learning styles are particular ways that individuals receive or process information.
- Cognitive, communication, relational, and motivational learning styles have a profound impact on classroom learning.
- Students who are limited in their English proficiency face various obstacles in the classroom.
- Teachers should be aware of what they bring to the classroom in terms of their strengths, weaknesses, and biases.
- Assessing the acculturation levels of the students in the classroom will help teachers determine how much their students are involved in their own culture as well as the Anglo-American culture.

# Activities

1. Develop some classroom exercises that might help students in a multicultural classroom overcome ethnocentrism.
2. Looking back upon your school experiences, make a plan that would integrate the various cultures in a multicultural classroom into a classroom community.
3. Explain how you would reconcile the learning styles of students in a sixth-grade classroom with the following student clientele: six Latinos, eight European Americans, five African Americans, four Japanese, and one Iranian.
4. Given the classroom described above, what kinds of communication problems would you anticipate at the beginning of the school year?

# Discussion Ideas

1. A college professor has a new student from China with excellent reading fluency in English but limited oral proficiency in her class. What factors should the professor consider when expecting full participation in classroom interaction?
2. In what ways does your current classroom setting embody American cultural values?
3. As an educational administrator, how would you handle a situation where a teacher maintains a classroom setting in which culturally diverse learning styles are ignored?
4. How can multicultural education be effective if it must deal with a large variety of learning styles and language differences?

## CHAPTER 10

# Cultural Influences on Context: The Health Care Setting

*If you are not in tune with the universe, there is sickness in the heart and mind.*

**NAVAJO SAYING**

*He who has health, has hope; and he who has hope has everything.*

**ARABIAN SAYING**

## Culture, Health Care, and Communication

Understanding the relationship between culture, health, and communication is essential for anyone involved in the health care professions. In the intercultural setting it is the health care provider that is given the task of communicating with people from a host of cultural backgrounds. Calderón and Beltrán emphasize this importance when they say that communication "is a fundamental ingredient in virtually every form of medicine and health."[1] If there is not clear and meaningful communication between health care providers and patients, the entire medical treatment process can be problematic. The potential for a serious crisis is of course compounded when the variable of culture is placed into the equation. Purnell and Paulanka emphasize this point when they suggest that global and multicultural populations produce a major impact on the ability of health care providers to provide an adequate level of service.[2] Kundhal and Kundhal echo this same concern when they write, "the cultural and ethnic backgrounds of patients can shape their views of illness and well-being in both the physical and spiritual realm and affect their perceptions of health care as well as the outcome of their treatment."[3]

Consequently, anyone involved with health care must consider cultural diversity in order to provide optimal care for all clients. In a multicultural society, people from dissimilar cultural backgrounds frequently have different expectations and employ disparate styles of communication. This important fact is often not recognized because, as Gropper tells you, "professional health care providers frequently assume that people's cultures are more similar than they actually are."[4] Consequently, misunderstandings arising from ineffective communication may result in misdiagnosis, risky procedures, unnecessary treatments, and needless suffering.[5] As a means of preventing these situations, Purnell and Paulanka advocate that health care providers "must be culturally sensitive and aware if they are to communicate culturally congruent health and treatment information."[6] They also believe that effective health care communication requires both health care providers and patients to freely share their thoughts and feelings with one another.[7]

The health care profession is one of the fastest-growing industries in the United States. If you are not already, you will someday be associated with a health care program as a provider or a recipient. And with the growing diversity of the U.S. population, in all likelihood that association will involve some degree of intercultural communication. At best, communication between health care professionals and clients is complex even when the two are from the same culture. The influx of immigrants from different ethnic and racial origins makes it even more difficult for health care professionals to provide safe, effective, and culturally congruent care. Kirkwood emphasizes this point when he says:

> The one area where all must be treated on equal terms is in the health care field. Health care workers have a reputation for being caring, understanding people. Because of this, they are aware that these newcomers have different beliefs and customs that need to be considered in the hospital setting. Different religious traditions have led to certain practices and behavior. These need to be respected, particularly when and where there is a person dying. Respect for these requirements is essential for the healthy grief of the relatives and friends.[8]

This requires that providers have knowledge about and understanding of a patient's cultural orientation, religion, language, interaction patterns, and attitudes toward health and illness. According to Donnelly, when health care workers are unaware of a person's cultural values as well as their family's expectations about roles and relationships, a communication disconnect can occur that may result in serious—if not fatal—outcomes.[9]

Kreps and Thornton believe that "human communication is the singularly most important tool health professionals have to provide health care to their clients."[10] But in an intercultural situation when people may not share the same language or the same culture, their attempts to communicate may not establish the necessary connection that facilitates healing. This lack of effective communication may be due to what Spector describes as a conflict between a health care provider's and a client's belief systems where the provider may be unable to recognize or understand there is a conflict, and hence, not find ways to minimize it.[11] Health care providers, therefore, must learn ways of caring for their clients that match the clients' perceptions of particular health problems and their treatment.[12] Communication becomes the tool by which health care providers can understand the cultural pressures and folk beliefs that are common to various cultures and co-cultures. It should be clear that understanding a client's belief systems is an important first step toward providing culturally competent health care. But the desire to provide culturally competent care often fails to recognize the impact of cultural diversity. Koenig and Gates-Williams make this important point when they say that many "calls for 'culturally competent care' ignore the dynamic nature of culture."[13]

As children grow up, they learn about culturally appropriate health care behaviors from their parents, families, and schools. Culture teaches children what makes people sick or causes injury. And, as Fitzgerald indicates, it also teaches them the language or words they should use to describe body parts and illness sensations, how they should behave when they are ill or injured, and what they need to say or do to feel better.[14]

It should be obvious that those who have grown up in diverse cultures have acquired very different sets of knowledge, beliefs, values, and attitudes about health. To help you understand these differences, this chapter explores six dimensions of cultural diversity that impact the health care system. First, we begin by looking at the relationship between diverse cultural worldviews and health care. Second, we consider health care belief systems. Third, we turn to diverse cultural beliefs about the causes of illness, how illness is treated, and how it can be prevented. Fourth, we explore some specific issues concerning religion, spirituality, and health care. Fifth, we examine communication patterns in the multicultural health care setting of the United States. And, finally, we offer some suggestions for improving intercultural health care communication.

# Culture and Health Care: Diverse Worldviews

Based upon our discussion of religions in Chapter 3, you should recognize that religious elements of culture account for many of the differences in how people view the world—including their views of health. Religion, however, is not the only worldview that influences health and illness. *Dualistic or holistic worldviews* and *mechanistic or non-mechanistic worldviews* also shape cultural perceptions of everything from the causes of illness to how illness is treated. We will discuss these views briefly before we proceed into the specifics of cultural diversity and the health care context.

## DUALISTIC AND HOLISTIC WORLDVIEWS

A dualistic worldview says that people and nature are two separate and distinct entities and thus values medical intervention carried out by physicians, nurses, and other health care practitioners. This dualistic relationship between humans and nature is found, according to Smart, among members of such religions as Judaism, Christianity, and Islam "because they see two separate parts to reality—God and creation."[15]

While dualism advocates a distinct separation of mind and body widely accepted in many Western cultures, you need to be aware that other cultures hold a different view. For example, Elgin points out that many Eastern cultures are profoundly nondualistic and hold a holistic vision of the world.[16] This philosophy sees the world as a unit—a world continuously creating and intimately infusing every aspect of the cosmos from its smallest detail to its grandest feature. Human beings in this orientation are held to be a unified body, mind, and spirit existing in a world that is holistic. This view would suggest that the person's entire body must be part of the healing process. In fact, "Chinese medicine teaches that health is a state of spiritual and physical harmony with nature."[17] In these cultures, many remedies and techniques are employed when a person becomes ill. In short, it is necessary to take care of the whole person, not just part of the person.

*In many cultures there is a belief that faith and prayer can create good health and even cure illness.*

## MECHANISTIC AND NON-MECHANISTIC WORLDVIEWS

A mechanistic worldview is common in the United States and is known by a variety of identifiers: *reason versus intuition, objectivity versus subjectivity,* or *science versus religion.* Regardless of the label, this aspect of the U.S. worldview deals with ways of knowing. Anthropologists Hoebel and Frost summarize this view in the following manner:

> American thought patterns are rational rather than mystic; the operative conception of the universe is mechanistic. The bedrock proposition upon which the whole worldview stands is the belief that the universe is a physical system operating in a determinate manner according to discoverable scientific laws. . . . Because they view the universe as a mechanism, Americans implicitly believe that individuals can manipulate it. Human beings need not accept it as it is; they may work on it, and as they gain in knowledge and improve their techniques, they even redesign it so that it will be more to their liking.[18]

Likewise, Paden believes that for many Westerners reasoning is considered to be humankind's "highest faculty and achievement."[19] For most Americans, facts are believed to be more reliable and dependable than subjective evaluations based on feelings and intuition. In short, the mechanistic worldview is orthodoxy and is a pervasive dynamic in Western culture.[20]

When the mechanistic view is applied to health care, there is a strong belief in the benefits of science and technology. Health care specialists use modern scientific tools such as x-rays, CAT, PET, MRI, or ultrasound scans, blood tests, and the like to discover why their clients are ill and to facilitate developing appropriate therapies that lead to cures.

The Eastern non-mechanistic worldview generally treats truth and reality quite differently than does the mechanistic worldview found in the West. Elgin explains that the non-mechanistic worldview is "a perspective that historically has emerged from such cultures as India, Tibet, Japan, China, and those of Southeast Asia. The non-mechanistic view is exemplified by spiritual traditions such as Buddhism, Hinduism, Taoism, and Zen."[21] Consequently, the roles of science and technology in the discovery and treatment of illness may be far less important than they are in the West. Whereas the Western view tends to place intellect and rationality above other traits, the Eastern view, according to Fisher and Luyster, often maintains that "intuition transcends the data of the senses and the manipulation of the mind to perceive truths that seem to lie beyond reason."[22] When dealing with illness, people who value an Eastern non-mechanistic worldview often believe that faith, magic, and supernatural forces can be employed as a means to good health.

In the next section, we are going to consider diversity in health belief systems. As you encounter these differing beliefs, we urge you to consider how the dualistic/holistic and mechanistic/non-mechanistic dimensions cause individuals from different cultures to differ significantly in their perception of health care.

# Health Belief Systems

Cultures are diverse in their understanding of what causes illness and how it should be treated and prevented. As Andrews explains:

> Generally, theories of health and disease/illness causation are based on the prevailing worldview held by a group. These worldviews include a group's health-related attitudes, beliefs, and practices and frequently are referred to as health belief systems.[23]

In Chinese medicine, for instance, a prevailing belief posits that "health is a state of spiritual and physical harmony with nature."[24] As a consequence, Hunter and Sexton indicate that the Chinese tend to be interested in health care that helps them attain this ideal.[25] In addition, many Africans and African Americans often perceive pain as a sign of illness or disease and often employ folk medicine to cure their illnesses.[26] Despite this diversity in worldviews, Andrews provides a paradigm in which all health belief systems can be divided into three major categories: *scientific/biomedical*, *magico-religious*, and *holistic*, each with its own corresponding system of health beliefs.[27]

## SCIENTIFIC/BIOMEDICAL SYSTEM

The scientific or biomedical system is derived from the dualistic and mechanistic viewpoint and is the dominant belief system in the United States, focusing on the objective diagnosis and scientific explanation of disease.[28] Andrews adds that under this paradigm is the belief that "life is controlled by a series of physical and biochemical processes that can be studied and manipulated by humans. Human health is understood in terms of physical and chemical processes.[29] This system disavows the metaphysical and usually ignores holistic approaches to medicine as well.[30] The biomedical health care system, as Luckmann relates, "is geared to conquer disease by battling the onslaught of microorganisms and diseased cells, as well as the breakdown of the body's organs due to aging."[31] Treatment in this approach seeks to destroy or remove the causative agent, repair the affected body part, or control the affected body system. And, as Angellucci adds, "Prevention of disease involves avoiding pathogens, agents, or activities known to cause abnormalities."[32]

## MAGICO-RELIGIOUS SYSTEM

The magico-religious system derives from a worldview in which the world is seen as an arena in which supernatural forces predominate.[33] Andrews describes this system as one where "the fate of the world and those in it, including humans, depends on the actions of God, or the gods, or other supernatural forces for good or evil."[34] Disease is perceived to result from the active intervention of supernatural beings (deity or gods), a nonhuman being (ghost or evil spirit), or a human (witch or sorcerer). The ill person is, therefore, a victim of punishment rendered by the supernatural agent. Treatment involves achieving positive association with spirits, deities, and so forth.[35]

Andrews believes that in the magico-religious perspective, "sorcery, breach of taboo, intrusion of a disease object, intrusion of a disease-causing spirit, and loss of soul are five widespread belief categories perceived to be responsible for illness."[36] Treatment involves calling forth and controlling supernatural forces for and against others and employs strategies that range from the use of "magic" by voodoo practitioners to the use of prayer by Christian Scientists.[37]

## HOLISTIC SYSTEM

The holistic perspective specifies that the universe is governed by natural laws that maintain order[38] and that "the forces of nature must be kept in natural balance or harmony."[39] Furthermore, well-being requires that a sense of equilibrium must be maintained between humans and the larger universe. Holistic approaches to medicine tend to be non-mechanistic and explain illness as a result of impersonal forces or conditions, including cold, heat, winds, dampness, and an upset in the balance of the basic body elements.[40] In this system, disease may result from disequilibria between the hot and cold elements of the body. "All foods, medicines, conditions, and emotions are ascribed hot and cold qualities."[41] The Vietnamese, says Nowak, frequently explain poor health as being the result of eating spoiled food or being exposed to inclement weather.[42] Treatment of illness involves restoring a person's hot/cold balance. This is done by prescribing remedies with hot forces to treat cold illnesses and using remedies with cold forces to cure hot illnesses. Additionally, as Angelucci explains, "Prevention of illness involves maintaining balance of the hot and cold forces within the mind, body, and environment."[43]

## ALTERNATIVE HEALTH CARE SYSTEMS

In addition to the three systems we just discussed, Luckmann[44] describes what she calls alternative health care systems. This approach differs significantly from the biomedical system, and its success cannot be conclusively determined by biomedical research. Alternative care includes diet therapy (macrobiotics and megavitamins), mind/body control methods (relaxation, counseling, prayer, hypnotherapy), working with the body structure (chiropractic, massage, and therapeutic touch), and pharmacologic and biologic therapies (antioxidants, oxidizing agents, and chelating therapy).[45]

Now that you have a basic understanding of the major categories of health belief systems, we will look at some of the cultural dynamics of these beliefs as they apply to the causes, treatment, and prevention of illness.

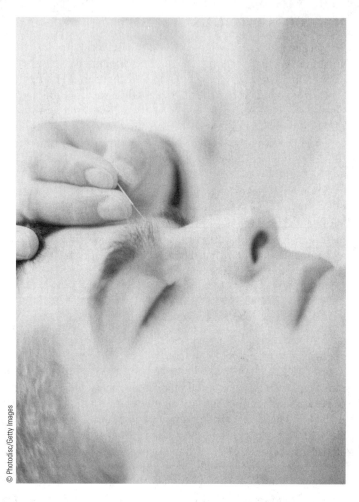

*Cultures differ in their understanding of the causes, treatments, and prevention of illness.*

# Cultural Diversity in the Causes of Illness

### SCIENTIFIC/BIOMEDICAL CAUSES

Most health care practitioners in Western cultures subscribe to the biomedical model of health and illness that we described above. This approach emphasizes biological concerns and is primarily interested in abnormalities in the structure and function of body systems and in the treatment of disease. Luckmann believes that adherents of this approach view the model as "more 'real' and significant in contrast to psychological and sociological explanations of illness."[46] Disease is believed to be present when a person's condition is seen to deviate from clearly established norms based on biomedical science. Treatments through surgery, medicine, or therapy are used to return the person to scientifically established norms.

### MAGICO-RELIGIOUS CAUSES

Magico-religious approaches to medicine are also sometimes called a supernatural approach[47] or a folk medicine approach.[48] This system "is widely accepted in traditional

Hispanic, Caribbean, African, and other cultures."[49] Cultural groups that follow this approach believe in a supernatural model that views illness as a sign of weakness, a punishment or retribution for shameful behavior such as lying, cheating, stealing, or a failure to show respect to elders.[50]

The Hmong, according to Giger and Davidhizar, "believe an individual's spirit is the guardian of the person's well-being. If the spirit is happy, then the person is happy—and well. A severe shock or scare may cause the individual's spirit to leave, resulting in unhappiness and ill health."[51] Laotians, as Dresser relates, hold a belief similar to the Hmong where "*Phi* (the spirits of nature) control people's lives and can cause illness."[52] For the Laotians, illness also may be caused by losing one of the body's thirty-two souls or by a sorcerer who can cast a spell by projecting foreign objects into a person's body. Often, examining the yolk of a freshly broken egg will tell a Laotian healer the exact cause of illness. In a similar manner, many Vietnamese also subscribe to magico-religious causes of illness.[53] For example, as Nowak indicates, many Vietnamese believe health problems such as the common cold, mild fever, and headache are caused by the natural element *cao gio*, which is associated with bad weather and cold drafts.[54]

Among some Latinos, health and disease are deemed to be consequences of God's approval or disapproval of one's behavior.[55] These Latinos are strongly influenced by their religious orientation from which they perceive God as the source of health.[56] Health, therefore, is seen as a gift from God and should not be taken lightly.[57] When illness does strike, their beliefs about its cause tend to reflect their religious beliefs. A fractured leg resulting from a fall, for instance, may be perceived as God's warning of future penalties for disobeying divine laws.[58]

One of the oldest and most widespread superstitions regarding the cause of illness is the *evil eye*, which is the belief that someone can project harm by gazing or staring at another.[59] Belief in the power of the evil eye exists in many parts of the world such as Southern Europe, the Middle East, and North America. Many ideas about the power of the evil eye were carried to the United States by immigrant populations where "these beliefs have persisted and may be quite strong among newer immigrants and heritage-consistent peoples."[60]

## HOLISTIC CAUSES

Holistic or naturalistic approaches to the cause of illness assume there are natural laws that govern everything and every person in the universe. For a person to be healthy, he or she must remain in harmony with nature's laws and willingly adjust and adapt to changes in their environment.[61]

In reviewing beliefs about holistic causes among Asian cultures, Giger and Davidhizar suggest that many people of Asian origin (Chinese, Filipinos, Koreans, Japanese, and Southeast Asians) do not believe they have control over nature. They possess a fatalistic perspective in which people adjust to the physical world rather than controlling or changing the environment.[62] Traditional Asian teachings stress a harmonious relationship with nature in which the forces of *yin* and *yang* are to be kept in balance. *Yin* represents a negative, inactive, feminine principle, while *yang* represents a positive, active, masculine force.[63] *Yin* and *yang* combine to produce every occurrence in life. Consequently, many Asians believe that an imbalance in this combination causes illness.[64]

Traditional Mexican and Puerto Rican medical beliefs are derived from the Greek humeral theory that specifies four humors of the body: "blood—hot and wet; yellow bile—hot and dry; phlegm—cold and wet; and black bile—cold and dry."[65] An imbalance of one of the four body humors is seen as a cause of illness.[66]

Spector suggests that people of African, Haitian, or Jamaican origin often view illness as a result of disharmony with nature.[67] Haitians, for instance, believe that both natural events such as viral infections and unnatural events such as spells, curses, magic, and evil people can cause others to become ill.[68]

In discussing American Indian views toward the causes of illness, Boyd explains that

Many American Indians with traditional orientations believe there is a reason for every sickness or pain. They believe that illness is the price to be paid either for something that happened in the past or for something that will happen in the future. . . . Everything is seen as being the result of something else, and this cause-and-effect relationship creates an eternal chain. American Indians do not subscribe to the germ theory of modern medicine. Illness is something that must be. Even the person who is experiencing the illness may not realize the reason for its occurrence, but it may, in fact, be the best possible price to pay for the past or future event(s).[69]

American Indians consider the earth "to be a living organism—the body of a higher individual, with a will and a desire to be well. For them, ill health is something that must be."[70] Spector continues to describe the American Indian belief system in this manner:

According to the American Indian belief system, a person should treat his or her body with respect, just as the earth should be treated with respect. When the earth is harmed, humankind is itself harmed, and conversely, when humans harm themselves they harm the earth. The earth gives food, shelter, and medicine to humankind, and for this reason, all things of the earth belong to human beings and nature.[71]

As you can see, cultural diversity in worldview results in multiple approaches to understanding the causes of illness. And, as you will see in the next section, cultural diversity leads to a variety of and sometimes contradictory ways of treating illness.

# Cultural Diversity in the Treatment of Illness

The English satirist Jonathan Swift wrote, "We are so fond of one another, because our ailments are the same." Notice he did not say that the treatments for ailments were the same. Just as cultures differ in their beliefs of what causes illness, they also differ in their views of what constitutes the proper treatment of illness. Thus, cultural diversity in the treatment of illness may also be understood by applying the *scientific/biomedical, magico-religious,* and *holistic* paradigms.

## SCIENTIFIC/BIOMEDICAL TREATMENTS

From the scientific/biomedical perspective, illness is an abnormality in the body's physical structure or its chemical functioning. Treatment attempts to return the body to its normal state through medical intervention that destroys or removes the cause of illness. In this approach, antibiotics may be administered to destroy illness-causing bacteria and antiviral vaccines may be used to treat viral infections. Surgery, chemotherapy, and radiation are employed to battle cancers. And nutritional supplements such as vitamins and minerals may be prescribed to help return the body to its normal state.

Scientific/biomedical treatments are the dominant form of treatment in the U.S. as well as many Western countries. In the United States, as elsewhere, some members of co-cultures may subscribe to a combination of beliefs about appropriate treatment and seek scientific/biomedical approaches for some illnesses and magico-religious or holistic forms for others. As Giger and Davidhizar point out, many Chinese Americans use both Western and Chinese medical services.[72] Many Filipinos are familiar with and accept Western medicine, although some Filipinos accept the efficacy of folk medicine and may consult with both Western-trained and indigenous healers.[73] Although Jewish Americans usually follow scientific/biomedical treatment protocols, their treatment may necessitate adjustment because of religious requirements. For instance, as Selekman relates, if an Orthodox Jew's condition is not life threatening, medical and surgical procedures should not occur on the Sabbath or holy days such as Yom Kippur.[74] Some Vietnamese may not seek scientific/biomedical treatment until they have exhausted their own resources. But, as Nowak points out, once a physician or nurse has been consulted, Vietnamese are usually quite cooperative and respect the wisdom and experience of biomedical practitioners.[75] Also, according to Chong, "Educated Latinos generally subscribe to the biomedical model of health as a state of complete physical, mental, and social well-being and not merely the absence of disease."[76]

## MAGICO-RELIGIOUS TREATMENTS

Many Asians—including Laotians, Hmong, and Vietnamese—as well as many people from Cuba, Puerto Rico, and Brazil believe that illness is in part caused by evil winds or spirits and seek treatments that are meant to induce the evil influence to leave the afflicted person. Many Asians employ a technique called "cupping" to drive out evil influences and cure illness. Cupping involves placing a heated glass upside down on the chest or back of the sick person and pulling it off after it has cooled and formed a vacuum. Another common treatment practiced by some Asians is called "spooning" or "coining." In the spooning treatment, a spoon is rubbed vigorously back and forth across the patient's body, most often on the back and the back of the neck. Coining involves the use of a coin about the size of a quarter rather than a spoon, which is rubbed on the back of the neck, the stomach, the chest, the upper arms, and even along the forehead and temples. Cupping, spooning, and coining are practices that are believed to "rub out" evil winds and spirits. They may, however, leave marks on the patient that the unaware Western practitioner may interpret as a form of physical abuse.

The Hmong employ folk healers to cure illness. These healers or shamans enter the spiritual world by chanting and summon good spirits who then diagnose illness and prescribe treatment to be carried out by the shamans. For members of the lu-Mein culture of Laos and Thailand, healing treatments may involve elaborate sacred ceremonies that require the sacrifice of a pig or chicken by a shaman in order to feed hungry spirits.[77]

Filipinos may hold magico-religious beliefs about illness that fit a general conceptualization of balance. Nydegger indicates that some Filipinos believe disease may be instigated by a sorcerer who causes a poison or noxious substance to be introduced into the body disturbing its normal equilibrium.[78] Filipinos also view pain as a part of living an honorable life and as an opportunity to attain a fuller spiritual life and atone for past transgressions leading them to appear stoic and able to be tolerant of a high degree of pain. Miranda, McBride, and Spangler believe that health care providers must recognize this mind set and both offer and encourage pain-relief medication for the Filipino who does not complain of pain.[79]

The perceived cause of an illness can often help determine which type of aid someone will seek. "Some Puerto Ricans, for instance, believe mental problems are caused by bad spirits and must therefore be dealt with by a person who specializes in spirits."[80] Many people of Latino descent utilize *curanderos* or folk healers along with institutionalized care. *Curanderismo* is a health treatment system with historical roots that combine Aztec, Spanish, spiritualistic, homeopathic, and scientific elements.[81] In addition, cultural beliefs can have a powerful influence on a patient's relationship with pain. Mexican women, for instance, have been known to refuse an epidural during childbirth because they (and their husbands) believe pain is part of becoming a mother.[82]

Many people from Cuba, Puerto Rico, and Brazil believe in *Santeria* (a type of religion). According to Dresser, when someone of this belief becomes sick, a *santero* is contacted, who consults an *Orisha* (saint-like deity) to assist in the cure.[83] Also, according to Galanti, it is not uncommon for Haitians to consult voodoo priests and priestesses for treatment that can involve candles, baths, charms, and spirit visits. Within the United States, some groups, particularly African Americans, rely on *pica*—a craving for nonfood substances—to treat illness. For example, an individual may eat laundry starch to "build up the blood" after an auto accident.[84] And, as Grossman relates, "Cubans may use traditional medicinal plants in the form of teas, potions, salves, or poultices. In the Little Havana community of Miami, *botanicas* sell a variety of herbs, ointments, oils, powders, incenses, and religious figurines to relieve maladies, bring good luck, drive away evil sprits, or break curses."[85]

## HOLISTIC/NATURALISTIC TREATMENTS

Holistic/naturalistic treatments are found in some Chinese medical practices. For example, Chinese medicine seeks to restore the balance between the *yin* and *yang* forces. Matocha explains this process in the following paragraph:

> The Chinese believe that health and a happy life can be maintained if the two forces of the *yang* and the *yin* are balanced. The hollow organs (bladder, intestines, stomach, and gallbladder), head, face, back, and lateral parts of the body are the *yang*. The solid viscera (heart, lung, liver, spleen, kidney, and pericardium), abdomen, chest, and the inner parts of the body are the *yin*. The *yin* is cold and the *yang* is hot. Health care providers need to be aware that the functions of life and the interplay of these functions, rather than the structures, are important to Chinese.[86]

Traditional methods of health protection among the Chinese include ingesting thousand-year-old eggs and following strict rules governing food combinations and foods that must be eaten before and after life events such as childbirth and surgery. Traditional cures include acupuncture, which is an ancient practice of applying needles to the body to cure diseases or relieve pain, moxibustion, which is a therapy based on the value of heat, and herbal remedies, such as ginseng, which are used widely by both Chinese and many Westerners.[87] Exercise is important, and many Chinese participate in formal exercise programs such as *tai chi.*

The Chinese are apt to self-medicate if they believe they know what is wrong or have been successfully treated by medicine or herbs in the past.[88] They may also rely on fortune-tellers to determine auspicious times to perform scheduled surgeries or other medical procedures.

Mexican folk medicine, which can be traced back to sixteenth-century Spain, is a common form of treating illness in Mexico. It looks beyond symptoms of illness and seeks to locate an imbalance in an individual's relationship with the environment, negative emotional states, and harmful social, spiritual, and physical factors. When one becomes ill, folk healers use foods and herbs to restore the desired balance. A hot disease is treated with cold or cool foods. A cold disease is treated by hot foods. Hot and cold do not refer to the temperature of the foods but to their intrinsic nature. Hot foods include chocolate, garlic, cinnamon, mint, and cheese. Cold foods include avocados, bananas, fruit juice, lima beans, and sugarcane.[89]

According to Burke, Wieser, and Keegan, the common folk healers in Mexico are *curanderos*, *yerberos*, and *sobadors*:

> *Curanderos* (healers), believed to be chosen and empowered by God, are the most respected folk healers. . . . *Yerberos* (herbalists) specialize in the use of herbs and spices to treat and prevent illness. . . . *Sobadors* (masseuses) attempt to correct musculoskeletal imbalances through massage or manipulation.[90]

Not all cultures subscribe to a specific approach in the treatment of illness. In Africa, for instance, there is no typical approach to seeking medical treatment. The effects of colonialism, spirituality, and ancestral traditions affect the varying perceptions toward health care. Many Africans differentiate health care into modern and traditional. Modern medicine follows the active biomedical model of Western medicine, while traditional medicine relies on folk healer practices. Depending on the type of illness, patients choose what they believe to be the most effective treatment.[91] In the U.S., as Campinha-Bacote relates, many African Americans will draw upon their ancestral roots and utilize folk practitioners selected from among spiritual leaders, grandparents, elders of the community, or voodoo doctors or priests.[92]

Although some of these treatments may seem unusual or even bizarre from a Western perspective, health care practitioners in other cultures have successfully employed these methods for centuries.

Now that you have developed a familiarity with cultural diversity in the causes and treatment of illness, we will turn your attention to how different cultures take steps to prevent illness.

# Cultural Diversity in the Prevention of Illness

Cultures differ in their beliefs and approaches to the prevention of illness. Unlike the causes and treatment of illness, where the methods are rather systematic, many cultures employ a combination of scientific/biomedical, magico-religious, and holistic approaches to prevent illness. In the United States and other highly technological cultures, good health is based on the ideals of annual physical examinations, immunizations at specified times, exercise, and good nutrition. Yet, many people also follow health regimens that may include stress-reducing massage and meditation as well as the ingestion of a variety of "natural" herbs to stimulate sexual performance, prevent or reduce memory loss, and promote energy. In addition, they may seek treatment from such health care practitioners as chiropractors, acupuncturists, or colon irrigationists as preventive measures.

In sharp contrast, many Muslim Afghanis rely on the Koran to protect them from illness. In a practice called *ta' wiz*, Koranic verses known as *shuist* or *dudi* are written on paper, wrapped in cloth, and worn by babies and the ill. Dressler reports that *shuist* verses may be written on paper, and then soaked in water that is drunk. *Dudi* verses might be written on paper and burned with rue close to the patient so the smoke will kill germs and ward off evil spirits.[93]

Many members of Mexican and Puerto Rican cultures, Giger and Davidhizar report, "believe that health may be the result of good luck or a reward from God for good behavior."[94] Consequently, they frequently depend on a variety of amulets or charms, often inscribed with magic symbols or sayings, to protect the wearer from disease or evil. Candles, herbs, crystals, statues of saints, shells, and herbal teas also are used to provide protection.

Many members of the Laotian culture may use a *Baci* ceremony of prayers and good wishes during pregnancy, birth, marriage, a change of location, illness, or surgery. Family members, including a *mor phorn* or wish priest, engage in group prayers while gathered around an altar of candles, incense, rice, folded banana leaves, holy water, flowers, and strings.[95] The Chinese, says Spector, often prepare amulets to ward off evil spirits and to protect their health.

> The amulets consist of a charm with an idol or Chinese character painted in red or black ink and written on a strip of yellow paper. These amulets are hung over doors or pasted on walls. They may be worn in the hair or placed in a red bag and pinned on clothing. Jade charms are particularly important because many Chinese see jade as the giver of children, health, immortality, wisdom, power, victory, growth, and food.[96]

Some cultures believe that violating cultural taboos can lead to illness. An example of this is found among several Native American cultures, who believe cutting a child's hair may cause the child to become sick and die. This belief can even extend to procedures on the child's head, such as stitches that require removal of the hair. The only way to avoid the death of the child is to counteract the violation of the taboo by attaching a medicine bundle to the child's chest.[97] In a similar manner, as Galanti explains, pregnant Hmong women ensure the health of their children by paying close attention to food cravings. It is their belief, for example, that if a woman "craved ginger and failed to eat it, her child will be born with an extra finger or toe."[98]

In our discussion about preventing and curing illness, we have so far examined some of the diverse ways in which cultures formally seek to prevent illness. Yet there are some cultures and co-cultures whose members may truncate their seeking preventive health care, may believe that the cure for their illnesses must be found within themselves, or may not attempt prevention at all.

Gays and lesbians, for instance, generally have lower rates of seeking preventive health care than the general population. Lesbian women are less likely than women in the general population to receive cancer-screening services such as mammography or Pap tests. Likewise, gay men are less likely to seek preventive health care than their heterosexual counterparts.[99] This reluctance may be due in part to societal homophobic views, which prompt gays and lesbians to keep their sexual identity secret. Many lesbians and gays report difficulty in communicating with their primary care provider, which causes delays in seeking health care.[100] Hesitancy to seek preventive medical care can be seen in other cultures as well. Such a tendency is expressed eloquently by a Yugoslavian proverb that says, "Good thoughts are half of health." This proverb implies that the act of thinking good thoughts wards against illness thus reducing the need to seek preventive medical care.

In other cultures, however, prevention may be a totally new concept. Many Haitians, for instance, do not believe in preventive health strategies and rarely engage in visits to physicians or obtain immunizations. They may eventually take ailing family members to the hospital but only when death is imminent.

Our examination of explanations, treatments, and prevention of illness clearly indicates that what a patient believes can profoundly affect the treatment process. While some of these health care beliefs and practices may seem strange, or even primitive, to you, remember that many cultures have not yet experienced the technological and economic benefits that are common in Western society. As a result, these less developed societies have little choice but to rely on their traditional health care customs that at times might be harmful to members of the culture. Western medicine, however, like the Western media, is rapidly reaching more people worldwide. As a consequence, many of the cultures we have discussed, while still adhering to their traditional medical practices, are becoming aware of and adapting Western scientific/biomedical approaches either alone or in conjunction with traditional cultural practices in the treatment of some illnesses.

Throughout our analysis of the link between health and culture, we have alluded to the impact of worldview, religion, and spirituality on health care. We now turn to those topics as a means of demonstrating how they actually get acted out.

# Religion, Spirituality, and Health Care

As we have mentioned throughout this chapter, religion, worldview, and spirituality are closely aligned with perceptions of health and illness.[101] Spector amplifies this position when he states:

> Religion strongly affects the way people interpret and respond to the signs and symptoms of illness. So pervasive is religion that the diets of many people are determined by their religious beliefs. Religion and the piety of a person determine not only the role that faith plays in the process of recovery but also in many instances the response to a given treatment and to the healing process.[102]

With regard to the role that religious beliefs play in health care, Kirkwood echoes Spector's view when he points out that within health care institutions socio-religious concerns are of great importance, no matter the country of origin or religion of the people involved. Of course, there are always some who are devout in their religious practice and others who are indifferent.[103] What we are suggesting is that religion and spirituality include all behaviors that give meaning to life and provide strength to the individual.[104]

In the Western scientific/biomedicine view of health, religion and magic have had limited explanatory power. Health care givers require no supernatural abilities, and for the most part, health tends to be segmented from religion and social relationships. Loustaunau and Sobo state that "biomedicine even divorces the mind from the body with different branches specializing in physical and mental health."[105] Yet, what has long been understood by many cultures around the world is now becoming recognized in Western society—a person's mental attitude and spirituality can help in the prevention and healing of illness. For people in many cultures, religion, spirituality, and health care are intertwined; religion provides solutions and solace when one is in ill health. As Spector tells you, "It [religion] dictates social, moral, and dietary practices that are designed to keep a person in balance and healthy and plays a vital role in a person's perception of the prevention of illness."[106]

As noted, a person's religious beliefs can have a significant effect on health care practices. For Hindus, Jews, Catholic, and Muslims, religion may be the primary focus underlying the manner in which certain health services and practices—such as seeking or limiting methods of birth control—are practiced. Dietary rules in the Jewish faith include specific methods for slaughtering animals and such strict proscriptions as not mixing meat and milk at the same meal.[107] The Koran provides guidelines for the Muslim diet, specifying what is permissible and what is not. And, as we mentioned earlier, Jews seek to avoid non-emergency medical procedures on the Sabbath or other holy days.

The Navajo believe wellness is related to their view of being in harmony with one's surroundings. When people are ill, a medicine man or woman will tell them what they have done to disrupt their harmony. Harmony is restored through the use of a healing ceremony. If a patient is being treated by a Western biomedical approach, according to Still and Hodgins, the healer may be summoned to conduct a healing ceremony before biomedical procedures are employed.[108]

You can see the connection between religion and health care in some African-American communities. Their religious behaviors are an integral part of life. African-American churches often play a major role in the development and survival of African Americans through prayers and rituals.[109]

The Catholic religion impacts strongly on the health-seeking behaviors of a large number of Catholic Latinos. Seeking the help of God to prevent or cure illness is common. Such help may be invoked by making promises, visiting shrines, offering medals and candles, and saying prayers.[110] Mexicans utilize two sayings that illustrate this view perfectly: "We submit to pain because it is inevitable, to bereavement because it is irreparable, and to death because it is our destiny," and "Man proposes and God disposes."

Miller reports that in many Eastern religions, people are portrayed as spiritual, and a sense of wellness or good health influences a person's spiritual journey.[111] In these cases, health and spirituality are reciprocal. Bhayana highlights this balance in the paragraph below:

> Quiet acceptance of one's fate, also pervasive in some Eastern philosophies, is difficult to reconcile with a commitment to preventive methods. Symptoms may be ignored because the fear of dying is lessened. Extraordinary efforts to preserve life may be hard to accept when a deep-rooted belief in reincarnation exists.[112]

Buddhism and Hinduism both offer examples of how religion influences health care practices. Although it is not a common practice, there are some Buddhists who do not accept responsibility for illness because they believe that illness is caused by spirits.[113] And, among some Hindu sects, people are not concerned about ill health because they believe it is a result of misdeeds committed in a past life. They also believe that praying for health is the lowest form of prayer because medical treatment, although useful, is transitory.[114]

For many Arabs, illness is often regarded as punishment for one's sins. Yet, according to Abu Gharbieh, by providing cures, Allah manifests mercy and compassion and supplies a vehicle for repentance and gratitude.[115]

By now, it should be obvious to you that religion and spirituality exert a strong influence on the way people define illness and choose to prevent it. In the United States, modern medicine and technology have often outweighed spiritual faith and alternative healing methods. Yet, as medical practices in other cultures become better known, some Western health care personnel are becoming more open to the influence of spiritual healing and acknowledging it as an effective form of recovery and prevention.

## Health Care Considerations for a Culturally Diverse Population

One of the major themes of this chapter has been that health care delivery in the United States may be hampered by cultural diversity. As Marquand says, "With the rising cultural diversity of individuals entering the United States comes increasing diversity in the health care beliefs and practices of those seeking health care."[116] In dealing with this diversity, agreeable ways of caring for all members of society must be discovered and practiced. Spector argues,

> In many situations, this is not difficult; in other situations, it seems impossible. . . . [T]he needs most difficult to meet are those of people whose belief systems are most different from the "mainstream" health-care provider culture.[117]

In health care, culture intervenes at every step of the process.[118] If optimal health care for all is to be a goal in the multicultural United States, then health care providers

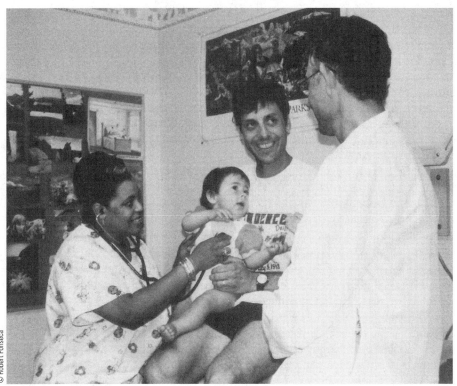

*Health care professionals need excellent intercultural communication skills.*

© Robert Fonseca

must be aware of the potential problems that may be caused by cultural differences. As Qureshi tells you:

> Ignorance of culture can lead to false diagnosis. Only by taking a full history and being sensitive to a patient's culture can a doctor make an accurate diagnosis, understand the patterns of illness in various ethnic groups, and isolate diseases which may or may not be specific to a particular ethnic group.[119]

We have clearly established that cultural diversity is a key consideration in providing effective health care. We will now examine *family roles, self-disclosure, language, nonverbal messages,* and *formality* as they relate to health care communication.

## FAMILY ROLES

As you learned in Chapters 2 and 3, cultures assign specific roles to various members of a family. These roles contribute structure and guidelines that tell family members how to perceive, communicate about, and deal with health care issues. The importance of knowing about family roles to health care communication is emphasized by Andrews:

> Knowledge of a client's family and kinship structure helps you to ascertain the values, decision-making patterns, and overall communication within the household. It is necessary to identify the significant others whom clients perceived to be important in their care and who may be responsible for decision making that affects their health care. For example, *familism*—which emphasizes interdependence over independence, affiliation over confrontation, and cooperation over competition—may dictate that important decisions affecting the client be made by the family, not the individual alone.[120]

We will now examine how family roles influence communication in the health care setting by discussing the impact of *dominance patterns, modesty and female purity,* and *pregnancy and childbirth.*

**Dominance Patterns.** In much of the world, gender roles are not as fluid as in the United States; many cultures make strong distinctions between what is appropriate behavior for men and for women. An awareness of family dominance patterns is important for determining whom the health care worker should include in the conversation. "In the African-American family, the traditional head of the household is the mother."[121] But this pattern is an exception. Within the structure of a traditional Latino family, for instance, "the father has the dominant role assuming responsibility for being head of the house and the decision maker."[122] In the Middle East, Asia, Latin America, Mexico, and Africa, men are in positions of authority both in and out of the home. If this cultural characteristic is misunderstood by health care providers, it can become a source of confusion and conflict in the health care setting.

Let us begin with a question: "Why might an East Indian Hindu woman refuse to answer personal questions about her health in the presence of her husband?" Reddy believes the answer lies in the assignment of family roles within the woman's culture. Traditionally, the role of East Indian Hindu women is faithfulness and servility to the husband.[123] The husband is regarded as the head of the family and serves as the primary spokesperson regarding family matters, including the health care of the individual members.[124] In a manner similar to the East Indian Hindu culture, Saudi Arabian men believe it is their duty to act as an intermediary between the world and their wives. When Saudi men (and others like them) take their wives to U.S. emergency rooms for treatment or to doctor visits, they usually answer all the questions directed to their wives. Abu Gharbieh says that even if the wife can speak English, the Saudi male will speak for her, usually relating the client's complaints with greater vehemence than the patient might.[125]

The traditional Vietnamese family is strictly patriarchal and is almost always an extended family with the male having the duty of carrying on the family name through his progeny. Some Vietnamese men, say Still and Hodgins, are not accustomed to female authority figures and may have difficulty relating to women as professional health care providers.[126] When dealing with patients from these and similar cultures, health care practitioners should expect the wife to defer all questions to her husband, although he may consult her before he answers the question. The practitioner who ignores the husband and seeks information directly from the wife may raise feelings of personal humiliation and disrespect of the husband in the eyes of the family.[127]

Gender misunderstandings can have severe consequences. At one extreme, routine procedures may be delayed, and at the other extreme, the life of the patient may be endangered. Galanti demonstrates this with the case of Rosa Gutierrez and her two-month-old son.

> Rosa had brought her son to the emergency room because he was having diarrhea and had not been nursing. The staff discovered that he was also suffering from sepsis, dehydration, and high fever. The physician wanted to perform a routine spinal tap, but Rosa refused to allow it. When asked why, she said she needed her husband's permission before anything could be done to the baby. The staff tried to convince her that this was a routine procedure, but Rosa was adamant. Nothing could be done until her husband arrived.[128]

The difficulty here is that in many traditional Mexican households the man makes most of the major decisions. Although Rosa could have legally signed the spinal tap consent form, from her cultural perspective she did not have the authority to sign it.

**Modesty and Female Purity.** The English essayist Joseph Addison wrote, "Modesty is not only an ornament, but also a guard to virtue." Modesty and female purity can affect exhibited behaviors in the health care setting. A woman from a culture in which modesty is highly valued may be reluctant to seek medical attention, follow medical advice, or undress for a medical examination because of these values. Unfortunately, Western practitioners do not always understand the possible consequences of violating these cultural norms, particularly if the woman is from an extremely traditional background.

The cultural importance placed on modesty and the reluctance to disrobe for examinations, as Abu Gharbieh reports, causes many Arab women to be reluctant about seeking health care.[129] Furthermore, in the Arabic culture, men must be treated by males and women by females. The impact of these cultural beliefs is demonstrated in an instance where flu shots were being administered to immigrant Somalis. Not only did male nurses have to give shots to the men and female nurses give them to women, but the shots had to be given to males and females in separate rooms.[130]

**Pregnancy and Childbirth.** Most of the world embraces the Irish saying, "Bricks and mortar make a house, but children make a home." We can say with some degree of accuracy that in every culture, childbearing and the gift of life are treated with celebration. All cultures have specific attitudes, practices, gender-related roles, and normative behaviors with regard to pregnancy and childbirth.[131] Although child-bearing is a deeply felt emotional experience, the meaning and significance of the experience are often dictated by culture. Child bearing is valued for distinct reasons in different cultures. In the Mexican culture, a woman's status is often derived from the number of children she has borne. In Asian cultures, children, especially males, are valued because they carry on the family name and traditionally care for their parents in old age. For Orthodox Jews, childbirth is valued because it is in obedience to biblical law to multiply and replenish the earth. In some cultures, children are valued because of the labor and support they can contribute to the family.

Whereas birth might be a private experience in one culture, it can be a social event in another. For North Americans, the birth experience is normally a private affair involving only the nuclear family. In many non-Anglo cultures, the birth experience is anticipated and shared by a large extended family. Often, some Asian, Mexican, and Roma families crowd outside delivery rooms awaiting the event. Attendance of the actual birth itself varies from culture to culture as well. In North America, it is not unusual for the woman's husband to assist her in the labor and delivery of their child, but in many cultures this is not done. Orthodox Jewish men rarely participate in childbirth because a man is forbidden to touch a woman during "unclean" times—when blood is present during menstruation or childbirth. Many Arab men feel that birthing is a female's job. Many Latinos feel this way as well, so the woman's mother usually accompanies her during a birth, and the husband does not see his wife or child until delivery is over and they have both been cleaned and dressed. In traditional Asian families, where couples reside with the husband's parents, the mother-in-law is often the birth attendant.[132]

**Self-Disclosure.** Closely related to cultural diversity in family roles are the cultural norms that govern self-disclosure. Effective health care demands that the patient trust the health care professional and both parties exchange essential medical information. Yet, cultural customs may strongly influence patient self-disclosure and communication. Although Americans tend to have few qualms about disclosing personal information, in other cultures personal information is considered private and may be difficult to obtain.

Cultural norms often dictate who can discuss what subject with whom. Some Latino women, for instance, may feel embarrassed or shy when talking about "female problems." Frequently, they will refrain from talking about birth control or childbirth with American physicians. When a Latina who spoke no English had to sign an informed consent form for a hysterectomy, she relied upon her son to act as a translator. When the son explained the procedure to his mother, he seemed to be translating accurately and indicating the proper body parts. The next day, however, his mother was very angry when she learned that her uterus had been removed and she could no longer bear children. Because of the cultural prohibition against the son discussing his mother's private parts, the uncomfortable son had explained that a tumor would be removed from her abdomen and pointed to the general area where the surgery would be performed. Thus, even when the same language is shared, communication may be ineffective. It is best to use same-sex interpreters when translating matters of a sexual or private nature.

As you learned in Chapter 5, Asian cultures are generally classified as high-context. For first- and second-generation Asian Americans, the problems associated with self-disclosure may be linked directly to this cultural characteristic. Among the Chinese, for instance, too much talk about personal matters is often considered in poor taste. The Japanese are expected to be shy and withdrawn—at least in public.[133] As a consequence, some Asian women may be reluctant to talk about or discuss female problems.

Germans value proper decorum and also are reluctant to disclose highly personal information in most settings. The proverb "A friend to everyone is a friend to no one" clearly underscores this view of superficial relationships. This reticent and reserved attitude often transfers to the health care context.

Communication characteristics among Russian immigrants have been fashioned by traditions and experiences over centuries of historical context. Their culture remains unique from that of other Europeans as well as Americans. Elliott indicates that Russians tend not to trust doctors. Many Russians fear nurses, physicians, and even receiving treatment, which leads to a lower reliance on health care professionals and a reluctance to talk about or disclose personal information.[134]

These examples demonstrate that not all patients are willing to talk to health care providers with the same degree of openness. Being familiar with these cultural variations regarding communication styles and self-disclosure can help the health care professional extract valuable information concerning the patient's health.

## LANGUAGE BARRIERS

The complexities of language were spelled out in Chapter 6, yet the role of language diversity in the health care setting needs to be explored because it can create seemingly impossible situations. How, for instance, does a young Latina woman who speaks no English explain to a medical team in a hospital emergency ward that the liquid drops she put into her baby's mouth (which were intended for the baby's ears) have made her child worse?

Elgin helps explain the difficulty of language barriers:

> Human languages around the world present very different models of what health and illness/injury/disability and medical care are, depending on the metaphors the language uses for these items and all their related phenomena. The range in medical models encoded in human languages around the world stretches from "All health problems are caused by evil spirits and bad thoughts" through "All health problems are punishments for sin" to "All health problems are caused by germs" and far beyond.[135]

Obvious problems such as language differences and the use of interpreters can complicate medical interactions. Think for a moment about the potential for confusion if a Western doctor speaks of a woman's "period" to someone whose culture does not use this metaphor. Also, a patient's literal translation of the phrase "have your tubes tied" may render an understanding that they can just as easily be "untied." Medical implications resulting from such miscommunication may be detrimental to the patient.

Subtle forms of communication behavior can have just as great an impact. In the following example, Galanti shows how the use of idioms can cause serious misunderstandings:

> A Chinese-born physician called the night nurse one evening to check on a patient scheduled for surgery the next day. The nurse advised the physician that she noticed a new hesitancy in the patient's attitude. "To tell you the truth, doctor, I think Mrs. Colby is getting cold feet." The physician was not familiar with this idiom, suspected circulation problems, and ordered vascular tests.[136]

The use of medical jargon may also complicate health care interaction. For example, the use of words like *rhinitis* rather than *hay fever*, *anosmia* instead of *loss of taste*, and *dementia* rather than *memory loss* can be confusing even to native-language speakers and even more so for individuals who speak a different language. In addition, Witte and Morrison relate that "it is sometimes difficult for members of diverse cultures to articulate their symptoms and feelings in a nonnative language."[137] As a result, vague symptoms and generalized descriptions of health may be conveyed.

Latinos are one of the most medically underserved co-cultures in the United States. Variation in language performance is a crucial determinant of health service utilization where not speaking English can deter Latinos from using health care services.[138] The seriousness of this problem is spelled out by Alcaley: "Compared with non-Hispanic whites in the United States, Hispanics, especially Mexican-Americans, underutilize preventive health services. They tend to forgo such routine procedures as physical checkups, dental and eye examinations, and prenatal care."[139] Within the Mexican-American community, a most obvious barrier to health care is language. In spite of the fact that Spanish-speaking people constitute one of the largest minority groups in this country, very few health care deliverers speak Spanish.[140]

Another factor important to consider about using Spanish when interacting with Latinos is to realize that language use varies among different Spanish-speaking communities. Osborn reported an instance when what was "considered to be a sensitive and acceptable translation of a safe-sex brochure from English into Puerto Rican Spanish would be highly offensive to those who spoke Mexican Spanish, for the very same words that were well chosen for one were considered rude in the other."[141]

## NONVERBAL MESSAGES

Cultural diversity in nonverbal behavior may seriously affect health care communication. Both health care practitioners and clients frequently express beliefs, feelings, and attitudes about illness and treatment nonverbally. Although it would be ideal if health care providers were knowledgeable about the nonverbal behavior of all cultures, it does not seem unreasonable to request they learn more about the meaning and use of nonverbal behavior across cultures.[142] There are four areas of nonverbal communication that are especially salient in health care communication: *eye contact, facial expressions, touch,* and *time.* Although these aspects of nonverbal communication were discussed extensively in Chapter 7, we will look at them again as they specifically apply to the health care context.

**Eye Contact.** Eye contact behavior is frequently a source of nonverbal confusion. Direct eye contact is prevalent in the dominant American culture, and lack of eye contact is often perceived as a sign of rudeness or an indication of inattention.[143] Many cultures and co-cultures, however, avoid direct eye contact because they hold it to be a sign of disrespect, especially when conversing with authority figures such as physicians and other medical professionals. According to Gleave and Manes, Central Americans, for instance, feel uncomfortable making immediate eye contact with strangers.[144] Chan reports that among the Japanese, avoidance of eye contact traditionally denotes respect, and direct or sustained eye contact with relative strangers may be interpreted as a sign of hostility.[145] American Indians often stare at the floor during conversations because they believe such behavior indicates that they are paying close attention to the speaker.[146] And many Vietnamese are uncomfortable with steady or direct eye contact and prefer fleeting glances.[147]

**Facial Expressions.** Facial expressions are commonly perceived as being a guide to a person's feelings. Many cultures and co-cultures such as Italians, Jews, African Americans, and Spanish-speaking people smile readily and use a wide variety of facial expressions. In other cultures, such as in England and Ireland, as well as in many northern European countries, fewer facial expressions are used.[148]

Smiling and laughing are indicative of happiness in the dominant American culture. In other cultures, however, smiles may reflect a variety of other emotions, including confusion, embarrassment, or politeness. Facial expressions may be used to express feelings that are the opposite of those being felt. In many Asian cultures, negative affect is often concealed with a smile. The Vietnamese, as Dinh and his associates report, have a tendency toward impassive facial expressions that make it difficult to know what the individual is thinking or how much is being understood.[149] In some cases, the recognition of facial displays of affect among members of cultural groups such as Native Americans may be difficult unless the observer has a deep understanding of both the person and her or his cultural norms.[150]

**Touch.** Cultural diversity in tactile behavior is yet another aspect of nonverbal communication that can affect health care. Although members of the dominant American culture are usually accustomed to being touched by their physicians and nurses, individuals from many other cultures may not. Vietnamese patients, for instance, prefer body touch be kept to a minimum.[151]

Cultural modesty also affects touching in the health care context. Although members of Latino cultures seem to engage in high levels of touching behavior, Brownlee indicates that many Latina women may be reluctant to expose their bodies to men or even other women and can become especially embarrassed during pelvic examinations.[152] Many Latino men may also feel threatened during physical examinations because of strong feelings about modesty.[153]

For members of some cultures, touch may have magical overtones. Among some Latinos and Native Americans, touch is used as a symbol for undoing an evil spell; it is seen as a means of preventing harm and promoting healing.[154] Some Vietnamese, on the other hand, believe their spirits may leave the body through physical contact, which can result in health problems.[155] Additionally, as Muencke points out, the Vietnamese perceive the human head to be the seat of life, and any procedure that violates the surface or an orifice of the head may cause strong feelings of fear.[156]

**Time.** In Chapter 7, we discussed the time orientations called monochronic time and polychronic time. These orientations are important in the health care setting because a patient's time perspective may affect when or whether he or she shows up for appointments. Time orientation may also affect how consistently a patient will take medicine according to a particular schedule or whether he or she will return for follow-up visits.

Differences in time orientations can also influence the amount of time health care professionals spend with patients. Members of the dominant American culture tend to follow an M-time orientation, and do not expect to spend much time with physicians establishing rapport or discussing the causes and cures of illness. Members of other cultures with a P-time orientation may hold different expectations and expect a physician or nurse to spend time building an appropriate interpersonal relationship as well as explaining all of the details of their illness and its cure.

## FORMALITY

Although we have already alluded to the importance of formality and informality elsewhere, the impact of these behaviors on the health care setting warrants a second examination. Members of those Asian, Latino, and European cultures, as well as others who value formality in language use, may be disturbed by the North American practice of addressing each other by first names. A physician who addresses an Asian by his or her first name rather than by title and last name may inadvertently diminish his or her credibility.

Formality is also reflected in varying degrees of politeness. Marks says, for example, that "Chinese politeness calls for three refusals before one accepts an offer."[157] In North America, however, "no" means "no" the first time. Imagine the confusion, misunderstanding, and suffering that could be experienced by a Chinese patient politely declining the first offer of pain medication from a North American nurse and then politely suffering while waiting for the second and third offers, which are not forthcoming.

In Chapter 5, we discussed how politeness is reflected in face-saving communication. In many cultures, authority figures are not to be disagreed with or challenged. Even if the patient does not concur with or understand the physician's advice, he or she may agree to comply because of politeness norms. Many Latinos, for example, believe that directly contradicting a physician is rude and disrespectful. They may indicate compliance in order not to embarrass the physician, but in actuality, they have no intention of following the instructions. Klessig warns that the physician who then perceives agreement can erroneously believe that a plan of action has been agreed upon.[158]

As all of our examples to this point have suggested, many misunderstandings in the health care setting can be traced to communication problems. Because of this, health care professionals need to have excellent intercultural communication skills. Let us look at some of those skills.

# Becoming a Better Intercultural Health Care Communicator

When you hear of multicultural issues, the reference is usually about racial and ethnic differences among people. Yet, as Luckmann indicates, there is a distinct medical and hospital culture in the United States that can be extremely disorienting and frightening to those on the outside.[159] Luckmann describes this culture in the paragraph below:

> In this culture technology is valued almost exclusively. Large amounts of data in the form of laboratory tests, invasive procedures, x-rays, body scans, and systems reviews are gathered in order to diagnose and treat the underlying pathophysiology. The goal is to rapidly resolve the patient's symptoms with biomedical interventions and ultimately to cure the patient's pathology. The strong, shared belief in the biomedical approach can result in

biomedical ethnocentrism which can be a serious impediment to effective communication between health care providers and patients. This ethnocentrism is often displayed in the derision that greets patients who show an interest in alternative health practices. Even using the term "alternative" suggests that such practices are outside the accepted biomedical approach.[160]

This medical culture may be overwhelming even to people who do understand Western medical practices. For example, as Gillmor tells you, there is a specialized language within this culture that makes many communications from medical staff unintelligible and perhaps even frightening to the uninitiated.[161] When awareness, acknowledgment, and action characterize the multicultural health care context, greater empathy is achieved.

It is important that you do not presume that the suggestions offered here are mutually exclusive or exhaustive. We recommend that you do not assume that the information contained in this chapter applies to all people associated with a particular culture. If you do so, you fail to acknowledge individuality. Additionally, acculturation and assimilation levels will affect a patient's response to illness and treatment. Despite these caveats, the suggestions we offer should be helpful in facilitating communication in the cross-cultural health care encounter.

## RECOGNIZE DIVERSE MEDICAL SYSTEMS

As we have indicated throughout this chapter, it is important to recognize that many cultures may have several medical systems on which they rely. Even in the United States, many alternative medical systems exist, including the mind-body and spiritual connections discussed earlier. Chiropractic, naturopathy, herbalism, and the laying on of hands may also be considered alternative medical systems.[162] In many instances, Western biomedicine when combined with an alternative method can result in great success. You can now, on occasion, find the same multiple approaches to medical treatment in other parts of the world. For example, in Mozambique, in addition to Western approaches to medicine, the government is embracing traditional healers as vital bearers of the safe-sex message. Because of the AIDS epidemic in the region, healers are using any means possible to reach the people. It is not unusual for a healer to begin an interaction by using such traditional behaviors as drum beating, rattle shaking, and making an appeal to a local god. Following this, the healer may approach the audience and ask, "Have you ever heard of condoms?"[163]

Successful communication with patients requires that their beliefs concerning the causes of illness, how illness should be treated, and how it can be prevented in the future must be acknowledged. Galanti makes much the same point when he writes, "Even in cases where Western scientific medicine is superior, if the patient believes it is insufficient for treating the problem, it probably will be."[164] This concept is clearly illustrated in the following narrative:

> An eighty-three-year-old Cherokee Indian woman was brought to a hospital emergency room after she passed out at home. X-rays revealed a bowel obstruction that required surgery. The woman refused to sign the consent form because she first wanted to see the medicine man on the reservation. At the request of the social worker, the woman's grandson drove to the reservation and returned with the medicine man in full traditional dress. He conducted a healing ceremony complete with bells, rattles, chanting, and singing for forty-five minutes. At the end of the ceremony, the medicine man indicated that the

woman was ready to sign the consent form. She did, and her immediate surgery was uneventful and without complications.[165]

Recognizing and being sensitive to patients' beliefs require a great deal of information. In addition to cultural knowledge and an awareness of communication patterns, certain knowledge of the individual is necessary. This means, when first treating a new patient, allowing them to "tell their story." "Initially, this may take more time, but it can save time in the long term. Do not anticipate where the client is leading, what the conclusion is, or how you will intervene."[166] Dennis and Small offer the following prompts and questions for gathering essential information:

1. How does the client/family identify itself? Do they call themselves American, Jamaican, Puerto Rican, Russian-American, Latino, etc.?
2. Are your questions answered by the client or by another family member?
3. Is there a family member who always speaks first?
4. Does the client or his or her family members speak to you in English and to each other in another language?
5. Will you need an interpreter? If so, select one that fits the family structure. For example, if only men respond to interview questions, a child or female would not be an appropriate interpreter.
6. Determine how respect is shown. Ask what titles of address should be used. First names may be regarded as disrespectful.
7. Here in the United States, maintaining eye contact shows interest and involvement. Is it the same or different in your client's culture?
8. Food is very cultural. What are the food choices of your client? Review a hospital menu with the client or family. Are ethnic dishes preferred? Can arrangements be made with the family based on the medical needs of the client?
9. Identify gender issues. Males/females may not be allowed to be present during the interview or during treatment.
10. Practice non-judgmental responses. These can open or close lines of communication.
11. What religion is practiced, if any? How will religious needs or requirements influence the health care agenda? Religion affects important aspects of life, including practices relating to euthanasia, autopsy, organ donation, amputations, burial, and prolongation of life.[167]

## RECOGNIZE ETHNOCENTRISM

Finally, embedded in all that we have said in this entire chapter is the fact that you must recognize that there is no single answer to all health care questions. When you behave as if you believe that your culture possesses that single answer, you are engaging in ethnocentrism. While we have discussed ethnocentrism elsewhere and will look at the concept again in later chapters, our point now is that ethnocentrism, if not kept in check, can influence issues related to health care. The first step in avoiding ethnocentrism is to identify any feelings you have about other cultures that might influence the health care setting. This same idea about starting with yourself is clearly articulated by Geist-Martin and her colleagues when they write, "The call to expand our understanding and appreciation of cultural communities implies that we need to acknowledge our own ethnocentrism."[168] Once you have acknowledged that you might possess ethnocentric notions, ask yourself if you are guilty of imposing your own views about illness and treatment on other people without ever considering their needs. In short, avoiding ethnocentrism demands that you take into consideration the cultural background of both patients and practitioners.[169]

Ludwick and Silva offer six suggestions that will help you determine whether your ethnocentric tendencies are at work during provider/client communication situations. These are:

1. Recognize that values and beliefs vary not only among different cultures but also within cultures.
2. View values and beliefs from different cultures within historical, health care, cultural, spiritual, and religious contexts.
3. Learn as much as you can about the language, customs, beliefs, and values of cultural groups, especially those with which you have the most contact.
4. Be aware of your own cultural values and biases, a major step to decreasing ethnocentrism and cultural imposition.
5. Be alert to and try to understand the nonverbal communications of your own and various cultures, such as personal space preferences, body language, and style of hair and clothing.
6. Be aware of bio-cultural differences manifested in the physical exam, in types of illnesses, in response to drugs, and in health care practices.[170]

Following these suggestions will help you become culturally sensitive to the effects of cultural diversity on the health care system. With the information we have provided in this chapter, you should be sensitive to the health care expectations of people whose cultural background is different from your own.

## Summary

- Cultures differ in the ways they explain, treat, and prevent illness.
- Health belief systems can be divided into three categories: scientific/biomedical, magico-religious, and holistic.
- Cultural diversity causes differences in beliefs about the causes of illness.
- Cultural diversity causes people to hold widely different beliefs about the appropriate treatment of illness.
- The way people approach the prevention of illness is culturally diverse.
- Religion, spirituality, and health care are often intertwined.
- Health care practices must accommodate a culturally diverse population.
- Family roles are culturally diverse and may affect communication in the health care setting. These roles deal with dominance patterns, modesty and female purity, and pregnancy and childbirth.
- Culturally diverse beliefs related to self-disclosure, language, nonverbal communication, and formality can influence the health care setting.
- If optimal health care is to be provided in a multicultural society such as the United States, you must recognize diverse medical systems, diverse approaches to treatment, and personal ethnocentrism.

# Activities

1. In a small culturally diverse group, identify and discuss the differences that exist between your various beliefs about the causes, treatment, and prevention of illness.
2. In a small group, discuss how spirituality is relevant to health care.
3. Interview members of your local health care community and determine what communication problems they have encountered when interacting with patients from diverse cultures.
4. Interview people from other cultures and ask them if they have encountered communication problems when seeking health care.

# Discussion Ideas

1. What is necessary to achieve effective intercultural communication in the health care setting? How might this be implemented?
2. How can health care professionals be trained to become effective intercultural communicators?
3. How does cultural diversity in language usage complicate the multicultural health care setting?
4. How does diversity in gender roles affect the giving and receiving of health care treatment?
5. Why might it be important to incorporate more than one medical belief system into the treatment of patients in a multicultural health care setting?

## CHAPTER 11

# Becoming Competent: Improving Intercultural Communication

*That is true culture which helps us to work for the social betterment of all.*

HENRY WARD BEECHER

*All persons are puzzles until at last we find in some word or act—the key to the man, to the woman; straightway all their past words and actions lie in the light before us.*

EMERSON

In 1963, President John F. Kennedy offered a fitting introduction to this chapter when he noted, "No problem of human destiny is beyond human beings." The appropriateness of his observation is germane because this is a chapter about many of the problems that you face when you engage in intercultural communication. The chapter is also about some of the methods you can employ to solve those problems. While this entire book has been about you becoming a more effective intercultural communicator, in this final chapter we explicitly focus on the actual act of engaging in communication.

Before we begin our discussion of potential communication problems, we must remind you of two interrelated concepts regarding the importance of intercultural communication. First, shifting demographics and changes in transportation, information systems, political dynamics, economics, disease, poverty, and global conflicts have brought people from diverse cultures and religions into contact with each other with a regularity and urgency that is unique to this period of history. Beamer and Varner underscore the frequency of these contacts as they apply to globalization and technology when they write, "The New Economy is active across national and ethnic boundaries in ways we did not begin to anticipate five years ago. Dramatic changes in technology, such as the growth of the Internet and the adoption around the planet of satellite and cellular telephony, make international communication even more commonplace today."[1] Smith echoes the same idea when he writes,

*Technology has created a world where intercultural contact has become more commonplace than ever before.*

© Thomas Nebbia/Woodfin Camp and Associates

"Lands around the planet have become our neighbors—China across the street, the Middle East at our back door."[2] Actually you do not have travel to China or the Middle East to see the interconnectedness of cultures. In the last decade there was a 57 percent increase in the United States foreign-born population.[3] What is happening is obvious: this new century has demonstrated that you will be communicating with people who may speak a language different from your own, have a boss or office mate from another culture, and talk on an Internet chat room with a partner thousands of miles away.

The second key concept of intercultural communication relates directly to *you*—for now we are referring to the manner in which you respond to these intercultural contacts. The importance of these contacts is clearly demonstrated by countless global conflicts throughout the world as well as serious environmental concerns related to pollution and severe shortages of both food and water.[4] When these and other issues are not addressed, the results can be grave. As Schneider and Silverman point out, "In today's global world, condemning other societies leads to misunderstanding and violence. The world's peoples need to learn about each other."[5] In an even more dramatic fashion, Hofstede echoes the same idea when he writes, "The survival of mankind will depend to a large extent on the ability of people who think differently to act together."[6] In this chapter we will attempt to make that "acting together" a little easier. First, we will offer a personal philosophy that reflects our optimism about your ability to improve the manner in which you communicate. Second, we will discuss the notion of communication competency. Third, we will examine some potential problems that often impede your efforts to be competent. Fourth, we turn our attention to some possible solutions to those problems. And some ethical guidelines will be offered as they apply to intercultural communication.

# A Philosophy of Change

When the Greek poet Euripides wrote, "All is change; all yields its place and goes," he was not only talking about nature and the universe changing, but he was also referring to how people change—in both body and mind. The inevitability of change, and what takes its place, is at the heart of this chapter. It is our belief that *you can shape that change*. This approach to improvement is not only expedient, but also possible. Our optimistic view is based on three interrelated assumptions about human communication: (1) *language is an open system*, (2) *we have free choice*, and (3) *communication has a consequence*.

## LANGUAGE IS AN OPEN SYSTEM

Our opening characteristic relates to your ability to learn and never stop learning. That is to say, there is not a "top end" to how many new words and how much new information a person can acquire. We present the following two examples to make our point. (1) The first word in our dictionary is *aal*, and it is an East Indian shrub, whose root is used to make a red dye. (2) We also want to tell you that Buddha was the son of a rich king born into the Shakyan clan. If these two facts were new information for you, our words, working in combination with your brain, would be adding to your fund of knowledge. These two specific examples are not what is important but rather the idea that you are capable of acquiring new knowledge for your entire life.

Inherent in our analysis is the fact that because you can learn, you are able to gain new information about other people and other cultures. You can, of course, also learn new ways of acting—you can change. We hope that by learning new information about intercultural communication, you will be able to make alterations to your own communication behavior.

## WE HAVE FREE CHOICE

Having just developed the idea that learning and change are inescapable, we now offer another truism about human behavior that adds support to our belief that improvement is possible. This supposition, although intricate in how it is acted out, is uncomplicated in its wording: *You have free choice*. While you might face biological limitations (you may not be as tall as you would like), nevertheless in most instances what you do in life is a matter of choices. From selecting a single word when you speak to deciding if you should drive over the posted speed limit, you have free will. Although many cultures have a strong belief in fate ("It is God's will"), and others limit the choices available to their members (arranged marriages), in most instances people choose what to do and what not to do. Reflect on the two examples we just used: selecting words and driving fast. We said that each word we choose is under our jurisdiction. We could, for example, have used the word *control* instead of *jurisdiction* in the last line, but we selected the word we wanted—it was our choice.

All of our examples underscore the degrees of freedom you enjoy in conducting your life. When you decide how to spend your time, or whom to select as a friend or a mate, you are reflecting free choice. Although selecting a lover might be harder than selecting what words to use, the principle is the same—you have free will. The key, of course, is how you use those choices. As the Irish novelist George Moore wrote, "The difficulty in life is the choice."

## COMMUNICATION HAS A CONSEQUENCE

Our final introductory edict concerning our positive view toward improvement is an idea that first appeared in Chapter 1 where we discussed how each of our actions produces a response in another human being. Some of the responses are obvious and others are subtle. But they all produce a result. Much like the Arab proverb that notes, "If you strike mud against the wall, even though it does not stick, it will leave a mark," when you communicate your actions "leave a mark." A part of improving your communication behavior demands that you take control of your actions—to stay with our metaphor—be aware of the mark you leave.

We are now ready to begin talking about improving intercultural communication by asking you to see the interconnective nature of the three points we developed in the last few pages: Language is an open system (you can learn), you have choices (you can communicate one way or another), and your actions produce a response (you do something to other people).

# Becoming Competent

Before we present specific techniques for improving intercultural skills, we will define intercultural communication competence and discuss several of its components.

## DEFINING INTERCULTURAL COMPETENCE

In its most unadorned form we would agree with Spitzberg, who suggests that intercultural communication competence is simply "behavior that is appropriate and effective in a given context."[7] Kim offers a more detailed definition when she notes that intercultural communication competence is "the overall internal capability of an individual to manage key challenging features of intercultural communication: namely, cultural differences and unfamiliarity, inter-group posture, and the accompanying experience of stress."[8] What these two definitions tell you is that being a competent communicator means you have the ability to analyze the situation and select the appropriate mode of behavior.

## BASIC COMPONENTS OF COMMUNICATION COMPETENCE[9]

Most of the research in the area of communication competence maintains that in selecting the most appropriate course of action (exercising free choice), effective communicators are those who are (1) *motivated*, (2) *have a fund of knowledge to draw upon*, (3) *possess requisite communication skills*,[10] and (4) *are of good character*. Let us look at

© A. Ramey/PhotoEdit

*Having the motivation to communicate is an important first step in overcoming violence and conflict.*

these four components as a general prologue to a detailed analysis of intercultural competence.

**Motivation.** Motivation as it relates to competence means that as a communicator you want to interact with someone from another culture. If you allow feelings of anxiety, ethnocentrism, and prejudice to control your actions, you will obviously lack the motivation necessary to be an effective communicator. Instead, you need to be committed to the entire communication process.

**Knowledge.** The knowledge dimension of communication competence means that you have a fund of knowledge about the other person and their culture. Luckmann points out the need for knowledge as it applies to the health care profession: "Nurses who are not knowledgeable about cultural differences risk misinterpreting patients' attempts to communicate. As a result, patients may not receive the proper care."[11] According to Morreale, Spitzberg, and Barge, you need two kinds of knowledge to be competent—content knowledge and procedural knowledge. "Content knowledge involves knowing what topics, words, meanings, and so forth are required in a situation. Procedural knowledge is knowing how to assemble, plan and perform content knowledge in a particular situation."[12] You need this knowledge so you can know what communication strategies to employ, what is proper protocol, and what customs need to be observed.

**Skills.** Skills are the actual application of specific behaviors that enable you to accomplish your goals. This point is further explained by Morreale, Spitzberg, and Barge when they observe, "Skills are goal directed because they must be designed to accomplish something."[13] According to Smith and Bond, the skills need to be adapted to the rules of interaction that are appropriate to the host culture.[14] You have learned those skills all your life so you can function effectively as a member of your culture. However, skills that are successful with one group, such as maintaining direct eye contact to show interest, may be inappropriate in cultures such as the Japanese, which finds such eye contact too obtrusive.

**Character.** While most of the literature dealing with communication competency includes only the three components we have just mentioned, it is our belief that one more feature needs to be added to the profile of a competent communicator. This attribute is *character*. The idea behind including character is simple—if you are not perceived by your communication partner as a person of good character your chances for success will be diminished. In many ways your character is composed of both your personal history and how you exhibit that history. As the American philosopher and teacher P. B. Fitzwater noted, "Character is the sum and total of a person's choices." The key, of course, is how you act out those choices when you interact with someone from another culture. Perhaps the single most important trait associated with people of character is their *trustworthiness*. Characteristics often associated with the trustworthy person are integrity, honor, altruism, sincerity, and goodwill.

# Potential Problems in Intercultural Communication

We have just offered a partial sketch of the competent communicator by noting that to accomplish your communication goals you must be motivated and knowledgeable, possess certain skills, and be of good character. We are now ready to talk about how you actually accomplish those goals. We will begin our detailed discussion of some of the major problems that can impede your efforts by reminding you of three important points.

First, in most instances, communication problems occur for an assortment of reasons. If you lose your temper while talking to a friend, a little introspection will often reveal that it was not solely your friend who prompted the anger but rather an accumulation of events and that your friend was merely a handy target. Although we will discuss potential problems one at time, they often occur in combination. Second, common sense tells you that the complex nature of human behavior produces many more communication problems than the list we have created in this section of the book. Third, although our discussion of potential problems and solutions has a strong theory base, it nevertheless is colored by our personal and cultural backgrounds. We are three white university professors born and raised in America, and although we have visited many countries and studied countless cultures, we have done so from our culture's perspective. Therefore, the "hidden grip" of culture has undoubtedly influenced the way we perceive and interact with the world. Although we have tried to assume a global orientation, we need to alert you to the Western bias that may occasionally, and we hope only accidentally, creep into our commentary.

## SEEKING SIMILARITIES

Walk around your campus and you will notice how people who share similar interests and cultures are usually clustered in groups. Or think for a moment about the meaning of the following proverb, which, in one form or another, is found in nearly every culture: "Birds of a feather flock together." The meaning of this proverb should be clear—most people seek to be near others with whom they share common outlooks, habits, and traits. Ask yourself the following two questions: What group of people do you choose to be around? How do you select those people? We are in no way passing a value judgment on the degree to which people seek out others who, consciously or unconsciously, remind them of themselves. Rather, we are drawing on the interpersonal communication research that maintains people gravitate toward people who are similar to themselves. For decades, the research in initial attraction and the development of friendships has revealed an overwhelming tendency among everyone to seek out people whom they perceive to be much like themselves.[15] It is a very natural inclination when meeting someone to talk about a topic that both parties might enjoy; and, should those talks prove interesting, it is equally natural for friendships to form and evolve. The more points of contact you can establish, the more comfortable you feel.[16]

The connection between intercultural communication and your inclination to solicit friends and acquaintances that mirror your personality should be obvious. The seriousness of this problem is seen globally as well as interpersonally. As the world gets more complex, and people feel overwhelmed by events, we find that "many millions of people believe that their best haven of certainty and security is a group based on ethnic similarity, common faith, economic interest or political like-mindedness."[17] We are not suggesting that there is anything wrong with seeking ethnic or cultural similarity; in fact, we already mentioned how common it is to seek out the familiar. The problem arises when the pull of similarities excludes those who are different. In short, many people deal with the unfamiliar by *withdrawing* from interaction with strangers or by experiencing feelings of *anxiety*.

## WITHDRAWAL

When we speak of withdrawal, we are referring to withdrawal on an interpersonal, intercultural, and international level. Problems occur when you withdraw from face-to-face interactions or when entire countries withdraw from the world community. Although it is a rather somber commentary of our times, it appears that "modern life," with its rapid pace, urbanization, massive institutions, and mediated contacts, has created a sense of bewilderment, alienation, and detachment. A common response to disaffection is to retreat rather than confront the cause of the separation.

Withdrawal, at both the international and domestic levels, has often been the rule rather than the exception. History is full of examples of how one nation or group of people has refused to engage in an international dialogue. For decades the governments of North and South Korea rebuffed each other, only to discover that talking to each other was beneficial to all parties. The relationships between East and West Germany, India and Pakistan, and Israel and Egypt represent three other vivid examples of choosing interaction over withdrawal. In each of those cases, it produced peaceful coexistence instead of carnage.

Perhaps if you examine your own behavior, you might discover instances when you withdraw from communication as do some governments, Cuba and the U.S. being an example. In an age when what happens in one part of the world affects the rest of the world, retreat and withdrawal can have devastating effects. As the philosopher Flewelling once wrote, "Neither province, parish, nor nation; family, nor individual, can live profitably in exclusion from the rest of the world."

## ANXIETY

Feelings of anxiety associated with the unknown represent yet another reason people are attracted to similarities and avoid the unfamiliar. As early as 1961, psychologists Herman and Schield summarized these often disquieting feelings when they wrote, "The immediate psychological result of being in a new situation is lack of security."[18] This lack of security can make you anxious. Thomas and Inkson, when applying anxiety to the intercultural situation, offer the following explanation:

> We may try not to be prejudiced against people from other cultures, but we notice, usually with tiny internal feelings of apprehension, the physical characteristics of others that make them different from us. All of us find differences threatening to some extent.[19]

While much of your communication behavior is habitual, with hard work and practice you can learn to control your feelings of anxiety. While the task is not easy, we agree with Barna when, writing about anxiety, she states, "For most people it takes insight, training, and sometimes an alteration of long-standing habits or cherished beliefs before progress can be made. The increasing need for global understanding and cooperation, however, makes the effort worthwhile."[20]

## UNCERTAINTY REDUCTION

Our next potential problem is in many ways a corollary of our first in that it too deals with the anxiety associated with communicating with strangers. However, in this instance the focus is on the uncertainties inherent at the beginning of an encounter. This familiar ritual of meeting someone has given rise to a theory known as *uncertainty reduction*.[21] Berger and Calabrese developed this theory and summarize it in the following manner: "Central to the present theory is the assumption that when strangers meet, their primary concern is one of uncertainty reduction or increasing predictability about the behavior of both themselves and others in the interaction."[22] According to the theory, people have a desire to reduce the uncertainty built into every new meeting. You know from personal experience that when you meet someone for the first time you can only *speculate* on how you should act and how the other person will respond to your action. In short, you try to imagine what the other person is like and predict how they will perceive you and your message. Berger offers a clear description of this process when he writes, "To interact in a relatively smooth, coordinated, and understandable manner, one must be able both to predict how one's interaction partner is likely to behave, and based upon these predictions, to select from one's own repertoire those responses that will optimize outcomes in the encounter."[23] The difficulty occurs when we add culture into the process of making predictions. As Gudykunst and Kim point out, "The problem is that we base our interpretations on our life experiences, cultures, or ethnic group memberships. Since our life experiences differ from the other person's, our interpretations of that person's behavior may be incorrect."[24] What is being suggested is that uncertainty is magnified when you meet people from cultures different from your own. As Luckmann notes, "Fear, dislike and distrust are emotions that all too often erupt when people from diverse cultures first meet."[25] Gudykunst also links this problem to intercultural communication when he adds, "If the amount of uncertainty present in initial interactions is not reduced, further communication between the people will, in all likelihood, not take place."[26]

There are certain strategies you can employ as you attempt to reduce uncertainty. Berger referred to these as passive, active, and interactive strategies.[27] *Passive strategies* ask you to take on "the role of unobtrusive observer of another."[28] This means you would watch and examine the other person in natural situations (restaurants, classrooms, talking to their friends) as a way of learning something about them. You would not be interacting with them directly, but rather learning about the other person by simply monitoring their actions. *Active strategies* call for a more active form of fact finding. There is still no direct contact with the other person, but instead you might ask a third party, such as a mutual friend, about the person and their culture. According to Banks and Rogers, *interactive strategy* "occurs when the observer and the other person engage in direct contact or face-to-face interaction—that is, conversation that may include self-disclosure, direct questions, and other information-seeking tactics."[29]

## STEREOTYPING

It is unfortunate, but stereotyping is a natural outgrowth of the preceding two problems we examined in this chapter. When there is a lack of familiarity and similarity, stereotyping often follows. As we noted earlier, "Psychologists conducting research in the area of interpersonal attraction have established an important principle: the more similar two people are to each other, the more likely they are to like one another."[30] Because you meet so many strangers, stereotyping is a common occurrence. The problem of stereotyping is compounded by the fact that most people fail to admit they hold negative stereotypes. As Taylor and Porter note:

> Most of us are reluctant to admit that we engage in stereotyping. We would rather prefer
> to believe that only racists and bigots stereotype other groups, yet all of us are guilty of
> stereotyping. Stereotyping then, is a universal process at both the group and individual
> level.[31]

**Defining Stereotypes.** Stereotyping is a complex form of categorization that mentally organizes your experiences and guides your behavior toward a particular group of people. Lippmann, who called attention to this concept as early as 1922, indicated that stereotypes were a means of organizing your images into fixed and simple categories that you use to stand for an entire collection of people.[32] In recent years, psychologists Abbate, Boca, and Bocchiaro have offered a more formal definition: "A stereotype is a cognitive structure containing the perceiver's knowledge, beliefs, and expectancies about some human social groups."[33] The reason for the pervasive nature of stereotypes is that human beings have a psychological need to categorize and classify. The world you confront is too big, too complex, and too transitory for you to know it in all its detail. Hence, you want to classify and pigeonhole. The main problem is not in the pigeonholing or categorizing, but rather "the difficulty lies with the overgeneralization and the often negative evaluations (attitudes and prejudices) that are directed toward members of the categories."[34] As you can observe, a problem with stereotypes is that they tend to be convenient, expeditious, and assist you with your classifications. Rapport and Overing underscore this point when they note that "stereotypes allow simplistic and fantastic claims to be made about a group's manifold memberships, claims which are all the more ambiguous and gross the higher the societal level to which the collective label is applied."[35]

**Variations in Stereotypes.** Because stereotypes are often a conglomerate of perceptions, emotions, and feelings, they vary in scope and magnitude. Let us pause for a moment and look at some of the variations that stereotypes can take.

First, according to Triandis, stereotypes can be characterized as *normative* or *personal*.[36] Normative stereotypes are those you might hold without any firsthand or direct experience with the group in question. You might have never been to France or even met a person from France, yet you most likely have a view (stereotype) of what the French are like from films, TV, or newspaper accounts. In personal stereotypes you actually have firsthand knowledge of the group—regardless of how limited that contact might be. If you met a French person on a bus and decided that the person was representative of all French people, you would be engaging in a personal stereotype.

Second, stereotypes, as Smith and Bond observe, "may be widely shared by others, even by the stereotyped persons themselves, or they may be idiosyncratic to the individual holding them."[37] What is being suggested is that one person or a large collection of individuals may hold stereotypes. This notion of how people may share the stereotype is often referred to as the "consensus variance" of stereotyping. In most instances, group stereotypes that cause the greatest damage in intercultural communication are those that have a wide consensus.

Third, stereotypes can be positive or negative. Stereotypes that refer to a large group of people as lazy, coarse, vicious, and moronic are obviously negative. There are, of course, positive stereotypes such as saying an entire group is hardworking, well mannered, kind, and intelligent. When stereotypes are accurate they are actually called a *sociotype*.[38] However, because stereotypes (as the word is currently defined) narrow our perceptions, they usually jeopardize intercultural communication and take on a negative tone.

A final variation in stereotyping deals with the intensity of the stereotype. Is the particular stereotype resolutely held, or is it temperate in its intensity? Examine your own catalogue of stereotypes and you will likely discover that some of them are strongly held while others are tentative and loosely held.

**Learning Stereotypes.** It should be clear that stereotypes, at least as we are defining them, represent a major stumbling block to successful interaction. Yet stereotypes are everywhere and they seem to endure. Why? Perhaps one way to understand the power and lasting impact of stereotypes is to examine how they are acquired. Remember, you are not born with stereotypes—*they are learned*. And like culture, they are learned in a variety of ways. Let us pause for a moment and look at some of the ways.

*Stereotypes and the Socialization Process.* The most obvious, and perhaps most important, agent of stereotypes is parents. While many parents might try to avoid teaching their children to think in stereotypes, we tend to agree with Schneider when he notes that many parents directly or indirectly promote them.[39] Children who hear their parents say, "It is too bad that all those Jews are in control of the film industry" are learning stereotypes. Once children enter school, peers become an important carrier of stereotypes. Of course the socialization process continues as the child becomes a member of various religious and social groups. These groups, intentionally and unintentionally, while teaching the virtues of a particular point of view might also be teaching stereotypes toward an opposite view. For example, learning but one particular view of religion and at the same time hearing of the "evils of religious terrorists," a child might be acquiring stereotypes toward Muslims.

***Stereotypes and Media.*** Many stereotypes are provided by the mass media. As Abbate and his associates point out, "Stereotypes are widely diffused through an incredible variety of media, such as movies, television programs, gossip, jokes, and advertisements to names of view."[40] Television has been guilty of providing distorted images of many ethnic groups, the elderly, and gays. Think for a moment of the stereotype embedded in the advertisement seen on television for e-mail that heralds the idea the product is so simple that "even Granny can use it." The problem is that for many people, these false facsimiles often become their private realities. In fact, numerous research studies show "that children as young as eight years old held primarily negative attitudes toward older persons."[41]

The perceptions of women and men are two other groups where media has played a role in perpetuating certain stereotypes. Wood offers an excellent summary of television's portrayal of men and women when she writes, "Media most often represents boys and men as active, adventurous, powerful, sexually aggressive, and largely uninvolved in human relationships, and represents girls and women as young, thin, beautiful, passive, dependent, and often incompetent.[42]

***Stereotypes and Fear.*** Finally, stereotypes may evolve out of fear of persons from groups that differ from your own. For example, many people view a person with mental illness as someone who is violence prone. This conflicts with statistical data, which indicates that persons with mental illness tend to be no more prone to violence than the general population. Yet because of well-publicized isolated cases of mentally ill persons killing other people, the stereotype is the rule instead of the exception. This is how many stereotypes develop in the first place: a series of isolated behaviors by a member of a group that unfairly becomes the generalized stereotype that represents all members of the group.

**Stereotypes and Intercultural Communication.** As we have pointed out, in most instances, stereotypes are the products of limited, lazy, and misguided perceptions. The problems created by these misperceptions are both serious and numerous.[43] Adler reminds you of the harmful effect stereotypes have on intercultural communication when she notes:

> Stereotypes become counterproductive when we place people in the wrong groups, when we incorrectly describe the group norm, when we inappropriately evaluate the group or category, when we confuse the stereotype with the description of a particular individual, and when we fail to modify the stereotype based on our actual observations and experience.[44]

Let us look at a few additional reasons why stereotypes hamper intercultural communication. First, stereotypes are a kind of filter—they only allow in information that is consistent with information already held by the individual. In this way, what might be the truth is never given a chance. For example, women were stereotyped for many years as a rather one-dimensional group. The stereotype of women as homemakers often keeps women from advancing in the workplace. As Sherman, Conrey, and Groom point out, "the principles of selective exposure suggest that people prefer to not attend to information that challenges their beliefs if they do not have the resources to counter argue that information."[45]

Second, it is not the act of classifying that creates intercultural problems; rather, it is assuming that all culture-specific information applies to all individuals from the cultural group.[46] Stereotypes assume that all members of a group have exactly the same traits. As Atkinson, Morten, and Sue note, "They are rigid preconceptions which are applied to all members of a group or to an individual over a period of time, regardless of individual variations."[47] This problem of assuming similarities at the expense of exceptions is the main reason we continue to remind you that your culture is one of the dynamics that determine attitudes, values, beliefs, and ways of behaving.

Third, stereotypes also keep you from being successful as communicators because they are oversimplified, exaggerated, and overgeneralized. As Pickering notes, "They distort the ways in which social groups or individuals are perceived, and obscure the more complex and finite particularities and subjectivities tangled up in the everyday lives of groups and individuals."[48] They distort because they are based on half-truths, and often-untrue premises and assumptions. Guirdham reaffirms this important point when he reminds you that stereotypes alter intergroup communication because they lead people to base their messages, their way of transmitting them, and their reception of them on false assumptions.[49]

Fourth, stereotypes are resistant to change. Because stereotypes are usually developed early in life, repeated and reinforced by the in-group, they grow in intensity each passing year. In fact, contact between in-groups and out-groups often only buttresses the stereotype. As Meshel and McGlynn point out, "Once formed, stereotypes are resistant to change, and direct contact often strengthens the pre-existing associations between the target group and the stereotypical properties."[50] Finally, Gudykunst notes, "Stereotypes can create self-fulfilling prophecies. Individuals tend to see behavior that confirms their expectations, even when it is absent."[51]

**Avoiding Stereotypes.** Although we move to solutions and remedies later in the chapter, it might be helpful if we paused at this stage and advanced a few ideas that can reduce stereotyping. Because culture and stereotypes are both learned early in life we recommend that the first stages of improvement begin with children. There is ample evidence that children who have positive face-to-face contact with other groups hold fewer negative stereotypes than those who are denied such contact.[52] In fact, research suggests that most positive contact can diminish many of the effects of stereotyping.[53] The assumption is that stereotypes can change when members of different groups increase their interaction with each other. Through this interaction, fictitious and negative stereotypes can be proven false.

We would also recommend that you might examine the stereotypes you currently hold. Ask yourself some of the following questions:

- Who is the target of my stereotype?
- What is the content of my stereotype?
- Why do I believe the stereotype is accurate?
- What is the source of my stereotype?
- How much actual contact do I have with the target of the stereotype?

Another effective method trying to control stereotypes is advanced by Toomey and Chung, who ask you "to learn to distinguish between inflexible stereotyping and flexible stereotyping."[54] As the word would indicate, *inflexible* stereotyping is rigid, intransigent, and occurs almost automatically. Because these stereotypes are so deeply entrenched you refuse to accept perceptions that run counter to the stereotype. When you try to engage in *flexible* stereotyping, you begin by being aware of your tendency to engage in categorization. The two most important aspects of being flexible are "being open to new information and evidence" and "being aware of your own zone of discomfort."[55]

## PREJUDICE

The French essayist Voltaire knew of the dangers associated with prejudice when he wrote that "prejudices are what fools use for reason." His rationale for this observation was simple—deeply felt prejudices, usually brought about by stereotyping, can cause serious communication problems. Let us examine some of those problems and make note as how they apply to intercultural communication.

**Defining Prejudice.** In its broadest sense, prejudices are deeply held negative feelings associated with a particular group. These sentiments often include anger, fear, aversion, and anxiety. Macionis offers a detailed definition of prejudice while at the same time explaining its damaging effect on intercultural communication:

> Prejudice amounts to a rigid and irrational generalization about a category of people. Prejudice is irrational to the extent that people hold inflexible attitudes supported by little or no direct evidence. Prejudice may target people of a particular social class, sex, sexual orientation, age, political affiliation, race or ethnicity.[56]

In a communication setting, according to Ruscher, the negative feelings and attitudes held by those who are prejudiced are often "displayed through facial expressions and peripheral nonverbal behaviors."[57] When expressed verbally, examples might include group labels, hostile humor, or speech that alleges the superiority of one group over another.[58]

As you can see, built into the idea of prejudice is the notion of hostility. This *hostility dimension* is explained by Levin, who believes that prejudice deals with "negative feelings, beliefs, and action-tendencies, or discriminatory acts that arise against human beings by virtue of the status they occupy or are perceived to occupy as members of a minority group."[59]

**Characteristics of Prejudice.** As was the case with stereotypes, beliefs linked to prejudices also have certain characteristics. First, they are *directed at a social group and its members*. Often those groups are marked by race, ethnicity, gender, age, and the like. Second, prejudices involve an *evaluative dimension*. According to Brislin, prejudices deal with "feelings about what is good and bad, right and wrong, moral and immoral and so forth."[60] These either/or feelings often see discussions of prejudice attitudes turning into heated debates. Third, *centrality* refers "to the extent to which a belief is important to an individual's attitude about others."[61] As you would suspect, the less intense the belief, the more success you would have in changing your prejudices or those of other people.

**Functions of Prejudice.** Prejudices serve various functions for the people who hold them. Levin underscores the importance of examining the functions of prejudice when he writes, "It follows that we can only reduce prejudice and attendant majority-minority inequities to the extent that we actually come to grips with the important functions that prejudice serves."[62] Let us spend a moment looking at four of the most common functions prejudices fulfill.[63]

***Ego-Defensive Function.*** The ego-defensive function of prejudice allows people to hold a prejudice without having to admit they possess these beliefs about a member of an out-group. An example of this type of prejudice might be found in someone who says, "My grades are low this semester because most professors feel sorry for those minority students and are giving them the higher grades." These types of remarks permit the person who utters them to articulate prejudicial statements while maintaining a sense of self instead of truly examining why their grades were low.

***Utilitarian Function.*** The utilitarian function of prejudice allows people to believe that they are receiving rewards by holding on to their prejudicial beliefs. The most vivid examples of this function are found in attitudes related to the economic arena. People often find it very useful, and to their economic advantage, to say, "Those poor people have so little education they are lucky to have the jobs we offer them." This sort of sentence reflects utilitarian prejudice because the holder of the prejudice can use the belief as a justification for offering minimal pay to the workers in question.

***Value-Expressive Function.*** We see people maintaining the value-expressive function of prejudice when they believe their attitudes are expressing the highest and most moral values of the culture. These usually revolve around values related to religion, government, and politics. A person who believes their God is the one and only true God is being prejudicial against people who hold different views.

***Knowledge Function.*** When carrying out the knowledge function of prejudice, a person is able to categorize, organize, and construct their perceptions of other people in a manner that makes sense to them—even if the sense-making is not accurate. In this way the world is easy to deal with in that people are not perceived individually but rather as members of a group. It is the knowledge level that produces an abundance of labels. People are seen not as persons with a variety of characteristics but rather as "Jews," "Mexicans," "gays," or "feminists," and these labels deny the existence of the individual's unique characteristics.

**Expressions of Prejudice.** Prejudices, like stereotypes, are learned. For some people, prejudices offer rewards ranging from feelings of superiority to feelings of power. Prejudice is expressed in a variety of ways—at times subtle and on other occasions overt. Allport discussed five of those expressions.[64] Although Allport's analyses were presented over forty years ago, they remain relevant today. In fact, many contemporary social scientists base their current theories on the work of Allport.[65]

First, prejudice can be expressed through what Allport refers to as *antilocution*. This level of prejudice involves talking about a member of the target group in negative and stereotypic terms. Someone would be engaging in this form of prejudice if he or she told a friend, "Those Germans did it once, so we can never trust any of them ever again." Another example of antilocution prejudice is the statement "Don't pay those immigrants very much. They don't have any education and will work for almost nothing."

Second, people act out prejudice when they *avoid and/or withdraw from contact* with the disliked group. The problems associated with this form of prejudice are obvious. How do you interact, solve problems, and resolve serious conflicts when you are separated from other people? On both the international and domestic levels, avoidance and withdrawal have often characterized an intercultural exchange. History is full of examples of how one nation or group of people refused to attend or withdrew from an important peace conference. For decades, the political leaders from East and West Germany and from Israel and Egypt rebuffed each other, only to discover decades later that talking benefited both parties. What is true with regard to governments is also characteristic of individual behavior. Have there been occasions when you, like governments, withdrew from communication because a person was a different color or spoke a different language?

Third, when discrimination is the expression of prejudice, the prejudiced person undertakes to *exclude all members of the group* in question from certain types of employment, residential housing, political rights, educational and recreational opportunities, churches, hospitals, or some other type of social institution. Often in cases of discrimination, we observe ethnocentrism, stereotyping, and prejudice coming together in a type of fanaticism that completely obstructs any form of successful intercultural communication. When discrimination replaces communication, you see overt and covert expressions of anger and hate that restrict one group's opportunity or access to opportunities that rightly belong to everyone. When a real estate agent will not show certain homes to African Americans, there is discrimination. When businesses promote less qualified males instead of competent women, you have discrimination.

Fourth, when prejudice moves to the next level of expression, you often see *physical attacks*. This form of prejudice often accelerates in hostility and intensity if left unchecked. From the burning of churches to the writing of anti-Semitic slogans in Jewish cemeteries, physical acts occur when minorities are the targets of prejudiced activity.

The fifth, and most alarming, form of prejudice is *extermination*. This expression of prejudice leads to acts of physical violence against the out-group. History is replete with examples of lynching, massacres, and programs of genocide. In cases such as Hitler's "master plan," the former Serbian "ethnic cleansing," tribal warfare in Africa, and the religious conflicts in Iraq and Afghanistan, you see attempts to destroy an entire racial or ethnic group.

**Causes of Prejudice.** There are no simple explanations for the causes of prejudice, which in most instances are multiple. Experts have isolated a few of the root motivations of prejudice. We will look at some of these in order to better understand how prejudice can be a major deterrent to successful interaction.

*Societal Sources.* A great deal of prejudice is built into the major organizations and institutions of a society. According to Oskamp, these organizations produce laws, regulations, and norms that create prejudice within a society. These laws and regulations help "maintain the power of the dominant groups over subordinate ones."[66]

*Maintaining Social Identity.* Early in this book, we set aside an entire chapter for the topic of identity (see Chapter 4). You will recall that we pointed out how important a person's identity was for connecting them to their culture. This connection is a very personal and emotional one. It creates a bond between the individual and their culture. Anything that threatens that bond, such as members of the out-group, can become the target of prejudice.

*Scapegoating.* History is replete with examples of how scapegoating can be a major cause of prejudice. Blacks, Jews, immigrants, gays, and others have been frequent scapegoating targets. Scapegoating occurs when a particular group of people, usually a minority, are singled out to bear the blame for events or circumstances, such as economic or social hardships, that adversely affect the dominant group. The role of scapegoating, and its link to prejudice, is made clear by Kaplan when he notes how scapegoating allows members of the in-group to act out their frustrations and hostilities by being prejudiced against the out-group.[67] Scapegoating generates arguments and justifications based on fear and imagined threats posed by the out-group. According to Stephan and Stephan, these assumed, unsubstantiated threats can be political, economic, or social concerns believed to threaten "the physical or material well being of the in-group or its members."[68]

**Avoiding Prejudice.** Avoiding prejudice is not an easy assignment, for like most aspects of cultural perceptions, racial and cultural prejudices are learned early and are reinforced through continued exposure. Nevertheless, research has revealed that two techniques are often successful in dispelling prejudicial views—*personal contact*[69] and *education*.[70] The research on the value of personal contact as a method of reducing prejudice has a history dating to the early 1950s. The rationale for the contact, at least in its expression, is a simple one—the greater the frequency of positive contacts between in-group and out-group individuals, the lower the level of perceived prejudice. The words "positive contact" should indicate to you that we are talking about more than two people coming together. According to Oskamp, the contact needs to meet certain conditions to be successful, the most important being "equal status between groups" and cooperation "toward common goals."[71]

There are two types of educational programs that psychologists have used to help reduce prejudice. The first type centers on what is called *multicultural education curricula*. According to Stephan and Stephan, this curricula "usually consists of materials on the history and cultural practices of a wide array of racial and ethnic groups."[72] The materials in multicultural classes are often presented from the point of view of the minority groups rather than from the perception of the dominant culture. *Cultural diversity training* is used mainly in business and organizational settings. Stephan and Stephan summarize this educational methodology when they note that these programs are used "to teach managers and employees to value group differences, increase understanding between groups, and help individuals recognize that their own behavior is affected by their background."[73] Regardless of the program selected, the explicit goals remain the same—to increase intergroup dialogue and reduce prejudice.

## RACISM

Early in this new century it appears that for most people of color Martin Luther King, Jr.'s dream that children "will be judged not by the color of their skin but by the content of their character" remains a dream because, as Dana points out, "Both subtle and overt racism still permeates mainstream American society."[74] This view is further articulated by Vora and Vora when they write, "Both blatant and very subtle forms of racism permeate organizational and personal levels of our society, from governmental, business, and educational institutions to our everyday interactions."[75] Racist acts in these institutions, and in society in general, target many groups and for a host of reasons. As Gold notes, "Forms of racism are experienced by groups such as Asian Americans, Latinos, Arabs, and American Indians, whose racialization is associated with factors such as religion, foreignness, clothing, culture, citizenship, gender and language."[76] Racism is not only a problem in the United States. Many studies point out that racism, throughout the world, is on the rise.[77] Although racism exists for many reasons, experts seem to agree that at its core racism is driven by "culture, economics, psychology and history."[78]

It is difficult to make a complete assessment of the consequences of racism because the effects are both conscious and subconscious. But what we do know is that racism is damaging to those who are the recipients of this destructive behavior as well as the racists themselves. It devalues the target person by denying their identity. It destroys the culture by creating divisions and making it less cohesive. As Leone notes, racism results "in the virtual isolation of a specific group or groups from the political, social and economic mainstream of a nation's life."[79]

What is sad but true about racism is that it seems to have been present throughout the world for thousands of years and history is full of examples. In the recent past we saw African Americans being forced to ride in the back of buses, Jews being required to wear a yellow Star of David, Japanese Americans being isolated in camps during the Second World War, American Indians having their land confiscated, and South African society divided along racial lines. Today we see manifestations of racism in the form of racial graffiti, property damage, intimidation, and even physical violence. There are also more subtle forms of racism such as uttering racial slurs or telling ethnic jokes. We will examine this harmful and insidious characteristic of racism so that you can work to eliminate it in your professional and private lives.

**Defining Racism.** Racism, in many ways, is an extension of stereotyping and prejudice, as you can see in the following definition advanced by Leone:

> Racism is the belief in the inherent superiority of a particular race. It denies the basic equality of humankind and correlates ability with physical composition. Thus, it assumes that success or failure in any societal endeavor will depend upon genetic endowment rather than environment and access to opportunity.[80]

It is important to notice the word "superiority" built into this definition. It is this idea of superiority that allows one group of people to mistreat another group on the basis of race, color, religion, national origin, ancestry, or sexual preference. A more detailed explanation of the unfounded beliefs and misleading arguments behind racism is offered by Nanda and Warms:

> There are biological fixed races; different races have different moral, intellectual, and physical characteristics; an individual's aptitudes are determined primarily by his or her race; races can be ranked on a single hierarchy; and political action should be taken to order society so that it reflects this hierarchy.[81]

The folly of the racist thinking described above is that it is not only unethical and cruel, but it is also constructed on false premises. It is now common knowledge, for those who are willing to be receptive to the knowledge, that "the big differences among human groups are the result of culture, not biological inheritance or race. All human beings belong to the same species and the biological features essential to human life are common to us all."[82] Yet in spite of this truth and wisdom, racism remains a major hindrance to successful intercultural communication.

**Expression of Racism.** As already mentioned, racism can be expressed in a variety of forms. Some of these are almost impossible to detect while others are blatant and transparent. In general these forms can be categorized as *personal* and *institutional*.

**Personal Racism.** "Personal racism consists of racist acts, beliefs, attitudes, and behaviors on the part of the individual persons."[83] Brislin identifies four of the most common types of personal racist views.

1. *Intense Racism*. In this form of racism, "Some people believe that virtually all members of certain out-groups are inferior in various ways and are not able to benefit fully from society's offerings such as education, good jobs, and participation in community affairs."[84] This form of racism begins with the belief that certain people (those of a race different from the person making and drawing the conclusion) are inferior, and hence are perceived as being of low worth.
2. *Symbolic Racism*. Some people hold racist views because "they feel that the out-group is interfering with important aspects of the culture."[85] This "interference" can be in the form of "creating problems" or "a greater economic advantage than they deserve."[86]
3. *Tokenism*. Tokenism occurs when one or two individuals from a particular minority group are placed in a large organization as symbolic representation of the entire minority group. Whether it be in the form of prejudice or racism, tokenism is difficult to detect. Normally, the minority person does not want to admit that he or she has been placed in a position because of race, ethnicity, or gender. Dominant group members will even engage in "token" activities to "prove" they are evenhanded in the treatment of other races.
4. *Arm's Length*. Brislin describes this negative behavior in the following manner: "Some people engage in friendly, positive behaviors toward out-group members in some social settings but treat those same out-group members with noticeably less warmth and friendliness in other settings."[87]

**Institutional Racism.** Earlier in this section we made reference to institutional racism by noting many institutions within a particular culture engage in racist practices. Blum is more specific when he writes, "*Institutional racism* refers to racial inferiorizing or antipathy perpetrated by specific social institutions such as schools, corporations, hospitals, or the criminal justice system as a totality."[88] While "institutional racism may be intentional or unintentional,"[89] its consequences have a detrimental effect on specific groups and society as a whole.

**Avoiding Racism.** Although views about race are deeply entrenched, there are four steps you can take to reduce racism in yourself and others. First, *try to be honest with yourself* when deciding if you hold some racist views. It is a simple point to state, but a difficult one to accomplish. Yet, confronting your racist views, if you hold any, is an important first step. Second, *object to racist jokes and insults* whenever you hear them. This daring, and at times courageous, act will send a message to other people that you denounce racism in whatever form it may take. Third, as straightforward as it sounds, we urge you to *respect freedom*. The United States Constitution states, "nor shall any state deprive any person of life, liberty, or property, without due process of law; nor deny to any person within its jurisdiction the equal protection of the laws." From this declaration it follows that to preserve liberty you must work to see that all individuals are free from political and social restrictions. Fourth, examine *the historical roots of racism*. The rationale for such an examination is clearly documented by Solomos and Back when they note that before the full impact of racism can be grasped and challenged you must be able to understand and explain "both the roots of contemporary racist ideas and movements and the sources of their current appeal."[90]

We conclude by reminding you that racism, stereotyping, and prejudice are pervasive because they are often learned early in life, and like much of culture, become part of your way of seeing the world. The African-American author Maya Angelou makes the same point when she writes, "The plague of racism is insidious, entering into our minds as smoothly and quietly and invisibly as floating airborne microbes enter into our bodies to find lifelong purchase in our bloodstreams."

## POWER

Much of what we have been talking about, whether it is stereotyping, prejudice, or racism, has its antecedent in issues related to power. Groups have employed guns, bombs, language, media, space, money, and even history as devices for gaining and keeping power over others. The reason is apparent, if not wholly justifiable—people who hold power achieve their will regardless of the type of relationship. Power, in one form or another, seems to be built into all human liaisons. The famous British philosopher Bertrand Russell made the same observation when he wrote, "The fundamental concept in social science is Power, in the same sense in which Energy is the fundamental concept in Physics."[91] Granting that there are many kinds of power (interpersonal, corporate, organizational, governmental, etc.), we will concentrate on power in the intercultural context.

**Defining Power.** Why do humans seek power? The answer to this question can be found in the very definition of power: Power is the ability to control what happens, to cause things you want to happen, and to block things you don't want to happen.[92] What makes power an important dimension in intercultural communication, and a potential problem, is that power usually means controlling not only your own life but also the lives of others. As Nanda and Warms tell you, "Power is thus the ability to make and carry out decisions affecting one's own life, control the behavior of other human beings, and transform objects and resources."[93] In many cultures this often means that the people in power can "follow their own interests at the expense of the goals of others."[94]

What is interesting about power is that the methods of power are as diverse as they are widespread. That is to say, power is present in nearly every human experience, from global politics to face-to-face interactions between the dominant culture and co-cultures. Therefore, the dynamics of power greatly influence all phases of intercultural communication. Martin and Nakayama offer an excellent summary of this point when they note, "We are not equal in intercultural encounters, nor can we ever be equal. Long histories of imperialism, colonialism, exploitation, wars, genocide campaigns, and more leave cultural groups out of balance when they communicate."[95]

**Degrees of Power.** It should be clear that power, both in definition and in practice, is complex. For example, not all power, either perceived or implemented, is the same.

Charon points out that it is best to view power on a continuum.[96] At one end of the spectrum, both parties hold some degree of control over the process and the outcome of the interaction. As you move along the continuum, one person would have a little influence over the other. At the opposite end of the scale, one person would have complete control. Here is where you find the idea of the "powerless." Again we turn to Charon for an explanation of what it means to be powerless:

> To be powerless means to be helpless in relation to others, to be determined by the will of others. Powerless means that one lacks control over one's own life, is unable effectively to resist the exertion of power by others, and lacks the ability to influence the direction of social organization, including society. Powerlessness brings dependence on others and exploitation (self use) by others, if they choose.[97]

**Power and Intercultural Communication.** The reason power is such an important consideration in the study of intercultural communication is that it can manifest itself in a variety of ways. In interpersonal communication the amount of power you have, or do not have, influences who you talk to, what you talk about, and how much control you have when you talk. Folb adds to the list when she tells us that the people in power have a major impact on what people "believe and do," and also influence the "rules of appropriate and inappropriate behavior, thought, speech, and action."[98] Carried to an extreme, and it often is, we find in many cultures that the following expression is true: "All men (perhaps even women) are created equal—some are just more equal than others."[99]

Your degree of power is contingent on the person(s) with whom you are interacting and the resources that you control. In intercultural communication, these two factors take on added significance, for the sources of power are culturally based. What one culture deems as a source of power, another culture may not consider a power variable. For example, in England, an individual's dialect is often a sign of potential power because it signals class and station. There also are instances when one culture believes that power is derived from simply being a member of that particular culture. African Americans have long expressed feelings of being controlled and manipulated by white males.[100] Many women in the United States have expressed this same view.[101] It is easy to see how this use, or misuse, of power, when employed to control and determine another's behavior, can restrict openness and communication. As Smith notes, "To allow customary subservience or power a place in human interaction is to introduce an inevitable obstruction."[102]

Although all cultures dislike the abuse of power, much of the world is composed of cultures that do not seek individual power. They believe that power resides outside of them and that fate, nature, or God has all the power. Power is not something they want, need, or have. Muslims use the phrase "It is God's will." For the Hindu, power is the acting out of individual karma, and in much of Mexico and Latin America, a strong belief in fatalism often replaces power. These cultures hold the view that, in most instances, the legitimacy of power is irrelevant.[103]

As an intercultural communicator, it is important that you become aware of each culture's approach to power. However, regardless of the culture you are interacting with, an adherence to the following philosophy advanced by Blubaugh and Pennington could greatly improve most intercultural transactions: "The ideal power relationship . . . is not concerned with the idea of control. . . . Rather, the desire is to attribute to all groups the credibility that allows them positive influence in communication."[104]

## ETHNOCENTRISM

People from one culture might view people who eat raw horse meat as being barbarous and abnormal. But the people who eat raw horse meat might consider people in other cultures as cruel and uncaring because they habitually confine the elderly to convalescent homes. Both attitudes are ethnocentric. At the core of ethnocentrism are judgments about what is right, moral, and rational. These judgments pervade every aspect of a culture's existence. Examples range from the insignificant ("Earrings should be placed on the ears, not on the nose") to the significant ("We need to enact trade quotas to protect our economy from cheap foreign imports"). What you see here is the very natural tendency to use one's own culture as a starting point when evaluating the behavior of other people and cultures.

**Defining Ethnocentrism.** Sumner, generally credited with introducing the term to the study of culture, defined *ethnocentrism* as "the technical name for the view of things in which one's own group is the center of everything, and all others are scaled and rated with reference to it."[105] Nanda and Warms offer a more contemporary explanation:

> Ethnocentrism is the notion that one's own culture is superior to any other. It is the idea that other cultures should be measured by the degree to which they live up to our cultural standards. We are ethnocentric when we view other cultures through the narrow lens of our own culture or social position.[106]

It is this "narrow lens" that links ethnocentrism to the concepts of stereotyping, racism, prejudice, and power that we just finished discussing.

© Robert Fonseca

*Ethnocentrism is learned early in life and is continuously being reinforced.*

## Characteristics of Ethnocentrism

**Levels of Ethnocentrism.** It is best to view ethnocentrism as having three levels: *positive, negative,* and *extremely negative*. The first, positive, is the belief that, at least for you, your culture is preferred over all others. This is natural, and inherently there is nothing wrong with it. In the negative level, you partially take on an evaluative dimension. You believe your culture is the center of everything and all other cultures should be measured and rated by its standards. As Triandis notes, "We perceive in-group customs as universally valid. We unquestionably think that in-group roles and values are correct."[107] Finally, in the extreme negative form, it is not enough to consider your culture as the most valid and useful, but now you perceive your culture as the most powerful and even believe that your values and beliefs should be adopted by other cultures.

**Ethnocentrism Is Universal.** Anthropologists generally agree that ethnocentrism, with varying degrees, is found in every culture in that "most peoples in the world regard their own culture as superior."[108] And like culture, ethnocentrism is usually learned at the unconscious level. For example, schools that teach mainly the history, geography, literature, and government of only their country and exclude others are encouraging ethnocentrism. When you study the accomplishments only of white males, you are quietly learning ethnocentrism. Students exposed to limited orientations develop the belief that America is the center of the world, and they learn to judge the world by American standards. What is true about American ethnocentrism is true about other cultures. As children in Iran learn only about the wisdom of Allah, they are learning to judge all religious truths by this singular standard. And when the Chinese, for thousands of years, "place themselves in the center of the world, referring to their nation using a Chinese character that literally means central state," they are teaching ethnocentrism.[109] Even the stories and folktales that each culture tells their young people contribute to ethnocentrism. Keesing described this subtle learning when he writes, "Nearly always the folklore of a people includes myths of origin which give priority to themselves, and place the stamp of supernatural approval upon their particular customs."[110]

**Ethnocentrism Contributes to Cultural Identity.** Another reason ethnocentrism is so pervasive is that it provides members of a culture with feelings of identity and belonging. As Rosen notes, "Belonging to this group, to this nation, or civilization, gives them self-esteem, makes them proud of the achievements of their own people."[111] The manner in which this idea translates into ethnocentrism is clearly articulated by Scarborough: "People have great pride in their culture; they must, because culture is their source of identity; they have difficulty understanding why others do not behave as they do, and assume that others would like to be them if they could."[112] Haviland echoes this same important function when he writes:

> To function effectively, a society must embrace the idea that its ways are the only proper ones, irrespective of how other cultures do things. This provides individuals with a sense of ethnic pride in and loyalty to their cultural traditions, from which they derive psychological support, and which binds them firmly to their group. In societies where one's self-identification derives from the group, ethnocentrism is essential to a sense of personal worth.[113]

Ethnocentrism is strongest in moral and religious contexts, where emotionalism may overshadow rationality and cause the type of hostility the world witnessed on

September 11, 2001. Explaining the link between ethnocentrism and devotion to one's culture, Brislin observes, "If people view their own group as central to their lives and as possessing proper behavioral standards, they are likely to aid their group members when troubles arise. In times of war the rallying of ethnocentric feelings makes a country's military forces more dedicated to the defeat of the (inferior) enemy."[114]

There can be serious consequences if you engage in negative ethnocentrism at the same time you are trying to practice successful intercultural communication. One of the major interpersonal consequences of ethnocentrism is anxiety—a problem we discussed earlier in the chapter. The argument is simple—and clearly enunciated by Gamble and Gamble: "The more ethnocentric you are, the more anxious you are about interacting with other cultures; when we are fearful, we are less likely to expect a positive outcome from such interactions, and less willing to trust someone from another culture."[115]

**Avoiding Ethnocentrism.** Avoiding ethnocentric perceptions and behavior is not an easy task. There are, however, some suggestions that we can offer that might help reduce the negative consequences of ethnocentrism. First, *try to avoid dogmatism*. You can begin by asking yourself to think about the following questions:

- Jews cover their heads when they pray, but Protestants do not—is one more correct than the other?
- The Catholic has one God, the Buddhist has no god, and the Hindu has many gods—is one more correct than the others?
- In parts of Iran and Saudi Arabia, women cover their faces with veils, whereas women in the United States do not—is one behavior more correct than the other?
- In Japan people eat with chopsticks, in the United States they use metal or plastic utensils—is one more correct than the other?

These sorts of rhetorical questions are limitless. We urge you to remember that it is not the questions that are important but rather the dogmatic manner in which people often answer them. The danger of ethnocentrism is that it is strongest in political, moral, and religious settings. In these contexts, it is easy to let culturally restricted views overshadow rationality. Hence, we again urge you to be alert to narrowness and intolerance in any form. St. Thomas Aquinas said much the same thing hundreds of years ago: "Beware of the man of one book."

Second, *learn to be open to new views*. Triandis converts this important idea into action when he writes: "When we make a comparative judgment that our culture is in some ways better than another, we need to learn to follow this judgment with two questions: Is that really true? What is the objective evidence?"[116] One of the main missions of this book has been to expose you to a variety of cultures so that you might be able to carry out the advice of Triandis by knowing the "truth" about other cultures. This lack of knowledge is a major cause of ethnocentrism. As Berry and his associates point out, "As a general rule the greater the cultural behavioral differences the greater is the potential for negative evaluations of the difference."[117]

## CULTURE SHOCK

The English Renaissance composer William Byrd once stated, "The song is best esteemed with which our ears are most acquainted." The adage simply underscores

*Major differences in perception can produce culture shock.*

© Alan Oddie/PhotoEdit

how everyone likes the familiar. As we pointed out at the beginning of this chapter, the familiar helps you reduce stress in that in most instances you know what you can expect from your environment and from those around you. When you leave these comfortable surroundings and journey into new areas, communication problems can occur.

It should not be surprising that dealing with a new culture can produce mental stress and create difficulty. As Nolan points out "Your new environment makes demands for which you have no ready-made responses; and your responses, in turn, do not seem to produce the desired results."[118] Smith and Bond offer a more specific summary of some of the problems of moving to a new location: "Separation from previous support networks, climate differences, increased health problems, changes in material and technical resources, lack of information about daily routines (e.g., how to travel from A to B), and so forth all exact their price."[119]

As we have emphasized throughout this book, contacts with other cultures are not only increasing in number and intensity, but they are taking a variety of forms. Millions of Americans are now traveling overseas, attending school, conducting business, or performing government service.[120] When you are thrust into another culture and experience psychological and physical discomfort from this contact, you experience culture shock.[121] Before we discuss the problems associated with culture shock, you need to realize that there is a difference between people who are temporary visitors (sojourners) and those who intend to take up permanent residence in a new country (immigrants, settlers). This distinction is relevant, as Bochner notes,

> because their respective contact experiences, and hence their reactions, differ. For instance, the two groups have different time frames. *Settlers* are in the process of making a permanent commitment to their new society, whereas *sojourners* are there on a temporary basis, although they may vary from a day with tourists to several years in the case of foreign students.[122]

Later in this chapter we will offer some advice concerning those individuals who are moving to a new country and facing the challenges of adapting to their new culture. However, at this time our focus is on the sojourner.

**Defining Culture Shock.** The term *culture shock* was first introduced by the anthropologist Oberg. In the following paragraph, he offers a detailed definition and account of this phenomenon:

> Culture shock is precipitated by the anxiety that results from losing all our familiar signs and symbols of social intercourse. These signs or cues include the thousand and one ways in which we orient ourselves to the situation of daily life: how to give orders, how to make purchases, when and where not to respond. Now these cues which may be words, gestures, facial expressions, customs, or norms are acquired by all of us in the course of growing up and are as much a part of our culture as the language we speak or the beliefs we accept. All of us depend for our peace of mind and efficiency on hundreds of these cues, most of which we are not consciously aware.[123]

While the above definition was the first one, it fails to mention that culture shock also involves a powerful disruption in one's routines, ego, and self image.[124] These feelings not only apply to businesspersons, students, and government employees, but, as Brislin notes, can "be experienced by individuals who have face-to-face contact with out-group members within their own culture."[125]

**Reactions to Culture Shock.** The reactions associated with culture shock vary from individual to individual and can appear at different times. For example, for the person who is constantly encountering other cultures, the anxiety period might be mild and brief. However, culture shock can generate a host of reactions that have the potential to create problems. Let us offer you a list of those reactions. The motivation behind our list is clearly noted by Lynch and Hanson when they say, "Understanding the concept of culture shock and its characteristics and stages provides a framework that enables individuals to recognize their feelings, analyze the cause, alter their approach, consciously manage their own behavior, and regain emotional equilibrium."[126] We should add that this list is not intended to overwhelm you or make you apprehensive about being a sojourner, but rather to help you be prepared if you experience some of these reactions.[127]

- Antagonistic toward new environment
- Sense of disorientation
- Feeling of rejection
- Upset stomach and headaches
- Homesickness
- Missing friends and family
- Believing in a loss of status and influence
- Withdrawal
- Perceiving members of host culture to be insensitive

**The Stages of Culture Shock (The U-Curve).** Although there might be great variations in how people respond to culture shock, and the amount of time needed for that adjustment, most of the literature in the area of culture shock suggests that people normally go through four stages. We should first mention that the seam separating the stages is almost impossible to see—that is to say, the transition from stage to stage is not as clear cut as our description might imply. You should view the stages as a U-shaped curve. "The U-curve depicts the initial optimism and elation in the host culture, the subsequent dip in the level of adaptation, and the following gradual recovery."[128] Let us examine these stages in more detail so that you will better understand the complex process of culture shock.

**Optimistic Phase.** The first phase, visualized as the top of the left side of the U, is usually filled with excitement, hopefulness, and a sense of euphoria as the individual anticipates being exposed to a new culture. Marx offers an excellent review of how this first phase might be perceived by someone undertaking an international management assignment:

> The new life is viewed as providing endless opportunities and the manager is usually in a state of exhilaration. There is openness and curiosity, combined with a readiness to accept whatever comes. Most importantly, at this stage judgment is reserved and even minor irritations are suppressed in favor of concentrating on the nice things about the job, the country, the colleagues, the food, etc.[129]

**Cultural Problems.** This second phase is when some initial problems begin to develop. For example, adaptation and communication difficulties begin to emerge. As Triandis notes, "The second phase is a period when difficulties of language, inadequate schools for the children, poor housing, crowded transportation, chaotic shopping, and the like begin taking their toll."[130] This phase is often marked by feelings of disappointment and discontent. It is the crisis period of culture shock. The person becomes confused and baffled by his or her new surroundings. This frustration can make them easily irritated, hostile, impatient, angry, and even incompetent. In extreme cases these uncomfortable feelings "can border on hating everything foreign."[131]

**Recovery Phase.** The third phase is characterized by gaining some understanding of the new culture. Here the person is gradually making some adjustments and modifications in how he or she is coping with the new culture. Events and people now seem much more predictable and less stressful.

**Adjustment Phase.** In the final phase, at the top of the other side of the U, the person now understands the key elements of the new culture (values, special customs, beliefs, communication patterns, etc.) and can now function with some degree of success. This ability to live within two cultures is often accompanied by feelings of enjoyment and satisfaction.

Some researchers suggest that there is also a kind of reverse culture shock that takes place when people return home. As Harris and Moran note, "Having objectively perceived his or her culture from abroad, one can have a severe and sustained jolt through reentry shock."[132] These expatriates often arrive home missing the new friends they made while overseas. Some bemoan the loss of prestige associated with foreign assignments. When this happens, the returnee experiences the same four phases of adjustment we discussed in the U curve. This gives rise to the term "W curve," because it joins two U curves together.

**Coping with Culture Shock.** This section on culture shock was predicated on two premises. First, each year millions of people go abroad to work, travel, and study. Second, many of those experiences end up producing stress, homesickness, and confusion. To help alleviate some of these problems we offer the following suggestions.

*Make Friends.* When we speak of making friends we are primarily talking about having contacts within the host culture. In fact, studies point out "that having friends among the nationals of the host country, rather than having contacts only with fellow expatriates, is an important determinant of satisfaction."[133] At the same time, it is important to have periodic interaction with other expatriates so you can share problems and solutions and find a degree of comfort in speaking your native language.

*Learn About the Host Culture.* One of the major themes of this book has been the notion that a fund of knowledge about other cultures is a useful first step toward improving intercultural communication. Here we return to that thesis. To avoid serious culture shock, we would urge you to learn about the culture's religious orientation, political system, key values and beliefs, verbal and nonverbal behaviors, family view organization, social etiquette, and the like. Learning as much of the language as possible is of particular importance.

*Be Patient.* You should allow some time when making the move from one culture to another. Be aware that there will be an adjustment period and prepare yourself for some of the reactions we discussed earlier.

*Participate in Cultural Activities.* An excellent way to learn about the new culture is to be an active participant in that culture. Attend social, religious, and cultural events. If possible you should try to interact with members of the host culture while attending these events. In most instances, members of the host culture will welcome the opportunity to learn about your culture while they are sharing theirs with you.

**The Lessons of Culture Shock.** Although we have placed the topic of culture shock under the category of "problems," we would be remiss if we concluded our discussion without emphasizing the idea that culture shock can be an explicit learning experience. In fact, as Adler notes, "Severe culture shock is often a positive sign indicating that the expatriate is becoming deeply involved in the new culture instead of remaining isolated in an expatriate ghetto."[134] This involvement helps people learn about themselves and, at the same time, other cultures. In a study examining culture shock, Kawano concluded that culture shock "gives the sojourners a chance to learn about themselves. In this sense experiencing culture shock has a strong potential to make people be multicultural or bicultural."[135]

To this point we looked at some potential problems that can arise when you engage in intercultural communication. We now shift our attention and offer some specific advice on how you may resolve some of those problems. Shakespeare expressed poetically the rationale for our sequence (moving from problems to solutions) in his play *Much Ado About Nothing,* where he wrote, "Happy are they that hear their detractions and can put them to mending." Having noted some "detractions" in the beginning of this chapter, we now progress to "mending."

# Improving Intercultural Communication

Although this entire book is aimed at improving intercultural communication, our suggestions, admonitions, counsel, and proposals in previous chapters have been only tangentially related to improvement. Our recommendations will now be very direct. And more importantly, all of the suggestions for improvement enable you to exercise your ability to make choices. Our propositions place *you* in the center of the activity. Whether we are asking you to learn more about a culture's view toward the elderly or appealing to you to develop some new skills, the power is all yours. What is being said here should be quite clear—you must act on what you have learned about other cultures. The Persian poet Sa'di said much the same thing over seven thousand years ago: "Whoever acquires knowledge and does not practice it resembles him who ploughs his land and leaves it unsown."

Before we offer our first bit of advice, we want to acknowledge a major danger in offering anyone personal advice. Whenever you tell another individual how to think or act, you run the risk—particularly if he or she listens to you—of making matters worse. The person may have been better off without your advice. For example, we believe that many of you already know a great deal about intercultural communication and, in fact, are very good practitioners of the art. In these cases, we run the risk of spoiling what has taken you years to develop. What we are saying is somewhat analogous to an old Chinese fable. In this fable, a monkey and a fish were very good friends. One day, however, a dreadful flood separated them. Because the monkey could climb trees, he was able to scramble up a limb and escape the rising waters. As he glanced into the raging river, he saw his friend the fish swimming past. With the best of intentions, he scooped his paw into the water, snatched his friend from the river, and lifted him into the tree. The result was obvious. From this modest story, you can see the dilemma we face. So please remember as we offer advice that, like the monkey, we have the best of intentions.

## KNOW YOURSELF

Earlier in the chapter we told you how important it was to identify the negative stereotypes and prejudices you carry around. We now expand that advice and suggest that an essential first step toward improvement is you. As obvious and simplistic as it sounds, what you bring to the communication event greatly influences the success or failure of that event—and what you bring is you. Knowing yourself is a crucial element in becoming a competent intercultural communicator. The novelist James Baldwin said it best when he wrote, "The questions which one asks oneself begin, at last, to illuminate the world, and become one's key to the experience of others." Baldwin's remarks serve as an ideal introduction for the portion of this book that urges you to begin your path to improvement with some self-analysis. As with many of the suggestions we offer in this section, it is easier to state the advice than to practice it. We can write the words "know yourself" with just a few strokes on our keyboard, but it will take a great deal of effort for you to translate this assignment into practice. We believe that the application of introspection should take four directions: (1) *know your culture*, (2) *know your perceptions*, (3) *know how you act out those perceptions*, and (4) *monitor yourself*. Although these four concepts work in tandem, it might be useful to examine them separately.

**Know Your Culture.** Your first step toward introspection should begin with your own culture. Remember, one of the major themes of this book has been that everyone sees the world through the lens of their culture. As Kim points out:

> Each of us is a product of our cultural background, including gender, ethnicity, family, age, religion, profession, and other life experiences. Our cultural inventory provides us with valuable insights for understanding our beliefs and attitudes, our values and assumptions. Thus, it is critical that we reflect on the various aspects of our own cultural identity and examine their positive and negative impacts on our personal and professional development.[136]

Stewart and Bennett, while speaking about the American culture, made a similar observation when they wrote: "An awareness of American culture along with examples of contrasting cultures contributes to the individual's understanding of her- or himself as a cultural being."[137] Novinger is even more specific in that she offers a listing of some influences your culture can have on your perceptions and communication behavior.[138] While most of the items she mentions have been alluded to in various parts of this book, they are nevertheless worth repeating here in the final chapter. Among other cultural components, you should examine your culture's key values, gender roles, thought patterns, worldview, social organizations, use of language, rules regarding specific contexts, common idioms, and nonverbal communication patterns.

**Know Your Personal Attitudes.** Not only do you need to know the values, attitudes, and perceptions of your culture, you also need to be aware of your own belief system. We are not referring to any mystical notions involving another reality, nor are we suggesting you engage in any deep psychological soul searching. Rather, we are asking you to identify those personal attitudes, prejudices, and opinions that you carry around that bias the way the world appears to you. If you hold a certain attitude toward gay men, and a man who is gay talks to you, your precommunication attitude will affect your response to what he says. Knowing your likes, dislikes, and degrees of personal ethnocentrism enables you to place them out in the open so you can detect the ways in which these attitudes influence communication.

**Know Your Communication Style.** The third step in knowing yourself is somewhat more difficult than simply identifying your prejudices and predispositions. It involves discovering the kind of image you portray to the rest of the world. Ask yourself, "How do I communicate and how do others perceive me?" If you perceive yourself in one way, and the people with whom you interact perceive you in another way, serious problems can arise. If, for instance, you see yourself as patient and calm, but you appear rushed and anxious, you will have a hard time understanding why people respond to you as they do.

As a starting point, we suggest that you learn to recognize your communication style—the manner in which you present yourself to others. Many communication scholars have attempted to isolate the characteristics that compose a communication personality. One such inventory, which Norton has proposed, has nine characteristics.[139] In Table 11.1, we offer a summary of each of these so that you can begin to evaluate your own communication style.

**TABLE 11.1** Communication Style

| TRAIT | COMMUNICATION CHARACTERISTICS |
| --- | --- |
| Dominant | Speaks frequently; interrupts, controls conversation |
| Dramatic | Expressive language; often exaggerates and embellishes |
| Contentious | Argumentative and often hostile |
| Animated | Energetic and expressive gestures and facial expressions |
| Impression-leaving | States ideas and feelings in an indelible fashion |
| Relaxed | Calm, comfortable, and seldom nervous around others |
| Attentive | Good listener; offers encouragement to the speaker |
| Open | Discloses personal information; shows emotions and feelings |
| Friendly | Offers positive feedback and encouragement |

Barnlund offers yet another insightful interpretation of what your individual communication style might include:

> By communication style is meant the topics people prefer to discuss, their favorite forms of interaction—ritual, repartee, argument, self-disclosure—and the depth of involvement they demand of each other. It includes the extent to which communicants rely upon the same channels vocal, verbal, physical for conveying information, and the extent to which they are tuned to the same level of meaning, that is, to the factual or emotional content of messages.[140]

Here again, asking yourself how you manifest Barnlund's characteristics can help you understand the manner in which you present yourself to your communication partner.

In addition to the challenges inherent in Norton's and Barnlund's descriptions, we also urge you to ask yourself some of the following questions:

- Do I seem at ease or tense?
- Do I often change the subject without taking the other person into consideration?
- Do I deprecate the statements of others?
- Do I smile often?
- Do I interrupt repeatedly?
- Do I show sympathy when someone has a problem?
- Do my actions tend to lower the other person's self-esteem?
- Do I employ a pleasant tone of voice when I talk to people?
- Do I tend to pick the topics for discussion or do I share topic selection?
- What does my tone of voice suggest?
- How do I react to being touched by a stranger?

**Monitor Yourself.** What should emerge from the last few paragraphs is that all of you have unique ways of interacting. Discovering how you communicate is not always an easy task. It is awkward and highly irregular for you to walk around asking people if they think you are relaxed, argumentative, friendly, animated, and the like. You must, therefore, be sensitive to the feedback you receive and candid in the reading of that feedback. The process of self-observation and analysis is often called "self-monitoring."[141] Some of the advantages of self-monitoring are discovering the appropriate behaviors in each situation, having control of your emotional reactions, creating good impressions, and modifying your behavior as you move from situation to situation.[142]

We conclude this section on self-awareness by once again reminding you that there is a vast difference between being self-aware and self-absorbed. The entire process of being a participant and an observer at the same time is not an easy assignment—it involves a balance of the two activities. As Morreale, Spitzberg, and Barge note, "The key to self-monitoring is to strike a balance between attention to your environment and your own motivation, knowledge and skills."[143] What they are saying is that being self-aware is not watching actions so that you can be the center of attention; rather, it is for the purpose of gaining honest and candid insight into your cultural and individual patterns of communication so that you can improve your intercultural skills. Shakespeare said it far more eloquently when he penned the often quoted line from *Hamlet*, "This above all: to thine own self be true, / And it must follow, as the night the day, / Thou canst not then be false to any man." And we would add, "Thou canst not then be false to yourself."

## EMPLOY EMPATHY

A well-known American Indian saying tells us, "We should not judge another person until we have walked two moons in his moccasins." Our next suggestion for improvement is about wearing those moccasins. Actually, what we should say is that it is about *your* trying to imagine wearing those moccasins. We used the word *imagine* because it is physically and psychologically impossible to ever really know what another person is actually experiencing. The process of empathy is of course much more complicated than merely imagining. Empathy is actually "the ability to recognize and understand another person's perceptions and feelings, and to accurately convey that understanding through an accepting response."[144]

Defining empathy in a cultural setting, Ting-Toomey describes it in the following manner: "Through empathy we are willing to imaginatively place ourselves in the dissimilar other's cultural world and to experience what she or he is experiencing."[145] While these two definitions might lead you to believe that empathy is a difficult process, it is in fact something everyone is capable of doing. Notice for example we used the heading "Employ Empathy" not "Learn to Empathize" to introduce this section of the book. Our reason is that you begin all communication encounters with the ability to empathize. It seems that being able to engage in empathy is innate. Even very young children seem to be able to empathize with the pain or happiness of other people. Speaking about this basic core of empathy, Katz writes, "A simple way to explain the origin of the empathic skill is to postulate that we are born to understand. Part of our biological heritage is the capacity to visualize and to apprehend the feelings of other members of our species."[146] The visualizing and apprehending is of course very limited when people are young. However, with age and experience a greater degree of empathetic feeling, understanding, and responsiveness develops.

The importance of empathy to the study of interpersonal and intercultural competence cannot be overstated. After reviewing the literature on the topic of empathy, Broome concluded, "Empathy has been recognized as important to both general communication competence and as a central characteristic of competent and effective intercultural communication."[147] Calloway-Thomas, Cooper, and Blake echo Broome's commentary when they write, "Empathy is the bedrock of intercultural communication."[148]

**Understanding Empathy.** Here, we need to mention two ideas that will aid you in understanding the role of empathy in intercultural communication. First, although we have focused primarily on culture, we also are concerned with the interpersonal aspects of intercultural communication. As Miller and Steinberg note, "To communicate interpersonally, one must leave the cultural and sociological levels of predications and psychically travel to the psychological level."[149] Simply put, empathy, while using knowledge about another's culture to make predications, also demands that the point of analysis be the individual personality. Second, it is best to view empathy as a complex activity composed of many variables. It involves a cognitive component (thinking), an affective (emotional identification) dimension, and a communication element (activity). Bell explains these three variables and how they interact with each other:

> Cognitively, the empathic person takes the perspective of another person, and in so doing strives to see the world from the other's point of view. Affectively, the empathic person experiences the emotions of another; he or she feels the other's experiences. Communicatively, the empathic individual signals understanding and concern through verbal and nonverbal cues.[150]

Before we look at some of the ways to improve our role-taking skills, it might be helpful to examine a few characteristics that can impede empathy.

### Hindrances to Empathy

*Different Cultural Backgrounds.* Our first hindrance reminds you that you approach each situation and individual from your own cultural perspective. Countless studies have verified the notion that individuals from similar cultures exhibit greater empathic concern than do those from dissimilar cultures.[151] What this means is that when confronting someone from a culture different from your own it would be useful to have as much knowledge of that culture as possible.

*Constant Self-Focus.* Perhaps the most common of all barriers to empathy is a constant self-focus. Attending to your own thoughts, or telling your own stories, uses much of the energy that you should direct toward your communication partner. At times everyone is guilty of behaving according to the German proverb "Everyone thinks that all the bells echo his own thoughts."

*Focusing on Details.* The tendency to note only some features of an individual to the exclusion of others can cause you to misuse the data you gather about another person. If, for example, you notice only a person's skin color or that his or her surname is Lopez, and from this limited information assume you know all there is to know about the person, you are apt to do a poor job of empathizing. Admittedly, color and names offer you some information about the other person, but you must add to this type of data. Although it is an overused analogy, you should remember that most outward features represent only the tip of the iceberg.

*Stereotyped Notions Concerning Gender, Race, and Culture.* We have already talked about the destructive nature of stereotypes, so now we only need to add that they also serve as potential stumbling blocks to empathy. If you believe that "all English people dislike the Irish," you might allow this stereotype to influence your view of an English person.

*Defensive Behavior.* People often engage in defensive behavior that keeps others from wanting to reveal information about themselves—information you need if you are going to engage in empathetic behavior. Because defensive behaviors are so common, it would be useful for you to examine how two of these actions inhibit your ability to empathize.

When you appear to be *evaluating other people*, whether by what you say or what you do, you are likely to make them feel defensive toward you. If you believe others are judging and evaluating you, you will hesitate to offer information that will foster empathy. Think about how awkward you feel when, after sharing some personal information, the other person quickly lectures you on the foolhardiness of your act. After a few minutes of criticism and ridicule, you probably would decide not to disclose any other information to that person.

An *attitude of superiority*, which produces defensive behavior, seldom elicits the kind of information you need for empathizing. Imagine how defensive you would become if someone from France told you that Americans used language in a very dull and unimaginative manner.

**Improving Empathy.** Up to this point, we have painted a rather dark picture of empathy and the difficulties related to practicing empathy in intercultural encounters. Although it is nearly impossible to know another person completely and accurately, you can develop the skills necessary to overcome the problems we have mentioned.

*Pay Attention.* Our first bit of advice grows out of a problem we mentioned earlier in this chapter; however, this time we will put a positive face on the topic of paying attention. Or as Trenholm and Jensen tell us: "The single most important thing you do is remind yourself to pay attention to the spontaneous emotional expressions of others."[152] As you know from personal experience, concentrating on one idea or one person is difficult. This high level of attention is even more strenuous when applied to empathy, for it, like our attention span, is dynamic. Barnlund underscores this idea when he writes, "Empathy tends to be a fleeting phenomenon, fluctuating from moment to moment and from situation to situation."[153] Thus, problems associated with concentration can be overcome if you work on staying focused on both the other person and the situation.

*Communicate Empathy.* Because empathy is a reciprocal act, you and your communication partner must be expressive (unless you are interacting with someone from a culture that values interpersonal restraint). You cannot expect individuals from other cultures to offer you verbal and nonverbal messages about their internal states if your behavior is not reciprocal with their efforts. Trenholm and Jensen also maintain that if your own expressive behavior encourages others to be more expressive and you pay attention to the wider range of nonverbal cues they are displaying, you should be more accurate in reading their emotional states.[154]

*Use Culturally Accepted Behaviors.* Empathy can be enhanced through awareness of specific behaviors that members of a particular culture or co-culture might find impertinent or insulting. For example, according to Rich, many African Americans find it offensive when they hear stereotypic statements ("All African Americans have good voices"), when they are called "boy" or "son," or when they are referred to as being "a culturally deprived minority."[155] And you would not receive vital information to use for empathy if you refused the hospitality offered by an Arab. In each of these examples, we have made the same point: to be successful as an intercultural communicator, you must develop empathy, and that can be cultivated only if you become sensitive to the values and customs of the culture with which you are interacting.

***Learn to Accept Differences.*** Our final proposal for improving your empathetic skills is perhaps the one that most closely parallels the main mission of this book. Again we remind you that empathy can be increased if you resist the tendency to interpret the other's verbal and nonverbal actions from your culture's orientation. The link between empathy and acceptance is mentioned by Lewis when he notes, "Empathy is based on accepting differences and building on these in a positive manner."[156] Learn to suspend, or at least keep in check, the cultural perspective that is unique to your experiences. Knowing how the frame of reference of other cultures differs from your own will assist you in more accurately reading what meaning lies behind words and actions. For example, in the Chinese culture, as a means of "saving face," people will often say one thing when they mean something else; knowing this difference can help you understand what is actually being expressed.[157]

## CULTURAL DIFFERENCES IN LISTENING

One of the major themes of this book has been that the ways in which we communicate, what we communicate, and our response to communication are greatly influenced by our culture. Listening is one of those ingredients embedded in all three of those important communication components because listening and culture are linked. Morreale, Spitzberg, and Barge speak to the importance of that connection when they write, "Cultural differences in how people engage in listening are a reality, so you need to recognize and respect such culturally based differences in listening style."[158] To help you better understand the role of culture in listening, let us look at a few ways the two work together.

**Direct and Indirect Listening.** Cultural differences in listening behavior have been classified as "direct" and "indirect."[159] While these two orientations represent two extreme approaches, they are nevertheless useful ways of looking at listening. Direct listening cultures such as France, Germany, and the United States listen primarily for facts and concrete information. In these cultures, listeners also confront speakers directly and feel comfortable asking questions. Indirect listening cultures such as Finland, Japan, and Sweden have a very different listening style. Interruptions do not occur while the speaker is talking and the politeness is part of the listener's behavior.

**The Value Placed on Listening.** As we have noted elsewhere, in many cultures in the Far East, the amount of time spent talking and the value placed on talking are very different from what happens in cultures that value conversation (Middle East, Latin America, and United States). Japan is a relatively homogeneous culture, and therefore most people have a pool of common experiences. This commonality helps them discern what the other is thinking and feeling without using words. Hence, silence is often valued over talk. Think about the connection between speaking, listening, and silence in the Buddhist expression "There is a truth that words cannot reach."

Place that against the Arab proverb that notes, "Your mouth is your sword." Two orientations—one favoring silence and one preferring talk.

**Nonverbal Communication and Listening.** Even the nonverbal responses to what you hear are often influenced by culture. In the United States it is often a sign of paying attention when you make the sound "mm-hmm" or "uh-huh" when someone is talking. Among the African-American co-culture the paralanguage responses on the part of the listener are even more pronounced with what is termed "call and response." When this technique is employed there is an active exchange between speaker and listener that is not found in most cultures.[160]

Eye contact is another nonverbal action that influences the listening process. In the United States and other Western cultures, a good listener is seen as paying attention if he or she makes direct eye contact with the person talking. But you will recall that direct eye-to-eye contact is not the correct custom in many Asian cultures or in the American Indian co-culture. In short, to be a good listener you need to know what nonverbal actions are appropriate and which might hamper the communication encounter.

**Encourage Feedback.** The interactive nature of communication brings us to our next suggestion: *encourage feedback*. Feedback is the information generated by the person who receives the message—information that is "fed back" to the person who sent the original message. This information may be a smile, the words "No, thank you," or even complete silence, void of any outward expression. As Wood points out, "Feedback may be verbal, nonverbal, or both and it may be intentional or unintentional."[161] Regardless of the form of the feedback, it allows you the opportunity to make qualitative judgments about the communication event while it is taking place. These judgments offer useful data that enables you to correct and adjust your next message. A competent communicator uses feedback both to monitor the communication process and to exercise some control over it. Feedback clearly manifests the three axioms we discussed at the beginning of this chapter—*you can learn, you can make choices*, and *you can act differently*.

Granting that feedback is critical, you must learn to create an atmosphere that encourages other people to provide you feedback. Therefore, we will review a number of communication skills that encourage other people to send you messages about the current situation—messages that might be useful as you continue the communication event.

*Nonverbal Feedback.* The first step in improving nonverbal feedback is recognizing that it takes many forms and its meanings are culture bound. This is perhaps best illustrated by relating a personal experience of one of your authors. After missing an exam, one of his Japanese students came to office hours. During the visit, the student continually giggled, averted her eyes, and held her hand over her mouth. From a Western perspective, the student's nonverbal behavior suggested she was not serious (laughing), deceptive (averting eyes), and very nervous (hand over mouth), further contributing to the impression of deceptiveness. The student offered no reason for missing the exam and did not ask for a retake. She simply apologized for not being there. A third party, however, had already told your author that the student's absence was due to the death of her grandfather. This demonstrates the importance of not assuming that nonverbal feedback in one culture carries the same meaning in another culture.

*Verbal Feedback.* Positive verbal behavior can also encourage feedback. In cultures that value conversation and openness, asking questions is an excellent method of encouraging feedback about the quality of your messages. You can ask questions such as "Perhaps we should start the meeting by introducing ourselves. Is that agreeable?" Or "How do you think we should start the meeting?" Further, questions can be used to seek additional clarification. If asked in a non-threatening manner, even the question "Am I clear?" assists in monitoring the level of comprehension. We should remind you before we leave this point that in some Asian cultures, the word *no* is often avoided. In Japan, for example, instead of responding negatively to your question, "they may simply apologize, keep quiet, become vague, or answer with a euphemism for no."[162] Your use of words also encourages feedback if you relate them directly to what the other person has just said. You know from your own experience that it is very disconcerting if you tell a friend that you do not feel well, and your friend responds that she or he just received an "A" on an examination.

*Silence as Feedback.* There are times when silence instead of words will inspire feedback. You have repeatedly seen that every culture has a unique communication style. Some cultural styles call for periods of silence and/or long pauses, and you must learn to respect these phases in the encounter. Giving the person this quiet period creates an atmosphere that promotes feedback once the silence is broken. As we noted elsewhere in the book, many Asian cultures do not enjoy being hurried when they are negotiating and/or solving problems. If you learn to remain silent, you will be sending them some positive feedback about the transaction. As we noted, in some cultures there is no positive compensation for a quick decision, particularly if you made that decision without sufficient feedback. Remember the French proverb "Patience is bitter but its fruit is sweet."

*Offer Non-Evaluative Feedback.* Although the idea of being non-judgmental might be an idea embedded in all our other suggestions, it is important to justify an independent category. The major advantage of non-evaluative feedback is that it sets a positive tone. As Gamble and Gamble point out, "When we provide non-evaluative feedback, we refrain from revealing our own personal opinions or judgments."[163] When you engage in non-evaluative feedback, you enable your communication partner to take part in the conversation without feeling that you are saying (verbally or nonverbally), "I don't think much of your ideas and beliefs."

Built into our last suggestion is the recommendation that you should try to *avoid negative feedback.* We will now list a few of the kinds of feedback that carry negative connotations. We should mention that while some of them might have a Western point of reference, your experiences should tell you they are common enough that they can have a negative outcome regardless of the culture. Hence we suggest you avoid (1) frequent shifting of your body as if you are bored with what the other person is saying, (2) a slouching posture, (3) engaging in other activities (talking to someone else, writing) while the other person is talking, (4) having your arms folded in front of your chest, and (5) frowning and scowling.

## DEVELOP COMMUNICATION FLEXIBILITY

Many experts in communication competence actually believe that one definition of competence is having the ability to adjust and fashion your communication behavior to fit the setting, the other person, and yourself.[164] A clear rationale for being amenable in the intercultural context, Gudykunst and Kim offer the following advice:

> To gather information about and adapt our behavior to strangers, we must be flexible in our behavior. We must be able to select strategies that are appropriate to gather the information we need about strangers in order to communicate effectively with them. This requires that we have different behavioral options for gathering information open to us.[165]

What is being said is that a competent intercultural communicator "must . . . develop a repertoire of interpersonal tactics."[166]

When speaking to the issue of how communication flexibility applies to international negotiations, Foster used an analogy:

> The better [international] negotiators are ultimately pragmatic. They are not oaks; rather, they are more like willows. Unable to predict every situation, every twist and turn, even in a domestic situation, they know that it is nearly impossible to do so in a cross-cultural one.[167]

An obvious component of being flexible is *developing a tolerance for ambiguity*. If your culture values competition and aggressive action, and you are around someone from a culture that values cooperation and interpersonal harmony, you might find his or her behavior ambiguous and confusing; yet coping with ambiguity is a key element in intercultural competence. As Ruben and Kealey note, "The ability to react to new and ambiguous situations with minimal discomfort has long been thought to be an important asset when adjusting to a new culture."[168]

There are some selective behaviors that the competent intercultural communicator can employ to increase tolerance for ambiguity. For example, Guirdham suggests some specific actions that might be helpful. First, "delaying the decision on how to approach a new person or situation until as much information as possible has been gained by observation."[169] Second, "using trial and error rather than the same formula until what works becomes clear."[170] Finally, perhaps the best advice on how to develop a tolerance for ambiguity is to be nonjudgmental, practice patience, and expect the unexpected, be adaptive. Remember the advice contained in the Spanish proverb—"I dance to the tune that is played."

## UNDERSTAND INTERCULTURAL CONFLICT

It is not an exaggeration to say that as long as people have been coming into contact with one another there has been conflict. Whether the conflict is over personality traits, a misunderstanding of the words being used, or a disagreement over goals, conflict seems to be a fact of life. Formally, when scholars speak of conflict in the communication context they are talking about a struggle between you and at least one or more individuals whom you perceive are frustrating and interfering with the achievement of your goals.[171] As it applies to an intercultural setting, Ting-Toomey defines conflict "as the perceived and/or actual incompatibility of values, expectations, processes, or outcomes between two or more parties from different cultures over substantive and/or relational issues."[172] The danger of conflict is that it can draw attention away from important activities, undermine morale support, polarize people and positions, magnify differences, and potentially lead to name-calling and even physical conflict. To help you improve your awareness of different ways that people manage conflict, we will

(1) *discuss some Western approaches for dealing with conflict*, (2) *look at how other cultures cope with conflict*, and (3) *offer some specific conflict skills that apply directly to intercultural communication.*

**Conflict: An American Perspective.** A substantial body of literature indicates that Americans usually employ five approaches to dealing with conflict.[173] Knowing these approaches will help you appreciate how you might deal with conflict. Later we will offer a cross-cultural comparison of these approaches so that you might be able to adapt to intercultural discord when it arises.

*Avoidance.* Also referred to as *denial or withdrawal*, avoidance is a strategy based on the assumption that a conflict will disappear if it is just ignored.[174] In some ways this is the easiest way to cope with conflict. Avoiding conflict can be either mental (being silent or not taking part in the interaction) or physical (removing yourself from the conflict). In either case the person is saying, "I do not want to get involved." Often when avoidance is the method used, the situation that created the conflict seems to intensify and worsen as the parties mull over what happened.

While avoidance is occasionally used by Americans, it is not a popular approach to conflict. Most Americans do not like unresolved problems and also have a need to "have their say." Therefore, for Americans, and other individualistic cultures, withdrawal "is rarely a satisfactory, long-term solution."[175]

*Accommodating.* Accommodating is a form of dealing with conflict that is closely related to avoidance, except this time you satisfy the other person's desires to the point that you are willing to give up your own needs and goals. These actions, according to Gamble and Gamble, "can precipitate an uneasy, tense relational state characterized by a weak, self-sacrificing approach and even nervous laughter."[176] As you would suspect, an attitude that tries to signal "I do not care what you do" has some other built-in weaknesses. First, it often leads to poor conclusions because only one point of view is being discussed. Second, accommodating can also create a situation where one person can take advantage of another.

*Competing.* The competing approach to conflict simply means winning at all costs. Forcing your wishes on another person as a means of resolving conflict can take a variety of forms. It can involve verbal aggression, intimidation, or manipulation. As you learned in Chapter 5 when we talked about values, competing is a fundamental American value. Hence, it is not surprising that competition is a characteristic of American conflict management.

*Compromise.* As Morreale, Spitzberg, and Barge note, "Compromise is about finding the middle course with each party agreeing to make concessions to the others."[177] In this approach people usually have to give something up or make a "trade" in order to resolve the conflict. The strategy is based on the simple belief that it is better to get something instead of nothing.

*Collaborating.* At the core of collaboration is the idea that all parties resolve conflict. DeFleur and her colleagues describe collaboration as an attempt to maintain a productive relationship that will resolve the disagreements while working collaboratively toward a common goal.[178] By employing creative devices, everyone's goals and needs can be satisfied. Because the conflict is viewed in a positive manner, collaboration is the most sought-after method of settling conflicts. It is also a popular method in North America in that you get to keep your goals in place while still cooperating with each other.

**Conflict: An Intercultural Perspective.** Although interpersonal conflict is a part of every social group, each culture's way of perceiving and dealing with conflict is part of their value system. For example, in the United States there is often a belief that conflict is part of competition and "self-awareness" and therefore can be useful. Roloff supports this view and claims that conflict in and of itself is not pejorative and, if handled properly, may actually lead to human growth and development.[179]

This positive view of conflict is also seen in other cultures. In the Middle East people perceive conflict as a natural way of life. People are expected to have intense feelings on many issues and to express those feelings in an animated and confrontational manner. Think for a moment of what is being said in the humorous Jewish proverb that venerates disputes and conflict by noting, "Where there are two Jews there are three opinions." Greeks also have an expressive approach to conflict and are proud of their long tradition of argumentation and debate. As Broome points out, for Greeks "challenges, insults and attacks are, within appropriate limits, almost synonymous with conversing."[180] Let us offer a few examples that underscore the point that culture and conflict are linked.

We begin with the Japanese and their perception of conflict. For the Japanese, conflict is seen as interpersonally embarrassing and distressing since it potentially disrupts social harmony.[181] For them, an indirect and passive approach to conflict would be the preferred method for dealing with social discord.[182] A similar view toward conflict can be found in the Chinese culture where social harmony is important.[183] This view, which is directly linked to the Confucian philosophy we discussed in Chapter 3, has the Chinese feeling more comfortable with avoidance and compromising when faced with a conflict situation. According to Ting-Toomey and Chung, this view of conflict even carries over to Asian Americans. They point out that "Asian Americans who adhere to traditional Asian values tend to use avoiding and obliging conflict style to deal with a conflict at hand. They sometimes also use 'silence' as a powerful, high-context conflict style."[184]

Latin cultures also perceive and deal with conflict in a manner that reflects many of their cultural values. Because Brazilian culture values friendships and positive interactions, conflict is seen as something to avoid. In the business context, for example, protocol requires that people feel comfortable with each other.[185] Interpersonal conflicts would disturb that comfort. Mexicans represent another group that does not enjoy direct confrontation.[186] For them, "an avoidance conflict style is sometimes preferred over a head-on confrontation style in dealing with minor or midrange conflict issues."[187]

Some European cultures also deal with conflict in ways that are dissimilar to the conflict style found in the United States. While interpersonal harmony is not the driving force, Germans do not engage in direct face-to-face conflict. Nees summarizes the German approach in the following manner: "Conflict is generally avoided, not by emphasizing harmony in personal relationships or by smoothing over differences of opinion, but rather by maintaining formality and social distance."[188] And for the French to lose control and outwardly engage in social conflict is "a sign of weakness."[189] Regardless of the motivation used to justify or avoid conflict, one thing should be clear by now—not all cultures display or deal with conflict in the same manner.

The conflict style favored by African Americans is quite different from that employed by the dominant culture. A forceful, dynamic, and emotionally expressive method of dealing with conflict is an accepted communication technique.[190] European-American women also respond to conflict differently than their male counterparts. Summarizing the research on conflict and gender, Wood indicates that most females would rather "defer and compromise to reduce tension."[191]

**Managing Intercultural Conflict.** As we have just noted, perceiving and dealing with conflict is rooted in your culture. However, some skills for responding to conflict can be employed regardless of the culture you are interacting with. Let us now examine some of these skills.

*Keep an Open Mind.* When we speak of trying to keep an open mind, we are not talking about blind allegiance to the other person's arguments. Rather, we are pointing out the advantages of learning new ideas. This notion of openness is expressed by Roy and Oludaja when they advise, "Approach the conflict with openness. Recognize that there is much to learn about the other participants as persons and the worldviews that shaped their positions."[192]

*Seek to Compromise.* In America there is often a notion that compromise is associated with defeat—avoid this idea when dealing with other cultures. Winning at all costs and placing that conflict in an either/or frame usually does not resolve the core of the conflict and with time the conflict resurfaces. In short, you need to suspend the belief that compromise is a form of appeasement. A healthier view is the one expressed by the British statesman Edmund Burke: "Every human benefit and enjoyment, every virtue and every prudent act, is founded on compromise and barter."

*Do Not Rush.* Do not rush to resolve the conflict when interacting with collective cultures. As Ting-Toomey notes, "Be sensitive to the importance of quiet, mindful observation."[193] Even more specifically, she offers the following non-Western advice for responding to conflict: "Use deep-level silence, deliberate pauses, and patient conversational turn taking in the conflict interaction process with collectivists."[194]

*Identify Key Issues.* Although taking time is important, it is just as crucial to realize that conflict cannot be managed unless you clearly identify the issues. Whether the conflict is over personalities or content, you must discover what the core of the disagreement is. Once you have clarified the issues, all parties can begin to focus on solutions to the controversy.

*Adjust to Cultural Differences.* If you are from a culture that values individualism, such as the United States, you must begin, according to Ting-Toomey, to "discard the Western-based model of effective communication skills in dealing with conflict situations in the collective cultures."[195] Ting-Toomey illustrates her point by offering some very specific skills that you can follow:

Individualists should learn to use qualifiers, disclaimers, tag questions, [and] tentative statements to convey their point of view. In refusing a request, learn to avoid using a blunt "no" as a response because the word "no" is typically perceived as carrying high face-threat value in collective cultures. Use situational or self-effacing accounts ("Perhaps someone else is more qualified than I am in working on this project"), counter questions ("Don't you feel someone else is more competent to work on this project . . ."), or conditional statements ("Yes, but . . .") to convey the implicit sense of the refusal.[196]

Learning to use collective pronouns can also help defuse conflict. Although at times you may have to refer to people by name, you should, when with a group of people, try to develop the practice of using group pronouns as a way of centering on content instead of people. Notice how words such as *we* and *our* focus the conversation on everyone instead of simply one person as is the case with *I, me,* or *you.*

Another adjustment strategy might be to simply ignore the conflict. Remember from Chapter 3, the Buddha taught that all things in life are transitory and will eventually fall away. There is even a Buddhist expression that relates directly to conflict. It is simply the phrase "Let it go." Ting-Toomey makes the same point in contemporary terms when she writes, "A cooling period sometimes may help mend a broken relationship and the substantive issue may be diluted over a period of time."[197]

## LEARN ABOUT CULTURAL ADAPTATION

Today the movement and relocation of refugees and immigrants is a fact of life. This impact and the importance of having to adapt to a new culture is clearly articulated by Kim:

> Each year, millions of immigrants and refugees change homes. Driven by natural disasters or economic need, or hoping for freedom, security, or economic betterment, people uproot themselves from their homes and embark on a new life in an alien and sometimes hostile milieu.[198]

In many ways the issue of cultural adaptation is related to our early discussion of communication flexibility. Except now we are talking about people who must adapt to all aspects of a new culture—and for a long period of time, perhaps permanently. Before we begin a more detailed analysis of the adaptation process, we should point out that the word *adaptation* is but one of a number of words the field of intercultural communication has used to represent this concept. Kim further develops this idea when she writes, "Cross-cultural adaptation embraces other similar but narrow terms, from assimilation . . . and acculturation . . . to coping and adjustment . . . as well as integration."[199] Because adaptation does embrace all the other concepts, and because in the final analysis the people involved have to learn to adapt, we will use the term *adaptation* in our discussion.

We start with these two questions: What problems hamper the adaptation process? What is the best way to adapt to a new culture if your exposure to that culture will be for an extended period? The answers to these questions are at the heart of the adaptation process. In this section we discuss cultural contacts that are not transitory but rather are sustained and ongoing. That is to say, we are now talking about people who need to cope with the cultural changes brought about by continuous firsthand contact with another culture. The problem is that on many occasions, these newcomers have a difficult time adapting to the host culture. As Mak, Westwood, Ishiyama, and Barker point out, "Newcomers may not be ready to learn and practice social behaviors appropriate to the new culture in the initial period of settlement. It is not unusual for recent arrivals to be overwhelmed by the immediate demands and challenges in the orienting to living in a new place."[200] To better deal with this problem, let us examine some challenges that face anyone who is attempting to adapt to a new culture and then conclude by offering a number of behaviors that can make the adaptation process a successful and rewarding experience.

**Challenges of Adaptation.** The problems facing anyone trying to adapt to a new and often quite different culture are numerous. During the adjustment period the new arrival might experience fear, feelings of being isolated, disliked, and even distrusted.[201] A review of some of the reasons behind these feelings is an excellent first step in developing the skills needed to adapt to a new culture.

*Language.* It is obvious that someone living in a new culture will usually face problems associated with having to learn and use a second language. Long-term sojourners and immigrants to the United States who have not mastered English experience social isolation and are, as Leong and Chou note, forced "into fields that require less mastery of English language and less interpersonal interaction."[202]

When we talk of problems associated with being exposed to a new language, we are talking about two ideas—language acquisition and the ways of speaking unique to the new culture. Both of these can delay the adaptation process. Harper summarizes this view when she notes, "Lack of language skills is a strong barrier to effective cultural adjustment and communication whereas lack of knowledge concerning the ways of speaking of a particular group will reduce the level of understanding that we can achieve with our counterparts."[203] The person trying to adapt to and interact with a new culture must face challenges associated not only with learning a second language but also the special and unique patterns found within every language. As we mentioned in Chapter 6, cultural variations in the use of language can mean everything from the use of idioms to different rules for turn taking, to linguistic ways of showing respect.

*Disequilibrium.* Successful adaptation demands a certain level of knowledge about the host country and making correct choices regarding that knowledge. Those choices can include everything from learning proper greeting behaviors (bowing, shaking hands, hugging, etc.) to deciding about eating utensils (chopsticks, knives and forks, fingers, etc.). As you would suspect, indecision creates problems. According to Kim, sojourners are "at least temporarily, in a state of disequilibrium, which is manifested in many emotional 'lows' of uncertainty, confusion, and anxiety."[204] The condition of disequilibrium complicates the adaptation process as the sojourner experiences a high level of apprehension as he or she attempts to decide what constitutes appropriate behavior.

*Ethnocentrism.* What is interesting about the role of ethnocentrism in adapting to a new culture is that it moves in both directions. As we pointed out earlier in this chapter, ethnocentrism is that cultural bias that leads people to judge another culture by the standards and practices that they are most familiar with and the one where their loyalty resides—their own. This means that members of the host culture pass judgment on outsiders while the person trying to adapt cannot, or will not, expunge their home culture. Hence, they bring some ethnocentrism to the host culture. Anderson makes this point very clear when he notes, "one of the chief characteristics of the adaptation process is that elements of the original culture can never be completely erased."[205] The key to effective adaptation is for both parties to recognize the strong pull of ethnocentrism and attempt to keep it in check.

**Improving the Adaptation Process.** Now let us turn our attention to a few strategies that will expedite and facilitate the adaptation process.

*Acquire Knowledge About the Host Culture.* Adaptation is less troublesome if you are aware of the characteristics of the culture with which you will be interacting. For someone coming to the United States, this means much more than learning how to order a Big Mac or rent an apartment. These assignments are easy compared to having to learn about the values, beliefs, and modes of behavior unique to each culture. Chen and Starosta note: "Culture awareness refers to an understanding of one's own and others' cultures that affect how people think and behave. This includes understanding commonalities of human behavior and differences in cultural patterns."[206]

As you have learned throughout this book, gathering a fund of knowledge about another culture takes a variety of forms, ranging from the apparent to the subtle. For example, as we just indicated, it is rather clear that learning the language of the host culture produces positive results. If you cannot learn the language of the host culture, you can at least try to master some of the basics of language such as greeting behaviors, proper polite responses, and words that deal with public transportation and shopping.

*Increase Contact with the Host Culture.* Direct contact with the host culture promotes and facilitates successful adaptation to a new culture. Begley accentuates the importance of direct contact when she notes, "Although insight and knowledge can be gained through prior intercultural study, additional practical wisdom is attained through everyday conversations with people from other cultures."[207] You should listen to Harris and Moran when they advise, "Immerse yourself in the host culture. Join in, whenever feasible, the artistic and community functions, the carnivals, the rites, the international and fraternal or professional organizations."[208] Although there are no substitutes for face-to-face interactions with host nationals, mediated communication such as radio, film, television, and the Internet can still moderately influence cross-cultural adaptation. Kim has pointed out that a host culture's mass communication "serves as an important source of cultural language learning, particularly during the early phases of the adaptation."[209] In addition to assisting in language learning, exposure to a culture's mass media can also aid in discovering some cultural values—at least as they are portrayed on television. When listening, watching, and interacting with people from the host culture, it is important to learn about what Althen calls "ritual social actions.[210] Althen offers a list of some of the "rituals" that contribute to understanding interaction in the host culture:

> Notice what people say (and how they say it) and what they do (and how they do it) when they greet an acquaintance, take leave of an acquaintance, are introduced to a new person, and take leave of a person they have just met. Watch for variations according to the age, sex, and apparent social status of the people involved.[211]

We end this section on improvement by reminding you that successful intercultural communication should always begin with your trying to understand the characteristics of the culture you will be interacting with. Once you acquire this understanding, you can then decide what constitutes appropriate and inappropriate behavior. Confucius said it far more eloquently: "The essence of knowledge is, having it, to apply it." We suggest you do both: have accurate knowledge and apply it.

*At the core of a meaningful intercultural ethic is the belief that all cultures share many of the same beliefs and values about children and families.*

© Robert Fonseca

# Ethical Considerations

Reflect for a moment on the following assertions: War is a viable option in some circumstances. War is always wrong. Abortion is right. Abortion is wrong. The killing of animals for food and clothing is okay. Animals should not be killed for food or clothing. Cheating on your income tax is acceptable because the government wastes so much of your money. Cheating on your income tax is dishonest. Sending jobs overseas (outsourcing) is good for the economy. Sending jobs overseas takes jobs away from Americans and exploits poor countries. All of the propositions we just advanced involve your having to make a decision that might contain some ethical implications. They focus on questions related to right, wrong, proper, and improper. These and countless other ethical decisions that you make are not based on chance or some impulse response, but rather on reasons that you believe to be sound. Therefore, ethics can be seen as a reflection of your convictions. Convictions are not only rooted in your culture, but are also guidelines that influence the manner in which you communicate with other people.

In short, ethics tells you what you ought do and how you ought to act, all of which have an impact on both you and the people you interact with. Remember, one of the premises of this book has been that communication is an instrumental act; whether it is used to sell cars, secure a mate, get elected to public office, teach children a foreign language, or secure directions, it will always have an impact, good or bad, desirable or undesirable, significant or insignificant. Put in slightly different terms, *communication creates effects—something happens when you send someone a message.* While what happens might be short term or long term, immediate or delayed, profound or subtle, public or private, you are producing change in another individual. This very fact speaks of the ethical component associated with communication. All cultures recognize the ethical dimensions of communication on a legal, religious, and interpersonal level. You will recall that in Chapter 3, when we discussed religion, we pointed out that one of the main functions of religion was to give its constituents ethical guidelines on how they ought to live their lives. In the United States, ethical principles are not only found in our religious institutions, but are also manifested in our libel, slander, truth-in-advertising, affirmative action, and campaign-practice laws.

Although most of your communication does not involve mass media or attorneys, this does not relieve you of considering the effects of your interpersonal actions. Whether the consequences of our messages are simple or profound, you cannot hide from the fact that your actions affect other people. As Shakespeare said in *The Comedy of Errors,* "Every why hath a wherefore." We now ask you to think about "why" and "wherefore"—to think about your actions and the results they produce. In the next section, we suggest an interpersonal ethic that will have beneficial consequences for you, for your interpersonal partners, and, because of the symbiotic relationship now existing in the world, for all humanity.

## A DEFINITION OF ETHICS

Ethics refers to judgments that focus "on degrees of rightness and wrongness, virtue and vice, and obligation in human behavior."[212] What ethics attempts to do is "provide the tools for making difficult moral choices, in both our personal and our professional lives."[213] These choices are made difficult when ethical practices collide—as they often do. Day identifies this problem when he writes: "The most difficult ethical dilemmas arrive when conflicts arise between two 'right' moral obligations. Thus, ethics often involves the balancing of competing rights when there is no 'correct' answer."[214] The relationship between making ethical choices and communication is clearly underscored by Angrosino when he points out that ethics come into play "when we act on our thoughts and our actions impinge on others."[215]

Religious thinkers, philosophers, and ordinary people have been struggling with the issues surrounding the consequences of our acts for thousands of years. From the Ten Commandments to the Buddha's Eightfold Path, to the writings in the Koran, to Epicurus's justification of egotistical behavior, to Martin Buber's "ethics with a heart," to Confucius's *Analects,* people have been trying to decide what their ethical obligations are to others and how they should treat them. Answers range from simplistic and selfish observations ("It's a dog-eat-dog world") to philosophical mandates that focus on our moral obligation to other people. This view is eloquently articulated by the great humanitarian Albert Schweitzer: "Just as the wave cannot exist for itself, but is ever a part of the heaving surface of the ocean, so must I never live my life for itself, but always in the experience which is going on around me."

You can see by the last paragraph that ethics is an elusive topic. As Griffin reminds us, "Ethics has to do with the gray areas of our lives. When moral decisions are black and white, knowing what we should do is easy."[216] But what about those countless occasions when the decision is not easy? Where do you turn when you need ethical guidance? To God, to family, to friends, to philosophers, to yourselves? What you find in many instances when seeking ethical advice is a multitude of approaches representing a variety of orientations. Let's briefly pause and look at two of these approaches—*relativism* and *universalism*—and discuss their application to intercultural communication.

## RELATIVISM

*Cultural relativism* grows out of the philosophical view that deciding what is right or wrong and good or bad behavior is not an absolute, but instead variable and relative. According to this ethical philosophy, there is no one correct moral code for all times and people, each group has its own morality relative to its wants and values, and all moral ideas are necessarily relative to a particular group of people. Wilson underscored this issue of multiple perspectives:

> Anthropologists believe that morality has no meaning outside the culture that defines it, philosophers argue that morality depends on a person's motives or the results he achieves, and ordinary people claim that personal freedom is supreme and that its exercise should be uninhibited unless it harms others.[217]

As you can see, by adding the issue of culture to the topic of ethics, we append yet another dimension to this already troublesome subject. Howell clearly summarizes some of the problems associated with a relativism (culture-specific) orientation to ethics when he writes:

> The fundamental connection between culture and ethics is this: Ethical standards are products of particular cultures. So it is not surprising that basic appropriate and inappropriate behavior important to a group varies from place to place. Consequently, we should not be surprised that one way of behaving has a high moral value—rightness—in one culture, has no ethical significance in a second culture, and in a third culture may be negatively moral, that is, considered by the majority of the population to be ethically wrong.[218]

People who find cultural relativism an appealing ethical standard appreciate the idea that under relativism no culture is superior to another and hence allows for a wide variety of cultures and practices to coexist. The argument also maintains that this acceptance of the behavior of others creates tolerance and understanding. Remember, under ethical relativism you try to refrain from making moral verdicts about other cultures, and therefore you must refrain from passing judgment.

We will now turn to the arguments advanced against ethical relativism by examining an opposite worldview.

## UNIVERSALISM

*Cultural universalism* takes the stance that regardless of the context or the culture, there are fixed and universal ethical precepts that apply to all cultures. While acknowledging differences in practices and beliefs, universalism still maintains that there is a set of values, standards, morals, and the like that weave their way in and out of every culture. Specifically it is an assertion that ethical principles hold for everybody and not simply for some. The underpinnings of the generalist approach to ethics can be found in the writings of the German philosopher Immanuel Kant. It was Kant's conviction that for action to be ethically correct, one must be able to will one's words or actions to be a universal law, that is, be willing to have everyone act in the same way.[219] This approach toward ethics is perhaps best summarized by Kant's single sentence: "Act only on that maxim whereby you can at the same time will that it should become a universal law." The problems related to the universalism approach seem rather obvious, and like relativism, underscore the difficulty of deciding on a standard of intercultural ethics that is applicable to all cultures in all situations. Think for a moment how problematic it would be even to somehow suggest that there is only one correct way for people to act. It should be clear by now that the study of ethics is complex and complicated. We cannot, however, let the difficulty of the issues keep us from searching for possible answers.

The remainder of the chapter will consider some ethical guidelines that you should bear in mind when interacting with people from different cultures. We will maintain that although there are cultural differences regarding specific ethical behaviors that cannot be condoned (honor killings, infanticide, *sati*, cannibalism, slavery, abuse of women, and the like), there are nevertheless universal codes of conduct that we believe apply to all people and all cultures. In short, it is our contention that you can develop a universal ethic that also grants the relativistic nature of cultures. Let us now look at those common codes.

# Guidelines for an Intercultural Ethic

## BE MINDFUL THAT COMMUNICATION PRODUCES A RESPONSE

In Chapter 1 and at the start of this chapter, we stressed the notion that the messages you send produce a response. In the intercultural environment, because of the diversity of backgrounds, it is much more difficult to assess and predict the type of response your messages will elicit. For example, people in the United States have learned, as part of their cultural endowment, how to thank someone for a compliment or a gift. They can predict, with some degree of accuracy, what others expect from them and how they will respond to their signs of veneration and appreciation. Forecasting the responses of other cultures is a far more difficult task. Let us stay with our simple example of thanking someone. In Arab cultures, one is expected to be profuse in offering thanks, whereas in England, one is expected to offer restrained thanks because too much exuberance is considered offensive. Because of the potential power of messages, you must always be aware of *the effects of that message on other people*. This focus on your actions and the results of those actions is called, in the Buddhist tradition, *being mindful*. "Mindfulness is the aware, balanced acceptance of the present experience."[220] It is, of course, more complicated than that. It is opening to and receiving the present moment. When practicing mindfulness during communication, you are giving your full attention to what is transpiring right now. By being mindful, you can adjust your messages to both the context and the person. You can, in short, be aware of what you are doing to another person. Tead links the need for mindfulness with the power of communication when he writes:

> Without indulging in too great refinements, let us remind ourselves that communication also has at bottom a moral aspect. It does, when all is said, anticipate a change in the

conduct of the recipient. If the change has any large significance it means an interposing or interference with the autonomy of the other person or persons. And the tampering with personal drives and desires is a moral act even if its upshot is not a far-reaching one, or is a beneficial result. To seek to persuade behavior into a new direction may be wholly justifiable and the result in terms of behavior consequences may be salutary. But the judgment of benefit or detriment is not for the communicator safely to reach by himself. He is assuming a moral responsibility. And he had better be aware of the area with which he concerns himself and the responsibility he assumes. He should be willing to assert as to any given policy, "I stand behind this as having good personal consequences for the individuals whom it will affect." That judgment speaks a moral concern and desired moral outcome.[221]

Mindfulness in intercultural communication takes on added importance due to cultural differences. The effort involved is illustrated by a Japanese woman who made a comment about talking in English to an American: "You have to have all your antennas out."

## RESPECT THE WORTH OF THE INDIVIDUAL

We begin this next ethical precept with this simple question: How do you feel when someone makes a fool of you, puts you down, or acts like you are insignificant? The answer is obvious. You do not like being diminished. Everyone wants some level of respect, dignity, and a feeling of worth. You certainly have no ethical responsibility to hold all people in high esteem, but you should respect all people equally. Burbulies calls the concept "the rule of reciprocity." This view asks you to develop a "reversible and reflexive attitude and reciprocal regard for others."[222] Burbulies is not alone in this conviction. Johannesen, in his book on ethics, uses words such as "devalues," "ridicule," and "excluding" when he speaks of ethical guidelines.[223] On a more universal scale we can turn to the United Nations Universal Declaration of Human Rights. There are a total of thirty articles, three of which directly relate to intercultural communication.

- **ARTICLE 1.** All human beings are born free and equal in dignity and rights. They are endowed with reason and conscience and should act toward one another in a spirit of brotherhood.
- **ARTICLE 18.** Everyone has a right to freedom of thought, conscience and religion.
- **ARTICLE 19.** Everyone has the right to freedom of opinion and expression.

What these proclamations are saying is that the ethical person respects people both physically and emotionally. Confucius said much the same thing when he told us, "Without feelings of respect, what is there to distinguish men from beasts?"

## SEEK COMMONALITIES AMONG PEOPLE AND CULTURES

We have spent considerable time in this book talking about differences that influence the intercultural setting. The way people move, pray, speak, raise their children, and countless other differences have been part of this book. Yet it is the similarities among people and cultures that can serve as an ethical guide. DeGenova has some words that we might be able to use as an illustration of this suggestion:

> No matter how many differences there may be, beneath the surface there are even more similarities. It is important to try to identify the similarities among various cultures.

Stripping away surface differences will uncover a multiplicity of similarities: people's hopes, aspirations, desire to survive, search for love, and need for family—to name just a few.[224]

This credo of similarity is important to the study of ethics in that it helps you look for common ground as a way of deciding how to treat other people regardless of their culture. It might be intriguing to know that "an American child sticks out his tongue to show defiance, a Tibetan to show courtesy to a stranger, and a Chinese to express wonderment,"[225] but it is more important to know that they share a series of more crucial characteristics that link them together. The similarities that unite people, and in a very real sense make everyone part of a single "community," range from the obvious to the subtle. For example, it is apparent that all seven billion people inhabit the same planet for a rather short period. And that all people share the same emotion and desire to be free from external restraint: The craving for freedom is basic. And there is nothing religious or metaphysical in the fact that all people seek to avoid physiological and psychological pain while searching for some degree of tranquility in life. As a species, not only do you have similarities in feelings and experiences, but there are values that are common to all cultures.

The world's great religious traditions have also recognized values that bind people together. They offer the same instructions to their members with regard to killing, stealing, bearing false witness, adultery, and the like. Variations of the "Golden Rule" are found in all cultures. Although the words are different, the wisdom contained within the words is universal.[226]

- **Buddhism:** "Hurt not others in ways that you yourself would find hurtful." Udana-Virga, 5:8
- **Christianity:** "All things whatsoever ye would that men should do to you, do ye even so to them." Matthew, 7:12
- **Confucianism:** "Do not do unto others what you would not have them do unto you." Analect, 15:23
- **Hinduism:** "This is the sum of duty: do naught unto others which would cause you pain if done to you." Mahabharatj, 5:1517
- **Islam:** "No one of you is a believer until he desires for his brother that which he desires for himself." Sunnah
- **Jainism:** "In happiness and suffering, in joy and grief, we should regard all creatures as we regard our own self." Lord Mahavira, 24th Tirthankara
- **Judaism:** "What is hateful to you; do not to your fellow man. That is the law: all the rest is commentary." Talmud, Shabbat, 31 a
- **American Indian:** "Respect for all life is the foundation." The Great Law of Peace

If it were not for space constraints, we could have included an even longer list of those cultures that exhort their members to the "oneness of the human family." On an interpersonal level, Kale counsels us regarding the "Rule" in the following fashion: "Ethical communicators address people of other cultures with the same respect that they would like to receive themselves."[227]

We believe that from this brief sample you should recognize that in all of the important human characteristics we are all very much alike. What is important is that in a multicultural world you begin to see their commonalities. Huntington expressed the same idea when he wrote, "People in all civilizations should search for and attempt to expand the values, institutions, and practices they have in common with people of other civilizations."[228]

## RECOGNIZE THE VALIDITY OF DIFFERENCES

Having just finished imploring you to see the similarities existing between people and culture, we now "turn the coin over." In this ethical canon, we ask you to think about the words of former Israeli Prime Minister Shimon Peres when he tells us, "All people have the right to be equal and the equal right to be different." In short, in this guideline we recommend that you become aware of and tolerant of cultural differences as a way of establishing an intercultural ethic. Put in slightly different terms, keep in mind one of our themes from Chapter 1—people are both alike and different. Barnlund wrote of this double-sided nature:

> Outwardly there is little to distinguish what one sees on the streets of Osaka and Chicago—hurrying people, trolleys and buses, huge department stores, blatant billboards, skyscraper hotels, public monuments—beneath the surface there remains great distinctiveness. There is a different organization of industry, a different approach to education, a different role for labor unions, and a contrasting pattern of family life, unique law enforcement and penal practices, contrasting forms of political activity, different sex and age roles. Indeed, most of what is thought of as culture shows as many differences as similarities.[229]

Thus, a complete and honest intercultural ethic grants similarities and recognizes differences. By accepting and appreciating both, you can better assess the potential consequences of your acts and be more tolerant of those of others. Thomas Jefferson said much the same thing about accepting differences when he wrote, "It does me no injury for my neighbor to say there are twenty gods, or no God."

## TAKE RESPONSIBILITY FOR YOUR ACTIONS

Earlier in the chapter we made reference to an axiom regarding free choice. We also mentioned that you should be aware (mindful) of what those choices do to other people. Our next ethical consideration places those two ideas into an intercultural context. We advocate a three-point declaration that grants *individual uniqueness, the ability to exercise free choice*, and *the interdependent nature of the world*. All your decisions, actions, and even your failures to act have consequences for yourself and countless other people. The obvious ethical consequence of this fact leads us to what the Dalai Lama called "our universal responsibility." Gomez-Ibanez spoke to that responsibility when he wrote: "If I am linked in some way to all this is, however tenuous the links may seem, then I am in some respect responsible for the welfare of all this is, also, I am responsible for the common good. That realization, it seemed to me, might be the foundation for all ethics."[230]

The central message is that if you are going to live in this crowded, interconnected world, and if this planet and you, its "temporary residents," are to survive, you must accept your individual roles within that world. Remember, as we have shown throughout this book, people and cultures are inextricably linked. As the English anthropologist Gregory Bateson noted, "What pattern connects the crab to the lobster and the orchid to the primrose and all four of them to me? And me to you?"

## BE MOTIVATED

We conclude this section on ethics with what is perhaps the most important of all our suggestions, the simplest to state, and the most difficult to put into operation. The proposition: *try to be ethical*. While those four words were effortless to type and uncomplicated for you to read, putting them into operation is an arduous and demanding assignment. Not only are your ethical decisions influenced by self-interest and your pursuit of happiness, they are also driven by your biology and culture.

It is only logical and natural that you are most motivated to care about the people who are close to you both physically and emotionally. Your primary concern is for your family. As your personal circle widens, it includes relatives and friends. Interest in other people then moves to neighbors and other members of the community. As you get farther and farther away from people in your immediate circle, you will find it difficult to empathize with them. Think for a moment about your reaction to the news that a member of your family has been seriously injured in an automobile accident versus your response to reading that 178,000 people have died in the tsunami in Asia and approximately 130,000 are still missing and presumed to be dead. In most instances you would be more motivated to learn about your family member than about the people thousands of miles away in Asia. Although this is a normal reaction, it often keeps you from trying to understand the experiences of people far removed from our personal sphere. For intercultural communication to be successful, you must go beyond personal boundaries and try to learn about the experiences of people who are not part of your daily life. This is no easy assignment, for as a Russian proverb states, "When you live next to the cemetery you cannot weep for everyone." We are not asking you to weep, just to care and not be unresponsive. As anthropologist Jane Goodall reminds us, "The greatest danger to our future is apathy."

As we leave this discussion of ethics we would urge you not to retreat from the difficult questions that focus on ethical issues. Even if thoughts of ethical behavior are not part of your consciousness you are, in reality, involved with ethical decisions all day long—decisions that by design or chance have an ethical component. To discount this component is to be deprived of free choice and for all you do to be governed by impulse or ignorance. It also denies the interlocking relationship between people and culture that has been a major theme of this book. To paraphrase the English poet Tennyson, "I am part of all that I have met, and they are part of me."

## Summary

- The belief that improvement in intercultural communication is possible is based on three assumptions: (1) language is an open system, (2) we have free choice, and (3) communication has a consequence.
- The basic components of communication competence are motivation, knowledge, skills, and character.
- Potential problems in intercultural communication include seeking similarities, anxiety, and the desire to reduce uncertainty, stereotyping, prejudice, racism, misuse of power, ethnocentrism, and culture shock.
- To improve intercultural communication, know yourself, employ empathy, be aware of cultural differences in listening, encourage feedback, develop communication flexibility, learn to manage intercultural conflict, and learn about cultural adaptation.
- Because communication is an activity that has a consequence, you must develop a communication ethic.
- An intercultural ethic asks you to be mindful of the power of communication, respect the worth of all individuals, seek commonalities among people and cultures, recognize the validity of differences, take individual responsibility for your actions, and be motivated.

# Activities

1. In small groups, discuss the following topic: Why is it difficult to know yourself and your culture?
2. In small groups, discuss the following topic: Granting the notion of individual and cultural differences, can we ever truly empathize with another person?
3. Do you see a future where people from different cultures become closer or a future where they become increasingly isolated from each other?
4. In small groups, discuss the following question: What should an intercultural ethic be?
5. With some members of your class, try to list some examples of what you believe to be examples of American ethnocentrism.
6. What is the relationship between stereotypes, prejudice, racism, and ethnocentrism?
7. Can you think of some intercultural communication problems that were not discussed in this chapter?
8. Discuss the following statement: "Prejudice can never be eliminated because it is so deeply rooted in human nature."
9. Do you believe there is still discrimination in the United States? If so, against which groups and why? Give examples.

# Discussion Ideas

1. Locate someone from a culture different from your own, and interview him or her regarding the characteristics of a successful communicator. Include some of the following questions in your interview:
   a. What are the characteristics of a highly credible person?
   b. What communication skills are associated with a person who has low credibility?
   c. What communication skills are less desirable in your culture?
   d. What communication skills are most valued in your culture?
2. Define your communication style to the best of your ability by answering these questions:
   a. Do I give my full attention to people?
   b. Do I seem at ease or tense?
   c. Do I often change the subject without taking the other person into consideration?
   d. Do I deprecate the statements of others?
   e. Do I smile often?
   f. Do I interrupt repeatedly?
   g. Do I show sympathy when someone has a problem?
   h. Do my actions tend to lower the other person's self-esteem?
   You may find it helpful to record yourself in conversation with another person or, if you have the means, to videotape yourself.
3. Discuss the pros and cons of the following proposition: There should be a constitutional amendment that English be declared the official language of the United States.
4. Because individual and cultural differences exist, can we ever truly empathize with another person? How do cultural differences compound the problem?
5. Can you think of some ways to improve intercultural communication that were not discussed in this chapter?
6. Find a newspaper or magazine article or story that you believe demonstrates a clash in cultural definitions of ethics. What are those differences? How can they be resolved?

# Where Have We Been? Where Are We Going?

*Our differences define us, but our common humanity can redeem us.*

KAREN ARMSTRONG

*Change is the constant, the signal for rebirth, the egg of the phoenix.*

CHRISTINA BALDWIN

## Where Have We Been?

We introduced the topic of intercultural communication by pointing out its importance both internationally and nationally. We started with a statement that has been at the heart of this book—*cultural diversity is a fact of life*. If you look around your everyday environment, peruse the daily newspaper, glance at the news channels, surf the Web, you will see the truth of that statement: cultural diversity is a fact, and it creates numerous social problems. Centuries before the tragic events of September 11, 2001, conflicts between ideologies and neighbors were pervasive throughout the world. But when those three planes struck the twin towers of the World Trade Center and the Pentagon, people were jolted into a realization that cultural or religious discord often leads to clashes anytime and anywhere. In a very real sense the abstract notion of the world being interconnected, for good and for evil, became a realization. In addition, people became aware of the fact that violent clashes were only one of many problems created by collisions of the world's cultures. In a single sentence Fleishman highlights some additional concerns when he writes, "We are afloat among resource depletion, terrorism, war, religious psychosis, population expansion, totalitarianism, and nuclear arms."[1] Huntington also speaks of these potential problems when he notes, "The world is indeed anarchical, rife with tribal and nationality conflicts, but the conflicts that pose the greatest dangers for stability are those between states or groups from different civilizations."[2] The world is full of examples of this growing strife. The violent actions taken in Europe by immigrants from the Middle East and Africa provide a recent example of culturally based problems.

While the world outside our national borders was becoming more problematic, the United States was experiencing escalating cultural diversity at a pace nearly matching the large influx of immigrants in the 1920s. Now nearly one in ten "Americans" was born outside of the country.[3] In addition, the immigrant population is reproducing 6.5 times faster than the native-born population. This rapidly increasing diversity is forcing Americans to think about intercultural communication in new terms. As Booth points out, "Today, the United States is experiencing its second great wave of immigration, a movement of people that has profound implications for a society."[4] Booth's "implications" are manifested in everything from increases in interracial marriages[5] to fights with racial overtones on high school campuses,[6] to aggressive acts against Arab-Americans, to calls for better employment, education, and health care, to calls for closing America's borders.

Once we examined the challenges we have just summarized, we defined intercultural communication. We suggested that intercultural communication occurs whenever a message sender belongs to one culture and the message receiver is of another culture. We also spent time early in the book looking at the role of communication in the study of intercultural communication and noted that communication is dynamic, symbolic, systemic, contextual, and has a consequence. When speaking of culture we pointed out that culture was the sum total of learned behavior of a particular group. As such culture is shared, transmitted, based on symbols, dynamic, and integrated.

The most important messages of culture, as we discussed, are carried by the institutions of family, history and religion. It is through these social organizations that members of a culture learn about the values, attitudes, and behaviors that are central to the particular culture. Values toward gender, age, work, the future, formality, time, power, individualism, collectivism, and the like were stressed. We also learned how a person's identity is directly linked to their culture.

Because people share cultural experiences in a symbolic manner, we explored the two most common symbol systems—verbal and nonverbal. Representing ideas and feelings by symbols is a complex and complicated procedure at best. When the dimension of culture is added to the encoding and decoding process, however, the act of sharing internal states becomes even more intricate.

Since intercultural communication always takes place within a social context, we looked at three social settings (business, education, health care) where a person's culture might influence the outcome of the meeting. By considering the issue of cultural differences in these three situations, we were able to demonstrate that perceptions and patterns of communication are modified by culture.

Next, we examined ideas and techniques that contribute to successful intercultural communication. We proceeded on the assumption that it is an overt activity. Intercultural communication is, in short, something people do to and with each other. We suggested actions that facilitate that interaction and identified some that impede it.

Finally, we concluded by pointing out that the inevitability of intercultural exchanges in the twenty-first century requires a careful analysis of the ethical implications of these contacts. Succinctly, what sort of intercultural and interpersonal ethic must be developed if people are to competently function in a mutually productive manner in this diverse new world?

# Where Are We Going?

We now move to the future of intercultural communication—its trends and challenges. We begin by noting that any attempt to chart the course of future events is a very tricky and perplexing assignment. It is obvious that no one knows with any degree of certainty what tomorrow will be like—let alone the next five, twenty, or hundred years. As Shakespeare wrote in *Hamlet,* "We know what we are, but know not what we may be." The same, of course, can be said for intercultural communication. We do know what we have been, so we might be able to use the past and present as a predictor of the future of intercultural communication.

If you use the past as a guide, the most apparent notion of the future is that your intercultural relationships and interactions will grow in intensity and magnitude. While there are countless trends that will impact intercultural communication in the future, we contend that there are three that demand our immediate attention: (1) *international problems,* (2) *technology,* and (3) *ethnic and cultural identity.* Although these trends are interconnected, for the sake of discussion we shall treat them one at a time. At the conclusion of our discussion we will advance our personal recommendations for the future.

## INTERNATIONAL PROBLEMS

**Hostility.** Hostility, tension, conflict, and enmity are not new to humankind. As Schlesinger has pointed out: "The hostility of one tribe for another is among the most instinctive human reactions."[7] When people of different nationalities and ethnic origins, who frequently speak different languages and hold different convictions, attempt to work and live together, conflicts easily arise. "Unless a common purpose binds them together," Schlesinger maintains that these "tribal hostilities will drive them apart. Ethnic and racial conflict, it seems evident, will now replace the conflict of ideologies

*World hunger continues to accelerate and therefore demands our immediate attention.*

© Alan Oddie/PhotoEdit

as the explosive issue of our times."[8] The increasing levels of terrorism and the potential spread of weapons of mass destruction sorely indicate the need for effective intercultural communication. When you add famine and worldwide pollution to the mix, you can appreciate why motivation and cultural understanding must replace apathy and ignorance.

**Famine.** As we noted in Chapter 1, world hunger is a major problem facing humankind. Yet, despite massive efforts by the food-producing nations, world hunger continues to accelerate. Haviland and his colleagues summarize the problem when they write:

> All told, about 1 billion people in the world are undernourished. Some 6 million children aged 5 and under die every year due to hunger, and those who survive often suffer from physical and mental impairment.[9]

This problem reveals that people from different cultures must interact with each other in the next decide. The reason is simple, and clearly stated by Haviland: "The immediate cause of world hunger has less to do with food production than with warfare and food distribution."[10] In short, both these causes have their roots in a lack of communication.

**Environmental Degradation.** Worldwide pollution is yet another reason that makes it necessary for cultures to interact. Global warming, deforestation, soil erosion, chemical poisoning of water and soil, acid rain, water scarcity, climate change, and the like know no boundaries. Pollution is indeed one of those topics that reflect our often truism that notes, "What happens in one part of the world happens in all parts of world." While people know the many causes and growing dangers of environmental degradation, most have refused to make any significant advances in dealing with this crisis. And we suggest the crisis is rapidly worsening. After analyzing a series of recent satellite pictures of the earth, Reuters news service reported, "The devastating impact of mankind on the plant is dramatically illustrated in pictures published on Saturday showing explosive urban sprawl, major deforestation and the sucking dry of inland seas over less than three decades."[11] This type of evidence makes it difficult to reject the proposition that in the future global pollution must be part of an international dialogue.

## TECHNOLOGY

It would appear that the Greek philosopher Plutarch was indeed a futurist when he wrote, "All things are daily changing." One of the most vivid examples of that change can be seen in the area of technology. As West and Turner point out, "The theme of technology is inescapable for anyone living today. Every day we are bombarded with messages from various technological innovations ranging from our telephones (cell and standard) to our computers, televisions, and fax machines."[12] This technology, and even newer innovations, is changing all phases of the communication process.[13] And as you should suspect, technological advancements have influenced—and will continue to influence—the future of intercultural communication. We believe that two issues regarding technology and intercultural communication must be addressed: (1) *cultural domination* and (2) *class disparity*. Let us begin with cultural domination.

**Cultural Domination.** As we discussed in Chapter 1, because of the rapid growth of information technology in the twenty-first century, we now have a situation where cultures, willingly or unwillingly, are exposed to messages from cultures other than their own. The sources of these messages are as diverse as the messages themselves. Cultures can "invade" each other with 24/7 news channels, CDs, films, television programs, high-powered radio stations, the Internet, mass media, and the like. This new exchange has created what Gross calls "a global flow of information."[14] With that flow comes numerous problems that must be solved in the future. Perhaps the main problem is that "many people feel that their culture's continued vitality and even long term existence may be threatened by new ways of living brought about by technology."[15] While this technology moves information in every direction, it is the United States that is currently dominating the flow and type of data. Command and control of the technology means that messages generated by the United States influence the socialization process in cultures other than its own. Kim offers an excellent example of this influence when she notes:

> Indeed, I have experienced the power of American culture wherever I have gone. *Titanic,* CNN, *Friends,* Oprah, and the Backstreet Boys have followed me to Japan, Korea, Thailand, Australia, France, and Italy. U.S. entertainment is the second largest export industry. American films, music, and books fascinate both young and old around the globe.[16]

Whether it be Iranians objecting to America's media transmitting immoral messages, or the French complaining about American commercialism, not everyone welcomes the American media thrusting its values on their culture. As we noted in Chapter 1, the media is an important component of how people learn—and much of the world is resentful of learning from the United States.

Those who rail against the power and influence of the United States note the rapid demise of many of the world's languages and the replacement of these languages with English. They also point to some other Western symbols and icons that dot their culture. In many cases their fear is that the United States is seeking domination of the world—and that the media is part of the controlling process. With the United States controlling the production and distribution of most entertainment media and media technology advancements, some people fear that we might be seeing a "United States of the World." Regardless of the merit of such arguments, it is nevertheless true that the future of intercultural interaction will have to confront the fears of those cultures that are apprehensive, and even hostile, toward the United States.

**Class Disparities.** The worries of class disparities brought about by technology, also known as the "digital divide," are simply and clearly stated by the RAND Corporation:

> As technology brings benefits and prosperity to its users, it may leave others behind and create new class disparities. Although technology will help alleviate some severe hardships (e.g., food shortages and nutritional problems in the developing world) it will create real economic disparities both between and within the developed and developing worlds.[17]

The basic premise behind the above argument is unadorned—at least in its explanation. What is being said is that it takes some level of technology to succeed in the twenty-first century, and if that technology, for whatever reason, is denied to poor countries, their economic development will suffer. Because most new business opportunities involve technology, poor populations and underdeveloped countries will not be able to compete with the more advanced nations. This technological inequality must be faced in the future or the gap between the rich and poor will only grow.

## ETHNIC AND CULTURAL IDENTITY

The third problem that confronts the future of intercultural communication is what we might call a backlash to the notion of a single homogeneous culture or a culture dominated by the United States. The idea of a single worldwide culture is an outgrowth of a line of reasoning that is summarized by Haviland and his associates:

> This idea is based largely on the observation that, due to technological developments in communication, transportation, and trade, peoples of the world are increasingly watching the same television programs, reading the same newspapers, eating the same foods, wearing the same type of clothes, and communicating via satellites and the Internet.[18]

There were even predictions that the world would see a single political system by the twenty-third century.[19] In response to the homogeneous culture position there has evolved a counter-hypothesis that suggests that the opposite dynamic is occurring throughout the world. This position holds that people and cultures, more than ever before, are resisting globalization, and instead, cultures and countries are turning inward. In short, it seems that there is now an "ethnic resurgence" sweeping through the globe.[20] One reason this so-called "turning inward" movement is gaining strength is that many people see the world as unpredictable, complex, and stressful. Heylighen offers a summary of this view in the following paragraph:

> Neither individual minds nor collective culture seem able to cope with the unpredictable change and growing complexity. Stress, uncertainty and frustration increase, minds are overloaded with information, knowledge fragments, values erode, negative developments are consistently overemphasized, while positive are ignored. The resulting climate is one of nihilism, anxiety and despair.[21]

A common response to these feelings of anxiety and uncertainty is that "many millions of people believe that their best haven of certainty and security is a group based on ethnic similarity, common faith, economic interests, or political likemindedness."[22] What appears to be happening is that people are retreating to the shelter of their own ethnic and cultural groups where they can find some sense of identity and feelings of worth and importance. In addition, ethnic groups are becoming nationalized, "with each group stressing its unique heritage and emphasizing differences with neighboring groups."[23]

Whether it be nationalism, cultural isolationism, or "tribalism," the consequences might well produce global conflict. As the philosopher Krishnamurti points out, "For safety and comfort we are willing to kill others who have the same kind of desire to be safe, to feel protected, and to belong to something."[24] Cleveland voices the same fear when he says, "Ethnic and religious diversity is creating painful conflicts around the world."[25] Ethnic discords are not confined to distant locations. As Ling-Ling tells us, there are "disturbing signs of rising racial and ethnic tension at home."[26]

The problem we face in the future is how we resolve the dilemma of culture's turning inward toward ethnocentrism when at the same time cultural interdependence has never been more important. As Smith and Bond remind us, there is an "increasing awareness of humanity's interdependence."[27] It is an inescapable fact that the world is interconnected because of a global economy, the sharing of the same environment, and the need to avoid wars. Herein lies the dilemma—how to balance self interest at the same time interdependence is a necessity. In the future, this quandary must be resolved. We believe that Cleveland does not overstate the point when he notes, "Finding ways to become unified despite diversity may be the world's most urgent problems in the years ahead."[28]

Perhaps the first step in seeking Cleveland's idea of marrying unification with diversity can be found in the words of the anthropologist Laura Nader when she says, "Diversity is rich."[29] We must all begin to realize that diversity can be rich without being threatening, for as we pointed out in the last chapter, in the end people are more alike than they are different. We all find the act of childbirth a dazzling and near mystical event. Nearly everyone belongs to a family, enjoys music and laughter, desires a mate, wants someone to love and care for them, expresses themselves aesthetically and socially, and must learn to cope with suffering and eventually must face death. These and other universal experiences support the notion that people are very much alike. We ask you, therefore, to reflect an attitude of mutual respect, trust, and worth. As John Comenius advised, "Let us have but one end in view, the welfare of humanity." We would urge those who claim that such a view is simplistic, fanciful, or unattainable to provide meaningful alternatives. In a world that can now destroy itself with powerful bombs, toxic gases, environmental degradation, or global pandemics, we do not consider it romantic or idealistic to issue an appeal that we strive to develop a greater understanding of people who may not be like us. The task is not simple, for Cleveland reminds us, "We do not yet quite know how to create 'wholeness incorporating diversity,' but we owe it to the world, as well as ourselves, to keep trying."[30] Because we agree with Cleveland, we add our voice to the call for you to keep trying.

# NOTES

**PREFACE**

1. Huston Smith, *The World's Religions* (New York: HarperCollins, 1991), 7.

**CHAPTER 1**

1. C. Shattuck, *Hinduism* (Upper Saddle River, NJ: Prentice Hall, Inc., 1999), 5–6.
2. *Newsweek*, July 22, 2002, 30F.
3. *U.S. News and World Report*, March 12, 2001, 12.
4. M. Lee, "U.N. Study Cites Value of Global Migration," *San Diego Union-Tribune*, December 5, 2004, A29.
5. D. Calbreath, "Boom Felt Across the Globe," *San Diego Union-Tribune*, March 21, 2005, B1.
6. J. Swomley, "When Blue Becomes Gold," *The Humanist*, September/ October 2000, 5.
7. Ibid., 6.
8. C. Tomlinson, "Why Can't Africa Feed Itself?" *San Diego Union-Tribune*, February 9, 2003, A3.
9. D. Gergen, "Averting Our Eyes," *U.S. News and World Report*, September 25, 2000, 76.
10. www.millenniumassessment.org (accessed May 9, 2005).
11. R. E. Schmid, "African Dust Could Be Killing Coral Reefs," *Las Vegas Review-Journal*, September 23, 2000, 16A.
12. L. Morrow, "Killing with Kindness?" *Time*, October 21, 2002.
13. *San Diego Union-Tribune*, December 10, 2004.
14. D. Mattern, "Humanity's Juncture: Abandoning the Road of War for the Road to Peace," *The Humanist*, March/April, 2000, 9.
15. A. Specter and C. Robbins, *Passion for Truth* (New York: HarperCollins, 2000), 531.
16. *San Diego Union-Tribune*, August 30, 2004, A11.
17. L. Beamer and I. Varner, *Intercultural Communication in the Workplace*, 2nd ed. (New York: McGraw-Hill Irwin, 2001), xiii.
18. G. Cowin, "Multiculturalism: Simply a Matter of Respect," *Australian Nursing Journal*, 10 (1), July 2002, 40.
19. M. Goldsmith, C. Walt, and K. Doucet, "New Competencies for Tomorrow's Global Leader," *CMA Management*, 73 (10), December 1999/January 2000, 20.
20. D. Guerrière, "Multiculturalism: American Success, Liberal Education, or Political Correctness?" *Modern Age*, Spring 2001, 175.
21. www.census.gov (accessed May 10, 2005).
22. www.cnn.printthis.com (accessed May 10, 2005).
23. *San Diego Union-Tribune*, March 13, 2001, A12.
24. www.cnn.com/2001/US/03/30/census.html (accessed March 30, 2005).
25. A. Acuña, "Changes in State's Ethnic Balance are Accelerating," *Los Angeles Times*, October 20, 1999, A20.
26. B. L. Rodriguez and L. B. Olswang, "Mexican-American and Anglo-American Mothers' Beliefs and Values About Child Rearing, Education, and Language Impairment," *American Journal of Speech-Language Pathology*, 12 (November 2003), 452.
27. I. R. Carlo-Casellas, "Marketing to U.S. Hispanic Population Requires Analysis of Cultures," *National Underwriter*, 14, January 2002, 9.
28. S. Gamboa, "Spanish-Language Political TV Ads Air Increasingly," *Las Vegas Review-Journal*, November 22, 2002, 14A.
29. www.census.gov/prod/2003pubs/pdf (accessed May 10, 2005).
30. R. Estrin, "Study Sees America Far from Color-blind," *The Sacramento Bee*, October 2, 1999, A10.
31. www.census.gov/prod/2003pubs/pdf (accessed May 10, 2005).
32. www.aaiusa.org/demographics.htl (accessed May 10, 2005).
33. R. N. Ostling, "First Detailed Survey of U.S. Muslims Find a Growing Faith," *Las Vegas Review-Journal*, April 27, 2001, 11A.
34. www.allied-media.com (accessed May 11, 2005).
35. S. D. McLemore, *Racial and Ethnic Relations in America* (Boston: Allyn and Bacon, 1994), 60.
36. www.census.gov/population/estimates/nation/infitle2-1.txt (accessed May 11, 2005).
37. E. A. Folb, "Who's Got Room at the Top? Issues of Dominance and Nondominance in Intracultural Communication," in *Intercultural Communication: A Reader*, 8th ed., L. A. Samovar and R. E. Porter, eds. (Belmont, CA: Wadsworth, 1997), 140.

38. Ibid., 140.
39. S. Victor, "Election 2000 and the Culture War," *The Humanist*, January/February, 2001, 5.
40. S. Lane, "Deafness Shouldn't Be Called Handicap," *Dallas Morning News*, March 5, 1995, 6-J.
41. J. Goodwin, "Sexuality as Culture," in *Handbook of Intercultural Training*, 2nd ed., D. Lanis and R. S. Bhagat, eds. (Thousand Oaks, CA: Sage Publications, 1996), 417.
42. J. T. Wood, "Gender, Communication, and Culture," in *Intercultural Communication: A Reader*, 7th ed., L. A. Samovar and R. E. Porter, eds. (Belmont, CA: Wadsworth, 1994), 57.
43. M. L. Hecht, S. Ribeau, and M. Sedano, "A Mexican American Perspective on Interethnic Communication," *International Journal of Intercultural Relations*, 14, 1990, 33.
44. C. F. Keating, "World Without Words: Messages from Face and Body," in *Psychology and Culture*, W. J. Lonner and R. S. Malpass, eds. (Boston: Allyn and Bacon, 1994), 175.
45. F. E. X. Dance and C. E. Larson, *Speech Communication: Concepts and Behavior* (New York: Holt, Rinehart, and Winston, 1972).
46. R. West and L. H. Turner, *Introducing Communication Theory: Analysis and Application* (Mountain View, CA: Mayfield Publishing Company, 2000), 5.
47. W. B. Gudykunst and Y. Y. Kim, *Communicating with Strangers: An Approach to Intercultural Communication*, 3rd ed. (New York: McGraw-Hill, 1997), 6.
48. S. Trenholm and A. Jensen, *Interpersonal Communication*, 2nd ed. (Belmont, CA: Wadsworth, 1992), 152.
49. J. T. Wood, *Gender Lives: Communication, Gender and Culture* (Belmont, CA: Wadsworth, 2005), 30.
50. S. W. Littlejohn, *Theories of Human Communication*, 3rd ed. (Belmont, CA: Wadsworth, 1989), 152.
51. S. Shimanoff, *Communication Rules: Theory and Research* (Beverly Hills, CA: Sage Publications, 1980), 57.

52. E. T. Hall and M. R. Hall, *Understanding Cultural Differences: Germans, French and Americans* (Yarmouth, ME: Intercultural Press, 1990), 18.
53. West and Turner, 2000, 5.
54. E. T. Hall, *Beyond Culture* (Garden City, NY: Anchor Doubleday, 1977), 14.
55. E. T. Hall, *The Silent Language* (New York: Doubleday, 1959), 169.
56. G. Hofstede, *Culture's Consequence: Comparing Values, Behaviors, Institutions, and Organizations Across Nations*, 2nd ed. (Thousand Oaks, CA: Sage Publications, 2001), 10.
57. R. W. Nolan, *Communicating and Adapting Across Cultures: Living and Working in the Global Village* (Westport, CT: Bergin and Garvey, 1999), 3.
58. G. Smith, Ed., *Communication and Culture: Readings in the Codes of Human Interaction* (New York: Holt, Rinehart, and Winston, 1966), 1.
59. H. C. Triandis, "Culture and Conflict," *International Journal of Psychology*, 35 (2000), 146.
60. T. Sowell, "Cultural Diversity: A World View," in *Intercultural Communication: A Reader*, 11th ed., L. A. Samovar and R. E. Porter, eds. (Belmont, CA: Wadsworth, 2006), 403.
61. W. A. Haviland, *Cultural Anthropology*, 10th ed. (Belmont, CA: Wadsworth, 2002), 34.
62. M. Harris, *Cows, Pigs, Wars, and Witches: The Riddles of Culture* (New York: Random House, 1974), 84.
63. S. Nanda, *Cultural Anthropology*, 5th ed. (Belmont, CA: Wadsworth, 1994), 50.
64. C. M. Parkes, P. Laungani, and B. Young, eds., *Death and Bereavement Across Cultures* (New York: Routledge, 1997), 15.
65. J. J. Macionis, *Society: The Basics*, 4th ed. (Upper Saddle River, NJ: Prentice Hall, 1997), 34.
66. Parkes, Laungani, and Young, 1997, 15.
67. Nolan, 1999, 3.
68. L. E. Harrison and S. P. Huntington, eds., *Culture Matters: How Values Shape Human Progress* (New York: Basic Books, 2000), xv.

69. A. L. Kroeber and C. Kluckhohn, "Culture: A Critical Review of Concepts and Definitions," *Harvard University Peabody Museum of American Archaeology and Ethnology Papers*, 47 (1952), 181.
70. W. J. Lonner and R. S. Malpass, "When Psychology and Culture Meet: Introduction to Cross-Cultural Psychology," in *Psychology and Culture*, W. J. Lonner and R. S. Malpass, eds. (Boston: Allyn and Bacon, 1994), 7.
71. H. Triandis, *Culture and Social Behavior* (New York: McGraw-Hill, 1994), 23.
72. Harrison and Huntington, 2000, xv.
73. S. P. Huntington, "The West Unique, Not Universal," *Foreign Affairs*, November/December 1996, 28.
74. R. Brislin, *Understanding Culture's Consequence on Behavior*, 2nd ed. (Fort Worth, TX: Harcourt College Publishers, 2000), 10.
75. H. L. Shapiro, *Aspect of Culture* (New Brunswick, NJ: Rutgers University Press, 1956), 54.
76. C. Kluckholn, *Mirror for Men* (New York: McGraw-Hill, 1944), 24–25.
77. D. G. Bates and F. Plog, *Cultural Anthropology*, 3rd ed. (New York: McGraw-Hill, 1990), 19.
78. E. A. Hoebel and E. L. Frost, *Culture and Social Anthropology* (New York: McGraw-Hill, 1976), 58.
79. H. W. Gardiner and C. Kosmitzki, *Lives Across Cultures: Cross-Cultural Human Development*, 2nd ed. (Boston: Allyn and Bacon, 2002), 67.
80. F. M. Keesing, *Cultural Anthropology: The Science of Custom* (New York: Holt, Rinehart, and Winston, 1965), 18.
81. B. Rubin, *Communication and Human Behavior*, 3rd ed. (New York: Macmillan, 1988), 384.
82. J. M. Sellers, *Folk Wisdom of Mexico* (San Francisco: Chronicle Books, 1994), 7.
83. E. G. Seidensticker, in *Even Monkeys Fall from Trees, and Other Japanese Proverbs*, David Galef, ed. (Rutland, VT: Charles E. Tuttle, 1987), 8.
84. Ibid.
85. W. Wolfgang Mieder, *Encyclopedia of World Proverbs: A Treasury of Wit and Wisdom Through the Ages* (New Jersey: Prentice Hall, 1986), xi.

86. Ibid., 1986, x.

87. Ibid., 1986, vii.

88. S. Nanda and R. L. Warms, *Cultural Anthropology*, 6th ed. (Belmont, CA: Wadsworth, 1998), 92.

89. Haviland, 2002, 294.

90. C. Tomlinson, "Myth of Invincibility Draws Children to Battles in Zaire," *San Diego Union-Tribune*, December 17, 1996, A-21.

91. R. Erdoes and A. Ortiz, eds. *American Indian Myths and Legends* (New York: Pantheon, 1984), xv.

92. Ibid., 1984, xv.

93. J. Campbell, *The Power of Myth* (New York: Doubleday, 1988), 5.

94. Ibid., 1988, 6.

95. W. A. Haviland, H. E. L. Prins, D. Walrath, and B. McBride, *Cultural Anthropology: The Human Challenge*, 11th ed. (Belmont, CA: Wadsworth, 2005), 369.

96. Nanda, 1994, 403.

97. E. H. Gombrich, *The Story of Art* (New York: Phaidon, 1955), 102.

98. A. Hunter and J. Sexton, *Contemporary China* (New York: St. Martin's Press, 1999), 158.

99. J. Campbell, *Myths to Live By* (New York: Penguin, 1972), 106.

100. Ibid., 106.

101. www.enchantedlearning.com (accessed May 23, 2005).

102. Keesing, 1965, 279.

103. www.artlex.com (accessed May 23, 2005).

104. Haviland, Prins, Walrath, and McBride, 2005, 369.

105. J. Thompson, "Mass Communication and Modern Culture: Contribution to a Critical Theory of Ideology," *Sociology*, 22 (1988), 359.

106. F. Williams, *The New Communications*, 2nd ed. (Belmont, CA: Wadsworth, 1989), 269.

107. F. P. Delgado, "The Nature of Power Across Communicative and Cultural Borders" (paper presented at the Annual Convention of the Speech Communication Association, Miami Beach, FL, November 1993), 12.

108. www.apa.org/pubinfo/violence.html (accessed May 24, 2005).

109. L. P. Stewart, A. D. Stewart, S. A. Friedly, and P. J. Cooper, *Communication Between the Sexes: Sex Differences and Sex-Role Stereotypes* (Scottsdale, AZ: Gorsuch Scarisbrick, 1990), 84–85.

110. Nanda and Warms, 1998, 47.

111. See M. J. Gannon, *Understanding Globe Culture: Metaphorical Journeys Through 23 Nations*, 2nd ed. (Thousand Oaks, CA: Sage Publications, 2001).

112. Ibid., vi.

113. Haviland, Prins, Walrath, and McBride, 2005, 321.

114. R. Brislin, *Understanding Culture's Influence on Behavior* (Fort Worth, TX: Harcourt Brace Jovanovich, 1993), 6.

115. J. M. Charon, *The Meaning of Sociology*, 6th ed. (Upper Saddle River, NJ: Prentice Hall, 1999), 4.

116. Ibid., 1999, 94.

117. Keesing, 1965, 28.

118. Haviland, Prins, Walrath, and McBride, 2005, 38.

119. J. J. Macionis, *Society: The Basics*, 4th ed. (Saddle River, NJ: Prentice Hall, 1998), 33.

120. Kluckhohn, 1944, 26.

121. H. L. Weinberg, *Levels of Knowing and Existence* (New York: Harper and Row, 1959), 157.

122. W. H. Goodenough, "Evolution of the Human Capacity for Beliefs," *American Anthropologist*, 92 (1990), 605.

123. Bates and Plog, 1990, 20.

124. P. Ethington, "Toward Some Borderlands Schools for American Urban Ethnic Studies?" *American Quarterly*, 48 (1996), 348.

125. Haviland, Prins, Walrath, and McBride, 2005, 46.

126. J. Luckmann, *Transcultural Communication in Nursing* (Albany, NY: Delmar Publishers, 1999), 22.

127. L. Beamer and I. Varner, 2001, 15.

128. D. C. Barnlund, *Communicative Styles of Japanese and Americans: Images and Realities* (Belmont, CA: Wadsworth, 1989), 192.

129. Nanda and Warms, 1998, 57.

130. Haviland, Prins, Walrath, and McBride, 2005, 39.

131. E. T. Hall, *Beyond Culture* (New York: Doubleday, 1976), 13–14.

132. R. Benedict, *Patterns of Culture*, 2nd ed. (New York: Mentor, 1948), 2.

133. R. Benedict, *Patterns of Culture* (Boston: Houghton Mifflin, 1934), 21–22.

134. S. Pinker, *The Blank Slate: The Modern Denial of Human Nature* (New York: Viking, 2002), 34.

135. K. S. Sitaram and R. T. Cogdell, *Foundations of Intercultural Communication* (Columbus, OH: Charles E. Merrill, 1976), 50.

136. J. Scarborough, *The Origins of Cultural Differences and Their Impact on Management* (Westport, CT: Quorum Books, 1998), 2.

137. Ibid.

138. "America's New Ambassador to South Africa," *Ebony*, August 1996, 82.

139. M. Weinberg, "Defining Multicultural Education," *Multicultural Newsletter* (California State University, Long Beach), December 1992, 2.

**CHAPTER 2**

1. J. G. Pankhurst and S. K. Houseknecht, "Introduction," in *Family, Religion and Social Change*, S. K. Houseknecht and J. G. Pankhurst, eds. (New York: Oxford University Press, 2000), 27.

2. "Racist Sect, Activists Square Off at Rally," *San Diego Union-Tribune*, July 5, 1999, A-8.

3. Y. Ling-Ling, "Ethnic Strife Is Not a Geographically Distant Phenomenon," *San Diego Union-Tribune*, June 10, 1999, B-11.

4. J. Leo, "War Against Warriors," *U.S. News and World Report*, March 8, 1999, 16.

5. J. Kahn, "Dozens Die in Ethnic Violence in Central China," *San Diego Union-Tribune*, November 1, 2004, A-16.

6. "Frontiers of Death," *Newsweek*, March 22, 2004.

7. G. Gedda, "Congo Violence Pat at 3,000 Deaths a Day," *San Diego Union-Tribune*, June 27, 2003, A 20.

8. P. Marshall and L. Gilbert, *Their Blood Cries Out: The Untold Story of Persecution Against Christians in the Modern World* (World Publishing, 1997).

9. S. P. Huntington, "The Clash of Civilizations," *Foreign Affairs*, 72 (1993), 22.

10. Ibid., 25.

11. W. A. Haviland, H. E. L. Prins, D. Walrath, and B. McBride, *Cultural Anthropology: The Human Challenge*, 11th ed. (Belmont, CA: Wadsworth, 2005), 77.

12. F. P. Delgado, "The Nature of Power Across Communicative and Cultural Borders" (paper delivered at the Annual Convention of the Speech Communication Association, Miami Beach, FL, November 1993), 11.

13. F. Ajami, "The Ancient Roots of Grievance," *U.S. News and World Report*, April 12, 1999, 20.

14. J. M. Charon, *The Meaning of Sociology*, 6th ed. (Upper Saddle River, NJ: Prentice Hall, 1999), 27.

15. S. P. Huntington, *The Clash of Civilizations and the Remaking of World Order* (New York: Simon and Schuster, 1996), 128.

16. W. B. Gudykunst and Y. Y. Kim, *Communicating with Strangers*, 4th ed. (New York: McGraw-Hill, 2003), 27.

17. S. Kakar, *The Colors of Violence: Cultural Identities, Religion, and Conflict* (Chicago: University of Chicago Press, 1996), 189.

18. S. P. Huntington, 1996, 21.

19. M. Guirdham, *Communicating Across Cultures* (West Lafayette, IN: Ichor Business Books, 1999), 63.

20. E. L. Lynch and M. J. Hanson, *Developing Cross-Cultural Competence: A Guide for Working with Young Children and Their Families* (Baltimore: Paul H. Brookes, 1992), 358.

21. D. E. Brown, *Human Universal* (New York: McGraw-Hill, 1991).

22. E. Y. Kim, *The Yin and Yang of American Culture* (Yarmouth, ME: Intercultural Press, 2001), 159.

23. Ibid.

24. B. G. Farrell, *Family: The Making of an Idea, an Institution, and a Controversy in American Culture* (Boulder, CO: Westview Press, 1999), 5.

25. F. I. Nye and F. M. Berardo, *The Family: Its Structures and Interaction* (New York: Macmillan, 1973), 3.

26. D. E. Smith and G. Mosby, "Jamaican Child-Rearing Practices: The Role of Corporal Punishment," *Adolescence*, 38 (2003), 369.

27. K. M. Galvin and B. J. Brommel, *Family Communication: Cohesion and Change*, 3rd ed. (New York: HarperCollins, 1991), 1.

28. A. Swerdlow, R. Bridenthal, J. Kelly, and P. Vine, *Families in Flux* (New York: Feminist Press, 1989), 64.

29. Haviland, Prins, Walrath, and McBride, 2005, 236.

30. P. Noller and M. A. Fitzpatrick, *Communication in Family Relationships* (Englewood Cliffs, NJ: Prentice Hall, 1993).

31. Haviland, 2002, 243.

32. J. Yerby, N. Buerkel-Rothfuss, and A. P. Bochner, *Understanding Family Communication*, 2nd ed. (Scottsdale, AZ: Gorsuch Scarisbrick Publishers, 1995), 13.

33. H. C. Triandis, *Culture and Social Behavior* (New York: McGraw-Hill, 1994), 159.

34. Haviland, Prins, Walrath, and McBride, 2005, 243.

35. Triandis, 1994, 159

36. R. M. Berko, L. B. Rosenfeld, and L. A. Samovar, *Connecting: A Culture-Sensitive Approach to Interpersonal Communication Competency* (Fort Worth, TX: Harcourt Brace Jovanovich, 1997), 331.

37. L. Schneider and A. Silverman, *Global Sociology: Introducing Five Contemporary Societies* (New York: McGraw-Hill, 1997), 77.

38. J. W. Berry, Y. H. Poortinga, M. H. Segall, and P. R. Dasen, *Cross-Cultural Psychology: Research and Application* (New York: Cambridge University Press, 1992), 22.

39. W. B. Gudykunst, *Asian American Ethnicity and Communication* (Thousand Oaks, CA: Sage Publications, 2001), 6.

40. K. J. Christiano, "Religion and the Family in Modern American Culture," in *Family, Religion and Social Change in Diverse Societies*, S. K. Houseknecht and J. G. Pankhurst, eds. (New York: Oxford University Press, 2000), 43.

41. M. I. Al-Kaysi, *Morals and Manners in Islam: A Guide to Islamic Abab* (United Kingdom: The Islamic Foundation, 1986), 36.

42. A. Burguiere et al., *A History of the Family* (Cambridge, MA: Harvard University Press, 1996), 9.

43. K. K. Lee, "Family and Religion in Traditional and Contemporary Korea," *Religion and the Family in East Asia*, G. A. De Vos and T. Sofue, eds. (Berkeley, CA: University of California Press, 1986), 185.

44. K. A. Ocampo, M. Bernal, and G. P. Knight, "Gender, Race, and Ethnicity: The Sequencing of Social Constancies," in *Ethnic Identity: The Formation and Transmission Among Hispanic and Other Minorities*, M. E. Bernal and G. P. Knight, eds. (New York: State University of New York Press, 1993), 106.

45. T. K. Gamble and M. W. Gamble, *Contacts: Interpersonal Communication in Theory, Practice, and Context* (New York: Houghton Mifflin, 2005), 422.

46. J. W. Whiting and I. Child, *Child Training and Personality* (New Haven: Yale University Press, 1953), 63–64.

47. G. L. Anderson, "The Family in Transition," in *The Family in Global Transition*, G. L. Anderson, ed. (St. Paul, MN: Paragon House, 1997), ix.

48. *Comparisons: Four Families* (Part I), film, I. MacNeill, writer and producer, National Film Board Production: McGraw-Hill Films, 1965.

49. M. McGoldrick, "Ethnicity, Cultural Diversity, and Normality," in *Normal Family Processes*, F. Walalish, ed. (New York: Guilford Press, 1973), 331.

50. M. McGoldrick, "Ethnicity and the Family Life Cycle," in *The Changing Family Life Cycle: A Framework for Family Therapy*, 2nd ed., B. Carter and M. McGoldrick, eds. (Boston: Allyn and Bacon, 1989), 69.

51. J. G. Pankhurst and S. K. Houseknecht, 2000, 28.

52. B. L. Rodriguez and L. B. Olswang, "Mexican-American and Anglo-American Mothers' Beliefs and Values About Child Rearing, Education, and Language," *American Journal of Speech-Language Pathology*, 12 (2003), 369.

53. J. T. Wood, *Gendered Lives: Communication, Gender, and Culture*, 6th ed., (Belmont, CA: Wadsworth, 2005), 154.

54. Ocampo, Bernal, and Knight, 1993, 14.

55. Berry, Poortinga, Segall, and Dasen, 1992, 25.

56. L. D. Purnell and B. J. Paulanka, "Purnell's Model for Cultural Competence," in *Transcultural Health Care: A Culturally Competent Approach*, L. D. Purnell and B. J. Paulanka, eds. (Philadelphia: F. A. Davis, 1998), 20.

57. C. Wade and C. Tavris, "The Long War: Gender and Culture," in *Psychology and Culture*, W. J. Lonner and R. S. Malpass, eds. (Boston: Allyn and Bacon, 1994), 125.

58. Ibid., 126.

59. M. Kim, "Transformation of Family Ideology in Upper-Middle-Class Families in Urban South Korea," *International Journal of Cultural and Social Anthropology*, 32 (1993), 70.

60. Ibid., 70.

61. W. R. Jankowiak, *Sex, Death, and Hierarchy in a Chinese City: An Anthropological Account* (New York: Columbia University Press, 1993), 166.

62. L. E. Davis and E. K. Proctor, *Race, Gender and Class: Guidelines with Individuals, Families, and Groups* (Englewood Cliffs, NJ: Prentice Hall, 1989), 67.

63. J. Hendry, *Understanding Japanese Society* (New York: Routledge, 1987), 5.

64. L. Beamer and Iris Varner, *Intercultural Communication in the Global Workplace*, 2nd ed. (New York: McGraw-Hill, 2001), 198.

65. M. Ferguson, *Feminism and Postmodernism* (Durham, NC: Duke University Press, 1994).

66. E. S. Kras, *Management in Two Cultures* (Yarmouth, ME: Intercultural Press, 1995), 64.

67. C. H. Mindel and R. W. Habenstein, *Ethnic Families in America: Patterns and Variations*, 2nd ed. (New York: Elsevier Science Publishing, 1981), 275.

68. Schneider and Silverman, 1997, 71.

69. Gannon, 2001, 394.

70. Mindel and Habenstein, 1981, 276–277.

71. R. H. Dana, *Multicultural Assessment Perspective for Professionals* (Boston: Allyn and Bacon, 1993), 70.

72. Gannon, 2001, 67.

73. Nanda, 1994, 137.

74. Anderson, 1997, 47.

75. S. K. Houseknecht, "Social Change in Egypt: The Roles of Religion and the Family," in *Family, Religion and Social Change in Diverse Societies*, S. K. Houseknecht and J. G. Pankhurst, eds. (New York: Oxford University Press, 2000), 79.

76. Al-Kaysi, 1986, 41.

77. M. S. Sait, "Have Palestinian Children Forfeited Their Rights?" *Journal of Comparative Family Studies*, 2 (2004), 214.

78. R. Patai, *The Arab Mind* (New York: Scribner's, 1973), 31

79. Ibid., 1994, 32.

80. S. Irfan and M. Cowburn, "Disciplining, Chastisement and Physical Abuse: Perceptions and Attitudes of the British Pakistani Community," *Journal of Muslim Affairs*, 24 (2004), 96.

81. Nanda and Warms, 1998, 221.

82. Lynch and Hanson, 1992, 161–162.

83. Triandis, 1994, 172.

84. R. West and L. H. Turner, *Introducing Communication Theory: Analysis and Application* (Mountain View, CA: Mayfield Publishing Company, 2000), 24.

85. D. C. Thomas and K. Inkson, *Cultural Intelligence: People Skills for Global Business* (San Francisco: Berrett-Koehfer Publishers, 2004), 31.

86. L. Veysey, "Growing Up in America," in *American Issues: Understanding Who We Are*, W. T. Alderson, ed. (Nashville, TN: American Association for State and Local History, 1976), 118.

87. F. M. Moghaddam, D. M. Taylor, and S. C. Wright, *Social Psychology in Cross-Cultural Perspective* (New York: W. H. Freeman, 1993), 73, 98.

88. K. McDade, "How We Parent: Race and Ethnic Differences," in *American Families: Issues in Race and Ethnicity*, C. K. Jacobson, ed. (New York: Garland Publishing, 1995), 283.

89. H. C. Triandis, *Individualism and Collectivism* (San Francisco: Westview Press, 1995), 63.

90. N. Nomura, Y. Noguchi, S. Saito, and I. Tezuka, "Family Characteristics and Dynamics in Japan and the United States: A Preliminary Report from the Family Environment Scale," *International Journal of Intercultural Relations*, 19 (1995), 63.

91. G. Althen, *American Ways: A Guide for Foreigners* (Yarmouth, ME: Intercultural Press, 1988), 5.

92. Ibid., 50.

93. S. Wolpert, *India* (Berkeley, CA: University of California Press, 1991), 134.

94. J. W. Santrock, *Life-Span Development*, 4th ed. (Dubuque, IA: Wm. C. Brown, 1992), 261.

95. Y. Sanchez, "Families of Mexican Origin," in *Families in Cultural Context: Strengths and Challenges of Diversity*, M. K. DeGenova, ed. (Mountain View, CA: Mayfield Publishing Company, 1997), 66.

96. M. B. Zinn and A. Y. H. Pok, "Traditional and Transition in Mexican-Origin Families," in *Minority Families in the United States: A Multicultural Perspective*, 3rd ed., R. L. Taylor, ed. (Upper Saddle River, NJ: Prentice Hall, 2002), 84.

97. T. Novinger, *Communicating with Brazilians: When Yes Means No* (Austin, TX: University of Texas Press, 2003), 82.

98. H. Carrasquillo, "Puerto Rican Families in America," in *Families in Cultural Context: Strengths and Challenges in Diversity*, M. K. DeGenova, ed. (Mountain View, CA: Mayfield Publishing Company, 1997), 159.

99. G. Asselin and Mastron, *Au Contraire! Figuring Out the French* (Yarmouth, MA: Intercultural Press, 2001), 62.

100. K. Peltzer, "Personality and Person Perception in Africa," in *Intercultural Communication: A Reader*, 11th ed., L. A. Samovar, R. E. Porter, and E. R. McDaniel, eds. (Belmont, CA: Wadsworth, 2006), 135.

101. Triandis, 1995, 65.

102. Gannon, 2001, 84.

103. Y. Richmond and P. Gestrin, *Into Africa: Intercultural Insights* (Yarmouth, ME: Intercultural Press, 1998), 3.

104. Schneider and Silverman, 1997, 73.

105. A. Valenzuela, "Liberal Gender Role Attitudes and Academic Achievement Among Mexican-Origin Adolescents in Two Houston Inner-City Catholic Schools," *Hispanic Journal of Behavior Sciences*, August 15, 1993, 294.

106. R. Shorto, "Made-in-Japan Parenting," *Health,* 23 (1991), 54.

107. Shorto, 1991.

108. J. J. Ponzetti, ed., *International Encyclopedia of Marriage and Family,* 2nd ed. (New York: The Gale Group, 2003), 1207.

109. G. C. Chu and Y. Ju, *The Great Wall in Ruins: Communication and Culture Change in China* (Albany, NY: State University of New York Press, 1993), 9–10.

110. Nydell, 1989, 75.

111. Haviland, Prins, Walrath, and McBride, 2005, 285.

112. J. F. Nussbaum, T. Thompson, and J. D. Robinson, *Communication and Aging* (New York: Harper and Row, Publishers, 1989), 21.

113. Haviland, Prins, Walrath, and McBride, 2005, 286.

114. H. W. Gardiner and C. Kosmitzki, *Lives Across Cultures: Cross-Cultural Human Development,* 2nd ed. (Boston: Allyn and Bacon, 2002), 100.

115. A. M. Lutfiyya, "Islam in Village Culture," in *Readings in Middle Eastern Societies and Cultures,* A. M. Lutfiyya and C. W. Churchill, eds. (Paris: Mouton, 1970), 55.

116. Kim, 2001, 163.

117. H. Wenzhong and C. L. Grove, *Encountering the Chinese: A Guide for Americans* (Yarmouth, ME: Intercultural Press, 1991), 6.

118. Gannon, 2001, 259.

119. Hendry, 1987, 24.

120. J. Carlson, et al., "A Multicultural Discussion About Personality Development," *The Family Journal: Counseling and Therapy for Couples and Families,* 12 (2004), 113.

121. T. Gochenour, *Considering Filipinos* (Yarmouth, ME: Intercultural Press, 1990), 19.

122. E. R. Curtius, *The Civilization of France* (New York: Vintage Books, 1962), 225.

123. Curtius, 1962, 226.

124. A. J. Rubel, "The Family," in *Mexican-Americans in the United States: A Reader,* J. H. Burma, ed. (New York: Canfield Press, 1970), 212.

125. V. Sanchez, 1997, 73.

126. Novinger, 2003, 84.

127. O. Still and D. Hodgins, "Navajo Indians," *Transcultural Health Care: A Culturally Competent Approach,* L. D. Purnell and B. J. Paulanka, eds. (Philadelphia: F. A. Davis, 1998), 430.

128. M. Yellowbird and C. M. Sniff, "American Indian Families," in *Minority Families in the United States,* 3rd ed., R. L. Taylor, ed, (Upper Saddle River, NJ: Prentice Hall, 2002), 240.

129. Ibid.

130. G. Arnold, "Living in Harmony: Makah," in *Stories of the People: Native American Voices,* National Museum of the American Indian, ed. (New York: Universe Publishing, 1997).

131. J. Campinha-Bacaote, "African-Americans," in *Transcultural Health Care: A Culturally Competent Approach,* L. D. Purnell and B. J. Paulanka, eds. (Philadelphia: F. A. Davis, 1998), 57.

132. Peltzer, 2006, 136.

133. J. M. Charon, *The Meaning of Sociology* (Upper Saddle River, NJ: Prentice Hall, 1999), 202.

134. M. H. DeFleur, P. Kearney, T. Plax, and M. L. DeFleur, *Fundamentals of Human Communication* (New York: McGraw-Hill, 2005) 157.

135. Galvin and Brommel, 1991, 22.

136. Anderson, 1997, 265.

137. Yerby, Buerkel-Rothfuss, and Bochner, 1995, 63.

138. L. H. Turner and R. West, *Perspectives on Family Communication* (Mountain View, CA: Mayfield, 1998), 10.

139. Berry, Poortinga, Segall, and Dasen, 1992, 67.

140. Moghaddam, Taylor, and Wright, 1993, 125.

141. Carrasquillo, 1997, 161.

142. N. Murillo, "The Mexican Family," *Chicanos: Social and Psychological Perspective,* C. A. Hernandez, M. J. Hang, and N. N. Wagner, eds. (Saint Louis, MO: C. V. Mosby, 1976), 19.

143. Moghaddam, Taylor, and Wright, 1993, 124.

144. McGoldrick, 1973, 341.

145. E. W. Ferna, "Childhood in the Muslim Middle East," in *Children in the Muslim Middle East,* E. W. Ferna, ed. (Austin, TX: University of Texas Press, 1995), 5.

146. R. Cooper and N. Cooper, *Thailand: A Guide to Customs and Etiquette* (Portland, OR: Graphic Arts Center, 1982), 83.

147. Kim, 2001, 181.

148. Ibid., 182.

149. A. Hunter and J. Sexton, *Contemporary China* (New York: St. Martin's Press, 1999), 150.

150. McGoldrick, 1973, 336.

151. Ibid., 1973.

152. W. C. Smith, *Modern Culture from a Comparative Perspective* (New York: State University of New York Press, 1997), vii.

153. Y. Yu, "Clio's New Cultural Turn and the Rediscovery of Tradition in Asia" (keynote address presented to the 12th Conference of the International Association of Historians of Asia, June 1991), 26.

154. "How the Seeds of Hate Were Sown," *San Diego Union-Tribune,* May 9, 1993, G5.

155. B. Lewis, *The Shaping of the Modern Middle East* (New York: Oxford Press, 1994), 11.

156. B. Lewis, *The Middle East: A Brief History of the Last 2,000 Years* (New York: Scribner, 1995), 67.

157. "Background Note: Rwanda," U.S. Department of State, www.state.gov/r/pa/ei/bgn/2861.htm (accessed October 31, 2005).

158. Ibid.

159. L. Banville. "Early History of the Region," *Conflict in Chechnya: Russia's Renegade Republic,* PBS Online NewsHour, www.pbs.org/newshour/bb/europe/chechnya/history.html (accessed October 31, 2005).

160. B. Kerblay, *Modern Soviet Society* (New York: Pantheon, 1983), 271.

161. J. H. McElroy, *American Beliefs: What Keeps a Big Country and Diverse People United* (Chicago: Ivan R. Dee, 1999), 51.

162. Ibid., 37.

163. Ibid., 1999, 220.

164. Van Doren, 1991, 224.

165. G. Althen, *American Ways,* 2nd ed. (Yarmouth, ME: Intercultural Press, 2003), 120.

166. J. H. McElroy, *Finding Freedom: America's Distinctive Cultural Formation* (Carbondale, IL: Southern Illinois University Press, 1987), 65.

167. S. D. Cohen, *An Ocean Apart* (Westport, CT: Praeger, 1998), 141.

168. E. C. Stewart and M. J. Bennett, *American Cultural Patterns*, rev. ed. (Yarmouth, ME: Intercultural Press, 1991), 136.

169. McElroy, 1987, 143.

170. R. G. Del Castillo, *The Treaty of Guadalupe Hidalgo: A Legacy of Conflict* (Norman, OK: University of Oklahoma Press, 1990), 4.

171. Steward and Bennett, 1991, 119–123.

172. R. V. Daniels, *Russia: The Roots of Confrontation* (Cambridge, MA: Harvard University Press, 1985), 55.

173. A. Esler, *The Human Venture*, 3rd ed. (Upper Saddle River, NJ: Prentice Hall, 1996), 668.

174. "Background Note: Russia," U.S. Department of State, www.state.gov/r/pa/ei/bgn/3183.htm (accessed October 31, 2005).

175. "The Uses and Abuses of History," *The Economist*, May 7, 2005, 43.

176. J. Kohan, "A Mind of Their Own," *Time*, December 7, 1992, 66.

177. Ibid.

178. "Victory Day Remembered," *The Economist*, May 7, 2005, 9.

179. J. Mathews and L. Mathews, *One Billion: A China Chronicle* (New York: Random House, 1983), 11.

180. "Background Note: China," U.S. Department of State, www.state.gov/r/pa/ei/bgn/18902.htm (accessed October 31, 2005.

181. L. K. Matocha, "Chinese Americans," in *Transcultural Health Care: A Culturally Competent Approach*, L. D. Purnell and B. J. Paulanka, eds. (Philadelphia: F. A. Davis, 1998), 164.

182. M. H. Bond, *Beyond the Chinese Face* (Hong Kong: Oxford University Press, 1991), 108.

183. S. Ogden, *China's Unresolved Issues: Politics, Development, and Culture*, 2nd ed. (Englewood Cliffs, NJ: Prentice Hall, 1992), 19.

184. Bond, 1991, 109.

185. Esler, 1996, 86.

186. Wenzhong and Grove, 1991, 1.

187. G. C. Chu and Y. Ju, *The Great Wall in Ruins: Communication and Cultural Change in China* (Albany, NY: SUNY Press, 1993), 272.

188. Bond, 1991, 7.

189. "The Chinese Examination System," *The Columbia Encyclopedia*, 6th ed., www.bartleby.com/65/ch/Chines-exa.html (accessed October 31, 2005). See also "Chinese Examination System," *Britannica Concise Encyclopedia*, 2005, Encyclopedia Britannica Online, www.britannica.com/ebc/article?tocId=9360615 (accessed October 31, 2005).

190. Bond, 1991, 28.

191. Huntington, 1996, 168.

192. "Background Note: China," March 2005.

193. "China," *The World Factbook*, www.cia.gov/cia/publications/factbook/rankorder/2001rank.html (accessed October 31, 2005).

194. "Muscle-flexing by China Not Called for: U.S.," *The Japan Times*, June 5, 2005, 3.

195. E. O. Reischauer and M. B. Jansen, *The Japanese Today: Change and Continuity* (Cambridge, MA: Harvard University Press, 1995), 31.

196. B. L. De Mente, *Behind the Japanese Bow* (Chicago: Passport Books), 1–2, 12.

197. Reischauer and Jansen, 1995, 32.

198. T. S. Lebra, *Japanese Patterns of Behavior* (Honolulu, HI: University of Hawaii Press, 1976).

199. "Background Note: Japan," U.S. Department of State, www.state.gov/r/pa/ei/bgn/4142.htm (accessed October 31, 2005).

200. Reischauer and Jansen, 1995, 15–16.

201. J. W. Dower, *Embracing Defeat: Japan in the Wake of World War II* (New York: W. W. Norton, 1999).

202. J. Hendry, *Understanding Japanese Society*, 3rd ed. (New York: RoutledgeCruzon, 2003), 18.

203. D. McCargo, *Contemporary Japan* (London: Palgrave, 2000), 169.

204. Del Castillo, 1990, xi.

205. C. McKiniss and A. Natella, *Business Mexico* (New York: Haworth Press, 1994), 70.

206. Schneider and Silverman, 1997, 60.

207. J. D. Cockcroft, *Mexico's Hope: An Encounter with Politics and History* (New York: Monthly Review Press, 1998), 13.

208. Schneider and Silverman, 1997, 60.

209. L. V. Foster, *A Brief History of Mexico* (New York: Facts on File, 1997), 2.

210. J. Norman, *Guide to Mexico* (Garden City: Doubleday, 1972), 53.

211. Cockcroft, 1998, 11.

212. Foster, 1997, 43.

213. Cockcroft, 1998, 19.

214. Foster, 1997, 65.

215. Ibid., 66.

216. Ibid., 96.

217. H. B. Parkes, *A History of Mexico*, 3rd ed. (Boston: Houghton Mifflin, 1969).

218. Foster, 1997, 111.

219. C. J. Johns, *The Origins of Violence in Mexican Society* (Westport, CT: Praeger, 1995), 202.

220. J. Eisenhower, "The War Nobody Knows," *On Air*, September 1998, 17.

221. "The Treaty of Guadalupe Hidalgo," Library of Congress, www.loc.gov/exhibits/ghtreaty/ (accessed October 31, 2005).

222. Del Castillo, 1990, xii.

223. J. Samora and P. V. Simon, *A History of Mexican American People* (London: University of Notre Dame Press, 1977), 98.

224. Ibid., 98.

225. Esler, 1996, 613

226. O. Najera-Ramirez, "Engendering Nationalism: Identity, Discourse, and the Mexican Charro," *Anthropological Quarterly*, 67 (1994), 9.

227. Foster, 1997, 156.

228. D. J. Weber, "Conflicts and Accommodations: Hispanic and Anglo-American Borders in Historical Perspective," *Journal of the Southwest*, 39 (1997), 1.

229. P. Lunde, *Islam* (New York: DK Publishing, 2002), 8.

230. J. L. Esposito, *What Everyone Needs to Know About Islam* (New York: Oxford University Press, 2002), 1.

231. "Background Note: Indonesia," U.S. Department of State, www.state.gov/r/pa/ei/bgn/2748.htm (accessed October 31, 2005).

232. M. M. Ayoub, *Islam: Faith and History* (Oxford: Oneworld Publications, 2005), 72–73.

233. F. M. Donner, "Muhammad and the Caliphate," in *The Oxford History of Islam*, J. L. Esposito, ed. (New York: Oxford University Press, 1999), 11.

234. Lunde, 2002, 8.
235. Donner, 1999, 11.
236. Ibid., 13.
237. S. H. Nasr, *Islam: Religion, History, and Civilization* (New York: HarperSanFrancisco, 2003), 10.
238. Esposito, 2002, 46.
239. Ibid., 47.
240. Lunde, 2002, 52, 61.
241. Ibid., 2002, 54.
242. Ibid., 2002, 54.
243. Ibid., 2002, 56.
244. J. I. Smith, "Islam and Christendom," in *The Oxford History of Islam*, J. L. Esposito, ed. (New York: Oxford University Press, 1999), 312, 337.
245. E. Rogers and E. M. Steinfatt, *Intercultural Communication* (Prospect Heights, IL: Waveland Press, 1999), 9.
246. Smith, 1999, 339.
247. B. Lewis, "The Revolt of Islam," *The New Yorker*, November 19, 2001, 53.
248. S. V. R. Nasr, "European Colonialism and the Emergence of Modern Muslim States, in *The Oxford History of Islam*, J. L. Esposito, ed. (New York: Oxford University Press, 1999), 552.
249. Lunde, 2002, 79.
250. Lewis, 2001, 51.
251. Ibid., 52.
252. Lewis, 1995, 17. See also J. Esposito, "Contemporary Islam: Reformation or Revolution?" in *The Oxford History of Islam*, J. L. Esposito, ed. (New York: Oxford University Press, 1999), 643.
253. Lewis, 2001, 52.
254. Ibid., 56.
255. Ibid., 59.
256. Esposito, 2002, 44.
257. W. Rahula, *What the Buddha Taught* (New York: Grove, 1974), 1.
258. Lewis, 1994, 27.
259. Esposito, 2002, 169.
260. Gergen, D. "One Nation, After All," *U.S. News and World Report*, March 16, 1998, 84.

**CHAPTER 3**

1. W. A. Haviland, H. E. L. Prins, D. Walrath, and B. McBride, *Cultural Anthropology: The Human Challenge*, 11th ed. (Belmont, CA: Wadsworth, 2005), 340.
2. N. Rapport and J. Overing, *Social and Cultural Anthropology: The Key Concepts* (New York: Routledge, 2000), 404.
3. E. A. Hoebel and E. L. Frost, *Cultural and Social Anthropology* (New York: McGraw-Hill, 1976), 324.
4. C. Kraft, "Worldview in Intercultural Communication," in *International and Intercultural Communication*, F. Casmir, ed. (Washington, DC: University Press of America, 1978), 407.
5. B. J. Hall, *Among Cultures: The Challenge of Communication* (Orlando, FL: Harcourt College Publishers, 2002), 29.
6. R. H. Dana, *Multicultural Assessment Perspectives for Professional Psychology* (Boston: Allyn and Bacon, 1993), 9.
7. E. A. Hoebel, *Man in the Primitive World* (New York: McGraw-Hill, 1958), 159.
8. R. O. Olayiwola, "The Impact of Islam on the Conduct of Nigerian Foreign Relations," *Islamic Quarterly*, 33 (1989), 19–26.
9. For a summary of the elements associated with worldview, see S. Ishii, P. Cooke, and D. Klopf, "Our Locus in the Universe: Worldview and Intercultural Misunderstandings/Conflicts," *Dokkyo International Review*, 12 (1999), 301–317.
10. D. L. Pennington, "Intercultural Communication," in *Intercultural Communication: A Reader*, 4th ed., L. A. Samovar and R. E. Porter, eds. (Belmont, CA: Wadsworth, 1985), 32.
11. T. Bianquis, *A History of the Family*, Vol. 4, A. Burguiere, gen. ed. (Cambridge, MA: Harvard University Press, 1996), 618.
12. *The Holy Bible: The New King James Version* (New York: American Bible Society, 1990), 1.
13. M. P. Fisher and R. Luyster, *Living Religions* (Englewood Cliffs, NJ: Prentice Hall, 1991), 153–156.
14. R. Bartels, "National Culture-Business Relations: United States and Japan Contrasted," *Management International Review*, 2 (1982), 5.
15. W. S. Howell, *The Empathic Communicator* (Belmont, CA: Wadsworth, 1982), 223.
16. P. Gold, *Navajo and Tibetan Sacred Wisdom: The Circle of the Spirit* (Rochester, VT: Inner Traditions, 1994), 60.
17. S. Ishii, D. Klopf, and P. Cooke, "Our Locus in the Universe: Worldview and Intercultural Communication," in *Intercultural Communication: A Reader*, 11th ed., L. A. Samovar, R. E. Porter, and E. R. McDaniel, eds. (Belmont, CA: Wadsworth, 2006), 32–38.
18. H. Helve, "The Formation of Religious Attitudes and Worldviews," *Social Compass*, 38 (1991), 373–392.
19. Haviland, Prins, Walrath, and McBride, 2005, 340.
20. S. Nanda and R. L. Warms, *Cultural Anthropology*, 6th ed. (Belmont, CA: Wadsworth, 1998), 275.
21. W. A. Haviland, *Cultural Anthropology* (Fort Worth, TX: Harcourt Brace Jovanovich, 1993), 346.
22. M. D. Coogan, "Introduction," in *The Illustrated Guide to World Religion*, M. D. Coogan, ed. (New York: Oxford University Press, 1998), 6.
23. A. Malefijt, *Religion and Culture: An Introduction to Anthropology of Religion* (Prospect Heights, IL: Waveland Press, 1968), 145.
24. S. Nanda, *Cultural Anthropology*, 5th ed. (Belmont, CA: Wadsworth, 1994), 349.
25. H. Smith, *The World's Religions* (New York: HarperCollins, 1991), 9.
26. H. Smith, *The Religions of Man* (New York: Harper and Row, 1986, 13.
27. M. Grondona, "A Cultural Typology of Economic Development," in *Culture Matters: How Values Shape Human Progress*, L. E. Harrison and S. P. Huntington, eds. (New York: Basic Books, 2000), 47.
28. M. B. McGuire, *Religion: The Social Context*, 5th ed. (Belmont, CA: Wadsworth, 2002), 1.
29. Haviland, 1993.
30. C. Lamb, "The Claim to Be Unique," in *Eerdmans' Handbook to the World's Religions*, R. Pierce Beaver et al., eds. (Grand Rapids, MI: Eerdmans, 1982), 358.
31. A. W. P. Guruge, "Survival of Religion: The Role of Pragmatism and Flexibility," paper presented at the Religious Studies Department, George Washington University, Washington, DC, November 1, 1995, 30.

32. R. L. Monroe and R. H. Monroe, "Perspectives Suggested by Anthropological Data," in *Handbook of Cross-Cultural Psychology: Vol. 1 Perspectives,* H. C. Triandis and W. W. Lambert, eds. (Boston: Allyn and Bacon, 1980), 259.

33. W. E. Paden, *Religious Worlds: The Comparative Study of Religion* (Boston: Beacon, 1994), 170.

34. K. E. Richter, E. M. Rapple, J. C. Modschiedler, and R. Dean, *Understanding Religion in a Global Society* (Belmont, CA: Wadsworth, 2005), 10.

35. "One Nation Under Gods," *Time,* vol. 142, issue 21, Fall 1993, 62.

36. www.adherents.com/Religions_By_Adherents.html (accessed March 3, 2005).

37. D. L. Carmody and J. T. Carmody, *In the Path of the Masters: Understanding the Spirituality of Buddha, Confucius, Jesus, and Muhammad* (New York: Paragon House, 1994), Preface.

38. N. Smart, *The World's Religions,* 2nd ed. (New York: Cambridge University, 1998), 541–546; 319–321.

39. Smith, 1991, 3.

40. K. Crim, *The Perennial Dictionary of World Religions* (New York: HarperCollins, 1989), 665.

41. Coogan, 1998, 9.

42. D. Crystal, *The Cambridge Encyclopedia of Language* (New York: Cambridge University Press, 1987), 384.

43. Ibid.

44. Richter, Rapple, Modschiedler, and Peterson, 2005, 92.

45. Ibid., 224.

46. McGuire, 2002, 17.

47. Malefijt, 1968, 193.

48. W. A. Haviland, *Cultural Anthropology* (Belmont, CA: Wadsworth, 2002), 274.

49. Coogan, 1998, 10.

50. Richter, Rapple, Modschiedler, and Peterson, 2005, 231.

51. M. V. Angrosino, *The Culture of the Sacred: Exploring the Anthropology of Religion* (Prospect Heights, IL: Waveland Press, 2004), 97.

52. Paden, 1994, 96.

53. Richter, Rapple, Modschiedler, and Peterson, 2005, 255.

54. J. Scarborough, *The Origins of Cultural Differences and Their Impact on Management* (Westport, CT: 1998), 3.

55. Smart, 1998, 18.

56. Ibid., 19.

57. H. Smith, *The Illustrated World's Religions: A Guide to Our Wisdom Traditions* (New York: HarperCollins, 1994), 210.

58. Ibid.

59. Ibid.

60. Coogan, 1998, 10.

61. J. J. Macionis, *Society: The Basics,* 4th ed. (Upper Saddle River, NJ: Prentice Hall, 1998), 319.

62. Smart, 1992, 23.

63. F. Ridenour, *So What's the Difference* (Ventura, CA: Regal Books, 2001), 7.

64. J. Hendry, *Understanding Japanese Society* (New York: Routledge, 1987), 103.

65. Coogan, 1998, 13.

66. W. C. Smith, *Modern Culture from a Comparative Perspective* (New York: State University of New York Press, 1997), 32.

67. *Newsweek,* April 16, 2001, 49.

68. B. Wilson, *Christianity* (Upper Saddle River, NJ: Prentice Hall, 1990) 16.

69. R. D. Hale, "Christianity," in *The Illustrated Guide to World Religions),* M. D. Coogan, ed. (New York: Oxford University Press, 1998), 54.

70. K. L. Woodward, "2000: Year of Jesus," *Newsweek,* March 29, 1999, 55.

71. D. S. Noss and J. B. Noss, *Man's Religions,* 7th ed. (New York: Macmillan, 1984), 412.

72. Wilson, 1999, 105.

73. Angrosino, 2004, 151.

74. *Prime Time School Television: The Long Search* (Chicago, 1978).

75. Carmody and Carmody, 1994, 116.

76. Ibid.

77. M. P. Fisher and R. Luyster, *Living Religions* (Englewood Cliffs, NJ: Prentice Hall, 1991), 228.

78. Smith, 1994, 212.

79. P. Novak, *The World's Wisdom: Sacred Texts of the World's Religions* (New York: HarperCollins, 1994), 242–243.

80. McGuire, 2002, 302.

81. Ibid.

82. Woodward, 1999, 56.

83. H. T. Blanche and C. M. Parkes, "Christianity," in *Death and Bereavement Across Cultures,* C. M. Parkes, P. Laungani, and B. Young, eds. (New York: Routledge, 1997), 145.

84. Woodward, 1999.

85. Ibid.

86. B. Storm, *More Than Talk: Communication Studies and the Christian Faith* (Dubuque, IA: Kendall/Hunt, 1996).

87. Wilson, 1999, 26.

88. Smith, 1994, 210.

89. Woodward, 1999, 55.

90. T. C. Muck, *Those Other Religions in Your Neighborhood: Loving Your Neighbor When You Don't Know How* (Grand Rapids, MI: Zondervan, 1992), 165.

91. Blanche and Parkes, 1997, 145.

92. C. Murphy, "The Bible According to Eve," *U.S. News and World Report,* August 10, 1998, 49.

93. J. L. Sheler, "Editing Peter and Paul," *U.S. News and World Report,* September 11, 2000, 88.

94. Woodward, 1999, 58.

95. Ibid., 57.

96. Murphy, 1998, 50.

97. Ibid., 49.

98. Carmody and Carmody, 1994, 104.

99. D. Crystal, ed. *The Cambridge Factfinder* (New York: Cambridge University Press, 1994), 343.

100. Smith, 1991, 271.

101. R. Banks, "The Covenant," *Eerdmans' Handbook to the World's Religions,* 278.

102. D. J. Boorstin, *The Creators* (New York: Random House, 1992), 43.

103. D. Prager and J. Telushkin, *The Nine Questions People Ask About Judaism* (New York: Simon and Schuster, 1981), 112.

104. C. S. Ehrlich, "Judaism," in *The Illustrated Guide to World Religion,* M. D. Coogan, ed. (New York: Oxford University Press, 1998), 16.

105. Malefijt, 1968, 69.

106. Ibid.

107. Smith, 1991, 287.

108. Fisher and Luyster, 1991, 175.

109. *Prime Time School Television,* 1978.

110. Ehrlich, 1998, 39.

111. C. Van Doren, *A History of Knowledge* (New York: Ballantine Books, 1991), 16.
112. Prager and Telushkin, 1981, 29.
113. Ibid.
114. Van Doren, 1991, 16.
115. F. E. Peters, *Judaism, Christianity and Islam: The Classical Texts and Their Interpretation* (Princeton, NJ: Princeton University Press, 1990).
116. Crim, 1989, 732.
117. L. Rosten, *Religions of America* (New York: Simon and Schuster, 1975), 143.
118. Rosten, 1975.
119. Novak, 1994, 179.
120. Prager and Telushkin, 1981, 46.
121. Smith, 1994, 189.
122. Rosten, 1975, 575.
123. Smith, 1991, 267.
124. D. Belt, "The World of Islam," *National Geographic*, January 2002, 77.
125. J. Blank, "The Muslim Mainstream," *U.S. News and World Report*, July 20, 1998, 22.
126. J. L. Sheler, "Muslim in America," *U.S. News and World Report*, October 29, 2001, 51.
127. Belt, 2002, 76.
128. Noss and Noss, 496.
129. E. E. Calverley, "World-Center of Islam," in *World-Center: Today and Tomorrow*, R. N. Anshen, ed. (New York: Harper and Brothers, 1956), 65.
130. *Qur'an*, 112:1–4.
131. J. Scarborough, *The Origins of Cultural Differences and Their Impact on Management* (Westport, CT: Quorum Books, 1998), 107.
132. C. E. Farah, *Islam*, 7th ed. (Hauppauge, NY: Barron's Educational Series, Inc. 2003), 120.
133. *Qur'an*, 3:145.
134. Ibid., 87:2–3.
135. K. L. Woodward, "In the Beginning, There Were the Holy Books," *Newsweek*, February 11, 2001, 52.
136. Van Doren, 1991, 20.
137. McGuire, 2002, 216.
138. M. S. Gordon, "Islam," in *The Illustrated Guide to World Religion*, M. D. Coogan, ed. (New York: Oxford University Press, 1998), 92.
139. Ibid., 91.
140. J. J. Elias, *Islam* (Upper Saddle River, NJ: Prentice Hall, 1999), 61.
141. Ibid.

142. Gordon, 1998, 100.
143. Fisher and Luyster, 1991, 278.
144. Crim, 1989, 346.
145. Elias, 1999, 62.
146. Ibid., 63.
147. Ibid.
148. Ridenour, 2001, 80.
149. Fisher and Luyster, 1991, 281.
150. Elias, 1999, 64.
151. Fisher and Luyster, 1991, 282.
152. Elias, 1999, 64.
153. Ibid., 65.
154. Fisher and Luyster, 1991, 282.
155. Ibid., 289.
156. Gordon, 1998, 115.
157. Nydell, 1987, 91.
158. L. Schneider and A. Silverman, *Global Sociology: Introducing Five Contemporary Societies* (New York: McGraw-Hill, 1997), 165.
159. Gordon, 1998, 116.
160. Ibid., 1998.
161. www.ubfellowship.org/archive/readers/601islam.htm (accessed April 12, 2005).
162. Nydell, 1987, 91.
163. Gordon, 1998, 116.
164. Elias, 1999, 71.
165. Ibid., 73.
166. *Middle East Quarterly*, June 1994, 50.
167. Gordon, 1998, 114.
168. Farah, 2003, 158.
169. Novak, 1994, 300.
170. J. L. Sheler, "Alive in the Presence of Their Lord," *U.S. News and World Report*, October 1, 2001, 38.
171. Gordon, 1998, 114.
172. Elias, 1999, 73.
173. Belt, 2002, 83.
174. Elias, 1999, 73.
175. K. Armstrong, *A History of God: The 4000-Year Quest of Judaism, Christianity and Islam* (New York: Knopf, 1994), 344.
176. Sheler, 2001, 38.
177. Gordon, 1998, 114.
178. www.islam-guide.com/ch3-7.htm (accessed April 11, 2005).
179. Belt, 2002, 82–83.
180. Novak, 1994, 282.
181. Elias, 1999, 21.
182. C. Wilson, "The Quran," in *Eerdmans' Handbook to the World's Religions*, 315.
183. Richter, Rapple, Modschiedler, and Peterson, 2005, 366.

184. M. K. Nydell, *Understanding Arabs: A Guide for Westerners* (Yarmouth, ME: Intercultural Press, 1987).
185. Novak, 1994, 282.
186. Angrosino, 2004, 149.
187. M. I. Al-Kaysi, *Morals and Manners in Islam: A Guide to Islamic Arab* (United Kingdom: The Islamic Foundation, 1986).
188. Smith, 1991, 189.
189. Angrosino, 2004, 208.
190. L. Beamer and I. Varner, *Intercultural Communication in the Global Workplace*, 2nd ed. (New York: McGraw-Hill, 2001), 93.
191. A. M. Lutfiyya, "Islam in Village Culture," in *Readings in Arab Middle Eastern Societies and Cultures*, A. M. Lutfiyya and C. W. Churchill, eds. (Paris: Mouton, 1970), 49.
192. A. Esler, *The Human Venture*, 2nd ed. (Englewood Cliffs, NJ: Prentice Hall, 1992), 257–258.
193. Ibid., 250.
194. Farah, 2003, 415.
195. Gordon, 1998, 122.
196. Elias, 1999, 105. See also Smith, 1994, 166–167, and Farach, 2003, 417.
197. Elias, 1999, 105–106.
198. Novak, 1994, 306.
199. Farah, 2003, 417.
200. Elias, 1999, 107.
201. Esler, 1992, 250.
202. Crim, 1989, 57.
203. L. Schmalfuss, "Science, Art and Culture in Islam," in *Eerdmans' Handbook to the World's Religions*, 328.
204. www.geocities.com/Athens/Forum/9410/hindu1.html (accessed November 7, 2004).
205. Esler, 1992, 80.
206. Scarborough, 1998, 131.
207. V. Narayanan, "Hinduism," in *The Illustrated Guide to World Religion*, M. D. Coogan, ed. (New York: Oxford University Press, 1998), 126.
208. Boorstin, 1992, 5.
209. Smart, 1998, 44.
210. C. Shattuck, *Hinduism* (Upper Saddle River, NJ: Prentice Hall, 1999), 17.
211. Ibid., 1998.
212. Ridenour, 2001, 89.
213. Richter, Rapple, Modschiedler, and Peterson, 2005, 89.
214. Scarborough, 1998, 31.
215. Narayanan, 1998, 130.

216. Shattuck, 1999, 20.
217. Richter, Rapple, Modschiedler, and Peterson, 2005, 114.
218. Crim, 1998, 785.
219. B. Usha, *A Ramakrishna-Vedanta Handbook* (Hollywood, CA: Vedanta Press, 1971), 79–80.
220. S. Prabhavanda and F. Manchester, *The Upanishads: The Breath of the Eternal* (Hollywood, CA: Vedanta Press, 1978), xvii.
221. www.religioustolerance.org/hinduism2.htm (accessed April 21, 2005).
222. Usha, 1971, 17–18.
223. Shattuck, 1999, 39.
224. Boorstin, 1992, 4–5.
225. R. Hammer, "The Eternal Teaching: Hinduism," in *Eerdmans' Handbook to the World's Religions,* 170.
226. R. S. Hegde, "Passages from Tradition: Communication Competence and Gender in India," paper presented at the Annual Convention of the Speech Communication Association, Miami Beach, FL, November 1993, 5.
227. T. K. Venkateswaran, "Hinduism: A Portrait," in *A Source Book for Earth's Community of Religions,* J. D. Beversluis, ed. (Grand Rapids, MI: Co Nexus Press, 1995), 40.
228. Narayanan, 1998, 128–129.
229. D. Jurney, ed., *Gems of Guidance: Selections from the Scriptures of the World* (Kidlington, Oxford: George Ronald, Publisher, 1992), 48.
230. G. Kolanad, *Culture Shock: India* (Portland, OR: Graphic Arts Center, 1994), 56.
231. Usha, 1971, 52.
232. Ibid., 1971.
233. Smart, 1998, 87.
234. Usha, 1991, 21–22.
235. N. Jain and E. D. Kussman, "Dominant Cultural Patterns of Hindus in India," in *Intercultural Communication: A Reader,* 9th ed., L. A. Samovar and R. E. Porter, eds. (Belmont, CA: Wadsworth, 2000), 83.
236. Hammer, 1982.
237. Jurney, 1992, 87.
238. Jain and Kussman, 2000, 84.
239. Ibid., 2000, 85.
240. M. K. DeGenova, *Families in Cultural Context: Strengths and Challenges in Diversity* (Mountain View, CA: Mayfield Publishing Company, 1997), 174.
241. Smart, 1998, 87.
242. S. Prabhavanda, *The Spiritual Heritage of India,* 2nd ed. (Hollywood, CA: Vedanta Press, 1969, 335.
243. Ibid.
244. McGuire, 2002, 166.
245. W. T. de Bary, *The Buddhist Tradition in India, China and Japan* (New York: Random House, 1972), vii.
246. N. Thera, *An Outline of Buddhism* (Singapore: Palelai Buddhist Temple Press, n.d.), 19.
247. H. Smith and Novak, *Buddhism: A Concise Introduction* (New York: HarperCollins, 2003), 4.
248. Van Doren, 1991, 21.
249. R. H. Robinson, W. L. Johnson, and T. Bhikku, *Buddhist Religions: A Historical Introduction,* 5th ed. (Belmont, CA: Wadsworth, 2005), 7.
250. Ibid.
251. Crim, 1989, 124.
252. M. D. Echel, "Buddhism," in *The Illustrated Guide to World Religion,* M. D. Coogan, ed. (New York: Oxford University Press, 1998), 166.
253. www.buddhanet.net/e-learning/history/bchron.htm (accessed November 3, 2005).
254. De Bary, 1972, xvii.
255. Smith and Novak, 2003, 3–4.
256. Ibid., 4.
257. W. Rahula, *What the Buddha Taught* (New York: Grove, 1974), 1.
258. Fisher and Luyster, 1991, 103.
259. Rahula, 1974.
260. Richter, Rapple, Modschiedler, and Peterson, 2005, 131.
261. Smith, 1991, 99.
262. W. Metz, "The Enlightened One: Buddhism," in *Eerdmans' Handbook of the World's Religions,* 231–232.
263. A. Solé-Leris, *Tranquility and Insight: An Introduction to the Oldest Form of Buddhist Meditation* (Boston: Shambhala, 1986), 14.
264. Rahula, 1974, 17.
265. Ridenour, 2001, 101.
266. www.buddhanet.net/e-learning/buddhism/bs-s04.htm (accessed April 26, 2005).
267. Smith, 1994, 71.
268. Eckel, 1998, 171.
269. Crim, 1998, 450.
270. Ibid., 1998, 540–541.
271. Rahula, 1974, 45.
272. Smith and Novak, 2003, 39.
273. Solé-Leris, 1986, 19.
274. Smith and Novak, 2003, 42.
275. www.wwzc.org/translations/TheEightfoldPaths.htm (accessed April 27, 2005).
276. www.dusers.drexel.edu/~buddha?Buddhism/Concepts/8FPath.htm (accessed April 27, 2005).
277. Robinson, Johnson, and Thanissaro, 2005, 30.
278. Fisher and Luyster, 1991, 110.
279. Rahula, 1974, 47.
280. Robinson, Johnson, and Thanissaro, 2005, 30.
281. Crim, 1998, 236.
282. Solé-Leris, 1986, 19.
283. Ibid., 1986.
284. www.wwzc.org/translations/TheEightfoldPaths.htm (accessed April 27, 2005).
285. Smith and Novak, 2003, 48.
286. Fisher and Luyster, 1991.
287. W. B. Gudykunst and Y. Y. Kim, *Communicating with Strangers: An Approach to Intercultural Communication* (New York: McGraw-Hill, 2003), 217.
288. R. Brabant-Smith, "Two Kinds of Language," *The Middle Way: Journal of the Buddhist Society,* 68 (1993), 123.
289. Smith, 1994, 68.
290. Thich-Thien-An, *Zen Philosophy, Zen Practice* (Emeryville, CA: Dharma, 1975), 17.
291. Jurney, 1992, 90.
292. B. Bodhi, *Nourishing the Roots and Other Essays on Buddhist Ethics* (Sri Lanka: Buddhist Publication Society, 1978), 7.
293. Smith and Novak, 2003, 56.
294. Ibid., 112.
295. www.sgi-use.org/buddhism/faqs/karma.html (accessed April 28, 2005).
296. Novak, 1994, 67.
297. De Bary, 1972, xix.
298. Smith, 1994, 68.
299. Oldstone-Moore, "Chinese Traditions," in *The Illustrated Guide to World Religion,* M. D. Coogan, ed. (New York: Oxford University Press, 1998), 200.
300. L. E. Harrison, "Promoting Progressive Cultural Change, in *Culture Matters: How Values Shape Human Progress,* L. E. Harrison and S. P. Huntington, eds. (New York: Basic Books, 2000), 296.

301. Gudykunst and Kim, 203, 80.

302. Malefijt, 1968, 197.

303. www.Ubfellowship.org/archive/readers/601_confucianism.htm (accessed November 2, 2005).

304. Crim, 1989, 188–189.

305. W. T. Barry, W. T. Chen, and B. Watson, *Sources of Chinese Tradition* (New York: Columbia University Press, 1960), 17.

306. Z. Lin, "How China Will Modernize," *American Enterprise, 2* (1991).

307. Schneider and Silverman, 1997, 15.

308. Ibid., 1997.

309. Scarborough, 1998, 27.

310. I. P. McGreal, *Great Thinkers of the Eastern World* (New York: HarperCollins, 1995), 3.

311. Crim, 1989, 192.

312. J. Oldstone-Moore, 1998, 205.

313. S. Dragga, "Ethical Intercultural Technical Communication: Looking Through the Lens of Confucian Ethics," in *Intercultural Communication: A Reader*, 11th ed., L. A. Samovar and R. E. Porter, eds. (Belmont, CA: Wadsworth, 2006), 421.

314. Angrosino, 2004, 148.

315. J. O. Yum, "Confucianism and Interpersonal Relationships and Communication Patterns in East Asia," in *Intercultural Communication: A Reader*, 9th ed., L. A. Samovar and R. E. Porter, eds. (Belmont, CA: Wadsworth, 2000), 64.

316. Oldstone-Moore, 1998, 212.

317. www.wckfc.com/article/ANALECT/analect.htm (accessed April 29, 2005).

318. McGreal, 1995, 4.

319. M. J. Gannon, *Understanding Global Cultures: Metaphorical Journeys Through 23 Nations* (Thousand Oaks, CA: Sage Publications, 2001), 423.

320. www.wckfc.com/article/ANALECT/analect.htm (accessed May 2, 2005).

321. Smith, 1994, 111.

322. Gannon, 2001, 424.

323. Smith, 1994.

324. Ibid., 110.

325. M. Soeng, *Trust Your Mind* (Boston: Wisdom Publications, 2004), 42.

326. Yum, 2000, 68.

327. G. Chen and J. Chung, "The Impact of Confucianism on Organizational Communication," *Communication Quarterly, 42* (1994), 97.

328. Novak, 1994, 120.

329. Beamer and Varner, 2001, 251.

330. Soeng, 2004, 43.

331. Gannon, 2001, 147.

332. G. Gao and Ting-Toomey, *Communicating Effectively with the Chinese* (Thousand Oaks, CA: Sage Publications, 1998), 75.

333. Yum, 2000, 70.

334. www.geocities.com/tokyo/springs/6339/Confucianism.html (accessed May 3, 2005).

335. T. L. Friedman, "A War We Can't Win with Guns Only," *San Diego Union-Tribune*, November 28, 2001, B-8.

336. Ibid., 2001.

**CHAPTER 4**

1. D. Tanno and A. Gonzales, "Sites of Identity in Communication and Culture," in *Communication and Identity Across Cultures*, D. Tanno and A. Gonzales, eds. (Thousand Oaks, CA: Sage Publications, 1998), 7.

2. J. S. Pinney, "A Three-Stage Model of Ethnic Identity Development in Adolescence," in *Ethnic Identity: Formation and Transmission Among Hispanics and Other Minorities*, M. E. Bernal and G. P. Knight, eds. (Albany, NY: State University of New York Press, 1993), 62.

3. J. N. Martin and T. K. Nakayama, *Experiencing Intercultural Communication: An Introduction*, 2nd ed. (Boston: McGraw-Hill, 2005), 80.

4. E. M. Greico and R. C. Cassidy, *Overview of Race and Hispanic Origin, Census 2000 Brief*, www.census.gov/prod/2001pubs/c2kbr01-1.pdf, p. 2 (accessed November 2, 2005).

5. A. Brittingham and P. de la Cruz, *Ancestry: 2000, Census 2000 Brief*, www.census.gov/prod/2004pubs/c2kbr-35.pdf, p. 9 (accessed November 2, 2005).

6. Ibid., 3.

7. Ibid., 9.

8. D. Brooks, "All Cultures Are Not Equal," *New York Times*, August 11, 2005, A23.

9. Ibid.

10. H. Cleveland, "The Limits to Cultural Diversity, in *Intercultural Communication: A Reader*, 11th ed., by L. A. Samovar, R. E. Porter, and E. R. McDaniel (Belmont, CA: Thomson-Wadsworth, 2006), 405.

11. M. L. Hecht, R. L. Jackson, II, and S. A. Ribeau, *African American Communication: Exploring Identity and Culture*, 2nd ed. (Mahwah, NJ: Lawrence Erlbaum, 2003), 62.

12. G. A. Yep, "My Three Cultures: Navigating the Multicultural Identity Landscape," in *Readings in Intercultural Communication*, J. N. Martin, T. K. Nakayama, and L. A. Flores, eds. (Boston: McGraw-Hill, 2002), 61.

13. S. Ting-Toomey, "Identity Negotiation Theory: Crossing Cultural Boundaries," in *Theorizing About Intercultural Communication*, W. B. Gudykunst, ed. (Thousand Oaks, CA: Sage Publications, 2005), 212.

14. Martin and Nakayama, 2005, 81.

15. G. Mathews, *Global Culture/Individual Identity* (London: Routledge, 2000), 17.

16. M. Fong, "Identity and the Speech Community," in *Communicating Ethnic and Cultural Identity*, M. Fong and R. Chuang, eds. (Lanham, MD: Rowman and Littlefield, 2004), 6.

17. Ibid.

18. M. W. Lustig and J. Koester, *Intercultural Competence: Interpersonal Communication Across Cultures* (Boston: Allyn and Bacon, 2003), 140.

19. S. Ting-Toomey and L. C. Chung, *Understanding Intercultural Communication* (Los Angeles: Roxbury, 2005), 93.

20. E. Jung and M. L. Hecht, "Elaborating the Communication Theory of Identity: Identity Gaps and Communication Outcomes," *Communication Quarterly, 52*, 2004, 265. See also J.-C. Deschamps and T. Deves, "Regarding the Relationship Between Social Identity and Personal Identity," in *Social Identity* by S. Worchel, J. F. Morales, D. Páez, and J.-C.

Deschamps (Thousand Oaks, CA: Sage Publications, 1998), 1, which states "Identity is a central concept in social psychology, probably because it is one of the main concerns of the field."

21. Lustig and Koester, 2003, 145.

22. Martin and Nakayama, 2005, 82.

23. J. C. Turner, *Rediscovering the Social Group: A Self-Categorization Theory* (Oxford: Basil Blackwell, 1987), 45.

24. B. J. Hall, *Among Cultures*, 2nd ed. (Belmont, CA: Thomson-Wadsworth, 2005), 108–109.

25. Ibid., 109.

26. W. B. Gudykunst, *Bridging Differences: Effective Intergroup Communication*, 4th ed. (Thousand Oaks, CA: Sage Publications, 2004), 77.

27. T. T. Imahori and W. R. Cupach, "Identity Management Theory: Face Work in Intercultural Relations," in W. B. Gudykunst, ed., *Theorizing About Intercultural Communication* (Thousand Oaks, CA: Sage Publications, 2005), 196.

28. M. J. Collier, "Researching Cultural Identity: Reconciling Interpretive and Postcolonial Perspectives," in *Communication and Identity Across Cultures*, D. V. Tanno and A. Gonzalez, eds. (Thousand Oaks, CA: Sage Publications, 1998), 127.

29. G. W. Allport, *The Nature of Prejudice* (Reading, MA: Addison-Wesley, 1954), 111.

30. Fong, 2004, 14.

31. T. Sowell, *Race and Culture: A World View* (New York: Basic Books, 1994), 6.

32. K. A. Ocampo, M. E. Bernal, and G. P. Knight, "Gender, Race, and Ethnicity: The Sequencing of Social Constancies," in *Ethnic Identity: Formation and Transmission among Hispanic and Other Minorities* (Albany, NY: State University of New York Press, 1993), 15.

33. A. D. Buckley and M. C. Kenney, *Negotiating Identity: Rhetoric, Metaphor, and Social Drama in Northern Ireland* (Washington, DC: Smithsonian Institution Press, 1995), 212.

34. Collier, 1998, 38; See also Ting-Toomey, 2005, 96–97.

35. V. Chen, "(De)hyphenated Identity: The Double Voice of *The Woman Warrior*" in *Our Voices*, 4th ed., A. González, M. Houston, and V. Chen, eds. (Los Angeles: Roxbury, 2004), 20.

36. Martin and Nakayama, 2005, 102.

37. Ting-Toomey, 2005, 213.

38. O. James, "Media's View of Beauty Is Not Good for Women," *Japan Times*, July 23, 2005, 19.

39. M. Fong and R. Chuang, *Communicating Ethnic and Cultural Identity* (Lanham, MD: Rowman and Littlefield, 2004), 30.

40. T. R. Reid, *The United States of Europe* (New York: Penguin Press, 2004), 200.

41. Allport, 1954, 116.

42. H. Hirayama, *Breakthrough Japanese* (Tokyo: Kodansha, 2004), 15–16.

43. H. Markus and S. Kitayama, "Culture and the Self: Implications for Cognition, Emotion, and Motivation," *Psychological Review*, 98 (1991) 224.

44. J. Suler, "Identity Management in Cyberspace," *Journal of Applied Psychoanalytic Studies*, 4 (2002), 455.

45. Ibid., 457.

46. "On-line Identity—Your 'Avatar,'" *On-Line Gamers Anonymous*, www.olganon.org/Gamer/Ideas_to_Help/Identity/identity.html (accessed November 2, 2005).

47. "Real-Life Character," *The Japan Times*, July 30, 2005, 4.

48. *Comic-Con 2005*, www.comic-con.org. Attendance for 2005 was obtained by an August 18, 2005, phone call to the Comic-Con headquarters in San Diego.

49. Ting-Toomey, 2005, 211.

50. Ibid., 212.

51. Phinney, 1993, 61–79.

52. Ibid., 66.

53. J. N. Martin, R. L. Krizek, T. K. Nakayama, and L. Bradford, "Exploring Whiteness: A Study of Self Labels for White Americans," *Communication Quarterly*, 44 (1996), 125.

54. Phinney, 1993, 69.

55. D. V. Tanno, "Names, Narratives, and the Evolution of Ethnic Identity," *Our Voices*, 4th ed., A. González, M. Houston, and V. Chen, eds. (Los Angeles: Roxbury, 2004), 39.

56. Phinney, 1993, 76.

57. Martin and Nakayama, 2005, 97–98.

58. Ibid., 99–100.

59. Hall, 2005, 117. See also Jung and Hecht, 2004, 265.

60. Hall, 2005, 119.

61. Yep, 2002, 63. See also Jung and Hecht, 2004, 266.

62. D. Molden, "Seven Miles from Independence: The War, Internee Identity and the *Manzanar Free Press*," dissertation, University of Minnesota, 1998, 21–22.

63. A. D. Buckley and M. C. Kenney, *Negotiating Identity: Rhetoric, Metaphor, and Social Drama in Northern Ireland* (Washington, DC: Smithsonian Institution Press, 1995).

64. J. A. Drzewiecka and N. Draznin, "A Polish Jewish American Story: Collective Memories and Intergroup Relations," in L. A. Samovar, R. E. Porter, and E. R. McDaniel, *Intercultural Communication: A Reader*, 11th ed. (Belmont, CA: Thomson-Wadsworth, 2005), 73.

65. H. C. Triandis, *Individualism and Collectivism* (Boulder, CO: Westview Press, 1995), 71. See also Martin and Nakayama, 2005, 84.

66. Y. Nemoto, *The Japanese Education System* (Parkland, FL: Universal Publishers, 1999), 47.

67. H. W. Gardiner and C. Kosmitzki, *Lives Across Cultures*, 2nd ed. (Boston: Allyn and Bacon, 2002), 74.

68. R. Resendes, *The Celebration of the Quinceañera*, gomexico.about.com/cs/culture/a/quinceanera.htm (accessed November 2, 2005).

69. Gardiner and Kosmitzki, 2002, 74.

70. A. Rajji-Kubba, "Living at the Crossroads of Cultures—East and West," *Salt Lake Tribune*, February 16, 2003, AA4.

71. G. David and K. K. Ayouby, "Being Arab and Becoming Americanized: Forms of Mediated Assimilation in Metropolitan Detroit," in *Muslim Minorities in the West*, Y. Y. Haddad and J. I. Smith, eds. (Walnut Creek, CA: Altamira Press, 2002), 131.

72. Ibid.

73. Ibid.

74. Ibid.

75. Hecht, Jackson, and Ribeau, 2003, 61.

76. Hall, 2005, 104.

77. Imahori and Cupach, 2005, 197.

78. M. J. Collier, "Cultural Identity and Intercultural Communication," in *Intercultural Communication: A Reader*, 11th ed., L. A. Samovar, R. E. Porter, and E. R. McDaniel, eds. (Belmont, CA: Thomson-Wadsworth, 2006), 59.

79. J. Brooke, "Embracing the Differences," *San Diego Union Tribune*, December 4, 2004, E-1.

80. "A Survey of America: The Americano Dream Forces," *The Economist*, July 16, 2005, 8.

81. "A Survey of America: Centrifugal Forces," *The Economist*, July 16, 2005.

82. R. Chuang, "Theoretical Perspective: Fluidity and Complexity of Cultural and Ethnic Identity," in *Communicating Ethnic and Cultural Identity*, M. Fong and R. Chuang, eds. (Lanham, MD: Rowman and Littlefield, 2004), 65.

83. J. N. Martin, T. K. Nakayama, and L. A. Flores, "Identity and Intercultural Communication" in *Readings in Intercultural Communication*, J. N. Martin, T. K. Nakayama, and L. A. Flores, eds. (Boston: McGraw-Hill, 2002), 33.

84. Brooke, 2004, E-4.

85. *Daughter from Danang*, www.daughterfromdanang.com (accessed November 2, 2005).

86. Brooke, 2004, E-1.

87. J. Kotkin and T. Tseng, "Happy to Mix It All Up," *Washington Post*, June 8, 2003, B-01.

88. Ibid.

89. J. Hitt, "The Newest Indians," *New York Times Magazine*, August 21, 2005, 38.

90. Ibid.

91. Ibid., 39.

92. L. E. Wynter, *American Skin: Pop Culture, Big Business and the End of White America* (New York: Crown, 2002), 1–10.

93. C. Onwumechili, P. O. Nwosu, R. L. Jackson II, and J. James-Hughes, "In the Deep Valley with Mountains to Climb: Exploring Identity and Multiple Reacculturation," *International Journal of Intercultural Relations*, 27 (2003), 42.

94. Ibid., 40, 50.

95. "A Spin with Carlos Ghosn," www.businessweek.com, October 4, 2004, www.businessweek.com/magazine/content/04_40/b3902020.htm (accessed November 2, 2005). See also "Nissan's Boss," www.businessweek.com, October 4, 2004, www.businessweek.com/magazine/content/04_40/b3902012.htm (accessed November 2, 2005).

96. C. Ghosn, "Creating Value Across Cultures," www.globalagendamagazine.com, www.globalagendamagazine.com/2004/carlosghosn.asp (accessed November 2, 2005).

97. Hitt, 2005, 40.

98. S. Worchel, " Developmental View of the Search for Group Identity," in *Social Identity*, S. Worchel, J. F. Morales, D. Páez, and J-C. Deschamps (Thousand Oaks, CA: Sage Publications, 1998), 56.

99. Adapted from G. Coombs and Y. Sarason, "Culture Circles: A Cultural Self-Awareness Exercise," *Journal of Management Education*, 22 (1998), 218–226.

100. Ibid.

## CHAPTER 5

1. N. Dresser, *Multicultural Manners* (New York: Wiley, 1996), 89–90.

2. M. Singer, *Intercultural Communication: A Perceptual Approach* (Englewood Cliffs, NJ: Prentice Hall, 1987), 9.

3. T. K. Gamble and M. Gamble, *Communication Works*, 5th ed. (New York: McGraw-Hill, 1996), 77.

4. Singer, 1987, 9.

5. J. W. Bagby, "A Cross-Cultural Study of Perceptual Predominance in Binocular Rivalry," *Journal of Abnormal and Social Psychology*, 54 (1957), 331–334.

6. G. Guilmet, "Maternal Perceptions of Urban Navajo and Caucasian Children's Classroom Behavior," *Human Organization*, 38 (1979), 87–91.

7. S. W. King, Y. Minami, and L. A. Samovar, "A Comparison of Japanese and American Perceptions of Source Credibility,"

*Communication Research Reports*, 2 (1985), 76–79.

8. R. B. Adler and G. Rodman, *Understanding Human Communication*, 5th ed. (Fort Worth, TX: Harcourt Brace Jovanovich, 1994), 37.

9. W. B. Gudykunst, *Bridging Differences: Effective Intergroup Communication*, 2nd ed. (Thousand Oaks, CA: Sage Publications, 1994), 67.

10. P. R. Harris and R. T. Moran, *Managing Cultural Differences: Leadership Strategies for a New World of Business* (Houston, TX: Gulf, 1996), 274.

11. H. C. Triandis, "Cultural Influences upon Perception," in *Intercultural Communication: A Reader*, 2nd ed., L. A. Samovar and R. E. Porter, eds. (Belmont, CA: Wadsworth, 1976), 119.

12. N. J. Adler, *International Dimensions of Organizational Behavior*, 4th ed. (Cincinnati, OH: South-Western College Publishing, 2002), 77.

13. Adler, 2002, 78.

14. E. M. Rogers and T. M. Steinfatt, *Intercultural Communication* (Prospect Heights, IL: Waveland Press, 1999), 81.

15. L. D. Purnell and B. J. Paulanka, "Transcultural Diversity and Health Care," in *Transcultural Health Care: A Culturally Competent Approach*, L. D. Purnell and B. J. Paulanka, eds. (Philadelphia: F. A. Davis, 1998), 3.

16. M. Rokeach, *The Nature of Human Values* (New York: Free Press, 1973), 161.

17. S. Nanda and R. L. Warms, *Cultural Anthropology*, 6th ed. (Belmont, CA: Wadsworth, 1998), 49.

18. G. Hofstede, *Culture's Consequence: Comparing Values, Behaviors, Institutions, and Organizations Across Nations*, 2nd ed. (Thousand Oaks, CA: Sage Publications, 2001), 5.

19. E. Albert, "Value System," in *The International Encyclopedia of the Social Sciences*, vol. 16 (New York: Macmillan, 1968), 32.

20. Hofstede, 2001, 6.

21. Rokeach, 1973, 5.

22. Hofstede, 2001, 6.

23. G. Gao and S. Ting-Toomey, *Communicating Effectively with the*

*Chinese* (Thousand Oaks, CA: Sage Publications, 1998), 39.

24. M. H. Bond, *Beyond the Chinese Face: Insights from Psychology* (New York: Oxford University Press, 1991), 41.

25. S. P. Huntington, "Cultures Count," in *Culture Matters: How Values Shape Human Progress*, L. E. Harrison and S. P. Huntington, eds. (New York: Basic Books, 2000), xiii.

26. L. Damen, *Culture-Learning: The Fifth Dimension in the Language Classroom* (Reading, MA: Addison-Wesley, 1987), 110.

27. E. W. Lynch, "Conceptual Framework: From Culture Shock to Cultural Learning," in *Developing Cross-Cultural Competence: A Guide for Working with Young Children and Their Families*, 2nd ed., E. W. Lynch and M. J. Hanson, eds. (Baltimore: Paul H. Brookes, 1998), 27.

28. Ibid., 24.

29. Ibid., 25.

30. L. P. Goodson, *Afghanistan's Endless War: State Failure, Regional Politics and the Rise of the Taliban* (Seattle: University of Washington Press, 2001), 12–13.

31. J. Challenger, "Career Pros: Women Taking Over by Degrees, *California Job Journal*, www.jobjournal.com/article_full_text.asp?artid=935 (accessed November 3, 2005).

32. M. J. Gannon, *Understanding Global Cultures*, 3rd ed. (Thousand Oaks, CA: Sage Publications, 2004), 11–14.

33. F. Trompenaars and C. Hampden-Turner, *Riding the Waves of Culture: Understanding Diversity in Global Business*, 2nd ed. (New York: McGraw-Hill, 1998), 8–11.

34. M. Grondona, "A Cultural Typology of Economic Development," in *Culture Matters: How Values Shape Human Progress*, L. E. Harrison and S. P. Huntington, eds. (New York: Basic Books, 2000), 44–55.

35. G. R. Weaver, "Contrasting and Comparing Cultures," in *Culture, Communication and Conflict*, 2nd ed., R. G. Weaver, ed. (Boston: Pearson, 2000), 72–77.

36. J. M. Charon, *The Meaning of Sociology*, 6th ed. (Upper Saddle River, NJ: Prentice Hall, 1999), 99.

37. Ibid.

38. E. Y. Kim, *The Yin and Yang of American Culture: A Paradox* (Yarmouth, ME: Intercultural Press, 2001), xv.

39. For a more detailed discussion of American values, see Adler and Rodman, 1994, 388–389; J. J. Berman, ed., *Cross-Cultural Perspectives* (Lincoln: University of Nebraska Press, 1990), 112–113; G. Althen, *American Ways*, 2nd ed. (Yarmouth, ME: Intercultural Press, 2003), 3–33; Kim, 2001; J. L. Nelson, *Values and Society* (Rochelle, NJ: Hayden, 1975), 90–95; E. C. Stewart and M. J. Bennett, *American Cultural Patterns: A Cross-Cultural Perspective* (Yarmouth, ME: Intercultural Press, 1991); Trenholm and Jensen, 1992, 156–158; R. M. Williams, *American Society: A Sociological Interpretation*, 3rd ed. (New York: Knopf, 1970).

40. Stewart and Bennett, 1991, 133.

41. Gannon, 2004, 209.

42. S. P. Huntington, "The West Unique, Not Universal," *Foreign Affairs*, November/December 1996, 33.

43. Kim, 2001, 35.

44. M. J. Hanson, "Families with Anglo-European Roots," in *Developing Cross-Cultural Competence: A Guide for Working with Children and Their Families*, 2nd ed., E. W. Lynch and M. J. Hanson, eds. (Baltimore: Paul H. Brookes, 1998), 103.

45. Althen, 2003, 15.

46. J. J. Macionis, *Society: The Basics*, 4th ed. (Upper Saddle River, NJ: Prentice Hall, 1998), 37.

47. Ibid.

48. Hanson, 1998, 104–105.

49. Stewart and Bennett, 1992, 119.

50. Althen, 2003, 27.

51. M. E. Clark, "Changes in Euro-American Values Needed for Sustainability," *Journal of Social Issues*, 51 (1995), 72.

52. Clark, 1995, 72.

53. Macionis, 1998, 36.

54. Hanson, 1998, 105.

55. Althen, 2003, 18.

56. Hanson, 1998, 105.

57. Althen, 2003, 19.

58. J. H. McElroy, *American Beliefs* (Chicago: Ivan R. Dee, 1999), 37.

59. "Winning isn't everything, it's the only thing," *The New Dictionary of Cultural Literacy*, 3rd ed., www.bartleby.com/59/3/winningisnte.html (accessed November 3, 2005).

60. Kim, 2001, 40.

61. Ibid.

62. Ibid., 42.

63. Harris and Moran, 1996, 316.

64. G. Hofstede, *Culture's Consequences: International Differences in Work-Related Values*, 2nd ed. (Beverly Hills, CA: Sage Publications, 2001). See also G. Hofstede, *Cultures and Organizations: Software of the Mind* (London: McGraw-Hill, 1991).

65. Hofstede, 2001, xix.

66. J. O. Yum, "The Impact of Confucianism on Interpersonal Relationships and Communication Patterns," in *Intercultural Communication: A Reader*, 8th ed., L. A. Samovar and R. E. Porter, eds. (Belmont, CA: Wadsworth, 1997), 78.

67. S. Ting-Toomey, *Communicating Across Cultures* (New York: Guilford Press, 1999), 67.

68. H. C. Triandis, *Individualism and Collectivism* (Boulder, CO: Westview Press, 1995). See also H. C. Triandis, "Cross-Cultural Studies of Individualism and Collectivism," in *Cross-Cultural Perspectives*, J. J. Berman, ed. (Lincoln: University of Nebraska Press, 1990), 41–133.

69. R. Brislin, *Understanding Culture's Consequence on Behavior*, 2nd ed. (Fort Worth, TX: Harcourt College Publishers, 2000), 53.

70. P. A. Andersen, M. L. Hecht, G. D. Hoobler, and M. Smallwood, "Nonverbal Communication Across Cultures," in *Cross-Cultural and Intercultural Communication*, W. B. Gudykunst, ed. (Thousand Oaks, CA: Sage Publications, 2003), 77.

71. Triandis, 1995.

72. D. Goleman, "The Group and Self: New Focus on a Cultural Rift," *New York Times*, December 22, 1990, 40.

73. D. A. Foster, *Bargaining Across Borders* (New York: McGraw-Hill, 1992), 267.

74. S. P. Morreale, B. H. Spitzberg, and J. K. Barge, *Human Communication: Motivation, Knowledge and Skills* (Belmont, CA: Wadsworth, 2001), 311.

75. P. Andersen, "In Different Dimensions: Nonverbal Communication and Culture," in *Intercultural Communication: A Reader,* 10th ed., L. A. Samovar and R. E. Porter, eds. (Belmont, CA: Wadsworth, 2003).

76. Hanson, 1998, 105.

77. R. D. Lewis, *When Cultures Collide: Managing Successfully Across Cultures* (London: Nicholas Brealey, 2000), 167.

78. Hofstede, 2001, 236.

79. Triandis, 1990, 52.

80. H. C. Triandis, "Collectivism and Individualism as Cultural Syndromes," *Cross-Cultural Research,* 27 (1993), 160.

81. Y. Richmond and P. Gestrin, *Into Africa* (Yarmouth, ME: Intercultural Press, 1998), 2.

82. D. Etounga-Manguelle, "Does Africa Need a Cultural Adjustment Program," in *Culture Matters: How Values Shape Human Progress,* in L. E. Harrison, ed. (New York: Basic Books, 2000), 71.

83. M. Meyer, *China* (Totowa, NJ: Rowman and Littlefield, 1994), 54.

84. M. L. Hecht, M. J. Collier, and S. A. Ribeau, *African American Communication: Ethnic Identity and Interpretation* (Newbury Park, CA: Sage Publications, 1993), 97.

85. J. Luckmann, *Transcultural Communication in Nursing* (Albany, NY: Delmar Publishers, 1999), 29.

86. M. Kim, W. F. Sharkey, and T. Singelis, "Explaining Individualist and Collective Communication—Focusing on the Perceived Importance of Interactive Constraints," paper presented at the Annual Convention of the Speech Communication Association, Chicago, October 1992.

87. S. Ting-Toomey and J. G. Oetzel, "Cross-Cultural Face Concerns and Conflict Styles," in *Cross-Cultural and Intercultural Communication,* W. B. Gudykunst, ed. (Thousand Oaks, CA: Sage Publications, 2003), 134–136.

88. G. Hofstede, "Cultural Differences in Teaching and Learning," *International Journal of Intercultural Relations,* 10 (1986), 301–319.

89. L. Schneider and A. Silverman, *Global Sociology: Introducing Five Contemporary Societies* (New York: McGraw-Hill, 1997), 48.

90. E. Marx, *Breaking Through Culture Shock* (London: Nicholas Brealey, 1999), 51.

91. Hofstede, 1986, 308.

92. Ibid., 301–319.

93. Hofstede, 2000, 169.

94. Lewis, 2000, 65

95. Harris and Moran, 1996, 217.

96. G. Hofstede, "The Cultural Relativity of the Quality of Life Concept," in *Cultural Communication and Conflict: Readings in Intercultural Relations,* 2nd ed., G. R. Weaver, ed. (Boston: Pearson, 2000), 139.

97. Foster, 1992, 265.

98. W. B. Gudykunst, *Asian American Ethnicity and Communication* (Thousand Oaks, CA: Sage Publications, 2001), 41.

99. D. Etounga-Manguelle, 2000, 68.

100. Adler, 2002, 56–57.

101. Brislin, 2000, 288.

102. C. Calloway-Thomas, P. J. Cooper, and C. Blake, *Intercultural Communication: Roots and Routes* (Boston: Allyn and Bacon, 1999), 196.

103. Hofstede, 2001, 107–108.

104. Adler, 2002, 61, 70.

105. Hofstede, 2001, 280.

106. "Ireland," *Global Database of Quotas for Women,* www.quotaproject.org/displayCountry.cfm?CountryCode=IE (accessed November 3, 2005).

107. Adler, 2002, 61.

108. Hofstede, 2000, 139.

109. "Sweden," *Global Database of Quotas for Women,* http://www.quotaproject.org/displayCountry.cfm?CountryCode=SE (accessed November 3, 2005).

110. Kim, 2001, 50.

111. Adler, 2002, 61.

112. Gudykunst, 2001, 47.

113. Hofstede 2001, 251.

114. Chinese Culture Connection, "Chinese Values and the Search for Culture-Free Dimensions of Culture," *Journal of Cross-Cultural Psychology,* 18 (1987), 143–164. See also G. Hofstede and M. H. Bond, "Confucius and Economic Growth: New Trends in Culture's Consequence," *Organizational Dynamics,* 16 (1988), 4–21.

115. Hofstede, 2001, 351.

116. Ibid., 360, 366–367.

117. F. R. Kluckhohn and F. L. Strodtbeck, *Variations in Value Orientations* (New York: Row and Peterson), 1960.

118. Stewart and Bennett, 1991.

119. R. L. Kohls, *Survival Kit for Overseas Living* (Chicago: Intercultural Network/SYSTRAN, 1979), 22.

120. M. L. Borrowman, "Traditional Values and the Shaping of American Education," in J. H. Chilcott, N. C. Greenberg, and H. B. Wilson, eds., *Readings in the Socio-Cultural Foundations of Education* (Belmont, CA: Wadsworth, 1968), 175.

121. L. Stevenson and D. L. Haberman, *Ten Theories of Human Nature,* 3rd ed. (New York: Oxford University Press, 1998), 4.

122. Ibid., 1998, 74–75.

123. Ibid., 1998, 28.

124. N. C. Jain and E. D. Kussman, "Dominant Cultural Patterns of Hindus in India," in *Intercultural Communication: A Reader,* 9th ed., L. A. Samovar and R. E. Porter, eds. (Belmont, CA: Wadsworth, 2000), 89.

125. L. D. Purnell, "Mexican Americans," in *Transcultural Health Care: A Culturally Competent Approach,* L. D. Purnell and B. J. Paulanka, eds. (Philadelphia: F. A. Davis, 1998), 411.

126. J. R. Joe and R. S. Malach, "Families with Native American Roots," in *Developing Cross-Cultural Competence,* 2nd ed., E. W. Lynch and M. J. Hanson, eds. (Baltimore: Paul H. Brookes, 1998), 137.

127. Adler, 2002, 25.

128. G. C. Chu and Y. Ju, *The Great Wall in Ruins* (Albany, NY: SUNY Press), 222–223.

129. E. T. Hall and M. R. Hall, *Understanding Cultural Differences* (Yarmouth, ME: Intercultural Press, 1990), 87.

130. A. C. Wilson, "American Indian History or Non-Indian Perceptions of American History?" in *Natives and Academics: Researching and Writing About American Indians,* D. A. Mihesuah, ed. (Lincoln, NE: University of Nebraska Press, 1998), 24.

131. Trompenaars and Hampden-Turner, 1998, 142.
132. Lewis, 2000, 65.
133. Ting-Toomey, 1999, 62.
134. Luckmann, 1999, 31.
135. N. J. Adler and M. Jelinek, "Is 'Organization Culture' Culture Bound?" in *Culture, Communication and Conflict: Readings in Intercultural Relations*, 2nd ed., G. R. Weaver, ed. (Boston: Pearson, 2000), 130.
136. Gannon, 2004, 74.
137. Kim, 2001, 115.
138. Gannon, 2004, 282.
139. R. Newman, "The Virtues of Silence," *Time*, June 2, 1997, 15.
140. Hecht, Collier, and Ribeau, 1993, 102–103.
141. L. Skow and L. A. Samovar, "Cultural Patterns of the Maasai," in *Intercultural Communication: A Reader*, 8th ed., L. A. Samovar and R. E. Porter, eds. (Belmont, CA: Wadsworth, 1997), 110.
142. E. T. Hall, *Beyond Culture* (Garden City, NY: Doubleday, 1976), 91.
143. Ibid., 85.
144. Hall and Hall, 1990, 6.
145. Hall, 1976, 91.
146. Hofstede, 2001, 30.
147. Hall and Hall, 1990, 6.
148. P. Andersen, "Cues of Culture: The Basis of Intercultural Differences in Nonverbal Communication," in *Intercultural Communication: A Reader*, 8th ed., L. A. Samovar and R. E. Porter, eds. (Belmont, CA: Wadsworth, 1997), 253.
149. Foster, 1992, 280.
150. Gudykunst, 2001, 32.
151. Hall and Hall, 1990, 7.
152. Lynch, 1998, 69.
153. Althen, 2003, 42.
154. S. Ting-Toomey, "Managing Intercultural Conflicts Effectively," in *Intercultural Communication: A Reader*, 8th ed., L. A. Samovar and R. E. Porter, eds. (Belmont, CA: Wadsworth, 1997), 394.
155. Harris and Moran, 1996, 25.
156. S. Ting-Toomey and A. Kurogi, "Facework Competence in Intercultural Conflict: An Updated Face-Negotiation Theory," *International Journal of Intercultural Relations*, 22 (1998), 187.
157. S. Ting-Toomey, "The Matrix of Face: An Updated Face-Negotiation Theory," in *Theorizing About*

158. B.-A. K. Cocroft and S. Ting-Toomey, "Facework in Japan and the United States," *International Journal of Intercultural Relations*, 18 (1994), 469.
159. Stewart and Bennett, 1991, 138.
160. W. B. Gudykunst and T. Nishida, *Bridging Japanese/North American Differences* (Thousand Oaks, CA: Sage Publications, 1994), 79.
161. R. M. March, *Reading the Japanese Mind* (Tokyo: Kodansha, 1996), 28.
162. G. Gao and S. Ting-Toomey, *Communicating Effectively with the Chinese* (Thousand Oaks, CA: Sage Publications), 54.
163. M.-S. Kim, *Non-Western Perspectives on Human Communication* (Thousand Oaks, CA: Sage Publications, 2002), 65.
164. Gudykunst and Nishida, 1994, 79.
165. S. Ting-Toomey and A. Kurogi, "Facework Competence in Intercultural Conflict: An Updated Face-Negotiation Theory," *International Journal of Intercultural Relations*, 22, (1998), 202.
166. March, 1996, 108.
167. Ting-Toomey and Kurogi, 1998, 202.

**CHAPTER 6**
1. N. Bonvillain, *Language, Culture, and Communication: The Meaning of Messages*, 4th ed. (Upper Saddle River, NJ: Prentice Hall, 2003), 1.
2. L. Thomas, *A Long Line of Cells* (New York: Book-of-the-Month Club, 1990), 68.
3. S. Pinker, *The Language Instinct: How the Mind Creates Language* (New York: Harper Perennial Classics, 2000), 1.
4. Ibid., 5.
5. M. Cartmill, "The Gift of Gab," *Discover*, November 1998, 56.
6. M. P. Orbe and T. M. Harris, *Interracial Communication: Theory into Practice* (Belmont, CA: Wadsworth, 2001), 50.
7. M. Saville-Troike, *The Ethnography of Communication: An Introduction*, 3rd ed. (Madden, MA: Blackwell Publishing, 2003), 13.
8. S. I. Hawakawa and A. R. Hawakawa, *Language and*

*Intercultural Communication*, W. B. Gudykunst, ed. (Thousand Oaks, CA: Sage Publications, 2005), 73.

*Translation*, 3rd ed. (Orlando, FL: Harcourt, 1990), 6.
9. G. Philipsen, "Speech and the Communal Function in Four Cultures" in S. Ting-Toomey and F. Korzenny, eds., *Language, Communication, and Culture: Current Directions*, International and Intercultural Communication Annual, vol. 13 (Newbury Park, CA: Sage Publications, 1989), 79.
10. Saville-Troike, 2003, 12–13.
11. P. Drew, "Conversation Analysis" in K. L. Fitch and R. E. Sanders, eds., *Handbook of Language and Social Interaction* (Mahwah, NJ: Lawrence Erlbaum, 2005), 74.
12. N. Rapport and J. Overing, *Social and Cultural Anthropology: The Key Concepts* (New York: Routledge, 2000), 88.
13. R. D. Coertze, "Intercultural Communication and Anthropology," *South African Journal of Ethnology*, 23, nos. 2–3 (2000), 117.
14. D. Crystal, *The Cambridge Encyclopedia of Language*, 2nd ed. (Cambridge, NJ: Cambridge University Press, 1997), 10.
15. Ibid., 13.
16. Ibid., 12.
17. R. Brislin, *Understanding Culture's Influence on Behavior*, 2nd ed. (Fort Worth, TX: Harcourt College Publishers, 2000), 112.
18. Crystal, 1997, 12.
19. Ibid., 13.
20. Ibid., 38.
21. G. Philipsen, "Speech and the Communal Function in Four Cultures" in S. Ting-Toomey and F. Korzenny, eds., *Language, Communication, and Culture: Current Directions*, International and Intercultural Communication Annual, vol. 13 (Newbury Park, CA: Sage Publications, 1989), 81.
22. Saville-Troike, 2003, 28.
23. Edwards, *Language, Society, and Identity* (Oxford, UK: Blackwell, 1985), 15.
24. Crystal, 1997, 34; *Wikipedia*, 2005, http://en.wikipedia.org/wiki/Basque_language (accessed November 8, 2005).
25. J. Andrews, "Cultural Wars," *Wired*, May 1995, 134.

26. *San Diego Union-Tribune*, February 13, 1997, A-20.
27. *Newsweek*, February 3, 1997, 4.
28. Andrews, 1995, 134.
29. Ibid.
30. B. D. Rubin, *Communication and Human Behavior*, 3rd ed. (Englewood Cliffs, NJ: Prentice Hall, 1992), 92.
31. Honig, *Handbook for Teaching Korean-American Students* (California Department of Education, 1992), 66.
32. California Department of Education, *Handbook for Teaching Vietnamese-Speaking Students* (California Department of Education, 1994), 29.
33. B. Honig, *Handbook for Teaching Filipino-Speaking Students* (California Department of Education, 1986), 27.
34. S. Nanda and R. L. Warms, *Cultural Anthropology*, 6th ed. (Belmont, CA: Wadsworth, 1998), 69.
35. J. C. Scott, "Differences in American and British Vocabulary: Implications for International Business Communication," *Business Communication Quarterly*, 63 (4), 2000 (extracted from *Proquest* database March 23, 2003), 1–2.
36. Ibid., 2.
37. Swain, "How to Communicate with People Who Speak English as a Second Language (ESL), *Et Cetera*, Summer 2000, 140, 12.
38. I. Reineke, *Language and Dialect in Hawaii* (Honolulu: University of Hawaii Press, 1969), 28–30.
39. W. Sloan, "Lapps' Ski-Doos Put Rudolph in Back Seat," *Christian Science Monitor*, December 7, 1995, 7.
40. Ibid.
41. W. V. Ruch, *International Handbook of Corporate Communication* (Jefferson, ND: McFarland, 1989), 174.
42. B. L. Whorf, *Language, Thought, and Reality: Selected Writings of Benjamin Lee Whorf*, I. B. Carroll, ed. (Cambridge, MA: MIT Press, 1940/1956), 239.
43. D. G. Mandelbaum, ed., *Selected Writings of Edward Sapir* (Berkeley and Los Angeles: University of California Press, 1949), 162.

44. B. I. Kodish, "What We Do with Language—What It Does to Us," *ETC: A Review of General Semantics*, Winter 2003–2004, 383–384.
45. Bonvillain, 2003, 61.
46. E. M. Rogers and T. M. Steinfatt, *Intercultural Communication* (Prospect Heights, IL: Waveland Press, 1998), 25.
47. S. Nanda, *Cultural Anthropology*, 4th ed. (Belmont, CA: Wadsworth, 1991), 120.
48. Rogers and Steinfatt, 1998, 25.
49. Nanda, 1991, 121.
50. Bonvillain, 2003, 46.
51. Nanda, 1991, 121.
52. Bonvillain, 2003, 46.
53. R. Young, "English as a Second Language for Navajos," in *A Pluralistic Nation*, M. Lourie and N. Conklin, eds. (Rowley, MA: Newbury House, 1978), 168.
54. Ibid., 121.
55. Bonvillain, 2003, 16.
56. Crystal, 1997, 15.
57. C. Shea, "White Men Can't Contextualize," *Linguafranca*, 11 (6), 2001, 44.
58. Ibid.
59. Ibid., 46.
60. Ibid., 47.
61. Ibid., 49.
62. E. Chaika, *Language: The Social Mirror*, 2nd ed. (New York: Newbury House, 1989).
63. C. Arensberg and A. Nichoff, *Introducing Social Change: A Manual for Americans Overseas* (Chicago: Aldine, 1965), 30.
64. E. S. Kashima and Y. Kashima, "Culture and Language," *Journal of Cross-Cultural Psychology*, 29 (1998), 461–487.
65. R. Ma, "Saying 'Yes' for 'No' and 'No' for 'Yes'" A Chinese Rule, *Journal of Pragmatics*, 25 (1996), 257–266.
66. Ibid., 260.
67. M. B. Marks, "Straddling Cultural Divides with Grace," *Christian Science Monitor*, November 15, 1995, 16.
68. R. Ma, "Language of Offense in the Chinese Culture: The Creation of Corrosive Effects," paper presented at the 92nd Annual Convention of the Speech Communication

Association, November 23–26, 1996, San Diego, California.
69. M. Park and K. Moon-soo, "Communication Practices in Korea," *Communication Quarterly*, 40 (1992), 200.
70. Ibid., 398.
71. Y. Richmond and P. Gestrin, *Into Africa: Intercultural Insights* (Yarmouth, ME: Intercultural Press, 1998), 85.
72. A. N. Miller, "Public Speaking Patterns in Kenya" in *Intercultural Communication: A Reader*, 11th ed., L. A. Samovar and R. E. Porter, eds. (Belmont, CA: Wadsworth, 2006), 238–245.
73. P. Matsumoto and M. Assar, "The Effects of Language on Judgments of Universal Facial Expression of Emotion," *Journal of Nonverbal Behavior*, 16 (1992), 87.
74. Crystal, 1997, 21.
75. Park and Moon-soo, 1992, 399.
76. Saville-Troike, 2003, 12.
77. Richmond and Gerstin, 1998, 75.
78. Ibid., 77.
79. A. N. Miller, "An Exploration of Kenyan Public Speaking Patterns with Implications for the American Introductory Public Speaking Course," *Communication Education*, 51, (2) 2002, 58.
80. Ibid., 59.
81. Richmond and Gerstin, 1988, 77.
82. J. Knappert, *The A–Z of African Proverbs* (London, UK: Karnak House, 1989), 3.
83. K. Yankah, *The Proverb in the Context of Akan Rhetoric: A Theory of Proverb Praxis* (New York: Peter Lang, 1982), 71.
84. Richmond and Gerstin, 1988, 77.
85. A. Almaney and A. Alwan, *Communicating with Arabs* (Prospect Heights, IL: Waveland Press, 1982), 84.
86. J. C. Condon, *Interact: Guidelines for Mexicans and North Americans* (Chicago: Intercultural Press, 1980), 37.
87. A. Riding, *Distinct Neighbors: A Portrait of Mexico* (New York: Knopf, 1985), 8.
88. S. N. Weber, "The Need to Be: The Socio-Cultural Significance of Black Language," in *Intercultural Communication: A Reader*, 7th ed., L. A. Samovar and R. E. Porter, eds.

(Belmont, CA: Wadsworth, 1994), 224.

89. B. Wallraff, "What Global Language?" *The Atlantic Monthly*, November 2000, 54.

90. Ibid., 54.

91. Ibid., 54.

92. D. M. Brown, *Other Tongue to English: The Young Child in the Multicultural School* (London: Cambridge University Press, 1979), 37.

93. S. H. Elgin, *The Language Imperative: How Learning Languages Can Enrich Your Life and Expand Your Mind* (Cambridge, MA: Perseus Books, 2000), xi–xii.

94. Nanda and Warms, 1998, 78.

95. I. R. Carlo-Casellas, "Marketing to U.S. Hispanic Population Requires Analysis of Cultures," *National Underwriter*, January 14, 2002, 9.

96. L. R. Arpan and L. S. Arpan, "Hispanic Connections," *Business and Economic Review*, October–December 2001, 3.

97. Ibid., 5.

98. Ibid., 6.

99. A. Bron, "From an Immigrant to a Citizen: Language as a Hindrance or a Key to Citizenship," *International Journal of Lifelong Education*, 22 (6), November–December 2003, 606.

100. B. L. Shade, "Afro-American Cognitive Style: A Variable in School Success," *Review of Educational Research*, 52 (1982), 219–244.

101. Bonvillain, 2003, 159.

102. M. L. Hecht, M. L. Collier, and S. A. Ribeau, *African American Communication: Ethnic Identity and Cultural Interpretation* (Newbury Park, CA: Sage Publications, 1993), 5.

103. Bonvillain, 2003, 159.

104. Nanda and Warms, 1998, 78.

105. G. Smitherman, *Talkin that Talk: Language, Culture, and Education in African America* (New York: Routledge, 2001).

106. Hecht, Collier, and Ribeau, 1993, 85.

107. J. R. Rickford, "A Suite for Ebony and Phonics," *Discover*, 18 (1997), 3.

108. Crystal, 1997, 35.

109. Rickford, 1997, 3.

110. Ibid.

111. Bonvillain, 2003, 161.

112. Smitherman, 2001, 23.

113. Rickford, 1997, 3.

114. Smitherman, 2001, 23.

115. Crystal, 1997, 35.

116. Rickford, 1997, 3.

117. Ibid.

118. Bonvillain, 2003, 160.

119. Crystal, 1997, 35.

120. Smitherman, 2001, 24.

121. Crystal, 1997, 35.

122. Bonvillain, 2003, 161.

123. Bonvillain, 2003, 181.

124. Ibid.

125. D. Tannen, *You Just Don't Understand: Women and Men in Conversation* (New York: William Morrow, 1990).

126. L. Elium and D. Elium, *Raising a Daughter* (Berkeley, CA: Celestial Arts, 1994), 21.

127. J. T. Wood, *Gendered Lives: Communication, Gender, and Culture* (Belmont, CA: Wadsworth, 1994).

128. Ibid., 142.

129. Ibid.

130. Ibid.

131. Ibid.

132. Ibid.

133. Ibid.

134. J. Holmes, "Hedges and Boosters in Women's and Men's Speech," *Language and Communication*, 10 (1990), 185–202.

135. Bonvillain, 2003, 192.

136. R. Lakoff, *Language and Woman's Place* (New York: Harper and Row, 1975).

137. B. Bate, *Communication Between the Sexes* (New York: Harper and Row, 1988); Holmes, 1990; J. T. Wood and L. F. Lenze, "Gender and the Development of Self: Inclusive Pedagogy in Interpersonal Communication," *Women's Studies in Communication*, 14 (1991), 1–23.

138. Wood, 1994, 143.

139. Holmes, 1990.

140. Tannen, 1990.

141. Wood, 1994, 144.

142. E. Aries, "Gender and Communication," in *Sex and Gender*, P. Shaver and C. Hendricks, eds. (Newbury Park, CA: Sage Publications, 1987), 149–176.

143. A. T. Beck, *Love Is Never Enough* (New York: Harper and Row, 1988); L. P. Steward, A. D. Steward, S. A. Friedley, and P. I. Cooper, *Communication Between the Sexes: Sex Differences and Sex Role Stereotypes*, 2nd ed. (Scottsdale, AZ: Gorsuch Scarisbrick, 1990).

144. Wood, 1994, 144.

145. Ibid., 145.

146. S. Romaine, *Communicating Gender* (Mahwah, NJ: Lawrence Erlbaum, 1999), 165.

147. J. Luckmann, *Transcultural Communication in Nursing* (Albany, NY: Delmar, 1999).

148. M. K. Nydell, *Understanding Arabs: A Guide for Westerners* (Yarmouth, ME: Intercultural Press, 1987), 21.

149. G. Geo and S. Ting-Toomey, *Communicating Effectively with the Chinese* (Thousand Oaks, CA: Sage Publications, 1998), 36.

150. Ibid.

151. Ibid., 36.

152. G. Asselin and R. Mastron, *Au Contraire: Figuring Out the French* (Yarmouth, ME: Intercultural Press, 2001), 37.

153. G. Chen and W. J. Starosta, "Intercultural Communication in the University Classroom" in *Intercultural Communication: A Reader*, 9th ed., L. A. Samovar and R. E. Porter, eds. (Belmont, CA: Wadsworth, 2000), 408.

154. J. Johnson, "The Press Should Show More Sensitivity to Disabled People," *Editor and Publisher*, February 22, 1986, 64.

155. E. W. Lynch and M. J. Hanson, *Developing Cross-Cultural Competence: A Guide for Working with Young Children and Their Families* (Baltimore: Paul H. Brookes, 1992), 44.

156. M. Guirdham, *Communication Across Cultures* (West Lafayette, IN: Purdue University Press, 1999), 243.

**CHAPTER 7**

1. D. C. Barnlund, *Interpersonal Communication: Survey and Studies* (Boston: Houghton Mifflin, 1968), 536–537.

2. M. L. Knapp and J. A. Hall, *Nonverbal Communication in Human Interaction*, 5th ed. (Belmont, CA: Wadsworth, 2002), 230.

3. J. K. Burgoon, D. B. Buller, and W. G. Woodall, *Nonverbal Communication: The Unspoken*

*Dialogue* (New York: Harper and Row, 1989), 9–10.

4. N. Pauronit, "The Role of Verbal/Nonverbal Cues in the Formation of First Impressions of Black and White Counselors," *Journal of Counseling Psychology,* 29 (1982), 371–378.

5. L. K. Guerrero, J. A. DeVito, and M. L. Hecht, *The Nonverbal Communication Reader: Classic and Contemporary Readings,* 2nd ed. (Prospect, IL: Waveland Press, 1999), 9.

6. E. Goffman, *The Presentation of Self in Everyday Life* (New York: Doubleday, 1957), 2.

7. L. A. Malandro and L. L. Barker, *Nonverbal Communication* (Reading, MA: Addison-Wesley, 1983), 13–15; see also P. Ekman and W. Friesen, "The Repertoire of Nonverbal Behavior: Categories, Origins, Usage and Coding," *Simiotica,* 1 (1969), 49–98, and M. L. Knapp and J. A. Hall, 2002, 12–18.

8. J. T. Wood, *Communication Mosaics: A New Introduction to the Field of Communication* (Belmont, CA: Wadsworth, 1998), 105.

9. S. Osborn and M. T. Motley, *Improving Communication* (Boston: Houghton Mifflin, 1999), 50.

10. L. Beamer and Iris Varner, *Intercultural Communication in the Global Workplace* (New York: McGraw-Hill, 2001), 160.

11. J. K. Burgoon, D. B. Buller, and W. G. Woodall, *Nonverbal Communication: The Unspoken Dialogue,* 2nd ed. (New York: McGraw-Hill, 1996), 5.

12. P. C. Rosenblatt, "Grief in Small-Scale Societies," in *Death and Bereavement Across Cultures,* C. M. Parks, P. Laungani, and B. Young, eds. (New York: Routledge, 1997), 36.

13. B. Vandenabeele, "The Need for Essences: On Non-verbal Communication in First Inter-Cultural Encounters," *South African Journal of Philosophy,* 21 (2002), 1.

14. E. T. Hall, *The Silent Language* (New York: Fawcett, 1959), 10.

15. P. Andersen, "Cues of Culture: The Basis of Intercultural Differences in Nonverbal Communication," in *Intercultural Communication: A Reader,* 9th ed., L. A. Samovar and R. E. Porter, eds. (Belmont, CA: Wadsworth, 2000), 258.

16. Andersen, 2000.

17. P. Ekman and W. Friesen, *Unmasking the Face: A Guide to Recognizing Emotions from Facial Expressions* (Englewood Cliffs, NJ: Prentice Hall, 1975). Also see P. Ekman, R. Sorenson, and W. V. Friesen, "Pan-Cultural Elements in Facial Displays of Emotion," *Science,* 64 (1969), 86–88.

18. Burgoon, Buller, and Woodall, 1996, 23.

19. J. J. Macaronis, *Society: The Basics,* 4th ed. (Upper Saddle River, NJ: Prentice Hall, 1998), 92.

20. V. P. Richmond, J. C. McCracken, and S. K. Payne, *Nonverbal Communication in Interpersonal Communication,* 2nd ed. (New Jersey: Prentice Hall, 1991), 13.

21. C. F. Keating, "World without Words: Message from Face and Body," in *Psychology and Culture,* W. J. Lonner and R. S. Malpass, eds. (Boston: Allyn and Bacon, 1994), 175.

22. P. A. Andersen, *Nonverbal Communication: Forms and Functions* (Mountain View, CA: Mayfield, 1999), 31.

23. "Obesity: A Heavy Burden Socially," *San Diego Union-Tribune,* September 30, 1993, A14.

24. J. Berg and K. Piner, "Social Relationships and the Lack of Social Relationships," in *Personal Relationships and Support,* S. W. Duck and R. C. Silver, eds. (London: Sage, 1990), 104–221.

25. B. D. Ruben, *Communication and Human Behavior,* 3rd ed. (Englewood Cliffs, NJ: Prentice Hall, 1992), 213.

26. L. A. Vazquez, E. Garcia-Vazquez, S. A. Bauman, and A. S. Sierra, "Skin Color, Acculturation, and Community Interest Among Mexican American Students: A Research Note," *Hispanic Journal of Behavioral Sciences,* 19 (1997), 337.

27. T. Novinger, *Intercultural Communication: A Practical Guide* (Austin, TX: University of Texas Press, 2001), 73.

28. Knapp and Hall, 2002, 200.

29. G. E. Codina and F. F. Montalvo, "Chicano Phenotype and Depression," *Hispanic Journal of Behavioral Sciences,* 16 (1994), 296–306.

30. F. Keesing, *Cultural Anthropology: The Science of Custom* (New York: Holt, Rinehart, and Winston, 1965), 203.

31. G. Griffen, "Laser Treatments Remove Immigrants' Tattoos, Stigma," *San Diego Union-Tribune,* June 26, 2001, E-7.

32. H. W. Gardiner and C. Kosmitzki, *Lives Across Cultures: Cross-Cultural Human Development,* 2nd ed. (Boston: Allyn and Bacon, 2002), 145.

33. Gardiner and Kosmitzki, 2002, 146.

34. Y. Richmond and P. Gestrin, *Into Africa: Intercultural Insights* (Yarmouth, ME: Intercultural Press, 1998), 45.

35. H. Wenzhong and C. L. Grove, *Encountering the Chinese* (Yarmouth, ME: Intercultural Press, 1991), 135.

36. M. S. Remland, *Nonverbal Communication in Everyday Life* (New York: Houghton Mifflin, 2000), 113.

37. Remland, 2000, 113–114.

38. R. B. Adler and G. Rodman, *Understanding Human Communication,* 8th ed. (New York: Oxford University Press, 2003), 171.

39. N. Joseph, *Uniforms and Nonuniforms: Communication Through Clothing* (New York: Greenwood Press, 1986), 1.

40. N. Dresser, *Multicultural Manners* (New York: Wiley, 1996), 58.

41. M. I. Al-Kaysi, *Morals and Manners in Islam: A Guide to Islamic Arab* (London: The Islamic Press, 1986), 84.

42. T. Gochenour, *Considering Filipinos* (Yarmouth, ME: Intercultural Press, 1990), 59.

43. E. T. Hall and M. R. Hall, *Understanding Cultural Differences: Germans, French and Americans* (Yarmouth, ME: Intercultural Press, 1990), 53.

44. W. V. Ruch, *International Handbook of Corporate Communication* (Jefferson, NC: McFarland, 1989), 166–167.

45. E. McDaniel, "Nonverbal Communication: A Reflection of

Cultural Themes," in *Intercultural Communication: A Reader*, 9th ed., L. A. Samovar and R. E. Porter, eds. (Belmont, CA: Wadsworth, 2000), 274.

46. Ruch, 1989, 242.

47. S. M. Torrawa, "Every Robe He Dons Becomes Him," *Parabola* (Fall, 1994), 21.

48. Torrawa, 1994, 25.

49. S. P. Morreale, B. H. Spitzberg, and J. K. Barge, *Human Communication: Motivation, Knowledge and Skills* (Belmont, CA: Wadsworth/ Thomson Learning, 2001), 125.

50. S. Ishii, "Characteristics of Japanese Nonverbal Communication Behavior," *Communication*, 2 (1973), 163–180.

51. R. Cooper and N. Cooper, *Culture Shock: Thailand* (Portland, OR: Graphic Arts Center, 1994), 14.

52. G. Kolanad, *Culture Shock: India* (Portland, OR: Graphic Arts Center, 1997), 114.

53. Novinger, 2001, 64.

54. G. Ness, *Germany: Unraveling An Enigma* (Yarmouth, ME: Intercultural Press, 2000), 93.

55. D. C. Thomas and K. Inkson, *Cultural Intelligence* (San Francisco: Berrett-Koehler Publishers, 2004), 114.

56. Remland, 2000, 229.

57. Ruch, 1989, 279.

58. Cooper and Cooper, 1994, 22–23.

59. For a more detailed account of posture and other nonverbal differences between males and females, see P. A. Andersen, 1999, 106–129; L. P. Arliss, *Gender and Communication* (Englewood Cliffs, NJ: Prentice Hall, 1991), 87; J. A. Doyle and M. A. Paludi, *Sex and Gender: The Human Experience*, 2nd ed. (Dubuque, IA: Wm. C. Brown, 1991), 235; J. C. Pearson, R. L. West, and L. H. Turner, *Gender and Communication*, 3rd ed. (Dubuque, IA: Wm. C. Brown, 1995), 126; L. P. Steward, P. J. Cooper, and S. A. Friedley, *Communication Between the Sexes: Sex Differences and Sex Role Stereotypes* (Scottsdale, AZ: Gorsuch Scarisbrick, 1986), 75; J. T. Wood, *Gendered Lives: Communication, Gender and Culture*, 6th ed. (Belmont, CA: Wadsworth, 2005), 138.

60. M. L. Hecht, M. J. Collier, and S. A. Ribeau, *African American Communication: Ethnic Identity and Cultural Interpretation* (Newbury Park, CA: Sage Publications, 1993), 102.

61. *San Diego Union-Tribune*, May 20, 1992, D4.

62. Thomas and Inkson, 2004, 115.

63. Dresser, 1996, 19.

64. R. G. Harper, A. N. Wiens, and J. D. Matarazzo, *Nonverbal Communication: The State of the Art* (New York: Wiley, 1978), 164.

65. E. W. Lynch and M. J. Hanson, *Developing Cross-Cultural Competence*, 2nd ed. (Baltimore, MD: Paul H. Brookes, 1998), 74.

66. A. Falassi and R. Flower, *Culture Shock: Italy* (Portland, OR: Graphic Arts Center, 2000), 42.

67. *Handbook for Teaching Korean-American Students* (Sacramento, CA: California Department of Education, 1992), 95.

68. M. K. Nydell, *Understanding Arabs* (Yarmouth, ME: Intercultural Press, 1987), 46.

69. Lynch and Hanson, 1998, 74.

70. R. D. Lewis, *When Cultures Collide: Managing Successfully Across Cultures* (London: Nicholas Brealey, 1999), 135.

71. Falassi and Flower, 2000, 42.

72. J. W. Berry, Y. H. Poortinga, M. H. Segall, and P. R. Dasen, *Crosscultural Psychology: Research and Applications* (New York: Cambridge University Press, 1992), 87–88.

73. T. Novinger, *Communicating with Brazilians* (Austin, TX: University of Texas Press, 2003), 173.

74. J. K. Winter, *Cultures of the World: Chile*, 2nd ed. (New York: Benchmark Books, 1994), 52.

75. Beamer and Varner, 2001, 166.

76. M. Kim, "A Comparative Analysis of Nonverbal Expression as Portrayed by Korean and American Print-Media Advertising," *Howard Journal of Communications*, 3 (1992), 321.

77. R. D. Lewis, 1999, 138.

78. Ruch, 1989, 191.

79. See P. A. Andersen, 1999, 118; Pearson, West, and Turner, 1995, 127.

80. Hecht, Collier, and Ribeau, 1993, 112.

81. M. Patterson, "Evolution and Nonverbal Behavior: Functions and Mediating Processes, *Journal of Nonverbal Behavior*, 3 (2003), 205.

82. Keating, 1994, 181.

83. D. G. Leathers, *Successful Nonverbal Communication: Principles and Applications*, 2nd ed. (New York: Macmillan, 1992), 32.

84. F. Davis, *Inside Intuition* (New York: Signet, 1975), 47. See also Ray L. Birdwhistell, *Kinesics and Context* (Philadelphia: University of Pennsylvania Press, 1970).

85. Ekman, "Face Muscles Talk Every Language," *Psychology Today*, September 1975, 35–39. Also see P. Ekman, W. Friesen, and P. Ellsworth, *Emotion in the Human Face: Guidelines for Research and an Integration of the Findings* (New York: Pergamon Press, 1972); Berry, Poortinga, Seagall, and Dasen, 1992, 81–86.

86. Andersen, 1999, 35.

87. R. E. Porter and L. A. Samovar, "Cultural Influences on Emotional Expression: Implications for Intercultural Communication," in *Handbook of Communication and Emotion: Research, Theory Applications, and Contexts*, P. A. Andersen and L. K. Guerrero, eds. (San Diego, CA: Academic Press, 1998), 454.

88. D. Matsumoto, *Unmasking Japan: Myths and Realities About the Emotions of the Japanese* (Stanford, CA: Stanford University Press, 1996), 54.

89. Matsumoto, 1996, 18–19.

90. Kim, 1992, 321.

91. Wenzhong and Grove, 1991, 116.

92. R. E. Kruat and R. E. Johnson, "Social and Emotional Messages of Smiling," in *The Nonverbal Communication: Classic and Contemporary Reading*, 2nd ed., L. K. Guerro, J. A. De Vito, and H. L. Hecht, eds.(Prospect Heights, IL: Waveland Press, 1999), 75.

93. Nees, 2000, 93.

94. E. R. McDaniel, "Japanese Nonverbal Communication: A Review and Critique of Literature," paper presented at the Annual Convention of the Speech

Communication Association, Miami Beach, FL, November 1993.

95. Matsumoto, 1996, 54.

96. Dresser, 1996, 21.

97. Cooper and Cooper, 1994, 18.

98. Remland, 2000, 193.

99. Pearson, West, and Turner, 1995, 123.

100. "The Evil Eye: A Stare of Envy," *Psychology Today,* December 1977, 154.

101. M. E. Zuniga, "Families with Latino Roots," *Developing Cross-Cultural Competence,* 2nd ed., E. W. Lynch and M. J. Hanson, eds. (Baltimore, MD: Paul H. Brookes, 1998), 231.

102. J. H. Robinson, "Communication in Korea: Playing Things by Ear," in *Intercultural Communication: A Reader,* 9th ed., L. A. Samovar and R. E. Porter, eds. (Belmont, CA: Wadsworth, 2000), 74.

103. D. Leathers, *Successful Nonverbal Communication: Principles and Applications* (New York: Macmillan, 1986), 42.

104. Remland, 2000, 274–275; also see T. K. Gamble and M. W. Gamble, *Contacts: Interpersonal Communication in Theory, Practice and Context* (New York: Houghton Mifflin, 2005), 184.

105. P. A. Andersen and H. Wang, "Unraveling Culture Cues: Dimensions of Nonverbal Communication Across Cultures," in *Intercultural Communication: A Reader,* 11th ed., L. A. Samovar and Richard E. Porter, eds. (Belmont: Wadsworth, 2006), 250–266.

106. H. Triandis, *Culture and Social Behavior* (New York: McGraw-Hill, 1994), 198.

107. E. W. Lynch, "From Culture Shock to Cultural Learning," in *Developing Cross-Cultural Competence: A Guide for Working with Young Children and Their Families,* E. W. Lynch and M. J. Hanson, eds. (Baltimore, MD: Paul H. Brookes, 1992), 19–33.

108. K. S. Verderber and R. F. Verderber, *Inter-Act: Interpersonal Communication Concepts, Skills, and Context,* 9th ed. (Belmont, CA: Wadsworth, 2001), 140.

109. H. Morsbach, "Aspects of Nonverbal Communication in Japan," in *Intercultural*

*Communication: A Reader,* 3rd ed., L. A. Samovar and R. E. Porter, eds. (Belmont, CA: Wadsworth, 1982), 308.

110. Richmond, McCracken, and Payne, 1991, 301.

111. Lewis, 1999, 137.

112. Dresser, 1996, 22.

113. Richmond and Gestrin, 1998, 88.

114. J. Luckmann, *Transcultural Communication in Nursing* (Albany, NY: Delmar, 1999), 57.

115. A. F. Meleis and M. Meleis, "Egyptian-Americans," in *Transcultural Health Care: A Culturally Competent Approach,* L. D. Purnell and B. J. Paulanka, eds. (Philadelphia: F. A. Davis, 1998), 221.

116. Lonner and Malpass, 1994, 180.

117. Beamer and Varner, 2001, 163.

118. Nees, 2000, 93.

119. For a discussion of homosexual nonverbal communication, see J. P. Goodwin, *More Man than You'll Ever Be* (Indianapolis, IN: Indiana University Press, 1989).

120. "Understanding Culture: Don't Stare at a Navajo," *Psychology Today,* June 1974, 107.

121. L. D. Purnell, "Mexican-Americans," in *Transcultural Health Care: A Culturally Competent Approach,* L. D. Parnell and B. J. Paulanka, eds. (Philadelphia: F. A. Davis, 1998), 400.

122. Morreale, Spitzberg, and Barge, 2001, 127.

123. For a more detailed account of gender differences in the use of eye contact and gaze, see P. A. Andersen, 1998, 106–128; M. L. Hickson and D. W. Stacks, *Nonverbal Communication: Studies and Applications,* 3rd ed. (Dubuque, IA: Brown and Benchmark, 1993), 20; D. K. Ivy and P. Backlund, *Exploring Gender Speak: Personal Effectiveness in Gender Communication* (New York: McGraw-Hill, 1994), 226; Remland, 2000, 158–159; J. T. Wood, *Gendered Lives: Communication, Gender, and Culture* (Belmont, CA: Wadsworth, 1994), 164.

124. D. C. Herberg, *Frameworks for Cultural and Racial Diversity* (Toronto, Canada: Canadian Scholars' Press, 1993), 48.

125. J. D. Salinger, *The Catcher in the Rye* (New York: Grosset and Dunlap, 1945), 103.

126. M. L. Knapp and J. A. Hall, *Nonverbal Communication in Human Interaction,* 3rd ed. (Fort Worth, TX: Harcourt Brace Jovanovich, 1992), 230.

127. P. A. Andersen, 1999, 46–47.

128. Ibid., 78.

129. W. B. Gudykunst and Y. Y. Kim, *Communication with Strangers,* 4th ed. (New York: McGraw-Hill, 2003), 256.

130. Dresser, 1996, 16.

131. J. Condon, *Good Neighbors: Communicating with the Mexicans* (Yarmouth, ME: Intercultural Press, 1985), 60.

132. C. Helmuth, *Culture and Customs of Costa Rico* (Westport, CT: Greenwood Press, 2000), 61.

133. L. K. Matocha "Chinese-Americans," in *Transcultural Health Care: A Culturally Competent Approach,* L. D. Parnell and B. J. Paulanka, eds. (Philadelphia: F. A. Davis, 1998), 184.

134. D. Rowland, *Japanese Business Etiquette* (New York: Warner, 1985), 53.

135. Adler and Rodman, 2003, 170.

136. Morreale, Spitzberg, and Barge, 2001, 128.

137. B. Bates, *Communication and the Sexes* (New York: Harper and Row, 1988), 62. See also Pearson, West, and Turner, 1995, 129; Wood, 1994, 162–163.

138. Novinger, 2001, 66.

139. Hecht, Collier, and Ribeau, 1993, 97. See also Burgoon, Buller, and Woodall, 1996, 230; Knapp and Hall, 2002, 293.

140. Leathers, 1986, 138–139.

141. V. P. Richmond, J. C. McCracken, and S. K. Payne, *Nonverbal Communication in Interpersonal Relations,* 2nd ed. (Englewood Cliffs, NJ: Prentice Hall, 1991), 94–109. Also see M. L. Knapp and J. A. Hall, 2002, 386–402.

142. Triandis, 1994, 202.

143. Novinger, 2002, 183.

144. Ruch, 1989, 191.

145. Remland, 2000, 227.

146. Cooper and Cooper, 1994, 31–32.

147. Hecht, Collier, and Ribeau, 1993, 113.

148. M. Houston, "When Black Women Talk with White Women: Why Dialogues Are Difficult," in *Our Voices: Essays in Culture, Ethnicity, and Communication*, 2nd ed., A. Gonzalez, M. Houston, and Victoria Chen, eds. (Los Angeles: Roxbury, 1997), 187–194.

149. A. W. Siegman and S. Feldstein, *Nonverbal Communication and Behavior*, 2nd ed. (Hillsdale, NJ: Lawrence Erlbaum, 1987), 355.

150. Pearson, West, and Turner, 1995, 131. Also see Wood, 1994, 164–165; Ivy and Backlund, 1994, 162–163.

151. M. Argye, "Nonverbal Vocalizations," in *The Nonverbal Communication: Classic and Contemporary Reading*, 2nd ed., L. K. Guerro, J. A. De Vito, and H. L. Hecht, eds. (Prospect Heights, IL: Waveland Press, 1999), 144.

152. Al-Kaysi, 1996, 55.

153. Lynch and Hanson, 1998, 26.

154. L. Skow and L. Samovar, "Cultural Patterns of the Maasai," in *Intercultural Communication: A Reader*, 9th ed., L. A. Samovar and R. E. Porter, eds. (Belmont, CA: Wadsworth, 2000), 97.

155. Richmond, McCracken, and Payne, 1991, 302.

156. McDaniel, 1993, 18.

157. E. T. Hall, *The Silent Language* (New York: Fawcett, 1959). See also Remland, 2000, 148–149.

158. W. B. Gudykunst, S. Ting-Toomey, S. Sudweeks, and L. P. Steward, *Building Bridges: Interpersonal Skills for a Changing World* (Boston: Houghton Mifflin, 1995), 325.

159. P. Andersen, "In Different Dimensions: Nonverbal Communication and Culture," in *Intercultural Communication: A Reader*, 10th ed., L. A. Samovar and R. E. Porter, eds. (Belmont, CA: Wadsworth, 2003), 239.

160. Triandis, 1994, 201.

161. Condon, 1985, 60.

162. Ruch, 1989, 239.

163. Richmond and Gestrin, 1998, 95.

164. Hall and Hall, 1990, 38.

165. M. J. Gannon, *Understanding Global Culture*, 2nd ed. (Thousand Oaks, CA: Sage Publications, 2001), 165.

166. Ibid., 122.

167. L. K. Matocha, 1998, 167.

168. McDaniel, 2000, 274.

169. N. Berkow, R. Richmond, and R. C. Page, "A Crosscultural Comparison of Worldviews: Americans and Fijian Counseling Students," *Counseling and Values*, 38 (1994), 121–135.

170. F. E. Jandt, *An Introduction to Intercultural Communication: Identity in a Global Community*, 4th ed. (Thousand Oaks, CA: Sage Publications, 2004), 140.

171. Chen and Starosta, 1998, 96.

172. A. L. S. Buslig, "Stop Signs: Regulating Privacy with Environmental Features," in *The Nonverbal Communication: Classic and Contemporary Reading*, 2nd ed., L. K. Guerro, J. A. De Vito, and H. L. Hecht, eds. (Prospect Heights, IL: Waveland Press, 1999), 243.

173. Hall and Hall, 1990, 91.

174. Beamer and Varner, 2001, 175.

175. McDaniel, 2000.

176. L. A. Samovar, "Prostitution as a Co-Culture: Speaking Well for Safety and Solidarity, Part II," paper presented at the Western States Communication Association Convention, Vancouver, 1999.

177. M. S. Remland, T. S. Jones, and H. Brinkman, "Interpersonal Distance, Body Orientation, and Touch: Effects of Culture, Gender and Age," *Journal of Social Psychology*, 135 (1995), 282.

178. Leathers, 1986, 236. Also see Andersen, 1998, 115; Remland, 2000, 157–160; Richmond, McCracken, and Payne, 1991, 132; Wood, 1994, 160–162; Pearson, West, and Turner, 1995, 121.

179. L. A. Siple, "Cultural Patterns of Deaf People," *International Journal of Intercultural Relations*, 18 (1994), 345–367.

180. N. Rapport and J. Overing, *Social and Cultural Anthropology: The Key Concepts* (New York: Routledge, 2000), 261.

181. K. L. Egland, M. A. Stelzner, P. A. Andersen, and B. H. Spitzberg, "Perceived Understanding, Nonverbal Communication and Relational Satisfaction," in *Intrapersonal Communication Process*, J. Aitken and L. Shedletsky, eds. (Annandale, VA: Speech Communication Association, 1997), 386–395.

182. A. Gonzalez and P. G. Zimbardo, "Time in Perspective," in *The Nonverbal Communication: Classic and Contemporary Reading*, 2nd ed., L. K. Guerro, J. A. De Vito, and H. L. Hecht, eds. (Prospect Heights, IL: Waveland Press, 1999), 227.

183. Lewis, 2000, 53.

184. D. I. Ballard and D. R. Seibold, "Time Orientation and Temporal Variation Across Work Groups: Implications for Group and Organizational Communication," *Western Journal of Communication*, 64 (2000), 219.

185. M. J. Gannon, *Understanding Global Culture*, 3rd ed. (Thousand Oaks, CA: Sage Publications, 2001), 216.

186. Novinger, 2003, 160.

187. M. Argyle, "Inter-cultural Communication," in *Cultures in Contact: Studies in Cross-Cultural Interaction*, Stephen Bochner, ed. (New York: Pergamon Press, 1982), 68.

188. S. Roraff and L. Camacho, *Culture Shock: Chile* (Portland, OR: Graphic Arts Center Publishing, 1998), 131.

189. Lewis, 2000, 56.

190. Richmond and Gestrin, 1998, 108.

191. Hall and Hall, 1990, 35.

192. E. Y. Kim, *The Yin and Yang of American Culture: A Paradox* (Yarmouth, ME: Intercultural Press, 2001), 115.

193. Andersen and Wang, 2005, 252.

194. G. Asselin and R. Maston, *Au Contraire! Figuring Out the French* (Yarmouth, ME: Intercultural Press, 2001), 233.

195. R. Brislin, *Understanding Culture's Influence on Behavior* (Fort Worth, TX: Harcourt Brace Jovanovich, 1993), 211.

196. P. R. Harris and R. T. Moran, *Managing Cultural Differences*, 4th ed. (Houston, TX: Gulf, 1996), 266.

197. Ruch, 1989, 278.

198. P. Abu Gharbieh, "Arab-American," in *Transcultural Health Care: A Culturally Competent Approach*, L. D. Purnell and B. J. Paulanka, eds. (Philadelphia: F. A. Harris, 1998), 140.

199. R. Levine, "Social Time: The Heartbeat of Culture," *Psychology Today*, March 1985, 35.

200. Richmond, McCracken, and Payne, 1991, 190.

201. S. A. Wilson, "Irish-American," in *Transcultural Health Care: A Culturally Competent Approach,* L. D. Purnell and B. J. Paulanka, eds. (Philadelphia: F. A. Harris, 1998), 357.

202. O. Still and D. Hodgins, "Navajo Indians," in *Transcultural Health Care: A Culturally Competent Approach,* L. D. Purnell and B. J. Paulanka, eds. (Philadelphia: F. A. Harris, 1998), 427–428.

203. J. Carlson et al., "A Multicultural Discussion About Personality Development, "*The Family Journal: Counseling and Therapy for Couples,* 12 (2004), 115.

204. Ibid.

205. N. J. Adler, *International Dimensions of Organizational Behavior,* 2nd ed. (Boston: PWS-KENT, 1991), 30.

206. E. T. Hall, *The Dance of Life: Other Dimensions of Time* (New York: Anchor Press/Doubleday, 1983), 42.

207. P. B. Smith and M. H. Bond, *Social Psychology Across Cultures: Analysis and Perspective* (Boston: Allyn and Bacon, 1994), 149.

208. Novinger, 2003, 161.

209. E. T. Hall, *The Silent Language* (New York: Fawcett, 1959), 19.

210. F. Trompenaars and C. Hampden-Turner, *Riding the Waves of Culture: Understanding Diversity in Global Business,* 2nd ed. (New York: McGraw-Hill, 1998), 143.

211. Smith and Bond, 1999, 147.

212. Gannon, 2004, 84.

213. Dresser, 1996, 26.

214. Richmond and Gestrin, 1998, 109.

215. Ibid., 110.

216. K. Burgoon and T. Saine, *The Unspoken Dialogue: An Introduction to Nonverbal Communication* (Boston: Houghton Mifflin, 1978), 131.

217. J. Horton, "Time and the Cool People," in *Intercultural Communication: A Reader,* 2nd ed., L. A. Samovar and R. E. Porter, eds. (Belmont, CA: Wadsworth, 1976), 274–284. Also see A. L. Smith, D. Hernandez, and A. Allen, *How to Talk with People of Other Races, Ethnic Groups, and Cultures* (Los Angeles: Trans-Ethnic Education, 1971), 17–19.

218. D. Crystal, *The Cambridge Encyclopedia of Language,* 2nd ed. (New York: Cambridge University Press, 1997), 174.

219. C. Braithwaite, "Cultural Uses and Interpretations of Time," in *The Nonverbal Communication: Classic and Contemporary Reading,* 2nd ed., L. K. Guerro, J. A. De Vito, and H. L. Hecht, eds. (Prospect Heights, IL: Waveland Press, 1999), 164.

220. J. Wiemann, V. Chen, and H. Giles, "Beliefs About Talk and Silence in a Cultural Context," paper presented at the Annual Convention of the Speech Communication Association, Chicago, 1986.

221. Beamer and Varner, 2001, 184.

222. Lewis, 1999, 13.

223. D. C. Barnlund, *Communicative Styles of Japanese and Americans: Images and Realities* (Belmont, CA: Wadsworth, 1989), 142.

224. S. Chan, "Families with Asian Roots," in *Developing Cross-Cultural Competence,* 2nd, ed., E. W. Lynch and M. J. Hanson, eds. (Baltimore, MD: Paul H. Brookes, 1998), 321–322.

225. A. Kerr, *Dogs and Demons: Tales from the Dark Side of Japan* (New York: Hill and Wang, 2001), 105

226. A. Jaworski, "The Power of Silence in Communication," in *The Nonverbal Communication: Classic and Contemporary Reading,* 2nd ed., L. K. Guerro, J. A. De Vito, and H. L. Hecht, eds. (Prospect Heights, IL: Waveland Press, 1999), 161.

227. Ibid.

228. N. J. Adler, *International Dimension of Organizational Behavior* (Cincinnati, OH: South-Western, 1997), 217.

229. N. Jain and A. Matukumalli, "The Functions of Silence in India: Implications for Intercultural Communication Research," paper presented at the Second International East Meets West Conference in Cross-Cultural Communication, Comparative Philosophy, and Comparative Religion, Long Beach, CA, 1993, 7.

230. Smith and Bond, 1999, 141.

231. R. L. Johannesen, "The Functions of Silence: A Plea for Communication Research," *Western Speech,* 38 (1974), 27.

232. Still and Hodgins, 1998, 427.

233. K. Basso, "'To Give Up Words:' Silence in Western Apache Culture," *Southwestern Journal of Anthropology,* 26 (1970), 213–230.

234. Pearson, West, and Turner, 1995, 134. Also see Doyle and Paludi, 1991, 226–228.

**CHAPTER 8**

1. M. K. Nydell, *Understanding Arabs: A Guide for Westerners* (Yarmouth, ME: Intercultural Press, 2002), 65.

2. T. Morrison, W.A. Conaway, and G. A. Borden, *Kiss, Bow, or Shake Hands: How to Do Business in Sixty Countries* (Avon, ME: Adams Media Corporation, 1994), 393.

3. A. Javidi and M. Javidi, "Cross-Cultural Analysis of Interpersonal Bonding: A Look at East and West," in *Intercultural Communication: A Reader,* 8th ed., L. A. Samovar and R. E. Porter, eds. (Belmont, CA: Wadsworth, 1997), 89.

4. G. Althen, *American Ways* (Yarmouth, ME: Intercultural Press, 2003), 17.

5. E. C. Stewart and M. J. Bennett, *American Cultural Patterns: A Cross-Cultural Perspective* (Yarmouth, ME: Intercultural Press, 1991), 160.

6. E. T. Hall and M. R. Hall, *Understanding Cultural Differences: Germans, French, and Americans* (Yarmouth, ME: Intercultural Press, 1990), 48.

7. Morrison, Conaway, and Borden, 1994, 171.

8. L. Schneider and A. Silverman, *Global Sociology: Introducing Five Contemporary Societies* (New York: McGraw-Hill, 1997), 70.

9. E. Gareis, *Intercultural Friendships: A Qualitative Study* (New York: University Press of America, 1995), 27.

10. E. Y. Kim, *The Yin and Yang of American Culture: A Paradox* (Yarmouth, ME: Intercultural Press, 2001), 143.

11. L. B. Nadler, M. K. Nadler, and B. Broome, "Culture and the Management of Conflict Situations," in *Communication, Culture and Organizational Processes,* W. B. Gudykunst, L. P. Stewart, and S. Ting-Toomey, eds. (Beverly Hills, CA: Sage Publications, 1985), 109.

12. H. Wenzhong and C. L. Grove, *Encountering the Chinese: A Guide to Americans* (Yarmouth, ME: Intercultural Press, 1991), 63.

13. L. Beamer and I. Varner, *Intercultural Communication in the Global Workplace* (Boston: McGraw-Hill Irwin, 2001), 199. See also, Morrison, Conaway, and Borden, 1993, 191.

14. T. Gochenour, *Considering Filipinos* (Yarmouth, ME: Intercultural Press, 1990), 23.

15. Ibid., 25.

16. Ibid., 24.

17. N. Yoshimura and P. Anderson, *Inside the Kaisha: Demystifying Japanese Business Behavior* (Boston: Harvard Business School Press, 1997), 83.

18. Schneider and Silverman, 1997, 9.

19. "Japan on the Brink," *The Economist*, April 11, 1998, 15.

20. G. Gao and S. Ting-Toomey, *Communicating Effectively with the Chinese* (Thousand Oaks, CA: Sage Publications, 1998), 61.

21. G. Chen and X. Xiao, "The Impact of Harmony on Chinese Negotiations," paper presented at the Annual Convention of the Speech Communication Association, Miami Beach, FL, November 1993, 4.

22. J. Condon, *Good Neighbors: Communicating with the Mexicans* (Yarmouth, ME: Intercultural Press, 1985), 44.

23. W. V. Ruch, *International Handbook of Corporate Communication* (Jefferson, NC: McFarland, 1989), 75.

24. G. P. Ferraro, *The Cultural Dimensions of International Business* (Upper Saddle River, NJ: Prentice Hall, 2002), 106.

25. Beamer and Varner, 2001, 118.

26. Ibid.

27. Morrison, Conaway, and Borden, 1994, 168.

28. C. Engholm, *When Business East Meets Business West* (New York: John Wiley and Sons, 1991), 10.

29. P. D. Curtin, *Cross-Cultural Trade in World History* (New York: Cambridge University Press, 1984), 65.

30. "Marco Polo and His Travels," Silk Road Foundation, www.silk-road.com/artl/marcopolo.shtml (accessed November 21, 2005).

31. F. Cairncross, *The Death of Distance* (Boston: Harvard Business School Press, 1997), 1.

32. M. Crutsinger, "Trade Deficit Hits All-Time Record." CBS News, February 10, 2005, www.cbsnew .com/stories/2005/02/10/ap/business/ printable672878.shtml (accessed November 21, 2005).

33. "Trade Deficit Increased in 2004," U.S. Census Bureau: Foreign Trade Statistics, www.census.gov/ foreign-trade/www/index.html (accessed November 21, 2005).

34. "Top Ten Countries with which the U.S. Has a Trade Deficit," 2005, U.S. Census Bureau: Foreign Trade Statistics, www.census.gov/ foreign-trade/top/dst/2004/12/ deficit.html (accessed November 21, 2005).

35. Crutsinger, 2005.

36. Ibid.

37. T. L. Friedman, "The Unseen Forces of Globalization," *San Diego Union-Tribune*, March 5, 2004, B8.

38. T. L. Friedman, "A Better World Through Outsourcing," *San Diego Union-Tribune*, March 2, 2004.

39. G. J. Bryjak, "Outsourcing the American Dream," *San Diego Union-Tribune*, February 4, 2004.

40. "Coca-Cola: Our Company, Around the World," www2.coca-cola.com/ ourcompany/aroundworld.html (accessed November 21, 2005).

41. McDonald's FAQ, www.mcdonalds .com/corp/about/mcd_faq.html (accessed November 21, 2005).

42. Starbucks Coffee International, www.starbucks.com/aboutus/ international.asp (accessed November 21, 2005).

43. T. R. Reid, *The United States of Europe* (New York: Penguin Press, 2004), 112–116.

44. D. C. Thomas, *Essentials of International Management* (Thousand Oaks, CA: Sage Publications, 2002), 3.

45. P. R. Harris and R. T. Moran, *Managing Cultural Differences: Leadership Strategies for a New World of Business*, 4th ed. (Houston: Gulf Publishing, 1996), 19.

46. Morrison, Conaway, and Borden, 1994, 168.

47. D. Endicott, "Doing Business in Egypt," *Bridge*, Winter 1981, 34.

48. Y. Richmond and P. Gestrin, *Into Africa: Intercultural Insights* (Yarmouth, ME: Intercultural Press, 1998), 128–129.

49. B. Zinzius, *Doing Business in the New China* (Westport, CT: Praeger, 2004), 182.

50. Ibid., 71.

51. Morrison et al., 1994, 326.

52. Zinzius, 2004, 53.

53. Harris and Moran, 1996, 256.

54. Zinzius, 2004, 62.

55. Ibid., 47.

56. Morrison et al., 1994, 118–119.

57. R. Desai, *Indian Business Culture* (Oxford: Butterworth-Heinemann, 1999), 112. See also S. Dunung, *Doing Business in Asia*, 2nd ed. (San Francisco: Jossey-Bass Publishers, 1998), 416, 435.

58. Dunung, 18–19.

59. E. McDaniel and S. Quasha, "The Communicative Aspects of Doing Business in Japan," *Intercultural Communication: A Reader*, 9th ed, L. A. Samovar and R. E. Porter, eds. (Belmont, CA: Wadsworth, 2000), 315.

60. Morrison et al., 1994, 134.

61. F. L. Acuff, *How to Negotiate Anything with Anyone Anywhere Around the World* (New York: American Management Association, 1997), 103.

62. Foreign Corrupt Practices Act (FCPA), www.usdoj.gov/criminal/ fraud/fcpa.html (accessed November 21, 2005).

63. Zinzius, 2004, 63.

64. Acuff, 1997, 104.

65. K. Nishiyama, *Doing Business with Japan* (Honolulu: University of Hawaii Press, 2000), 61.

66. Morrison et al., 1994, 54, 87.

67. Ibid., 145, 208.

68. Dresser, *Multicultural Manners* (New York: Wiley, 1996), 94.

69. J. Scarborough, *The Origins of Cultural Differences and Their Impact on Management* (Westport, CT: Quorum, 1998), 5.

70. D. Thomas, *Essentials of International Management* (Thousand Oaks, CA: Sage Publications, 2002), 27.

71. P. C. Earley and S. Ang, *Cultural Intelligence: Individual Interactions Across Cultures* (Stanford, CA:

Stanford Business Books, 2003), 231.

72. Scarborough, 1998, 64.
73. C. Gordon, *The Business Culture in France* (Oxford: Butterworth–Heinemann, 1996), 164.
74. J. Mattock, ed., *Cross-Cultural Communication* (London: Kogan Page, 2003), 164.
75. Information on contracts comes from a number of sources: Acuff, 1997, 86; N. J. Adler, *International Dimensions of Organizational Behavior*, 4th ed. (Cincinnati, OH: South-Western: Thomson Learning, 2002), 65; C. Cellich and S. C. Jain, *Global Business Negotiations* (Mason, OH: South-Western: Thomson, 2004), 38–39; D. W. Hendon, R. A. Hendon, and P. Herbig, *Cross-Cultural Business Negotiations* (Westport, CT: Quorum Books, 1996), 113; S. C. Schneider and J.-L. Barsoux, *Managing Across Cultures*, 2nd ed. (New York: Prentice Hall, 2003), 30; Zinzius, 2004, 72.
76. Acuff, 1997, 87; see also Hendon, Hendon, and Herbig, 1996, 114.
77. Hendon, Hendon, and Herbig, 1996, 3.
78. L. Drake, "Negotiation Styles in Intercultural Communication," *The International Journal of Conflict Management*, 6 (1), 1995, 76.
79. M. Spangle and M. Isenhart, *Negotiation: Communication for Diverse Settings* (Thousand Oaks, CA: Sage Publications, 2003), 97.
80. A. Goldman, *Doing Business with the Japanese* (Albany: State University of New York Press, 1994), 153.
81. C. Cellich and S. Jain, *Global Business Negotiations* (Cincinnati, OH: South-Western: Thomson Learning, 2004), 12.
82. Hendon, Hendon, and Herbig, 1996, 12. See also R. Lewis, *When Cultures Collide*, 2nd ed. (London: Nicholas Brealey, 1999), 314, and Thomas and K. Inkson, *Cultural Intelligence: People Skills for Global Business* (San Francisco: Berrett-Koehler, 2004), 119.
83. Zinzius, 2004, 48.
84. Hendon, Hendon, and Herbig, 1996, 174.
85. Lewis, 1999, 399.

86. L. Pye, *Chinese Negotiating Style* (New York: Quorum, 1992), 23.
87. Beamer and Varner, 2001, 262.
88. Ibid., 257.
89. Hendon, Hendon, and Herbig, 2004, 140.
90. Pye, 1992, 23.
91. J. W. Salacuse, *The Global Negotiator* (New York: Palgrave Macmillan, 2003), 20.
92. Zinzius, 2004, 72; Pye, 1992, 23.
93. Hendon, Hendon, and Herbig, 2004, 173.
94. Thomas, 2002, 94.
95. Hendon, Hendon, and Herbig, 24.
96. E. R. McDaniel and S. Quasha, "The Communicative Aspects of Doing Business in Japan," in *Intercultural Communication: A Reader*, 9th ed., L. A. Samovar and R. E. Porter, eds. (Belmont, CA: Wadsworth, 2002), 318.
97. T. Kume, "Managerial Attitudes Toward Decision-Making," in *Communication, Culture, and Organizational Processes*, W. B. Gudykunst, L. P. Stewart, and S. Ting-Toomey, eds. (Newbury Park, CA: Sage Publications, 1985), 232.
98. Beamer and Varner, 2001, 236–237.
99. Zinzius, 2004,190.
100. Hendon, Hendon, and Herbig, 210.
101. E. S. Krauss, T. P. Rohlen, and P. G. Seinhoff, "Conflict and Its Resolution in Postwar Japan," in E. S. Krauss, T. P. Rohlen, and P. G. Steinhoff, eds., *Conflict in Japan* (Honolulu: University of Hawaii Press, 1984), 382.
102. F. Cairncross, *The Company of the Future* (Boston: Harvard Business School, 2002), 5.
103. E. R. McDaniel, *Changing Japanese Organizational Communication Patterns* (San Diego, CA: SDSU Center for International Business Education and Research, 2004), CIBER Working Paper Series – Publication No. C04-016.
104. R. J. Fouser, "'Culture,' Computer Literacy, and the Media in Creating Public Attitudes toward CMC in Japan and Korea," in C. Ess, ed., *Culture, Technology, Communication: Towards an Intercultural Village* (Albany, NY: State University of New York, 2001), 269.
105. McDaniel, 2004, 17.

106. "Ability to Speak English, 2000," U.S. Census Bureau: American FactFinder, http://factfinder.census.gov/servlet/QTTable (accessed November 21, 2005).
107. "Hispanic and Asian Americans Increasing Faster than Overall Population," U.S. Census Bureau News, www.census.gov/Press-Release/www/releases/archives/economic_census/000372.html (accessed November 21, 2005).
108. "Los Angeles County, California, 2003 American Community Survey," http://factfinder.census.gov/servlet/SAFFFacts, then search for Los Angeles data (accessed November 21, 2005).
109. Ibid.
110. "Bossing the Big Tortilla," *The Economist*, May 14, 2005, 31.
111. "Working in the 21st Century," U.S. Department of Labor: Bureau of Labor Statistics, www.bls.gov/opub/working/page4a.htm (accessed November 21, 2005).
112. M. Toossi, "A Century of Change: The U.S. Labor Force, 1950–2050," *Monthly Labor Review*, May 2002, 16.
113. "Minority-Owned Firms Grow Four Times Faster Than National Average, Census Bureau Reports," U.S. Census News: U.S. Department of Commerce, www.census.gov/Press-Release/www/releases/archives/economic_census/000372.html (accessed November 21, 2005).

**CHAPTER 9**

1. J. Tapia, "Living the Dream: The Cultural Model of School in Latino Communities," *Latino Studies Journal*, 9 (1), Winter, 1998, 9.
2. M. Saville-Troike, *A Guide to Culture in the Classroom* (Rosslyn, VA: National Clearinghouse for Bilingual Education, 1978).
3. K. A. Bruffee, "Taking the Common Ground: Beyond Cultural Identity," *Change*, February 2002, 15.
4. J. Henry, "A Cross-Cultural Outline of Education," in *Educational Patterns and Cultural Configurations*, J. Roberts and S. Akinsanya, eds. (New York: David McKay, 1976).
5. J. S. Keohane and J. S. Nye, Jr., "Globalization: What's New? What's

Not? (And So What?)," *Foreign Policy*, 118, Spring 2000.

6. P. M. Brannon, "Diversity," *Human Ecology*, June 2004.

7. J. Malveaux, "A Multicultural Globalism," *Black Issues in Higher Education*, 18 (24), January 17, 2002.

8. Bruffee, 2002, 15.

9. B. R. Singh, "Multicultural Education—Social Aspects," *Educational Review*, 4 (1), 1995, 11–25.

10. Ibid.

11. J. Holland, "Enhancing Multicultural Sensitivity through Teaching Multiculturally in Recreation," *Parks and Recreation*, 323 (5), May 1997.

12. Singh, 1995, 11–25.

13. N. P. Stromquist and K. Monkman, "Defining Globalization and Assessing Its Implications on Knowledge and Education," in *Globalization and Education: Integration and Contestation across Cultures*, N. P. Stromquist and K. Monkman, eds. (Lanham, MD: Rowman and Littlefield, 2000), 1.

14. S. Lu, "Culture and Compliance Gaining in the Classroom: A Preliminary Investigation of Chinese College Teachers' Use of Behavior Alteration Techniques," *Communication Education*, 46, January 1997, 13–14.

15. Y. Nemoto, *The Japanese Education System* (Parkland, FL: Universal Publishers, 1999), 23.

16. M. J. White, *The Japanese Educational Challenge: A Commitment to Children* (New York: Free Press, 1987), 150.

17. Nemoto, 1999, 11.

18. Ibid., 15.

19. H. Grossman, *Educating Hispanic Students: Cultural Implications for Instruction, Classroom Management, Counseling, and Assessment* (Springfield, IL: Charles C. Thomas, 1984).

20. Ibid., 85.

21. Nemoto, 1999, 20.

22. S. Ting-Toomey, *Communicating Across Cultures* (New York: Guilford Press, 1999), 216–217.

23. Grossman, 1984.

24. S. Headden, "One Nation, One Language," *U.S. News and World Report*, September 25, 1995, 38–42.

25. H. L. Hodgkinson, "Diversity Comes in All Sizes and Shapes," *School Business Affairs*, 1997, 3.

26. H. Jones, "A Research-Based Approach on Teaching to Diversity," *Journal of Instructional Psychology*, 31 (1), 2004, 13.

27. D. M. Golnick and P. C. Chinn, *Multicultural Education in a Pluralistic Society*, 6th ed. (Upper Saddle River, NJ: Merrill Prentice Hall, 2002), 4–5.

28. G. Gay, "The Importance of Multicultural Education," *Educational Leadership*, December 2003/January 2004, 30.

29. J. A. Banks, P. Cookson, G. Gay, W. D. Hawley, J. J. Irvine, S. Niego, J. W. Schofield, and W. G. Stephan, "Diversity Within Unity: Essential Principles for Teaching and Learning in a Multicultural Society," *Phi Delta Kappan*, November 2001, 196–203.

30. Bruffee, 2002, 12

31. Gollnick and Chinn, 2002, 5.

32. G. Althen, *American Ways: A Guide for Foreigners in the United States* (Yarmouth, ME: Intercultural Press, 2003), 102–103.

33. J. Le Roux, "Effective Educators Are Culturally Competent Communicators," *Intercultural Education*, 13 (1), 2002, 37.

34. Ibid., 30.

35. C. Calloway-Thomas, P. J. Cooper, and C. Blake, *Intercultural Communication: Roots and Routes* (Boston: Allyn and Bacon, 1999), 199.

36. E. R. Hollins, J. E. King, and W. C. Haymen, *Teaching Diverse Populations: Formulating a Knowledge Base* (New York: State University of New York Press, 1994).

37. Calloway-Thomas et al., 1999, 199.

38. Gay, 2000, 147.

39. Calloway-Thomas et al., 1999, 199.

40. B. J. Shade, C. Kelly, and M. Oberg, *Creating Culturally Responsive Classrooms* (Washington, DC: American Psychological Association, 1997), 21.

41. Ibid.

42. M. Yehieli and M. A. Grey, *Health Matters: A Pocket Guide for Working with Diverse Cultures and Under-served Populations* (Yarmouth, ME: Intercultural Press, 2005), 9.

43. R. D. Lewis, *The Cultural Imperative: Global Trends in the 21st Century* (Yarmouth, ME: Intercultural Press, 2002).

44. Yehieli and Grey, 2005, 10–11.

45. D. M. Golnick and P. C. Chinn, *Multicultural Education in a Pluralistic Society* (New York: Macmillan, 1994), 306.

46. B. P. Leung, "Culture as a Study of Differential Minority Student Achievement," *Journal of Educational Issues of Language Majority Students*, 13, 1994.

47. J. C. Kush, "Field-Dependence, Cognitive Ability, and Academic Achievement in Anglo American and Mexican American Students, *Journal of Cross-Cultural Psychology*, 27 (5), September 1996, 563.

48. Grossman, 1984.

49. Hollins, King, and Hayman, 1994, 19.

50. L. M. Cleary and T. D. Peacock, *Collected Wisdom: American Indian Education* (Boston: Allyn and Bacon, 1998).

51. Grossman, 1984.

52. Cleary and Peacock, 1998.

53. S. Reese, "Understanding Our Differences," *Techniques*, January 2002, 21.

54. Shade, Kelly, and Oberg, 1997, 63.

55. Ibid.

56. Ibid.

57. Ibid., 63–64.

58. Reese, 2002, 21.

59. H. Grossman, *Teaching in a Diverse Society* (Boston: Allyn and Bacon, 1995), 270.

60. Gollnick and Chinn, 1994, 306.

61. Grossman, 1995.

62. Grossman, 1984.

63. Cleary and Peacock, 1998.

64. Ibid., 160.

65. Grossman, 1995.

66. M. E. Franklin, "Culturally Sensitive Instruction Practices for African-American Learners with Disabilities," *Exceptional Children*, 59 (1992), 115–122.

67. E.L. Yao, "Asian-Immigrant Students—Unique Problems that Hamper Learning," *NASSP Bulletin*, 71 (1987), 82–88.

68. Grossman, 1995.

69. Ibid., 273.

70. M. J. White, *The Japanese Educational Challenge: A*

*Commitment to Children* (New York: Free Press, 1987).

71. B. J. Walker, J. Dodd, and R. Bigelo, "Learning Preferences of Capable American Indians of Two Tribes," *Journal of American Indian Education* (1989 Special Issue), 63–71.

72. Ibid.

73. Shade, Kelly, and Oberg, 1997, 23.

74. Gay, 2000, 90

75. Ibid., 90–91.

76. Shade, Kelly, and Oberg, 1997, 23.

77. Ibid.

78. Ibid., 27.

79. S. Nelson-Barber and T. Meier, "Multicultural Context a Key Factor in Teaching," *ENC Online*, Spring 1990, www.enc.org/topics/equity/articls/document.shtm?imput-ACQ-111465-1465.oo.sh (accessed November 18, 2004).

80. Shade, Kelly, and Oberg, 1997, 30.

81. J. J. Irvine, *Educating Teachers for Diversity: Seeing with a Cultural Eye* (New York: Teachers College Press, 2003).

82. R. R. Gann, "Language, Conflict and Community: Linguistic Accommodation in the Urban US," *Changing English*, 11 (1), March 2004, 105.

83. U.S. Census Bureau, American Community Survey, www.census.gov/acs/www/index.html (accessed December 2, 2005).

84. Ibid.

85. P. Leppert, *Doing Business with Mexico* (Fremont, CA: Jain, 1996), 13.

86. J. Abrams and J. Ferguson, "Teaching Students from Many Nations," *Educational Leadership*, December 2004/January 2005, 89.

87. Ibid., 274.

88. Le Roux, 2001, 274

89. Ibid., 274–275.

90. S. J. Dicker, *Languages in America: A Pluralist View* (Philadelphia: Multilingual Matters, Ltd., 1996), 2.

91. Ibid., 4.

92. Ibid.

93. D. McKeon, "When Meeting Common Standards is Uncommonly Difficult," *Educational Leadership*, 51 (1994), 45–49.

94. Ibid.

95. Ibid.

96. E. K. Ngwainmbi, Communication in the Chinese Classroom," *Education*, 125 (1), 2004, 63–76.

97. Banks et al., 2001, 197

98. V. D. Menchaca, "Multicultural Education: The Missing Link in Teacher Education Programs," *Journal of Educational Issues of Language Minority Students*, Special Issue, 17, Fall 1996, 2.

99. R. White-Clark, "Training Teachers to Succeed in Multicultural Classrooms," *The Education Digest*, April 2005, 26.

100. Ibid.

101. E. R. Hollins, *Culture in School Learning: Revealing the Deep Meaning* (Mahwah, NJ: Lawrence Erlbaum, 1996), 2.

102. Ibid., 23.

103. Le Roux, 2001, 279.

104. R. D. Rhine, "Pedagogical Choices in the Teaching of Communication and Multicultural Diversity," paper presented at the annual meeting of the Speech Communication Association, San Antonio, TX, November 1995.

105. Banks et al., 2001, 197.

106. G. Wan, "The Learning Experience of Chinese Students in American Universities: A Cross-Cultural Perspective," *College Student Journal*, 35 (1), March 2001.

107. A. S. Jazayeri, "Immediacy and Its Relationship to Teacher Effectiveness: A Cross-Cultural Examination of Six Cultures," paper presented at the annual meeting of the National Communication Association, Chicago, 1999.

108. K. N. Robins, R. B. Lindsey, D. B. Lindsey, and R. D. Terrell, *Culturally Proficient Instruction: A Guide for People Who Teach* (Thousand Oaks, CA: Corwin Press, 2002), 130.

109. Nelson-Barber and Meier, 1990, 9.

110. Ibid.

111. M. Ramsey, "Monocultural versus Multicultural Teaching: How to Practice What We Preach," *Journal of Humanistic Counseling, Education, and Development*, 38 (3), 2000.

112. Y. A. M. Leeman, "School Leadership for Intercultural Education," *Intercultural Education*, 14 (10), 2003, 37–38.

113. Shade, Kelly, and Oberg, 1997, 42–55.

114. Leeman, 2003, 40.

115. L. Murry and J. Williams, "Diversity and Critical Pedagogy in the Communication Classroom," paper presented at the annual meeting of the Western States Communication Association, Pasadena, CA, February, 1996.

116. Le Roux, 2002, 42.

117. S. D. Johnson and A. N. Miller, "A Cross-Cultural Study of Immediacy, Credibility, and Learning in the U.S. and Kenya," *Communication Education*, 52 (3), July 2002, 289.

118. Ibid.

119. Jazayeri, 1999.

120. P. J. Cooper and C. J. Simonds, *Communication for the Classroom Teacher*, 7th ed. (Boston: Allyn and Bacon, 2003), 67.

121. Ibid.

122. Ibid., 68.

123. I. G. Malcolm, "Invisible Culture in the Classroom: Minority Pupils and the Principle of Adaptation," in *English Across Cultures, Cultures Across English: A Reader in Cross-Cultural Communication*, O. Garcia and R. Otheguy, eds. (New York: Mouton de Gruyter, 1989), 134.

**CHAPTER 10**

1. L. Calderón and R. A. Beltrán, "Pitfalls in Health Communication: Health Care Policy, Institution, Structure, and Process," *Medscape General Medicine*, 6 (1), 2004, 1 (www.medscape.com, print accessed January 13, 2005).

2. D. Purnell and B. J. Paulanka, eds., *Transcultural Health Care: A Culturally Competent Approach* (Philadelphia: F. A. Davis, 1998), xiii.

3. K. K. Kundhal and P. S. Kundhal, "Cultural Diversity: An Evolving Challenge to Physician-Patient Communication," *Journal of the American Medical Association*, 298 (1), January 1, 2003, 94.

4. R. C. Grooper, *Culture and the Clinical Encounter: An Intercultural Sensitizer for the Health Professions* (Yarmouth, ME: Intercultural Press, 1996), 2.

5. L. Haffner, "Translation Is Not Enough: Interpreting in a Medical Setting," *Western Journal of Medicine*, 157, (1992), 225–230.

6. Purnell and Paulanka, 1998, xiii.

7. Ibid.

8. N. A. Kirkwood, *A Hospital Handbook on Multiculturalism and Religion* (Harrisburg, PA: Morehouse Publishing, 1993), 6.

9. P. J. Donnelly, "Ethics and Cross-Cultural Nursing," *Journal of Cross-Cultural Nursing*, 11 (23), April 2000, 19.

10. G. L. Kreps and B. C. Thornton, *Health Communication: Theory and Practice* (Prospect Heights, IL: Waveland Press, 1992), 2.

11. R. E. Spector, *Cultural Diversity in Health and Illness*, 4th ed. (Stamford, CT: Appleton and Lange, 1996), 4.

12. Ibid.

13. B. Koenig and J. Gates-Williams, "Understanding Cultural Differences in Dying for Dying Patients," *Western Journal of Medicine*, 163 (1995), 246.

14. M. H. Fitzgerald, "Multicultural Clinical Interactions," *Journal of Rehabilitation*, April/June 1992, 39.

15. R. Smart, "Religious-Caused Complications in Intercultural Communication," in *Intercultural Communication: A Reader*, 5th ed., L. A. Samovar and R. E. Porter, eds. (Belmont, CA: Wadsworth, 1988), 65.

16. D. Elgin, *Voluntary Simplicity* (New York: William Morrow, 1981), 225.

17. R. E. Spector, *Cultural Diversity in Health and Illness*, 6th ed. (Upper Saddle River, NJ: Pearson/Prentice Hall, 2004), 212.

18. E. A. Hobel and E. L. Frost, *Cultural and Social Anthropology* (New York: McGraw-Hill, 1967), 331.

19. W. E. Paden, *Religious Worlds: The Comparative Study of Religion* (Boston: Beacon, 1994), 26.

20. W. W. Cobern, "College Students' Conceptualization of Nature: An Interpretive Worldview Analysis," *Journal of Research in Science Teaching*, 30 (1993), 937.

21. Elgin, 1981, 225.

22. M. P. Fisher and R. Luyster, *Living Religions* (Englewood Cliffs, NJ: Prentice Hall, 1991), 22.

23. M. M. Andrews, "The Influence of Cultural and Health Belief Systems on Health Care Practices," in *Transcultural Concepts in Nursing Care*, 4th ed., M. M. Andrews and J. S. Boyle, eds. (Philadelphia:

Lippincott Williams and Wilkins, 2003), 75.

24. Spector, 2004, 312.

25. A. Hunter and J. Sexton, *Contemporary China* (New York: St. Martin's Press, 1999), 155.

26. J. Camphinha-Bacote, "African Americans," in *Transcultural Health Care: A Culturally Competent Approach*, J. D. Purnell and B. J. Paulanka, eds. (Philadelphia: F. A. Davis, 1988), 68.

27. Andrews, 2003, 75.

28. J. N. Giger and R. E. Davidhizar, *Transcultural Nursing: Assessment and Intervention*, 2nd ed. (St. Louis, MO: Mosby, 1995), 21.

29. Andrews, 2003, 76.

30. Ibid.

31. J. Luckmann, *Transcultural Communication in Nursing* (Albany, NY: Delmar Publishers, 1999), 49.

32. P. Angelucci, "Notes from the Field: Cultural Diversity: Health Belief Systems," *Nursing Management*, 26 (August 1995), 8.

33. Andrews, 2003, 75.

34. Ibid.

35. Angelucci, 1995, 8.

36. Andrews, 2003, 75.

37. Ibid.

38. Ibid., 77.

39. Angelucci, 1954, 8.

40. Andrews, 2003, 77.

41. Angelucci, 1954, 8.

42. T. T. Nowak, "Vietnamese Americans," in L. D. Purnell and B. J. Paulnaka, eds., *Transcultural Health Care: A Culturally Competent Approach* (Philadelphia: F. A. Davis, 1998), 468.

43. Angelucci, 1995, 8.

44. Luckmann, 1999, 49.

45. Ibid., 50.

46. Luckmann, 1999, 47.

47. Andrews, 2003, 75.

48. Giger and Davidhizar, 1995, 217.

49. Luckmann, 1999, 47.

50. Ibid.

51. Giger and Davidhizar, 1995, 456.

52. N. Dresser, *Multicultural Manners: New Rules of Etiquette for a Changing Society* (New York: John Wiley and Sons, 1996), 236.

53. Giger and Davidhizar, 1995, 465.

54. Nowak, 1998, 468.

55. N. Chong, *The Latino Patient: A Cultural Guide for Health Care

Providers* (Yarmouth, ME: Intercultural Press, 2002), 27.

56. Ibid.

57. Spector, 2004, 256.

58. Chong, 2002, 47.

59. C. Maloney, ed. *The Evil Eye* (New York: Columbia University Press, 1976), 14.

60. Ibid., vi–vii.

61. Luckmann, 1999, 49.

62. Giger and Davidhizar, 1995, 404.

63. Ibid.

64. Ibid.

65. I. Murillo-Rhode, "Hispanic American Patient Care," in *Transcultural Health Care*, G. Henderson and M. Primeaux, eds. (Menlo Park, CA: Addison-Wesley, 1981), 59–77.

66. Dresser, 1996, 246.

67. R. E. Spector, "Cultural Concepts of Women's Health and Health-Promoting Behavior," *JOGNN*, March/April 1995, 243.

68. Giger and Davidhizar, 1995, 510–511.

69. D. Boyd, *Rolling Thunder* (New York: Random House, 1974).

70. Spector, 2004, 189.

71. Ibid.

72. Giger and Davidhizar, 1995, 404.

73. B. F. Miranda, M. R. McBride, and Z. Spagler, "Filipino-Americans," in *Transcultural Health Care: A Culturally Competent Approach*, L. D. Purnell and B. J. Paulanka, eds. (Philadelphia: F. A. Davis, 1988), 267.

74. J. Selekman, "Jewish-Americans," in *Transcultural Health Care: A Culturally Competent Approach*, L. D. Purnell and B. J. Paulanka, eds. (Philadelphia: F. A. Davis, 1988), 389.

75. Nowak, 1998, 462.

76. Chong, 2002, 47.

77. N. Saelaw, "Lu-Mein Ceremonies," ASU Newsletter, www.savannanet.com/baci.htm (accessed December 4, 2005).

78. C. N. Nydegger, "Multiple Causality: Consequences for Medical Practice," *Western Journal of Medicine*, 138(3), 1983, 430–435.

79. Ibid.

80. Chong, 2002, 58.

81. Spector, 2004, 262–263.

82. A. S. Collins, D. Gullette, and M. Schnepf, "Break Through,"

*Nursing Management*, August 2004, 34–38.

83. Dresser, 1996, 238.
84. G. A. Galanti, *Caring for Patients from Different Cultures: Case Studies from American Hospitals* (Philadelphia: University of Pennsylvania Press, 1991), 101.
85. D. Grossman, "Cuban Americans," *Transcultural Health Care: A Culturally Competent Approach*, L. D. Purnell and B. J. Paulanka, eds. (Philadelphia: F. A. Davis, 1998), 208.
86. L. K. Matocha, "Chinese Americans," in *Transcultural Health Care: A Culturally Competent Approach*, L. D. Purcell and B. J. Paulanka, eds. (Philadelphia: F. A. Davis, 1988), 181.
87. Spector, 2004, 217–219.
88. Ibid.
89. Murillo-Rhode, 1981.
90. M. E. Burk, P. C. Wieser, and L. Keegan, "Cultural Beliefs and Health Behaviors of Pregnant Mexican-American Women: Implications for Primary Care," *Advances in Nursing Science*, 17 (4) June 1995, 27–52.
91. P. A. Twumasi, "Improvement of Health Care in Ghana: Present Perspectives," in *African Health and Healing Systems: Proceedings of a Symposium*, P. S. Yoder, ed. (Los Angeles: Crossroads Press, 1982).
92. Campinha-Bacote, 1998, 69.
93. Dresser, 1996, 249.
94. Giger and Davidhizar, 1995, 216.
95. "Lao Custom—Baci Ceremony," www.savannanet.com/baci.htm (accessed December 5, 2005).
96. Spector, 2004, 217–218.
97. Galanti, 1996, 106.
98. A. Fadiman, *The Spirit Catches You and You Fall Down* (New York: Farrar, Strauss and Giroux, 1997), 4.
99. K. A. Bkonviciniu and M. J. Perlin, "The Same but Different: Clinician-Patient Communication with Gay and Lesbian Patients," *Patient Education and Counseling*, 51 (2003), 115–122.
100. Ibid., 117.
101. Spector, 2004, 104.
102. Ibid., 105.
103. Kirkwood, 1003, 8.
104. Purnell and Paulanka, 1998, 39.
105. M. O. Loustaunau and E. J. Sobo, *The Cultural Context of Health,*

*Illness and Medicine* (Westport, CT: Bergin and Garvey, 1997), 93.
106. Spector, 1995, 244.
107. Purnell and Paulanka, 1998, 39.
108. O. Still and D. Hodgins, "Navajo Indians," in *Transcultural Health Care: A Culturally Approach*, L. D. Purnell and B. J. Paulanka, eds. (Philadelphia: F. A. Davis, 1988), 442.
109. Campinha-Bacote, 1998, 66.
110. Chong, 2002, 59.
111. M. A. Miller, "Culture, Spirituality, and Women's Health, *JOGMN*, March/April 1995, 256–263.
112. B. Bhayana, "Healthshock," *Health Sharing*, 12 (3), 1991, 28–31.
113. Miller, 1995.
114. C. G. Helman, *Culture, Health, and Illness*, 2nd ed. (London: Wright, 1990).
115. P. Abu Gharbieh, "Arab Americans," in *Transcultural Health Care: A Culturally Competent Approach* (Philadelphia: F. A. Davis, 1998), 154.
116. R. Marquand, "Healing Role of Spirituality Gains Ground," *Christian Science Monitor*, December 6, 1995, 18.
117. Spector, 1996, 4.
118. L. Payer, *Medicine and Culture: Varieties of Treatment in the United States, England, West Germany, and France* (New York: Henry Holt, 1988), 26.
119. B. Qureshi, *Transcultural Medicine: Dealing with Patients from Different Cultures*, 2nd ed. (Lancaster, UK: Kluwer Academic Publishers, 1994), vii.
120. Andrews, 2003, 24.
121. Campinha-Bacote, 1998, 56.
122. Giger and Davidhizar, 1995, 213.
123. G. Reddy, "Women's Movement: The Indian Scene," *Indian Journal of Social Work*, 46 (4), 1986, 507–514.
124. Giger and Davidhizar, 1995, 487.
125. Abu Gharbieh, 1998, 144.
126. Still and Hodgins, 1998, 454.
127. Giger and Davidhizar, 1995, 487.
128. Galanti, 1991, 63.
129. Abu Gharbieh, 1998, 154.
130. *San Diego Union-Tribune*, October 23, 1998, B-6.
131. L. C. Callister, "Cultural Meaning in Childbirth," *JOGNN*, May 1995, 327–331.
132. Galanti, 1991.
133. Purnell and Paulanka, 1998, 18.

134. R. L. Elliott, "Cultural Patterns in Rural Russia," *Journal of Multicultural Nursing and Health*, 3 (1), Winter 1997, 22–28.
135. S. H. Elgin, *The Language Imperative* (Cambridge, MA: Perseus Books, 2000), 82.
136. Galanti, 1991, 17.
137. K. Witte and K. Morrison, "Intercultural and Cross-Cultural Health Communication," in *Intercultural Communication Theory*, R. L. Wiseman, ed. (London: Sage, 1995).
138. R. Alcalay, "Perceptions About Prenatal Care Among Health Providers and Mexican-American Community Women," *International Quarterly of Communication Health Education*, 13 (2), 1992, 107–118.
139. Alcalay, 1992.
140. Spector, 1996.
141. J. E. Osborn, "Communication and the Health of the Public," *Patient Education and Counseling*, 41, 2000, 127–136.
142. E. W. Lynch, "From Culture Shock to Culture Learning," in *Developing Cross-Cultural Competence: A Guide for Working with Young Children and Their Families*, E. W. Lynch and M. J. Hanson, eds. (Baltimore, MD: Paul H. Brookes, 1992), 19–33.
143. Giger and Davidhizar, 1995.
144. D. Gleave and A. S. Manes, "The Central Americans," in *Cross-Cultural Caring: A Handbook for Health Professionals in Western Canada*, N. Waxler-Morrison, J. Anderson, and E. Richardson, eds. (Vancouver, BC: The University of British Columbia Press, 1990), 36–67.
145. S. Chan, "Families with Asian Roots," in *Developing Cross-Cultural Competence: A Guide for Working with Young Children and Their Families*, E. W. Lynch and M. J. Hanson, eds. (Baltimore, MD: Paul H. Brookes, 1992), 181–258.
146. M. M. Andrews, "Transcultural Nursing Care," in *Transcultural Concepts in Nursing Care*, M. M. Andrews and J. S. Boyle, eds. (Philadelphia: J. B. Lippincot, 1995), 49–96.
147. D. Dihn, S. Ganesan, and N. Waxler-Morrison, "The Vietnamese," in *Cross-Cultural*

Caring: A Handbook for Health Professionals in Western Canada, N. Waxler-Morrison, J. Anderson, and E. Richardson, eds. (Vancouver, BC: The University of British Columbia Press, 1990), 181–213.

148. Giger and Davidhizar, 1995.

149. Dihn et al., 1990.

150. G. Althen, American Ways: A Guide for Foreigners in the United States (Yarmouth, ME: Intercultural Press, 1988).

151. Dihn, et al., 1990.

152. A. T. Brownlee, Community, Culture, and Care (St. Louis, MO: C. V. Mosby, 1978).

153. N. Murillo, "The Mexican American Family," in Chicanos: Social and Psychological Perspectives, C. A. Hernandez, J. H. Haug, and N. N. Wagner, eds. (St. Louis, MO: C. V. Mosby, 1978), 15–25.

154. A. Montagu, Touching: The Significance of the Human Skin (New York: Columbia University Press, 1971).

155. L. Rocereto, "Selected Health Beliefs of Vietnamese Refugees," Journal of School Health, 15 (1981), 63–64.

156. M. Muencke, "Caring for Southeast Asian Refugee Parents in the USA," American Journal of Public Health, 74 (1983), 431–438.

157. M. B. Marks, "Straddling Cultural Divides with Grace," Christian Science Monitor, November 15, 1995, 16.

158. J. Klessig, "The Effect of Values and Culture of Life Support Decisions," Western Journal of Medicine, 157 (1992), 316–322.

159. Luckmann, 1999, 81.

160. Ibid.

161. M. Gilmor, "The Hospital: A Foreign Culture," International Journal of Childbirth Education, 16 (1), March 2001, 18.

162. Fitzgerald, 1992.

163. R. L. Swarms, "Mozambique Enlists Traditional Healers in War on AIDS," San Diego Union-Tribune, December 11, 1999, A-25.

164. Galanti, 1991, 109.

165. Ibid., 102.

166. B. P. Dennis and E. B. Small, "Incorporating Cultural Diversity in Nursing Care: An Action Plan,"

The ABNF Journal, January/February, 2003, 20.

167. Ibid.

168. P. Geist-Martin, E. B. Ray, and B. F. Sharf, Communicating Health: Personal, Cultural and Political Complexities (Belmont, CA: Wadsworth, 2003), 69.

169. Ibid.

170. R. Ludwick and M. C. Silva, "Nursing Around the World: Cultural Values and Ethical Conflicts," Online Journal of Issues in Nursing, August 14, 2000, www.nursingworld.org (accessed December 14, 2004).

**CHAPTER 11**

1. L. Beamer and Iris Varner, Intercultural Communication in the Global Workplace (New York: McGraw-Hill, 2001), vii.

2. H. Smith, The Illustrated World's Religions (New York: Harper San Francisco, 1994), 13.

3. Time, December 20, 2004, 27.

4. Time, August 26, 2002, 8–10.

5. L. Schneider and A. Silverman, Global Sociology: Introducing Five Contemporary Societies (New York: McGraw-Hill, 1997), xxi.

6. G. Hofstede, Culture's Consequences: Comparing Values, Behavior, Institutions, and Organizations Across Cultures, 2nd ed. (Thousand Oaks, CA: Sage Publications, 2001), xv.

7. B. H. Spitzberg, "A Model of Intercultural Communication Competence," in Intercultural Communication: A Reader, 9th ed., L. A. Samovar and R. E. Porter, eds. (Belmont, CA: Wadsworth, 2000), 375.

8. Y. Y. Kim, "Intercultural Communication Competence: A Systems-Theoretic View," in Cross-Cultural Interpersonal Communication, S. Ting-Toomey and R. Korzenny, eds. (Newbury Park, CA: Sage Publications, 1991), 259.

9. S. P. Morreale, B. S. Spitzberg, and J. K. Barge, Human Communication: Motivation, Knowledge and Skills (Belmont, CA: Wadsworth/Thomson Learning, 2001), 37–40.

10. B. Spitzberg and W. Cupach, Interpersonal Communication

Competence (Beverly Hills, CA: Sage Publications, 1984).

11. J. Luckmann, Transcultural Communication in Nursing (Albany, NY: Delmar, 1999), 64.

12. Morreale, Spitzberg, and Barge, 2001, 39–40.

13. Ibid., 2001, 40.

14. P. B. Smith and M. H. Bond, Social Psychology Across Cultures, 2nd ed. (Boston: Allyn and Bacon, 1999), 284.

15. E. Griffin, A First Look at Communication Theory, 2nd ed. (New York: McGraw-Hill, 1994), 173.

16. Ibid.

17. H. Cleveland, "The Limits of Cultural Diversity," in Intercultural Communication: A Reader, 9th ed., L. A. Samovar and R. E. Porter, eds. (Belmont, CA: Wadsworth, 2000), 427.

18. S. Herman and E. Schield, "The Stranger Group in a Crosscultural Situation," Sociometry, 24 (1961), 165.

19. D. C. Thomas and K. Inkson, Cultural Intelligence: People Skills for Global Business (San Francisco: Berrett-Koehler Publishers, 2004), 11.

20. L. Barna, "Stumbling Blocks in Intercultural Communication," in Intercultural Communication: A Reader, 6th ed., L. A. Samovar and R. E. Porter, eds. (Belmont, CA: Wadsworth, 1991), 351.

21. See C. M. Berger and R. J. Calabrese, "Some Explorations in Initial Interaction and Beyond," Human Communication Research, 1 (1975), 99–112; and C. R. Berger and J. J. Bradac, Language and Social Knowledge: Uncertainty in Interpersonal Relations (London: E. E. Arnold, 1982).

22. Berger and Calabrese, 100.

23. C. R. Berger, "Communicating Under Uncertainty," in Interpersonal Processes: New Directions in Communication Research, M. E. Roloff and G. R. Miller, eds. (Newbury Park, CA: Sage Publications, 1987), 41.

24. W. B. Gudykunst and Y. Y. Kim, Communication with Strangers: An Approach to Intercultural

*Communication,* 4th ed., (New York: McGraw Hill, 2003) 13.

25. J. Luckmann, *Transcultural Communication in Nursing* (New York: Delmar Publishers, 1999), 66.

26. W. Gudykunst, *Bridging Differences: Effective Intergroup Communication,* 3rd ed. (Thousand Oaks, CA: Sage Publications, 1998), 272.

27. C. R. Berger, "Inscrutable Goals, Uncertain Plans, and the Production of Communication Action," in *Communication and Social Process,* C. R. Berger and M. Burgoon, eds. (East Lansing: Michigan State University Press, 1995), 1–28.

28. E. Banks and M. Rogers, "Uncertainty Reduction Theory," in *Introducing Communication Theory: Analysis and Application,* R. West and L. H. Turner, eds. (Mountain View, CA: Mayfield Publishing Company, 2000), 140.

29. Ibid.

30. D. M. Taylor and L. E. Porter, "A Multicultural View of Stereotyping," in *Psychology and Culture,* W. J. Lonner and Roy S. Malpass, eds. (Needham Heights, MA: Allyn and Bacon, 1994), 87.

31. Ibid., 85.

32. W. Lippman, *Public Opinion* (New York: Macmillan, 1957), 79–103.

33. C. S. Abbate, S. Boca, and P. Bocchiaro, "Stereotyping in Persuasive Communication: Influence Exerted by Disapproved Source," *Journal of Applied Social Psychology,* 34 (2004), 1192.

34. J. W. Berry, Y. H. Segall, and P. R. Dasen, *Cross-Cultural Psychology: Research and Application* (New York: Cambridge University Press, 1992), 299.

35. N. Rapport and J. Overing, *Social and Cultural Anthropology: The Key Concepts* (New York: Routledge, 2000), 343.

36. H. C. Triandis, *Culture and Social Behavior* (New York: McGraw-Hill, 1994), 138.

37. P. B. Smith and M. H. Bond, *Social Psychology Across Cultures: Analysis and Perspectives* (Boston: Allyn and Bacon, 1994), 169.

38. Triandis, 1994, 138.

39. D. J. Schneider, *The Psychology of Stereotypes* (New York: Guilford Press, 2004), 341.

40. Abbate, Boca, and Bocchiaro, 2004, 1192.

41. D. S. Meshel and R. P. McGlynn, "Intergenerational Contact, Attitudes, and Stereotypes of Adolescents and Older People," *Educational Gerontology,* 30 (2004), 458.

42. J. T. Wood, *Gendered Lives: Communication, Gender and Culture* (Belmont, CA: Wadsworth/Thomson Learning, 2005), 234.

43. For a detailed discussion of the problems associated with stereotyping, see Y. Lee, L. J. Jussim, and C. R. McCawley, eds., *Stereotyping Accuracy: Toward Appreciating Group Differences* (Washington, DC: American Psychological Association, 1995).

44. N. J. Adler, *International Dimensions of Organizational Behavior,* 2nd ed. (Boston: PWS-KENT, 1991), 74.

45. J. W. Sherman, F. R. Conrey, and C. J. Groom, "Encoding Flexibility Revisited: Evidence for Enhanced Encoding of Stereotypes— Inconsistent Information Under Cognitive Load," *Social Cognition* 22 (2004), 215.

46. E. W. Lynch and M. J. Hanson, *Developing Cross-Cultural Competence: A Guide for Working with Young Children and Their Families* (Baltimore, MD: Paul H. Brookes, 1992), 44.

47. D. R. Atkinson, G. Morten, and D. Wing Sue, "Minority Group Counseling: An Overview," in *Intercultural Communication: A Reader,* 4th ed., L. A. Samovar and R. E. Porter, eds. (Belmont, CA: Wadsworth, 1982), 172.

48. M. Pickering, *Stereotyping: The Politics of Representation* (New York: Palgrave, 2001), 10.

49. M. Guirdham, *Communicating Across Cultures* (West Lafayette: Purdue University Press, 1999), 163.

50. Meshel and McGlynn, 2004, 461.

51. W. B. Gudykunst, *Asian American Ethnicity and Communication* (Thousand Oaks, CA: Sage Publications, 2001), 140.

52. Meshel and McGlynn, 2004, 462.

53. W. Stephan, *Reducing Prejudice and Stereotyping in Schools* (New York: Teachers College Press, 1999), 17–19.

54. S. Ting-Toomey and L. C. Chung, *Understanding Intercultural Communication* (Los Angeles: Roxbury Publishing Company, 2005), 238

55. Ibid., 239.

56. J. J. Macionis, *Society: The Basics,* 4th ed. (Upper Saddle River: NJ: Prentice Hall, 1998), 217.

57. J. B. Rusher, *Prejudice Communication: A Social Psychological Perspective* (New York: Guilford Press, 2001), 4.

58. Ibid., 6.

59. J. Levin, *The Functions of Prejudice* (New York: Harper and Row, 1975), 13.

60. R. Richard Brislin, *Understanding Culture's Influence on Behavior,* 2nd ed. (New York: Harcourt College Publishers, 2000), 209.

61. H. D. Fishbein, *Peer Prejudice and Discrimination: The Origins of Prejudice* (Mahwah, NJ: Lawrence Erlbaum, 2002), 61.

62. Levin, 1975, 10.

63. For a more detailed account of the functions of prejudice, see Brislin, 2000, 208–213; D. Katz, "The Functional Approach to the Study of Attitudes," *Public Opinion Quarterly* 24 (1960), 164–204; B. Hall, *Among Cultures: The Challenge of Communication* (New York: Harcourt College Publishers, 2002), 224–227.

64. A. G. Allport, *The Nature of Prejudice* (Cambridge, MA: Addison-Wesley, 1954).

65. J. Feagin, *Racial and Ethnic Relations,* 3rd ed. (Englewood Cliffs, NJ: Prentice Hall, 1989).

66. S. Oskamp, "Multiple Paths to Reducing Prejudice and Discrimination," in *Reducing Prejudice and Discrimination,* S. Oskamp, ed. (Mahwah, NJ: Lawrence Erlbaum, 2000), 3.

67. A. Kaplan, "Equality," in *Bigotry, Prejudice and Hatred: Definitions, Causes and Solutions,* R. M. Baird and S. E. Rosenbaum, eds. (Buffalo, NY: Prometheus Books, 1992) 24.

68. W. G. Stephan and C. W. Stephan, "An Integrated Threat Theory of Prejudice," in *Reducing Prejudice and Discrimination*, S. Oskamp, ed. (Mahwah, NJ: Lawrence Erlbaum, 2000) 25.

69. Oskamp, 2000, 7.

70. Stephan and Stephan, 2000, 40–41.

71. Oskamp, 2000, 9.

72. Stephan and Stephan, 2000, 40.

73. Ibid.

74. R. H. Dana, *Multicultural Assessment Perspectives for Professional Psychology* (Boston: Allyn and Bacon, 1993), 23.

75. E. Vora and J. A. Vora, "Undoing Racism in America: Help from a Black Church," *Journal of Black Studies*, 32 (2002), 389.

76. S. J. Gold, "From Jim Crow to Racial Hegemony: Evaluating Explanations of Racial Hierarchy," *Ethnic and Racial Studies*, 27 (2004), 957.

77. L. D. Bobo and C. Fox, "Race, Racism, and Discrimination: Bridging Problems, Methods, and Theory in Social Psychology Research," *Social Psychology Quarterly*, 66 (2003), 324.

78. Gold, 2004, 953.

79. B. Leone, *Racism: Opposing View Points* (Minneapolis, MN: Greenhaven Press, 1978), 1.

80. Ibid.

81. S. Nanda and R. L. Warms, *Cultural Anthropology*, 6th ed. (Belmont: CA: Wadsworth, 1998), 9.

82. Ibid., 10.

83. L. Blum, *I'm Not a Racist, But . . .* (Ithaca, NY: Cornell University Press, 2002) 9.

84. R. Brislin, *Understanding Culture's Influence on Behavior* (Fort Worth, TX: Harcourt Brace Jovanovich, 2000), 214.

85. Ibid., 215.

86. R. W. Brislin, "Prejudice in Intercultural Communication," in *Intercultural Communication: A Reader*, 6th ed., L. A. Samovar and R. E. Porter, eds. (Belmont, CA: Wadsworth, 1991), 386.

87. Brislin, 2000, 220.

88. Blum, 2002, 9.

89. Gudykunst and Kim, 2003, 143.

90. J. Solomos and L. Back, *Racism and Society* (New York: St. Martin's Press, 1996), 216.

91. B. Russell, *Power* (New York: W. W. Norton, 1938), 10.

92. R. A. Barraclough and R. A. Stewart, "Power and Control: Social Science Perspectives," in *Power in the Classroom*, V. P. Richmond and J. McCroskey, eds. (Hillsdale, NJ: Prentice Hall, 1991), 1–4.

93. Nanda and Warms, 1998, 226.

94. Ibid.

95. J. N. Martin and T. K. Nakayama, *Intercultural Communication in Context* (Mountain View, CA: Mayfield, 1997), 103.

96. J. M. Charon, *The Meaning of Sociology*, 6th ed. (Englewood Cliffs, NJ: Prentice Hall, 1999), 152–153.

97. Ibid., 153.

98. E. Folb, "Who's Got the Room at the Top?" in *Intercultural Communication: A Reader*, 9th ed., L. A. Samovar and R. E. Porter, eds. (Belmont, CA: Wadsworth, 2000), 122.

99. E. Folb, 2000, 122.

100. M. L. Hecht, M. J. Collier, and S. A. Ribeau, *African American Communication: Ethnic Identity and Cultural Interpretation* (Newbury Park, CA: Sage Publications, 1993), 135–137, 144. Also see A. Smith, *Transracial Communication* (Englewood Cliffs, NJ: Prentice Hall, 1973), 118–119.

101. Wood, 2005, 296–297.

102. Smith, 1973, 71.

103. G. A. Borden, *Cultural Orientation: An Approach to Understanding Intercultural Communication* (Englewood Cliffs, NJ: Prentice Hall, 1991), 116.

104. J. A. Blubaugh and D. L. Pennington, *Crossing Differences: Interracial Communication* (Columbus, OH: Charles E. Merrill, 1976), 39.

105. W. G. Sumner, *Folkways* (Boston: Ginnand, 1940), 13.

106. Nanda and Warms, 1998, 6.

107. Triandis, 1994, 252.

108. Nanda and Warms, 1996, 7. Also see D. G. Bates and F. Plog, *Cultural Anthropology*, 3rd ed. (New York: McGraw-Hill, 1990), 17; W. A. Haviland, *Cultural Anthropology*, 7th ed. (Fort Worth, TX: Harcourt Brace Jovanovich, 1993), 48.

109. Macionis, 1998, 48.

110. F. M. Keesing, *Cultural Anthropology: The Science of Custom* (New York: Holt, Rinehart, and Winston, 1965), 45.

111. J. Rusen, "How to Overcome Ethnocentrism: Approaches to a Culture of Recognition by History in the Twenty-First Century," *History and Theory, Theme Issues*, 43 (December 2004), 121.

112. J. Scarborough, *The Origins of Cultural Differences and Their Impact on Management* (Westport, CT: Quorum Books, 1998), 14.

113. W. A. Haviland, *Cultural Anthropology* (Belmont, CA: Wadsworth, 2002), 470.

114. R. Brislin, 2000, 45.

115. T. K. Gamble and M. W. Gamble, *Contacts: Interpersonal Communication in Theory, Practice, and Context* (Boston: Houghton Mifflin Company, 2005), 281.

116. Triandis, 1994, 39.

117. J. W. Berry, Y. H. Poortinga, M. H. Segall, and P. R. Dasen, *Cross-Cultural Psychology: Research and Application* (New York: Cambridge University Press, 1992), 9.

118. R. W. Nolan, *Communicating and Adapting Across Cultures* (Westport, CT: Bergin and Garvey, 1999), 19.

119. Smith and Bond, 1994, 192.

120. C. Storti, *The Art of Coming Home* (Yarmouth, ME: Intercultural Press, 1997), 2.

121. A. Furnham and L. Bochner, *Culture Shock—Psychological Reactions to an Unfamiliar Environment* (New York: Methuen, 1986).

122. S. Bochner, "Culture Shock," in *Psychology and Culture*, W. J. Lonner and R. S. Malpass, eds. (Needham Heights, MA: Allyn and Bacon, 1994), 246.

123. K. Oberg, "Culture Shock: Adjustments to New Cultural Environments," *Practical Anthropology*, 7 (1960), 176. Also see P. K. Bock, *Culture Shock* (New York: Knopf, 1970).

124. A. Furnham and S. Bochner, *Culture Shock: Psychological Reactions to Unfamiliar Environments* (New York: Routledge, 1989), 250.

125. R. W. Brislin, *Cross-Cultural Encounters: Face-to-Face Interactions*

(New York: Pergamon Press, 1981), 155.

126. Lynch and Hanson, 1992, 23.

127. For a discussion of the reactions produced by culture shock, see S. Bochner, 1994, 249; W. B. Gudykunst and Y. Y. Kim, 2003, 377; J. T. Gullahorn and J. E. Gullahorn, "An Extension of the U-Curve Hypothesis," *Journal of Social Science,* 17 (1963), 33–47; and Triandis, 1994, 264.

128. Gudykunst and Kim, 2003, 379.

129. E. Marx, *Breaking Through Culture Shock* (London: Nicholas Brealey, 1999), 7.

130. Triandis, 1994, 265.

131. Ibid., 7.

132. P. R. Harris and R. T. Moran, *Managing Cultural Differences: Leadership Strategies for a New World of Business,* 4th ed. (Houston, TX: Gulf, 1996), 142.

133. Berry, Poortinga, Segall, and Dasen, 1992, 340.

134. N. J. Adler, *International Dimensions of Organizational Behavior,* 3rd ed. (Cincinnati, OH: South-Western College Publishing, 1997), 238.

135. I. Kawano, "Overcoming Culture Shock: Living and Learning in Japan Through the JET Program," paper presented at the Annual Convention of the Western States Communication Association, Monterey, CA, February, 1997, 25.

136. E. Y. Kim, *The Yin and Yang of American Culture* (Yarmouth, ME: Intercultural Press, 2001), 207.

137. E. C. Stewart and M. J. Bennett, *American Cultural Patterns: A Cross-Cultural Perspective* (Yarmouth, ME: Intercultural Press, 1991), 175.

138. T. Novinger, *Intercultural Communication: A Practical Guide* (Austin, TX: University of Texas Press, 2001), 24.

139. R. Norton, *Communication Style: Theory, Application and Measures* (Beverly Hills, CA: Sage Publications, 1982).

140. D. C. Barnlund, *Public and Private Self in Japan and the United States: Communication Styles of Two Cultures* (Tokyo: Simul Press, 1975), 14–15.

141. See M. Snyder, *Public Appearance, Private Realities: The Psychology of Self-Monitoring* (New York: Freeman), 1987.

142. M. Guirdham, *Communication Across Cultures* (West Lafayette, IN: Purdue University Press, 1999), 243.

143. Morreale, Spitzberg, and Barge, 2001, 256.

144. L. A. Haynes and A. W. Avery, "Training Adolescents in Self-Disclosure and Empathy Skills," *Journal of Community Psychology,* 26 (1979), 527.

145. S. Ting-Toomey, *Communicating Across Cultures* (New York: Guilford Press, 1999), 160.

146. R. L. Katz, *Empathy: Its Nature and Uses* (New York: The Free Press of Glencoe, 1963), 62.

147. B. J. Broome, "Building Shared Meaning: Implications of a Relational Approach to Empathy for Teaching Intercultural Communication," *Communication Education,* 40 (1991), 235.

148. C. Calloway-Thomas, P. J. Cooper, and C. Blake, *Intercultural Communication: Roots and Routes* (Boston: Allyn and Bacon, 1999), 106.

149. G. R. Miller and M. Steinberg, *Between People: A New Analysis of Interpersonal Communication* (Chicago: Science Research Associates, 1975), 167.

150. R. Bell, "Social Involvement," in *Personality and Interpersonal Communication,* J. McCroskey and J. Daly, eds. (Newbury Park, CA: Sage Publications, 1987), 205.

151. D. W. Nelson and R. Baumgarte, "Cross-Cultural Misunderstandings Reduce Empathic Responding," *Journal of Social Psychology,* 34 (2004), 398.

152. S. Trenholm and A. Jensen, *Interpersonal Communication,* 2nd ed. (Belmont, CA: Wadsworth, 1992), 254.

153. D. C. Barnlund, *Communication Styles of Japanese and Americans* (Belmont, CA: Wadsworth, 1989), 162.

154. Trenholm and Jensen, 1992, 255.

155. A. L. Rich, *Interracial Communication* (New York: Harper and Row, 1974), 35–36.

156. R. D. Lewis, *When Cultures Collide: Managing Successfully Across Cultures,* (Yarmouth, ME: Intercultural Press, 1999), 443.

157. H. Wenzhong and C. Grove, *Encountering the Chinese: A Guide for Americans* (Yarmouth, ME: Intercultural Press, 1991), 114.

158. Morreale, Spitzberg, and Barge, 2001, 160.

159. Lewis, 1999, 101–105.

160. M. K. Asante and A. Davis, "Encounters in the Interracial and Intercultural Workplace," in *Handbook of International and Intercultural Relations,* M. K. Asante and W. B. Gudykunst, eds. (Newbury Park, CA: Sage Publications, 1989), 374–391.

161. J. T. Wood, *Communication Mosaics: A New Introduction to the Field of Communication* (Belmont, CA: Wadsworth, 1998), 25.

162. D. Rowland, *Japanese Business Etiquette* (New York: Warner, 1985), 47.

163. Gamble and Gamble, 2005, 127.

164. R. Hart, R. E. Carlson, and W. F. Eadie, "Attitudes Toward Communication and the Assessment of Rhetorical Sensitivity," *Communication Monographs,* 47 (1980), 1–22.

165. Gudykunst and Kim, 2003, 290.

166. S. Trenholm, *Human Communication Theory* (Englewood Cliffs, NJ: Prentice Hall, 1986), 112.

167. D. A. Foster, *Bargaining Across Borders: How to Negotiate Successfully Anywhere in the World* (New York: McGraw-Hill, 1992), 253.

168. B. D. Ruben and D. J. Kealey, "Behavioral Assessment of Communication Competency and the Prediction of Cross-Cultural Adaptation," *International Journal of Intercultural Relations,* 3 (1979), 19.

169. Guirdham, 1999, 242.

170. Ibid.

171. R. M. Berko, L. B. Rosenfeld, and L. A. Samovar, *Connecting: A Culture-Sensitive Approach to Interpersonal Competency,* 2nd ed. (New York: Harcourt Brace College Publishers, 1997), 372.

172. S. Ting-Toomey, "Managing Intercultural Conflicts Effectively," in *Intercultural Communication: A Reader,* 9th ed., L. A. Samovar and R. E. Porter, eds. (Belmont, CA: Wadsworth, 2000), 388.

173. See R. H. Kilman and K. W. Thomas, "Developing a

Forced-Choice Measure of Conflict Handling Behavior: MODE Instrument," *Educational and Psychological Measurement*, 37, 1977, 309–325; R. S. Lulofs and D. D. Cahn, *Conflict: From Theory to Action*, 2nd ed. (Boston: Allyn and Bacon, 2000); Morreale, Spitzberg, and Barge, 2001, 364–366; W. W. Wilmont and J. L. Hocker, *Interpersonal Conflict*, 5th ed. (Boston: McGraw-Hill, 1998).

174. Berko, Rosenfeld, and Samovar, 1997, 386.

175. Beamer and Varner, 2001, 239.

176. Gamble and Gamble, 2005, 330.

177. Morreale, Spitzberg, and Barge, 2001, 365.

178. M. H. DeFleur, P. Kearney, T. G. Plax, and M. L. DeFleur, *Fundamentals of Human Communication* (New York: McGraw-Hill, 2005), 341.

179. M. Roloff, "Communication and Conflict," in *Handbook of Communication Science*, C. Berger and S. H. Chaffee, eds. (Beverly Hills, CA: Sage Publications, 1990), 484–534.

180 B. J. Broome, "Palevome: Foundations of Struggle and Conflict," in *Intercultural Communication: A Reader*, 9th ed., L. A. Samovar and R. E. Porter, eds. (Belmont, CA: Wadsworth, 2000), 110.

181. S. Miyagi, B. Spitzberg, and L. Samovar, "Dealing with Conflict: A Study of Japanese and American Strategies," paper presented at the Annual Convention of the Western States Communication Association Convention, Vancouver, Canada, 1999.

182. D. Barnland, *Public and Private Self in Japan and the United States* (Tokyo: Simul Press, 1975), 35.

183. Gao and Ting-Toomey, 1998, 60.

184. Ting-Toomey and Chung, 2005, 278.

185. T. Novinger, *Communicating with Brazilians: When "Yes" Means "No"* (Austin, TX: University of Texas Press, 2003), 138.

186. Ting-Toomey and Chung, 2005, 278.

187. Ibid.

188. G. Ness, *Germany: Unraveling the Enigma* (Yarmouth, ME: Intercultural Press, 2000), 63.

189. G. Asselin and R. Mastron, *Au Contraire: Figuring Out the French* (Yarmouth, ME: Intercultural Press, 2001), 186.

190. Ting-Toomey and Chung, 2005, 276. See also W. L. Splicher, "Intercultural Conflict: Attribution and Cultural Ignorance," *Howard Journal of Communication*, 5 (1995), 195–213.

191. Wood, 2005, 186.

192. A. Roy and B. Oludaja, "The Role of Dialogue in Managing Intergroup Conflict," in *Intercultural Communication: A Reader*, 11th ed., L. A. Samovar and R. E. Porter, eds. (Belmont, CA: Wadsworth, 2006), 384.

193. S. Ting-Toomey, "Managing Intercultural Conflicts Effectively," in *Intercultural Comunication: A Reader*, 9th ed., L. A. Samovar and R. E. Porter, eds. (Belmont, CA: Wadsworth, 2000), 396.

194. Ibid.

195. Ting-Toomey, 2000, 397.

196. Ibid.

197. Ibid., 397.

198. Y. Y. Kim, "Adapting to a New Culture," in *Intercultural Communication: A Reader*, 8th ed., L. A. Samovar and R. E. Porter, eds. (Belmont, CA: Wadsworth, 1997), 404.

199. Y. Y. Kim, "Cross-Cultural Adaptation: An Integrative Theory," in *Theories in Intercultural Communication*, R. L. Wiseman, ed. (Thousand Oaks, CA: Sage Publications, 1995), 171.

200. A. S. Mak, M. J. Westwood, and F. I. Ishiyama, "Optimising Conditions for Learning Sociocultural Competencies for Success," *International Journal of Intercultural Relations*, 23 (1999), 80.

201. R. L. Rothenburger, "Transcultural Nursing: Overcoming Obstacles to Effective Communication," *AORN Journal*, 51 (1990), 1349–1363.

202. F. T. Leong and E. L. Chou, "The Role of Ethnic Identity and Acculturation in the Vocational Behavior of Asian Americans: An Integrative Review," *Journal of Vocational Behavior*, 44 (1994), 165.

203. A. M. Harper, "Cultural Adaptation and Intercultural Communication: Some Barriers and Bridges," paper presented at the Annual Convention of the Western Speech Communication Association, Monterey, CA, February 1997, 13.

204. Kim, 1995, 177.

205. E. Anderson, "A New Look at an Old Construct: Cross-Cultural Adaptation," *International Journal of Intercultural Relations*, 18 (1994), 293–328.

206. G. M. Chen and W. J. Starosta, "Intercultural Communication Competence: A Synthesis," in *Communication Yearbook*, vol. 19, B. R. Burleson and A. W. Kunkel, eds. (Thousand Oaks, CA: Sage Publications, 1996), 365.

207. P. A. Begley, "Sojourner Adaptation," in *Intercultural Communication: A Reader*, 9th ed., L. A. Samovar and R. E. Porter, eds. (Belmont, CA: Wadsworth, 2000), 404.

208. P. R. Harris and R. T. Moran, *Managing Cultural Differences: Leadership Strategies for a New World of Business*, 4th ed. (Houston, TX: Gulf, 1996), 143.

209. Kim, 1995, 172.

210. G. Althen, *American Ways* (Yarmouth, ME: Intercultural Press, 1988), 165.

211. Ibid.

212. R. K. Johannesen, *Ethics in Human Communication*, 4th ed. (Prospect Heights, IL: Waveland Press, 1996), 1.

213. L. A. Day, *Ethics in Media Communications: Cases and Controversies*, 3rd ed. (Belmont, CA: Wadsworth, 2000), 3.

214. Ibid., 2.

215. M. V. Angrosino, *The Culture of the Sacred* (Prospect Heights, IL: Waveland Press, 2004) 147.

216. E. Griffin, *A First Look at Communication Theory*, 2nd ed. (New York: McGraw-Hill, 1994), 458.

217. J. Q. Wilson, *San Diego Union-Tribune*, November 29, 1993, B5.

218. W. S. Howell, *The Empathic Communicator* (Belmont, CA: Wadsworth, 1982), 179.

219. Johannesen, 1996, 244.

220. S. Boorestein, *It's Easier Than You Think: The Buddhist Way to Happiness* (New York: HarperCollins, 1995), 60.

221. O. Tead, *Administration: Its Purpose and Performance* (New York: Harper and Row, 1959), 52.

222. N. Burbules, *Dialogue in Teaching* (New York: Teachers College Press, 1993), 81–82.

223. Johannesen, 1996, 257.

224. M. K. DeGenova, *Families in Cultural Context: Strength and Challenges in Diversity* (Mountain View, CA: Mayfield Publishing Company, 1997), 6.

225. Y. Chu, "Six Suggestions for Learning About People and Cultures," in *Learning About Peoples and Cultures*, S. Fersh, ed. (Evanston, IL: McDougal and Littell, 1974), 52.

226. J. Beversluis, *A Source Book for Earth's Community of Religions* (New York: Global Education Associates, 1995), 138.

227. D. W. Kale, "Peace as an Ethic for Intercultural Communication," in *Intercultural Communication: A Reader*, 9th ed., L. A. Samovar and R. E. Porter, eds. (Belmont, CA: Wadsworth, 2000), 452.

228. S. Huntington, *The Conflict of Civilizations and the Remaking of World Order* (New York: Simon and Schuster, 1996), 320.

229. Barnlund, 1989, 92–93.

230. D. Gomez-Ibanes, "Moving Toward a Global Ethic," in *A Source Book for Earth's Community of Religions*, J. Beversluis, ed. (New York: Global Education Associates, 1995), 128.

## EPILOGUE

1. P. R. Fleischman, *Cultivating Inner Peace* (Seattle: Pariyatt Press, 2004).

2. S. Huntington, *The Conflict of Civilization and the Remaking of World Order* (New York: Simon and Schuster, 1996), 36.

3. W. Booth, "Diversity and Division," *Washington Post*, March 2, 1998, 6.

4. Ibid.

5. B. Willingham, "Interracial Relationships Make Gains," *Albany Times Union*, June 3, 2004, E-3, E-12.

6. "Campus Fights Spark Resignation," *San Diego Union-Tribune*, June 2, 2005, A-5.

7. A. Schlesinger, Jr., *The Disuniting of America: Reflections on a Multicultural Society* (New York: Norton, 1992).

8. Ibid., 10.

9. W. A. Haviland, H. E. L. Prins, D. Walrath, and B. McBride, *Cultural Anthropology: The Human Challenge*, 11th ed. (Belmont, CA: Wadsworth, 2005), 446.

10. W. A. Haviland, *Cultural Anthropology*, 10th ed. (Belmont, CA: Wadsworth, 2002), 476.

11. "Environment Atlas Reveals Planetwide Devastation," CNet News, http://news.com.com/2100-1028_3-5732050.html (accessed December 6, 2005).

12. R. West and L. H. Turner, *Introducing Communication Theory: Analysis and Application* (Mountain View, CA: Mayfield Publishing Company, 2000), 424.

13. Ibid., 425.

14. L. S. Gross, *The International World of Electronic Media* (New York: McGraw-Hill, 1995), 1.

15. www.rand.org/publications/MR/MR1307/MR1307.sum.html (accessed November 22, 2005).

16. E. Y. Kim, *The Yin and Yang of American Culture: A Paradox* (Yarmouth, ME: Intercultural Press, 2001), 2.

17. www.rand.org/publications/MR/MR1307/MR1307.sum.html (accessed November 22, 2005).

18. Haviland, Prins, Walrath, and McBride, 2005, 426.

19. H. Cleveland, "The Limits to Cultural Diversity," *Futurist*, March–April 1995.

20. Haviland, Prins, Walrath, and McBride, 2005, 430.

21. F. Heylighen, "What Is a World View?" http://pespmc1.vub.ac.be/WORLVIEW.html (accessed December 6, 2005).

22. Cleveland, 1995, 23.

23. Haviland, Prins, Walrath, and McBride, 2005, 431.

24. 131. J. Krishnamurti, *Krishnamurti to Himself* (San Francisco: HarperCollins, 1987), 60.

25. Cleveland, 1995, 23.

26. Y. Ling-Ling, "Ethnic Strife Is Not a Geographically Distant Phenomenon," *San Diego Union-Tribune*, June 10, 1999, 11.

27. R. B. Smith and M. H. Bond, *Social Psychology across Cultures*, 2nd ed. (Boston: Allyn and Bacon, 1999), 312.

28. Cleveland, 1995, 23.

29. V. Lynch Lee, ed., *Faces of Culture* (Huntington Beach, CA: KOCE-TV Foundation, 1983), 69.

30. Cleveland, 1995, 26.

# PHOTO CREDITS

# INDEX

## A

AAVE. *See* African-American
    vernacular English
Abraham, 79, 86
Activity orientation in Kluckhohns and
    Strodtbeck's value orientations,
    156–157
Addison, Joseph, 301
Adoptions, international, 124
Adult white males in the
    United States, 10
Aeschylus, 2
Aesthetics in learning, 270
Affect and language, 166, 167, 179
African-American vernacular English
    (AAVE), 184–185
African Americans
    age and, 51
    as co-culture in United States, 7–8
    subjugation of, 54
Age
    and families, 49–51
    *see also* Elderly
Allah, 79, 88
Alternative health care systems, 289
Alternative views of reality.
    *See* Cultural values
Ambiguity in nonverbal
    communication, 199–200
Ambiguity tolerance versus
    intolerance, 269, 347
American Community Survey (2003),
    United States Census
    Bureau, 253
American English versus British
    English, 170–171
Analects, 79, 80, 105
Analytical learning approach, 270
Angelou, Maya, 256, 329

Anti-Semitism, 87
Antilocution prejudice, 324
Anxiety, 318
Appearance in nonverbal
    communication, 201–202, 242
Aquinas, St. Thomas, 333
Arab cultures
    and age, 49–50
    collectivism in, 48
    gender roles in, 45–46
    loyalty in the family, 49
Aristotle, 226, 266
Armed conflicts, 110
Arm's length racism, 328
Armstrong, Karen, 363
Art and culture, 25–26
Asian Americans as co-culture in
    United States, 7–8
Asians
    age and, 50
    gender roles, 44–45
    and loyalty, 49
    social skills and, 52
Assertiveness, 233–234
Attire in nonverbal communication,
    203–204
Aural preferences, 271
Authoritarian orientation, 157

## B

Bacon, Francis, 138
Baldwin, Christina, 363
Balkan states, 38, 54, 69
Basic needs, 18
Bateson, Gregory, 360
Beauty judgments in nonverbal
    communication, 202–203
Beecher, Henry Ward, 311
Being-in-becoming orientation, 156

Being orientation, 156
Beliefs, 130–131
    *see also* Values
Benedict, Ruth, 30
Berlin Wall, 237
Bhagavad Gita, 79, 96, 97, 98
Bible, 79, 89
Bicultural identities, 110
Biologic therapies, 289
Body appearance and
    behavior in nonverbal
    communication, 201–208
Body movement in nonverbal
    communication, 204–205
Body structure therapies, 289
Bolshoi Ballet, 59
Bond, Michael Harris, 150
Brahman, 97
Bribery, 242
British English versus American
    English, 170–171
Buber, Martin, 355
Buddha, 79, 99
Buddhism, 29, 74, 80, 99–104
    in China, 61
    in Japan, 61
Burke, Edmund, 35
Burton, Robert, 32
Bush, George W., 135
Business, 229–255
    assessing the context, 231–236
    communication rules, 230–232
    conflict management,
        251–252
    culturally diverse settings, 7
    decision making, 249–251
    the domestic context, 253–254
    gift giving, 242–243
    greeting behaviors, 240–241

Business (*continued*)
  information technology (IT)
    influence, 252–253
  initial contacts, 239–240
  intercultural communication
    and, 237–238
  and Islam, 94
  management styles, 243–245
  multinational context, 238–253
  negotiation styles, 245–249
  personal appearance, 242
  protocol in, 238–240
  and worldview, 74
Byrd, William, 333
Byzantine emperors, 58

# C

Cage, John, 227
Carlyle, Thomas, 225
Caucasoid race, 113
Cellular telephony, 311
Centrality dimension of prejudice, 323
Change, philosophy of, 313–314
Character, 316
Chavez, Cesar, 54–55
Chechnya, 54, 59
Chesterfield, Lord Philip, 31
Chief Joseph, 227
Child-rearing practices, 46
Childbirth, 301–302
Chinese culture, 23, 25
Chinese history, 59–61
Christianity, 29, 54, 68, 82–85
Chung Tzu, 23
Church
  and culture, 22
  *see also* Religion
Cicero, 53, 194
Civil Rights Act of 1964, 8
Civil rights movements, 54, 87, 113
Class disparities and technology, 367–368
Classrooms
  multicultural competency
    in, 277–282
  *see also* Education; Learning
Clinton, Bill, 54, 235
Co-cultures, defined, 11
Coca-Cola, 238
Codes of ethics, 74
Cognition styles, 268–270
Collective consciousness, 54
Collectivism, 158, 161, 162
  and families, 47–49
  in Hofstede's value dimensions,
    141–142
  Japan and U.S. compared,
    116–117, 122
Comenius, John, 369

Communal function of language, 166
Communal identity, 112
Communication, 11–16
  as complex, 16
  defined, 12
  as dynamic process, 12
  and the family, 42–43
  flexibility in, 346–347
  as having consequences, 15–16, 314
  and health care, 284–310
  information technology (IT)
    influence, 252–253
  and language, 164–168
  making inferences in, 14–15
  principles of, 12–16
  responses in, 15–16, 357
  rules of, 230–231
  as symbolic, 12–13
  as systemic, 13–14
  *see also* Intercultural communication
Communication context, 229–236
Communication strategies, 281–282
Communism
  in China, 61
  and Confucianism, 104
  in Russia, 58
Community, 36
  *see also* History
Competition, 122
Complementing in nonverbal
  communication, 198
Complexity of communication, 16
Conflict. *See* Intercultural conflict
Conflict management, 251–252
Conflict resolution, 161–162
Conflicts, global, 311, 312
Confucianism, 29, 44, 104–107
  in China, 61
  in Japan, 61
Confucius, 1, 23, 80, 104–105
Congruency in communication, 282
Constructive learning, 270
Contextualization in language, 175
Contradicting in nonverbal
  communication, 199
Conversation, 165–167, 179–182
Cooperation versus competition, 268–269
Core values, 32
Country, 36
  *see also* History
Credibility and silence, 226
Cross-communication, 200
Cross-cultural trade, 237
Crusades, 68
Cultural adaptation, 351–353
  disequilibrium, 352
  ethnocentrism, 352–353
  improving, 353
  language, 352

Cultural diversity training and
    prejudice, 326
Cultural domination and
    technology, 367
Cultural identities, 38–39, 109–126,
    368–369
  establishing and enacting, 121–123
  and the family, 42
  and intercultural communication,
    123–124
  and multiculturalism, 124–125
  *see also* Identity
Cultural interdependence, 368–369
Cultural isolation, 368
Cultural patterns, 130, 132–162
  diverse, 140–162
  in dominant U.S. culture, 135–140
  Hall's high-context and low-context
    orientations, 158–160
  Hofstede's value dimensions,
    140–151
  Kluckhohns and Strodtbeck's value
    orientations, 151–158
  obstacles in studying, 132–134
  selecting, 134–135
  Ting-Toomey's face and facework,
    160–162
  *see also* Perception; Values
Cultural quotas, 169
Cultural values. *See* Values
Cultural variations in the use
    of language, 189
Culture, 16–20
  basic functions of, 16–18
  and the business setting, 229–255
  characteristics of, 20–30
  and context, 229
  deep structure of, 29
  defined, 19–20
  dynamic nature of, 29–30
  and education, 256–283
  elements of, 18–19, 27
  and families, 22
  as group worldview, 17
  and health care, 284–310
  influence of, 1–2, 16
  as an integrated system, 30
  and language, 164–193
  learned nature of, 21–27
  learning through art, 25–26
  learning through folktales/legends/
    myths, 24–25
  learning through mass media, 26–27
  learning through proverbs, 23–24
  and nonverbal communication,
    200–201
  and objectivity, 32
  and perception, 129–130
  shared nature of, 27–28

sources of learning, 22, 27
and stereotyping, 31–32
symbolic basis of, 28–29
transmitted from generation to
generation, 28
unconscious or hidden dimension
of, 22, 73
Culture shock, 333–337
coping with, 337
defining, 335
lessons of, 337
reactions to, 335
stages of, 335–336
Cyber and fantasy identity, 118–119

**D**

DaimlerChrysler, 238
Dalai Lama, 360
Darwin, Charles, 208
Deaf culture as a co-culture, 9, 11
Decision making, 249–251
Deep structure of culture, 29, 35–39
background and history, 35–37
emotional nature of, 38
enduring nature of, 37–38
forms cultural identities, 38–39
important beliefs in, 37
see also Families; History; Worldview
Defensive behavior, 242–243
Deforestation, 5, 6, 366
Demographics, changing, 311
Dependency/independence relational
style, 270
Derived needs, 18
Descartes, René, 138, 153
Dharma, 98
Diaz, Porfirio, 66
Diet therapy, 289
"Digital divide," 367–368
Directive function of language, 166
Directness and indirectness in language,
176–177
Disabled people as a co-culture, 9, 11
Discrimination, 32
Disease, 5, 311
Disraeli, Benjamin, 12
Diverse cultural patterns, 140–162
Diversity
cultural, 4
and education, 259–264
understanding, 278–279
and unification, 369
Dogmatism, 333
Doing orientation, 84, 156–157
Domestic contact in intercultural
communication, 7–9
Dominance patterns, 300–301
Dominant culture, defined, 10

Dualistic worldview, 286
Durant, Ariel, 35
Durant, Will, 35
Dylan, Bob, 210

**E**

Earth's health, 5
Eban, Abba, 260
Economics, 311
Ecosystems, 5
Education, 256–283
cognition styles, 268–270
communication strategies, 281–282
and cultural diversity, 259–264
cultural interaction styles, 273–275
and globalization, 258
importance in studying, 256–258
and language diversity, 275–277
learning and cultural styles, 267–268
limited English proficiency (LEP)
students, 276–277
motivational styles, 272–273
multicultural competency in the
classroom, 277–282
and multiculturalism, 258–259,
264–275
relational styles for learning, 270
Educational level, 133
Egalitarian relationships, 235–236
Eightfold Path, 101–102
Einstein, Albert, 138
Elderly
treatment of, 41
see also Age
Emerson, Ralph Waldo, 167, 210,
225, 311
Empathy, 341–344
in communication, 281–282
defining, 341–342
hindrances to, 242–243
improving, 343–344
Enculturation, 21–22
and language, 168
Energy/calmness styles, 271–272
English ethnicity, 10
English-language education, 184
Enlightened One, 99
Entrepreneurs, minorities as, 253
Environmental problems, 5–6, 312, 366
Ethics, 354–361
codes of, 74
commonalities among people and
cultures, 358–359
definition of, 355–356
guidelines for intercultural,
357–361
individual worth, 358
relativism, 356

and religion, 81
responsibility for own actions, 360
universalism, 356–357
validity of differences, 360
Ethnic cleansing, 325
Ethnic hatreds, 36
Ethnic identity, 113–114, 368–369
"Ethnic resurgence," 368
"Ethnic shopping," 124
Ethnocentrism, 95, 227, 260
avoiding, 333
characteristics of, 332–333
and cultural identity, 368–369
defining, 331
in defining family, 40
and objectivity, 32
recognizing, 308–309
Euripides, 313
European Americans, 10
European Union, 61
Evaluative dimension of prejudice, 323
Evaluative values, 132
Extended families, 40, 41
Extermination in prejudice, 325
Extrinsic motivation, 273
Eye contact and gaze in nonverbal
communication, 209–212,
304–305

**F**

Face and facework, 160–162
Facial expressions in nonverbal
communication, 206–208, 305
Families, 36, 37, 39–52
age and, 49–51
collectivism and, 47–49
and culture, 22
definition of, 40
extended, 40, 41
forms of, 40–41
functions of, 41–42
and gender roles, 44–46
and health care, 300–303
importance of, 39–40
individualism and, 46–47
social skills and, 51–52
universal nature of, 39
variants within a culture, 43
Famine, 365, 366
Fantasy identity, 118–119
Fear and stereotypes, 321
Fellini, Federico, 164
Female circumcision, 46
Feng shui, 218
Field independence versus field
sensitivity, 268
Fishing rights, 5
Fitzwater, P. B., 316

Floods, 5
Folktales in culture, 24–25
Food sources, 5, 312
Forecasting, 357
Foreign Corrupt Practice Act, 242
Formal learning, 22
Formality, 306
    as cultural dimension, 232–233
Four Noble Truths, 100–101
Frankfurter, Felix, 137
Franklin, Benjamin, 136–137, 204
Free choice, 13–14, 350
Freedom, respect of, 328
Freire, Paulo, 256
Furniture arrangement in nonverbal
    communication, 218–219
Future orientation, 222–223

**G**

Gandhi, Mahatma, 127
Gates, Bill, 55
Gautama, Siddhartha, 99
Gays and lesbians as a co-culture, 9, 11
Gender
    in Christianity, 85
    and families, 44–46
    Islam and, 94–95
Gender identity, 115
Generalizations (stereotyping) and
    culture, 31–32
Generational transmission of culture, 28
Genuineness in communication, 282
Gestures in nonverbal communication,
    206–208
Ghosn, Carlos, 125
Gift giving, 242–243
Global conflicts, 311, 312
Global economy, 6–7
Globalization, 311
    in cultural identity, 109–110, 124
    and education, 258
    resisting, 368
Godparenting (compadrazgo), 48, 50
"Golden Rule," 359
Goodall, Jane, 361
Goodman, Paul, 260
Grant, Richard, 109
Greeting behaviors, 240–241
Group membership and cultural
    identity, 119
Guadalupe Hidalgo Treaty, 65
Gypsies, 87

**H**

Hadith, 73
Hall, Edward T., 135, 216–217, 223
Hall's high-context and low-context
    orientations, 158–160

Han Dynasty, 60
Hasan al-Zayyat, Ahmad, 180
Health care, 284–310
    belief systems in, 288–295
    causes of illness, 290–295
    considerations for a culturally diverse
        population, 299–306
    family roles in, 300–303
    formality and, 306
    importance of culture and
        communication in, 284–286
    improving intercultural
        communications, 306–309
    language barriers and, 303–304
    nonverbal messages and, 304–306
    prevention of illness, 295–297
    religion and spirituality in, 297–299
    self-disclosure in, 302–303
    treatment of illness, 292–295
    and worldviews, 286–288
Heraclitus, 29, 196
Hesse, Hermann, 128
Heterogeneity in cultural patterns,
    133–134
Hierarchical relationships, 236
High-context orientation of Hall, 158–159
Hidalgo Y Costilla, Miguel, 65
Hinduism, 95–98
History, 52–70
    background and definition, 52–55
    Chinese history, 59–61
    as element of culture, 18, 53
    Islamic civilization history, 66–70
    Japanese history, 61–63
    Mexican history, 64–66
    Russian history, 58–59
    United States history, 55–57
Hofstede's value dimensions, 140–151
Holistic system in health care, 289,
    291–292, 294–295
Holistic worldview, 286
Homogenous culture position, 368
Hoover, Herbert, 137
Host cultures, 353
Hostility, 32, 365–366
Hostility dimension of prejudice, 323
Human communication.
    See Communication
Human identity, 112
Human nature orientation in Kluckhohns
    and Strodtbeck's value
    orientations, 151–153
Huxley, T. H., 99
Huygens, Christian, 219

**I**

Identity, 109–121
    acquiring and developing, 119–121

communal, 112
cyber and fantasy, 118–119
defining, 110–112
ethnic, 113–114
gender, 115
human, 112
and language, 276
models of identity development, 120
national, 115–116, 122
organizational, 116–117
personal, 112, 117–118
racial, 110, 113
regional, 116
relational, 112
social, 112
typology of, 113–119
    see also Cultural identity
Identity expression and language, 168
Idioms, 190
Illegal immigrants, 66
Illness. See Health care
Immediacy in communication, 281
Immigration
    as cause of problems, 2
    in cultural identity, 109, 110, 113,
        114, 124
    illegal, 66
    and language, 190
Impulsivity/reflectivity style, 271
Inclusiveness, 32
Independence/dependence relational
    style, 270
India
    gender roles in, 45
    and silence, 226
Individual worth, 358
Individualism, 158, 161–162
    as American value, 27, 47, 55–56
    in Christianity and Judaism, 84
    and families, 46–47
    in Hofstede's value dimensions,
        141–142
    and space and distance, 217
Individuals. See Cultural identity
Industrialization, 5
Informal learning, 22
Informal time, 220–222
Informality as cultural dimension, 232
Information systems, 311
    and international interaction, 4
Information technology (IT), 235
    influence on business, 252–253
Initial contacts, 239–240
Institutional racism, 328
Integrative needs, 18
Intense racism, 328
Interaction management with nonverbal
    communication, 197
Interaction rules and language, 175–182

Interaction styles, 273–275
Intercultural communication
    challenge and importance of, 1–4
    competence in, 314–316
    and cultural identities, 123–124,
        368–369
    defined, 9–10
    domestic contact, 7–9
    future of, 365–369
    improving, 338–354
    intercultural contact, 3–4, 36
    and international problems,
        365–366
    problems in, 316–337
    and stereotypes, 321–322
    study of, 31–32
    and technology, 366–368
    see also Communication; International
        interaction
Intercultural conflict, 347–351
    management of, 350–351
    Western approaches, 348–349
Intercultural marriage in cultural
    identity, 109, 110, 124
Intercultural transients, 124, 125
Internal states and nonverbal
    communication, 196
International adoptions, 124
International conflict, 6, 36
International interaction, 4–7
    global economy and, 6–7
    population and, 4–6
    technology and information systems
        and, 4
International market, 238
International problems, 365–366
    environmental degradation, 366
    famine, 365, 366
    hostility, 365–366
Internet, 311
    and culture, 27
    in cyber and fantasy identities,
        118–119
    genealogical research, 125
    impact on communication, 2, 4
Interpersonal harmony, 234–235
Interrelatedness of cultural
    patterns, 133
Intimate distance, 217
Intrinsic motivation, 272–273
Intuition in learning, 270
Intuitive problem solving, 74, 82
Invisible aspect of nonverbal
    communication, 200
Iran, Muslims in, 67
Iraq, 54
    Muslims in, 67, 68
    United States involvement in, 9
Isaac, 86

Islam, 29, 88–95
    and ethics, 81
    gender roles in, 46, 73
Islamic civilization history, 66–70
IT. See Information technology
Iyer, Pico, 1

J

Jacob, 86
James, William, 21
Japan
    as collectivistic culture, 116–117
    interaction styles in schools, 122
    and loyalty, 49
Japanese history, 61–63
Japanese tea ceremony, 80
Jerusalem, 68, 92
Jesus, 80, 82, 90
Jews, 54, 78, 79
Jihad, 92–93
Johnson, Lyndon, 156
Judaism, 68, 85–88
    and ethics, 81

K

Kant, Immanuel, 152, 357
Karma, 98, 103
Kennedy, John F., 254, 311
Kinesics in nonverbal communication,
    204–205
King, Martin Luther, Jr., 54, 326
Kluckhohns and Strodtbeck's value
    orientations, 151–158
Koran, 45–46, 79, 88, 90, 91, 93
Korea, 44

L

Language, 164–193
    affect expression, 166, 167, 179
    African-American vernacular English
        (AAVE), 184–185
    barriers in health care, 303–304
    clarity in intercultural interaction, 191
    communal function of, 166
    and communication, 164–168
    contextualization in, 175
    conversation, 165–167, 179–182
    cultural variations in the use of, 189
    and culture, 19, 168–173
    culture bound words, 190–191
    defined, 164
    directness and indirectness, 176–177
    diversity and co-cultures in the U.S.,
        182–188
    diversity in, 275–277
    female versus male communication
        patterns, 187–188

functions of, 166
    and identity, 276
    identity expression and, 168
    idioms, 190
    and interaction rules, 175–182
    learning languages of other cultures,
        188–189
    limited English proficiency (LEP)
        students, 276–277
    as open system, 313
    preserving culture, 166, 167
    and reality control, 167
    sensitivity to diverse coding
        systems, 191
    social relationships and, 177–178
    socialization and enculturation, 168
    societal function of, 166
    Spanish-speaking Americans, 184
    and thought, 167, 173
    understanding diverse message
        systems, 188–191
    verbal processes, 169–170
    and women, 186–188
    word and pronunciation diversity,
        170–171
    word meanings, 171–173
    see also Symbols
Lao-tzu, 23
Latin Americans, gender roles, 45
Latinos
    as co-culture in United States,
        7–8, 253
    see also Mexican Americans
Learning
    and cultural styles, 267–268
    on demand, 273
    formal, 22
    informal, 22
    relational styles for, 270
    when interested, 273
    see also Education
Learning culture, 21–27
    through art, 25–26
    through folktales/legends/myths, 24–25
    through mass media, 26–27
    through proverbs, 23–24
    see also Education
Legends in culture, 24–25
LEP. See Limited English proficiency
    (LEP) students
Limited English proficiency (LEP)
    students, 276–277
Lincoln, Abraham, 24, 54
Linear-active cultures, 267
Listening, 344–346
    direct and indirect, 344
    and feedback, 345–346
    and nonverbal communication, 345
    value placed on, 344–345

Listening and receiving learning style, 269
Location in communication, 14
Locke, John, 135–136, 138
Lombardi, Vince, 140
Long- and short-term orientation in
    Hofstede's value dimensions,
    150–151
Low-context orientation
    of Hall, 159–160
Loyalty, 38
Lu Wang, 143
Luther, Martin, 83

# M

Machado, Antonio, 130
Magico-religious system in health care,
    289, 290–291, 293–294
Mainstream culture, 10
Malnutrition, 5
Management styles, 243–245
Manifest Destiny principle, 57, 65
Mao Zedong, 61
Marceau, Marcel, 194
Marriage in cultural identity, 109, 110
Masculinity/femininity in Hofstede's value
    dimensions, 148–150
Mass media
    and cultural identity, 119
    in culture, 26–27
    and stereotypes, 321
Mass social learning, 27
McDonald's, 235, 238
Mead, Margaret, 43
Meaning of life, 73, 78
Mecca, 92
Mechanistic worldview, 287–288
Media. See Mass media
Meditation, 74, 98, 99
Men
    adult white males in the United
        States, 10
    female versus male communication
        patterns, 187–188
Mencius, 23
Metalinguistic function of language, 166
Metaphysical worldview, 75
Mexican-American War, 64, 65
Mexican Americans
    as a co-culture, 11
    age and, 50
    social skills and, 51–52
    see also Latinos
Mexican culture, collectivism in, 47–48
Mexican history, 64–66
    United States and, 57
Middle East, 38, 54
    gender roles in, 46
    and oil resources, 5, 69

Migration of populations, 5
Miller, Henry, 139
Mind/body control therapies, 289
Mindfulness, 357
Minorities
    as entrepreneurs, 253
    in the United States, 7–9, 253
Modesty and female purity, 301
Mongoloid race, 113
Monochronic (M-time), 223, 224
Moore, George, 314
Moses, 79, 86, 87
Motivational styles in learning,
    272–273
Muhammad, 67, 79, 89, 90, 93
Multi-active cultures, 167–168
Multicultural workforce, 7
Multiculturalism
    competency in the classroom, 277–282
    and cultural identities, 124–125
    and education, 258–259, 264–275
    education curricula and prejudice, 326
    and health care, 306–309
Multinational corporations, 46
Multiple cultural identities, 110
Muslim Americans as co-culture in
    United States, 7–8
Muslims, 54
    in world population, 66–67
Myths in culture, 24–25

# N

Nader, Laura, 369
NAFTA. See North American Free Trade
    Agreement
Nation, 52
    see also History
National identity, 115–116, 122
Nationalism, 38, 81–82, 368
Native Americans, 25, 26, 125
    as a co-culture, 9
    age and, 50
    nature orientation of, 73, 154
    and silence, 227
    social skills and, 52
    subjugation of, 54, 57, 113
    time orientation of, 155
Natural resources, limited nature of, 5
Nature, perception of, 73
Nature/person orientation in Kluckhohns
    and Strodtbeck's value
    orientations, 153–154
Navajo language, 174
Need satisfaction nature of culture, 18
Negative behavior, 32
Negative feedback, 346
Negotiation process, 245–249
    expected outcomes, 248–249

external factors, 246–248
    participant perspective, 246
Negroid race, 113
Nirvana, 97, 98
Nixon, Richard, 61
Non-Hispanic whites (Caucasians), 7
Non-mechanistic worldview, 287–288
Nonverbal communication, 194–228
    ambiguity in, 199–200
    body appearance and behavior,
        201–208
    classifications of, 201–227
    creating impressions with, 196–197
    and culture, 200–201
    defining, 197–198
    functions of, 198–199
    in health care, 304–306
    interaction management with, 197
    and internal states, 196
    invisible aspect of, 200
    of students, 282
    study of, 199–200
    universal nature of, 196
Normative values, 132
North American Free Trade Agreement
    (NAFTA), 66
Nuclear families, 41, 47
Number of people in communication, 14
Nursing homes, 41, 49

# O

Objectivity
    and culture, 32
    versus subjectivity, 287–288
Occasion in communication, 14
Occupation, 133
Oil, 5
Organizational identity, 116–117
Ottoman Empire, 67
Ovid, 140

# P

Pace and time in nonverbal
    communication, 221–222
Paine, Thomas, 72
Palestinian problem, 69
Pali Canon, 79
Paralanguage in nonverbal
    communication, 214–216
Parks, Rosa, 54
Participation/passivity relational
    style, 270–271, 274
Particularism in religion, 89
Passivity/participation relational
    style, 270–271, 274
Past orientation, 222
Pasternak, Boris, 59

Paz, Octavio, 264
Perception, 128–130
    and culture, 129–130
    defining, 128–129
    and nature of reality, 73
Peres, Shimon, 360
Person/nature orientation in Kluckhohns
        and Strodtbeck's value
        orientations, 153–154
Personal appearance and business, 242
Personal contact and prejudice, 326
Personal experience, 133
Personal identity, 112, 117–118
Personal racism, 328
Personal space, 216–218
Peter the Great, 58
Pharmacologic therapies, 289
Phatic function of language, 166
Philosophy, 82
    of change, 313–314
    see also Worldview
Physical attack in prejudice, 325
Pillars of Faith, 89–91
Pinker, Steven, 164
Plato, 226
Plutarch, 366
Poetic function of language, 166
Political dynamics, 311
Polychronic (P-time) time, 223–224
Population, 4–6
    and environmental problems, 5–6
    growth in, 4–5, 264
    and international conflict, 6
    migration of, 5
    and natural resources, 5
Posture in nonverbal
        communication, 205
Poverty, 5, 311
Power, 329–331
    defining, 329
    degrees of, 329–330
    and intercultural communication,
        330–331
Power distance in Hofstede's value
        dimensions, 146–148
Pregnancy, 301–302
Prejudice, 323–326
    avoiding, 326
    causes of, 325–326
    defining, 323
    expressions of, 324–325
    functions of, 323–324
Present orientation, 222
Presley, Elvis, 55
Prevention of illness, 295–297
Primary values, 131
Productive land, 5
Protocol in business, 238–240
Proverbs and culture, 23–24

Proximics, 216
Public distance, 217
Puerto Rico, 48, 51
Punctuality, 220–221
Putin, Vladamir, 59

Q

Qur'an, 73, 90, 91

R

Racial identity, 110, 113
Racism, 9, 66, 326–329
    avoiding, 328–329
    defining, 327
    expressions of, 327–328
    historical roots of, 329
    institutional, 328
    personal, 328
Reactive cultures, 268
Reagan, Ronald, 235
Reality, perception and nature of, 73
Reality control and language, 167
Reason versus intuition, 287–288
Reflecting and clarifying feelings, 282
Regional identity, 116
Regulating in nonverbal
        communication, 199
Reincarnation, 98
Relational identity, 112
Relational (social) orientation in
        Kluckhohns and Strodtbeck's
        value orientations, 157–158
Relational styles for learning, 270
Relativism, 356
Religion
    authority in, 79–80
    Buddhism, 99–104
    Christianity, 82–85
    Confucianism, 104–107
    as element of culture, 18, 29
    and ethics, 81
    and health care, 297–299
    Hinduism, 95–98
    as human universal, 75
    importance of, 75–76
    Islam, 88–95
    Judaism, 85–88
    numbers, diffusion, and relevance, 78
    sacred scriptures, 78–79
    and security, 81
    selection of traditions for study, 77–78
    similarities in, 78
    statistics of, 78
    and the study of intercultural
        communication, 77
    traditional rituals, 80
    as worldview, 75–81
    see also Church; Worldview

Repeating in nonverbal
        communication, 198
Retirement communities, 41, 49
Rites of passage, 80, 121, 122
Rituals in religion, 80
Russell, Bertrand, 138, 329
Russian history, 58–59

S

Sacred scriptures, 78–79
Saddam Hussein, 54
Sa'di, 338
Santayana, George, 139
Satellite telephony, 311
Scapegoating in prejudice, 325–326
Schools
    and cultural identity, 119
    and culture, 22
Schweitzer, Albert, 355
Science versus religion, 287–288
Scientific/biomedical system in health
        care, 288, 290, 292–293
Scientific method, 74, 82
Scientific worldview, 75
Seating in nonverbal
        communication, 218
Secondary values, 131
Secular worldview, 81
Security and religion, 81
Self-disclosure, 302–303
Self-knowledge, 338–341
    communication style, 339–340
    culture, 339
    monitoring yourself, 340–341
    personal attitudes, 339
Self-understanding, 278
September 11 terrorist attacks, 9, 66, 88,
        92, 332–333, 363
Shakespeare, William, 214, 337, 355, 365
Shang Dynasty, 59
Shared nature of culture, 27–28
Shaw, George Bernard, 72
Shiite Muslims, 54, 67–68, 89
Silence
    in feedback, 346
    in nonverbal communication,
        225–227
Silone, Ignazio, 127
Similarities
    seeking, 316–317
    see also Universalism
Sitting in nonverbal communication,
        205–206
Skin color in nonverbal
        communication, 202
Slaves from Africa, 70, 113
Social distance, 217
Social identity, 112

Social organizations
    as element of culture, 19
    *see also* specific organizations
Social relationships and language,
        177–178
Social skills and families, 51–52
Socialization, 21–22, 38
    by the family, 41, 51–52
    and language, 168
    and stereotypes, 320
Societal function of language, 166
Societal sources of prejudice, 325
Socioeconomic status, 133
Sociotypes, 320
Socrates, 226, 278
Solzhenitsyn, Alexander, 59
Sophocles, 154
Space and distance in nonverbal
        communication, 216–219
Spanish-speaking Americans, 8, 184
Spirituality and health care, 297–299
Stalin, Joseph, 58
Starbucks, 238
Starvation, 5
State, 22, 36
    *see also* History
Statistics of religion, 78
Status relationships, 235–236
    egalitarian relationships, 235–236
    hierarchical relationships, 236
Stereotyping, 319–323
    avoiding, 322–323
    and culture, 31–32
    defining, 319
    and empathy, 342
    learning, 320–321
    variations in, 320
Stone, Elizabeth, 109
Subcultures. *See* Co-cultures
Substituting in nonverbal communication,
        198–199
Sunni Muslims, 54, 67–68, 89
Swift, Jonathan, 292
Symbolic racism, 328
Symbols
    in communication, 12–13
    in culture, 28–29, 51
    in nonverbal communication, 195
    *see also* Language
Systemic nature
    of communication, 13–14
    of culture, 30

**T**

Tactile/kinesthetic learning, 270
Talmud, 87
Technology, 311, 366–368
    and class disparities, 367–368

cultural domination and, 367
    and international interaction, 4
Tehyi Hsieh, 259
Television, violent programs on, 27
Ten Commandments, 81, 83, 86
Tennyson, Lord Alfred, 172, 361
Terrorism, 3, 6, 366
Tertiary values, 131
Thayer, William, 39
Thoreau, Henry David, 28
Thought and language, 167, 173
Time in communication, 14
Time in nonverbal communication,
        219–224, 305–306
Time orientation in Kluckhohns and
        Strodtbeck's value orientations,
        154–156
Ting-Toomey's face and facework, 160–162
Tocqueville, Alexis de, 83, 138
Tokenism, 328
Torah, 86
Touch in nonverbal communication,
        212–214, 305
Tourism, 3, 4
Traditional rituals in religion, 80
Transportation, 311
Treatment of illness, 292–295
Trial and error versus "watch,
        then do," 269
Tribal groups, 2
Tribalism, 368
Truman, Harry, 54
Trustworthiness, 316
"Turning inward" movement, 368
Twentieth century, conflicts in, 3
Twenty-first century, intercultural
        challenges in, 4

**U**

U-curve in culture shock, 335–336
Umbrella culture, 10
Uncertainty avoidance in Hofstede's value
        dimensions, 145–146
Uncertainty reduction, 318–319
Unconscious or hidden dimension of
        culture, 22, 73
Unification and diversity, 369
United Nations Universal Declaration of
        Human Rights, 358
United States
    adult white males, 10
    business in, 253–254
    co-cultures in, 7–9, 54, 253, 282
    competition in, 140
    and conflict approaches, 348–349
    cultural diversity in, 110, 125, 364
    cultural patterns in dominant
        culture, 135–140

dominant culture, 7, 9, 23, 54
    English values, 55
    equality in, 137
    first immigrants, 55
    history of, 55–57
    immigration to, 2, 7, 8, 55, 190
    individualism in, 27, 47, 55–56,
        116–117, 135–137
    interaction styles in schools, 122
    labor force in, 253
    language and co-cultures in
        the U.S., 182–188
    Manifest Destiny principle, 57, 65
    materialism in, 137–138
    minorities in, 7–9, 253
    as multicultural nation, 55
    population changes in,
        7, 264, 311
    progress and change in, 138–139
    proverbs in dominant culture, 23
    science and technology in, 138
    separation of church and state, 55
    violence and wars, 56
    western frontier, 56
    work and leisure in, 139
United States Census 2000, 110
United States Census Bureau,
        American Community Survey
        (2003), 253
United States Constitution, 238
Universalism
    of ethics, 356–357
    and ethnocentrism, 332
    of families, 39
    in nonverbal communication, 196
    and proverbs, 23
    of religions, 75, 78
Upanishads, 96, 98

**V**

Values, 127–163
    and beliefs, 130–131
    core, 32
    defined, 131–132
    as element of culture, 19
    and the family, 41
    *see also* Cultural patterns;
        Perception
Vedas, 79, 96
Verbal preferences, 271
Villaraigosa, Antonio, 8
Visual preferences, 271
Vocal characteristics in nonverbal
        communication, 215–216
Vocal qualities in nonverbal
        communication, 215
Vocal segregates in nonverbal
        communication, 216

**W**

Water crisis, 5, 312
Weapons of mass destruction, 3, 6, 366
Western bias, 316
"Whiteness" in positions of
    privilege, 114
Whorf, Benjamin Lee, 173
Wiesel, Elie, 87
Williams, Tennessee, 145, 212
Withdrawal, 317

Women
    as a co-culture, 9, 11
    female versus male communication
        patterns, 187–188
    and language, 186–188
Word and pronunciation diversity,
    170–171
Word meanings, 171–173
Workforce, multicultural, 7
World Trade Center terrorist attacks, 6, 9,
    66, 88, 92, 363

Worldview, 72–108
    defined, 73
    and health care, 286–288
    importance of, 72–73
    manifestations of, 73–74
    of nature, 73–74
    religion as, 75–81
    scientific, metaphysical, and
        religious, 75
    secular, 81
    *see also* Church; Religion

# Helping students become effective, culturally aware communicators in today's world!

The latest edition of **Communication Between Cultures** is packed with current and respected research and theories on intercultural communication and offers fresh examples that are certain to get students thinking about their own assumptions and cultural biases. Timely and engaging coverage of religion, cultural identity, gender, prejudice, and racism, along with the work of a new coauthor, Dr. Edwin R. McDaniel, illustrate the subtle and profound ways culture affects communication with all people.

The Sixth Edition is enhanced with a variety of new features, including:

- A new chapter on cultural identity and its influence on intercultural communication
- An entire chapter on religion, which demonstrates how one's world view gets translated into daily life—including interactions with people from different cultures
- A new section that helps you adapt your language to various intercultural settings
- An expanded section on ethics
- Updated information on values and cultural patterns and a new section on the Asian notion of "face saving"
- A wealth of new examples and references that keep this text on the cutting-edge of the discipline

**Communication Between Cultures is enhanced with a robust suite of teaching and learning resources:**

### Instructor's Resource Manual
0-495-09265-7
This teaching resource includes strategies for managing sensitive issues in classroom discussions, chapter outlines, discussion questions, and sample test items.

### ExamView; Computerized Testing
0-495-09264-9
Create, deliver, and customize tests and study guides (both print and online) in minutes with this easy-to-use assessment and tutorial system. **ExamView** offers both a Quick Test Wizard and an Online Test Wizard that guide you step by step through the process of creating tests.

### Turnitin®
Access packaged with the text 0-495-15822-4
This proven online plagiarism-prevention software promotes fairness in the classroom by helping students learn to correctly cite sources and allowing instructors to check for originality before reading and grading papers. Turnitin quickly checks student papers against billions of pages of Internet content, millions of published works, and millions of student papers and within seconds generates a comprehensive originality report.

### Resources for your students:

### NEW!
### Intercultural Communication: A Reader, Eleventh Edition
*by Larry A. Samovar, Richard E. Porter, and Edwin R. McDaniel*
0-534-64440-6 • packaged with the text 0-495-05597-2
The perfect partner to enhance your course! This reader includes a balance of articles with readings that discuss the classic ideas that laid the groundwork for this field. Please visit http://www.thomsonedu.com/communication for more information on this market-leading reader.

### Companion Website
http://thomsonedu.com/communication/samovar
The **Communication Between Cultures** website presents many skill-building resources to help your students master their intercultural communication skills. The site features interactive activities, tutorial quizzes, web links, research information, and much more. Encourage your students to visit this site today.

ISBN 0-495-17219-7

9 780495 172192

9000

## THOMSON
## WADSWORTH

Visit Thomson Wadsworth at **www.thomsonedu.com**